A Companion
to Ethics

Blackwell Companions to Philosophy

This outstanding student reference series offers a comprehensive survey of philosophy as a whole. Written by many of today's leading figures, each volume provides lucid and engaging coverage of the key figures, terms, and movements of the main subdisciplines of philosophy. Each essay is fully cross-referenced and supported by a selected bibliography. Taken together, it provides the ideal basis for course use and an invaluable work of reference.

Already published:

1 **A Companion to Ethics**
   Edited by Peter Singer

2 **A Companion to Aesthetics**
   Edited by David Cooper

3 **A Companion to Epistemology**
   Edited by Jonathan Dancy and Ernest Sosa

4 **A Companion to Contemporary Political Philosophy**
   Edited by Robert E. Goodin and Philip Pettit

5 **A Companion to the Philosophy of Mind**
   Edited by Samuel Guttenplan

6 **A Companion to Metaphysics**
   Edited by Jaegwon Kim and Ernest Sosa

Forthcoming:

7 **A Companion to the Philosophy of Law and Legal Theory**
   Edited by Dennis Patterson

8 **A Companion to the Philosophy of Religion**
   Edited by Philip Quinn and Charles Taliaferro

9 **A Companion to the Philosophy of Language**
   Edited by Crispin Wright and Bob Hale

Blackwell
Companions to
Philosophy

A Companion
to Ethics

Edited by

PETER SINGER

BLACKWELL
Publishers

Copyright © Blackwell Publishers Ltd, 1991, 1993

First published 1991
First published in paperback (with corrections) 1993
Reprinted 1993 (twice), 1994 (twice), 1995, 1996

Blackwell Publishers Ltd
108 Cowley Road
Oxford OX4 1JF, UK

Blackwell Publishers Inc.
238 Main Street
Cambridge, Massachusetts 02142, USA

British Library Cataloguing in Publication Data
A CIP catalogue record for this book is available from the British Library

Library of Congress Cataloging in Publication Data
A Companion to ethics/edited by Peter Singer.
p.   cm. — (Blackwell companions to philosophy)
Includes bibliographical references and index.
1. Ethics. 2. Social ethics. I. Singer, Peter. II. Series.
BJ1012.C62   1991   90–23456
170—dc20   CIP

ISBN 0–631–16211–9 — ISBN 0–631–18785–5 (Pbk)

Typeset in 10.5 on 12.5pt Photina
Printed and bound in Great Britain by Hartnolls Ltd, Bodmin, Cornwall

This book is printed on acid-free paper

Introduction

The title *A Companion to Ethics* may suggest a volume with short entries, in alphabetical order, providing summary information about leading theories, ideas and people in the academic discipline of ethics. As a glance at the outline of the volume (following this introduction) will show, this book is very different. It consists of 47 original essays. These essays deal with the origins of ethics, with the great ethical traditions, with theories about how we ought to live, with arguments about specific ethical issues, and with the nature of ethics itself. (In accordance with current usage, in this book 'ethics' will usually be used not only for the study of morality (that is, as a synonym for 'moral philosophy') but also to refer to the subject matter of that study, in other words as meaning 'morality'.)

I have chosen to organize the book in this way because it is vital that ethics not be treated as something remote, to be studied only by scholars locked away in universities. Ethics deals with values, with good and bad, with right and wrong. We cannot avoid involvement in ethics, for what we do – and what we don't do – is always a possible subject of ethical evaluation. Anyone who thinks about what he or she ought to do is, consciously or unconsciously, involved in ethics. When we begin to think more seriously about these questions, we may begin by exploring our own underlying values but we will also be travelling over roads that have been trodden by many other thinkers, in different cultures, for well over two thousand years. For such a journey it is helpful to have a guide with information about the path we shall tread, how it came to be laid out, the major forks where people have taken alternative routes, and who has been there before us. More valuable still, however, is the kind of companion who will stimulate our thought about the route we are taking and warn us of the traps and culs-de-sac that have stopped others making progress.

So the best way to use this book is to go first to the Outline of Contents, a kind of map of the book, with explanatory notes at points where the map might otherwise be unclear to those who do not already know the territory. Then, depending on your interests, you may wish to start at the beginning and work your way through, or you may prefer to read specific essays on subjects that interest you. To find any subject not mentioned in the Outline of Contents, consult the Index. It is designed to make it easy to find not only specific concepts or theories, for example justice, or utilitarianism, but also particular aspects of topics. Thus under 'killing' you will find not a single heading, but also sub-headings that will lead you to discussions of ethical aspects of killing in Buddhism, Hinduism and Jainism; to the distinction between killing and letting die; to euthanasia and killing in war; to the treatment of killing by consequentialist, deontological, utilitarian and virtue-based ethical theories; and to killing in small-scale societies. In addition you will find cross-references to capital punishment and to murder, which have separate entries in the index. In this way I hope that the aim of producing a book that is readable will not have been achieved at the cost of rendering the book less helpful as a work of reference.

The selection of a companion is a personal matter; so too with the selection of topics (and authors) for this *Companion*. I have tried to be broad in my tastes, covering traditions that are certainly not mine, and inviting contributions from authors with whom I expected to disagree (and my expectations were not disappointed). Nevertheless, there can be no totally objective and impartial selection of topics or contributors. Another editor might have produced a very different volume. I was brought up in a Western English-speaking society, and educated in the Western philosophical tradition; I would not even be competent to edit a volume that gives equal space to other traditions. Within that Western philosophical tradition, although no-one can claim to be immune from intellectual trends, I have tried to focus on the timeless questions of Western ethical thought, in preference to the issues that are currently fashionable.

P.S.

Acknowledgements

I owe thanks to many. First, obviously, thanks are due to the contributors, not only for taking the time to write their articles, but even more for being willing to revise them in the light of my views as to what this volume should be like. Less obviously, Stephan Chambers, of Basil Blackwell, persuaded me to do the volume; without his initiative, it would not have existed at all. Alyn Shipton then took over the production process, and has been an invaluable source of encouragement and advice. Richard Beatty handled the desk editing with great skill and commendable attention to detail. Finally, Dale Jamieson and R. M. Hare have acted as informal editorial advisors at every stage of the book. Without them the task of editing would have been more difficult, and the final product, I am sure, of a lower standard.

PETER SINGER
December 1990

Contents

ix

CONTENTS

PART II: THE GREAT ETHICAL TRADITIONS

There are many distinct ethical traditions. The essays in this part outline some of the major ones: Indian, Buddhist, Chinese, Jewish, Christian and Islamic. (Western philosophical, as distinct from Christian, ethics is the subject of Part III.) These ethical traditions are, for much of the world's population, the living ethical systems to which they look for guidance.

The essays present, for each tradition, the answers to such questions as: how did this tradition arise? What is distinctive about it? How does it answer such basic questions as: Where does ethics come from? How can I know what is right? What is the ultimate criterion of right action? Why should I do what is right? The essays also indicate what each tradition shares with other ethical traditions, especially with contemporary Western ethics.

PART III: WESTERN PHILOSOPHICAL ETHICS: A SHORT HISTORY

The dominant position of Western civilization today means that the Western tradition of philosophical thinking about ethics exerts a strong influence on all contemporary discussions of ethics. The three articles that follow cover the history of Western philosophical ethics from ancient Greece to the present day.

PART IV: HOW OUGHT I TO LIVE?

The articles in this part discuss ethical theories that attempt to answer the fundamental practical questions of ethics: What ought I to do? How ought I to live? These theories make up the more abstract part of what is known as normative ethics – that is, the part of ethics concerned with guiding action.

One ancient answer to the question 'How ought I to live?' is: 'In accordance with human nature'. In tracing the changes in the meaning of this answer since Greek and Roman times, this essay provides a background to many later ethical theories. At the same time it indicates some problems for subsequent attempts to appeal to natural law in order to argue that specific kinds of conduct (for example, the use of contraception) are wrong.

Many modern ethical theorists invoke ideas that have their origins in the ethical writings of Kant. Kant's claim that all rational beings ought to obey a 'categorical imperative' derived from a universal law of reason has been much acclaimed, but also much criticized. Here Kant's position is explained, and the common charges against it are considered.

Can morality be thought of as an implicit agreement we make with our fellow human beings in order to gain the benefits of a co-operative social life? This initially attractive view must face several objections: attempts to meet these lead to distinctive modern variations on the idea of a social contract as it was developed in the seventeenth and eighteenth centuries.

Egoism tells us to live so as to further our own interests. Psychological egoists think that we all do this anyway, and so it scarcely needs to be advocated. Other philosophical egoists advocate the pursuit of one's own interest as the rational, and even the ethical, way to live. Despite doubts about whether egoism is properly classified as an ethical theory, it does provide a challenging answer to the fundamental practical question of how we ought to live.

Perhaps 'What ought I to do?' is the wrong question to ask. We might ask instead: 'What kind of person should I be?' Virtue theory focuses on this latter question, and on the virtues that make up good character. But can a theory of the virtues replace alternative approaches to ethics?

Some hold that a morality can be based on rights; others regard them as derivative from a more fundamental moral principle or principles. Whatever the view taken on this question, it is widely thought that at least a partial answer to the question of how we ought to live is given by the injunction to respect the rights of others.

PART V: APPLICATIONS

The application of ethical reasoning to specific issues or areas of practical concern – sometimes known as applied ethics – is the practical counterpart of the more abstract theories of normative ethics discussed in Part IV. In the last two decades the development of applied ethics has been so great that it is impossible to cover it here in any systematic way. Instead, this Part consists of articles on issues selected on the basis of the practical importance of the issue, and the extent to which the issue is amenable to ethical reasoning. (Ethical reasoning can do little to resolve an issue if the parties are at one on all the value-questions, and differ only in their views of the facts.) The titles of the articles indicate their subject-matter clearly enough to make further description unnecessary.

PART VI: THE NATURE OF ETHICS

Despite the many ethical theories that have been developed with a view to guiding our conduct, and the considerable body of writing on the application of these theories to practical issues, there is uncertainty about what exactly we are doing – and are justified in doing – when we make ethical judgements, or engage in ethical argument. Are we trying to get the facts right, as a scientist might do? Or simply expressing our feelings, or perhaps the feelings of our society as a whole? In what sense, if any, can moral judgements be true or false? The study of these questions has led to the development of theories that differ from the normative theories discussed in Part IV, because they are not intended to guide conduct. They are not so much theories *of* ethics, as theories *about* ethics. For that reason this branch of moral philosophy is known as meta-ethics; a term that suggests that we are not engaged in ethics, but are looking at it, and considering what exactly ethics is, what rules of argument can apply to it, in what way it is possible for ethical judgements to be true or false, and what (if anything) can provide a grounding for them.

Moral realism is the view that in some sense there is an objective moral reality; realism thus asserts that morality is objective. It also seems undeniable, however, that morality provides us with reasons for action. But the standard picture of human psychology suggests that to have a reason for action we must have a desire; and desires seem to be subjective, in that one person's desire may not resemble the desires of another. That difficulty for realism is the theme of this article.

moral decisions that combine elements of Kantian and utilitarian thinking. Unlike the other meta-ethical theories discussed in this Part, universal prescriptivism is of relatively recent origin; it is here outlined by its creator and leading exponent.

Do we develop morally, as we develop psychologically? This may not seem to be a question about the nature of ethics, but the answer we give is directly relevant to central issues about the nature of ethics. If human beings generally pass through stages of moral development corresponding to their psychological development, and if it could be shown that these stages are the same for all of us, this would be persuasive evidence that morality is not purely subjective or culturally relative.

The final essay in this section differs from the others, in that its topic is not the nature of ethics, but the nature of moral theory: that is, of the kinds of theories of ethics put forward in Part IV of this volume. How can we construct such theories, and argue that one is better than another? Two different models are proposed and discussed. The widespread use of hypothetical and imaginary examples in deciding between theories is also addressed.

PART VII: CHALLENGE AND CRITIQUE

Subjectivism and relativism, discussed in Part VI, deny that ethics has any objective or universal validity; but these are not the only challenges that defenders of ethics have had to meet. There have been other attempts, based on specific philosophical positions, to show that morality is merely the instrument of the dominant group in society, or is all an illusion, or is meaningless in the absence of religion. The articles in this Part take up some of these challenges.

Is there something distinctively male about ethics, or about the way in which we currently understand ethics? The suggestion that there is has been made by recent feminist writers; but what would a 'female ethic' be like? Is ethics really something that can properly take forms that differ according to gender?

Darwin's theory of evolution tells us that we owe our existence to millions of years of evolution in which organisms that left more descendants survived, and those that did not perished. Can we reconcile ethics with such a process? Does evolution imply that our morality should allow the weak to go under? Or more drastically, that we should reject morality altogether?

According to Marx, the morality of a society reflects its economic basis, and serves the interests of the ruling class. At the same time Marx condemned capitalism in terms that suggest strongly-held values. Is Marx inconsistent? If not, what substance is there in the Marxist challenge to morality?

It is often said that without God, there can be no morality. This essay examines different grounds for holding that belief: that the very meaning of 'good' and 'bad' stem from God's will; that only through God can we come to know what is good; and that only belief in God can serve to motivate us to act morally.

The entire apparatus of moral decision-making, praise and blame, reward and punishment, seems to be premised on the assumption that in normal circumstances we are responsible for what we freely choose to do. Determinists maintain that there is a causal explanation for everything that happens in the universe, human behaviour included. This seems to suggest that we do not freely choose to do anything, and this in turn appears to imply that we are not morally responsible for anything we do. Are ethics and determinism incompatible?

Contributors

Brenda Almond is Reader in Philosophy and Education at the University of Hull. She is Joint Editor of the *Journal of Applied Philosophy*. Her books include *Moral Concerns* and *The Philosophical Quest*.

Kurt Baier teaches in the Department of Philosophy at the University of Pittsburgh. He is the author of *The Moral Point of View*, and works in the field of moral, political and legal philosophy.

Raymond A. Belliotti is a philosophy professor at S U N Y Fredonia State University, and is also an attorney. His articles in the areas of philosophy of law, political philosophy and ethics have appeared in numerous journals.

Jonathan Berg is a Lecturer in Philosophy at the University of Haifa and works mainly in philosophical logic and applied philosophy.

Puruṣottama Bilimoria teaches in the School of Humanities at Deakin University in Victoria, Australia. He is the author of *Sabdapramāña: Word and Knowledge*. He works in the fields of Indian philosophy, ethics, cross-cultural hermeneutics and philosophy of religion, and edits a book series on *Indian Thought*.

Bernard Boxill teaches in the Department of Philosophy at the University of North Carolina at Chapel Hill. He is the author of *Blacks and Social Justice*, and works in the field of political philosophy.

Stephen Buckle is a Lecturer in Philosophy at La Trobe University, Victoria, Australia. He is the author of *Natural Law and the Theory of Property: Grotius to Hume*, and co-editor of *Embryo Experimentation*.

C. A. J. Coady is Boyce Gibson Professor of Philosophy and Director of the Centre for Philosophy and Public Issues at the University of Melbourne. He has published extensively in epistemology, ethics and political philosophy and has a particular interest in questions to do with political violence.

Jonathan Dancy is Reader in Philosophy at the University of Keele. He is the author of *An Introduction to Contemporary Epistemology* and *Berkeley: an Introduction*, and of a forthcoming book on moral theory.

Nancy Davis (who publishes under 'Nancy' but answers to 'Ann') is an Associate Professor of Philosophy and an Associate of the Center for Values and Social Policy at the University of Colorado at Boulder. Her interests and publications lie primarily in moral theory, applied ethics (including bioethics) and moral methodology.

M. W. Padmasiri de Silva, formerly Professor of Philosophy at the University of Peradeniya, Sri Lanka, now teaches philosophy at the National University of Singapore. His publications include *Buddhist and Freudian Psychology*, *An Introduction to Buddhist Psychology* and *Tangles and Webs*.

Nigel Dower teaches in the Department of Philosophy at the University of Aberdeen. He is the author of *World Poverty – Challenge and Response*, and editor of *Ethics and Environmental Responsibility*, and has a general interest in the ethics of international relations.

Robert Elliot teaches in the Department of Philosophy at the University of New England, Armidale, Australia. He is a co-editor of *Environmental Ethics: A Collection of Readings*, and has published articles on environmental ethics, meta-ethics, philosophy of education and philosophy of mind.

Robert Goodin is Professorial Fellow in Philosophy at the Research School of Social Sciences, Australian National University. He is Associate Editor of the journal *Ethics*, and author of various books in political theory and applied ethics, including most recently *No Smoking: The Ethical Issues*.

Jean Grimshaw teaches in the Department of Humanities, Bristol Polytechnic. She is the author of *Feminist Philosophers: Women's Perspectives on Philosophical Traditions*, and works in the fields of philosophy, cultural studies and women's studies.

Lori Gruen is currently working on a Ph.D. in Philosophy at the University of Colorado, Boulder, where she is affiliated with the Center for Values and Social Policy. She is the co-author of *Animal Liberation: A Graphic Guide*; has published articles on ethical issues concerning women, animals, and the environment; and has written on feminism and science.

John Haldane is Reader in Moral Philosophy at the University of St Andrews, where he is also Director of the Centre for Philosophy and Public Affairs. He has published widely in many areas of philosophy.

Chad Hansen is a professor of Philosophy at the University of Vermont. He has spent over seven years in Asia and speaks Cantonese, Mandarin and Japanese. His publications include *Language and Logic in Ancient China* and *A Daoist Theory of Chinese Thought*, along with numerous articles on Chinese philosophy.

R. M. Hare is Graduate Research Professor in the University of Florida and White's Professor of Moral Philosophy Emeritus in the University of Oxford. His books include *The Language of Morals*, *Freedom and Reason*, and *Moral Thinking*.

Dale Jamieson is Associate Professor and Director of the Centre for Values and Social Policy at the University of Colorado. He has published many articles in various areas of philosophy, and is co-editor of *Interpretation and Explanation in the Study of Animal Behavior*.

Menachem Kellner teaches in the Department of Jewish History and Thought at the University of Haifa. He is the editor of *Contemporary Jewish Ethics*, translator of *Isaac Abravanel's Principles of Faith*, and author of *Dogma in Medieval Jewish Thought, Maimonides on Human Perfection, Maimonides on Judaism and the Jewish People*, and essays on medieval and modern Jewish thought.

Helga Kuhse is a Senior Research Fellow at the Centre for Human Bioethics at Monash University. She is the author of *The Sanctity-of-Life Doctrine in Medicine* and (with Peter Singer) of *Should the Baby Live?*

Will Kymlicka holds a Canada Research Fellowship at the University of Toronto. He is the author of *Liberalism, Community, and Culture* and *Contemporary Political Philosophy*.

Hugh LaFollette is Professor of Philosophy at East Tennessee State University. He has published essays in ethics and political philosophy and is currently completing a book entitled *Just Good Friends*.

Gerald A. Larue is Emeritus Professor of Biblical History and Archaeology, and Adjunct Professor of Gerontology at the University of Southern California, Los Angeles. His most recent publication is *Ancient Myth and Modern Life*.

Jeff McMahan is Assistant Professor of Philosophy at the University of Illinois at Urbana. He is currently working on two forthcoming books, *The Ethics of Killing* and *The Ethics of War and Nuclear Deterrence*.

Mary Midgley, formerly Senior Lecturer in Philosophy at the University of Newcastle on Tyne, is the author of *Beast and Man, Wickedness* and other books on problems concerned with ethics, evolution and human nature.

Azim Nanji is Professor and Chair in the Department of Religion at the University of Florida. He specializes in the study of Muslim culture and thought and is the author of various books, chapters and articles on Islam and comparative topics. His most recent publications deal with Muslim ethical and cultural values in historical and modern contexts.

Onora O'Neill teaches in the Department of Philosophy at the University of Essex. She is the author of *Faces of Hunger* and *Constructions of Reason*, and works on ethics, political philosophy and the philosophy of Immanuel Kant.

Gregory Pence holds joint appointments in Medicine and Philosophy at the University of Alabama. He has published *Classic Cases in Medical Ethics* and a critical survey of work on virtues.

Philip Pettit holds a Personal Chair at the Research School of Social Sciences at the Australian National University. Among his recent publications is a book entitled *Not Just Deserts: A Republican Theory of Criminal Justice*, co-authored with John Braithwaite.

Charles R. Pigden teaches in the Department of Philosophy at the University of Otago. His papers include 'Logic and the autonomy of ethics' and 'Anscombe on "ought"'. He is interested in meta-ethics, the philosophy of logic, and the philosophy of literature.

Ronald Preston, formerly Canon Theologian of Manchester Cathedral, is Professor Emeritus of Social and Pastoral Theology at the University of Manchester. His books include *Religion and the Persistence of Capitalism, Church and Society in the Late Twentieth Century,* and *The Future of Christian Ethics.*

James Rachels is Professor of Philosophy at the University of Alabama at Birmingham. He is the author of *The End of Life: Euthanasia and Morality* and *Created from Animals: The Moral Implications of Darwinism.*

Christopher Rowe holds a Personal Chair in Ancient Philosophy and Greek at the University of Bristol. He is the author of *Plato* and a commentary on Plato's *Phaedrus;* his work is mainly on Plato, and on Aristotle's ethical and political philosophy.

Michael Ruse teaches in the Philosophy and Zoology Departments at the University of Guelph, Ontario. His most recent book is *The Darwinian Paradigm: Essays on its History, Philosophy and Religious Implications.* At the moment he is writing a book on the concept of progress in evolutionary biology.

J. B. Schneewind, Chair of the Philosophy Department at The Johns Hopkins University, is author of *Sidgwick's Ethics and Victorian Moral Philosophy* and editor of *Moral Philosophy from Montaigne to Kant.*

George Silberbauer, formerly a District Commissioner and Bushman Survey officer in Botswana, is now in the Department of Anthropology and Sociology at Monash University. He is the author of *Bushman Survey Report, Hunter and Habitat in the Central Kalahari Desert* and *Cazadores del Desierto,* and works in the areas of disaster management, socio-ecology and philosophy of social science.

Peter Singer is Professor of Philosophy and Director of the Centre for Human Bioethics at Monash University, Melbourne. His books include *Democracy and Disobedience, Animal Liberation, Practical Ethics, The Expanding Circle, Marx, Hegel, The Reproduction Revolution* (with Deane Wells) and *Should the Baby Live?* (with Helga Kuhse). With Helga Kuhse he now edits *Bioethics,* an international journal published by Basil Blackwell.

Michael Smith teaches in the Department of Philosophy at Monash University, and has taught previously at the University of Oxford and Princeton University. He is the author of *The Moral Problem* (forthcoming), as well as several papers in ethics and moral psychology.

Robert C. Solomon is Quincy Lee Centennial Professor of Philosophy at the University of Texas at Austin. He is the author of several books about business ethics including *Above the Bottom Line, It's Good Business* and *Ethics and Excellence.* He is also the author of *The Passions, In the Spirit of Hegel, About Love* and *A Passion for Justice.*

C. L. Ten is Reader in Philosophy at Monash University. He is the author of *Mill on Liberty* and *Crime, Guilt, and Punishment*.

Laurence Thomas teaches in the Philosophy and Political Science Departments at Syracuse University, and is the author of *Living Morally: A Psychology of Moral Character* (Temple University Press, 1979), as well as numerous articles in moral and social philosophy.

Mary Anne Warren teaches in the Department of Philosophy at San Francisco State University. Her publications include *The Nature of Woman: An Encyclopedia and Guide to the Literature* and *Gendercide: The Implications of Sex Selection*.

David B. Wong teaches in the Department of Philosophy at Brandeis University. He is the author of *Moral Relativity*, and works in ethical theory, the history of philosophy, comparative ethics and Chinese philosophy.

Allen Wood is Professor of Philosophy at Cornell University. He is the author of numerous books and articles, chiefly in the field of the history of eighteenth- and nineteenth-century German philosophy, including *Kant's Moral Religion, Kant's Rational Theology, Karl Marx* and *Hegel's Ethical Thought*.

Robert Young is a member of the Department of Philosophy at La Trobe University, Melbourne. His publications have been in the philosophy of religion, metaphysics, ethics, social and political philosophy.

PART I
THE ROOTS

I

The origin of ethics

MARY MIDGLEY

i The search for justification

WHERE does ethics come from? Two very different questions are combined here, one about historical fact and the other about authority. Anxiety about both questions has been active in shaping many traditional myths about the origin of the universe. These myths describe, not only how human life began, but also why it is so hard, so painful, so confusing, so conflict-ridden. The primal clashes and disasters they tell of are intended – perhaps often primarily intended – to explain why human beings have to live by rules which can frustrate their desires. Both these questions are still pressing. And in the last few centuries, theorists have tried strenuously to answer them in more literal and systematic terms.

This quest does not flow just from curiosity, nor just from the hope of proving the rules unnecessary, though both are strong motives. It perhaps arises centrally from conflicts within ethics, or morality, itself. (I shall make no distinction between these two words for the very general purposes of this article.) In any culture, accepted duties sometimes clash, and deeper, more general principles are needed to arbitrate between them. People look for the point of the different rules involved, and try to weigh these points against each other. This search often forces them to look, more widely still, for a supreme arbiter – the point of morality as a whole.

This is why our original question is so complex. Asking where ethics comes from is not like asking the same question about meteorites. It is asking why we should now obey its rules. (Rules are not actually the whole of morality, but we can concentrate on them for the moment, because they are often the point where conflicts arise.) In order to answer this question, it is necessary to imagine what life would be like without these rules, and this inevitably does raise questions about origins. People tend to look backwards, asking whether there was once an 'unfallen' conflict-free state before the rules were imposed, a state where rules were not needed, perhaps because nobody ever wanted to do anything bad. They then ask 'How did we come to lose this pre-ethical condition? Can we get back to it?'

In our own culture, two sweeping answers to these questions have been widely accepted. One – coming predominantly from the Greeks and from Hobbes – explains ethics simply as a device of egoistic prudence; its origin-myth is the social contract. It sees the pre-ethical state as one of solitude; the primal disaster being that people ever began to meet each other at all. Once they did, conflict was inevitable, and the state of nature was then, as Hobbes put it, 'a war of every man against every man' (Hobbes, 1651, Part One, Ch. 13, p. 64) even if, as Rousseau insisted, they had not been actually hostile to each other before colliding (Rousseau, 1762, pp. 188, 194; 1754, Part One). Survival itself, let alone social order, became possible only through rules arrived at by a reluctant bargain. (This story was of course usually seen as symbolical, not as literal history.) The other account, which is Christian, explains morality as our necessary attempt to bring our imperfect nature in line with the will of God. Its origin-myth is the Fall of Man, which has produced that imperfection in our nature in the way described – again symbolically – in the Book of Genesis.

Simplicity itself is always welcome in a confusing world, so the popularity of these two accounts is not surprising. But simple accounts cannot really explain complex facts, and it has already become clear that neither of these sweeping formulae can really deal with our questions. The Christian account shifts the problem rather than solving it, since we still need to know why we should obey God. Christian teaching has of course plenty to say about this, but what it says is complex, and cannot keep its attractive simplicity once the question about authority is raised. I cannot discuss further here the very important relations between ethics and religion (see Article 46, HOW COULD ETHICS DEPEND ON RELIGION?). But it is important that this Christian answer does not just derive our duty to obey God naively from his position as an all-powerful being who has created us – a derivation which would not confer moral authority. If a bad being had created us for bad purposes, we should not think we had a *duty* to obey that being, whatever prudence might dictate. The idea of God is not just the idea of such a being, but crystallizes a whole mass of very complex ideals and standards that lie behind moral rules and give them their meaning. But the authority of these ideals and standards is just what we are enquiring about. So that question is still with us.

ii The lure of egoism and the social contract

The notion that ethics is really just a contract based on egoistic prudence is indeed much simpler, but for that very reason it is far too unrealistic to account for the actual complexities of ethics. It may be true that a society of perfectly consistent prudent egoists, if it ever existed, would invent institutions for mutual insurance which would look like many of those found in actual human societies. And it certainly is true that these careful egoists would avoid many of the atrocities that actual human beings commit, because human rashness and folly notoriously and constantly magnify the bad effects of our vices.

But this cannot mean that morality, as it actually exists anywhere, arises only from this calculating self-interest. There are several reasons why this is impossible, but I shall mention only two. (For further discussion, see Article 16, EGOISM.)

(1) The first rests on an obvious human defect. People simply are not so prudent or consistent as this account would imply. Even the very moderate amount of deliberately decent conduct that is actually found in human life would not be possible if it relied solely on these traits.

(2) The second is an equally well-known range of human good qualities. People who do make an effort to behave decently plainly are often moved by a quite different set of motives, arising directly out of consideration for the claims of others. They act from a sense of justice, from friendship, loyalty, compassion, gratitude, generosity, sympathy, family affection and the like – qualities that are recognized and honoured in most human societies. Egoist theorizers such as Hobbes sometimes explain this by claiming that these alleged motives are unreal, only empty names. But it is hard to see how names could ever have been invented, and have become current, for non-existent motives. And it is still more puzzling how anyone could ever have successfully pretended to be moved by them.

I have mentioned this egoistic explanation at once because, in spite of its crying defects, it is very influential today. In asking about the origin of ethics, modern people are quite likely to find themselves unthinkingly using its language. They will pose their question in the Hobbesian form, 'How did an original society of egoists ever come to find itself lumbered with rules that required consideration for others?' The crippling difficulties that infest this approach will become clearer as we go on.

iii   Moral and factual arguments

We might be asked to accept extreme individualism on strictly scientific grounds, as a factual discovery. It then appears as a piece of information about how human beings are actually constituted. Today, the most usual form for this argument rests on the idea of evolution as proceeding, for all species, by the 'survival of the fittest' in unmitigated cut-throat competition between individuals. That process is held to have shaped them into isolated, wholly egoistic social atoms. This picture is often conceived to rest so directly on evidence as to be – unlike all earlier stories about origins – not a myth at all but wholly scientific.

We should be sceptical about this claim. In the crude form just cited, the pseudo-Darwinian myth contains at least as much emotive symbolism from current ideologies and as much propaganda for limited, contemporary social ideals as does its predecessor the Social Contract story. It does also incorporate some genuine scientific evidence and principles, but it ignores and distorts a great deal more than it uses. It is particularly remote from current science on two issues: first, its fantasy-ridden, over-dramatized notion of competition, and second, the strangely predominant place that it gives to our own species in the evolutionary process.

(1) It is essential to distinguish the mere fact of happening to 'compete' from the complex of human motives which current ideology endorses as fitting for competitors. Any two organisms may be said to be 'in competition' if they both need or want something they cannot both get. But they are not acting competitively unless they both know this and respond by deliberately trying to defeat each other. Since the overwhelming majority of organisms are plants, bacteria etc. which are not even conscious, the very possibility of deliberate, hostile competition is an extremely rare thing in nature. Moreover, both at the conscious

5

and the unconscious level, all life-processes depend on an immense background of harmonious co-operation, which is necessary to build up the complex system within which the much rarer phenomenon of competition becomes possible. Competition is real but necessarily limited. For instance, the plants in a particular ecosystem normally exist in interdependence both with each other and with the animals that eat them, and those animals are equally interdependent with each other and with their predators. If there had really been a natural 'war of all against all', the biosphere could never have developed in the first place. It is not surprising therefore that conscious life, arising out of such a background, acts in fact in a way that is much more often co-operative than competitive. And when we come shortly to consider the motivation of social creatures, we shall clearly see that co-operative motivations supply the main structure of their behaviour.

(2) Many popular versions of the pseudo-Darwinian myth (though not all) present the evolutionary process as a pyramid or ladder existing for the purpose of producing MAN as its apex, and sometimes as programmed to develop MAN further to some distant 'omega point' which will further glorify contemporary Western human ideals. This notion has no basis in today's genuine biological theory (Midgley, 1985). Current biology depicts life-forms quite differently, on the pattern sketched out by Darwin in the *Origin of Species*, as spreading, bush-like, from a common source to fill the available niches, without any special 'upward' direction. The pyramid picture was proposed by J.-B. Lamarck and developed by Teilhard de Chardin; it does not belong to modern science at all but to traditional metaphysics. Of course that does not refute it. But since the views of human nature associated with it have been widely seen as 'scientific', the point is of some importance for us in assessing the standing of these views, and relating them to our questions about the origin of ethics.

iv Dualistic fantasies

These questions have begun to look harder since it became generally accepted that our species took its rise from others which we class as merely 'animals'. In our culture, the species-barrier has commonly been seen as being also the boundary of the moral realm, and metaphysical doctrines have been built to protect this boundary. Christians, unlike Buddhists, have believed that souls, the seat of all the faculties that we honour, belong only to human beings. Any emphasis on the relationship between our own and other species was seen as degrading us, as suggesting that our spirituality was 'really' only a set of animal reactions. This idea of animality as a foreign principle quite alien to spirit is an ancient one, often used to dramatize psychological conflicts as raging between the virtues and 'the beast within'. The human soul then appears as an isolated intruder in the physical cosmos, a stranger far from its home.

This sharp and simple dualism was important to Plato, and to early Christian thinking. It is probably much less influential today. Its contemptuous attitude to natural motives has not worn well, and on the theoretical side it faces enormous difficulties in explaining the relation between soul and body. Yet dualism still seems to be used as a background framework for certain topics, notably for our thought about other animals. Aristotle countered Plato by proposing a much less divisive, more reconciliatory metaphysic to bring together the various aspects both of human individuality and of the outside world. St Thomas followed this lead, and recent thought has in general been moving the same way. But this more monistic approach has encountered great difficulty in conceiving how human beings could actually have developed out of non-human animals. The trouble was that those animals were viewed as symbols of anti-human forces, indeed often simply as embodied vices (wolf, pig, raven). Until this view was challenged, only two alternatives seemed open – either a depressed, reductive view of humans as 'no better than the other animals', or a purely other-worldly view of them as spirits inserted during the evolutionary process into bodies to which they were quite unrelated. (See Midgley, 1979, Ch. 2.)

Hence come the two simple ideas mentioned earlier about the origin of ethics. On the social contract pattern all animate beings equally were egoists, and human beings were distinctive only in their calculating intelligence. They were merely the first *enlightened* egoists. On the religious view, by contrast, the insertion of souls introduced, at a stroke, not just intelligence but also a vast range of new notivation, much of it altruistic. To Darwin's distress, his collaborator A. R. Wallace adopted this second view, arguing that God must have added souls to emerging primate bodies by miraculous intervention during the course of evolution. And today, even among non-religious thinkers, there is still often found an intense exaltation of human capacities which treats them as something totally different in kind from those of all other animals, to an extent which seems to demand a different, non-terrestrial source. Indeed, science-fiction accounts of a derivation from some distant planet are occasionally invoked with apparent seriousness to meet this supposed need.

v The advantages of ethology

We can, however, avoid both these bad alternatives today by simply taking a more realistic, less mythical view of non-human animals. In our own time, their behaviour has at last been systematically studied, and the rich, complex nature of social life among many birds and mammals is now becoming a matter of common knowledge. People indeed have long known something about it, though they did not use that knowledge when they thought of animals as incarnations of evil. Thus, two centuries ago Kant wrote, 'The more we come in contact with animals the more we love them, for we see how great is their care for their young. It is then difficult for us to be cruel in thought even to a wolf.'

Social traits like parental care, co-operative foraging and reciprocal kindness show plainly that such creatures are not in fact crude, exclusive egoists, but beings who have evolved the strong and special motivations needed to form and maintain a simple society. Mutual grooming, mutual removal of parasites and mutual protection are common among social mammals and birds. They have not produced these habits by using those powers of prudent selfish calculation which the Social

Contract story views as the mechanism necessary for such a feat, since they do not possess them. Wolves, beavers, jackdaws, and other social creatures, including all our primate relatives, do not build their societies by wily calculation from a Hobbesian 'state of nature', an original war of all against all. They are able to live together, and sometimes to co-operate in remarkable tasks of hunting, building, joint protection or the like, simply because they are naturally disposed to love and trust one another.

This affection becomes evident in the unmistakable misery of any social animal, from a horse or a dog to a chimpanzee, if it is kept in isolation. Though they often ignore each other and will indeed in certain circumstances compete with and attack each other, they do this against a wider background of friendly acceptance. Devoted care of the young, often including real self-denial over food, is widespread and is often shared by other helpers besides the parents. (It may perhaps be seen as the original matrix of morality). Some creatures, notably elephants, will adopt orphans. Defence of the weak by the strong is common and there are many well-attested examples of cases where the defenders have paid for it with their lives. Old and helpless birds are sometimes fed. Reciprocal help among friends is often seen. All this is by now not a matter of folklore but of detailed, systematic, well-researched record. And there surely is every reason to accept that in this matter human beings closely resemble all their nearest relatives. (For the anthropological evidence of this, see Konner, 1982.)

vi Two objections

Before we examine the link between these natural dispositions and human moral-ity, two possible contrary ideological objections to this approach must be considered. There is the behaviourist thesis that *human beings have no natural dispositions at all*, being blank paper at birth, and the sociobiological reply that *social dispositions do exist, but are all in some sense 'selfish'*. (Readers not interested in these ideologies could skip this discusssion.)

(1) The behaviourist thesis was, I think, always an obvious exaggeration. The idea of a purely passive, motiveless infant never made sense. The exaggeration had a serious moral point – namely, to reject certain dangerous ideas about just what the innate tendencies were, ideas which were used to justify institutions such as war, racism and slavery. But these were ideological *misrepresentations* of the human heritage. It has proved much better to attack them on their own ground, without the crippling difficulties imposed by espousing so unconvincing a story as the Blank Paper theory.

(2) Over sociobiology, the trouble is really one of wording. Sociobiologists use the word 'selfish' in a quite extraordinary way, to mean, roughly, 'gene-promoting; likely to increase the future survival and spread of an organism's genes'. They are saying that the traits actually transmitted in evolution must be ones which do this work, which is true. By using the language of 'selfishness' however, they inescapably link this harmless idea to the still powerful egoist pseudo-Darwinian myth, since the word *selfish* is entirely a description of motive –

not just of consequences – and its central meaning is the negative one that one does *not* care for others. Sociobiologists do sometimes point out that this is a technical use of the word, but nearly all of them get carried away by its normal meaning and may be heard preaching egoism as ardently as Hobbes. (See Wilson, 1975, also Midgley, 1979 – index s.v. Wilson – and Midgley, 1985, Ch. 14.)

vii Sociability, conflict and the origins of morality

Having said something to meet these objections to the idea that humans have natural social dispositions, we ask next, what relation have these dispositions to morality? They do not constitute it, but they surely do contribute something essential to making it possible. Do they perhaps supply, as it were, the raw material of the moral life – the general motivations which lead towards it and give it its rough direction – while still needing the work of intelligence, and especially speech, to organize it, to contribute its form? This suggestion was sketched out by Darwin, in a remarkable passage which uses central ideas from Aristotle, Hume and Kant (Darwin, 1859, Vol. 1, Part 1, Ch. 3. This discussion has so far had little attention because versions of the noisy pseudo-Darwinian myth were widely accepted as the only evolutionary approach to ethics).

By this account, the relation of the natural social motives to morality would be much like that of natural curiosity to science, or of natural wonder and admiration to art. Natural affections do not of themselves create rules – indeed, it might seem that in an unfallen state they would make rules unnecessary. But in our actual, imperfect state, these affections often conflict with each other, or with other strong and important motives. In non-human animals, those conflicts may be settled simply by further second-order natural dispositions. But beings who reflect much on their own and each others' lives, as we do, need to arbitrate these conflicts somehow in a way that makes their lives feel reasonably coherent and continuous. To do this we set priorities between different aims, and this means accepting lasting principles or rules. (It is, of course, not clear at all that other social creatures are totally non-reflective, since much of our own reflection is non-verbal, but we cannot discuss their situation here. On the very complex primate situation, see Desmond 1979.)

Darwin illustrated the difference between the reflective and non-reflective predicaments in the case of a swallow, which can desert the young it has been devotedly feeding without apparent hesitation when its flock migrates. (Darwin, 1859, pp. 84, 91.) As he points out, someone blessed or cursed with a much longer memory and a more active imagination could not do this without agonizing conflict. And there is a most interesting difference between the two motives involved. An impulse which is violent but temporary – in this case migration – is opposed to a habitual feeling, much weaker at any one time, but stronger in that it is far more persistent and lies deeper in the character. Darwin thought that the rules chosen would tend to arbitrate in favour of the milder but more persistent motives, because violating them would lead to much longer and more distressing remorse later on.

9

In searching, then, for the special force possessed by 'the imperious word *ought*' (p. 92), he pointed to the clash between these social affections and the strong but temporary motives which often oppose them. Intelligent beings would, he concluded, naturally try to produce rules which would protect the priority of the first group. He therefore thought it exceedingly likely that 'any animal whatever, endowed with well-marked social instincts, would inevitably acquire a moral sense or conscience, as soon as its intellectual powers had become as well-developed, or anything like as well-developed, as in man' (p. 72). Thus 'the social instincts – the prime principle of man's moral constitution – with the aid of active intellectual powers and the effects of habit, naturally lead to the Golden Rule, "As ye would that men should do unto you, do ye to them likewise" and this lies at the foundation of morality' (p. 106).

viii   The problem of partiality

How convincing is this? Of course we cannot test Darwin's generalization empirically; we have not communicated well enough with any non-human species that we recognize as sufficiently intelligent. (It might be immensely helpful, for instance, if we could hear something from the whales ...) We must simply compare the cases. How suitable do these traits in other social creatures seem to be to furnish material that could develop into something like human morality?

Some objectors rule them out of court entirely because they occur fitfully, and their incidence is strongly biased in favour of close kin. But this same fitfulness and this same bias towards kin prevail to some extent – often very powerfully – in all human morality. They are strong among the small hunter-gatherer societies that seem closest to the original human condition. People growing up in such circumstances are of course in general surrounded – just as young wolves or chimpanzees are – by those who actually *are* their kin, so that the normal attitude they acquire to those around them is, in varying degrees, one which makes wider concern and sympathy possible.

But it is important to notice that this bias does not vanish, it does not even become noticeably weaker, with the development of civilization. It is still fully active in our own culture. If any modern parents were to give no more care and affection to their own children than they did to all others, they would be perceived as monsters. We quite naturally spend our resources freely on meeting even the minor needs of our close families and friends before considering even the grave needs of outsiders. It strikes us as normal for human parents to spend more on toys for their children than they spend in a year on aid to the destitute. Human society does indeed make some provision for outsiders, but in doing so it starts from the same strong bias towards kin which shapes animal societies.

This same consideration applies to another, parallel objection often brought against treating animal sociability as a possible source of morality, namely the bias towards reciprocity. It is true that, if we were dealing with calculating egoists, the mere returning of benefits to those who had formerly given them might be nothing but a prudent bargain. But again, in all existing human moralities this transaction appears in quite a different light, not just as insurance for the future but as appropriate gratitude owed for kindness shown in the past, and as flowing naturally from the affection that goes with it. There is no reason why this should not be equally true of other social creatures.

It is quite true that these narrowing biases need to be – and gradually are – systematically corrected by the recognition of wider duties as human morality develops (see Singer, 1981). This widening, however, is surely the contribution of the human intelligence, gradually developing wider social horizons as it devises institutions. It is not and cannot be a substitute for the original natural affections themselves. A certain narrowness in those affections is only to be expected, since in evolution they have served the essential function of making possible strenuous and devoted provision for the young. This could not have been effectively done if all parents had cared as much for every passing infant as they did for their own. In such a casual, impartial regime, probably few warm-blooded infants would survive. Thus, as the sociobiologists rightly point out, heritable altruistic dispositions are not easily passed on unless they make possible an increase in the survival of the altruist's own kin, who share the gene that gives rise to them. But when that does occur, it becomes possible for such traits to develop and to spread through 'kin selection', in a way that did not seem conceivable on the older, crude model that only considered competition for survival between individuals.

ix Is morality reversible?

If, then, these dispositions are indeed not disqualified by their narrowness from serving as essential material for the development of morality, does Darwin's picture become a convincing one? There is surely great force in his suggestion that what makes morality necessary is conflict – that an 'unfallen' harmonious state would not require it. If this is right, then the idea of 'immoralism' as the proposal to get rid of morality (Nietzsche, 1886, 1, section 32) would involve making everybody somehow conflict-free. Unless that were done, we need priority-rules, not just because they make society smoother, nor even just to make it possible at all, but also more deeply, to avoid lapsing individually into states of helpless, conflict-torn confusion. In some sense, this is 'the origin of ethics' and our search need take us no further.

It may, however, seem less clear just which kind of priorities these rules are bound to express. Is Darwin right in expecting them on the whole to favour the social affections, and to validate the Golden Rule? Or is this just a cultural prejudice? Might a morality be found which was the mirror-image of our own, counting our virtues as vices and our vices as virtues, and demanding generally that we should do to others just what we would least want done to ourselves (a suggestion for which also Nietzsche sometimes wished to make room)?

Now it is of course true that cultures vary vastly, and since Darwin's day we have become much more aware of that variation. Yet anthropologists, who did the world a huge service by demonstrating that variability, are now pointing out that it should not be exaggerated (Konner, 1982; Mead, 1956). Different human societies do have many deep structural elements in common. If they did not, no mutual understanding would be possible at all, and indeed it would scarcely have been possible to do anthropology. Among those elements, the kind of consideration and sympathy for others that is generalized by the Golden Rule plays a central part, and if we ask 'Could there be a culture without that attitude?' we may find real difficulty in imagining how it would count as a culture at all. The mere mutual terror of co-existing egoistic solitaries that Hobbes invoked for his Social Contract could certainly never produce one. Common standards, common ideals, common tastes, common priorities that make a common morality possible, rest on shared joys and sorrows and all require active sympathy. Morality needs, not just conflicts, but a willingness and a capacity to look for shared solutions to them. As much as language, it seems to be something that could only occur among naturally social beings. (For more discussion of the common elements of human culture, see Article 2, ETHICS IN SMALL-SCALE SOCIETIES.)

x Conclusion

This account of the origin of ethics is intended to avoid on the one hand the unrealistic, reductive abstractions of egoist theorizing, and on the other the equally unreal, moralistic boasting that tends to make the whole origin of human beings as a terrestrial primate species look incomprehensible. It does not equate human morality with anything found among other social creatures. It is always a fallacy (the 'genetic fallacy') to equate any product with its source – to say 'that flower is really only organized dirt'. Morality as it emerges from this matrix is what it is.

References

Darwin, C.: *The Descent of Man* (1859); (London: Princeton University Press, 1981).
Desmond, A.: *The Ape's Reflexion* (London: Blond and Briggs, 1979).
Hobbes, T.: *Leviathan* (London: 1651); Everyman edition (London: Dent and Dutton 1914).
Kant, I.: *Lectures on Ethics*; trans. L. Infield (London: Methuen, 1930), p. 239.
Konner, M.: *The Tangled Wing; Biological Constraints on the Human Spirit* (London: Heinemann, 1982).
Mead, M.: *New Lives for Old* (London: Gollancz, 1956).
Midgley, M.: *Beast and Man, The Roots of Human Nature* (Harvester Press: Hassocks, 1979).
——: *Evolution As A Religion* (London and New York: Methuen, 1985).
Nietzsche, F.: *Beyond Good and Evil* (1886); trans. R. J. Hollingdale (Harmondsworth: Penguin Classics, 1973).
——: *On The Genealogy of Morals* (1887); trans. Walter Kaufman and R. J. Hollingdale (New York: Vintage Books, 1969).
Rousseau, J.-J.: *The Social Contract* (1762) and *Dissertation on the Origin of Inequality* (1754); Everyman edition (London: Dent and Dutton, 1930).
Singer, P.: *The Expanding Circle; Ethics and Sociobiology* (Oxford: Clarendon Press, 1981).
Wilson, E. O.: *Sociobiology, The New Synthesis* (Cambridge, Mass.: Harvard University Press, 1985).

Further reading

Bellah, R. et al.: *Habits of the Heart; Middle America Observed* (London: Hutchinson, 1988).

Kohn, A.: *No Contest; The Case Against Competition, Why We Lose in our Race to Win* (Boston: Houghton Mifflin Co., 1986).

2

Ethics in small-scale societies

GEORGE SILBERBAUER

A SMALL-SCALE society is one whose members are to be counted in tens of thousands, or even hundreds, rather than in millions. Largely or wholly-non-industrial, its technology is centred on agricultural or pastoral production for consumption within the society, or on hunting and gathering. No society is isolated but those of small scale tend to be more nearly self-contained and inward-looking than are societies of our own type which are extensively connected to others. Their social relationships are more integrated and close-knit than are ours; people interact with one another in a wider range of roles which requires a more coherent ordering of behaviour. Any one relationship has a wider range of functions – bears a greater 'load' – and its state or condition is correspondingly more important than is the case in our society where many relationships are single-purpose and impersonal, e.g. that between bus-conductor and passenger. But how different it would be if the conductor were also my sister-in-law, near neighbour and the daughter of my father's golfing partner – I would never dare to tender anything other than the correct fare. In a small-scale society every fellow member whom I encounter in my day is likely to be connected to me by a comparable, or even more complex web of strands, each of which must be maintained in its appropriate alignment and tension lest all the others become tangled. My father's missed putts or my inconsiderate use of a motor-mower at daybreak will necessitate very diplomatic behaviour on the bus, or a long walk to work and a dismal dinner on my return.

Social life of this complexity cannot be governed by a book of laws with any more success than mere knowledge of the rules of tennis will improve my rabbit's performance on the court. Relationships are dynamic, not static, and co-ordination of their processes requires many techniques and skills and also direction. As a means of evaluating behaviour in gradations of good or bad a society's ethical and moral system provides some of that direction.

The institutions of small-scale societies, in keeping with the multi-purpose, many-stranded nature of relationships, are also versatile and unspecialized, serving many functions simultaneously. Their ethics are comparably diffuse. These are not to be found formulated in a unitary doctrine, nor are they necessarily explicitly stated as values or principles. The anthropologist studying a small-scale society must go through the slow process of discovering and learning the content, and vernacular view of its members' joint cultural and social creations before finding the ethical meanings carried in, to us, unconventional vehicles like proverbs, riddles, folktales or myths, which initially seem to have significances quite other than the ethical. Eventually, with skill and serendipity the anthropologist can derive the values which the society's members hold in common, the rules of their transformation as principles and precepts and their parameters of relevance as well as the protocols of precedence of one over another. These are peculiar to each society – there are parallels and correspondences but each set of trans-formations is unique. Consequently, although there are values which can be seen as common to nearly all societies, there are sometimes strong contrasts in the ways in which they are expressed in precepts, principles and evaluations of behaviour. Comparison of different societies' ethics must, therefore, take full account of cultural context and vernacular social meaning if it is to be anything more than idle collecting of curiosities.

The task of anthropology is to explain human social and cultural behaviour. In the early stages of its history the discipline was concerned only with small-scale societies, it then being assumed that we knew enough of our own kind of society not to have to explain this kind of behaviour of its members. As research into individual tribes, peasant communities and other small-scale social formations amassed, comparison became increasingly rewarding and revealing. At the same time progress in other social sciences, (particularly sociology, politics and econ-omics) made it clear that there was, indeed, a great deal of social and cultural behaviour in our, and other large-scale societies that called for explanation and that the problems were similar to those which had excited the attention of anthropologists. Anthropology has not only broadened its scope to that of the whole phenomenon of social and cultural behaviour; it has also been much enriched by being able to take the concepts and theories developed from con-templation of our own circumstances and apply them to other societies, and test its own constructs on our own social and cultural behaviour.

The study of the ethics and morals of small-scale societies did not benefit from this cross-fertilization until rather late. One's own morality lies deeply internalized, and it is not easy to overcome ethnocentric prejudice when con-fronted by behaviour which prima facie offends against it. Early anthropolo-gists reacted by dismissing the 'savages' as immoral or, at best, amoral or 'the slaves of custom'. Later fieldwork showed the falseness of this view but the tendency was to consider a people's morality only as a part of their religion. As I have mentioned, and will return to later, the ethics of a small-scale society are not easily fractionated out of the mass of standards and precepts governing the behaviour of its members. It is principally from the attempt to understand vernacular epistemologies and logics of action that the realization has grown that there are well-developed moral and ethical systems embedded in the cultures of small-scale societies.

The constructs of Western moral philosophy cannot be applied to other cultures without some modification. Culture is learned behaviour (and its prod-ucts) to which social meaning is accorded. Meaning is somewhat arbitrary; what is mechanistically the same behaviour will have different meanings in different societies. Even in the same society the meaning will change with context (I may be beaten to pulp in the boxing ring and have to lose with such grace as I can pretend; outside the ring such treatment constitutes criminal battery).

Anthropology interprets behaviour in a culturally relativistic way, in the terms of the society and context in which it occurs. Direct comparisons between cultures cannot be made. When the matrices of meaning of the behaviour have been understood, generalizations can be formulated in an abstract manner analogous with an algebraic equation's standing for a range of particular arithmetic calculations. Only at this generalized level can comparison proceed, including comparison of moralities.

To proceed with direct comparisons is either to abandon one's own moral standards or to condemn the observed practice as immoral. The obligatory brother–sister royal marriages of dynastic Egypt, old Hawaii or the Venda of the northern Transvaal in South Africa, or the ritual incest of the Ronga of southern Mozambique appear abhorrent to foreigners.

The moral significance of behaviour in any society is strongly culture-bound. To choose a cousin as a spouse is, to the Tswana of Botswana, a good and sensible thing to do. A Shona of Zimbabwe would be disgusted by this suggested incest. Greatly simplified, the explanation of this contrast is that the relationship between nieces and nephews and their respective aunts and uncles is of such a nature that Shona cousins are regarded almost as brothers and sisters. Tswana cousins are bound by ties of affection of a different kind; their respective families know each other, and each others' children, thoroughly, and can competently and confidently assess the compatibility of the prospective spouses. In their respective contexts the two opposing moral evaluations of cousin marriage make sense.

With the possible exception of ancient Egypt (see Article 3, ANCIENT ETHICS) the royal brother–sister marriages referred to above were statements of the purity and uniquely exalted status of the couples. Theirs was a purely social and economic, not a sexual, relationship. A royal baby was recognized as the offspring and heir of the king but was not begotten by him. Among the Ronga ritual incest was a mimic performance in which actual intercourse did not occur. Rather than a breach of what is, in fact, a strictly-observed prohibition, the ritual was an indirect affirmation of their sexual morality. To compare directly and judge the ritual by our own values would be as naïvely grotesque a distortion as would be equating a communicant's partaking of the body and blood of Christ with cannibalism.

Anthropologists use many techniques for studying societies. The strategy within which they are applied is that of participant observation. One lives in the society, looking and listening and using the repertoire of theory and research techniques to give direction and enhance the extent and accuracy of seeing and hearing. Consistent with the cultural-relativistic approach and to broaden exploration of the unknown, the anthropologist participates in as many of the ongoing activities as circumstances, the researcher's abilities and the measure of her or his acceptance permit. Fieldwork is largely a matter of learning what everybody else in the society already knows (without necessarily being aware of having that knowledge). It is a survey of a 'space' of unknown dimensions with no prior knowledge of how much there is to be learned. A discovery made today may recast the perceptions and interpretations of all the yesterdays.

Whether a society has an ethical system can be recognized by its having a mental construct of values which are expressed as principles to be invoked and interpreted in guiding social behaviour (i.e. that which has significance and meaning for others) and in judging it in gradations of good or bad. All known societies, judged by this criterion, have ethical systems. It is not necessary that the principles be always successfully invoked, nor that everybody invoke the same ones in coming to judgement, nor is it necessary that judges always concur. It is sufficient that those concerned have shared knowledge of the values, etc. and of their meanings.

In complex, large-scale societies like our own, social institutions are highly elaborated and specialized and, although integrated as components of the whole socio-cultural system, are relatively separate from, and impervious to one another. (However much some may wish it otherwise, business is an economic pursuit; ethics in business are important, but not central to the firm's operations.) In small-scale societies institutions are versatile, serving many functions simultaneously, and are not readily separable, having high levels of mutual relevance. (In such societies an economic exchange may be more highly valued for its social kudos than for the material gain it brings.) The moral system of one of these societies is not to be found in a single, readily identifiable, coherent body of thought. As a category of thought the concept of a moral system is an artefact of our own, and a small number of similar traditions (as is the concept of a philosophy, for that matter). The presence of a notion of good and bad may be diagnostic of the existence of a moral system but its contents will not necessarily be a unitary entity. It is for the culturally-relativistic anthropologist to sort through what is known and understood of the inventory of values, principles and rules governing the people's repertoire of regular, patterned behaviour in order to select functional equivalents of what the moral philosophers include in their domain.

It is easy for the anthropologist to overlook corners of the culture or fail to recognize the ethical in its vernacular guise of what we see as economics, theology, politics, law, etiquette or everyday folk wisdom. Moreover, many values and principles are distilled and crystallized as aphorisms, proverbs or even as riddles. In many non-literate societies such crystallization amounts to an art-form, the terse products of which have many facets and depths of meaning. The Shona proverb, *Murao ndishe*, translates literally as 'the law rules'. One level of its meaning is that none may rule without reck of law and custom; not only must it be followed, it must also be fostered. At a deeper level, custom is the shield of the people against both tyrants and their own self-destructive folly. Customs and laws are made by the people and are the symbolic, as well as organizational embodiment of their unity.

An appropriate equivalent is the Tswana proverb, *Kgosi kekgosi kabatho*, 'the king is (made) king by the people'. In this society, until recently dynastically ruled, the words seem nonsensical. The hidden irony appeals to Tswana humour. There would always be a number of princes qualified for the throne; what gained it for

17

any particular one was the support of the people for him against his royal rivals who would never unite among themselves against him. While kingmakers could also become kingbreakers the proverb served to remind them that it was their choice that the king ruled, and if it had been a poor one, it was their fault as much as the king's. Power of both kings and kingmakers is undone by its inherent vulnerability unless it is used for good.

Sociability appears to be a universal human trait. Hermits are a possible exception but it could be argued that they surround themselves with remembered and imaginary others for comfort and reference. Whether sociability is an instinctual drive as the sociobiologists would have it, or a learned, acquired dependence on others cannot be decided by present knowledge and is fortunately not an issue here.

An apparently necessary condition of sustained relationships in all societies is that that which is done, or given to one should be returned in some way. What varies among and within societies are the vectors of reciprocation (i.e. direct or indirect and, if the latter, via which categories of persons or groups) and methods of evaluating the goods, services or other presentations (e.g. emotional responses) which constitute the exchanges.

Although reciprocity appears to be a universal value from which a variety of principles are derived, not all reciprocations are necessarily included in a society's scheme of morals and ethics. Some forms or contexts of exchange are considered to be of purely economic, political or legal significance. This distinction is less common in small-scale societies. Exchanges which might appear to us as being of solely economic nature are also means of creating, expressing or modifying relationships. As such, the transactions would be judged in gradations of good or bad, i.e. exchange is also an ethical matter. Relationships are more important in small-scale societies than are the rather casual, comparatively attenuated acquaintanceships of suburbia or the workplace. We tend to perceive self and personal identity as autonomous, self-contained attributes of individuals. In a smaller society they are seen and felt as including the individuals' kin and friends and enemies. That is to say that, as a Mushona of Zimbabwe or a Motswana or G/wi of Botswana, what I am is also a matter of what relationships I am involved in, and my state of well-being, or otherwise, is much affected by the health of those relationships. Health here is not a simple function of amity; it is the orderedness of those relationships. In friendship I should know what my friend expects of me, and why, and should behave accordingly. Similarly, I have expectations of my friend's behaviour, including her or his reactions to what I do. My enemy should behave and react in comparable fashion. Health of a relationship is thus reflected by my level of confidence in my expectations of others' behaviour. Our shared concepts of good and bad are important cardinal points in orienting ourselves in agreed evaluations of behaviour. This function of morality is not, of course, peculiar to small-scale societies. In these, however, moral orientation may be effected in a somewhat different way. In their restudy of Schapera's compilation of Tswana custom and law, Comaroff and Roberts argue that, for the Tswana, these 'represent a symbolic grammar in terms of which reality is continually constructed and managed in the course of everyday interaction and confrontation' (Comaroff and Roberts, 1981, p. 247). They are not (as is often supposed) precepts for ideal behaviour. Rather, they are a code for interpreting the meanings of actions. Also, importantly, the shared knowledge of customs and laws creates expectations of consequences and reactions to acts which amount to something akin to a multi-dimensional, dynamic and relativistic conceptual map of the possible states of relationships. By choosing appropriate routes on this map people can manoeuvre their relationships around hazards, or conduct them from one state to another. I do not wish to misrepresent custom and law as a programme for social action; it is, if you like, a navigational aid. Like seafarers' and fliers' aids to navigation its use requires judgement, experience and purpose, and where custom and law do not maintain the health of a relationship, 'pilot error' is often the cause.

In the context of relationship hygiene there is a dialectic of cardinal value and negotiation which, in a crude and not very satisfactory way, may be compared with negotiating the monetary value of a transaction in our society. If, for instance, a dealer and I haggle over the trade-in of my old car for a newer one, we start by referring to the agreed value of a dollar, pound or kina and use it as a cardinal point in our arguing the value of our respective vehicles. By the time we have arrived at agreement we have, in effect, altered the dollar (or whatever) value of the two cars with respect to one another and, thus, changed the value of the dollar itself for this transaction. (I emphasize that moral negotiation is not conducted in the conventions of cut-throat secondhand car trading.)

The G/wi (the oblique stroke represents a click consonant) Bushmen of the central Kalahari desert in Botswana provide a case-study of a moral system's operation in an unusually small social formation. Until the last decade they were hunters and gatherers, living in bands of 40 to 80 men, women and children. These were autonomous, making their own social, political and economic order, each in its own territory over which it controlled the use of resources it contained. The G/wi should not be taken as living examples of early mankind. It is true that all our ancestors lived by hunting and gathering until about ten thousand years ago, and that this means of subsistence has given way to the technology of raising, and living off crops and domesticated animals, inventing and using machines to wrest more materials and energy from the environment, which has enabled people to live in very much larger groupings. Because the G/wi did not do these things does not indicate that they stood still for ten thousand years. Their ancestors and they had as long to devise and experiment with different cultural solutions as did ours and ourselves. They are of interest here not as a relic of the Stone Age but as a contemporary people whose lifestyle, although so different from our own, nevertheless illustrates the commonality of human cultural themes in a context of singularly small and intimate social groupings beset by the severe environmental stress of a desert. This stress they successfully contended with by using a small inventory of material culture and a large corpus of knowledge with ingenuity and elegant, efficient simplicity. Plainly they did not value the acquisition of power and material wealth as we do. They found for themselves a social and psychological

19

security very different from that which is our lot. But they did it by using essentially the same cultural apparatus which we have and the way they used it gave them security and stability under very trying circumstances.

In G/wi exchanges the service or good given to another was evaluated by the recipient's need for it, discounted by the donor's capacity to give. 'You do not give meat to a man who has a full pot' epitomizes the standard. Among people who had no means of preserving and storing meat, any more than enough was worthless. Allowing somebody opportunity to show her or his generosity and capability to do a favour was to confer a grace, which is why there was the discounting factor. Nothing was subtracted from the value of what was given from small store, or from what was done with difficulty and the rule inhibited exploitation of a differential in advantage.

Any needed good or service might have been given in return for what had been received. It was clearly in the giver's interest to choose what was most needed by the recipient (had the highest value) rather than simply that which was most easily given (incurred the highest discount). Profit and opportunity tended to cancel one another and the result was a gradient from the haves to the have-nots along which goods and services flowed, reducing inequalities in the distribution of wealth and ability.

From the viewpoint of a capitalist society these ethics and this economic logic seem improbably virtuous and ruinously profligate. However, there was another value being pursued, namely the establishing and maintaining of harmonious relationships. Again and again in discussion and in general conversation this stood out as a desired and enjoyed end in itself, often as the ultimate rationale for action.

G/wi bands were egalitarian; that is, there were as many valued social positions as there were those who sought them. Statuses were not ranked (with the exception of the culturally limited authority which parents had over their children). Economic egalitarianism, encouraged by the equalizing tendency of exchange valuation, was favoured by G/wi theology which held the world and its resources, together with humans and other creatures, to be the property of N!adima, the creator. Things were only susceptible to ownership by people once they had been collected, hunted or made, and it was an affront to N!adima (the exclamation mark represents a different click consonant) to take more than was sufficient for one's needs. He is a deity who cannot be favourably influenced so there was no practice of prayer, sacrifice or anything that was clearly worship. There was consequently no cadre of priests who might otherwise have had exclusive access to resources or other dimensions of power.

Politics, the conduct of affairs of public policy, were similarly non-exclusive in the distribution of power and advantage. Political process was a series of consensus decisions in which all adults and near-adults could, and usually did participate. Consensus is neither unanimity nor majority will; it is consent to the judgement of those who make it. In this case it was the band that judged what course action would take, or which position would prevail. It was sometimes the case that the wishes of a single member prevailed against all others, who agreed to the will of a minority-of-one because they could tolerate adjustment to the dissenter's position and she or he could not move to theirs. A requirement of consensus is that all are bound by the eventual decision and that all have access to a common pool of information, including the rules, subject, reason and foreseen consequences of making the decision.

An example illustrates the scope that this system provided for 'negotiating' values. A woman had left her husband for his closest friend. Divorce was not normally a shattering event, the spouses usually finding new partners within a year and settling down happily. But this man would not; he mourned the undoing of both the marriage and the friendship with so much sorrow as to disturb everybody in the band. His lot thus became a public, hence political matter and the band saw itself as having to solve an intolerable problem. The man could not be condemned; he had done no wrong, but was unbearable. His former wife and friend had moved away, so were beyond the blame or other direct influence of the band. Enquiries found that they were happy together but the man missed his former friend. Delicate diplomacy uncovered the couple's willingness to return and try out the unprecedented arrangement of a *ménage à trois*. Polyandry was completely unknown; it appeared to constitute adultery but, if all acquiesced, was it? All did acquiesce, it was deemed not to be adultery and the band, the couple and the deserted husband lived more happily.

Despite their enthusiasm for harmony and order the G/wi are volatile and passionate and conflict was common. Men and women committed adultery, kin stinted their relatives or were tardy in returning favours and gifts. People are lazy and thoughtless. Everybody relishes gossip, but some lacked discretion and feelings would run high. Then morals and ethics had plenty of private and public use and reference in attacking, defending and judging behaviour.

Healthy relationships help to avoid much conflict; one can confidently expect that behaviour of this sort or that sort will be well received, or that other behaviour will provoke antagonism. But life apparently cannot be so structured as to avoid all oppositions of interest and there is a need for ways in which disagreement, outrage and resentment can be meaningfully and acceptably expressed. Many societies have institutionalized what is termed the joking relationship, in which certain categories of kin have licence to (among other things) criticize with broad latitude one another's conduct. It is a spear with a point at each end as the right of reply is automatically unsheathed. Anger to white heat is permitted, but to allow the flame of temper to ignite is deeply shameful. Where a direct exchange may be too inflammatory or excessively confrontationary, the flanking assault of 'talking at' is used: A loudly informs B of her or his complaint against C, resorting to more or less oblique allusion. C responds by addressing to D an equally indirect answer or rebuttal, with a counter-charge. In G/wi bands the joking treatment was frequently used to nip in the bud any growing tendency to commit nuisance and, quite commonly, as a punishment. In these instances the sting of satire ridiculing the offender would be sharpened by an appreciative audience's derisive response.

Some conflicts could be left to the adversaries to fight out alone. Violence was mainly verbal with occasional light blows being struck with fists or pieces of firewood. Physical violence beyond this was a terrifying and shameful matter.

Recidivists were subjected to the 'wrong-footed' treatment; a conspiracy of action to keep the victim out of tune with whatever was going on. Requests, suggestions, jokes, whatever were misunderstood and the ensuing outbursts of frustration were met with puzzled incomprehension. The object was to induce in the wrongdoer a disgust with the band and the general obtuseness of its members, leading her or him to seek other company in another band.

Judgement was never framed in terms of outright condemnation and rejection of a wrongdoer. This seems to be a common inhibition in small communities. (Until becoming an academic anthropologist at near to middle age, I had spent all my working life in a variety of small, rather closed and remote groups which were part of either large-scale or small-scale societies.) Heinous offences were redefined as being of lesser severity – a father's murder of his son became ostensibly a shooting accident. Irreducible wrongs like incest, of which there are not degrees, disappeared behind a conspiracy of disavowal of the correct facts, even where evidence was irrefutable. Preventive and compensatory measures were applied, but informally, and outwardly for reasons unconnected with the offence. A third alternative was to declare the wrongdoer insane but without involving competent psychiatric opinion, even when it was available. This radically changed the offender's status, moral and social responsibilities and capacity for future relationships. The society at large may well have a concept of elimination by banishment or judicial execution, but the isolated community itself lacks the social and moral structures which could bear the burden that actual elimination would impose. When we all come face to face every day, how shall I become reconciled with my brother's hangman? This way I can make atonement to the victim's children. With the efficiency of communication that can be achieved in a small community, negotiation of moral values can produce tolerable satisfaction. The arithmetic of *lex talionis* inflicts on the wrongdoer the pain and loss suffered by the victim, but the latter cannot see with the eye, nor bite with the tooth that the former renders up. In the calculus of negotiation the principle of restitution complements that of retaliation.

A Tswana villager, A, contracted to drive B's two cows to market, a week's walk distant. Many misadventures befell A and one cow died the night before getting to market. He butchered the carcase and sold the meat for a higher price than the remaining cow fetched. All the money was paid to B, who, however, felt aggrieved by the death of his cow and took A before the village headman's court. He was fined an amount equal to half the proceeds of the butchered meat. In discussing the case with the headman I argued that B had benefitted from A's initiative in turning a carcase into marketable cuts. The headman challenged me, 'If I tear your old shirt while beating your back in an assault would you be content if I gave you a new shirt?' To these villagers cattle were not simply commodities to be converted into money. The cows were B's darlings, of his prideful breeding, and one of them had been belittled in the market. Here negotiation required that retaliation be added to restitution and I had been the only one in the village who had not understood why and how. A's initiative *had* been acknowledged; without it the fine would have been heavier.

A widely-held value is that, having taken into account all known and relevant factors, members of a social group will seek to prolong the lives of those recognized as belonging to the group. In expressing the value in action, there is broad variation of what constitutes known and relevant factors and of the boundaries of recognition of membership of the group. G/wi theology has N!adima as a capricious deity who may decide to take a life because he 'has grown tired of that person's face', and will bring some lethal mishap to pass. Little, or no effort would be made by others to save the victim. In one episode a lion made uncharacteristically repeated attacks on one of a group of hunters. His companions decided it must be N!adima's agency and did little to intervene. When the victim survived the first few attacks they changed their minds, reasoning that N!adima would have been more efficient and had the lion kill in the first or, at least second onslaught. They then made strenuous efforts to drive off the lion. The man survived.

Edward Nelson, writing of the Bering Strait Malemut a century ago, described how one of a party camped near a Kuskokwim village took umbrage at being slighted by a villager and went to his tent to fetch a weapon to kill him. Two of his Malemut companions tried unsuccessfully to dissuade him and one then drew his knife and disembowelled him. In speaking of it afterwards, the man who had done the killing said that if they had been among their own people he would not have interfered, but added: 'We were only a few among the Kuskokwim men, and if our companion had killed one of their men they would have killed all of us and it was better that he should die' (Nelson, 1899 (1983), pp. 302–3).

Judicial execution is practised in both large and small-scale societies. Its rationale in many of these is a confused mixture of discouraging example, retribution, defence and rejection of wrongdoing which had placed its perpetrator beyond the pale of society. Nowhere do people behave consistently in their defence of other's lives but expediently juggle with 'known and relevant factors' or recognition boundaries to decide whether intervention shall be for, or against, prolonging a threatened life. In the 1930s the Nuer of the Sudan were faithful to the blood feud, it being the duty of the deceased's kin in the male line to avenge the death by taking the life of the killer or of one of his kin. In many instances it would become necessary for men who were related through the male line to both killer and victim to choose which side they belonged to. This was done by locating one's kinship standing as being closer to one or the other group. Those who were allies in one feud could become mortal enemies in another (Evans-Pritchard, 1940). The principle remains valid but perception of the frame in which it operates has changed. Although the context is very much a moral matter (it is good to seek vengeance for the wrong killing of another) the logic of the application of the moral principle is entirely amoral. I remark this not to accuse the Nuer of muddled thinking but to illustrate the universality of moral conundrums arising from the seemingly inevitable application of combinations of differently oriented principles (here, ethics and amoral logic) to the solution of moral problems.

In our society we have stoically become accustomed to chafing under the rough edges of the rule of rules. The absurdity of the logical consequence of inflexible obedience to a rule is satirized by some (*vide* W. S. Gilbert, A. P. Herbert, on law or C. Northcote Parkinson on bureaucracy), railed against by others and haphazardly juggled by legislators and administrators, but it is endured, nor cured. In small-scale societies the latitude allowed by negotiating the application of principles tempers the rigidity of the rule of rules without challenging their validity. Principle and goal are thus kept in alignment and absurdities are avoided or, at least, ameliorated in their extent, frequency or both.

Many values are expressed in the form of virtues by which to live and vices to eschew. It is recognized that these are simplifications. All Shona are taught that the truth must be told, and that it is wrong to lie. But not all persons are entitled to the truth; should a man ask a question beyond what is seen as the legitimate scope of his business, he is properly answered, '*Hameno*' (I don't know). This is not to lie, nor culpably to fail to tell the truth but to say, with face-saving politeness, 'I'm not going to tell you.' In some situations the extolled virtues appear contradictory; in punishing wrongdoers fine judgement is needed in achieving the right proportions of strength and compassion. To use too much strength is to be viciously vengeful and to be too compassionate is weakness. Shona do not see these oppositions as contradictory, double binds or no-win traps. Virtues, and the values they represent are standards of good, not absolutes which are in themselves the essence of good. The real good is the enjoyment of what the attainment or observance of values brings. In small-scale societies morality is ultimately about states of affairs and the health of relationships rather than a concern with abstract ideals. Not in a lotus-eating, hedonistic way, but as a striving for the most comfortable arrangements to which people can come in their shared joys and sorrows, pleasures and pains.

This is not to say that that endeavour is always successful. Every anthropologist encounters much behaviour that causes (and, often, is intended to cause) bad consequences for others. No society has been reported to be free of horrid individuals and unhappiness caused by horrid behaviour. Evans-Pritchard's account of the Nuer is far from adulation of their good fellowship. The reader is left with an impression of their enthusiasm for scoring off one another whenever they think they can get away with it.

But all know the rules and meta-rules and can competently perform the calculus of the consequences of action and reaction and, in their bruising style, maintain the health of relationships between friend and friend and enemy and enemy.

In many societies morality has divine, or other supernatural authority. To the Huli of the south highlands of Papua New Guinea, Datagaliwabe is a deity in the pantheon whose 'special province is punishing breaches of kinship and for this purpose he continually observes social behaviour ... punishes lying, stealing, adultery, murder, incest, breaches of exogamy and of taboos relating to ritual. He also penalizes those who fail to avenge the deaths of slain kin. He has no concern, however, with the behaviour of unrelated persons' (Glasse, 1965).

Among the Manus of the Admiralty Islands the moral life of the household is watched over by the ghost of a recently dead male relative. His skull is kept in the house and the ghost punishes various offences by sending sickness and misfortune (Mead 1963). Among many southern African Bantu-speaking peoples the semi-divine spirits of ancestors both punish wrongdoers and reward good behaviour.

The G/wi avoid greed for fear of N!adima's wrath, but also despise it as socially disruptive. However, their theology holds that any action which is likely to disturb the order of the world will anger him as that order is part of his creation. As none could be confident that he would restrict his punishment to the actual wrongdoer and not visit it upon the whole band or, indeed, the whole world, anything likely to anger N!adima was dangerous to all and therefore immoral in its recklessness. In G/wi eyes an exact parallel would be for a man to have left his poisoned hunting arrows within reach of a young child. It would therefore be misleading to claim that G/wi morality has religious origins. Their design for living, they say, is of their own devising, as is that of any other living creature. N!adima created life-forms, including mankind, each with its particular characteristics, and it is up to each species to explore its capabilities and devise a *modus vivendi* within them. Explicitly, N!adima did not dictate *how* they should live.

The Pitjantjatjara of central Australia faithfully maintain their relationship with *tjukurpa*, the mystical past and its supernatural heroes, by performing rituals and other observances. To imperil this relationship will diminish and otherwise harm the people, and carries its own fitting punishment. But, as with the G/wi case above, many will suffer for the neglect or other wrongdoing of one, or a few. If the wrong is severe enough in its foreseeable consequences, the punishment may be death. Unlike the small communities I referred to earlier, Pitjantjtatjara society *does* have the structural means of accommodating the burden that execution places on the social order. The problem of the executioner's having to face the wrongdoer's kin and friends and maintain normal relations with them after having had to perform his dreadful duty is solved. Elimination is secret, and is anonymously done by one or more of a group of senior men whose experience and advancement in ritual knowledge qualify them to make decisions and act on behalf of society with faithfulness to its values and principles and with wise concern for the circumstances of the offence. Unlike the requirement of British justice that it be seen to be done, the righting of wrongs in Pitjantjatjara society is achieved by means in which all have trust and do not require public scrutiny for their validation. The processes of judgement and punishment are mysterious but their rationale is known to all.

Lesser wrongs, deserving of less momentous punishments than death, are judged and dealt with in public. As is commonly, if not universally the case in small-scale societies, the essence of the process is that the wrongdoer should proclaim her or his acknowledgement of the wrong and of submission to judgement and punishment. For some offences, a guilty man will present himself for spearing, standing out in the open, clear of bystanders, and wait for his aggrieved plaintiff to hurl a spear through his thigh. Here the health of the relationship between enemy and enemy is of exquisite importance; if the guilty victim does not stand absolutely still he will spoil the other's aim and risk being speared through an artery or the bone with fatal result. Should the plaintiff miss the small part of the thigh which can be speared relatively harmlessly, he will be guilty of murder. Each participant *must* meet the other's expectations and in so doing symbolically respect public morality.

I have stressed that the social meaning, hence moral significance of behaviour is culture-bound. The integrity of the system of meanings depends on the stability of the culture. Change in one area or component of a people's culture will bring changes of meaning which may spread well beyond the area of initial change. If the rate and nature of change are such that the society can accommodate them without loss of cultural coherence (not every society has a generation gap!) then the attendant changes in moral values will probably not cause great distress. They may even be seen as progressive and beneficial (e.g. such emancipation and liberation of women and children as have occurred in our society in the last 150 years). We do not know enough of the early social history of many of the peoples studied by past anthropologists to say whether or not they experienced cataclysmic internal upheaval in their distant past, so we cannot judge their previous stability. We do, however, have a plethora of evidence of the effects that contact with the industrialized West has had on small-scale societies. It has almost always been violently disruptive, destroying traditional social order and invalidating established systems of meaning and morality, leaving the people confused and deeply distressed.

The Ik of northern Uganda, as described in Colin Turnbull's *The Mountain People*, are a deeply disturbing example of the corrosive effects of social dislocation on a people's moral system. They were displaced from the favourable, fruitful part of their land when it was declared a game park. Abandoned in almost barren mountain country, they discarded their social and moral order, once comparable with that of the G/wi, for a dog-eat-dog existence. Turnbull's description is not of brutal violence but of tragic, cold indifference. Among the Ik the boundary of the life-respecting group appears to have contracted to closed self-interest. Their rationale of social order was negated by dislocation from the matrix of meanings given, and sustained by the activities these hunters and gatherers had previously engaged in, the interlocking roles, exchanges and interdependencies they had developed and once maintained. The effect on the Ik of the loss of their fruitful valley was to leave them not only without game to hunt and plants to gather but was also to alienate them from their own lexicon of social meanings. Relationships were no longer characterized by confident expectations of others' behaviour and reactions. Dislocation was all the more devastating because it befell the whole society at once, leaving it bereft of any means of repair and sense of direction in which to turn for adaptation to the new conditions. At the time Turnbull wrote they had not even managed to devise stable, respectful and even minimally affectionate relationships between spouses or parents and children.

It seems that the Ik have 'ethical knowledge' in that they are quite aware of the deleterious consequences for others of harmful actions. However, they choose

26

to act anyway, without concern for the cost to another. Does this mean that they have no morals? *The Mountain People* could almost be an allegory of driver behaviour on our roads; behind the wheel I behave like a pig when I think I can get away with it, and the difficulties I cause others are *their* problem. I know I am being horrid but feel safe in the anonymity of traffic.

Are the Ik a people without society and thus disqualified from generalizations about universal ethical and moral values? That would be special pleading leading to the circularity: no society without morality, therefore all societies have morals. They *do* have social order but it is fragile and unstable, being based on the exploitation of the weak by the momentarily strong, who forbear to exploit to extinction only because the weak will be needed again tomorrow for more exploitation. Perhaps this could be seen as minuscule respect for life, but it has more the appearance of ruthless, cold-blooded recognition that an unextinguished life might bring benefit to the exploiter. This is a rare, perhaps singular instance to validate Hobbes; their life is, indeed 'nasty, brutish and short', but only because what Turnbull describes is the wreckage of a society.

Among the characteristics common to all moralities, with the possible exception of such special cases as the Ik, it seems that sociability is a universal human trait and reciprocity appears to be a functional necessity of sustained relationships. Respect for human life could perhaps also be regarded as a universal value, but is subject to wide variation in the extent of recognition and of priority accorded to life preservation relative to other interests. In all societies there is a fear of chaos but this is not necessarily manifested as an insistent desire for order. Were that the case it is difficult to see how change could occur because, in anything as complex as even the simplest society, any change brings a measure of disorder. It is probably the case that there is a general need to maintain order (or contain disorder) at a level at which confidence of expectations is not intolerably low. The threshold of tolerance is culturally defined and is also perceived subjectively. Many societies have theologies (i.e. doctrines of humanity's relationship with a supernatural final cause) but many theologies are irrelevant to the people's morality (as would be, for instance, a set of scientific beliefs about their relationship with the sun).

If there is a difference between the moralities of small-scale societies and those of societies like ours, I suggest it stems from the greater importance of interpersonal relations in the former. In these, morality is less of an end in itself but is seen more clearly as a set of orientations for establishing and maintaining the health of relationships. Morality, then, is a means to a desired, enjoyed end. In complex, large-scale societies relationships are less intense and less significant in the lives of individuals and in the structures of the societies. Morality certainly provides a set of orientations and thus helps to create and maintain coherent expectations of behaviour, but operates impersonally in that there is not the same capacity for negotiation. Morality thus tends to be valued more as an end in itself and less as a means to an end. This is not to conclude or imply that small-scale societies would therefore have less developed moral systems. The opposite could well be argued, on the grounds that a moral system which is viewed and used as a means to an end, and in which there is the additional dimension of complexity which negotiation entails, is constantly under practical test and public scrutiny.

References

Comaroff, J. L. and Roberts, J.: *Rules and Processes: The Cultural Logic of Dispute in an African Context* (University of Chicago Press, 1981).

Evans-Pritchard, E. E.: *The Nuer* (Oxford: Oxford University Press, 1940).

Glasse: 'The Huli of the Southern Highlands', in *Gods, Ghosts and Men in Melanesia;* ed. P. Lawrence and M. J. Meggitt (Melbourne: Melbourne University Press, 1965).

Nelson, E. W.: *The Eskimo about Bering Strait* (1899); reprinted (Washington, DC: Smithsonian Institution, 1983). A pioneering ethnography of excellent quality by a US Army weather observer.

Turnbull, Colin: *The Mountain People* (St Albans: Paladin, 1984).

Further Reading

Edel, M. and A.: *Anthropology and Ethics* (Illinois: C. C. Thomas, 1959). Much detail, less analysis.

Evans-Pritchard, E. E.: *Nuer Religion* (Oxford: Oxford University Press, 1956).

Gelfand, M.: *The Genuine Shona – Survival Values of an African Culture* (Salisbury (i.e. Harare): Mambo Press, 1973). Rich descriptive detail of the Shona ethical code.

Hogbin, I.: *The Island of Menstruating Men* (Scranton, Penn: Chandler, 1970).

Mead, M.: *Growing Up in New Guinea* (Harmondsworth: Penguin, 1963).

Radin, P.: *Primitive Man as Philosopher* (New York: Dover, 1957). An undeservedly neglected discussion of philosophical thought in small-scale societies.

Silberbauer, G. B.: *Hunter and Habitat in the Central Kalahari Desert* (Cambridge: Cambridge University Press, 1981).

3

Ancient ethics

GERALD A. LARUE

SOMETIME between the twelfth and tenth millennia BCE (Before the Common Era, the universal designation replacing BC, 'Before Christ'), human life patterns in the ancient Near East began to change from migratory existence or dwelling in caves to habitation in settled communities. In this new setting, humans produced their own food, developed skills in pottery making and the building of permanent structures, all the while moving from hamlet and town environments to cities and city-state organizations. By the end of the fourth millennium BCE, the two great river civilizations, Mesopotamia and Egypt, had invented and were using writing. This essay utilizes some of the surviving written materials from the ancient Near East, including stories about heroes who exemplified virtues most admired, legal codes that defined acceptable and non-acceptable conduct and instructional formulations, all of which inform us about the nature of ethics as it first developed into something sufficiently explicit to be the subject of reflection and discussion. As we shall see, later Western ethics has its roots in these ancient approaches to the problems of regulating a settled society. (For discussion of early ethical writings in India and China, see Article 4, INDIAN ETHICS, and Article 6, CLASSICAL CHINESE ETHICS.)

i Ethics in ancient Mesopotamia

Although the exposition of ethical principles as such was not of primary concern in the ancient Near East, value concepts can be discerned from commercial documents, law codes, wisdom sayings, hero stories and myths. Many of the earliest known textual materials from Mesopotamia relate to business and are little more than 'laundry lists' dealing with land sales, contracts or explaining that so-and-so brought his beast as an offering to such-and-such a temple where it was received by priest so-and-so. The greatest number of recovered texts is from the early second millennium, but from earlier records, beginning in the late fourth millennium BCE, we learn that societies in the Tigris–Euphrates valleys were organized along bureaucratic lines.

Royal archives provide the boasts of monarchs who conquered and often devastated neighbouring territories. Obviously, no universal declaration of human rights protected vanquished people. Personal property became booty and men, women, and children were chattels. Oaths of fealty were demanded and given,

and the conquered territory, now governed by vassals, became part of an expanding empire.

Mesopotamian legal texts and codes reflect monarchical and temple-state
settings which reveal the union of church and state for control of the land and
the people. Territorial boundaries provided citizen identity. Temples to various
deities abounded within the cities but each city-state had its own ruling deity and,
ideally, the land belonged to him. The local ruler, as the god's personally chosen
steward, controlled the divine estate. The people were deemed to be in the service
of the gods to keep them at ease – a notion that is specifically stated in the
Babylonian creation epic *Enuma elish* (Speiser, 1958; Pritchard, 1958, vi. 33–6;
131). The king governed according to a code which was supposed to have been
revealed to him by the chief deity but which, in each instance, is clearly a
projection of current social ethics and practice. Regulations were presented as
case laws reading 'If a man . . .' Of course the god could be consulted for guidance
on immediate problems by way of temple omens – a system that vested tremendous
power in the temple priesthood.

The temple functioned much in the manner of a modern city hall, and was
the centre for the administration of justice. Violations of divinely revealed codes
were interpreted as offences against the gods. Cases were heard at the temple gate
but when opponents or witnesses were required to swear oaths in the name of
the god, the case was moved indoors to the temple proper.

Despite the temple-state control of the land, secularization and privatization
of property did occur. Different social classes were recognized, and local economy
rested largely on slave labour. Most slaves were acquired by conquest, others were
natives who had fallen on hard times. Such individuals became property to be
bought and sold, bequeathed or given away.

One of the earliest monarchs in ancient Sumer, Gilgamesh, the third-mil-
lennium BCE king of Uruk, posthumously assumed legendary status and was said
to be the product of the union of a high priest and the goddess Ninsun. The epic
story of his life reveals much about the values of ancient Sumer. In the fragmentary
contemporary textual references to him there is no indication that this legend was
current during his lifetime. A contemporary incantation text characterized him
as one who did 'inquire, examine, judge, perceive and lead aright' (Heidel, 1949).

In the legend that portrayed him as a semi-divine hero, he was introduced as
a brutal tyrant who ignored human rights and who, by virtue of rank and strength,
sought meaning through unbridled power as he bullied men and possessed virgins
prior to marriage (Pritchard, 1958; I, ii, 23–27). When the people complained to
the gods, a companion named Enkidu was formed and Gilgamesh's antisocial
behaviour was modified. Instead of using his authority and strength against his
own subjects, he redirected his energies into heroic exploits involving the conquest
of territory beyond Uruk. This value system faltered when Enkidu and Gilgamesh
violated sacred precincts and offended the gods. Enkidu was condemned to die.
Now Gilgamesh became aware of his personal mortality. Never doubting the
validity of an ethic based on strength and authority, he determined to defeat
death. As he began his venture, he paused for refreshments at an ale-house where

the barmaid commented on the folly of his quest and suggested a different value system:

> Gilgamesh, where are you running?
> You won't find the immortal life you are seeking.
> When the gods created humankind
> They ordained death for humans
> And retained immortality for themselves.
> So Gilgamesh, let your belly be full.
> Be merry every day and night.
> Make each day a day of joy.
> Dance, play, by day and by night.
> Wear clean clothes.
> Let your head be washed and your body bathed with water.
> Cherish the little child who grasps your hand.
> Let your wife rejoice in your arms
> For this is the destiny of mankind ...

Gilgamesh ignored her logic. An ethical system that developed out of the recognition that one's lifetime was limited and that proposed that life best be spent in companionship, love and enjoyment did not coincide with his quest.

Ultimately, he met with his ancestor Utnapishtim who had preserved all life during the flood and who had, unlike his biblical counterpart Noah, been granted immortality by the gods. Gilgamesh received instruction concerning the impermanence of human life and accomplishments and learned that despite his power as a semi-divine king, he, like all mortals, would die. As compensation, Utnapishtim directed him to a magic plant that grew at the bottom of the sea which, when eaten, would make 'the old man become as the young man'. Gilgamesh obtained the plant with the rejuvenating power, but decided to delay eating it. As he was bathing, the plant was consumed by a snake, which explains why the snake sheds its skin and renews itself while humans are destined to wrinkle and age. Gilgamesh returned to Uruk to become the great king, a shepherd to his people and the builder of the ancient walls.

The Gilgamesh legend, which was known throughout the ancient Near East, presented, in the adventures of the monarch, a commentary on finding meaning in life. If an ethic that ignored the rights of others or exhausted itself in heroics failed when performed by a semi-divine king, obviously such an ethic would fail for ordinary humans. Even the simple, hedonistic, day-by-day joy in living and loving recommended by the barmaid was rejected. If neither immortality nor the secret of rejuvenation were available to humans and only the grave lay ahead, how should one live?

The ethical stance that gave meaning and purpose to Gilgamesh's life was not stated but implied. He built the walls of Uruk that provided security for his people. He refurbished the temples of Anu, the patron god of the city, which would secure divine blessing for the people, and also those of Ishtar, the goddess of love and fertility, which would promote amicable relationships and fecundity of crops, flocks, herds and families. In other words, he lived up to the responsibilities of his divinely appointed task to be king in charge of the god's people and estates. The ethic that emerges from the story is the familiar work ethic. One fulfils one's destiny through service and through fidelity to whatsoever becomes one's responsibility. Each reader was encouraged, implicitly, to build his own walls of Uruk.

The law code of the Semitic King Lipit-Ishtar of the city of Isin, composed during the early nineteenth century BCE. is one of several early royal prescriptions recovered by archaeologists. The prologues in these codes are alike in that each ruler declared that he was divinely chosen for office, thereby linking earthly rule to divine wishes. Lipit-Ishtar claimed to have been selected by the sky god, Anu, and the wind or storm god, Enlil,

to establish justice in the land, to rectify complaints, to eliminate hostility and armed insurrection and to bring peace to the Sumerians and Akkadians.

Royal hymns exalt the period of peace. The focus on family law reflected concern for family values and stability by providing guidelines for the rights of, and the inheritance of property by, children produced by a legal wife or wives, a female slave or a harlot. There was no recognition of equality among men or sexes. Some men and women were affluent estate owners, other were slaves to be bought, sold or traded although freedom could be earned. Other laws in the damaged text dealt with business ethics. Lipit-Ishtar appears to have remitted debts, established business controls to prevent social injustice and to have tried to put ceilings on accumulated private wealth. In an epilogue, the king boasted that he had eliminated enmity, rebellion, weeping and lamentations, and had brought righteousness and truth to his kingdom.

The most famous Mesopotamian law code, that of Hammurabi of Babylon (1728–1646 BCE) echoes much that appeared in earlier codes. He was divinely appointed to promote the welfare of his subjects by ensuring justice through the elimination of evil and the wicked so that the 'strong might not oppress the weak'. Justice, which meant 'the straight thing', referred primarily to economic justice (Saggs, 1962, p. 198ff) and many of the laws dealt with property, law suits, business practice and contracts. Justice was not blindfolded and distinctions were made between social classes and family members. Personal injuries to members of the aristocracy called for the *lex talionis*, an eye for an eye. For injury to freemen and slaves, fines sufficed and, in the case of injury to a slave, the fine was paid to the master as recompense for damage to property. Family law established the primacy of the father. If a member of the aristocracy encountered financial difficulties, he could sell his wife and children into slavery for a four year period. A wife acquired without a contract had no legal standing. Rape of a betrothed virgin of aristocratic standing resulted in the death of the rapist. Women accused of infidelity were thrown into the river where, it was assumed, the river god would attest to innocence or guilt.

False accusations were harshly dealth with and to accuse another falsely of murder resulted in the death penalty for the accuser. Careless or inefficient behaviour could result in payment for damages but a surgeon who operated with a bronze lancet on a man of standing and caused his death or opened up his eye-socket and caused blindness had his hand cut off. If the operation was successful, the doctor was paid ten shekels of silver. If the patient was a slave, the physician replaced a slave for the dead slave and for the loss of a slave's eye, paid the owner one-half the value of the slave. If the slave recovered, the physicians received two shekels of silver. If a man struck the pregnant daughter of a freeman causing her to miscarry, he paid ten silver shekels for the loss of the fetus. Should his blow cause the woman to die, the striker's daughter was killed. Should the woman be of a lower class or a slave, the killer paid a fine. The laws protected the male over the female, the aristocrat over the freeman and slave.

ii Ethics in ancient Egypt

As ethical patterns were developing in Mesopotamia, an ethical emphasis that both differed from, and at times paralleled, Mesopotamian thought, was emerging in Egypt. At the heart of the Egyptian ethic was *ma'at*, a word that signified justice, balance, the norm, order, truth, what is correct and right action, all of which were established in the beginning by the gods and were presently guaranteed by the pharaoh. From the Fifth Dynasty (*c.* 2450–2300 BCE) onward, public officials appointed by the king to deal with legal matters were called 'priests of *ma'at*' (Morenz, 1973, pp. 12ff). No law codes defining *ma'at* have been recovered and the concept appears to have functioned as a basic value providing the foundation for moral behaviour and judgement. It is clear that there must have been commonly accepted regulations based on *ma'at* which could be augmented from time to time by pharaonic edicts. Justice and truth were not vague concepts, they were to be spoken and lived. In courts of law, justices were to manifest *ma'at* in what they said and in how they determined cases (Morenz, 1973, p. 125). Individual Egyptians were expected to operate in harmony with *ma'at*, not in terms of prescribed legal precepts, but rather broadly and freely, although in later times, the tendency was to conform to rules (Wilson, 1958).

Ethical norms that sustained *ma'at* were taught in scribal schools by wise men. Schoolboy copies of the aphorisms, maxims and advice, some from around 2000 BCE, have been found. They stress the importance of following precepts for success in business, governing, holding administrative and state offices. The reasons given for adherence to the ethical norms were essentially practical: to ignore them was to court failure, to violate them was to invite punishment and social disaster (Larue, 1988, pp. 70–73).

Pupils were encouraged to marry. The basic social unit was the family, including the father, one or more wives and their children. Incestuous marriages were accepted as normal. Property was inherited through families and when a mother died, the father stood to lose because the daughter assumed control of the property. To keep holdings within the family, it was not uncommon for a father to marry his daughter or for a brother to marry his sister. There can be no doubt that many of these unions were formal arrangements, designed purely to protect property; however, there is some debate as to whether or not such marriages were ever sexually consummated. The term 'sister-wife' is often mentioned in inscriptions and it is possible that some incestuous marriages reflect genuine love and affection between siblings. 'The gods Osiris and Set married their sisters Isis and Nephthys respectively, and Osiris begat Horus by Isis and Set begat Anubis by Nephthys; therefore the marriage of brothers and sisters was sanctioned by the gods, and there is no doubt that they existed in the earliest times in Egypt' (Budge, 1977, p. 23). Manchep White points out that 'To safeguard the purity of succession it was advisable that the king should procreate as many children as possible within what is called the forbidden degree. To this end he not infrequently married his own daughters' (White, 1970, p. 15).

Regarding non-incestuous marriage, pupils were advised to choose a wife carefully, to provide her with food, clothing and ornaments to keep her content, because she was the source of children, in particular sons who would inherit the father's office and carry on the family name. The husband was cautioned to avoid legal disputes with his wife and to avoid other men's wives. Because of inheritance laws, women in Egypt enjoyed a status and a freedom denied them elsewhere in the ancient Near East.

Rebellion against parental authority was discouraged. A son should be humble, willing to accept counsel, should avoid dishonest or fraudulent acts and develop good manners. According to the wise vizier, Ptah-hotep (twenty-fifth century BCE), filial misbehaviour could be the basis for disowning the son. The wise teacher, Amen-em-opet, (fourteenth century BCE) counselled against greed for power and wealth through theft, fraud or dishonesty in business, urged his pupils to think before speaking and warned against association with disruptive or quarrelsome persons. His ideal was the temperate man who performed good deeds and kindly acts, who did not mock the deformed or the elderly, who would assist an elderly drunk rather than strike him and who, when reproached by an elder, accepted the abuse and kept his composure.

Some dimensions of Egyptian ethics are related to their belief in an afterlife. 'No other nation of the ancient world made so determined an effort to vanquish death and win eternal life' (Lichtheim, 1975, I, p. 119). The mode was through preservation of the body and the use of magic combined with a concept of ethical judgement. Chapter 125 of 'The Book of the Dead' contains a negative confession in which the deceased recited before a panel of 42 divine judges a list of 42 sins not committed. The crimes included mistreatment of persons or animals, blasphemy, theft, maligning a servant to his master, causing pain or tears or suffering, killing another, theft, illicit sex or masturbation, cheating in business, and so forth. The protest ended with the repeated affirmation 'I am pure!' In an additional statement made in the Hall of Ma'at, the deceased claimed to have given bread to the hungry, water to the thirsty, clothing to the naked and river transportation to the man without a boat (Budge, 1913, p. 587). Clearly, one of the most powerful forces motivating adherence to accepted social values was fear of judgement in the afterlife.

The prohibition of cruelty to animals, which represents an unusual ethical stance in the ancient world, rests in part on the Egyptian belief that when Ptah, the creator god of Memphis, brought life into being by his spoken word, all creatures were manifestation of the divine. All that was, including the other gods, were projections of Ptah. Thus, Egyptians could imagine the creatures of the world welcoming and praising the rising sun as it was reborn each day, just as each Egyptian would do. Moreover, some gods assumed animal form. For example, Thoth could be either a baboon or an ibis, the sacred animal of the goddess Bast was the cat, Tauret was a hippopotamus goddess, Sebek a crocodile and so on. The list of sacred animals was extensive and included the vulture, hawks, swallows, turtles, scorpions, serpents, and so forth. Despite the respect and veneration given to these creatures (some were mummified), Egyptians did not hesitate to use them for food, but because the animals were valuable and also because of the Egyptian veneration of life, humans were expected to treat other creatures with respect and, in the case of domestic animals, with kindness, for in the afterlife the treatment of animals would be included in actions to be judged.

Of course there were those who were sceptical of the promise of afterlife. Entertainment at Egyptian feasts was furnished, in part, by a harpist who encouraged the guests 'to surrender themselves to pleasure, because they can have no certainty that earthly diligence will lead to eternal bliss' (Wilson, 1958, p. 467). The harpist noted that the pyramidal graves of the divine Pharaohs and their nobles had been violated, and it was as if they had never existed. He pointed out that no one ever returned from the grave to assure the living of immortality. Like the barmaid who counselled Gilgamesh, the harpist advised his audience:

> Follow your desires as long as you live.
> Put myrrh on your head and wear fine linen . . .
> Don't hesitate to seek personal pleasures and your own good.
> Satisfy your earthly needs as your heart desires
> Until your day of mourning comes.

He added that one can't take one's goods with one, that mourning and wailing won't save one from the grave from which there is no return.

So far as the world outside Egypt was concerned, Egyptian notions of their own superiority were obvious. Egyptians saw themselves as humans as distinct from gods and above animals. The term for foreigner suggested a category not up to the Egyptian category of human, for according to Egyptian thinking foreign influence was responsible for social breakdown. Foreigners, living in the outlands away from the bounty of the Nile and the normality of life in Egypt (*ma'at*), were even grouped in some literature together with animals. However, should a foreigner make his home in Egypt, that person joined the ranks of humans.

iii Ethics in the Hebrew Scriptures

When the Hebrews entered Canaan, probably in the late thirteenth century BCE, the land was controlled by local monarchies that paid tribute to Egypt. According to biblical legend, the Hebrew kingship, like that of Mesopotamia, was established in the tenth century BCE through divine choice by the Hebrew god, Yahweh. Saul was selected and then rejected (1 Sam. 10: 17–25; 13: 13–14). David was chosen and established the Judean line of rulers (1 Sam. 16: 1–13; 2 Sam. 7: 5–17). The king was protector of Yahweh's kingdom (1 Sam. 8: 20), a shepherd to Yahweh's people (2 Sam. 5: 2; 2 Kings 11:17), a participant in some of the cultic rites (1 Kings 3: 4, 8: 62, etc.), and in some instances was involved in the judicial process (2 Sam. 12: 1–6) but was not entirely above the law (2 Sam. 12: 7–14; 1 Kings 21).

Biblical law echoes motifs found in Mesopotamian legislation. Yahweh's rules were revealed to his chosen vassal, Moses, in a personal encounter on Mount Sinai (Horeb). The Torah, which represents a compilation of prescriptions – some borrowed and some original – developed between the tenth and the fifth centuries BCE. Like Mesopotamian law, it provided an identity for worshippers as a chosen people bound to their deity in a binding convenantal and legal relationship (Deut. 14:2). Even after the sixth century BCE, when Yahweh was presented as a universal, rather than a territorial, god, the Jews retained a particularism within the univeralist expression (Isa., Chs. 40–55). The convenantal sign, circumcision, was uniquely male, and non-circumcision or any attempt to obscure the sign was tantamount to abandonment of the covenant (1 Maccabees 1:15).

The aim of the law was *sedeq* which is usually interpreted as 'justice' or 'righteousness' and which signifies 'the right way' or that which is normal. The Deuteronomist wrote:

Sedeq, sedeq you shall pursue so that you may live and inherit the land which Yahweh, your god, gives to you. (Deut. 16:20)

Sedeq as expressed in biblical law came in both casuistic (case law) and apodictic (thou shalt/not) form. When the law was sanctified as holy and adquate for all time and all generations, it assumed the binding, inflexible form of 'rule book ethics'.

The relationship between deity and people was based on a *do ut des* (I give so that thou mayest give) principle by which Yahweh promised rich blessings in proportion to obedience to his rules, which covered everything from acceptable food, clothing, and sexual practices to offerings and ritual enactments. In other words, obedience earned rewards, disobedience caused punishment, so that when an individual or group suffered pain or loss it could be attributed to unethical behaviour (Deut. 7:12–14; 28).

The cohesive nature of the family produced a concept that has been labelled 'corporate personality' (Robinson, 1936). Evil done in one generation could be punished in another (Deut. 5:9). Thus, an unethical ancestor might escape punishment and a good descendant might suffer misfortune. This belief, which reflected a defective sense of individualism, was challenged in Ezekiel where each person was held responsible for personal evil (Ezek. 18).

The relationship between sin and punishment was challenged in the story of Job. The hero, a righteous individual who had faithfully observed all the rules, suffered not because of his or another's sin but because of a wager made in heaven. Since Job could not know the reason for his misery and because traditional theories did not explain his circumstance, questions were implied concerning the proper way to live. The answer in Job was that one should unquestionably obey the revealed rules whether or not the consequences made sense. A different response was given in Ecclesiastes.

Ecclesiastes echoes themes familiar from Gilgamesh and the songs of the harpist in Egypt. The author, posing as Solomon, assumed the title Qoheleth (teacher). His opening cry is that life is meaningless. By virtue of status, wealth and power (as Solomon), he could indulge his every whim, from participation in the ways of wisdom to pleasure (wine, women and song), from accumulation of wealth and investment in building projects to madness and folly. All were void of significance. Indeed, the fate of humans, whether wise or foolish, good or evil, was perceived to be no different from that of other living creatures (Eccl. 2: 14–16; 3: 18–21; 7:15; 8:8). The mystery of what life was all about remained hidden (8:17). How then should one live? Qoheleth recommended acceptance of whatever lot was given to humans and, like the barmaid in the Gilgamesh legend, advised his pupils:

Go then, eat your bread with enjoyment, and drink your wine with a merry heart, for God has already approved what you do. Wear white garments and anoint your head with oil. Enjoy life with the woman you love, all the fleeting days of your meaningless life span, because that is your lot in life as you toil at your tasks beneath the sun. Whatever your hand finds to do, do it with your might, for in Sheol (the grave), where you will be going, there is neither work nor thought nor knowledge nor wisdom. (Eccl. 9: 7–10)

Qoheleth's ethic suggested a one-day-at-a-time approach to life. Unlike the Egyptians, he had no belief in judgement in an afterlife. This life was all there is. The work ethic remained at the core of his teaching and the significance of the responsible life with joy in existence was not ignored. Some things are better than others: wisdom is preferred to stupidity, decency to indecency, life rather than death, but ultimately, when death comes, whatever one has chosen is meaningless.

Hebrew wisdom teachings (Proverbs) recognized two classes of men: the wise who adhered to the divine law and who were good citizens, discreet, prudent, reliable, honest, of gentle speech, humble, conforming, industrious, and impartial in judgement, and the evil who were stupid and ignored the law. There were two classes of women: the good who were ideal wives whose major concerns where the welfare of family and husband and who worked diligently as home managers and astute business women (Prov. 31: 10–31), and the evil who were wanton adventuresses representing the way of folly and disaster (Prov. 7: 6–27; 9: 13–18). The reason for following the teaching was practical – one way led to success, the other to failure and trouble.

Despite the regulation in Exodus 12: 49 'You shall have but one law for the home-born and for the outsider who lives among you', distinctions were made. There were citizens and there were slaves, sojourners who passed through the land and resident aliens, and there were men and there were women. All were not equal. Social concern was expressed for orphans and widows and sojourners (Deut. 10: 18–19). Enslaved Hebrews were to be released after six years and treated generously (Deut. 15: 12–18). Intermarriage with outsiders was forbidden (Deut. 7: 3–4); Neh. 13: 23–27). Social and political inequities were accepted.

Familial ethics emphasized the significance of the male family line. There was no belief in an afterlife and 'immortality' consisted in the continuance of identity through male offspring.

Of course *sedeq* was ignored by some. Prophetic protests decry the violation of the rights of the poor and of widows and orphans by the rich and powerful. Micah, in the eighth century BCE, called upon the people to 'do justice, to love kindness and to walk in humility with your God' (6: 8). The prophetic threat of disaster made to the nation during that same period might have terrified some but was ignored and mocked by others (Isa. 28: 14–22).

By the close of the sixth century BCE, the threatened disasters had occurred: Jerusalem had been destroyed, Jewish leaders and skilled artisans had been taken to Babylon as exiles, and Cyrus of Persia had, in turn, conquered Babylon. Persian policy permitted Jewish exiles to return and rebuild the ruined city of Jerusalem and the temple. In the fifth century BCE, powerful Jewish leaders emerged, including Ezra and Nehemiah, who sought to establish Jewish identity, not only through the physical restoration of the city and temple, but also on the basis of a faith system. During this period, final additions were made to the Torah. This law code, which comprises the first five books of the Bible, became the basis for a covenantal ethic, based on a relationship between deity and the people – a relationship which tradition traced back through Moses to Abraham. Nehemiah's and Ezra's interpretation of this covenant demanded the separation of Jews from all others, forbade intermarriage between Jews and non-Jews (Neh. 10: 30) and even went so far as to insist that intermarriages already consummated be dissolved (Ezra 10: 18–19). These two leaders were convinced that intermarriage not only polluted the purity of Judaism (Neh. 13: 23–26) but violated scriptural prescriptions (Neh. 13: 1–3) and provoked divine anger (Ezra 10: 14).

Not everyone agreed with the separationist policy. The author of the book of Ruth, which was composed in the late fourth century BCE, noted that King David was descended from a Moabite-Hebrew marriage. The novella Jonah made clear the concern of the Jewish deity for other people and hence the responsibility of the Jew for foreigners – even the despised Assyrians (Jonah 4: 11)

While the struggle concerning separationist ethics was in progress, another element influenced Jewish thought. It stemmed from the Persian religion of the prophet Zoroaster and introduced into Judaism the Aryan notion of cosmic dualism. Zoroastrian theology taught that Ahura Mazda, the all-knowing creator and sustainer of the world of good, truth, purity, and light was pitted against Angra Mainyu, the epitome of evil, the lie and darkness. Each human was endowed with free choice and each could choose whether to follow light or darkness. Within this bipolarity, Zoroastrianism envisaged history as moving toward an end-time, a final epoch in which truth and goodness would triumph. In the *eschaton*, each human soul now united with its body would approach a Bridge of Separation over which the righteous would pass to paradise and from which the wicked would be turned away. Ultimately, both wicked and righteous would be tested by passing through a stream of molten metal. To the righteous it would be like taking a warm bath, for the evil it would mean extinction. The eschatological ethics were concerned with the problem of theodicy, the righteousness of God. If the deity was good and righteous and all powerful, how could evil be so prevalent and successful in the world? The response was that evil was the result of the activity of Angra Mainyu (who foreshadowed the devil), and although evil seemed to triumph in this world, balance would be restored in the world to come when right behaviour would be rewarded and evil punished. The focus was on the individual whose good behaviour would earn eternal paradise.

These concepts entered into Jewish ethics. They form the central teachings of the book of Daniel, written about 168 BCE when persecution of the Jews by the Seleucid Greeks was most intense and vicious (see 1 Maccabees 1; 2 Maccabees 6–7; Josephus, *Antiquities* XII. v, vi). Daniel provided the Jews with a new answer to the problem of theodicy: if the righteous suffer on earth despite their goodness and fidelity to the Law, they will be rewarded in the afterlife. Should evil people seem to prosper and grow in power and wealth and authority, the pious knew that in the afterlife they would be punished in proportion to their evil deeds, for all the power, wealth and authority gained in this life mattered nothing in the world to come. The righteous knew that the end was at hand, they had only to hang on to their faith despite persecution, torture and death. Yahweh was an ethical deity, his regulations represented a positive ethic, and his obedient followers knew they were living according to the highest ethic, a divinely revealed code of behaviour.

The book of Daniel symbolized a failure of nerve. The good life, the decent life, the ethical life was no longer important for the creation of an ethical society. That was impossible among humans, for evil was dominant and besides, the end was at hand. Only in the afterlife, when the kingdom of the righteous came into being, could the full ethical society emerge. To be part of that idealized society, one must focus on individual righteousness in this life. Whereas Judaism had taught that ethical behaviour in this life could be recognized as fulfilling the covenant regulations and thereby earned rewards in divine blessing for the individual and the nation, now the emphasis was upon personal reward and punishment.

Some Jewish sects, including the Pharisees and the monks who lived by the Dead Sea (who are believed to have been Essenes) accepted the eschatological teachings; it may have been through these sects that this view of the world became part of Christianity and Christian ethics.

References

Budge, E. W.: *The Dwellers on the Nile* (London: Religious Tract Society, 1926); (New York: Dover Publications, Inc., 1977).

——: *The Book of the Dead* (London: Medici Society, 1913); (New York: University Books, 1960).

Heidel, A.: *The Gilgamesh Epic and The Old Testament* (Chicago: University of Chicago Press, 1949).

Josephus: *Antiquities*.

Larue, G. A.: *Ancient Myth and Modern Life* (Long Beach, Cal.: Centerline Press, 1988).

Lichtheim, M.: *Ancient Egyptian Literature*, 2 vols. (Berkeley: University of California, 1975/76).

Morenz, S.: *Egyptian Religion*, trans. by Ann E. Keep (Ithaca, NY: Cornell University Press, 1973).

Pritchard, J. B., ed.: *Ancient Near Eastern Texts Relating to the Old Testament* (Princeton, NJ: Princeton University Press, 1958).

Robinson, H. W.: 'The Hebrew conception of corporate personality', *Werden und Wesen des Alten Testaments*, ed. J. Hempel, *Beiheft zur Zeitschrift für die Alttestamentliche Wissenschaft*, LXVI (1936), pp. 49ff.

Saggs, H. W. F.: *The Greatness That Was Babylon* (New York: Hawthorne Books, 1962).

Speiser, E. A.: 'The creation epic', *Ancient Near Eastern Texts Relating to the Old Testament*, ed. James B. Pritchard (Princeton University Press, New Jersey, 1958), pp. 60–72.

White, J. E. Manchep: *Ancient Egypt, Its Culture and History* (New York: Dover Publications, Inc., 1970).

Wilson, J. A.: 'Egyptian secular literature and poems', *Ancient Near Eastern Texts Relating to the Old Testament*, ed. J. B. Pritchard (Princeton, NJ: Princeton University Press, 1958), pp. 467–70.

Further reading

Bottero, J., Cassin, E. and Vercoutter, J., eds.: *The Near East: The Earliest Civilizations*, trans. by R. F. Tannenbaum (New York: Delacorte Press, 1967).

Breasted, J. H.: *Development of Religion and Thought in Ancient Egypt* (New York: Charles Scribner's Sons, 1912).

Breasted, J. H.: *The Dawn of Conscience* (New York: Charles Scribner's Sons, 1933).

Clark, R. T. R.: *Myth and Symbol in Ancient Egypt* (New York: Grove Press, 1960).

Erman, A.: *Life in Ancient Egypt* (1894); trans. by H. M. Tirard (London: Benjamin Blom, 1969).

Frankfort, H., et al.: *The Intellectual Adventure of Ancient Man* (Chicago: University of Chicago Press, 1946).

Jacobsen, T.: 'Primitive democracy in Mesopotamia', *Journal of Near Eastern Studies*, II (1943), 159ff.

——: 'Mesopotamia', *The Intellectual Adventure of Ancient Man* (Chicago: University of Chicago Press, 1946).

——: *The Treasures of Darkness* (New Haven: Yale University Press, 1976).

Kaster, J.: *Wings of the Falcon* (New York: Holt, Rinehart and Winston, 1968).

Kramer, S. N.: *History Begins at Sumer* (New York: Doubleday, Anchor, 1959).

——: *Sumerian Mythology* (New York: Harper & Row, 1961).

——: *The Sumerians* (Chicago: University of Chicago Press, 1963).

Larue, G. A.: *Old Testament Life and Literature* (Boston: Allyn & Bacon, 1968).

Murray, M. A.: *The Splendor That Was Egypt* (New York: Hawthorn Books, Inc., 1963).

Oppenheim, A. L.: *Ancient Mesopotamia* (University of Chicago Press, 1964).

PART II
THE GREAT ETHICAL TRADITIONS

4

Indian ethics

PURUṢOTTAMA BILIMORIA

Preamble

IT IS often asked: 'Has there ever been "ethics" in India?' Can one meaningfully speak of "Indian ethics"?' 'Isn't the idea of "ethics" a Western invention – like anthropology?' Or, alternatively, does not the Indian mystical and 'life-denying' world-view rule out the use of ethics? There is no gainsaying that the Indian tradition did concern itself with a quest for the 'morally good life' and the attendant principles, laws, rules, etc. that might help achieve this goal. And like their counterparts elsewhere, Indian thinkers did not shy away from enquiring into the nature of morality, of 'right' and 'wrong', 'good' and 'bad', even if they went no further than describing or codifying the prevailing *'ethos'*, mores, customs and habitual traditions – that is to say, giving expression to what in Sanskrit is termed *dharma*, meaning, very roughly, the moral and social order.

The questions we began with do, however, point to one difficulty, namely, that of locating in the Indian tradition the sort of ahistorical, abstract and formal theorizing in ethics that we have become accustomed to in the West. In India it was recognized that ethics is the 'soul' of the complex spiritual and moral aspirations of the people, co-mingled with social and political structures forged over a vast period of time. And this is a recurrent *leitmotif* in the culture's profuse wisdom literature, legends, epics, liturgical texts, legal and political treatises.

As with any other major civilization whose origins lie in antiquity, one can naturally expect there to be a variety of ethical systems within the Indian tradition. To cover all of these positions would be an impossible task. Also, to speak of 'Indian tradition' is to refer rather loosely to an incredibly diversified collection of social, cultural, religious and philosophical systems, which have also changed over time. The present discussion has to be selective and it will be confined to the Brahmanical–Hindu and Jaina traditions, concluding with a brief look at Gandhian ethics. (Buddhist ethics, whose Indian career would normally be part of such a chapter, is discussed in Article 5.) The use of Sanskrit terms is inevitable, in view of the lack of English equivalents (and vice versa), but they will be explained.

General remarks about early Indian ethics

To start with the most general remark, the early Indian people in their practical moral judgements, placed on the side of the 'good': happiness, health, survival, progeny, pleasure, calmness, friendship, knowledge and truth; and on the side of 'bad' more or less their opposites or disvalues: misery or suffering, sickness and injury, death, infertility, pain, anger, enmity, ignorance or error, untruth, etc. And these are universalized for all sentient beings, for it is thought that the highest good is possible when the whole world can enjoy the good things the cosmos has to offer. The highest good, however, is identified with the total harmony of the cosmic or natural order, characterized as *rita*: this is the creative purpose that circumscribes human behaviour. The social and moral order is thus conceived as a correlate of the natural order. This is the ordered course of things, the truth of being or reality (*sat*) and hence the 'Law' (*Rigveda* 1.123; 5.8).

One therefore does that which is consistent with, or which promotes, the good so perceived, and desists from doing that which produces the bad things or effects, so that overall the *order* is not unduly disturbed. One may also attempt to prevent or overcome the untoward effects of certain actions. An act is therefore right if it conforms to this general principle, and an act is wrong if it contravenes it, and hence is *anrita* (disorder) (*Rigveda* 10.87.11). Since to do what is right safeguards the good of all qua *rita* (the factual order), it is assumed that it is more or less obligatory to do or perform the right acts (the 'ought' or moral order). This convergence of the cosmic and the moral orders is universally commended in the all-embracing category of *dharma*, which becomes more or less the Indian analogue for ethics.

'Right' or rightness is identified with 'rite', i.e. it is formalized as ritual, with varying content. In other words, the obligation derived from a value, say, survival of the race, becomes the value itself, e.g. sacrifice, regardless of what is offered in the act. Rite now comes to possess an intrinsic moral worth. But it also assumes a power all its own, and people are disposed to pursuing rites or rituals for egoistic ends. One group may claim entitlement and therefore advantage over others as to the prescribed rites, their content, correct performance, utility, and so on. This leads to the working out of differential duties and moral codes for the different groups in the larger social complex. Differentiation is superimposed on the organic unity of nature and individuals alike.

What counts as *ethics*, then, although in appearance naturalistic, is largely normative; the justification usually is that this is the 'divined' ordering of things, and hence there is a tendency also to absolutize the moral law.

That is not, however, to say that genuine issues, concerns and paradoxes of ethical relevance do not get raised, even if these appear to be couched in religious, mythical or mythological terms. To give an illustration: scriptures prescribe avoidance of flesh; but a priest would wrong the gods if he refuses to partake of a certain ritual offering involving an animal. With the gods wronged, *order* can't be maintained: which then should he do? (Kane, 1969, I. 1.) Here we are led into an ethical discussion. What we have sketched above is, admittedly, a sweeping account that basically covers the very early period (*c.* 1500–800 BCE), during which time the Brahmanical tradition grew and flourished. This also outlines a broad framework for looking at how moral consciousness, various ethical concepts and often competing moral schemes develop and become articulated in later periods, which we may identify as the 'Hindu' ethical tradition.

i Brahmanical–Hindu ethics

First we shall make three concrete observations about the Brahmanical society.

1 The Vedas, the canonical collection of texts, is its ultimate authority. There is no one 'Supreme Revealer' who is the source of the scriptures. Their contents are simply 'seen' or 'heard' (*shruti*); and the principles invoked are embodied in the gods, who are models for human conduct.

2 A particular principle of social ordering is adopted (probably introduced in India by Aryans around 1500 BCE), according to which society is organized into a functional division of four 'classes', called *varna* (literally, 'colour'). These are, with their respective tasks:

brahmana (brahmin)	religious, instructional
kshatriya	sovereign, defence
vaishya	agriculture, economic
shudra	menial, labour

Ideally, the sources of power are distributed justly at different places; and also, differences in function need not entail differences in interests, rights and privileges. But the outcome in practice appears to be otherwise. A system of subdivisions or 'castes' (*jati*) further complicates the class functions, gradually turning them into a discriminatory institution based on birth. The brahmins profit most from the system and they hold the power-base. A life-affirming but rigidly authoritarian morality develops. Because of this, Max Weber judged that the Vedas 'do not contain a rational ethic' (Weber, 1958, pp. 261, 337).

3 Despite the overall ritualistic worldview, the Vedic hymns do praise certain humanistic virtues and moral ideals, such as truthfulness (*satya*), giving (*dana*), restraint (*dama*), austerities (*tapas*), affection and gratitude, fidelity, forgiveness, non-thieving, non-cheating, giving others their just desert, and avoiding injury or *himsa* to all creatures. (*Rigveda*, 10; vedas, *Atharvaveda*, 2.8.18–24; cf. Kane, 1969, I.1:4.)

Classical Hindu ethics

Vedic authority becomes normative in the later periods; the Vedas, which now extend beyond hymns and rituals, are invoked as the source or as symbols of ethics. Another important institution, *ashrama*, and two morally significant concepts, namely, *dharma* and *karma* emerge, and these culminate in the ethical concept of *purusharthas* (ends), which are all central to classical Hindu ethics, as we shall now describe.

Ashrama (life-cycle).   Life is conceived as progressing through four relative stages in concentric circles, each with its own codes of conduct. Namely, *studentship*, requiring discipline, continence and dedication to the teacher; the *householder* stage, entailing marriage, family, and their obligations; the *semi-retreat* stage, entailing gradual withdrawal from worldly pursuits and pleasures; and *renunciation*, leading to total withdrawal and contemplation. The last stage marks the preparation for final liberation and shedding of egoistic as well as altruistic tendencies, since the renunciant has to exercise extreme disinterestedness. It also involves breaking with the customary patterns of family and society and becoming an autonomous individual.

Dharma (duty).   *Dharma*, as we said, is an all-embracing conception and is perhaps unique to Indian thought. But the term is also rather diffuse as it has many and varying meanings, beginning with 'fixed principles' in the Vedas and ranging from 'ordinance, usage, duty, right, justice, morality, virtue, religion, good works, function or characteristics' to 'norm', 'righteousness', 'truth' and much else (Kane, 1969, I.1: 1–8). The word is derived from the Sanskrit root *dhr*, meaning to form, uphold, support, sustain, or to hold together. It certainly connotes the idea of that which maintains, gives order and cohesion to any given reality, and ultimately to nature, society and the individual. As will be noticed, *dharma* takes over from the Vedic idea of organic unity (*a lá rita*) and shifts more towards the human dimension. In this respect it parallels Hegel's idea of *Sittlichkeit* (the actual ethical order that regulates the conduct of the individual, family, civil life, and state) more than it does Kant's ideal conception of the Moral Law. Nevertheless, to a Hindu *dharma* suggests a 'form of life' whose sanction lies beyond individual and even group or collective preferences.

Law makers brought the notion of *dharma* more down to earth by devising a comprehensive system of social and moral regulations for each of the different groups, subgroups (caste, rulers, etc.) within the Hindu social system, as well as specifying certain universal duties encumbent on all. Vocational niches, duties, norms, and even punishments are differently arranged for different groups, and the roles and requirements also vary in the different *life-cycle* stages for the different groups. Thus, while the wife of a 'twice-born' (the three higher classes) may take part in certain Vedic rites, a *shudra* (toiler) would be risking punishment if he or she so much as hears the Vedas recited – to say nothing of those who fall outside the class-caste order, and aliens like us! (Manu, 2.16, 67; 10.127.)

More often than not though, *dharma* is invoked as though it were an objective possibility, when in fact it merely gives an overall form to a system of positive law, mores and regulations which are cultural imperatives, the contents of which are determined by various factors, more particularly the voice of tradition, convention or custom, and the conscience of the learned. *Dharma* then provides a 'frame' for what is ethically proper or desirable at any one time. What gives coherence to the conception itself is perhaps its appeal to the need to preserve the organic unity of being, to 'make' justice where justice is due, and to minimize the burden of *karma*, if not also to free the individual from its encumbrances. But what do we understand by the concept of *karma*?

Karma (action-effect).   The basic idea here is that every conscious and volitional action an individual engages in generates conditions for more than the visible effect, such that the net effect of an action X may manifest itself at a later time, or perhaps its traces remain in the 'unconscious' and get distributed over another time. X may combine the residual effect of Y to generate a compounded effect in some future moment. And this in turn becomes a determinant of another action, Z, or a state of affairs pertaining to that particular individual (perhaps even a collective). The effect of Z might be pleasurable (*sukha*) or it might be painful and induce suffering (*dukkha*), but this is the retribution entailed in the causal network that is itself an inexorable manifestation of *dharma*.

Further, the idea of an infinite possibility of action-retribution suggests to the Indian mind the idea of rebirth, for merit or virtue appears to be in need of being rewarded, and demerit punished, according to the Law of Karma. Thus merit or demerit achieved in one lifetime could well continue to determine one's capacities, temperament and circumstances in another birth. Hindu thought generally espouses the idea of a more substantial theory of rebirth, meaning that something like the 'soul' carries with it the latent potential (*karma*) of all that constitutes the person. However, some Hindu philosphers, such as Shankara (eighth century CE) do away with the idea of a permanent self by asserting the identity of the individual self, *atman*, with the ultimate reality, *Brahman*; hence what really transmigrates is something nearer to an illusory self, which has lost sight of its true identity, namely its oneness with *Brahman*.

The linkage of *dharma* and *karma* (action–effect) has the following consequences: there are no 'accidents of births' determining social iniquities; mobility within one lifetime is excluded; one has one's *dharma*, both as endowment and as a social role (Creel, 1984, p. 4). One either accumulates an improvement in *karma* aiming towards a higher, re-birth, or one tries to cut the Gordian knot and opts to step off, once and for all, the wheel of cyclical existence (*samsara*). But this is not achieved as simply as it is willed. Indeed, this freedom is placed as the fourth and the most difficult of goals in the scheme of the fourfold deontological ends of *purusharthas*, literally, 'things sought by human beings'.

Purushartha (human ends).   According to the Hindu view, there are four pursuits in life which are of intrinsic value, namely: *artha*, material interests; *kama*, pleasure and affective fulfilment; *dharma*, again, social and individual duties; and *moksha*, liberation. They may or may not be continuous with each other, though one goal might prove to be of instrumental value for achieving another; *dharma* is often thought to be of instrumental value in connection with liberation. Thus an ascending scale might be admitted, and the fixing of the relative status of each could lead to vigorous debate, as it has in Indian philosophy.

What is significant is that the above conception of human ends provides the context and criteria for determining the rules, conduct and guidelines in respect of the institutes of class and life-cycle stages. For an individual will want to strive towards achieving the best in terms of these ends within the limits of his or her temperament, circumstances, status and so on. Sometimes it is a question of balance; at other times it is a question of which interests get priority.

For example, a brahmin in the semi-retreat stage might consider that he has discharged all his family and social obligations, so that his remaining interest is to edge towards liberation, by becoming a full-time renunciant. What he should do and what he should not do in pursuit of this end is left entirely to his own determination, for which he relies on his meditative and cognitive insights. His particular *dharma* is the correlate of his innate constitution, of which he alone is the master: thus an inward-attentive praxis is the source of the principles for his ethic. Here, it may be observed, the gap between intuition and ethics is very nearly closed over. This is another salient feature of Indian ethics.

Upanishadic ethics

The *Upanishads* (post 500 BCE), perhaps the key philosophical texts of the Hindus, presuppose in principle the authority of the earlier Vedas (while being cynical regarding Vedic ritualism with its promises for utilitarian returns, such as cows and progeny), however, develop this alternative scheme with much finesse for a more universal application. Here metaphysical knowledge is placed above worldly pursuits. But this scheme also allows for the possibility of, indeed encourages, a detached and asocial pursuit of spiritual ends removed from the challenges of the world.

That this tendency develops in the hands of yogis and ascetics, and that it influences Indian ethical thinking cannot be denied. It appears almost as though *dharma* could be dispensed with. As the virtuoso Yajnavalkya, justifying his hasty decision to leave behind his wealth, home and two wives, puts it: It is not for the sake of the husband, wife, sons, wealth, gods, Vedas, brahminhood, kshatriyahood, etc., that these are dear, but for the sake of the Self, all these are the Self, one knows all in the Self ... Work cannot increase nor diminish the greatness of this knowledge (*Brihadaranyaka Upanishad* 5.5.6–7; 4.4.24). Virtue is deemed necessary for knowledge, and the Socratic dictum, 'knowledge is virtue' rings through here also. The ideal Upanishadic person is expected to overcome emotions, feelings, inclinations and sentiments in pursuit of a higher, nonetheless self-centred, 'calling'. But there are few rules.

It is, however, just for these sorts of reason that there have been charges, from within and without the tradition, that all we have here is an ethically bankrupt, quietistic and mystically-grounded morality (Danto, 1972, p. 99). At least this is what is said of the Vedanta and Yoga systems.

True as this charge might be, there is a list of three comprehensive virtues extolled in the Upanishads (and familiar to readers of T. S. Eliot) which is worthy of mention, namely, '*damyata, datta, dayadhvam*', signifying, self-restraint, giving or self-sacrifice, and compassion. But again, there are no rules other than exemplars, and no virtues to worry about after attaining liberation. Still, one moral ramification of the Upanishadic worldview is that all life, as indeed the whole world, is to be looked upon as a whole, where the ego sets aside its own narrow self-interests and even effaces itself.

Smarta ethics

There occur parallel and subsequent developments among the more doctrinaire and legalistic advocates of the rule of *dharma*, in what we shall call *smarta* (derivative) ethics. The school of Mimamsa champions a rigidly categorical reading of the scriptural imperatives. The implication is that all duties – religious as well

48

as secular – could be divided into those that are optional or prudential and those that are obligatory, and that all ensuing actions are instrumental towards some result or end (even if not indicated). But if there is a mandate one does it out of a sense of obligation. The Mimamsa developed the thorough going hermeneutic of *dharma* for which the school is best known, and which proved instructive for later ethical and legal discourses.

The more populist texts known as *Dharmashastras*, of which the most relevant are Manu's 'Law Books' and Kautilya's treatise on politics, overstress the legalistic side (Manu, 1975; Kane; 1969). Thus Kautilya (*c.* 200 CE) justifies the rigid reign of the 'rod' (*danda*) wielded by the king on the grounds that unless there are calculated controls the (natural) law of the small fish being swallowed by the big fish would prevail. Jurisprudence, ordinances for regulating civil life, and the governance and security of the state are his chief objectives. But he also highlights the use of reasoning (*anvikshiki*) in the study and deliberation on these matters (Kane, 1969, I.1:225) Both he and Manu make it mandatory for the king to attend first to the welfare of the citizens, and they seek to protect the rights and interests of the individual within a group framework, although not in the most egalitarian manner. Manu even admits that there are different *dharmas* in different epochs, which is suggestive of relativity in ethics (Manu, 1975, I, 81–86). Manu decrees some ten virtues, namely contentment, forgiveness, self-restraint, non-anger, non-appropriating, purity, sensual-control, wisdom, self-knowledge, and truth. Again, these are common to Indian ethics.

The Epics and the Gita

The popular epics of the *Ramayana* and *Mahabharata*, through their moving narratives and anecdotes, explore the struggles, paradoxes and difficulties of coming to grips with the evolving idea of *dharma*. The *Ramayana*, which presents the heroic Rama and his chaste wife Sita as the paragons of virtue, is somewhat dogmatic on its stance of 'righteousness', while the voluminous *Mahabharata* is less sanguine about exactness in matters of duty, as it turns over every conceivable ethical stance the culture has hitherto known. For instance, the sage Kaushika, who in the *Mahabharata* courts censure for his insistence on telling the truth to a bandit – because it leads to the killing of an innocent man – might well be acclaimed in the *Ramayana* for his uncompromising adherence to principle – as Rama indeed is for giving priority to his father's promise over his royal and family obligations.

The *Bhagavad Gita*, however, which is part of the *Mahabharata*, appears to be more decisive in its ethical pronouncements and perhaps for that reason has had an extraordinary impact on the modern Hindu–Indian mind. The *Gita* locates itself in the middle of two opposing traditions: *Nivritti* (abstinent), the austere path of anti-action (echoing non-Vedic asceticism), and *Pravritti* (performative), the doing of social and moral duties. Each had ethical ramifications for its time and their respective codes and rules were in competition and conflict.

While the *Gita* is recognized for the ingenuity with which it raises a host of

49

ethical issues (e.g., should I kill my own kin for the sake of regaining my rightful sovereignty?), its judgements have not satisfied all and sundry. The deep conflict of traditions is resolved through a synthesis of asceticism and duty in the unique concept of *nishkama karma* or disinterested action. What this implies is that one does not forsake one's apportioned duties but performs them in complete disregard of their fruits or consequences. Action is a universal necessity, and the individual has a 'right' (*adhikara*) only to the performance of the action and not to its fruit (2.47). The argument is that it is not acting that enslaves, but rather the thought that one is the cause, the agent and enjoyer of the act; stripped of this linear causal thinking no action can be binding on the self, which is *free* to start with.

This *disinterested action* ethics might look somewhat like Kant's ethic of 'duty for duty's sake', or acting from respect for the Law (hence the Categorical Imperative), but the precise rational-universalizable formulation of Kant is absent here. The *Gita*'s motivation is not so much to make the 'Good Will' the determinant of moral actions but to conserve the Brahmanical cultural base (its performative ideal) while integrating the threatening asocial ethic of ascetic renunciation, and also accommodating the influence of a nascent devotionalism, with its theistic orientation. The *Gita*'s ethics is both formal and material: one must do one's duty according to one's 'nature'; but this duty is determined by virtue of the individual's place in the larger social whole, i.e. by dint of the class he or she finds himself belonging to. Thus the maxim: better one's duty (though) imperfect, than another's duty well-performed (3.35). As to the specific content of the duty and the criterion by which its validity is to be judged, the text remains largely obscure. Nonetheless, the promise of liberation lies in disinterestedly pursued action, and a crude 'work ethic' (*karmayoga*), rid of egoism, is suggested, which might appear to justify prescribed ritual activity (sacrifice, austerities and giving) (18.5) and killing alike (18.8).

But the *Gita* does not overlook the significant role that a quasi-rational discerning faculty plays in such a process. For this it develops the *yogas* (paths) of *buddhi* or intelligent-willing and *jnana* or knowledge ('*gnosis*'). That the 'will' could at once be intelligent and practical (i.e. socially-attuned), making for its moral autonomy, is itself an interesting idea canvassed here. Apart from these teachings, truth, continence and non-violence (*ahimsa*), (16.2; 17.14) as well as 'welfare of all' (*lokasamgraha*) and 'desiring the good of every living creature' are underscored in the *Gita* (3.20; 5.25). The *Gita*'s model of an ethical person, in Krishna's words, is one who is:

without hatred of any creature, friendly and compassionate without possessiveness and self-pride, equable in happiness and unhappiness ... who is dependent on nothing, disinterested, unworried ... and who neither hates nor rejoices, does not mourn or hanker, and relinquishes both good and evil.

(12.13–17)

But as to why one should follow these principles, and what one should do if the consequences of one's action or duty are detrimental to the interests of another, the *Gita* seems to have little to say. (Cf. Rama Rao Pappu, 1988.) Also, if good and evil are transcended and the distinction obliterated can there any longer be an ethic to speak of? (Can we each be like Nietzsche's Superman?) Modern Indian reformers, such as Gandhi, have tried to fill in some of the lacunae in the traditional ethical teachings, symbolized in the *Gita*. But before that we'll look at another, contrasting, Indian ethical system.

ii Jaina ethics

One of the lesser known ethical traditions of India is that of the Jainas. Jainism, which is both a philosophical system and a way of life in its own right, was founded around 500 BCE by Mahavira, an ascetic and unorthodox teacher thought to be a contemporary of the Buddha, to whom he is often compared. Jainism is decidedly non-theistic, rejecting, like Buddhism, belief in a 'supremely personal God'. Very early on a dispute and rift arose over the charge that Jainas had concerned themselves far too much with individual morality and monastic life. This gave way to two distinct Jaina sects, the Digambaras (non-clad) and Shvetambaras (white-clad); the latter shifting towards a more pragmatic approach to lay life in contrast to the strictly austere life continued by the former.

The source of Jaina teachings is identified with a much older ascetic group of 'great teachers' (*tirthankaras*) called Nirgranths. Their teachings were codified and systematized in canonical texts known as *Nigantha pavayana*, most of which are no longer extant (Jaini, 1979, p. 42). The basic philosophic belief of the Jainas is that every entity in the world has *jiva* or a sentient principle, whose distinguishing feature is consciousness along with vital energy and a happy disposition. The idea is that consciousness is continuous and nothing in the universe is without some degree of sentiency at varying levels of conscious and apparently unconscious existence, from its more developed form in adult human beings to invisible embryonic modes at 'lower' animal and plant levels. (Here sentiency is not determined merely by pain–pleasure responses.)

Each and every sentient principle however, subsists in a contingent relation to the quantity of *karma*, which is described as a 'nonconscious immaterial' *matter* of the most subtle form that determines the relative nature of the being. Activity, of both volitional and non-volitional kinds, induces *karma* and by association conditions the development of the sentient being, resulting in the eventual death and reembodiment of the particular 'soul'. If *karma* can be prevented and exhausted the bondage could be broken, the cyclical process arrested, and the sentient principle could grow to its fullest possible realization – a belief Jainism shares with much of Hindu and Buddhist thought (Jaini, 1979, pp. 111–14).

The ethical implication of this 'spiritual' worldview is that there has to be a rigid discipline of renunciation, which entails an individual and a collective mode of life, *dharma*, conducive to this principle. A monastic community (*samgha*) is the preferred model, although a social life that aims to maximize this principle in a secular environment is acceptable. The life of a monk, particularly of an *arhant*, a philosopher–ascetic, who through his stoic practices has attained a 'near-omniscient' state, becomes the normative standard for the layperson, who would have to be born as a monk in the next round to attain that glorious final liberation (*moksha*) which is the end of Jaina life. Thus the duties of the layperson in civil life are derived, with due concessions and modifications, from those observed by the monk in a monastic *samgha*. But this rules out the possibility of an independent social ethics, for as with Hindu Yoga, self-culture and personal 'salvation' take priority over all else. Paradoxically, this end is not attainable without the annihilation of all self-interest and self-centred desires and inclinations. The sentient principle in that state is both disinterested and inactive. It goes without saying that for the Jaina all ethics is perceived by reference to monastic ethics.

The Jaina ethical life becomes almost synonymous with the observance of a list of vows and austerities, and abstention from useless and untoward activities. But the Jainas gave no real reasons why a certain practice X, e.g. the painful uprooting of every hair from the body, is deemed essential to an ascetic life, save to say that hair represents pleasure. So all pleasure is evil, and pain is at least endurable: which in effect turns classical utilitarianism on its head! The practical manual of Jaina ethics defines right conduct in terms of the observance of vows of restraint, progressively geared towards the complete renunciation of the ascetic. This is their axiological scheme. There are five such 'vows', namely, *ahimsa, satya, asteya, brahmacharya, apigraha*, which we shall describe briefly.

Ahimsa refers to non-injury or non-harming of sentient beings and is perhaps the most fundamental concept of Jaina ethics. With its broad understanding of sentience, Jaina ethics inevitably reflects an uncompromising 'reverence for all life'. The restraints comprise rigid dietary habits, such as non-consumption of meat, alcohol, and foods of certain kinds, and rules against the abuse, ill-treatment, exploitation, etc. of all 'breathing, existing, living, sentient creatures'. There are prohibitions against injurious treatment of animals, such as beating, mutilating, branding, overloading and deprivation of food and space. Meat-eating is strictly prohibited on the grounds that this requires killing of animals.

These concerns make the Jainas among the earliest protagonists of 'animal liberation' and they surpassed the Hindus and Buddhists on this moral stance and in expounding vegetarianism (Jaini, 1979, p. 169). Furthermore, Jainas were so sensitive to the killing, both intentional *and* accidental, of living matter that they would strain water to avoid drinking any creatures that might be in it, brush ants and insects from the path, and wear masks over the mouth to prevent minute '*nigodas*' (fungus-like entities) from being inhaled. The logical extreme of this ethic would be to curtail all movement and starve oneself (to death), as indeed some Jaina monks did – a sure antidote to eudaimonism! In cases of extreme or terminal illness, this practice may also be opted for by a Jaina.

One important qualification, however, has to be noted here. While the vow of *ahimsa* or non-injury may appear to have been practised on altruistic grounds, the concern here is as much with the motive of avoiding injury or harm to *oneself*, which could occur through any number of actions, not just in acts that lead to the suffering of others. Thus if one told lies this could be harmful to oneself for it hinders the development of one's 'soul'. Thus a Jaina monk will maintain silence where lying to the bandit could well save the life of his innocent prey. A layperson, however, may be inclined to place the interest of the victim above his or her own minimally threatened interest. This rather negatively articulated virtue has had an influence on the wider Indian ethical tradition.

The other vows pertain to being truthful (*satya*); not appropriating what is not one's own (*asteya*); exercising sexual continence (*brahmacharya*) – which legitimizes the institution of marriage for the laity; and non-possessiveness (*apigraha*), which encourages disinterested dealings in daily life. Fasting, giving alms, forgiveness, compassion and kindness towards others are some of the positive virtues that are encouraged. It could be said that the question of 'rights' and interests of others is not raised, except marginally under *ahimsa* (non-injury), for the ultimate justification for all ethical practices is that they should raise the moral stature of the practitioner, not necessarily of others. One even pardons another for this reason. In the stark absence of other beings, a lonesome Jaina might not accumulate much meritorious *karma*! Sometimes monks appeal to adverse social consequences to explain the evils of the non-observance of vows, but such prudential and utilitarian considerations are merely expedient rationalizations rather than their justification.

It has been claimed, somewhat contentiously, by some modern writers that virtues such as *ahimsa* have intrinsic value and that their justification lies in their being derived, not from objective facts (such as 'life is dear'), but from some experience which is self-evident. What is 'right' is in harmony with this experience. *Ahimsa*, in their example, is an experience related to the occurrence of pain and suffering among living beings and is universalized for others from one's own experience of pain. *Ahimsa* stands as the 'good' to which other values tend (Sogani, 1984, p. 243).

Overall, one gets the sense that Jaina ethics strives to be autonomous; it is not naturalistic but normative, and it admits the possibility of objective values, of which *ahimsa* seems to be its most significant and distinctive contribution.

iii Gandhian ethics

M. K. Gandhi, or Mahatma Gandhi as he is popularly known, is all but forgotten in India; and yet he, more than most in recent times, has struggled to advance Indian ethics beyond the pale of its apparently diminishing relevance in a modern, civilizing, world. Perhaps Gandhi doesn't have much to offer as an ethical theoretician. But, it is said, his genius lay in his practical wisdom, especially his ability to take an idea from a traditional practice or context (e.g. fasting) and apply it to contemporary issues or situations, whether on dietary matters or in an act of civil disobedience. For this he would attract criticism from both traditionalists and modernists alike.

Gandhi led a nationalist struggle against British sovereignty in India, which sparked off a spate of anti-colonial movements throughout the globe. The *way* or means by which he was able to achieve this feat, and how this ties in with the particular ethics he gave voice to, is particularly significant. That in the process he also ended up questioning many of the traditional (Hindu) values and customary practices, as well as a host of modern (Western) values, though perhaps not overturning them, is also significant. So, for example, he grew up a vegetarian on customary Hindu grounds; but after a short lapse he switched his moral justification for vegetarianism to ethical consideration for animals.

Gandhi is a curious mix of the radical and the conservative. For example, he takes up the cause of civil rights in South Africa, but his struggle does not extend much beyond rights for the Indian community. Still, he set an example of 'civil resistance' which some Black leaders and their Christian sympathizers of the time followed. Returning to India, Gandhi is much anguished by the injustices of the caste, class and religious divisions that had taken deep root in the Indian society. He becomes a champion of the cause of the 'untouchables', whom he gives the name *Harijan* (People of the Lord), and he rails against the prejudices and 'the evils of the caste system'. It looks as though Gandhi is set to have the entire structure dismantled.

In the long run, however, Gandhi defends the *varna* class structure, on the grounds that it is (1) different from the divisive caste system, (2) a sensible scheme for demarcation of work, (3) a law of human nature, and hence part of *dharma*. What he doesn't find agreeable is the inordinate privileges one class, especially the brahmin, has arrogated to itself. Inequality, he thinks, is not an issue in the design, but it becomes a problem when the structure gets tilted vertically (Gandhi, 1965, pp. 29, 80.) The enigma of *dharma* oddly places constraints on the otherwise splendid idea of civil and human rights that Gandhi awakens to rather early in his career; but it also helps him forge a principle of human action which itself has buttressed the struggle for rights of one kind or another in different quarters. That principle is non-violent action or, as Gandhi also called it, *ahimsa*.

Gandhi first toys with non-co-operation, an idea which he discovers in Tolstoy and Henry Thoreau, and which is reinforced by his Quaker friends in South Africa. It underpins the idea of 'non-resistance' (or 'resist not evil'), meaning the renunciation of all opposition by force, when faced with evil, injustices and oppression. Gandhi initially calls this 'passive resistance'; although he modifies his strategy, and coins a new term, *satyagraha* ('truth-force'), which he says better reflects the Indian basis of this technique. What this implies is that Gandhi, no longer content with simply 'turning the other cheek' or just withholding taxes and obligations, or advocating 'go slow', looks for a method by which to bring the adversary to (1) confront the situation and meet 'eye-to-eye' on the issue in dispute, and (2) redress the evil or wrong without coercing or inflicting injury or violence onto the other party.

In developing this method, what Gandhi does in effect is to combine three cardinal notions that had long currency in Hindu, Jaina and Buddhist ethics, namely, *satya*, *ahimsa*, and *tapasya*. The last of these came up in our discussion of the austere practices associated with asceticism (*tapas*, 'spiritual heat'). For Gandhi this concept provides a framework for the cultivation of courage, fortitude, stamina and most importantly *disinterestedness* (here invoking the *Gita*), necessary for the successful deployment of the ensuing technique.

Satya has to do with 'truth', but truth in three senses, namely, of being truthful, the truth of knowledge and the truth of being or reality. Its original sense is of course derived from *sat*, which means the 'IS' of existence, the really existent truth; whether this is identified with Non-being, Brahman, *Nirvana*, or God is a matter for philosophy to determine. For Gandhi *Truth* is God, by which he means we should continue to strive for truth beyond all human conception, in a spirit of creative tolerance.

On the practical level, *satya* means *truth as action*, or *satyagraha*, which suggests the idea of 'seizing' or 'holding firmly to a good cause'; thus *satyagraha* is a categorical attitude or 'force' by which one holds firmly to, grasps and hangs in there until truth triumphs in the situation. And this truth-force, he argues, must meet the needs of society at large beyond the individual's selfish ends (Gandhi, 1968, 6, pp. 171ff).

There lurks in the idea of *satyagraha* all the connotations of a *force*, or exertion, of pushing oneself, or doggedly putting one's foot down, and so on. The force could be a subtly coercive one, or an overtly injurious or violent one. This is where Gandhi finds the Jaina precept of *ahimsa* or 'not causing injury or harm to another being' to be most instructive. Of course, we shouldn't overlook the Buddhist emphasis on just the same precept. Gandhi acknowledges as much and uses this negative precept of non-injury to qualify *satyagraha* so that no hurt or harm should arise.

But Gandhi does more: he transforms *ahimsa* into a dynamic condition for a stratagem that does not stop until the goal of the action is achieved! In other words, far from a passive 'do not' injunction, *ahimsa* (non-injury), when intertwined with *satyagraha* (truth-force), becomes a positive mode of action that raises the *intent* of this injunction to a much higher ethical level: it seeks to bring about what is *right* in the situation at hand. Further, the interest of the other party is not compromised, for activists would rather suffer injury or violence on themselves than have it inflicted on the other; and compassion or 'love', as Gandhi calls it, as well as utter humanity or humility, must accompany the action. This, Gandhi believes, can be universalized to form a principle of disinterested non-violent action.

This principle is then put to use in social and political action, in a civil disobedience movement, in non-violent freedom and civil rights struggles, some of which have achieved remarkable results. One can argue whether the application of this principle in some instances does or does not entail coercion, and whether this would nullify the principle; or whether the inadvertent violence unleashed in the process defeats the purpose altogether. The consensus of those who have been influenced by this principle, such as Martin Luther King, Jr., in leading the struggle for the rights of Afro-Americans in North America, is that the purpose is never defeated. This will perhaps go down as the most significant development of Indian ethics in the twentieth century.

iv   Concluding remarks

What our enquiry shows is that the Indian culture, like any civilization, strives for ethically right conduct as well as a theoretical understanding of ethics. It may not succeed in achieving the goal, or it may lose sight of its goal, or even fail to reach a stage of clarity in its ethical discourse. But there are some important ideas and a few principles that emerge; these helped the society to survive, and to develop, even aesthetically. For us in the modern era, edging towards the twenty-first century, they may seem inadequate; but they might at least provide some useful metaphors, or *analogues*, to engage with our own notions, ideas, theories and analysis.

Dharma, with its roots in *rita* or 'natural order', can open up a more holistic, organic and ecologically enlightened perspective as a contrast to the more individualistic, competitive, nature-subjugating, and technocratic environment in which we try and think ethics. *Karma* or 'action-effect', and even the Indian ideas of concentric life-cycles and human ends, may suggest other possibilities of integrating the disparate and finite features of human life into this organic whole. And last but not least, the principle of disinterested non-violent action may prove effective in the continuing struggles towards justice and peace in the world.

References

Bhagavadgita in the Mahabharata, The; trans. and ed. J. A. B. van Buitenen (Chicago: University of Chicago Press, 1985).

Creel, A.: 'Dharma and justice: comparative issues of commensurability' (Paper read at Honolulu: Society for Asian and Comparative Philosophy Research Conference, 1985).

Danto, A. *Mysticism and Morality* (Harmondsworth: Pelican, 1972).

Eliot, T. S.: *The Waste Land* (London: 1922); (London: Faber & Faber, 1935).

Gandhi, M. K.: *My Varnashrama Dhama* (Bombay: Bharatiya Vidya Bhavan, 1965).

——: *The Selected Works of Mahatma Gandhi* (Ahmedabad: Navajivan Publishing House, 1968).

Jaini, P.: *The Jaina Path of Purification* (Delhi: Motilal Banarsidass, 1979).

Kane, P. V.: *History of Dharmasastra: Ancient and Medieval Religious and Civil Law in India*, Vols. I–V (Poona: Bhandarakar Oriental Research Institute, 1969).

Kautilya: *Kautilya's Arthasastra*; trans. R. Shamasastry (Mysore: Mysore Printing and Publishing House, 1960). Also in *History of Dharmasastra*, ed. P. V. Kane (Poona: Bhandarakar Oriental Research Institute, 1969).

Mahabharata, The, Books 1–5; trans. J. A. B. van Buitenen (Chicago: University of Chicago Press, 1978–80).

——, *A Play*; adapted by J.-C. Carrière, trans. from French by Peter Brook (New York: Harper & Row, 1985).

Manu: *The Manusmrti*; ed. S. B. Yogi (Delhi: Motilal Banarsidass, 1975).

Rama Rao Pappu, S. S.: 'Detachment and moral agency in the *Bhagavadgita*', in his *Perspectives on Vedanta: Essays in Honor of P. T. Raju* (Leiden: E. J. Brill, 1988).

Ramayana, The; trans. A. Menen (New York: Scribner's, 1954).

Rigveda, The Hymns of the; trans. R. T. H. Griffiths (Delhi: Motilal Banarsidass, 1973).

Sogani, K. C.: 'Jaina ethics and the meta-ethical trends', *Studies in Jainism*, ed. P. M. Marathe et al. (Poona: Indian Philosophical Quarterly Publication No. 7, 1984), pp. 237–47.

Upanishads, The Principal; ed. and trans. S. Radhakrishnan (New York: The Humanities Press, 1974).

Vedas: *The Vedic Experience Mantramanjari, An Anthology*; compiled and trans. R. Panikkar et al. (London: Darton, Longman and Todd, 1977).

Weber, M.: *The Religion of India* (Illinois: Free Press, 1958).

Further·reading

Bilimoria, P.: 'Gandhian ethics of nonviolence', *Prabuddha Bharata*, Vol. 93 (Calcutta: May 1988), 184–91.

Bowes, P.: *Hindu Intellectual Tradition* (Delhi: Allied Publishers, 1978).

Crawford, C.: *The Evolution of Hindu Ethical Ideals* (Honolulu: University of Hawaii Press, 1982).

Creel, A.: '*Dharma* as an ethical category relating to freedom and responsibility', *Philosophy East and West*, 22 (Honolulu: 1972), 155–68.

deNicolas, A. T.: *Avatara: The Humanization of Philosophy Through The Bhagavadgita* (New York: Nicolas Hays Ltd, 1976).

Erikson, E. H.: *Gandhi's Truth: On the Origins of Militant Nonviolence* (New York, London: W. W. Norton & Co, 1969).

Hindery, R.: *Comparative Ethics in Hindu and Buddhist Traditions* (Delhi: Motilal Banarsidass, 1978).

Koller, J.: '*Dharma*: an expression of universal order', *Philosophy East and West*, 22 (1972), 131–44.

Matilal, B. K.: *Logical and Ethical Issues of Religious Belief* (Calcutta: University of Calcutta, 1982).

O'Flaherty, W. D.: 'Separation of heaven and earth in Indian mythology', *Cosmology and Ethical Order*, ed. R. W. Lovin and F. E. Reynolds (Chicago: University of Chicago Press, 1985), pp. 177–99.

Schubring, W.: *The Doctrine of the Jainas* (Delhi: Motilal Banarsidass, 1962).

Thakur, S.: *Christian and Hindu Ethics* (London: George Allen & Unwin, 1969).

5

Buddhist ethics

PADMASIRI DE SILVA

i Introduction

THE Buddha's personal name was Siddhartha and his family name was Gotama. His father was the ruler of the kingdom of the Sakyas in North India. As a prince living in north India during the sixth century BCE, Siddhartha was caught in the intellectual ferment of the times, of ascetics and seers and philosophers of various brands, materialists, sceptics, nihilists, determinists and theists. He was also highly disturbed by the rigidities of caste, by animal sacrifices and by the uncritical attitudes of rulers regarding these issues. But he was even more disturbed by the perennial human issues of sickness, anguish and suffering, and the riddle of life and death. Thus in the young Siddhartha who left the royal palace at the age of 29 to become an ascetic, we find the profile of a rebel as well as a philosopher.

In addition to inquiring into these issues, Siddhartha experimented with different lifestyles. He immersed himself in the different techniques of meditation current at the time. He learnt from the teachers of meditation at the time the practices leading to states of meditative absorption referred to as *jhānas*. But he wished to go beyond these current practices and developed a comprehensive system of meditation, including both the practice of tranquillity meditation to reach a stage of calmness and the development of insight. The development of insight was focused on the three important realities of impermanence, suffering and egolessness. By the practice of meditation, he attained enlightenment at the age of 35 years, and preached thereafter to his fellow men. For 45 years after his enlightenment he taught and spoke to all types of men and women, peasants, carpenters, Brahmins and outcastes, kings and criminals, as well as ascetics and philosophers. It is these discourses which have been preserved in the Pali canon and are the primary sources for our study of the ethics of Buddhism.

The teachings of the Buddha were handed down in the form of an oral tradition, and it was many years later (first century BCE) that the monks wrote the discourses in ola leaves. They remained so till during recent times they were edited and printed by the Pali Text Society. Of these discourses, the group of discourses called the *Vinaya Piṭaka* deal with the rules of discipline for the monks, while the *Sutta Piṭaka* contains the basic teachings of the Buddha. A systematization of the doctrine by later commentators is called the *Abhidhamma Piṭaka*. Together they are called the three baskets and provide the primary sources for the study of Buddhism as well as the guidelines for the practical codes of conduct.

The very early tradition of Buddhism often called *Theravāda* Buddhism took root in South East Asia, specially in Sri Lanka, Thailand, Burma and Cambodia. The later traditions, *Mahāyāna* (meaning the Greater Vehicle) developed in Nepal, China, Korea and Japan, while the tradition called the *Tantrayāna* (the Esoteric Vehicle) emerged in Tibet and Mongolia. The *Mahāyānist* referred to the early Buddhist tradition as *Hīnayāna* (the lesser vehicle). In this article we are concerned with the common ethical teachings of the Buddha. Some of the differences of emphasis brought out by the different traditions in relation to ethics will be dealt with in the final section of this analysis.

ii Ethical concerns in the Buddhist tradition

When we refer to 'Buddhist ethics', we refer to the Buddha's analysis and insights into ethical issues, found dispersed over his discourses, as well as the reflections on ethical issues found in the later traditions. The discourses, however, provide the common doctrinal core for the analysis of ethical issues from a Buddhist perspective. Though he did not present a well-knit treatise on philosophical ethics, the discourses contain theoretical perspectives on major ethical issues. But beyond the rational scrutiny of ethical issues, he showed an abiding interest in ethics as a practical concern, a way of life and a well-defined ethical path towards liberation from suffering.

While the Buddha often emphasized the social dimensions of ethics, he also saw it as a personal quest marked by leading a good life, practising virtues and following meditational exercises. The practice of meditation emphasized the importance of paying attention to whatever one is doing while doing it, without the intrusion of distracting thoughts. Developing awareness of this sort laid the foundation for meditational exercises with specific objects for concentration. The development of meditation promoted its expansion into daily activities and enhanced individual morality. Thus in Buddhist ethics there is a close integration of the ethical as a rational engagement of analysis and argument, as a normative recommendation of conduct and a way of life, as a social expression and as an intense personal quest and mode of character development.

To understand how ethical concerns originate in the Buddhist traditions, one has to focus attention on the Four Noble Truths, which in a sense summarize the basic message of the Buddha. An understanding of the Four Noble Truths and the orientation of the Buddhist world-view helps us to place Buddhist ethics in a proper setting. At the core of the Buddha's doctrine is the notion of *dukkha*, a sense of *unsatisfactoriness* which lies at the heart of the perilous condition of human suffering, of physical pain and sickness, psychological conflict, anxiety and anguish and a deeper feature of the world described as insubstantiality. This latter feature of insubstantiality is related to the Buddhist doctrine of egolessness and the doctrine of change and impermanence. What we call an 'individual' or 'I' is, according to the Buddha, a combination of physical and psychological factors which are in constant change. By projecting a sense of 'permanence' onto a process which is in constant flux, man becomes disappointed when he faces change, destruction and loss. This complex which we consider as an 'individual' is liable to constant suffering, and if we project and anticipate a continuous life of pleasure and joy in terms of our sense of an individual person, we find it difficult to accept that we are liable to sickness, grief and suffering. Thus in this manner the three doctrines of impermanence, suffering and egolessness are interrelated. The Four Noble Truths, and the Noble Eightfold Path as a component of the Four Noble Truths, are related to the diagnosis of the human predicament described by the Pali word *dukkha*. Reflections on morality and society cannot be severed from this basic concern.

Some see the notion of *dukkha* as indicating a pessimistic outlook. Yet the ideal that the Buddha offers for man in following the ethical system is an ideal of happiness. While *nibbāna* represents the ideal of ultimate happiness for man as a moral ideal, the Buddha also offers a qualified notion of happiness for the householder who lives a harmonious and righteous life. Just as there are various expressions of pain, there are also diverse grades of pleasure and well-being. While the righteous and harmonious life permits the householder to seek wealth by lawful means, without greed and longing, to get ease and pleasure for him or herself and do meritorious deeds, the recluse exercises a more stringent control over desires and wants and is more earnestly committed to the ideal of release from all suffering (*nibbāna*). Both the life ideals of the householder as well as those of the recluse are highly critical of the life of pure sensuality devoid of any ethical constraints. A life of pure pleasure by its inner nature ends up in boredom and dissonance, and interferes with the healthy functioning of family and community life. The Buddha condemned pure hedonism on psychological and ethical grounds. The Buddha was also critical of some materialists who did not believe in an afterlife and thus supported a hedonistic lifestyle without any moral values.

The Buddha was critical of the way of pure sensuality and the way of self-mortification, and considered his own way as the middle path. The first Noble Truth is the truth of suffering, the second deals with the arising of suffering, the third deals with the cessation of suffering (*nibbāna*), and the fourth with the way to end suffering (the Noble Eightfold Path). The Noble Eightfold Path has the following aspects: (1) right understanding; (2) right thought; (3) right speech; (4) right bodily action; (5) right livelihood; (6) right effort; (7) right mindfulness; (8) right concentration. An important point about the path is that the items fall under three divisions: items 3–5 come under ethical conduct (*sīla*), items 6–8 come under mental training (*samādhi*), and items 1 and 2 come under wisdom (*paññā*). Thus it is a threefold scheme of moral training, consisting of the practice of virtues and the avoidance of vices, the practice of meditation and the development of wisdom. It is through the Eightfold Path that one can attain the ultimate moral ideal of Buddhism.

iii The moral philosophy of Buddhism

Philosophically, the first prerequisite for a system of ethics, according to the Buddha, is the notion of free will, secondly the distinction between good and bad, and thirdly the notion of causation in relation to moral action. The third concept, as indicating the good and bad consequences of actions which can be morally assessed, is also related to a specifically Buddhist notion, survival after death.

Of these, the most crucial concept necessary for the evaluation of human action is the notion of *kamma*, based on the notion of moral causation. The Pali term *kamma* is used to refer to volitional acts which are expressed by *thought*, *speech* and *bodily action*. The oft-quoted statement 'I call the motive to be the deed' provides a focus for the evaluation of human action from a moral point of view. Volitional acts which come within the purview of moral evaluation can be good, bad or neutral, and could also be of a mixed nature.

When we evaluate an action, we can look at its genesis. If the action has as its roots greed, hatred and delusion, it is an unwholesome or bad action, and if it was generated by the opposite roots of liberality, compassionate love and wisdom, it is a good action. But we have also to see its consequences to others as well as oneself, as they also play a part in moral evaluation.

The Pali word '*cetanā*, usually translated as motive, is a complex term covering intention and motive as well as the consequences of action dependent on the motive or intention. According to the law of moral causation, if a person gives some money to a needy person several consequences follow in the form of psychological laws: it is a good thought and stabilizes the tendency to repeat such thoughts, it is a good action, and it is said that the greatest blessing of a good action is the tendency to repeat it, that it becomes a part of one's character. This psychological dimension is believed to extend over several births and to be carried over to another life.

There is another aspect to the consequences of good and bad actions. According to the law of moral causation, a person who gives for charity expects to get something in return, comforts in future life, and a person who steals or is miserly will be repaid by being subjected to poverty. These are two aspects of the moral consequences of action. We may describe the first aspect of character-building as the *craftsmanship model* of action and the second aspect, which focus on rewards and punishments, as the *judicial model* of action.

Another dimension of these two models is that disinterested character-building may be *nibbāna*-oriented, as it is basically an attempt to rid oneself of greed, hatred and delusion, and the attempt to accumulate merit is directed towards a better life in the future. It has been observed by scholars who have gone into the terminology that 'good' and 'bad', used in the context of *nibbāna*-oriented action, may be translated by the words *kusala* and *akusala*, and 'good' and 'bad', when speaking of the wish for a better existence in the future lives, may be translated by the terms *puñña* and *pāpa*. If *puñña* is rendered as merit and *pāpa* as de-merit, a meritorious action paradoxically helps us to collect more fuel for a longer journey in *saṃsāra* (the wheel of existence), while a good action in the form of *kusala* shortens our journey and speeds our approach to *nibbāna*.

The Buddha will not limit the evaluation of actions to the narrow concept of a motive alone, as the act has to be performed, and the manner in which it is done and the consequences are important. In this sense this is a consequentialist or a teleological ethics. (See Article 19, CONSEQUENTIALISM.)

Within the consequentialist orientation, Buddhist ethics lays very great emphasis on working towards the material and spiritual welfare of others. The Buddha himself was described as a person concerned with the well-being and happiness of mankind. In general, Buddhist ethics has a utilitarian stance, but the Buddhist utilitarianism is not a hedonistic utilitarianism. (Varieties of utilitarianism are discussed in Article 20, UTILITY AND THE GOOD.) Certainly the Buddha would be critical of the pursuit of pure sensuality and also of any attempt to reduce human pleasures to a hedonistic calculus. As one proceeds on the path of meditation, the *jhānas* (states of deep meditative absorption) are associated with states of pleasure and happiness, not of a mundane nature but rather states of joy, zest and rapture. There are certain refinements in these states which go beyond the pleasures we normally associate with hedonism (the view that pleasure is or ought to be the goal of all our actions). Against the background of these jhānic states, concepts like hedonism and eudaimonism (in which 'happiness' plays the role that 'pleasure' does in the hedonistic doctrine) used in the context of Western ethics may lose clear application.

Buddhism may be described as a consequentialist ethic embodying the ideal of ultimate happiness for the individual, as well as a social ethic with a utilitarian stance concerned with the material and spiritual well-being of mankind. In keeping with this stance, Buddhism also has a strong altruistic component, specially embodied in the four sublime virtues of lovingkindness, compassion, sympathetic joy and equanimity.

The Buddha also emphasizes the role of duties and obligations in relevant contexts. The *Sigālōvāda Sutta* discusses the duties and rights of parents and children, husband and wife, teachers and pupils as well as one's obligations to friends and recluses. But what is described here are reciprocal relations of mutual obligations, rather than any concept of human rights. First, the Buddhist approach to duties and rights is more a humanistic than a legalistic one. Second, while considering duties and rights as important, the Buddha never elevated them into an ethic of duty and obligation as found in Western ethical systems. (See, for example, Article 18 AN ETHIC OF PRIMA FACIE DUTIES.) In ethical systems emerging in the Judeo-Christian tradition, a breach of duties is tied to the notion of feeling guilty about wrongdoing. Sin and guilt and worry over past offences are not concepts that fit into the Buddhist analysis of wrong-doing. In fact it is a difficult task to find a Pali equivalent in the discourses for notions like guilt in the context of wrongdoing. In general wrongdoing is described as unskilled action, as unwholesome, as a defilement etc. In fact, worry and restlessness, as well as unhealthy fears regarding wrongs done, are considered as obstructions to the leading of a morally good life. Thus while concepts of duty and obligations, as well as of justice and righteousness, play a part in Buddhist ethics, they are integrated within the broader humanistic and consequentialist ethics of Buddhism.

iv   A Buddhist perspective on the place of knowledge and truth in ethics

In ordinary everyday situations, statements like 'There is a red book on my table' can be checked regarding their truth and falsity. But in ethics we get statements like 'Killing is wrong', 'Stealing is bad', 'He did wrong in not going to the appointment' and so on. Though these statements are grammatically similar to the other statement cited above, they appear to lack any cognitive content. Thus it is said that it is illogical to apply notions like knowledge and truth in the field of ethics. (For further discussion see Articles 35 and 38, REALISM and SUBJECTIVISM.)

Such problems did not disturb the Buddha and there is no explicit discussion in his discourses of the relationship between facts and values. Yet the Buddha upheld the relative objectivity of moral utterances as crucial to his system against the sceptics and the relativists of his time. There is a broad-based naturalistic stance in Buddhist ethics, and it can be said that *certain types of facts are* relevant as support for moral utterances. Thus in Buddhist ethics, there is no relationship of logical entailment between facts and values, but a relationship of specific kinds of relevance according to which facts will provide a *kind* of grounding for values.

But yet from another perspective it appears that a concept like *dukkha* seems to lie at the point of intersection between a range of facts and their evaluation. A word like *dukkha* is a description of a state of affairs, the nature of the human predicament, but in the context of the Four Noble Truths, it carries with it the notion that it has to be *known, abandoned* and *realized*. The first Noble Truth suggests that *dukkha* has to be realized, the second that it has to be abandoned, the third that it has to be realized and the fourth that knowledge about *dukkha* has to be developed and gradually refined so that it culminates in knowledge of *dukkha*. Thus in Buddhist ethics, in one sense facts are relevant for understanding values, but in another sense some of the central concepts like that of *dukkha* seem to lie at the point of intersection between values and facts.

It is also necessary to point out that the Buddha's use of the notion of 'fact' goes beyond its usage in Western ethical reflections. A 'fact' for the Buddha can be found out by the avenues of our normal senses, but he also upholds the acquaintance with facts through extra-sensory perception. Let us take an example like 'Killing is bad'. Killing is considered bad or wrong for several reasons. (1) The genesis of the action show that it is clearly associated with the effective root of hatred, sometimes with greed and also with the cognitive root of having wrong views; (2) It has harmful consequences to oneself and is an obstruction to attaining *nibbāna* or will have bad consequences in another life; (3) Here and now, it hardens one's character in transgressing the ideal of non-injury, makes one develop a heavy conscience, comes into conflict with other people and can be punished by the law.

Now, some of the information relevant to the normal utterances may be had by sensory observation, by self-analysis, by the observation of others, etc. But certain types of information like the consequences for a future life go beyond our normal powers. Buddhism also accepts that there are levels of spiritual development and that the differences between normal perception and extra-sensory perception are merely a difference of degree, not of kind.

The Buddha's notion of facts and the relevance of facts to values is something which emerged from the nature of the world in which he lived. Sometimes we convert ordinary usages into excessively difficult riddles by trying to impose a formal rigour into them. The Buddha himself said that he was neither a traditionalist nor a rational metaphysician who considers that logic can solve all the problems, but an experimentalist who respects facts as they are found in the world. But facts to him also have some *significance* in the light of his doctrine. That significance is something which emerges from the natures of things and is not imposed from outside.

v Buddhism as an ethics of virtues and vices

As an ethics concerned with the moral development of man, Buddhist ethics deal both with the nature of the evil states which darken the mind, as well as the wholesome mental states which illumine the mind. The sutta on the *Simili of the Cloth* cites sixteen such defilements: greed, covetousness, malevolence, anger, malice, hypocrisy, spite, envy, stinginess, deceit, treachery, obstinacy, impetuosity, arrogance, pride and conceit. The most well-known and important analysis is the tenfold evil actions, which are in turn related to the three roots of evil: killing, stealing, enjoying sensual pleasures of a wrong nature, false speech, slanderous speech and frivolous talk, as well as intense greed, malevolence and wrong view.

The Buddha requested people not only to refrain from such evil states, but also to practise positive moral virtues. Following the analysis of Wallace (*Virtues and Vices*, 1978), we can say that the virtues fall into three groups:

1   virtues of conscientiousness:
      veracity, truthfulness and righteousness
2   virtues of benevolence:
      lovingkindness, compassion, sympathetic joy and equanimity
3   virtues of self-restraint:
      self-control, abstinence, contentment, patience, celibacy, chastity, purity

The arrangement of the recommended moral qualities shows that Buddhist ethics brings into play a wide variety of virtues for the building up of human character. Some of them are closely welded to the natural feelings humans have for fellow beings, others apply to the needs of social organization and community living, and yet others are demanded by the path of moral development and self-restraint. Virtues and vices also refer to our emotional aspect. In addition to making a close analysis of the negative emotions like anger, malevolence, lust, envy and worry, the Buddha gave a central place to the positive and creative emotional responses which had a great moral relevance, like compassion, generosity and gratitude. His analysis shows that there is a great range and variety of emotional responses sharpening and expanding our moral sensibility. The link between moral psychology and ethics is a central feature of the ethics of Buddhism and makes it appropriate to consider it as an ethic of virtue. (See Article 21, VIRTUE THEORY.)

vi   Buddhist social ethics

The social ethics of Buddhism revolve around two important ethical perspectives, which may be referred to as 'the ethic of care' and the 'ethic of rights'. It is a blend of the principles of humanistic altruism and the notion of a *righteous* social, moral and political order which provide the ethical foundations of society. Though the ethical path as a path towards liberation is basically a consequentialist ideal, the social and political ethics of Buddhism has a deontological strand as an ethics of duty and rights, which is, however, integrated into Buddhist social ethics in its own way.

The family forms a central unit in Buddhist social ethics. Within the family there are reciprocal duties that link up all members of the family. This notion of reciprocity in human relations means that talk of sexual equality and the rights of men and women is somewhat misplaced. The concept of equality was raised when the question of admission of women to the order became a practical issue. Regarding the moral and spiritual excellence of women, there is a well documented tradition of references in the discourses and the Buddha gave permission to initiate a separate order of nuns. Within the family it was accepted that a woman brings stability, care, patience and compassion. While women attained the state of sainthood (*arahat*), the concept of a Buddha was limited to men and this became a point of debate within the later traditions.

In rejecting caste and race the Buddha said that distinctions based on birth are artificial and the only worthwhile distinctions are based on character. In admitting people to the order he did not pay any attention to distinctions based on caste and socio-economic status.

The Buddha also showed concern regarding all forms of life. The Buddhist concept of society would in a deeper ethical sense include all living beings, not only those who are human but animals and lower creatures as well. Unlike most Western systems of ethics, the cultivation of socio-moral virtues covers behaviour in relation to all living beings.

The Buddha expected the universal monarch to govern justly and impartially. There are three components of the concept of righteousness; impartiality, just requital and truthfulness. While impartiality and fair play are emphasized for kings, their rule is expected to be pervaded by the spirit of benevolence. Above the social and political order was the Buddhist concept of *dharma*, the cosmic order in the universe, and the king had not merely to respect this order but also as the 'wheel-turning monarch' to see that this order was reflected in his regime. In general it may be said that though in the political order the concepts of rights and fairness are important, the Buddhist social ethics is centred on human relations, where the ethic of responsibility and the recognition of differences in need play an important part.

65

vii Buddhist perspectives on practical ethics

If one is to search for the existence of any core moral values in Buddhism, they are to be found in the five precepts: abstention from killing and hurting living creatures, abstention from stealing, abstention from wrong indulgence in sensual pleasures, abstention from lying and abstention from taking intoxicants. These precepts embody basic requirements for the living of a good life and the establishment of a good community. The respect for life and property, the acceptance of a lifestyle which rejects excessive, illegitimate and harmful pleasures, truthfulness and an awareness of the danger of certain social evils like alcoholism and drug addiction are the basic moral concerns of a Buddhist society.

During the time of the Buddha as well as during later debates, questions relating to these precepts have been discussed. We shall briefly take two of these issues, questions concerning the respect for life in relation to animals and the accumulation of wealth.

Even kings were expected to provide protected territory not only for human beings but also for beasts of the forests and birds of the air. Deliberate infliction of torture and hurt to animals and killing were condemned by the Buddha.

There are four topics in the discourses which are relevant to issues pertaining to the values of life: animal sacrifices, warfare, agriculture and meat-eating. The Buddha did not hesitate to condemn both the performance of animal sacrifices and the pleasures of hunting. He also pointed out the futility of warfare. He prohibited the monks from joining the army and also from digging the ground, as in this process there was the danger of injuring insect life. But regarding meat-eating he left it as an open possibility that if one practises compassion one would be inclined to practise vegetarianism. Also there is a social context where the Buddha himself and other monks went for their food with the begging bowl and walked silently through the streets and the marketplace. The Buddha had asked the monks not to ask for any particular food unless the monk was sick but collect what was offered. As far as the rules are concerned the monk may accept meat that is offered for a meal if the monk is convinced that it was not specially killed and prepared for a monk's meal. Though the Buddha rejects professions like the selling of armaments and the killing and selling of animals, he did not restrict the monk's food, unless it was forbidden because it was poisonous. It is also important that the Buddha did not want to make eating into a fad or a fetish through which recluses would seek purification. It appears that vegetarianism is a positive practice that can emerge through the practice of compassion, but in the context of the monks collecting the food that was given to them, there was no rule forbidding them from taking meat under all conditions.

The problem about the accumulation of wealth is of course well understood in terms of the lifestyles recommended by the Buddha. While the monk lives with no possessions except the robes and the begging bowl, the layman is encouraged to contribute to his economic stability. The layman is asked to concentrate on the production of wealth through skilled and earnest endeavour, and protecting wealth through savings and living within one's means. The Buddha condemned both miserliness and extravagance and provided the guidelines for contented living. The layman has a right to property and to accumulate wealth to ensure a decent existence for his family, but not to develop greed and avarice for wealth. Also, the idea that the needy should be helped and that wealth should be given to the have-nots was accepted even by the kings who ruled according to the advice of the Buddha. Whatever moral values we take in terms of the five precepts, there was a pragmatism and realism in the Buddha's outlook, which provide useful resources for dealing with conflicts between human needs and moral ideals.

viii Contributions to ethics in the later Buddhist traditions

The later Buddhist traditions of *Mahāyāna*, the *Tantrayāna* and Zen Buddhism are all rooted in the original teachings of the Buddha, and with the *Hīnayāna* tradition share his basic doctrines of egolessness, impermanence and suffering. But their techniques of communication and points of emphasis took different directions.

In relation to the ethics of Buddhism a central point on which both the *Mahāyāna* and the *Tantrayāna* traditions opened up a fresh line of inquiry was on the question whether everyone should aspire to be a Buddha or whether one should be contented with the cessation from suffering by attaining the state of perfection called the *arahant*. The *Mahāyānist* felt that instead of attaining enlightenment as a disciple of the Buddha, everyone should aspire to be a Buddha, so that one could help others. The *Mahāyānist* felt, like the followers of *Tantrayāna*, that there was a higher ideal, that of the *Bodhisatva*, which indicated an infinite commitment to others and was an expression of the widest limits of altruism. The Buddha is an enlightened one and a *Bodhisatva* is one who aspires to be a Buddha. The different lives of the Bodhisatva are dedicated to the practice of special virtues like charity, patience, effort, meditation and wisdom. The *Bodhisatva* attempts to identify himself with the liberation of others.

The *Tantrayāna* added a strong devotional strand into the religious practices with an emphasis on symbolism and rituals. As these were associated with esoteric teachings they do not appear to have any specific contribution to ethics which differs from the Mahayanist perspective.

The word Zen is an equivalent of the Sanskrit word *dhyāna* meaning meditation. It emerged from the Chinese soil and was deeply centred on the practice of meditation. But it was critical of moral codes and rituals which were practised through the force of convention. When a tradition gets too much stuck in rules, codes and procedures an intended 'means' can become an 'end' in itself. Also, the prolific philosophical and scholastic distinctions which emerged in the Indian tradition after the Buddha seemed to submerge the deep meditative tradition which the Buddha initiated. Thus the Zen masters used stories, paradoxes, parables, and meditational exercises called *koans* to shock the conventional mind stuck in rules and procedures. This is a useful perspective for the practice of morality rather than a theory of ethics, but it does emphasize that the practice of morality is intrinsically related to the inner transformation of the individual. Thus the Zen masters come out with the paradox that Zen begins where morality ends.

Both the early and later traditions of Buddhism continue as living traditions in different parts of the Eastern world and their impact has spread to the West. While the ethics of Buddhism influence the daily lives of its adherents, there is a great admixture of rituals and conventional practices of each culture, which can both be an aid to the development of the teachings of the Buddha as well as an obstruction. Thus Buddhism continues to live in the minds of people at different levels, of routine practice and rituals, intellectual reflection and debate, and a deeper personal quest rooted in Buddhist meditation.

References

The reader who is interested in reading the discourses of the Buddha may follow up by reading the following texts:

Gradual Sayings; Vols. I, II, V, trans. F. L. Woodward; Vols. III, IV, trans. E. H. Hare (London: Pali Text Society, 1932–6).
Dialogues of the Buddha; Part I, trans. T. W. Rhys Davids; Parts II and III, trans. T. W. and C. A. F. Rhys Davids (London: Pali Text Society, 1956–7).
Middle Length Sayings; Vols. I, II, III, trans. I. B. Horner (London: Pali Text Society, 1954–9).
Kindred Sayings; Parts I and II, trans. C. A. F. Rhys Davids; Parts III, IV, V, trans. F. L. Woodward (London: Pali Text Society, 1917–56).

Also referred to:
Wallace, J.: *Virtues and Vices* (Ithaca, NY: Cornell University Press, 1978).

Further reading

Conze, E.: *Buddhism: Its Essence and Development* (Oxford: Bruno Cassirer, 1951).
de Silva, P.: *An Introduction to Buddhist Psychology* (London: Macmillan Press, 1979).
Dharmasiri, G.: *Fundamentals of Buddhist Ethics* (Singapore: The Buddhist Research Society, 1986).
Jayatilleke, K. N.: *Ethics in Buddhist Perspective* (Kandy: Buddhist Publication Society, 1972).
Premasiri, P. D.: 'Moral evaluation in early Buddhism', *Sri Lanka Journal of Humanities*, 1, 1 (1975).
Saddhatissa, H.: *Buddhist Ethics* (London: Allen and Unwin, 1970).
Tachibana, S.: *The Ethics of Buddhism* (Colombo: The Baudha Sahitya Sabha, 1943).
Webb, R.: *An Analysis of the Pali Canon* (Kandy: Buddhist Publication Society, 1975). This book contains information about the sources of the Buddha's teachings used in this article.
Wijesekera, O. H. de A.: *Buddhism and Society* (Colombo: Baudha Sahitya Sabha, 1952).

6

Classical Chinese ethics

CHAD HANSEN

THIS essay focuses on the classical period of Chinese thought (550–200 BCE) which spawned the main Chinese philosophical positions. We will forgo a comprehensive treatment of the entire civilization's history, which includes both a Buddhist and a neo-Confucian epoch, for a more detailed analysis of the classical views.

The differences between Chinese and Western ethics are broad and deep. Our inherited Greek psychology divides the ego into the rational and the emotional. It explains all human mental processing via belief and desire. Our concept of morality involves reference to the human faculty of reason. Chinese thinkers view human action in a different way. They appeal to no such faculty nor to beliefs and desires as reasons for action.

The Chinese approach is initially more social. Humanity is social. A social *dao* ('way') guides us. Chinese ethical thinkers reflect on how to preserve, transmit or change this way – the public, guiding discourse. When modern Chinese writers sought a translation for 'ethics', they chose the compound term *dao de* – ways and virtues. *Dao* is public, objective guidance. *De* ('virtue') consists of the character traits, skills, and dispositions induced by exposure to a *dao*. *De* is the physical realization of *dao* in some part of the human system – a family, a state, or an individual. We may get virtue either by internalizing a way or it may be inborn.

Both *dao* and *de* encompass more than morality proper. There are ways of fashion, etiquette, archery, economics, and prudence. Both *dao* and *de* can have negative connotations, e.g. when speaking of the ways of one's opponents. Most Chinese writers, however, use *dao* in speaking of their own system for guiding behaviour and most take the social point of view. Translations, as a rule therefore, treat *dao* as a definite description. They write '*The* Way' when they find *dao* in a text. (Classical Chinese has no definite article.) This causes no difficulty if we remember that the different schools disagreed about *which* way was *the* way.

i The positive Dao period: Confucius and Mozi

1 *Confucius and the conventional Dao*

Confucius (551–479 BCE) was the first and most famous thinker from the classical period. He alleged, however, that he was merely transmitting a code of social conduct – the *li* ('ritual') inherited from ancient sage-kings. The *Book of Li* makes up the Confucian *dao*. Confucius taught his disciples the *dao* in all the classic texts. He did not see himself as a philosopher but as a historical scholar. His task was not justifying or systematizing the code but learning and relaying it.

Confucius' disciples collected dialogues and exchanges that they remembered having with Confucius. These make up the aphorisms in the book known as *The Analects*. His disciples disagreed about Confucius' *dao*. Some focused on *li* ('ritual') and others on *ren* ('humanity'). *Ren* occurred often and somewhat mysteriously in *The Analects*.

Confucius treated the code of ritual as consisting of names and role descriptions. His pronouncements included no explicitly prescriptive *ought*-statements. He did not segment the *li* into sentence-like rules which generate duties. For Confucius, the basic role of all language is to guide our acts. We hear, study and learn the way of the sage-kings via transmitted texts, inherited traditions and conventional strings of words. They used language to regulate behaviour. Their guidance is still available to us now because they recorded and relayed their words.

We detect the *li* in explicit written form. *Li* epitomizes a positive, cultural *way* conveyed in literature. Translations of *li* include 'ritual', 'etiquette', 'manners', 'ceremonies' and 'propriety'. The most general term we might use for *li* is 'conventions'. *Li* guide, for example, forms of address, funeral wear, even how to sit at meals. Confucius' attachment to *li* is uncritical. He never raises the Socratic ethical question, 'Why follow just these conventional norms?' Yet he does seem aware that conventional norms vary in different areas and at different times.

Classical Chinese philosophers expressed their disputes as accounts of *i* ('morality'). Translations normally translate *i* puritanically as 'righteousness' or deontologically as 'duty'. I avoid 'duty' since Chinese thinkers do not segment their systems of guidance into sentential rules. They do not individualize obligations and duties as we do. Think of *i* ('morality') as the ideally correct social guidance in language. Confucius thus has a conventional morality (*li i*) in contrast to Mozi's utilitarian morality (*li i* – a different *li* character) and Mencius' intuitive morality (*ren i*).

Confucius argued for neither the content of the *Book of Ritual* nor for its guiding authority. He fixed instead on an intriguing practical concern. How do we correctly extract guidance from the language in the text? How do we use the book in building the human virtues that would result in our following the sages' intended way?

Confucius addressed the intellectual problem of interpretation of the guiding texts. His was a *dao* of education. The key to communicating a literary *dao*, he argued, was to rectify names. (*Analects* 13:3.) The first step is study – ingest the content. Confucius had his disciples study the classics. They contained both the guiding codes and the accepted description of historical models of appropriate virtue.

We learn to embrace these cultural roles and play them by studying models in life and literature. We learn to play music or act out our parts from models. The society must provide us with example of rulers, ministers, fathers, and sons, and correctly identify them. Only then can we learn from their interpretations of their parts. The desire to internalize roles flows from our nature as social beings. We make ourselves fully human by expanding our repertoire of roles. We show our excellence by the quality of our interpretation of our parts.

Interpretation of ritual, thus, shares the sense it has when we speak of musical interpretation. Confucius often pairs *yue* ('music') with *li* ('ritual'). Given any piece of music used as a guide, we may perform it well or badly. We call our performance an interpretation of the piece. Building good character requires that we *interpret* the *li* in playing our roles. The mysterious concept *ren* ('humanity') guarantees a correct performance of the guiding *dao*.

The interpretive ability must be separate from the code which we interpret and yet closely tied to it. Humanity is an interpretive intuition. We cannot teach *ren* by explicit instructions, since we have to interpret those instructions. This makes it look as if humanity must be inborn. Yet we do get better at interpretation as we learn and practice. Without this interpretive skill, the ritual code cannot function correctly.

Thus humanity must be the ability to rectify names. We rectify a name when we make the right discrimination, apply it to the right setting. Think of the code as an internalized programme. To execute the programme containing the term X, we have to discriminate whether *this* is a case of X or non-X. We must rectify any term that occurs in the code book. To rectify a name is to see that people use it of the right objects. Otherwise the code book's instructions will misdirect people. Since he regards the tendency to convey and receive a *dao* as natural, the main political concern for Confucius is rectifying names. 'If names are not rectified ... affairs cannot be accomplished ... and the people will not know how to move hand or foot.'

The ruler rectifies names in appointing people to status positions. Most of the code's content directs proper action toward people filling social roles – father, brother, ruler, minister etc. The names are primarily social, hierarchical roles. The ruler *dubs* someone *minister*. We then all conform in using that title to guide our behaviour toward the person filling the role. Similarly, Confucius argues, the political system should identify model fathers and sons. This gives us our link to the code. It also gives us our models of how to act out the role patterns described in the ritual code. Without an accepted, shared social pattern of name use, the code could not guide us.

Plainly, rectifying names requires something beyond the code book itself, since we must rectify names to use the code book. *Ren* ('humanity') is the intuitive ability to interpret the *li* correctly. We may apply *ren* either in our own action or in guiding others. Rectifying the use of language requires *ren*. Without people to model roles and rulers to *recognize* and title a fine performance, we cannot relay the role-based way intended by the sage-kings.

Some passages suggest Confucius pointedly would not teach about this nurtured interpretive intuition he called *ren*. He used the term often, but was notoriously elusive about it. In response to his students' frustration Confucius twice hinted without explanation that all the details of his guiding *dao* had some unifying core. 'Confucius said, "My *dao* has a single thread". Zengzi replied, "I hear you". Confucius left. The other asked "What did he refer to?" Zengzi answered, "Our master's *dao* is loyalty and reciprocity".' (*Analects* 4:15.) Most Confucians accept Zengzi's guess. Confucius himself bequeathed little of his theory of either loyalty or reciprocity.

Confucius *does* formulate a *negative* version of the Golden Rule, 'What you do not desire, do not effect on others.' This may count as a gloss on 'reciprocity'. In its simplicity, it conflicts with the elaborate code of *li* which Confucius usually stresses. It is implausible that Confucius meant the Golden Rule to replace his role-based morality – the way Christ repealed 'the law' with his Golden Rule. Still, such passages suggest that while the code is conventional, interpretation of the code appeals to more universal, moral considerations. Confucius' refusal to elaborate on *ren* invites speculation that it is a universal moral sense intended to guide interpretation. The conventional translations – 'humanity' or 'bene-volence' – suggest a universal utilitarian standard for interpretation. Confucians would find this result uncomfortable. The orthodoxy treats Confucius as an anti-utilitarian because his most vociferous critic advocated utility.

Apart from pointing to a developed intuition for interpreting, Confucius did not theorize about abstract axioms of conduct. He bases his explicit normative system on roles. He does not assign a normative value to persons apart from their social relationships. All your duties are duties of your station towards other socially described persons or things. These roles are natural and the family roles are the core examples. This leads Confucianism to characterize itself as a system of 'partial' or 'graded' love. We deal with people qua 'mother', 'neighbour', 'mentor', 'daughter'. Contrast this with the Kantian respect for individuals as bare persons or agents. The basis for this special Kantian status of moral respect is the rationality of moral agents (persons). (See Article 14, KANTIAN ETHICS.)

Confucius also exhibits little sense of desert in moral theory. Nor does he exhibit familiar deontological attitudes such as categorical requirements to tell the truth or keep promises, to be just or to respect an agent's autonomy. He strongly opposes the rule of law. In part he objects to the tendency of punishment to induce egoism. Confucians also oppose the role-corroding egalitarianism of a legal code. In place of law, Confucius would have social education – modelling of name use and role performance, together with a traditional socio-cultural *dao* set in the classics. The basis for normative relations among people is social role relations, not some bare rational agency.

2 Mozi and the utilitarian Dao

Mozi, the first rival philosopher, adopts much of the structure of Confucius' normative scheme. He too discusses how names in codes guide behaviour rather than discussing *ought* sentences. We use a name by making a *shi* ('this:right') or a *fei* ('not this:wrong') assignment. To know the name is to know to *shi* what should have the name and *fei* what should not. This ability to divide things in response to language triggers a tendency to treat each discriminant in the proper way. Still Mozi raises familiar philosophical doubts about the explicit linguistic content of the guidance. He asserts that we need an argument for the traditional content. Why should we regard our specific traditions or customs as *i* ('morality')? Why regard *ren* ('humanity') as merely an intuitive interpretive ability applied to a *customary dao* ('way')? Any such ability should also guide us to create new moral codes – to revise social morality. Thus he directly questions the authority of the ancestral guiding *dao*s.

Customs can be very wrong. (Mozi recites or invents a story of a tribe who customarily eat their first-born sons. That should shock good Confucians!) So, he argues, we must have a gauge for selecting among different *dao* contents. He proposed utility as the measure. He treated this norm as the standard of *shi* ('this:right') and *fei* ('not this:wrong). Thus it became a model both for ordering and rectifying the terms in the *dao*.

Mozi argued that his criterion came from a natural or heavenly *will* – the natural preference for benefit over harm. This naturally guiding name pair (*benefit-harm*) becomes the basis for using all other guiding name pairs. If we do not start from that distinction, Mozi says, we can never be clear on *shi-fei*. So a correct, positive *dao* should contain whatever passages will increase benefit when appropriately engaged in guiding our behaviour. Mozi is a language utilitarian. We should use a single criterion to choose both the code we follow and the discriminations we make with the terms in that code. We should choose both in ways that *constantly* or reliably advance *li* ('benefit') and diminish *hai* ('harm').

Mozi thinks this proposal entails that we should use the phrase 'universal love' in public discourse rather than the Confucian 'partial love'. A *dao* that includes frequent use of the phrase partial love will not be constant. It will guide someone who adopts it to prefer that *others* have a more universal attitude. (*Mozi*, Section 16.) The question for Chinese ethics is what *dao* should we instil in people to guide their *de*. Partial love doctrines will entail that we ought to instil a universal love *dao*. Since it is self-condemning in this way, the Confucian *dao* is not a constant *dao*.

Mozi assumes that we should make both our name assignments *and* the patterns of *shi-fei* judgements uniform throughout society. Thus we should curtail a host of wasteful orthodox Confucian ritual practices such as elaborate funerals, expensive concerts and especially aggressive warfare. They waste resources that could be better used to benefit the people. He condemns Confucians for being able to separate morality from immorality in small matters, while in large matters, such as a state's going to war, they praise the ruler and call him 'moral'. He likens it to calling a little bit of white 'white' and a lot of white 'black'. Confucians set a bad example of moral term use.

Mozi's way is utilitarian. He does not link his utility to subjective states such as pleasure, happiness or desire satisfaction. Utility is a matter of objective, material well-being. In other ways as well, Mozi's viewpoint is less individualistic than a typical Western moral theory. His version of the Socratic philosophical question is social rather than individual. Socrates asks whether *he* should obey socially accepted codes. Mozi asks if *society* should accept or change its public code.

ii The anti-language period: Yangzhu, Mencius and Laozi

1 *Mencius: innate guidance*

Mencius lived after Mohism, the school of Mozi, had become a large school and a powerful political force. He saw it as a rival to Confucian influence and power. He bemoaned the spread of the *language* of Mozi and another consequentialist, Yangzhu. Mencius takes Yangzhu's language to embody egoism. Yangzhu used heaven-nature as his touchstone for guiding conduct. However, he took heaven's *mandate* to be implicit in our natural capacities rather than natural will. Heaven mandates that I live a fixed time by endowing me at birth with a fixed quantity of *qi* ('breath'). To die before my organically intended death is to go against heaven's command. Thus, I must avoid any activity (particularly politics) that might result in exhausting my *qi* before heaven wants me to die. Our life is a command from heaven and self-preservation, therefore a duty.

Mencius absorbed both his opponents' views about the need for a natural or heavenly standard to ground the social, conventional *dao*. He argues, however, that heaven's guidance comes as inborn feelings or inclinations to behaviour. These are neither merely inclinations to egoistic preservation nor even a general inclination for altruistic benefit. Heaven's endowment is a fully instinctive morality in *seed* form. Each of us is born with genetic inclinations to behaviour. As we mature, these inclinations grow in strength and sensitivity to the moral setting. Barring deprivation or distortion from external influences, they will eventually yield sage-like Confucian moral character. The heart can be thought of as similar to *conscience* in Western theories except that the moral discrimination capacity postulated by Mencius grows in accuracy throughout life.

The inclinations to behaviour make up the *xin* ('heart-mind') – the ruler of the body. Its role is to guide human behaviour. Mencius identifies four seeds or hearts which develop into the four primary virtues. The first seed is the human proclivity Mozi wanted to inculcate. We react out of sympathy for other humans. That, fully developed, becomes the virtue of humanity. The second is our penchant to feel shame, which motivates the development of *i* ('morality'). The third is our disposition to show respect and deference toward social superiors. This motivates conformity to *li*. Finally, we have a congenital tendency to discern *shi-fei*. We distinguish in action and attitude between something approved in the context (*shi*) and something not approved (*fei*). This tendency to have pro-con, action-guiding attitudes grows into practical wisdom, *zhi* ('knowledge').

These seeds, in the normal course of development, generate their associated virtues. We can impede their normal healthy development, however. Political, economic and social conditions can interfere with proper maturation of the organic moral traits. People made desperate by war or economic deprivation will not develop normal moral character. People influenced by the language of Mozi and Yangzhu will also fail to develop. They try to *force* their plant's growth using words and language. Both heretics claim a natural basis for their discriminations. However, each uses a basic distinction (benefit-harm or self-other) to change the natural inclination to moral guidance. They advocate adopting linguistic practices to alter the natural pattern of *shi-fei* assignments. The seeds, finally, might also fail to develop because we ourselves do not diligently attend to and encourage them. If we could erase all these distorting influences, human moral perfection would be the rule, not the rare exception.

Mencius alleges that their spontaneous origin vindicates the conventional practices. The burial rituals come about as a natural response. We cannot bear to see insects and wild animals feasting on a dead parent's corpse. Thus, indirectly, heaven commands the funeral ritual via the natural feelings and behavioural biases in the heart. The attitudes of special affection for family and clan (partial love) are also natural. Heaven programmes all moral behaviour in us at birth. It also programmes the ritual code of etiquette and the ability to sort types in guiding action – the interpretive ability to *shi-fei*. Any *spontaneous* sorting is a correct sorting. A sorting generated by a specific, deliberate criterion can only distort that natural spontaneous way of sorting.

Mencius thus launched a radical departure from the assumptions Confucius and Mozi shared. Our motivation to ethical conduct, our character, comes from nature not nurture. (Although we must cultivate it.) Morality is not a product of civilization. It is hereditary. It is organic. Fully matured, these *seed* propensities culminate in sage-like moral character. Since the motivations are natural, they are mystically continuous with the entire order of nature. The sage can, therefore, take the whole world as the subject of his moral concern. Fully ripened, the heart's organic constitution puts us in harmony with a cosmic moral force – the 'flood-like' *qi* ('breath'). We simultaneously use and are used by it.

Mencius similarly vindicates the code of *li*. Since produced by the sage-kings, that code represents the best imaginable linguistic summary of the correct *dao*. But the definitive criterion of moral behaviour is the mind of the sage, not any code book. (*The Mencius*, 4A:2) The question in each predicament is 'What would a sage do here?' Each action position is unique. Thus a developed intuition is preferable to any language-based moral system. Without the intuition, we would misinterpret the guiding discourse. So Mencius stresses *ren* and *i* where Confucius stressed *li*.

His opposition to the *language* of Mozi and Yangzhu becomes an opposition to language itself. Language is a chief source of distortion of the natural inclinations to moral behaviour. Mencius makes moral pronouncements freely. He pointedly avoids formulating a normative theory, however. If you guide yourself with any contrived moral language you have 'two bases' of your behaviour. You both rely on your moral instincts and try to change them to fit some linguistic blueprint – some explicit *dao*. This can only retard or damage the natural moral instincts. You can no more force their growth by studying a criterion for discrimination than you can hurry the growth of rice plants by pulling on them.

2 Laozi: primitive innatism

Mencius was not the only anti-language moral philosopher. Laozi, the mythical author of the *Daode-jing* (*Tao-te Ching*), presents another anti-distinction view. Both agree that no linguistic guide to behaviour can give *constantly* adequate advice. As Mozi showed, etiquette Confucianism cannot be a constant *dao*. Without some interpretive instinct, its guidance is indeterminate and its partial love condemns itself as a collective guide. And Mozi may be no better off. His appeal to universal utility may be inconstant too. Mencius argued that a *dao* based on utility might not be able to justify appealing *publicly* to utility. (Mencius 1A:1.) Promoting talk of benefit may not benefit society. Further, even if we accept a certain linguistic content, as Confucius noted, the interpretive problem still faces us. We need an extra-linguistic guide to use a linguistic one. We need a moral intuition to interpret the terms of a guiding code. The code itself can never guarantee constant patterns of conduct.

The *Daode-jing* gives an explicit linguistic rationale for its scepticism that any *dao* can be constant. No *dao* can be constant because no *ming* ('names') can be constant. We can interpret any *dao* in various ways because the application of *any* name contained in a *dao* requires both an interpretive distinction and preference induced response. Mozi merely assumed the *li-hai* ('benefit-harm') distinction provides guidance. It may also be interpreted, and the interpretation would likely vary in different utilitarian theories. He seemed to ignore something. If social discourse can modify our preference for our own family, it can modify our preference for benefit. Furthermore, social discourse can instil different ways to calculate benefit. Each will generate different courses of action – different *daos*. One could even have an anti-benefit *dao*. Thus *benefit* is not a constant *dao*.

Names supply all (linguistic) moral ways with their capacity to guide in the real world. A name guides discrimination, desires, and action. Learning a name guides because, when we add it to our vocabulary, we become disposed to make a socially approved distinction. Our social superiors, our teachers and models, approve when we discriminate as they would with a given term. This training is an integral part of our socialization. Our social models train us to choose ways of acting toward the object named. In a particular context, they teach us to treat some thing as *shi* and other things as *fei*. To learn any name is to learn to *shi-fei* with it.

These learned inclinations to select and reject things are conventional or acquired desires. An internalized linguistic *dao* translates into a body of inclinations to classify things. We use the classification in executing our internalized guiding programme. We select or avoid those things in conduct. Thus language guides our *wei* ('deeming:actions'). Actions based on deeming things to be this or not-this are unnatural, conventional actions. Laozi's famous slogan, *wu-wei* ('avoid deeming action') enjoins us to vacate this social, linguistic, conditioning. The contrasting ideal is spontaneous, natural action. Whenever conventional categories generate the actions, the actions are unnatural. Natural actions, by contrast, do not require any artefact terms. No one needs to teach us to eat, sleep, or procreate.

To *wei* – engage in discriminating behaviours guided by names – interferes with our natural spontaneity. Laozi's theory explains Mencius' criticism of language-based ways. He also adopts a more realistic view of the range of natural behaviour. Mencius had assumed that our intuition was potentially rich enough to make us sage-kings of a unified moral empire. Laozi's version of pre-linguistic inclinations remains strongly optimistic from a Western individualist perspective but less idealistic than Mencius. He assumes that without language and cultural accumulation, we would be social enough only to form small farming villages. We would live in peace because, without language, we would lack curiosity to interact with the other villages. That natural primitive behaviour is the only *chang* ('constant') *dao*. We follow that natural path when we refuse to act by deeming – *wu-wei*.

As we saw with Mozi and Confucius, conflicting ways use the same terms, e.g. good and bad, beautiful and ugly, high and low. However, they disagree about how to draw the distinctions in guiding our behaviour. Laozi's *Daode-jing* invites us to contemplate an anti-conventional way. That way reverses all the conventional pairs of opposing guiding terms. The *dao* of reversal reverses valuation. We normally value dominance, the male, the active, having, benevolence, wisdom, and clarity. Laozi presents considerations for valuing submissiveness, the female, the passive, lacking, non-benevolence, and dullness. For each pair of opposite guiding terms, the text tries to motivate reversing the conventional choice. This is enough to show that these names do not give constant guidance.

Once we see the inconstancy of social guidance by names or language, what follows? Here the *Daode-jing* becomes enigmatic. Confucian interpretations treat Laozi as recommending his negative way as the constant way. Legalism also treats the advice as a serious guide, expecially in its political reversal sections. Legalist writers draw quotations from the text justifying Machiavellian 'scheming methods' of government – keeping people ignorant, finding benevolence unnatural.

I recommend a different view of Laozi. He urges, as Mencius does, that we abandon all language guides to behaviour. The issue between Mencius and Laozi lies in their view of the content of our genetic mechanisms. On Laozi's account, our natural bent, unembellished by culture and language, would only support society at the level of the agrarian village. Call this primitive Daoism.

We may also take the point of reversing values associated with names to express pure scepticism. This pairs him with Zhuangzi. Finally, Buddhists read the text as entailing mystical monism and, like the metaphysics of the Buddha-nature, justifying stoic resignation. There may be other possibilities. The *Daode-jing* alleges simply that no statement of a way can be constantly sound. It could not coherently tell us what constant, practical conclusion to draw.

iii   The schools of names: formal meta-ethics

The obvious importance of names and language in Chinese ethical doctrines led to a period of intense analysis of names. Three schools of thought emerged. One conclusion was that we should reform language along ideal theoretical lines. Ethical guidance, using names, should be unambiguous to be *chang* ('constant'). This proposal is a formal version of Confucius' doctrine of rectifying names. It adopts the slogan of one-name-one-thing.

Another school, the neo-Mohists, noted that natural language does not and need not conform to the one-name-one-thing. Our ordinary ways of speaking do not follow any consistent principle. We ordinarily do think a white horse is a horse. We also agree that riding a white horse is riding a horse. But sometimes we do not think doing something to an object under one description is the same as doing it under another description. We think a thief is a person, but we treat executions (killing thieves) as different from murders (killing people).

This school thought that we could perfectly well make sense of our language *as long as* we based it on what we knew of reality. Given common sense and the external similarities and differences, we can rest the patterns of name use on an external, constant reality. This school, an outgrowth of Mozi's thought, thus developed a linked theory of linguistic and moral realism. The world provides the grounds of assertability of our *shi*s and *fei*s.

The third school challenged even this qualified realism. Similarities and differences among things do guide our naming, but we can count and group similarities in unlimited ways. Reality privileges no constant classification scheme. Reality cannot settle our disputes about how to draw distinctions. Interpretation of any *dao* ('way') must capriciously adopt one of a limitless range of perspectives.

iv   Zhuangzi: Daoist relativism

That third position underwrote the Daoism of Zhuangzi. He could no longer follow the anti-language views of Mencius and Laozi. The realists had shown that any statement of an anti-language position was incoherent. To say 'all language distorts the *dao*' was to distort the *dao*. They had further argued that in any disagreement about *shi-fei* one party must be correct.

Zhuangzi reversed Laozi's Daoism. Do not reject language for natural, spontaneous action. Instead he dropped the assumption that 'heavenly', 'natural', or 'reality' provides a coherent standpoint for constructing *dao*s. Zhuangzi likened all the warring schools to 'pipes of heaven'. Each claims to be expressing the *natural* or *heavenly* point of view. Trivially, each does. They are, as *actual* points of view, natural. In their naturalness, however, none is superior to the others. All the actual points of view about *shi-fei* are equal from the point of view of heaven or reality.

Of course, once we take this lofty cosmic view, we must grant the same status to the points of view of animals. The cosmos assigns no special significance to the life or death of the human species.

The goal of deriving guidance out of natural make-up fails, Zhuangzi shows. It always assumes some prior interpretive *shi* ('this:right'). Consider, for example, how Mencius tried to get guidance out of the natural qualities of the heart-mind. He presumes that the heart-mind *should* rule the other natural inclinations. He imagines that sage-like taste is this:right and the fool's taste in cultivating his heart-mind is not this:wrong. The whole idea that the heart-mind can be a distorted standard – the distinction between a natural and deficient development of the heart-mind – presupposes some standard for developing the heart. It must be other than appeal to the natural, organic heart. No mature heart-mind yields a *shi-fei* judgement without having accumulated and assumed a prior arbitrary *shi-fei* standard of judgement.

Thus Zhuangzi arrives at a sceptical view of guidance by language. We can show that natural or evaluative distinctions among types are correct only when we presuppose an evaluative point of view. All assignments of *shi* are indexical. What is *shi* (from one vantage point or intellectual lineage) is *fei* (from another). Anyone trying to resolve a difference takes a third point of view. Knowledge neither reaches all the way down nor all the way out. Our lives do end. To pursue what has no limit (perfect knowledge) with what has a limit (our lives) is foolish. Even if we had knowledge, we would not know it. We would not know if we had found the *constant* knowledge-ignorance distinction.

So what conclusion would Zhuangzi have us adopt from this non-cognitivist analysis? (For an account of non-cognitivism in Western ethics, see Article 38, SUBJECTIVISM.) Zhuangzi seems, with some hesitation, to draw three practical conclusions. First, he extols flexibility and tolerance – openness to other perspectives. He seems aware that even this advice also presupposes a point of view – a point of view on points of view. Once we take Zhuangzi's perspective, we lose the motivation to condemn *all* alternative ways of guiding discourse and behaviour. Some new way of assigning categories and guiding action, e.g. science, might turn out to give us amazing powers – like the ability to fly. Being open to new conceptual schemes is characteristic of youth and flexibility. Being closed and rigid is characteristic of old age and impending death. Zhuangzi, of course, worries that our preferring life to death might arise from ignorance.

Second, we *can* go with 'the usual' since it provides the basis for useful co-operation and interchange with others. We could practically, intelligibly require little more of a point of view or a way. Finally, given any guiding way we ingest – even being a butcher – we can hone it to artistic perfection. We can develop any skill to the point of *second* nature. We lose ourselves in our practice. When we have that trained intuition guiding our actions, our inner view is that an external force evokes and guides the skill. We can make any learned activity into skilled artistry and create satisfying beauty in practice. Of course to cultivate any such skill is to ignore others. Perfected at one thing, we are tragically condemned to be flawed at another.

v Xunzi: pragmatic Confucianism

Xunzi also learns from the analytic theories of language and sees in their analysis a way to resurrect Confucianism. As Hui Shi and Zhuangzi have argued, we have no natural basis for *shi-fei* distinctions. The only legitimate grounds of correct and incorrect language are the very conventions from which Mencius and Laozi fled. Only a fixed social pattern of *shi-fei* can make the use of names correct. The world cannot do it alone. Humans are linguistically social animals and the standards of acceptability are social. Our impulses impel us to adopt, preserve, and transmit such guiding conventions. Rather than undermine them, any responsible person would strive to accord with them. Thus, society should punish those who mis-construe names, make new distinctions, and sow conceptual confusion.

The ancestral Confucian way, based on ritual, is thus the only appropriate guide to action. Wonderfully intelligent sage-kings wrote it and all the ages have followed it successfully. To muddle it invites anarchy and disaster in an already dangerous world. The evidence of history is that the ancestral *dao* secures human survival. It works because it coincides with *natural* human feelings. On the other hand, it *instils* orderly feelings and desires. The use of ritual in the state results in instilling desires in a population. The desires are different for each hierarchical role. People of higher ranks learn a different set of desires and inclinations. If people have different desires, then society can distribute scarce resources while satisfying all desires. If all desire silk, the result will be competition, strife, chaos and disaster. We instil the desire for silk only in the higher classes. A differentiated ability to classify and desire will thus encourage widespread satisfaction. Inequality will lead to equality.

Humans have a natural tendency to make such discriminations and to adopt conventional, invented moral systems. Mencius' idealist assumption that nature disposes us to the specific *content* is the mistake. People *are* naturally moral, but only in the sense that they are natural language users. We have tendencies to adopt *some* conventional structure *or other*. Xunzi still asserts we all have the abstract capacity to be sages because we can learn any role, together with its desires. If we could get rid of distorting obsessions, passions and distractions, any of us could apprehend the right way as the sages did. Still, given the strength of our other motivations, giving up on historic standards of behaviour would lie somewhere between imprudent and insane.

vi The Dark Ages: the end of the Hundred Schools

Xunzi's most famous disciples became the leaders of a legalist school. It accepted Xunzi's *language* – minus his passion about traditional norms. We do need con-ventional standards of behaviour, but they need not be *old* conventions. Their usefulness as conventions does not require a sage-king ancestry. Modern kings can perfectly well formulate them. A contemporary way will be more realistic.

This view served the First Emperor of Qin particularly well. He succeeded in conquering China, burying rival scholars, burning books and bringing the exciting classical period of China to a thundering halt.

That first dynasty lasted barely longer than the First Emperor's reign.

vii The continuing impact of classical thought

The Emperors of the later Han Dynasty adopted Confucianism as the official *dao* in the midst of the Philosophical Dark Age. Buddhism, imported from India, introduced elements of a more Western conceptual scheme and dominated early medieval China. Later as Buddhism declined, a Mencian version of Confucianism re-emerged. This neo-Confucian orthodoxy divided into disputing interpretive factions, but all accepted the orthodoxy of Mencius. They are competing interpretations of natural intuitionism in ethics.

The contact with the West has faced the Chinese tradition with its second barbarian invasion of ideas. Socialism and pragmatism were the most attractive Western systems to Chinese intellectuals. Mao Zedong, however, liked to compare himself to the legalist First Emperor as a reformer of tradition. Deng Xiaoping represents the resurgence of the pragmatic impulse. Whatever *dao* follows next in China will show more Western influence, but China is not likely to interpret it via the ethical scheme of deontological individualism. Chinese reformers may well try the rule of law, but, like the classical political thinkers, they may always prefer character inculcation to punishment.

References

All quotations translated by the author. Most of these passages can be found in:

Chan, Wing-tsit: *A Source Book in Chinese Philosophy* (Princeton: Princeton University Press, 1963).

For longer quotations and elaboration:

Hansen, C: *A Daoist Theory of Chinese Thought* (New York: Oxford University Press, 1990).

Further reading

Fingarette, H.: *Confucius – The Secular as Sacred* (New York: Harper & Row, 1972).
Fung, Yu-lan: *A Short History of Chinese Philosophy*, trans. D. Bodde (New York: The Macmillan Company, 1958).
Graham, A.: *Chuang-tzu: The Inner Chapters* (London: George Allen & Unwin, 1981).
——: *Later Mohist Logic, Ethics and Science* (Hong Kong and London: Chinese University Press, 1978).
Hansen, C.: *Language and Logic in Ancient China* (Ann Arbor: University of Michigan Press, 1983).
Mote, W.: *Intellectual Foundations of China* (New York: Alfred A. Knopf, 1971).
Munro, J.: *The Concept of Man in Early China* (Stanford: Stanford University Press, 1969).
Smullyan, R.: *The Tao is Silent* (New York: Harper & Row, 1977).

7

Jewish ethics

MENACHEM KELLNER

THE very concept 'Jewish ethics' raises a number of problems, some of them
inherent in the notion of any parochial ethic (be it Christian ethics, Navajo ethics,
Marxist ethics, or whatever) and some of them unique to Jewish ethics. But, these
problems aside, there exists a substantial body of literature which by common
consensus is called 'Jewish ethics'. A separate essay in this volume is devoted to
an analysis of the relation between religion and ethics (see Article 46, HOW COULD
ETHICS DEPEND ON RELIGION?); the general problems raised, therefore, by the
notion of Jewish ethics as an example of a religious ethic will not be addressed
here. There remain, however, a number of problems unique to Jewish ethics. This
essay, then, will be divided into two parts. In the first I will describe some of the
problems raised by the notion of Jewish ethics while in the second I will describe
that body of literature ordinarily denoted by the term.

What is Jewish ethics? Answering this question presupposes being able to
answer the antecedent question, 'What is Judaism?' This is not so simple a task.
As the old saw has it, 'Two Jews, three views'. The well-known propensity of Jews
to disagree on matters theological while not definitively excluding each other from
the faith or from the community may reflect the typical Jewish concentration on
matters concrete and practical. This concentration elevates matters of behaviour
(including most emphatically ethical issues) to a centrality of importance which
may be unique among Western monotheistic faiths. Thus, for example, we find
the Talmud quoting God as saying, 'Would that they [the Jewish people] had
abandoned Me but kept my Torah!' (T. J. *Hagigah*, I. 7). This emphasis on how to
behave as opposed to what to believe makes it difficult to define 'Judaism' as a
system of beliefs in a simple fashion.

In the contemporary world, for example, Judaism can be defined in both
secular and religious terms. The secular definition can itself be either nationalist
or cultural. The secular nationalist definition can either be Zionist (calling for the
resettlement of the Jews in their ancient homeland) or non-Zionist. The Zionist
definition of Judaism is itself defined in a plethora of ways. Defining Judaism in
religious terms is no simpler today. Four different major movements (Orthodoxy,
Conservatism, Reconstructionism and Reform) each claim to be the normative
interpretation of Judaism. Many of the approaches mentioned here can also be
combined (as, for example, in forms of religious Zionism).

It is immediately evident, then, that no one definition of Jewish ethics is
possible, since there are so many varieties of Judaism. Since, however, we cannot

possibly hope to settle this issue here we will simply ignore it henceforth. But, even assuming that we know what the term 'Jewish' means in the expression 'Jewish ethics', there are still fundamental problems which need clarification.

Judaism is very much a religion oriented towards practical perfection in this world (a 'religion of pots and pans' in the words of its nineteenth-century Protestant derogators). This practical orientation finds its concrete expression in the codified norms of Torah-based behaviour called *Halakhah* or Jewish law. While much of Halakhah is given over to what we would today call religious or ritual law, it encompasses, civil, criminal and moral law as well. The moral component, however, is not distinguished in any way from the other components of Halakhah and, at least from within the system, is seen as drawing its authority, as does the rest of the Torah, from God's command. Since Halakhah contains an ethical component it must be asked whether 'the Jewish tradition recognizes an ethic independent of Halakhah' (see Aharon Lichtenstein's article by this name in Kellner, 1978). Can there be, that is, significantly *Jewish* ethical norms not included in Halakhah?

This is a thorny problem. If Judaism recognizes the existence of two authentically Jewish yet independent realms, one of Halakhah and one of ethics, how do they interrelate? Can Halakhah be corrected on the basis of Jewish ethical considerations? This possibility is abhorrent to those Jews who maintain that Halakhah is the unchanging expression of God's will on earth. Can ethics be corrected on the basis of halakhic considerations? This possibility would probably be unacceptable to those Jews who see Halakhah as an expression of an early stage of God's dynamic and ongoing revelation. This issue may be rephrased as follows: if Halakhah and Jewish ethics are both authentically Jewish, is one superior to the other? If not, what do we do when they conflict? If they never conflict, in what sense are they different?

And there are yet further problems; if there exists a supra-halakhic Jewish ethic, what is its relationship to non-Jewish civil law? What is the obligation of the Jew with respect to imposing that ethic upon or offering it to non-Jews?

More questions arise: if morality must be universally recognizable, then not only must Jewish ethics apply to all human beings, but it must be available to them as well. If a supra-halakhic Jewish ethic exists, is it really universally available, and, if it is, what is specifically *Jewish* about it?

So much for the problems raised by the notion of Jewish ethics generally. If, as is often maintained, Jews are like everybody else, only more so, it is appropriate that the notion of Jewish ethics be as problematic as the notion of religious ethics, only more so. But since, as the Yiddish expression has it, no-one has ever died from having an unsolved philosophical problem, we can turn to the second part of our discussion and describe what in fact has been passing as Jewish ethics all these many years.

Following the lead of Isaiah Tishby and Joseph Dan we may divide the literature of what is ordinarily called Jewish ethics into four main categories: biblical, rabbinic, medieval and modern. Certain recent scholars (such as Israel Efros and Shubert Spero) have maintained that the (Hebrew) Bible is self-consciously aware of a distinct area of human activity parallel to what we call ethics. I do not agree; while the Bible is surely permeated with ethical concern, it does not see the laws mandating ethical behaviour as being in any significant sense distinct from its laws governing civil, criminal, and ritual matters: they all 'are given from one Shepherd' (Eccl. 12: 11). Biblical Hebrew does not even have a word for 'ethics' in our sense of the term. The Bible, then, teaches ethics, but not self-consciously and as such: it is a *source* of Jewish ethics while not seeing itself, so to speak, as an ethical text. (On biblical ethics, see also Article 3, ANCIENT ETHICS.)

This said, the question remains, what are the ethical teachings of the Bible? The question presupposes that the Bible is, at least in moral and theological terms, a single unit. While that assumption may be rejected by historians of the Bible, it reflects the traditional Jewish approach to the text and will be adopted here.

Perhaps the best-known of the ethical teachings of the Bible is the so-called 'Ten Commandments' ('so-called' because there are many more than ten specific commandments in this passage), found in Exodus 20. Of the ten discrete statements in this text, at least six have direct ethical import: (a) honour thy father and thy mother; (b) thou shalt not murder; (c) thou shalt not commit adultery; (d) thou shalt not steal; (e) thou shalt not bear false witness against thy neighbour; and (f) thou shalt not covet thy neighbour's possessions (which include thy neighbour's wife, which indicates that the Decalogue is not exactly a monument to feminist sensibilities). The remaining four ('I am the Lord thy God . . .', that God alone may be worshipped, that God's name must not be taken in vain, and the observance of the Sabbath) relate to matters of theological and ritual importance. This division of subject matter reflects a division which later rabbis read out of (or into) the Bible: that between obligations between human individuals and obligations between human individuals and God.

Much of biblical legislation involves this first group and herein may lie one of the basic contributions of Judaism to the Western religious tradition: that one worships God through decent, humane, and moral relations with one's fellows. (As the later rabbis were to put it, God is ideally worshipped in three ways: study of Torah, sacrifice and prayer, and acts of lovingkindness.) In other words, whatever morality might be, its basis is in God's will. God can be no more irrelevant to morality than he can be for religion. The basis for this demand that God makes upon his creatures to treat each other properly is the biblical teaching that man is created in the image of God (Gen. 1: 27).

Since human beings are created in the image of God, it is obvious that one achieves the highest possible level of perfection or self-realization by becoming as similar to God as humanly possible. This is the basis for what may be the single most important ethical doctrine of the Hebrew Bible, that of *imitatio Dei*, the imitation of God (on which, see the essays by Shapiro and Buber in Kellner, 1978).

The biblical doctrine of *imitatio Dei* finds expression in verses such as the following: 'Ye shall be holy, for I the Lord your God am holy' (Lev. 19: 2); 'And now, Israel, what doth the Lord thy God require of thee, but to fear the Lord thy God, to walk in all His ways, and to love Him, and to serve the Lord thy God with all thy heart and with all thy soul' (Deut. 10: 12); and 'The Lord will establish thee for a holy people unto Himself, as He hath sworn unto thee; if thou shalt keep the commandments of the Lord thy God, and walk in His ways' (Deut. 28: 9). For our purposes here, these verses involve two explicit commandments: to be holy, because God is holy, and to walk in the ways of God. How does one make oneself holy and thus God-like? The Bible couldn't be clearer. Leviticus 19: 2 is an introduction to a list of commandments combining matters moral (honour of parents, charity, justice, honesty, kindness to the disadvantaged, etc.), ritual (Sabbath observance, sacrifices, etc.), and theological (not taking the name of the Lord in vain). One achieves holiness, that is, by obeying God's commandments, or, in the words quoted above from Deuteronomy, by walking in his ways.

It should come as no surprise that when Judaism, which so clearly emphasizes the practical over the metaphysical, introduces a doctrine which seems so clearly to beg for a metaphysical interpretation, it immediately insists on interpreting it in practical terms. The imitation of God, that is, is not a metaphysical issue in Judaism but a practical, moral one. Jews are not commanded (and it must not be forgotten that the imitation of God, as the verses adduced above clearly show, is a *commandment* of the Torah and was so construed by most later authorities) literally and actually to transcend their normal selves and become in some sense *like* God; rather, they are commanded to act in certain ways. It is through the achievement of practical, moral perfection, that Jews imitate God and thus fulfil their destiny as individuals created in the image of God.

This point can be made sharper if we contrast the Jewish approach to the imitation of God to two others, that of Plato and that of Christianity. In the *Theaetetus* (176) we find Socrates saying, 'We ought to fly away from earth to heaven as quickly as we can; and to fly away is to become like God, as far as this is possible: and to become like him is to become holy, just, and wise.' Far from flying away from earth, the Torah calls upon Jews to imitate God here on earth, through the fulfilment of his commandments. One does not then become *like* God; one walks *in his ways*, i.e. acts in a God-like manner so far as this is possible for a human being. In Christianity we find an even clearer emphasis on the actual, literal, and therefore metaphysical interpretation of the imitation of God. The God of Christianity is so eager to allow human beings to become like him that he actually performs an act of *imitatio humani* and incarnates himself in the body of an actual living breathing human being. The imitation of God is then performed through an intermediary and becomes *imitatio Christi*, which finds its expression, not in the fulfilment of the six hundred and thirteen commandments of the Torah, but in attitudes of faith and trust, and, before its self-destructiveness became evident, through the imitation of Christ's passion. (For a Jewish view of this, see Buber in Kellner.)

The moral implication of humanity's having been created in the image of God underlies both specific laws (such as 'Thou shalt love thy neighbour as thyself' (Lev. 19: 18) – because your neighbour is no less created in the image of God than you are) and the general universalistic thrust of the Hebrew Bible, something particularly evident in the classical literary prophets (Isaiah, Jeremiah, Ezekiel). It also lies at the basis of rabbinic discussions of what we would call moral issues.

85

I wrote above that the Hebrew Bible is not self-consciously aware of morality as a distinct religious or intellectual category. This is also true, I would maintain, of the corpus of rabbinic writings which centres on the Mishnah and those texts which developed around it. Here, too, we have no separate, distinct text dealing with ethics in an explicit fashion, and no apparent recognition of ethics as a department of thought which must be treated independently of other concerns. This is even true of the well-known Mishnaic tractate *Avot*, a compilation of maxims and homilies, many of which embody what we call ethical teachings. The point of this treatise, as Herford suggests, is to describe the ideal personality of the Mishnah; it is therefore much more concerned with piety than with ethics.

Even more than the Bible, the vast corpus of rabbinic writings is basically concerned with one issue: how we ought to live our lives so as to fulfil the command to make ourselves holy by walking in God's ways. The rabbinic response to this was the delineation of a body of detailed law designed to govern every aspect of our behaviour. That body of law is called 'Halakhah' (homiletically if not etymologically derived from the Hebrew word for 'the way' – compare the Chinese concept *dao*, discussed by Chad Hansen in Article 6, CLASSICAL CHINESE ETHICS – and thus taken as the specification of how one walks in God's ways) and includes, but by no means is limited to, moral concerns.

Fully aware, however, that no specification of legal obligations can cover every moral dilemma, the rabbis of the Mishnah and Talmud rely on a number of broad spectrum biblical commands such as 'Righteousness, righteousness, shalt thou pursue' (Deut. 17: 20) and 'Thou shalt do what is right and good in the sight of the Lord' (Deut. 6: 18) – and on one of their own devising, the *obligation* to go beyond the letter of the law in the fulfilment of God's will – to demand super-erogatory behaviour from the Jews. Such a demand may be justified on the grounds that one never fully satisfies the obligation to imitate God.

The centrality of the doctrine that human beings are created in the image of God (the basis, as noted above, for the commandment to imitate God) is emphasized in the well-known debate between two mishnaic rabbis: Akiba and Ben Azzai. Their debate centred on the question, 'What is the great[est] maxim of the Torah?' Rabbi Akiba's nominee was 'Thou shalt love thy neighbour as thyself' (Lev. 19: 18) while Ben Azzai insisted on 'This is the book of the generations of man, in the image of God created He him' (Gen. 5: 1). (*Sifra*, VII.4. On this debate, see the article by Chaim Reines in Kellner, 1982.) The important point for our purposes here is that there is no actual debate. Both Rabbi Akiba and Ben Azzai agree that the doctrine of humanity's having been created in the image of God is the central teaching of the Torah. Ben Azzai cites the doctrine itself, Akiba, its clearest moral implication. Given the Jewish tradition's preference for practice over preaching, it is no surprise that in the popular Jewish mind, at least, Rabbi Akiba is thought to have won the argument.

This emphasis on the respect for others based on their having been created in the image of God also finds expression in what may be the best-known rabbinic moral teaching, Hillel's so-called 'Golden Rule'. When a non-Jew asked Hillel to teach him the entire Torah while he (the non-Jew) stood on one foot, Hillel replied, 'What you dislike don't do to others; that is the whole Torah. The rest is commentary. Go and learn.' (B.T. Shabbat 31a). It is perhaps only a personal idiosyncrasy (I don't like to be nagged) but I like to think that Hillel's formulation of this principle is superior to that of a well-known contemporary of his who phrased the same idea in positive terms ('Do unto others as you would have them do unto you') since I think that one can show no higher respect to one's fellows than to leave them alone if their behaviour harms no-one.

In sum, despite the importance of moral teachings in the Bible and Talmud, these texts know of no self-consciously worked-out moral system; they are not even aware of ethics as a distinct religious, intellectual, or human category. It is only in the Middle Ages, under the apparent impress of Greek categories of thought as mediated through Islam, that we first find a distinct corpus of Jewish literature self-consciously and explicitly devoted to ethics. The form may have been essentially Greek; the concern with right behaviour is obviously not new. What is new is the composition of texts which deal with moral behaviour outside of the strict context of Torah and Halakhah.

The literature of this period has been divided by Tishby and Dan into four categories: philosophic, rabbinic, pietistic, and kabbalistic. In terms of literary genre we find ethics being taught in philosophical or mystical texts, sermons, homilies, wills and letters, stories and fables, poetry, commentaries on Bible and Mishnah, and in manuals of ethical behaviour.

Turning to the first of the four categories of medieval Jewish ethical literature, it would seem that the basic issue which underlay discussions of ethics among medieval Jewish philosophers had to do with the nature of God: the importance one attaches to ethical behaviour (the *vita activa* as over against the *vita contemplativa*) depends upon one's assessment of human nature. Since Judaism teaches that human beings are created in the image of God and reach their most perfect self-realization through the imitation of God, it follows that our estimation of human nature depends to a great extent upon our estimation of divine nature. If God is construed as essentially active, then we should find our perfection in activity and ethics becomes a very important department of human endeavour; if, on the other hand, God is essentially contemplative, then we should find our perfection in contemplation and ethics plays a correspondingly less important role in our lives, often being seen as a propaedeutic to intellectual (contemplative) perfection.

The issue is highlighted in the work of the most important of the medieval Jewish philosophers, Moses Maimonides (1138–1204). In a semi-popular work, 'Laws of Character Traits', Maimonides presented a slightly modified version of Aristotle's doctrine of the 'Golden Mean' as the ethical teaching of Judaism. In his philosophic work, *Guide for the Perplexed*, however, he seems to advance a purely intellectualist interpretation of Judaism, reducing ethical (and, concomitantly, halakhic) perfection to the level of a necessary propaedeutic for the achievement of intellectual perfection. At the very end of the book, however, the moral, practical orientation of Judaism wins out and Maimonides informs his reader that the truest perfection involves the imitation of God's lovingkindness, justice, and righteousness after having achieved the highest achievable level of intellectual perfection.

87

Maimonides the philosopher, one might say, urges us to imitate God through metaphysical speculation; Maimonides the rabbi cannot leave it at that and insists that such imitation have practical impact on our lives in the community.

Perhaps in response to the ethical writings of medieval Jewish philosophers (on which see the Introduction to Kellner, 1978) writers rooted deeply and often exclusively in the rabbinic tradition began writing ethical treatises based entirely on mishnaic and talmudic texts, in an attempt to prove that these texts provided all that one needed in order to produce a complete ethical system. Accepting the rabbinic injunction to turn and turn in the Torah 'because everything is included in it' (*Avot*, V. 25), they felt that there was no need to turn to Aristotle for instruction in either the form or content of ethics. Rather, all one need do is search through the Torah and the rabbinic compilations. Rabbinic ethics is not a uniquely medieval phenomenon and works continue to be written to this day in this framework. A whole movement, which started in the last century and which has about it remarkable elements of modernity, the so-called 'Mussar Movement' (on which see Hillel Goldberg) is perhaps best understood as a version of medieval rabbinic ethics.

Pietistic ethical literature is associated with a circle of Jewish mystics and pietists called Hasidei Ashkenaz, who were active in twelfth- and thirteenth-century Germany. This literature, by and large, is concerned with specific problems and actual situations, rather than with the search for general principles. It is marked by deep piety, by superstitious elements typical of Jewish folk as opposed to elite religion, and by an emphasis on the effort involved in the performance of a moral or religious action: the greater the difficulty in performing an action, the more praiseworthy it is. This idea, and the parallel notion that the pietist (*hasid*) is marked by his adherence to the 'law of Heaven', which is stricter and more demanding than the 'law of the Torah' to which all others must adhere, may not have been totally unprecedented in Judaism, but were surely given new emphasis by the Hasidei Ashkenaz. This call for supererogatory ethical behaviour had great influence on subsequent developments in European Jewry.

One of the most striking intellectual developments in the history of medieval Judaism was the rise and spread of a Jewish mystical movement called Kabbalah (on which see Scholem, 1946, and Moshe Idel, 1988). A Kabbalistic idea which had important influence on Jewish ethics was the notion that religious actions can have a profound impact on the very structure of the universe. This, of course, makes sense in the context of a world-view which sees the physical and the spiritual in a constant state of active interpenetration. On this understanding there is no problem with maintaining that a definite interdependence can exist between the deeds of human beings and developments in the world.

Not until 1789 in Europe and much later in the Muslim world were Jews allowed, to all intents and purposes, fully to take part in the cultures of the societies around them. When such participation was made possible, the Jews dove in enthusiastically. This openness to and involvement in the broader culture is one of the crucial distinguishing marks of modern as opposed to medieval Judaism. A second distinguishing mark of modern Judaism is the way in which it has become fractured into many competing movements, trends, and even, perhaps, denomi-nations. Judaism today, therefore, is distinguished from medieval Judaism by virtue of its being open to the entire problematic of modernity, and in that it no longer speaks with one voice (or with many different but still essentially har-monious voices, for those who insist that Judaism was always marked by plural-ism) in its attempt to answer that complex of problems.

This situation is particularly clear in the case of ethics. One can find Jewish thinkers who maintain that Jewish ethics is essentially autonomous in the Kantian sense and others who glory in the fact that it is, was, and should be absolutely heteronomous (see Article 14, KANTIAN ETHICS). Every possible position on the question of the relation between ethics and Halakhah is forcefully maintained by different thinkers as being the authoritative position of the Jewish tradition. On a more concrete level, you have rabbis who can boast of impressive credentials as experts in the fields of Jewish law and ethics testifying before congressional committees studying the question of abortion and presenting diametrically opposed positions on the Jewish attitude towards abortion. (On all these matters see the essays in Kellner, 1978, and S. Daniel Breslauer's important annotated biblio-graphies.)

Jews and Judaism are not, of course, unique in this respect. They are like everyone else, only more so. The fractured Jewish response to the problems posed by the modern world is as much a reflection of the nature of modernity as it is a reflection of the nature of Judaism.

References

Avot; see Herford, 1962.

Breslauer, S. D.: *Contemporary Jewish Ethics: A Bibliographical Survey* (Westport, Conn.: Greenwood Press, 1985).

——: *Modern Jewish Morality: A Bibliographical Survey* (Westport, Conn.: Greenwood Press, 1986).

Dan, J.: 'Ethical Literature', *Encyclopaedia Judaica* (Jerusalem: Keter, 1971), vol. 6, columns 922–32.

Efros, I.: *Ancient Jewish Philosophy* (Detroit: Wayne State University Press, 1964).

Goldberg, H.: *Israel Salanter: Text, Structure, Idea* (New York: Ktav, 1982).

Herford, R. T.: *The Ethics of the Talmud: Sayings of the Fathers* (New York: Schocken Books, 1962). (This is an edition of *Avot*.)

Idel, M.: *Kabbalah* (New Haven: Yale University Press, 1988).

Kellner, M. M., ed.: *Contemporary Jewish Ethics* (New York: Hebrew Publishing Company, 1978).

Maimonides: see Weiss and Butterworth, 1983.

Plato: *Theaetetus;* trans. Benjamin Jowett (New York: Random House, 1953).

Scholem, G.: *Major Trends in Jewish Mysticism* (New York: Schocken, 1946).

Spero, S.: *Morality, Halakhah, and the Jewish Tradition* (New York: Ktav, 1983).

Tishby, I. and Dan, J.: *Mivhar Sifrut ha-Mussar* (Jerusalem: Neuman, 1971).

Weiss, R. and Butterworth, C., eds.: *Ethical Writings of Maimonides* (New York: Dover, 1983).

Further reading

Agus, J. B.: *The Vision and the Way: An Interpretation of Jewish Ethics* (New York: Ungar, 1966).

Fox, M., ed.: *Modern Jewish Ethics: Theory and Practice* (Columbus: Ohio State University Press, 1975).

Lamm, N.: *The Good Society: Jewish Ethics in Action* (New York: Viking, 1974).

Rosner, F. and J. D. B.: *Jewish Bioethics* (New York: Hebrew Publishing Company, 1979).

Schwarzschild, S. S.: 'Moral radicalism and "middlingness" in Maimonides' ethics', *Studies in Medieval Culture* 11 (1977), 65–94.

8

Christian ethics

RONALD PRESTON

CHRISTIAN ethics can most simply be differentiated as the way of life appropriate to those who accept the Christian faith. However, in the course of nearly two thousand years Christianity has become a worldwide protean phenomenon. Therefore there are many points of view from which Christian ethics could be analysed, and many ways in which its history could be charted. This account is written by one who can reasonably be said to be in the mainstream of Christianity, as it has been historically expressed. So the plan of this article is to begin with an overall view of the phenomenon of Christian ethics, then to deal with its foundation in New Testament times in the ministry of Jesus and the interpreter of Jesus of whom we have most evidence, St Paul, and conclude with a brief mention of criticisms of Christian ethics made in recent years.

i A survey of Christian faith and ethics

The Christian faith, as its name implies, is specifically related to Jesus Christ. It can be said to rest on two presuppositions. The first is the reality of God. But when the question is raised, what sort of God? (since there have been many and diverse gods in human history), the second presupposition is that God is as disclosed in the ministry of Jesus Christ. This has become a single name in common usage, though the term Christ is rooted in the Jewish faith within which he lived. It refers to an expected Deliverer who would be sent by God to put the world to rights. The earliest Christians were those Jews who believed that this had indeed happened in the ministry of Jesus.

The Jewish faith is a strongly ethical one, quite unlike the various mystery religions which were current in the Roman Empire at the time of Jesus. So it is no surprise that the Christian faith is also strongly ethical. Its sources are found first of all in the Bible. The Old Testament is seen as preparing for and being fulfilled (though also in many respects negated) by the ministry of Jesus; the New Testament is seen as a witness to the life, death, and triumph over death of Jesus, and to the new community, or People of God, which came into existence as a result of his ministry. Experiences after his death led the closest disciples to worship God through him, an extraordinary thing for strictly monotheistic Jews to do; and that is why the Christian church commonly ends prayers with the phrase 'through Jesus Christ our Lord'. However, even the term 'resurrection' which the Christians used to interpret Jesus' triumph over death is drawn from the vocabulary of Judaism in the last few centuries BCE.

Initially the traditions about Jesus were transmitted to and within the new Christian congregations by word of mouth, and in ways relevant to their situation. Later they were incorporated into the four gospels, each author having his own theological stance. Mark is the earliest, about forty years after Jesus' death. Prior to that we have letters from St Paul to various churches, several of which he founded. These cover both his basic understanding of Christian faith and ethics, and his answers to specific ethical problems which had arisen in the life of these young churches.

It took three or four centuries before it became quite clear which books would be regarded by the Church as included in the Canon (or Rule) of Scripture, and thus in the Bible as we know it. So the sources of Christian ethics also include the tradition of ethical reflection in the community of the Church down the centuries as it was brought to bear on the changing situations it faced. And the data themselves of these problems became another source of Christian ethics. Underlying all is the conscience (or power of reasoning on ethical questions) which Christians share with all human beings.

The questions which had to be raised ranged from the intimately personal to the complexities of economic and political life, including those of war and peace. A classic typology of five characteristic attitudes to the whole realm of human culture which continually appear in Christian history is that of Richard Niebuhr (*Christ and Culture*, 1951). These are (1) Christ against culture, a kind of other-worldly pietism; (2) the Christ of culture, a Christianity which casts a gospel glow over the existing order and hardly challenges it; (3) Christ and culture in paradox, which makes a sharp separation between God's kindly rule in the Church and his stern rule (for the sake of order) in public life; (4) Christ above culture, meaning a triumphalist church which seeks control over public life; (5) Christ transforming culture, a leaven in the lump of personal and public life which allows for a legitimate autonomy of secular disciplines and seeks to influence but not necessarily to control institutions. All five positions refer back to the same biblical material, showing how important is the way it is decided to move from the Bible to the modern world. These five types have usually not been exemplified in totally pure ways; they are what the sociologist Max Weber called 'ideal types', in which an attempt is made to distil the distinctive elements and different tendencies in each. But it is suggested that since they have reappeared so constantly in Christian history each is likely to have some basic cogency. For instance the Christ against culture type speaks powerfully when Christians find themselves against hostile and oppressive governments; or perhaps a small minority in a particularly alien environment. However, this is not to say that all five are equally plausible. All of them originally developed against the background of a social order relatively stable compared to that which the world has known since the scientific and technological changes which we call the Industrial Revolution. This has produced a new kind of civilization, and one involving rapid social change over almost the whole world. Today the fifth type, Christ transforming culture, seems to be much the most cogent, and more so than in the days of St Augustine and Calvin whom Richard Niebuhr finds to be two of the most notable examples of it.

This typology illustrates the protean nature of Christianity. Beginning as a reform movement, associated with a charismatic figure in the Jewish countryside, it rapidly became a predominantly urban movement as it spread along the great road routes of the Roman Empire. The direct Jewish influence soon ceased (particularly after the fall of Jerusalem to Rome in 70 CE), and that of the pervasive Hellenistic culture increased, with its legacy of Greek philosophy and ethics. After the fall of Rome itself four centuries later, Christianity became heir to the rickety Roman Empire, and in due course embodied itself closely in the institutions of one civilization, that of Europe and its later offshoots in the 'new world'. Christianity has now spread globally and this presents it with new doctrinal and ethical issues.

Living through these changes, Christianity has split into five broad confessional traditions, each of which has achieved a certain stability and each with a doctrinal and ethical style of its own. (1) The Orthodox, primarily in eastern Europe and Russia; (2) the Roman Catholic, by far the most numerous; (3) the Lutheran; (4) the Calvinist or Reformed, met with in the English-speaking world in the form of Presbyterian, Congregationalist and Baptist; (5) the Anglican, to which must be added Methodism as an offshoot bigger than the parent. In addition there are hundreds of other churches; a few are historic, like the Society of Friends or Quakers and other Peace Churches, whilst many are the products of this century, notably indigenous African churches. The Ecumenical Movement is bringing greater coherence and mutual understanding into both doctrinal and ethical reflection among this variety, though there remains a sizable minority which is either anti-ecumenical or so far unaffected by it.

To come closely to grips with Christian ethics, against this general background, it is worth noting that the term is commonly used in Protestant circles, whereas in Catholic ones the more common term is moral theology. There is no agreed differentiation between the use of the terms nor any essential difference in subject matter. Both are concerned with the two basic issues in ethics, how to act from the right motive and how to find what is the right action in particular circumstances. In essence the methods and procedures of Christian ethics are no different from those of moral philosophy; the difference in Christian ethics is its starting point in the Christian faith. (Other systems of ethics will have other starting points, either religious or some form of humanism, for all must have some presuppositions before they can get going.) It will be found that at many points there will be an overlap between different systems of ethics, and this is important in a growingly interconnected but plural world whose inhabitants must learn to live together.

That the two basic issues in ethics are right motive and right action seems obvious, but it is not always realized that they are. For instance Samuel Butler in his nineteenth-century novel *The Way of All Flesh* has this passage, 'The more I see the more sure I am that it does not matter why people do the right thing so long as they do it, nor why they may have done wrong if they have done it. The result depends upon the thing done and the motive goes for nothing.' St Paul, in

93

a benevolent mood in the first chapter of *Philippians*, seems to take the same view. He says some people are preaching Christ out of envy but nevertheless he rejoices that Christ is preached. However, he would not have agreed with Butler that 'motive goes for nothing'. In furthering action from the right motive Christian ethics is concerned with what is often called 'spiritual formation'. By that is meant a growth in character through private prayers and public worship (both of which involve reflection on the Bible), and discussion with fellow Christians (and others where appropriate) so that one's insight or powers of discernment deepen. Bringing motivation to bear on particular decisions is traditionally known as casuistry. This got a bad name at the time of the Counter-Reformation because its aim seemed to be a series of rules for the evasion of obvious moral duties rather than to find out and fulfil what was the right action in particular circumstances. For instance mental restriction, equivocation and perjury were said to be legitimate if the welfare of the person, including honour or possessions, was at stake; whilst the doctrine of 'philosophic sin' held that no action was morally sinful unless the agent was actually thinking of God at the moment of committing it. Such absurdities were excoriated in Pascal's *Lettres Provinciales* (1656) and they were soon condemned by the Papacy. It was a passing phase. The abuse of a procedure does not mean that the procedure is wrong in itself. 'Casuistry', whether known by that name or not, is essential. But it can no longer be tied to the precise demarcation of sins, associated with the confessional, as recent Roman Catholic moral theology recognizes. Nor is it to be supposed that there are clear, specific, 'Christian' answers to all the ethical problems that the world throws up. More likely there is a range of possibilities, with some ruled out. Recognizing the ambiguities of choice is part of the task of Christian ethics.

ii Jesus

We turn to the roots of Christian ethics in the ministry of Jesus, especially the teaching in the so-called synoptic gospels, Mark, Matthew and Luke. The fourth, John, can best be regarded as a selective and mature series of meditations on the main themes of the first three, whether the author knew them or only the oral traditions behind them. The crux of Jesus' teaching concerns the Kingdom of God, or the way God exercises his rule as King over the world. Jesus saw it as exemplified in his own life and teaching. He reflected on the traditions of his people which were available to him through the synagogues as he grew up, and interpreted them in a new and original way in terms of his own mission. He saw the weight of God's purpose for the world through Israel resting upon himself. The intimacy of his understanding of God comes clearly through the gospels. His understanding of God's kingly rule was highly paradoxical by conventional standards, so he expressed it less by doctrinal affirmations than by indirect means, parables and pithy sayings (as well as by choice of actions), related to everyday experiences but designed to startle the assumptions of the hearers and viewers and shift them to a new dimension. In particular God's rule is seen not in the punishment of wrongdoers but in bearing the consequences of their wrongdoing. Equally para-doxical ethical teaching followed.

It may be asked how far we can be sure that these teachings go back to Jesus. The broad answer is that the gospels have been put through a more meticulous and widespread critical examination than any other writings of the ancient world and that, allowing for elements of uncertainty in places, there is no doubt that from them we can know a great deal about Jesus' teaching, even though it has come to us filtered through the concerns of the earliest Christian congregations. One of the indirect evidences for this is that two great themes of post-resurrection (Pauline) Christianity, the dynamism of the Holy Spirit and the universality of the gospel, were not read back into the life of Jesus but only appear as anticipatory hints in the written gospels.

What is conduct appropriate to a citizen of the Kingdom of God? Some of it is at the level of 'natural' morality, for instance the Golden Rule, 'Always treat others as you would like them to treat you' (Matt. 7: 12), which is found in some similar form in other ethics, and which can be taken at different levels provided one is consistent between oneself and others. Some of Jesus' words appear to follow 'natural' human judgements in offering rewards for good conduct and threatening penalties for bad. We shall return to this. But the distinctive feature of Jesus' ethical teaching is the way it radicalizes common morality. For instance there is to be no limit to the forgiveness for injuries (Matt. 18: 21ff), not on the grounds that it will win over the offender but because it corresponds to God's forgiveness of us. Similarly love of enemies is enjoined (Matt. 6: 14ff) not because it will win over the enemy (although of course it might) but because God loves his enemies. There is to be no restriction on neighbour love (Luke 10: 29ff). Anxiety is the surest sign of lack of trust in God (Matt. 6: 19–34), especially anxiety over possessions. So far from motive not being important provided the right action is done, Jesus was penetratingly critical of the self-love of 'good' people (Luke 18: 9–14), and it is clear from many passages in the gospels that he thought bad people to be not nearly so bad as the 'good' thought them. Underlying all this teaching lies the fact that Jesus was a man of faith (trust). Faced with the ambiguities of existence he looked at the weather, sun shining and rain falling alike on good and bad, and saw it as a sign of the unconditional goodness of the creative power of God. A sceptic would have drawn from the same evidence the conclusion that the universe is quite indifferent to moral worth. In this respect Jesus is an archetype for his followers.

His ethics is very different from an everyday ethic of doing good turns to those who do good turns to you; that is to say an ethic of reciprocity. This is invaluable as far as it goes. Social life requires a level of mutuality on which we can normally rely. One of the perils of international relations is that governments have not sufficient confidence in their relations with one another for mutuality to be relied upon. However, in our lives as citizens we do usually count on it. Some people behave better than the rule of reciprocity requires. Some keep it exactly on a fifty-fifty basis. Some get by with the minimum of co-operation. Some who do not even do that are likely to end in prison. Jesus goes much deeper, explicitly warning

95

against loving only those who love you, and saying that there is nothing extra-ordinary in that, the Gentiles do it; rather, what do you do more? (Matt. 5: 45ff). He goes beyond the world of claims and counter-claims, of rights and duties or something owed to others, as St Paul clearly sees when in Romans (13: 8) he says, 'Owe no-one anything but to love one another'. Jesus calls for a certain flair in life, a certain creative recklessness at critical points.

It might be thought that another emphasis in the gospels, that on rewards, is incompatible with this non-reciprocal ethic. Indeed it has continually been misunderstood. It is true that there is one passage in the gospels, about taking the lower seat in order to be promoted to the higher (Luke 14: 7ff) which is presented as pure prudential morality, presumably teaching that egoism is self-defeating, as a traditional proverb might. But it is most uncharacteristic. The usual teaching on rewards is found in such passages as Matthew 19: 29, where it is eternal life, or Luke 18: 22 where it is treasure in heaven, and especially the Beatitude in the Sermon on the Mount, 'Blessed are the pure in heart for they shall see God' (Matt. 5: 8). This teaching, as that on punishments, must be taken as a statement of fact. In the Kingdom of God there is only one reward whether, as in the parable of the labourers in the vineyard, you have worked all day or began only at the eleventh hour (Matt. 20: 1ff). The thrust of the teaching is towards a self-forgetfulness which results in an unselfconscious goodness. Writers on spirituality often call it disinterestedness. Jesus spoke severely against self-conscious goodness, as we noted when referring to Luke 18: 9ff. In the allegory of the sheep and the goats the sheep are unconscious of either their goodness or of rewards. The rewards Jesus spoke of cannot follow from the direct pursuit of them. Indeed consciously to pursue disinterestedness is self-defeating. One cannot *pursue* self-forgetfulness. *If* God is as Jesus said he is, it must be the case that following his way of life brings us to God; and to turn our backs on it must bring us to destruction, vividly symbolized by the perpetual burning rubbish dump outside the walls of Jerusalem (Gehenna). The fact that one can be tempted to do the right thing for the wrong reason, which was the fourth and most insidious temptation of Becket in T. S. Eliot's play *Murder in the Cathedral*, cannot alter that reality. The reward of God's presence must be for those who follow 'the way of the Lord Jesus' for love's sake, not the reward's sake. Indeed only they will be able to appreciate the reward. Whether anyone with full knowledge will turn their back on the vision of goodness lived and taught by Jesus is a question to which we have no answer. If there is a hell of destruction, is it empty?

This teaching on rewards has often not been followed or understood. Alms-giving is a litmus test. Donations and bequests have often been made with the motive of securing God's favour now and after death, and not as a joyful response to a graciousness of God already known.

It is significant that Jesus did not give a precise ruling on detailed ethical issues. When asked whether tribute should be given to Caesar (Matt. 22: 25ff) he said that what was due to God should be rendered to God and what due to Caesar should be rendered to him, without saying which was which. This has had continually to be worked out in varying circumstances. Education is a key area.

When asked by two brothers to divide an estate he refused (Luke 12: 14). There is truth in Richard Robinson's contention (*An Atheist's Values*, 1964, p. 149): 'Jesus says nothing on any social questions except divorce, and all ascriptions of political doctrine to him are false. He does not pronounce about war, capital punishment, gambling, justice, the administration of law, the distribution of goods, socialism, equality of income, equality of sex, equality of colour, equality of opportunity, tyranny, freedom, slavery, self-determination or contraception. There is nothing Christian about being for any of these things nor about being against them if we mean by 'Christian' what Jesus taught according to the synoptic gospels.'

Some have thought that the passage in the Sermon on the Mount concerning 'turning the other cheek' is an injunction to pacifism as a political technique (Matt. 5: 39ff), but this is to ignore its literary character as well as the nature of Jesus' ethical teaching. It occurs along with the command to pluck out an eye or cut off a hand rather than fall into evil, and also to give your cloak as well to anyone who asks for your coat (and thus be naked, for only two garments were worn). Like paradox, hyperbole is a way of giving concreteness to abstract ideas. The passage is neither for nor against pacifism as a political technique; Robinson is right.

Divorce is the one apparent exception to the fact that Jesus did not give detailed ethical rulings, but it is very doubtful if it is so. The key passage is Mark 10, 1–12 which deals with God's basic intention for marriage, without any direct reference to ecclesiastical, still less state, law. In Matthew 5: 32 and 19: 9 this is modified to include a clause forbidding divorce except on the grounds of *porneia*, usually translated as adultery. There has been an immense discussion of these texts. Apart from the inherent improbability that Jesus would give a detailed rule on only one issue, it seems clear that Matthew has made him arbitrate between the two rival contemporary rabbinic schools of Hillel and Shammai on what justified divorce in terms of the Mosaic ruling in Deuteronomy 24: 1.

The fourth gospel reflects in its own way the distinctive features of Jesus' ethical teaching. There is no ruling on any specific issue. The concentration is on the radical challenge Jesus brings to accepted ways. All is darkness except the white light focused on him, and through him on his intimate disciples. Indeed mutual love in the first instance is restricted to them, but it is only a provisional restriction, for the world is to be saved and not abandoned (17: 20ff). Love in word, will and action is stressed, even as a condition of knowledge (7:17). There is a parallel here with classical Marxism, which has been picked up by recent liberation theology, that only those who are actively committed to the cause of the poor will understand the Christian faith. It is certainly the case that Jesus challenged society's standards by the standards of the Kingdom of God in his attitude not only to the poor, but to heretics and schismatics (Samaritans), the immoral (prostitutes and adulterers), the politically compromised (tax collectors), society's rejects (lepers), those whom society neglected; and to women as a sex.

What is the meaning of love to which Jesus referred when he said that the Old Testament law (Torah) could be summarized in two commandments, love to God

97

and to one's neighbour as oneself? (Matt. 22: 34ff). Without going into a detailed word study, it is well known that the one English word love covers several different Greek words, notably *eros* (a yearning for satisfaction at any level up to the heights of beauty, truth and goodness), *philia* (friendship), and *agape*. This last was a relatively colourless Greek word which Christians took over to express the heart of Jesus' teaching. The two loves are not univocal, for adoration and worship are involved in our attitude to God, but not to our neighbour. Briefly, love of neighbour means being responsible for our fellow human beings, not because of their idio-syncratic qualities but because of their humanity as made in the image of God (Gen. 1: 22). It does not depend on natural affection in the one who loves nor natural attractiveness in the one loved. It does not imply identical treatment, but putting oneself in the neighbour's shoes. It is not a question of what *you* would want if you were in the neighbour's shoes. It does not mean submission to being exploited; for one thing it would not be for the good of the neighbour to be allowed to exploit you. Nor is it in the first instance concerned with self-sacrifice; it is service to the neighbour, not a loss to the self which is important. Indeed an affirmation of the self is needed. Those who hate or despise themselves cannot love their neighbour. It is pride, sloth and anxiety which are the enemies of the self, and thus the enemies of *agape*.

When more than two people are involved the expression of *agape* involves being fair to each of them. Questions of corrective and distributive justice are in the background of the New Testament, but the relation of them to *agape* is not systematically worked out because it is not a systematic work on ethics. The focus is on the new community of the church. Response in neighbour love to the love of God requires life within a community of love, a fellowship of repentance, forgiveness and reconciliation. The New Testament is very rich in its picture of the church in this respect, and very sharp in its criticism of the church when it fails to be such a community. But questions of justice remain. Suppose, for instance, parents have two children. They love both equally; but children of the same parents can differ greatly and it is still necessary to be *fair* between them. If this is so in the intimacy of family relations it is just as necessary and far more difficult to arrive at what is fair, in the wider collective relationships in which humans are involved. These extend even to issues of war. St Thomas Aquinas' brief discussion of the rudiments of a 'just war' doctrine occurs in the framework of his treatment of love. (*Summa Theologiae*, 2a, 2ae, q40 articles 1–3.)

The relation of justice and love is complex. It quickly brings in questions which are discussed in moral philosophy, like the place of special obligations. At least it must be said that love presupposes justice; it cannot require less than justice even if it transcends it; otherwise it degenerates into sentimentality.

Love as motivation does not give detailed content to ethical decisions. That requires knowledge and discernment, a combination of skills and perceptiveness. A love which is unwilling to be formed in this way and is content to 'mean well' is irresponsible and potentially dangerous. Some of the worst sins against love have been perpetrated by those who 'meant well'.

One theological tradition, the Lutheran, has particularly emphasized the gratuitous and unceasing love of God, his 'amazing grace', which is not dependent in any way on the merits of the loved one. It does this because it wants to remove any possibility of human boasting, any trace of a religion of works which thinks it can earn acceptance by God, that a credit balance of meritorious deeds is a prior condition of being 'right with God', rather than the Christian life being a response to God's prior graciousness. In a major modern work, *Agape and Eros*, Anders Nygren ends by comparing human beings to tubes or channels through which God's grace flows to the neighbour. Something has gone wrong when humans are compared to tubes. Rather they are called to share in God's non-reciprocal love which yearns for a response from the neighbour but does not give up when it fails to elicit it. In this it differs from friendship, which is more mutual and changeable, and needs *agape* to save it from self-centredness. *Eros* also, which can move from the instinctive level of sexual libido to the highest levels of aspiration, needs to be set in the context of *agape* to save it from self-centredness.

The Church has had trouble in holding to this radical understanding of love. It is focused in the question of how to interpret the very radical sayings found in the Sermon on the Mount (Matt. 5–7), the most considerable collection of Jesus' teaching. Several ways have been adopted, all having the effect of neutralizing these radical elements and bringing them nearer to common-sense morality. One has been to say that Jesus expected the imminent end of the world and that the ethic was meant only for the short time left. This is probably correct about Jesus' expectation, but it does not follow that the ethic is irrelevant now that the world has not ended. Another way has been to siphon off the more radical elements as 'counsels of perfection' to which a few are called. They are usually to be found in monasteries and nunneries, having taken vows of poverty, chastity and obedience, and are called the Religious with a capital R. The rest are called to follow the basic ethical 'precepts' which are binding on all. One way of expressing this is to say that one *must* be just and one *may* be loving. It is a kind of Honours and Pass course in Christian living. A serious feature of it has been to make the married state a second best. Whilst Religious communities still flourish, they are rarely advocated to-day, even by their members, on such grounds. Still another way is to make a sharp separation between the realm of love in the church and the stern realm of justice and order in the world, or to say that the purpose of Jesus' radical ethic is to convict us of sin and prevent the development of spiritual pride. None of these attempts will do. The radical elements in Jesus' ethic are an authentic corollary of the radical stance of the Kingdom of God, calling us past the necessary struggles with justice to a fuller realization of love. It is the more challenging because the more serious sins feed on moral achievements, not on the more coarse and flamboyant ones. Both with individuals and collectives corruption can feed on moral achievement, so that if there is a moral collapse it can be greater than if the achievement had been less. Nazi Germany is the great example of this in the twentieth century. Hence the question has been raised, Is there any point in such a radical ethic which is always being ignored? Would not a less drastic and more practical one be better? It is a question which is frequently asked in this century by adherents of other faiths, such as Jews and Muslims.

One of the first Jewish writers to make a sustained effort to get behind the polemics and persecutions of the centuries and take a new look at Jesus was Joseph Klausner (*Jesus of Nazareth*, 1925). He has had a number of successors. This is a remarkable change. Christian scholarship at the same time has become alert to the deep Jewishness of Jesus. Klausner's verdict is that all Jesus' ethical teaching is to be found somewhere in Jewish sources but nowhere else gathered together without any commonplace matter. However, it is an ethic for the days of the Messiah and impossible short of them. It breaks up the family, ignores justice, and would disrupt social stability. More than that it has been ignored by all except priests and recluses; and in its shadow every kind of wickedness and vice has flourished. How much better the practical, corporate ethic of Judaism! For instance the Rabbis would have been likely to agree with Jesus that 'the sabbath was made for man and not man for the sabbath' (Mark 2: 27), but they wanted a rule for breaking the normal sabbath rules and this he did not give. This is not because life can be lived without rules or codes, like an extemporare speaker, but because Jesus' ethic is in a different dimension. It always seeks an adequate expression of *agape* whilst transcending particular instances of it.

To these charges Christians tend to make two replies. One is to say that it is indeed fortunate that Jesus did not give us detailed ethical instructions or we would be forever trying to relate them to very different and changing cultures and involved in tortuous exegesis in doing so. Second, and more important, they stress the relevance of an impossible ethic. Its point is to bring us to see that the reward of loving is to learn more of the depth and range of love, so that even those who we consider the most 'saintly' are those who are most conscious of the gulf in their lives between what *is* and what *ought to be* the case; and this not because they are morbid but because they have grasped more of the inexhaustible nature of love.

Such a perspective is meant to be a spur to action, with both a personal and social reference, and not an excuse for a spurious otherworldliness (as distinct from a hope beyond this life which is involved in following Jesus' understanding of human destiny). To paraphrase the rather prosaic words of a modern New Testament scholar, the Christian ethic does not provide a law for either the individual or society, but creates a tension which has transforming results. (*Jesus the Messiah*, William Manson, 1943).

That is how it should work out. What did the earliest Christians make of it? Here our best witness is St Paul; and his later years lead on to post-apostolic Christianity and the latest books of the New Testament.

iii   St Paul

St Paul is a controversial figure because of the controversies in which he was involved, and those which have focused on him since, not least at the time of the Reformation. Because of his Pharisaic background and his split from it he cannot be considered apart from the question of the self-definition of the Christian community as against Judaism, particularly after the fall of Jerusalem to the Romans in 70 CE. By then the number of Jews in the Christian community was small. The kind of character that Jews and Christians admired was very similar, and hence Christianity attracted admirers of Judaism in the Gentile world because it commended the virtues of Judaism but without circumcision and the food laws. The dominant gospel picture of Jesus' controversies with the Pharisees must not be taken as a complete picture; indeed there are indications in them of a positive relationship between him and some Pharisees. The Pharisees were not a uniform party. In an effort to find and follow God's way in every detail of life they were argumentative. Moreover arguments were not finally resolved; minority opinions continued as part of the tradition. Some Pharisees were like the dominant gospel picture, but it has been a Christian travesty to say of all of them that they were content with a religion of outward observance of moral rules as a means of establishing their moral worth in God's eyes, whereas Jesus probed to inward motives. This travesty was intensified by Luther's struggle against the spirit of late medieval Catholicism, as he encountered it, which often became attributed to Pharisaism. Wherein, then, lay the difference between Jesus and the various parties of Judaism, particularly the Pharisees? In the first place it was their exclusiveness, and in the second their understanding of the range and depth of love was not radical enough. But with respect to St Paul, he was a complex thinker and these issues are still much discussed and by no means resolved.

It is clear, however, that St Paul grasped that the basis of Jesus' ethic is a joyful response in life to the overflowing graciousness of God. 'Freely you have received, freely give' (Matt. 10: 8). The Kingdom of God in the first three gospels is witnessed to in St Paul's letters as the new life in Christ, which he understood as essentially a community experience. A typical expression is 'We who are many are one body in Christ' (Rom. 12: 5). The 'law of Christ' is Christ himself (Rom. 10: 4). The Kingdom of God is both a present reality and a leaven in the lump of history (Rom. 14: 7), and yet it is still to come in its fullness (1 Cor. 15: 24 and 50). Love is the cornerstone of it. The characteristics of love are spelled out in 1 Corinthians 13, which is somewhat like a Stoic diatribe but quite different in spirit. Jesus was the model for this passage. St. Paul does not directly quote incidents from his life but assumes they are known to his hearers and readers by referring in passing to his birth, teaching, crucifixion, burial and resurrection. He assumes that the young Christian congregations know in their own experience that the work of Christ has led to an outpouring of God's spirit which has broken down barriers between people which humans have created; between Jews and Gentiles, men and women, slaves and free. He uses this shared assumption to chide them when they fail to express this reality. In Romans 13 he sums up the Christian ethic as one of love, as has been mentioned.

Moreover what makes St Paul so important for us is that he is the first Christian of whom we are aware who was called upon to bring his understanding of the Christian ethic to bear on particular problems thrown up by the churches, as when a deputation from Corinth puts to him various questions about marriage which he answers in 1 Corinthians 7. In dealing with them he shews on occasion, as we would expect, that not every corner of his mind was instantly converted to understand all the implications of his new faith. Some of his teaching with respect to women is incompatible with his best insights. Too often the church has taken his instructions as a permanent rule so that, to take a trivial example, it is only in this century that women have been able to enter churches without hats because of what St Paul wrote in 1 Corinthians 12.5ff. Again as we would expect, his advice has to be put in the context of the situation of the early Christians in the first century AD. His expectation of the imminent end of the world influenced his advice on marriage. However, he took a typically robust attitude in urging the Christians to get on with their daily lives and work just because time is short, and not sit about waiting for it to end. By the close of the first century the church had made a major change of view in this matter (though the attitude has continued among some to this day). The fourth gospel re-interprets the return of Christ and the end of time as the gift of the Spirit within the community. Cosmically St Paul accepted the current view that superhuman powers affect human affairs (though the exalted Christ had now drawn their sting). These ideas have to be translated by us into a realistic sociology. As to earthly powers, Christians were in no position to alter human institutions or affect public policy. In this situation St Paul takes a favourable view of the pagan Roman state, of which he was proud to be a citizen and to which he had reason to be grateful. The abolition of slavery does not enter his view, though he does show how Christians can transcend its structures (note the letter to Philemon). In short he gave to people oppressed with a fear of change and of a fate decreed by the stars a present security and a future hope because of his belief in the lordship of Christ.

The problem of Christians in the later years of the first century, as of all Christians since, was to sustain the radical rigour of the gospel ethic without an expectation of the imminent end of time. The ongoing life of the local churches produced a number of standard problems, particularly in the realm of marriage and the family. In the later books of the New Testament we find codes of conduct inserted, often taken from Greek ethics and Christianized with biblical illustrations. Examples can be found in Colossians (3. 18–4.1), Ephesians (5.12–6.9), 1 Peter (2.11–3. 12 and 5.1–5), Titus (2.1–3.2), and 1 Timothy (2.1–6.19). There is here a difference in emotional tone as well as in content from that of earlier letters; piety and perserverance are stressed, and love becomes one virtue in a list of others. There is no reason to object to codes of conduct to cover standard situations, provided the radical ambience of the gospel is kept. However, some of it was lost. The church is settling down too easily in the current social and political order. An unfortunate feature of some of the codes is a stress on the duties of the 'inferior' to the 'superior' party, wives to husbands, children to parent, and slaves to masters, without any corresponding stress on the duties of the 'superior' party. Such an ethic of patience and submission is hardly adequate for our world, which is more and more conscious of personal responsibility and the need for social structures which encourage it, or even in some situations of oppression begin to make it possible for the first time.

However, periodic persecutions prevented the church settling down too easily, and we can find elements of a challenge to those who tried to do so in these later

New Testament writings. It takes the form of a rigorist reaction against mere conforming, in the shape of references to sins which cannot be forgiven. We do not know what was the 'sin unto death' of John 5: 16 (perhaps apostasy), but we are forbidden even to pray for anyone who commits it. In three places Hebrews refers to sins which cannot be forgiven (6: 4–6; 10: 26–31; 12: 16ff), whilst Revelation never considers that any of those who suffer the fearful penalties of John's visions will repent, nor hopes that they will; rather it exults in their punishment. These two tendencies continued. Conformism in the church, especially after the 'conversion' of Constantine, as it is usually referred to – it is not clear how far he was using Christianity as a weapon in his political struggle – led to the rigorist reaction of the Desert Fathers, and then to the beginnings of communal monasticism and to the double standard of counsels of perfection and precepts. Thus by the end of the New Testament period the creative tension established by Jesus had largely been dissolved into disparate elements, though it has always remained as a source of renewal in the church, challenging distortions.

iv   Criticisms of Christian ethics

Problems of moving from the Bible to the modern world continue to be explored, as do the different traditions in thinking about ethical issues which have developed in Christian history. Notable among these has been the incorporation of Natural Law thinking into Christian ethics; on this see Article 11, MEDIEVAL AND RENAISSANCE ETHICS, and Article 13, NATURAL LAW.

It is necessary, however, that mention should be made of some common contemporary criticisms of Christian ethics.

(1)   Christian ethics is intolerant and breeds intolerance. There is much evidence to support this charge. All the major confessional traditions have at times persecuted each other. Indeed it was only at the second Vatican Council (1962–5) that the Roman Catholic Church finally abandoned the position that 'error has no rights'. Anti-semitism was also a major disease of Christendom (though also found outside it). Toleration came into the 'Christian' world largely through the influence of those who were appalled by Christian intolerance, and Christians learned through the sceptical tolerance of a man like Voltaire to distinguish tolerance from an indifference to truth. There have always been Christians who understood this. Bitter lessons this century have brought it home.

(2)   Christian ethics is immoral because it works on a system of rewards (heaven) for good behaviour and threats (hell) for bad; and not on doing what is right simply because it is right and for no other reason. The question of rewards has already been mentioned and seen to be overdone. (See also Article 14, KANTIAN ETHICS.)

(3)   Instead of leading to self-fulfilment Christian ethics is repressive. Most modern psychological analyses of human growth and development advocate as an ethical norm an altruistic, autonomous character. They do not look to Christianity to produce it; rather they think it leads to defensive and restrictive behaviour, and to a static social conformism. This is connected to a further criticism.

(4)   Christian ethics keeps people at an immature level, because it leads to stock moral reactions regardless of circumstances. It prevents people from learning from experience. Many immature people are 'religious'. At its worst Christian ethics has certainly had this effect, but at its best its effect has been quite the reverse, as in its traditional teaching on conscience. The traditional teaching has been that it is reasons which justify moral judgements, and conscience has been the name given to the power of reason and discernment brought to bear on moral issues. This is so central to the integrity of the person that the teaching is that 'conscience must always be obeyed'. In saying this no claim is made for the infallibility of conscience, or for more certainty than the very nature of the uncertainties of ethical decisions can provide. The teaching is accompanied by a call for the formation of an informed and sensitive conscience by living in the Christian community, and making use of the resources for the education of conscience which have already been mentioned. Differences between Christians on ethical issues often arise from different weights attached to these different sources. Sometimes this whole teaching has been suspect as leading one to put one's own unregenerate judgements in the place of the guidance of God. Hence sometimes conscience has been seen as the 'voice of God' within the self, but the problems and dangers of this, as of all forms of intuitionism, are obvious. (On intuitionism see Article 36, INTUITIONISM, and Article 40, UNIVERSAL PRE-SCRIPTIVISM.) Once the complexities of the moral life are faced, the traditional teaching on conscience is seen to lead to vigorous, creative and hopeful Christian living.

Within the spectrum of attitudes among Christians to Christian ethics there is a strong, though not universal, stress on the dignity of the human person, the reality and universality of the community of the church, and a concern for its contribution to the holding together of humanity in a pluralistic world. Christianity must not add to its divisions, but exert a healing influence. These convictions are in conflict in many respects with the 'possessive individualism' which has had a wide influence in Western circles in the late twentieth century. It has produced in some circles a version of Christian ethics in its own image, but one which is not accepted by the majority of contemporary Christian ethicists, certainly not those influenced by the Ecumenical Movement. Rather there has been a growing emphasis on giving preference to the needs of the poor. These two emphases, concern for the unity of mankind and for 'a preferential option for the poor', mark the end of the embodiment of the Christian ethic in Church and State which for centuries characterized its heartland, Christendom.

References

Aquinas, Thomas: *Summa Theologiae*.
Butler, S.: *The Way of All Flesh* (London: 1903); (Harmondsworth: Penguin, 1947).
Eliot, T. S.: *Murder in the Cathedral* (London: Faber & Faber, 1935).
Klausner, J.: *Jesus of Nazareth* (London: Allen & Unwin, 1925).
Manson, W.: *Jesus the Messiah* (London: Hodder & Stoughton, 1943).

Niebuhr, H. R.: *Christ and Culture* (New York: Harper & Brothers, 1951).
Nygren, A.: *Agape and Eros* (London: SPCK, 1953).
Pascal, B.: *Lettres Provinciales* (Paris: 1656); (Harmondsworth: Penguin, 1967).
Robinson, R.: *An Atheist's Values* (Oxford, Clarendon Press, 1964).

Further reading

Beach, W. and Niebuhr, H. R., eds.: *Christian Ethics: Sources of the Living Tradition* (New York: Ronald Press, 1955).
D'Arcy, M. C.: *The Mind and Heart of Love* (London: Faber and Faber, 1946).
Donnelly, J. and Lyons, L., eds.: *Conscience* (New York: Alba House, 1973).
Furnish, V. P.: *The Love Commandment in the New Testament* (Nashville, Tenn.: Abingdon Press, 1972).
Le Roy Long Jr., E.: *A Survey of Christian Ethics* (New York: Oxford University Press, 1967).
——: *A Survey of Recent Christian Ethics* (New York: Oxford University Press, 1982).
Macquarrie, J. and Childress, J., ed.: *A New Dictionary of Christian Ethics* (London: S.C.M. Press, 1986).
Nelson, E. E., ed.:*Conscience: Theological and Psychological Perspectives* (New York: Newman Press, 1973).
Oppenheimer, H.: *The Hope of Happiness: a Sketch for a Christian Humanism* (London: S.C.M. Press, 1983).
Outka, G.: *Agape* (New Haven, Conn.: Yale University Press, 1972).
Ramsey, I. T., ed.: *Christian Ethics and Contemporary Philosophy* (London: S.C.M. Press, 1966).
Robinson, N. H. G.: *The Groundwork of Christian Ethics* (London: Collins, 1971).
Smart, Ninian: *The Phenomenon of Christianity* (London: Collins, 1979).
Thielicke, H.: *Theological Ethics* Vol. 1, *Foundations* Vol. 2, *Politics* (London: E. T. A. & C. Black, 1968 and 1969).

9

Islamic ethics

AZIM NANJI

i Introduction

ISLAM is among the youngest of the world's major religions, belonging to the family of monotheistic faiths that also includes Judaism and Christianity. From its beginnings in what is now Saudi Arabia over 1,400 years ago, it has grown and spread to include almost a billion adherents, living in virtually every corner of the world. Though the majority of Islam's followers, called Muslims, are found in the continents of Africa and Asia (including the Asian republics of the Soviet Union and north-west China), there has been a substantial increase in the number of Muslims living in the Americas, Australia and Europe in the last quarter of the twentieth century. More recently, the various nation-states and communities that constitute the global Muslim *ummah* (community), are expressing a need, in varying degrees, to relate their Islamic heritage to questions of national and cultural self-identification. Where this phenomenon has become allied to domestic or international reaction and conflict, it has caused a great deal of confusion and misunderstanding regarding the role of Islam. It is therefore important to develop historical insight into how the whole spectrum of Islamic values and their underlying moral and ethical assumptions have been shaped in the course of Muslim history, in order to appreciate the diversity of Islam's heritage of ethical thought and life.

ii Beginnings and development: foundational values

The norms and assumptions that have characterized belief and action in Islam have their initial inspiration in two foundational sources. One is scriptural, embodying the message revealed by God to the Prophet Muhammad (d. 632) and recorded in the Quran. The second is the exemplification of that message in the perceived model pattern of the Prophet's actions, sayings and norms, collectively called the *Sunnah*. Muslims regard the Quran as the ultimate closure in a series of revelations to humankind from God, and the *Sunnah* as the historical projection of a divinely inspired and guided human life in the person of the Prophet Muhammad, who is also believed to be the last in a series of messengers from God.

The late Fazlur Rahman, noted University of Chicago scholar of Islamic thought and modernist Muslim thinker, argued that in its initial phase Islam was moved by a deep rational and moral concern for reforming society, and that this moral intentionality was conceived in ways that encouraged a deep commitment to reasoning and rational discourse. Like other religous traditions, and particularly Christianity and Judaism, Islam, in answering the question 'What ought or ought not to be done?' thus had a clearly defined sense of the sources of moral authority. While revealing his will to humankind in the Quran, God also urges them to exercise reason in understanding revelation. One part of this rational inquiry into the meaning of revelation led Muslims to elaborate rules for ethical behaviour and the principles upon which such rules could be based. In time, the relationship between the Quran and the life of the Prophet, as a model of behaviour, would also be elaborated, to extend the framework within which values and obligations could be determined. The process of determination and elaboration, however, involved the application of human reasoning, and it is this continuing interaction between reason and revelation, and the potential and limits of the former in relation to the latter, that provided the basis for formalized expressions of ethical thought in Islam.

In one of the chapters of the Quran, entitled the Criterion (*Furqan*: Sura 25), revelation – to all humanity – becomes the point of reference for distinguishing right from wrong. The same chapter goes on to cite examples of past biblical prophets and their role as mediators of God's word to their respective societies. Like Judaism and Christianity, Islam's beginnings are thus rooted in the idea of the divine command as a basis for establishing moral order through human endeavour. (See Article 46, HOW COULD ETHICS DEPEND ON RELIGION?) Elsewhere in the Quran, the same term also indicates the concept of a revealed morality that presents humanity with a clear distinction between right and wrong which is not subject to human vicissitude. By grounding a moral code in divine will, an opportunity is afforded to human beings to respond by creating a rational awareness that sustains the validity of revelation. Thus a wider basis for human action is possible, if rationality comes to be applied as a result of revelation to elaborate criteria for encompassing the totality of human actions and decisions. These themes are played out in the Quranic telling of the story of Adam's creation and regress.

Adam, the first human, is distinguished from existing angels, who are asked to bow down to him, by virtue of his divinely endowed capacity to 'name things', that is to conceive of knowledge capable of being described linguistically and thereby codified, a capacity not accessible to angels, who are seen as one-dimensional beings. This creative capacity carries with it, however, an obligation not to exceed set limits. Satan in the Quran exemplifies excess, since he disobeys God's command to honour and bow before Adam, thus denying his own innate nature and limits. In time, Adam too fails to live within the limits set by God, loses his honourable status, which he will have to recover subsequently by struggling with and overcoming his propensities on earth, the arena that allows for choice and action. Ultimately he does recover his former status, attesting to the capacity to return to the right course of action through rational understanding of his failure and by transcending the urge to set aside that rationality and test the limits set by divine command. Adam's story therefore reflects all of the potential for good and evil that is already built into the human condition and the unfolding saga of human response to a continuous divine revelation in history. It exemplifies the ongoing struggle within humanity to discover the mean that allows for balanced action and submission to the divine criterion. It is in that sense that the word *Islam* stands for the original revelation, requiring submission to achieve equilibrium, and that a *muslim* is one who seeks through action to attain that equilibrium in personal life as well as society.

The human quality that encompasses the concept of the ideal ethical value in the Quran is summed up in the term *taqwa*, which in its various forms occurs over two hundred times in the text. It represents, on the one hand, the moral grounding that underlies human action, while on the other, it signifies the ethical conscience which makes human beings aware of their responsibilities to God and society. Applied to the wider social context *taqwa* becomes the universal, ethical mark of a truly moral community:

O humankind! We have created you out of male and female and constituted you into different groups and societies, so that you may come to know each other – the noblest of you, in the sight of God, are the ones possessing *taqwa*. (49: 11–13)

More specifically, when addressing the first Muslims, the Quran refers to them as 'a community of the middle way, witnesses to humankind, just as the Messenger (i.e. Muhammad) is a witness for you' (2: 132).

The Muslim *ummah* or community is thus seen as the instrument through which Quranic ideals and commands are translated at the social level. Individuals become trustees through whom a moral and spiritual vision is fulfilled in personal life. They are accountable to God and to the community, since that is the custodian through whom the covenantal relationship with God is sustained. The Quran affirms the dual dimension of human and social life – material and spiritual – but these aspects are not seen in conflictual terms, nor is it assumed that spiritual goals should predominate in a way that devalues material aspects of life. The Quran, recognizing the complementarity between the two, asserts that human conduct and aspirations have relevance as acts of faith within the wider human, social and cultural contexts. It is in this sense that the idea that Islam embodies a total way of life can best be understood.

An illustration of one aspect of such a vision is the Quran's emphasis on the ethics of redressing injustice in economic and social life. For instance, individuals are urged to spend of their wealth and substance on:

1 family and relatives
2 orphans
3 the poor
4 the travelling homeless
5 the needy
6 freeing of the enslaved.

Such acts define a Muslim's responsibility to develop a social conscience and to share individual and communal resources with the less privileged. They are institutionalized in the Quran through the duty of *zakat*, a term connoting 'giving', 'virtue', 'increase' and 'purification'. In time, this became an obligatory act, assimilated into the framework of the ritual pillars of the faith, including prayer, fasting and pilgrimage. The Quran also sought to abolish usurious practices in the mercantile community of Mecca and Medina, stigmatizing such practices as reflecting the lack of a work ethic and an undue exploitation of those in need.

At the social level, the Quran's emphasis on the family includes a concern for ameliorating the status of women, through the abolition of pre-Islamic practices such as female infanticide and by according women new rights. Among these were the rights of ownership of property, inheritance, the right to contract marriage and to initiate divorce, if necessary, and to maintain one's own dowry. Polygyny, the plurality of wives, was regulated and restricted, so that a male was permitted to have up to four wives, but only if he could treat them with equity. Muslims have traditionally understood this practice in its seventh-century context, as affording the necessary flexibility to address the social and cultural diversity that arose with the expansion of Islam. Some modern Muslims, however, maintain that the thrust of the Quranic reform was in the direction of monogamy and an enhanced public role for women. They also hold that the development and occurrence of customs and practices of seclusion and veiling of women were a result of local tradition and customs, occasionally antithetical to the spirit of emancipation of women envisaged in the Quran.

Since Muslims had been privileged by the Quran as the 'best of communities', whose function it was to command the right and prevent wrong, the Prophet Muhammad's mission, like that of some past prophets, involved the creation of a just, divinely ordained polity. The struggle towards this goal involved Muslims in warfare, and the term in the Quran that encompasses this effort as a whole is *jihad*. Often simply and erroneously translated as 'holy war', *jihad* carries a far wider connotation that includes striving by peaceful means, such as preaching, education, and in a more personal and interiorized sense, as struggle to purify oneself. Where it refers to armed defence of a justly executed war, the Quran specifies the conditions for war and peace, the treatment of captives and the resolution of conflict, urging that the ultimate purpose of God's word was to invite and guide people to the 'ways of peace'.

As the Muslim polity took shape it also became necessary for it to address the question of its relationship and attitude towards non-Muslims with similar scriptural traditions, particularly Jews and Christians. In the Quran they are referred to as 'People of the Book'. Where they lived among Muslims, as subjects, they were to be granted 'protected' status through a mutual agreement. They were to be subject to a poll tax and their private and religious property, law and religious practices were to be protected. They could not, however, proselytize among Muslims. While recognizing the particularity of the Muslim community and its pre-eminent status, the Quran encourages a wider respect for difference and otherness in human society, while favouring common moral goals over mutually divisive and antagonistic attitudes:

For each community, we have granted a Law and a Code of Conduct. If God wished, He could have made you One community, but he wishes rather to test you through that which has been given to you. So vie with each other to excel in goodness and moral virtue. (5: 48)

The need for congruence between the divine moral imperative and human life is also reflected in the preserved Prophetic tradition, which is perceived as explaining and confirming Quranic values and commands. The recording of episodes of the Prophet's life, his words, actions and habits, came in time to represent for Muslims a timeless model pattern for daily life. It also assumed an authoritative role in explaining and complementing the Quran. His personal character, struggle, piety and eventual success, enhance for Muslims Muhammad's role as the paradigm and seal of prophecy. A rich tradition of poetry in praise of the Prophet exists in virtually all the languages spoken by Muslims, enhancing both the commitment to emulate his behaviour and a sense of personal affinity and love for his person and family. For Muslims, the message of the Quran and the example of the Prophet's life thus remain inseparably related through all of history as paradigms for moral and ethical behaviour. They formed the basis for Muslim thinkers subsequently to develop legal tools for embodying moral imperatives. The elaboration of the legal sciences would lead to a codification of norms and statutes that gave form to the concept of law in Islam, generally referred to as the *Shari'a*. Among the forms that developed to encompass the moral imperative are the various schools of law in Islam, each of whom, through the legal discipline of *fiqh* (jurisprudence), elaborated legal codes to embody their specific interpretation of how Muslims should respond to God's commands in conducting their daily lives.

Parallel to the developing legal expressions, there also emerged a set of moral assumptions that articulated ethical values, rooted in a more speculative and philosophical conception of human conduct as a response to the Quran and the Prophet's life. Groupings in Islam, as well as schools of law, were not as clearly circumscribed in the first three centuries of Muslim history as is generally thought. Most were still crystallizing and their subsequent boundaries and positions were yet to be fully defined and elaborated. Public, legal and educational institutions in the Muslim world of the time had not achieved the classical forms or purposes that came to be associated with them. A key to this process of definition and distinction is the nature of public discourse that characterized the growing Muslim society in its first three centuries. Muslim conquest and expansion had resulted in contact with cultures whose intellectual heritages were in time selectively appropriated by Muslims, then refined and further developed. The integration of the intellectual and philosophical legacies of Greece, India and Iran among others, created conditions and a tradition of intellectual activity that would lead to the cosmopolitan heritage of an emerging Islamic civilization. Christian and Jewish scholars, who had already encountered the above legacies in varying degrees, played a crucial mediating role as 'translators', particularly since they were also aware that the moral disposition of Muslims, like theirs, was shaped by common monotheistic conceptions based on divine command and revelation. The term *adab* has come to be used to define the wide connotation of meanings implied by the moral, ethical, intellectual and literary discourse that emerged. It was also during this period, from the eighth to the tenth centuries, that we see the emergence of what later came to be clearly identifiable theological and intellectual positions, within the Muslim community identified with traditions such as the Sunni, Shi'a, Mu'tazila and the Muslim philosophers.

The main features of the moral environment and perspective based on the Quranic message are defined by general ethical stances that came to be regarded as normative through their expression in legal language and terms. In the early period of Muslim intellectual history, these values also provided a frame of reference for the selective appropriation and development of philosophical, moral and ethical assumptions from other traditions, such as the Hellenistic, and served as a basis for widening the scope and application of an Islamic frame of reference to articulate ethical and moral values outside of merely juristically defined values. Since clear-cut distinctions in Islam between religion, society, and culture are hard to sustain, it seems appropriate, in discussing Muslim ethics, to let the whole spectrum of tendencies, legal, theological, philosophical and mystical, act as resources for disclosing moral assumptions and commitments in order to appreciate both development and continuity across the whole spectrum of Muslim thought and civilization.

iii The theological and traditionalist approaches

The transition towards what Marshall Hodgson has termed the 'Islamicate' civilization marked two types of moral and intellectual beginnings. Both derived their inspiration from Islam's foundational texts and the unfolding of self-reflexive rational processes. The first involved, on the part of the early Muslims, a shift from a pre-Islamic Arab culture bound primarily by local, oral tradition, to one based on a revealed text, whose preservation and recording, in Arabic, created the conditions for the emergence of a new Islamic culture, based on the Quran and incorporating and extending the monotheistic imperative reflected in Judaism and Christianity. The second 'beginning' was influenced in part by the translation into Arabic and study of works of ancient philosophy, medicine and the sciences (to a lesser extent including those of ancient Iran and India). The moral discussions and intellectual forces that emerged from the juxtaposition and integration of these into fresh beginnings, facilitated to a certain extent by the presence of Jewish and Christian scholars, stimulated a concern for how moral and religious perspectives could be reconciled with intellectual modes of inquiry.

The emergence of an intellectual tradition of inquiry based on the application of rational tools as a way of understanding Quranic injunctions led to the use among Muslims of a formal discipline devoted to the study of *kalam*, literally speech, i.e. the word of God. The goals of this discipline were theological, in the sense that the application of reason was to make comprehensible and justify the word of God. The discussions involved Muslims in the elaboration and definition of certain ethical concerns, namely:

1 the meaning of Quranic ethical attributes such as 'just', 'obligatory', 'good', 'evil', etc.
2 the question of the relationship between human free will and divine will
3 the capacity of human beings to derive, through reason, the knowledge of objective ethical norms and truths.

Without doing too much injustice to the process of debate and discussion among various Muslim groups, it can be maintained that, in general, two clear positions emerged; one associated with the *Mu'tazila* and the other a traditionalist approach (generally associated with the Sunni tradition in Islam).

The Mu'tazila argued that since God is just and rewards and punishes within that context, human beings must possess free choice in order that they might be held fully accountable. They denied that acts could therefore be predestined. Secondly, they maintained that since ethical notions had objective meaning, human beings possess the intellectual capacity to grasp these meanings. Reason therefore was a key attribute capable, independently of revelation, of making empirical observations and drawing ethical conclusions. Natural reason, however, must be supplemented and confirmed by divine revelation. Related to this was another Mu'tazili conviction, that God's just nature precluded any belief that he might deliberately lead believers to sinful acts.

Historically, the Mu'tazila school of thought died out and its views were not deemed acceptable to the majority of the traditionalists. The latter's refutation of the main points suggest a differing orientation towards the sources from which ethical values are derived, and the context of faith in which they have meaning. The traditionalist position, as embodied, for example, in the classic work of one founder of a Muslim juridical school, al-Shafi'i, was that the foundations of faith were a matter of practice, not speculation. Over against the Mu'tazila belief that natural reason enabled good and evil to be determined, al-Shafi'i emphasized revelation as the ultimate source of definition. Since the principle of human accountability was also the cornerstone of juridical thought – obligations implied the capacity to undertake them – good and evil were to be determined on the basis of textual proof, Quranic and by extension that contained in Prophetic tradition. Acts and obligations were good and evil ultimately because divine commands defined them as such.

On the question of human freedom for action, the Mu'tazili portion was combated, in one respect, through a notion of 'acquisition'. It was argued that the human power to perform acts was not one's own, but came from God. Human beings 'acquire' responsibility for their actions, thus making them accountable. It must be underlined that traditionalist thinkers were not opposed to the use of reason, quite the contrary; they parted company with rationalists only over the value placed on reason. They regarded it as an aid and tool for affirming issues of faith, but purely secondary in its relation to the definition of ethical obligation.

In summing up the traditionalist position, George Makdisi has emphasized that the final basis for moral obligation, from its perspective, was the data of Islam's foundational texts, the Quran and the *Sunnah*, elaborated and applied as God's commands and prohibitions, conceived as the *Shari'a*, formulated through the respective Muslim juridical schools. Such formulations of commands and prohibitions in Muslim books of law are expressed in ethical terms. Five categories are employed for evaluating all acts:

1 Obligatory acts, such as the duty to perform ritual prayer, paying of *zakat* and the practice of fasting.
2 Recommended acts, which are not considered obligatory, such as supererogatory acts of charity, kindness, prayer, etc.
3 Permitted actions, regarding which the law adopts a neutral stance, that is there is no expectation of reward or punishment for such acts.
4 Acts that are discouraged and regarded as reprehensible, but not strictly forbidden; Muslim jurists differ about what actions to include under this category.
5 Actions that are categorically forbidden, such as murder, adultery, blasphemy, theft, intoxication, etc.

These categories were further set by jurists within a dual framework of obligations: towards God and towards society. In each instance transgression was perceived in both legal and theological terms, as constituting a crime as well as a sin. Such acts were punishable under the law and the jurists attempted to specify and elaborate the conditions under which this could occur. For example, one of the punishments for theft or highway robbery was the cutting off of a hand and in minor instances, flogging. Traditionally, jurists attempted to take into account active repentance to mitigate such punishment, following a tradition of the Prophet to restrict the applicability of such punishments to extreme cases.

Some of these categories have received attention in several Muslim countries in recent times, where traditional juristic procedures have been reinstated, but there is a great deal of divergence in the Muslim world about the necessity and applicability of some of these procedures. Where applied, such punishment is meted out through *Shari'a* courts and rendered by appointed Muslim judges. Jurists or legal experts also function as interpreters of the *Shari'a* and are free to render informed legal opinions. Such opinions may be solicited by individuals who wish to be certain about the moral intentionality of certain acts, but among most Muslim schools of law such opinions need not be binding. The four major Sunni schools of law consider each other to reflect normative stances on matters of legal and ethical interpretation. For these Muslim jurists, both law and ethics are ultimately concerned with moral obligations, which they believe are the central focus of the Islamic message.

iv Philosophical approaches

The integration of the philosophical legacy of antiquity in the Islamic world was a major enabling factor in the use of philosophical tradition among Muslim intellectuals. It gave rise to figures such as al-Farabi, Ibn Sina (Avicenna), Ibn Rushd (Averroes), and others, who became well-known to medieval Europe as philosophers, commentators and exponents of the classical tradition going back to Plato and Aristotle. The public discourse of *adab*, grounded in philosophical and moral language and concerns, represents a significant part of the cosmopolitan heritage of ethics in Islam and reflects efforts to reconcile religiously and scripturally derived values with an intellectually and morally based ethical foundation. The Muslim philosophical tradition of ethics is therefore doubly significant: for its value in continuing and enhancing classical Greek philosophy and for its commitment to synthesizing Islam and philosophical thought.

Al-Farabi (d. 950 CE) argued for harmony between the ideals of virtuous religion and the goals of a true polity. Through philosophy, one is able to arrive at an understanding of how human happiness is to be achieved, but the actual recourse to moral virtues and acts involves the instrumentality of religion. He compares the founding of religion to the founding of a city. Citizens ought to acquire the traits which enable them to function as residents of a virtuous polis. Similarly the founder of a religion establishes norms that must be upheld through action, if a proper religious community is to be established. The thrust of Farabi's argument, particularly as it is articulated in his classic work, *The Virtuous City*, suggests a communal framework for attaining ultimate happiness, and therefore significant social and political roles for religion as well as an engagement in similar concerns by politicians. In this respect, the emphasis on virtue and its ethical connotations suggests a common focus for both Greek and Muslim philosophy, namely the application of such standards and norms to political societies. The greater the wisdom and virtue of the rulers and the citizens, the greater the possibility of attaining the true goal of philosophy and religion – happiness.

Ibn Sina (d. 1037) develops the argument that the Prophet embodies the totality of virtuous action and thought, the best of which is reflected in the attainment of moral virtue. The Prophet has acquired the moral characteristics needed for his own development which, having resulted in a perfect soul, not only imbues in him the capacity of a free intellect, but also makes him capable of laying down rules for other people, through laws and the establishment of justice. This implies that the Prophet goes beyond the philosopher and the virtuous ruler, who possess the capacity for intellectual development and practical morality, respectively. The establishment of justice is, in Ibn Sina's view, the basis for all human good. The combination of philosophy and religion encompasses harmonious living in both this world and in the hereafter.

Ibn Rushd (d. 1198) was faced with the daunting task for a Muslim philosopher of defending philosophy against attacks, the most well-known being by the great Sunni Muslim theologian Al-Ghazāli (d. 1111). The latter, through a work entitled *The Incoherence of the Philosophers*, had sought to represent philosophers as self-contradictory, anti-scriptural and in some cases as affirming heretical beliefs. Ibn Rushd's defence was based on his contention that the Quran enjoined the use of reflection and reason and that the study of philosophy complemented traditionalist approaches to Islam. He asserted that philosophy and Islam had common goals, but arrived at them differently. There is thus a basic identity of interest between

Muslims who adopt philosophical frames of inquiry and those who affirm juridical ones.

In summary, the various Muslim philosophers in their extension and occasional revision of earlier classical notions linked ethics to theoretical knowledge, which was to be acquired by rational means. Since human beings were rational, the virtues and qualities that they embraced and practised were seen as furthering the ultimate goal of individuals and the community. This goal was the attainment of happiness.

v Ethics in the Shi'a tradition

Among the Shi'a, who differed from the Sunni group in attributing legitimate authority after the Prophet Muhammad's death to his cousin and son-in-law 'Ali, and subsequently to his designated descendants, known as Imams, there developed the notion of rationality under the guiding instruction of the Imam. The Imam, who was believed to be divinely guided, acted in early Shi'a history as both custodian of the Quran and the Prophet's teaching, and interpreter and guide for the elaboration and systematization of the Quranic vision for the individual as well as society. Shi'ism, like the early theological and philosophical schools, affirmed the use of rational and intellectual discourse and was committed to a synthesis and further development of appropriate elements present in other religions and intellectual traditions outside Islam.

An example of a work on ethics by a Shi'a writer is the well-known *Nasirian Ethics* by Nasir al-din Tusi (d. 1275). Developing further the philosophical approaches already present among Muslims and linking them to Shi'a conceptions of guidance, Tusi draws attention to the need for ethical enactments to be based on superiority of knowledge and preponderance of discrimination, i.e. by a person 'who is distinguished from others by divine support, so that he may be able to accomplish their perfection' (Tusi, 1964, pp. 191–2). Wilferd Madelung has tried to show that Tusi blended into his ethical work elements of Neoplatonic as well as Shi'a Ismaili and Twelver Shi'a philosophical and moral perspectives.

The Twelver Shi'a are so-called because of their belief that the twelfth in the line of Imams they recognized had withdrawn from the world, to reappear physically only at the end of time to restore true justice. In the meantime, during his absence, the community was guided by trained scholars called *mujtahids* who interpreted for individual believers right and wrong in all matters of personal and religious life. In the Twelver Shi'a tradition therefore, such individuals, called *mullahs* in popular parlance, play a significant role as moral models and, as in recent times in Iran, have assumed a major role in the political life of the state, seeking to shape it in line with their view of a Muslim polity.

Among Ismaili groups that give allegiance to a living Imam, the Imam's presence is considered necessary to contextualize Islam in changing times and circumstances and his teachings and interpretation continue to guide followers in their material as well as spiritual lives. An example is the role of the current Imam of the Nizari Ismailis, the Aga Khan, who leads a worldwide community.

Among the Shi'a continuity with Muslim tradition and values thus remains tied to the continuing spiritual authority vested in the *Imam* or his representatives.

vi   Sufi perspectives

Sufism is the mystical and esoteric dimension of Islam, emphasizing the cultivation of an inner personal life in search of divine love and knowledge. Since a major part of Sufi teaching was to enable an individual Muslim to seek intimacy with God, it was felt that such seekers must embrace a commitment to an inner life of devotion and moral action that would lead to spiritual awakening. The observances of the *Shari'a* were to be complemented by adherence to a path of moral displine, enabling the seeker to pass through several spiritual 'stations', each representing inner, spiritual growth, until one had understood the essential relationship of love and union between seeker and God. Since the inner meaning of action was a significant aspect of Sufi understanding of ethical and moral behaviour, Sufis emphasized the linkage between an inner, experiential awareness of morality and its outward expression, so that a true moral action was one embracing and penetrating the whole of life.

In institutional settings organized Sufi groups taught conformity to traditional Muslim values but added the component of discipline and inner purification. Since the practices that instilled discipline and moral awareness varied across the range of cultures and traditions encountered by Islam, many local practices were appropriated. These included, for example, the acceptance of the moral customs and practices adhered to in local tradition, such as in Indonesia and other countries, where large scale conversions had occurred. Sufi ethical practices thus provided a bridge for incorporating into Muslim moral behaviour the ethical values and practices of local traditions illustrating the universality of Sufi Muslim perspectives on the oneness of the inner dimension of various faiths. Al-Ghazāli, the Sunni jurist and theologian mentioned earlier, became a supporter of Sufi thought, but sought to synthesize the moral perspectives of the *Shari'a* with the notion of inner piety developed by Sufis. He conceived of divinely ordained obligations as a starting point for cultivating a moral personality, provided that it led to an inwardly motivated sense of ethics in due course. He was, however, reluctant to accept the emphasis of some Sufis on a purely experiential and subjectively guided basis for moral action.

vii   Muslim ethics in the contemporary world

The practice and influence of the diverse ethical heritage in Islam has continued in varying degrees among Muslims in the contemporary world. Muslims, whether they constitute majorities in the large number of independent nation states that have arisen in this century, or where they live in significant numbers and communities elsewhere, are going through an important transitional phase. There is growing self-consciousness about identification with their past heritage and a recognition of the need to adapt that heritage to changing circumstances and a globalization of human society. As with the rest of the issues, ethical questions cannot be reflected in unified and monolithic responses. They must take into account the diversity and pluralism that has marked the Muslims of the past as well as the present.

Ethical criteria that can govern issues of economic and social justice and moral strategies for dealing with questions of poverty and imbalance have taken up the greater share of Muslim attention in ethical matters. Whether such responses are labelled 'modernist' or 'fundamentalist', they all reflect specific readings of past Muslim symbols and patterns and in their rethinking and restating of norms and values, employ different strategies for inclusion, exclusion and encoding of specific representations of Islam. In terms of broad moral and ethical concerns, this ongoing discourse seeks to establish norms for both public and private life, and is therefore simultaneously cultural, political, social and religious.

Since the modern conception of religion familiar to most people in the West assumes a theoretical separation between specifically religious and perceived secular activity, some aspects of contemporary Muslim discourse, which does not accept such a separation, appear strange and often retrogressive. Where such discourse, expressed in what appears to be traditional religious language, has become linked to radical change or violence, it has unfortunately deepened stereotypical perceptions about Muslim fanaticism, violence, and cultural and moral difference. As events and developments in the last quarter of the twentieth century indicate, no one response among the many Muslim societies in the world, can be regarded as normative for all Muslims.

In the pursuit of a vision that will guide Muslims in decisions and choices about present and future ethical matters, the most important challenge may be not simply to formulate a continuity and dialogue with its own past ethical underpinning but, like the Muslims of the past, to remain open to the possibilities and challenges of new ethical and moral discoveries.

References

Al-Farabi: 'The attainment of happiness'; trans. M. Mahdi in *Al-Farabi's Philosophy of Plato and Aristotle* (New York: The Free Press, 1962).

Al-Ghazāli, Abu Hamid: *Tahafut Al-Falasifah*; trans. S. A. Kamali, *The Incoherence of the Philosophers* (Lahore: Pakistan Philosophical Congress, 1963).

Hodgson, M. G. S.: *The Venture of Islam: Conscience and History in World Civilization*, 3 vols., (Chicago: University of Chicago Press, 1974).

Houvannisian, R. ed.: *Ethics in Islam*, Ninth Levi Della Vida Conference (Malibu, Cal.: Undena Publications, 1985). In addition to the main presentation by Fazlur Rahman, the book contains articles by K. Faruki, G. Hourani, W. Madelung, G. Makdisi and F. Denny.

Madelung, W.: 'Nasir-al-Din Tusi's ethics'; in Houvannisian, 1985.

Makdisi, G.: 'Ethics in Islamic traditionalist doctrine'; in Houvannisian, 1985.

Quran, The: *The Meaning of the Glorious Koran*, an explanatory translation by M. M. Pickthall (New York: Mentor, 1964).

Rahman, F.: *Major Themes in the Quran* (Minneapolis: Bibliotheca Islamica, 1980).
Ibn Rushd (Averroes): *Averroes on Plato's 'Republic'*; trans. Ralph Lerner (Ithaca, NY: Cornell University Press, 1974).
Schimmel, A.: *Mystical Dimensions of Islam* (Chapel Hill: University of North Carolina Press, 1976).
Al-Shafi'i, Muhammad: *Islamic Jurisprudence: Shafi'i's Risala*; trans. M. Khadduri (Baltimore: Johns Hopkins University Press, 1961).
Ibn Sina: *Isharat wa al Tanbihat*; trans. S. C. Inati, *Remarks and Admonitions* (Toronto: Pontifical Institute of Medieval Studies, 1984).
Al-Tusi, Nasir al Din: *The Nasirean Ethics*; trans. G. Wickens (London: Allen and Unwin, 1964).

Further reading

Arkoun, M.: *Islam, Morale et Politique* (Paris: Desclee de Brouwer, 1986).
Hourani, G.: *Reason and Tradition in Islamic Ethics* (Cambridge: Cambridge University Press, 1985).
Journal of Religious Ethics, 11/2 (Fall, 1983), contains several excellent articles dealing with Islamic ethics.
Khadduri, Majid: *The Islamic Conception of Justice* (Baltimore: Johns Hopkins University Press, 1984).
Lapidus, I.: 'Knowledge, virtue and action: the classical Muslim conception of *Adab* and the nature of religious fulfilment in Islam', *Moral Conduct and Authority*, ed. B. Metcalf (Berkeley: University of California Press, 1984).
Mottahedeh, R.: *The Mantle of the Prophet* (New York: Pantheon Books, 1985).
Nanji, A.: 'Medical ethics and the Islamic tradition', *Journal of Medicine and Philosophy*, 13 (1988), 257–75.
Nasr, S. H.: *Ideals and Realities of Islam* (Cambridge, Mass.: Beacon Press, 1972).
Walzer, R., trans.: *Al-Farabi on the Perfect State* (Oxford: The Clarendon Press, 1985).

PART III

WESTERN PHILOSOPHICAL ETHICS:
A SHORT HISTORY

10

Ethics in ancient Greece

CHRISTOPHER ROWE

i Historical outline

THE tradition of Western ethical philosophy – if that is generally understood as
the search for a rational understanding of the principles of human conduct –
began with the ancient Greeks. From Socrates (469–399 BCE) and his immediate
successors, Plato (c. 427–347) and Aristotle (384–322), there is a clear line
of continuity, through Hellenistic (i.e., broadly, post-Aristotelian), Roman, and
medieval thought to the present day. While it is true that the problems and
interests of modern ethical philosophers frequently diverge from those of their
Greek counterparts, their discussions are still recognizably the descendants of
those that were already taking place in the fifth and fourth centuries BCE. Nor is
the connection purely historical. The study of the ancient texts, at least in the
English-speaking world, is nowadays largely the preserve of scholars who are
themselves philosophers, and who recognize in them an immediate relevance and
vivacity which belies their age. The process is two-way; on the one hand, modern
insights repeatedly give an extra dimension to our understanding of Greek thought;
on the other, Greek ideas retain the power directly to shape, or at any rate to
sharpen, contemporary reflections – and not least in the sphere of ethics (for two
recent examples, albeit of somewhat different kinds, see Bernard Williams's *Ethics
and the Limits of Philosophy*, and Martha Nussbaum's *The Fragility of Goodness*).

It is a moot point where ancient Greek ethics ends. Lucretius and Cicero, for
example, the two most important early writers of philosophy in Latin aim chiefly
to interpret Greek sources for a Roman audience, and it was Greek thinking –
chiefly Stoicism, in various forms – which dominated intellectual life at Rome
from the late Republic onwards. But in the present context 'Greek ethics' will
mean the period from Socrates down to Epicurus himself (341–271) and the
founding fathers of Greek Stoicism, Zeno of Citium (334–262), Cleanthes (331–
232), and Chrysippus (c. 280–c. 206).

Chrysippus was especially prolific, and is said to have produced more than
seven hundred 'books' (i.e. papyrus scrolls); Epicurus wrote about a third as many.
But of all this vast output hardly anything remains: we possess none of Chrysippus'
works, and only three summaries and a collection of 'key doctrines' from Epicurus.
Lucretius' poem *On the Nature of Things* gives us a fairly complete account of the
principles of Epicureanism, though with little reference to the ethical doctrines,
and Cicero provides what appear to be highly competent accounts of the central

features of the Epicurean system, of Stoicism, and also of the brand of scepticism adopted by Plato's Academy in the third and second centuries. For the rest, the evidence for the Hellenistic era – which also includes other minor schools like the Cynics – has mostly to be gathered from scattered reports and references in later writers, many of whom are distinctly hostile witnesses.

But in the case of Socrates, Plato, and Aristotle, who on any account are likely to appear as the most influential representatives of Greek ethics, we are fortunately better off. Socrates himself in fact wrote nothing, but a clear picture of his distinctive ideas and methods emerges from – among other sources – the earlier dialogues of Plato like the *Euthyphro* or the *Laches*, whose chief purpose seems to have been to continue the Socratic tradition of oral philosophy in written form. In later works like the *Republic* (for which the important *Gorgias* may be regarded as a kind of preliminary sketch), Plato goes on to develop a series of ideas which increasingly distance him from Socrates, although he would no doubt have seen them as legitimate extensions of the Socratic approach: most notably, what has come to be known as the 'theory of forms', and a theory of government closely based on it. Aristotle, for his part, will have nothing to do with Platonic form-theory, which he seems to have rejected soon after he joined the Academy at the age of seventeen. But with that main exception his two ethical treatises, the *Eudemian* and *Nicomachean Ethics* (both written after the foundation of his own school, the Lyceum or Peripatos), build directly on his Academic inheritance, as does his treatise on *Politics*. Indeed later writers like Cicero saw no essential difference between Platonic and Aristotelian philosophy, although that was largely from the perspective of a contrast between them and Epicurus. The relationship of the Hellenistic philosophers to Aristotle, and to Socrates and Plato, is a more complex question, but there is little doubt that in general they wrote with a fair knowledge of their predecessors.

ii Themes and issues in Greek ethics

Greek ethics in all periods essentially revolves around two terms, *eudaimonia* and *arete*; or, as they are traditionally rendered, 'happiness' and 'virtue'. These translations are probably as good as can be managed, but in many contexts – as we shall see – are likely to be thoroughly misleading. It will be as well, then, to begin by getting clear about the real meanings of these two central terms.

Let us take *eudaimonia* first. 'Happiness', the English term, now perhaps primarily connotes a subjective feeling of contentment or pleasure (as in 'happy as a sand-boy'). The Greeks, however, attributed *eudaimonia* to someone with reference rather to what would normally be the *source* of such feelings, i.e. the possession of what is thought to be desirable, which looks more like an objective judgement. Thus someone may be called *eudaimon* because he or she is rich, powerful, has fine children, and so on; if such things may very well make for contentment, the ascription of *eudaimonia* need not strictly imply it. (If it did, Solon's maxim 'Call no man happy until he is dead' would be literally nonsense; as would Plato's suggestion that the good man would be *eudaimon* even if impaled on a stake –

although this is a less secure example, since it is in any case a deliberate paradox.) 'Happiness' too, of course, may be used in something like this 'objective' sense, but probably only by derivation from the other sense: if 'Happiness is a warm puppy', that is just because being warm makes one, or the puppy, *feel* happy.

The relationship between 'virtue' and *arete* is rather more complex. Firstly, things as well as people can be described as possessing their appropriate *arete* ('excellence'?). But secondly, and more importantly, the list of the *aretai* (plural) of a human being may include qualities which are not 'virtues' at all – that is, not *moral* qualities: so for example Aristotle's list includes 'wittiness', and the capacity for successful philosophizing, both of which seem in themselves clearly to lie outside the sphere of morality. On the other hand, most of what we do count as virtues – though not all of them – are there, and indeed what Socrates and Plato mean by *arete* seems largely to be restricted to these. (Their basic list runs: wisdom, justice, courage, and moderation, with 'piety', which relates to right behaviour towards the gods, often added as a fifth. Wisdom, from our point of view, might be the odd one out, as at most a condition of some types of morally respectable behaviour. But Socrates, at any rate, seems to take a different view, insofar as he makes the claim that each of the other virtues is somehow identical to wisdom or knowledge.)

The importance of these issues about translation becomes obvious as soon as we encounter the fundamental question which preoccupied all the Greek ethical philosophers. It is first framed by Socrates (or rather by Socrates as reported by Plato): how should a man live, in order to achieve *eudaimonia*? Now if the question meant merely 'What makes for an enjoyable life?', it would be entirely uninteresting, since almost anything might turn out to fit that description. Perhaps more importantly, it would imply that Socrates took a fundamentally hedonistic position, which is certainly untrue: if in any sense he died for his beliefs, it was not the pleasure of doing so that motivated him. (Plato's *Protagoras* indicates a way in which his views *could* be represented in hedonistic terms, but the historical Socrates should not be held to that.) Epicurus alone among the major figures identifies *eudaimonia* with pleasure; for all the rest it is in principle an open question whether pleasure or enjoyment is even a part of the *eudaimon* life. But even for Epicurus himself, '*Eudaimonia* is pleasure' is something which has to be argued for, not a mere tautology. If so, and if 'pleasantly' is Epicurus' answer to Socrates' question, that question cannot itself contain any essential reference to pleasure. It is rather a request for reflection about what is *really* desirable in human life: how should a man live in order that we may reasonably say of him that he has lived successfully?

Socrates' own answer, which is echoed by nearly everyone else in the Greek tradition, gives pride of place to *arete*. If *arete* were equivalent to 'virtue', this could be taken as a simple assertion that the good life is, necessarily, a good *moral* life. As it happens, this might fairly respresent the core of Socrates' position – and of Plato's, to the extent that we can distinguish the two. But Aristotle seems finally to adopt a quite different view: for him, the life 'in accordance with' *arete* in the highest sense turns out to be the life of the intellect, in which the 'moral' and the other 'virtues' play a role only insofar as the human intellect – unlike its divine counterpart – is an aspect of a more complex entity (the whole human being), which has more complex needs and functions. In this case, plainly, *arete* means something rather different from 'virtue'; if we do translate it in that way, Aristotle's conclusion will look strange indeed – and there is no clear indication that he thinks of himself as applying the term in any radically new way.

We can get closer to an idea of the true meaning of *arete* by looking at the type of argument which Plato and Aristotle use to connect it with *eudaimonia*. It is assumed, first, that human beings – seen either as complexes of soul and body (Aristotle), or as souls, temporarily united with bodies (Plato) – are like other things in the world in that they have a 'function' or activity which is peculiar to them. The second assumption is that the good life, *eudaimonia*, will consist in the successful performance of that function. But, thirdly, nothing can perform its peculiar function successfully unless it possesses the relevant *arete*, i.e. unless it is *good of its kind* (so, to use two Platonic examples, the only horses that will be able to win races, and the only pruning-knives which can successfully be used to cut vines, will be *good* ones). But this then raises two questions: what is the 'function' of human beings, and what is the *arete* which relates to that? Plato's answers are, respectively, 'governing and the like' (i.e. the governing by the soul of its union with the body), and 'justice'; Aristotle's, 'an active life of that which possesses reason', and 'the best of the *aretai*'. It is a matter of dispute whether Aristotle is here already referring to the *arete* of the intellect functioning in isolation, or whether he means something else – perhaps the combination of this with the kind of *arete* which he sees as necessary to the conduct of practical life, and which forms the main subject of the *Ethics* (practical wisdom, together with the relevant dispositions of *ethos* or 'character', justice, courage, wittiness and the rest). But for present purposes what is significant is that for both Plato and Aristotle the content of *arete* depends on some prior notion of what it is to be human. In this respect it is quite different from the concept of 'virtue', which already marks out a more or less well defined area for investigation by the 'moral philosopher' – the category of 'morality' itself. The modern philosopher can start by asking about the relationship between moral and non-moral considerations, about the nature of moral reasoning, or about substantive moral issues. Such a category hardly exists in the Greek context. The subject of investigation is not morality, but the nature of the good life for man; and since different views can be taken about what human nature is, so different views can also be taken about what it might be to live a good human life, and about the role to be played in such a life – if any – by the sorts of questions which we are likely to regard from the beginning as central to the concerns of philosophical ethics.

In one respect, this is perhaps an overstatement. Justice, courage, moderation, 'piety', liberality – all of these form part of the civic ideal in the Greece of the fifth and the fourth centuries BCE; and at first sight this hardly seems different from our own general presumption in favour of the 'virtues'. But the point should not be pressed too hard. To us, perhaps, the concept of virtue is likely in the cir-cumstances of ordinary life to appear as self-justifying, in the sense that if in some particular situation this or that is agreed to be the right and virtuous thing to do, that already constitutes at least a prima facie reason for choosing it; and if people who are in a position to choose it fail to do so, our natural reaction is to say either that they are insufficiently principled, or that they have not sufficiently thought the matter through. In Plato's *Gorgias*, Socrates proposes what looks like a similar analysis in relation to *arete*: in calling unjust actions 'shameful', he suggests, he and anyone else will implicitly be saying that there is a powerful reason for avoiding them (since otherwise the description 'shameful' will amount to a meaningless noise). But what he is up against is the view that behaving unjustly or unfairly is often *better for the agent*, which to Socrates' opponent seems an even more powerful consideration. Indeed Socrates only manages to persuade him in the end by demonstrating – albeit by somewhat devious means – that 'shameful' is itself to be understood in the same terms. The rules of justice, from this point of view, are merely a limitation on one's freedom to act, imposed either by society, or as Thrasymachus puts it in the *Republic*, by whatever government happens to be in power, as a means of furthering its own interests. If this looks, and is, an extreme position, it accurately reflects a widely felt ambivalence not only about justice but about all the civic 'virtues'. That one had obligations to one's city, and one's fellow-citizens, was of course recognized; but there were also competing sets of obligations to other groupings within the city – one's associates, friends, family. Even more crucially, the male citizen had a strong sense of his own worth, and of being in a state of permanent competition with others. In the absence of any notion of a moral imperative, of an 'ought' which somehow carries with it (in however vague a sense) its own stamp of authority, the question was always likely to arise why one should honour obligations whose strength appeared to stand in inverse proportion to their distance from home. (The same attitude may of course arise in other societies; in present-day Britain and the United States, for example, politicians, publicists and other allies of the conservative right sometimes appear anxious to encourage it. But it is likely to have been far more marked in a society like that of ancient Athens, which had never known a liberal moral consensus of any kind.)

Nor, when in the *Gorgias* Socrates adopts the criterion of self-interest, is he merely taking on the colouring of his opponent, or arguing *ad hominem*. Although he saw himself – again, if we can believe Plato's evidence – as having spent a lifetime of service to the Athenians, attempting to stir them into active thought about the conduct of their lives, the idea that service to others might be an end in itself hardly seems to have surfaced at all in his explicit arguments. If, as he believed, we all seek *eudaimonia*, that means our own, not someone else's. For him too, therefore, the fact that certain types of behaviour seemed to involve preferring the interests of others to one's own was itself the problem, not a solution; and any successful case for justice and the rest had somehow to show that they were, after all, in the interests of the agent. It is in this sense that we are to understand the famous Socratic paradoxes, that '*Arete* is wisdom', and 'No-one goes wrong deliberately'. 'Think hard enough', he is saying, 'and you will always find that doing the right thing is best for you' – and if anyone does do wrong, that is because they have not thought enough. The good that is supposed to come of right action is not of a material kind, although it will include the right use of material goods; rather it is the living of a successful life, of which right action, based on the use of reason, is the chief (or only?) ingredient. ('No-one goes wrong deliberately' – or, as the Greek is usually translated, 'No-one does wrong willingly': this is Socrates' famous denial of the existence of *akrasia*, or 'weakness of will'. Aristotle's characteristic comment on this claim, in *Nicomachean Ethics* VII, is that it is 'manifestly at odds with the observed facts', though he then proceeds – again characteristically – to concede that Socrates was in a sense right. What Socrates denied was that one could act contrary to one's knowledge of right and wrong. True, says Aristotle, in the sense that what is 'dragged about', or obscured, by pleasure in the weak-willed man is not knowledge in the primary sense, i.e. knowledge of the relevant general principle, so much as his awareness of the particular fact that *this now* falls under it.)

Something like this general strategy of Socrates' is adopted by most of his successors, although only the Stoics are tempted to connect the good life so single-mindedly with rational processes. For Plato and Aristotle the use of reason is a necessary, not a sufficient, condition of living the life of practical *arete*. In effect, they point out that not all actions allow for reflection. Suppose that I see an old lady (not my grandmother, or Aunt Lucy) about to walk under a ten-ton truck: if I stop to reason things out, then the decision which Socrates would probably have thought right would have been pre-empted by the truck. What is clearly needed, and what Plato and Aristotle provide, is a parallel emphasis on the dispositional aspect of behaviour. If I do the right thing, and put myself at risk by doing something to save the old lady, that is partly because I have acquired the disposition to act in that sort of way, or because I have become that sort of person (i.e. courageous), even though when I do have time to pause and think, reason will confirm the rightness of my action. Perhaps Socrates would have agreed with this as a sensible modification of his position. Alternatively, he might have offered a different model of reasoning which would somehow include instantaneous decisions, as the Stoics seem to have done: the Stoic sage, if he ever existed, would evidently *know* under any circumstances exactly what it was appropriate to do, and act accordingly. In any case, all those who followed old Socrates – even, in his way, the pleasure-seeking Epicurus – were happy to accept two basic points from him. First, they accepted that the ways of man both can be and need to be justified by rational means. Second, they accepted that that justification must ultimately be in terms of the individual's self-interest. There is also widespread agreement that the Socratic *aretai* are indispensable to the good life. Except when he turns, surprisingly, to eulogy of the purely intellectual life, this seems to be Aristotle's position; hedonists like Epicurus, too, insist that these cardinal 'virtues' have a place, insofar as they contribute to the sum of pleasure. If pleasure is the only rational goal in life, and if pleasure is broadly defined – as Epicurus defined it – as the absence of pain, doing the just thing will be the most efficient way of avoiding painful injuries to oneself, a moderate attitude towards pleasures (in the ordinary sense) will spare one both the frustration of unfulfilled desire and the consequences of over-indulgence, and the courage which comes from reasoning about the things we fear will remove the most potent form of mental anguish.

By itself, the emphasis on self-interest may seem like a kind of egoism, and indeed in Epicurus that would be exactly the right way to describe it. But the interpretation put on 'self-interest' by the other philosophers, which treats even necessarily other-regarding qualities like justice as good for their possessors, makes it nothing of the sort (despite Aristotle's paradoxial claim that someone who acts for others, like the man who dies for friends or country, is *philautos*, a lover of self, insofar as 'he claims a greater share of what is fine for himself'). It was in plain fact the only means available for the defence of such qualities in a society which – notwithstanding the lofty pronouncements by public figures like Pericles, in the Funeral Speech attributed to him by Thucydides – continued to place a primary value on individual status and achievement. The rise of Greek ethics can be seen in large part as a reflection of the overlaying of a fundamentally individualistic ethos with the demands for co-operative behaviour implied by the political institutions of the city-state. What the philosophers attempt to show is that there is, in the end, no conflict between the two. Their faith in reason also had deep roots in fifth- and fourth-century Greek culture, both insofar as it expressed the habit of argument and debate, ingrained in a form of political society which presupposed a fair degree of individual involvement, and as a reaction against less rational forms of persuasion which the rhetorical theoreticians of the time had already developed into a high art. The hedonists alone advocated retirement from the political sphere, as altogether too dangerous; all the rest see man, to use Aristotle's famous phrase, as a 'political animal', or rather as a creature destined by his nature to participate, in a rational way, in the life of the larger community. Nowhere, perhaps, is this clearer than in Stoicism, which counts the realization of our relatedness to other members of the human race as itself part of our growth to maturity as rational beings.

But if fine or right actions matter to us, how do we come to know what fine and right actions are? This question, which overlaps with the modern question about the sources of moral knowledge, inevitably became a major preoccupation of the Greek philosophers, not least because they themselves tended to emphasize how difficult it was. Only the hedonists found it easy: 'right action' was merely what was generally considered to be right, and since it was only justified by its contribution to pleasure, any grey areas could in principle be illuminated by reference to that criterion, which was recognizable by anyone. By contrast, Socrates seems to claim neither to know himself how to give a proper account of this thing, *arete*, which he values so highly, nor to be able to find anyone else who knows about it. At the same time, Plato represents him as behaving as if anyone might *discover* what it was, for the Socrates of the earlier dialogues – who, as I have said, seems to be meant to stand close to the historical Socrates – is apparently happy to discuss the subject with all and sundry. In later dialogues, on the other hand, where authentic Socratic ideas begin to fade into the background, Plato begins to treat such knowledge as accessible even in principle only to a few. His general theory of knowledge (the 'theory of forms') has much in common with theories of innate ideas. What is known, at the highest and most general level, is a collection of objects, with which we have all had direct acquaintance prior to birth (the 'forms' or 'ideas'). All of us, therefore, may have some inkling of general truths; but only those whose rational capacities are especially well developed – in short, philosophers – can fully reactivate their memories. The consequence is that *arete* itself is fully accessible only to these few, insofar as it involves the exercise of reason and deliberate choice (one cannot choose what one does not know), and the majority, if they are to be able at all to imitate the harmonies discovered by their intellectual superiors, must be robbed of their autonomy. That, at any rate, is the view which Plato proposes in the *Republic*. In later dialogues, the idea of the possibility of discovering ethical truths by rational introspection largely disappears, to be replaced by a greater emphasis on the need for a consensus among the citizens about public and private values. But throughout all its phases the Platonic project always has more to do with establishing the foundations of such values than with examining them in themselves, and understanding their implications for the conduct of everyday life. He tells us a good deal about the *sort* of person we should aim to be, and why (broadly, because being like that is in harmony both with our nature as human beings, and with nature as a whole), but relatively little which might help to solve the particular problems which the individual actually faces in life.

Plato himself shows some signs of recognizing this gap in his account, but has no way of filling it. The fact is that no amount of gazing on eternal truth, or the structure of the universe, can tell me how to act *now*. The Stoics, in effect, follow him up the same blind alley by putting all their money on the impossible ideal of the sage, whose attitude and actions will somehow unfailingly answer to his predetermined role in the cosmic drama. At first sight, Aristotle seems to offer us something more promising. He begins by rejecting the theory of knowledge of the *Republic* outright, and erects in its place a theory which locates the source of ethical insight in experience of life itself. Knowing how to act, the possession of practical wisdom, means having an 'eye' for solutions; and that can only be developed through a combination of training in the right habits and direct acquaintance with practical situations. This is in itself an attractive proposal, which accords at least with our more optimistic intuitions about human beings: that our sensitivity, and our ability to make appropriate decisions on our own account, gradually increase through a process of trial and error. The trouble is that Aristotle stops there. Like Plato, he describes types of correct behaviour – as for example in his famous 'doctrine of the mean', which locates each of the 'virtues' between corresponding 'vices' of excess and defect. Courage will be a matter of striking the right balance between fear and confidence; moderation lies between excessive indulgence and complete insensitivity to pleasure; wittiness between boorishness and a crass lack of humour, and so on. He also stresses, far more than Plato did, how difficult it will be to apply these descriptions to cases, and in general how imprecise a science ethics is. But our reaction is likely to be that this is just the point at which ethical philosophy becomes interesting, and useful. The world is full of problems – about forms of war, about war itself, life and death, sex, race and religion – to which Aristotle's bland assurance, 'Maturity will bring an answer', scarcely seems an adequate response.

A further difficulty about Aristotle's position is that it ties his conclusions to pre-existing patterns of behaviour. Aristotelian man is a creature of fourth-century Greece, in many respects incapable of being transported into any other cultural environment. Socrates and Plato are somewhat less liable to this criticism, insofar as they seem to set out partly to *reform* existing attitudes. Thus if Socrates is dissatisfied with the answers he gets to his questions about justice, or piety, that is not only because his fellow-citizens are unable to articulate their ideas, but also because they frequently say things with which he fundamentally disagrees. So Euthyphro's understanding of piety turns out to be predicated on an unacceptable view of the nature of the gods; and the plain man's account which Polemarchus gives of justice in the *Republic*, as doing good to one's friends and harm to one's enemies, meets with the reasonable objection that harming anyone *per se* seems rather to be a matter of injustice. In this way Socrates and Plato – for it is after all Plato who is here reconstructing or inventing Socrates' arguments for him – appear as thoroughgoing radicals. But this is in part an illusion. The emphasis of Socrates' arguments is not on pointing out the error in other people's ways, but on revealing the lack of clarity in their ideas, and the way in which they so often turn out to believe things which are actually mutually contradictory. His whole method, in fact, presupposes that the truth can be discovered from them: what he wants to know is something that is common to everyone, if only it could be properly articulated. This idea in a way prefigures the Platonic doctrine of learning as recollection, which similarly implies that ethical truth is a matter of common property (even if not commonly accessible). It also implies, of course, that this truth – as both Socrates and Aristotle would have agreed – is *objective*, and not merely culturally determined. (Several other essays in this volume take up this issue: see especially Article 35, REALISM; Article 38, SUBJECTIVISM; and Article 39, RELATIVISM.) The fact is, however, that what any of the three philosophers thinks of as being 'discovered', whether through questioning, through introspection, or through experience, has overwhelmingly to do with the resolution of the tension between civic and individualistic values which I earlier identified as a basic feature of Greek society of the period.

If they were to return from the dead, Socrates and company might plead in mitigation that such tensions are likely to exist to some degree in any society; for good measure, they might then try to turn the charge of cultural relativism against their modern counterparts for their obsession with that puzzling special category of considerations labelled 'moral'. But neither move would be effective. The complaint against them is not that they have nothing to say which is of relevance to any other society (far from it), but rather that they are so impressed with the need to defend the basis of civilized life that they fail to consider how civilized that life really is. Plato, for example, takes the institution of slavery for granted, while Aristotle justifies it in the most question-begging way. Neither raises a voice against the subordinate position of women in Greek society (except, in Plato's case, on pragmatic grounds: *some* women are clearly outstanding, so that it would be a waste not to put their talents to use). 'Man' in Socrates' question – 'How should a man live?' – is automatically regarded as referring exclusively to the (adult, free) male of the species, and the parallel question about the female is assumed, strangely, to be adequately answered by her actual role in a male-dominated society. (Or perhaps it is not so strange: after all, the issue arises in relation to men chiefly because society seems to offer them the possibility of living in more than one kind of way.) Again, both typically endorse a narrow nationalism, and the easy assumption of the inferiority of non-Greek races; and so on. There are of course some elements in modern society with which such ideas strike a ready chord, and which are happy to cite Plato and Aristotle as their authority. But that some people, however great, happened to express unargued prejudices similar to one's own is hardly a useful justification for continuing to repeat them. What is sometimes conveniently forgotten is that it is a guiding principle of Greek philosophy itself that a position is only as good as the arguments that support it. It is this that represents its real and lasting legacy to the modern world. Plato's Socrates repeatedly warns us against taking any proposition what-ever as authoritative; and in doing so he not only entitles but invites us to apply the same criterion either to him or to anyone else. We may notice and deplore the fact that he and his successors in some respects remained prisoners of their culture. But at the same time they provided the only means by which it is possible to break free from the assumptions foisted on us either by society or by temporarily fashionable ideologies. Or, to put it in a more generous way, we may deplore the fact that they expended so much energy on exploring the foundations of the subject that they had none left for discussing the substantive issues that constitute the subject itself – rather as if a mathematician were to become so obsessed with the problem of the nature of mathematical truth as to forget to do any mathematics. But this is to speak with hindsight. In the context in which the ancient Greek philosophers wrote, it was the fundamental questions – about the sort of life one should live (if I may here write anachronistically in a gender-neutral way), and about the criteria to be used in answering questions of that sort – which really mattered. In any case, it will be a poor mathematician who fails to worry about the status of the things with which he plays his complex games.

A postscript: I said that Socrates and nearly everyone after him 'gave pride of place to *arete*' in the good life. This phrase was intended to be sufficiently vague to include a variety of different positions: that *arete* is sufficient by itself for *eudaimonia*, which is complete without anything being added to this one ingredient; that it is sufficient, but that other things – good fortune, material goods – may enhance the degree of one's *eudaimonia*; and that while *arete* is the most important ingredient in *eudaimonia*, other things are also necessary. The first position is that of the Stoics, the last that of Plato and Aristotle (for the mature Plato, the good life will include the moderate satisfaction of our irrational impulses, while for Aristotle material goods are the necessary means of excellent activity, whether practical or intellectual – and who, he asks rhetorically, would attribute *eudaimonia* to someone who encountered the misfortunes of a Priam?). All three positions, however, can and have been plausibly attributed to Socrates. This example will serve as a general indication of the degree of disagreement which often exists between different interpreters of Greek ethics; my own brief account should be read with this in mind, although I have not deliberately adopted any outrageously radical views.

References

Primary sources

Aristotle: *Eudemian Ethics*; trans. Ross (revised by Urmson); and *Nicomachean Ethics*; trans. Solomon, in Barnes, J., ed., *The Complete Works of Aristotle: The Revised Oxford Translation*, Vol. II (Bollingen Series LXXI. 2) (Princeton, NJ: Princeton University Press, 1984).

Long, A. A. and Sedley, D. N., eds., *The Hellenistic Philosophers*, Vol. I: *Translations of the Principal Sources, with Philosophical Commentary* (Cambridge: Cambridge University Press, 1987).

Lucretius: *On the Nature of Things*; trans. Lakham (as *The Nature of the Universe*) (Harmondsworth: Penguin Books, 1951).

Plato: *Euthyphro*; trans. Tredennick, in *The Last Days of Socrates* (Harmondsworth: Penguin Books, 1969).

—— *Laches*; trans. Lane, in *Plato: Early Socratic Dialogues* (Harmondsworth: Penguin Books, 1987).

—— *Gorgias*; trans. Irwin, in the *Clarendon Plato* series (Oxford: Oxford University Press, 1979). Includes commentary.

—— *Republic*; trans. Grube (Indianapolis: Hackett, 1974, and London: Pan Books, 1981).

Other references

Nussbaum, M. C.: *The Fragility of Goodness* (Cambridge: Cambridge University Press, 1986).

Williams, B.: *Ethics and the Limits of Philosophy* (London: Fontana/Collins, 1985).

Further reading

Commentaries

Annas, J.: *An Introduction to Plato's Republic* (Oxford: Oxford University Press, 1981).

Cross, R. C. and Woozley, A. D.: *Plato's Republic: A Philosophical Commentary* (London: Macmillan; New York: St Martin's Press, 1964).

Geach, P. T.: 'Plato's Euthyphro. An analysis and commentary', *Monist*, 51 (1966).

Hardie, W. F. R.; *Aristotle's Ethical Theory*, 2nd edn (Oxford: Oxford University Press, 1980).

Stokes, M. C.: *Plato's Socratic Conversations: Drama and Dialectic in Three Dialogues* (including the *Laches*) (London: Athlone Press, 1986).

Urmson, J. O.: *Aristotle's Ethics* (Oxford: Blackwell, 1988).

Woods, M.: *Aristotle's Eudemian Ethics Books I, II, and VIII* (Oxford: Oxford University Press, 1982).

Other secondary reading

Barnes, J.: *Aristotle*, in the *Past Masters* series (Oxford: Oxford University Press, 1981).

Barnes, J., Schofield, M. and Sorabji, R., eds., *Articles on Aristotle*, Vol. II: *Ethics and Politics* (London: Duckworth, 1977).

Dover, K. J.: *Greek Popular Morality in the Time of Plato and Aristotle* (Oxford: Blackwell, 1974).

Gulley, N.: *The Philosophy of Socrates* (London: Macmillan; New York: St Martin's Press, 1968).

Guthrie, W. K. C.: *A History of Greek Philosophy*, Vols. III–VI (Cambridge: Cambridge University Press, 1969–81).

Irwin, T.: *Plato's Moral Theory: The Early and Middle Dialogues* (Oxford: Oxford University Press, 1977).

Long, A. A.: *Hellenistic Philosophy*, 2nd edn (London, Berkeley, Los Angeles: Duckworth, 1986).

Rist, J. M.: *Epicurus: An Introduction* (Cambridge: Cambridge University Press, 1972).

Rowe, C. J.: *Plato*, in the *Philosophers in Context* series (Brighton: The Harvester Press; New York: St Martin's Press, 1984).

Sandbach, F. H.: *The Stoics* (London: Chatto and Windus, 1975).

Vlastos, G., ed.: *The Philosophy of Socrates: A Collection of Critical Essays* (New York: Anchor Books, 1971).

——, ed.: *Plato: A Collection of Critical Essays*, Vol. II (New York: Anchor Books, 1971).

11

Medieval and Renaissance ethics

JOHN HALDANE

The Human will is subject to three orders. Firstly, to the order of its own reason, secondly to the orders of human government, be it spiritual or temporal, and thirdly, it is subject to the universal order of Divine rule.

ST THOMAS AQUINAS, SUMMA THEOLOGIAE, Ia, IIae, q8, a1

i Introduction

THE central timespan covered in this essay extends from the eleventh to the sixteenth centuries – a period of half a millennium of considerable philosophical activity only matched in its variety and vigour by the modern and contemporary periods. Yet, somewhat surprisingly, between the end of the Renaissance and the middle of the twentieth century the philosophy of those five hundred years was largely forgotten. Indeed, it is only in the last twenty or so years that philosophers in the English-speaking world have begun to appreciate the intrinsic quality of medieval and Renaissance thought, and its relevance for the continuing effort to understand the central issues in philosophy.

Part of the difficulty in evaluating the philosophy of the Middle Ages, and to a lesser extent that of the Renaissance, is that it is couched in a largely unfamiliar theoretical vocabulary. This is connected with the nature of *scholasticism* – the dominant philosophical tradition – which was uncompromisingly technical. A further problem for understanding and assessing the argument and conclusions presented by authors of these periods arises from the very different assumptions about the nature of the universe and the situation of mankind within it that they and we are apt to make.

In order, then, to make sense of the patterns of ethical thought which developed through the medieval and Renaissance periods, it is necessary to begin with an account of the historical and philosophical background to the emergence of scholasticism towards the end of the eleventh century. Following that, I shall discuss some of the ideas and disputes of the one-hundred-year period falling roughly between the middle of the thirteenth and that of the fourteenth centuries. This was without doubt the high point of medieval thought, a period in which intellectual seeds were sown and entire philosophical gardens grew up, flourished and bloomed. The authors of the great works of this era were members of two religious orders – the *Dominicans* and the *Franciscans* – whose activity determined much of the character of a fruitful age in the history of Western culture.

Following upon this, however, was a period of relative infertility. Significantly, not a single historically important philosopher was born in the fourteenth century. (The best candidate for this status, namely John Wyclif (1320–84), was too much a theologian and churchman to qualify.) Yet by its close, new growth had begun which in due course produced several new species of ideas and transformations of older ones. Discussion of this period will lead on to an examination of the main elements in Renaissance ethics, which can be divided into two traditions: first that of the late scholastics, who elaborated and synthesized the products of the geniuses born in the thirteenth century, and second that of the humanists who looked back to classical antiquity and forward to a secularized political future.

ii From the Church Fathers to the scholastics

The earliest post-classical origins of medieval philosophy lie in the patristic period of Christianity, in the writings of the Church Fathers. These works were produced between the second and fifth centuries by religious teachers belonging to the Eastern and Western Churches. The aim of these theological authors was to interpret Judeo-Christian scriptures and traditions with the assistance of ideas derived from Greek and Roman philosophy. Although the Fathers were not themselves speculative thinkers, they introduced into their theistic ethics notions of considerable importance which recur throughout medieval and Renaissance philosophy.

The first of these, which appears in the writings of Clement of Alexandria (150–215) and in subsequent authors, is the idea that, by the exercise of natural reason, some of the philosophers of antiquity had arrived at conclusions concerning the kind of life fitting for human beings which were coincident with parts of Christian moral teaching. This concurrence was later to become a theme in the defence of philosophy, and of the study of pagan writers, that scholastics would offer to the charge that their enquiries endangered faith. The particular discovery of Greek philosophy which interested the Fathers was that of practical reasoning (ratio practica) or 'right reason' (recta ratio in the Latin, orthos logos in the Greek). Both Plato and Aristotle had argued that there is a faculty of rational judgement concerned with choosing the right way of acting. Excellence in the exercise of this power constitutes the intellectual virtue of practical wisdom – phronesis (Latin: prudentia) – and conduct in accord with its deliverances is moral virtue.

Generally there was little concern with the philosophical arguments supporting these suggestions. The points of interest were rather that some of the conclusions about how to live concurred with religious teachings derived from revelation, and, implicit in this, that an alternative model of moral knowledge might be available. In addition to knowing how to act by having received public instruction, it might be that an individual could think his own way towards moral rectitude. This possibility would relieve the difficulty with the idea of public revelation: that, through no fault of their own, those who have not received it directly, or had it communicated to them, are deprived of the means of salvation. For if the pagans could reason their way to virtue, then perhaps all men have the same innate resource to lead good lives. This indeed became a model of *universal salvific grace*; that is, of the idea that each man is given sufficient means for his salvation – though, of course, he may choose not to follow the route this grace prescribes.

Notice, however, that the idea of an innate power of moral knowledge is open to at least two interpretations. On the first, men are endowed with a capacity for rational thought, and starting from certain premises, knowledge of which is not dependent on revelation, they can arrive at conclusions about right conduct. On the second interpretation, the relevant endowment is one of a faculty of moral sense by which men can simply intuit what it is right or wrong to do. Borrowing from the vocabulary of later theories it may be useful to describe these views as 'rationalist' and 'intuitionist', respectively.

Following the introduction of the term by St Jerome (347–420), writers of the earlier and later Middle Ages referred to the innate power of distinguishing good from evil as *synderesis*. Jerome himself describes this as the 'spark of conscience ... by which we discern that we sin', but it later became usual to reserve the term 'conscience' (*conscientia*) for the ability to distinguish good from bad at the level of particular actions. In the thirteenth century, for example, St Thomas Aquinas (1224–74) argues that the first principle of thought about conduct is that good is to be done and pursued and evil avoided. This *'synderesis* rule' is, he maintains, a self-evident principle, such that anyone who understand it must assent to its truth. What it concerns, however, is not the rightness or wrongness of this or that particular action, but rather the polarity of the axis on which conduct lies and the intrinsic attraction of one pole and repulsion of the other. Even granting the truth of the principle, however, knowledge of it will not suffice to guide one through life without a more specific capacity to distinguish good from bad courses of action, and it is this capacity which Aquinas follows tradition in identifying with *conscientia*. Furthermore, given his distinctly rationalistic account of moral knowledge (which I discuss below) it should come as no surprise to learn that he regards conscience as equivalent to practical or 'right' reason (*recta ratio*). In the pre-scholastic period, however, the tendency was to take an intuitionist view of moral thinking. On this account, versions of which are to be found in the writings of St Jerome and St Augustine (354–430), conscience is an innate faculty which reveals God's moral law as this is inscribed in men's souls. Something of this idea persists today in contemporary Christian discussions which (adapting the sense analogy) speak of conscience as if it were the mind's 'inner ear' by which one may attend to the word of God.

In Augustine's moral theology this account of conscience is connected to a line of thinking which constitutes the second major contribution from earlier tradition to later medieval moral philosophy. This is the idea of moral purification as resulting in a 'flight of the soul' away from the world. The more distant origins of this notion lie in Plato's *Republic* and in equally ancient mystical traditions. It features in the writings of Plotinus (204–69) but was introduced into patristic thought by his Christian fellow-student Origen (185–255). Indeed it was a widely held doctrine, advanced in one form or another by St Gregory of Nyssa (335–95),

Dionysius the pseudo-Areopagite (fifth century) and John Scotus Eriugena (810–77), and it was taken up again with some enthusiasm in the Renaissance period by Mirandola (1463–94) and other Neoplatonists. According to Augustine, God endows each man with a conscience whereby he may know the moral law. However, this knowledge is not sufficient for virtue, which requires that the will should also be turned towards the good. In order to achieve this benevolent orientation God illuminates the soul by a revelation of his own goodness, and this induces virtue as the soul becomes charged with love for God's perfection and strives to be united with him. This psychology of grace is less prosaically expressed by Augustine in the claim that love draws a soul to God as weight draws a body to the earth; but, of course, since God is 'above' all things, the direction of pull is upwards and so the movement effected by grace becomes a flight of the soul away from the world.

A further issue raised by this theory of moral knowledge concerns the nature of that which conscience reveals. Earlier it was said that conscience discloses the moral law, but this latter notion is in turn open to at least two interpretations, both of which influenced medieval and Renaissance thought. The expression 'law' translates the Latin word *ius*, which may mean either order or ordinance, systematic regularity or prescribed regulation. Hence the claim that conscience is a form of knowledge of the moral law could be read as holding that it is a means of discerning states of affairs and properties which constitute moral facts and values, just as science is a method for discovering those facts which are constitutive of the laws of physics, for instance. Alternatively, the claim could be interpreted as maintaining that conscience is a way of coming to know what God commands, much as consulting a textbook may be a way of discovering the content of a nation's law.

Writers of classical antiquity, of the patristic period and of the early and later Middle Ages often use the expression 'natural law' (*ius naturale*) to refer to whatever principles are taken to govern human conduct, other than those which originate in human legislation or positive law (*ius positivum*). To the modern reader the expression 'natural law' probably suggests the idea of an objective moral order independent of the mind or will or any being. It should be clear, however, that for those living in these earlier periods if might signify a number of distinct ideas. The common element is the contrast with human legislation, but beyond that lie differences. It was held by some that natural law pertains to the ordered structure of the world into which each kind of thing fits and by reference to which a proper pattern of its development may be determined. On this view, the idea that natural law yields *prescriptions* for human conduct is a metaphorical way of referring to preconditions of man's natural development, but it has no implication that their prescriptivity issues from the will of a legislator. They are not in that sense *commands*. According to a second view, however, natural law is precisely the set of rules legislated by God and promulgated to mankind via the presentation of the decalogue to Moses, and via the revelation afforded to individuals through their exercise of conscience.

The first of these views partly originates in the pre-Socratic period of Greek philosophy and was known to authors of the early Middle Ages in the form of the Stoic doctrine that all processes are governed by cosmic reason (*logos*), and that law (*nomos*) is what this universal rational principle dictates concerning the various spheres of activity. This idea was usually combined with two others which, taken together, yielded a more theologically acceptable account of natural law as metaphysical order. The first of these additional notions was the Platonic theory that individual entities and characteristics are instances of ideal forms (*eide*), and are better or worse of their kind to the extent that they approximate to, or deviate from, these perfect paradigms. The second related notion derived from patristic exegeses of Chapter 1 of Genesis, which suggested that in creating the world God gave material instantiation to a plan which pre-existed as an eternal idea (*ratio aeterna*) in his mind. (This notion, sometimes referred to as 'divine exemplarism', was undoubtedly influenced by the previously mentioned element of Plato's metaphysics and by the creation myth he presents in the dialogue *Timaeus*, in which the supreme God or Maker (*demiurge*) is attributed with the desire to create a world that embodies the forms.) Put together, these ideas provided an account of natural law as the proper pattern of activity in accord with the rational order of creation.

It is important to appreciate that in the foregoing account the role of God in relation to the moral law is an indirect one. An action is good because fitting, given the nature of things – a nature owing to God's design and manufacture. But according to the second view mentioned above, God's role is wholly direct, for the natural law is nothing other than a body of legislation willed into existence by God for the governance of human affairs. And this law need have no relation to the design of the created world.

In the thirteenth century there was a major dispute between proponents of these two views of the universal moral law. I shall return to this in the next section. For now, however, it is enough to point out that there are further complexities in the structure of pre-scholastic theories which were transmitted to later periods. For example, as was previously noted, it was held by some that the innate capacity to determine the requirements on conduct is the ability to discover the proper nature of things, most centrally of man himself, and to reason to conclusions about how to perfect these natures. For others, while the truths discovered by the exercise of *synderesis* and *conscientia* are indeed those pertaining to self-perfection, their discovery is not a matter of empirical investigation and practical reasoning but simply apprehension of prescriptions pronounced to the soul by God. (In a famous passage in his work *On the Trinity*, Augustine writes that 'men see the moral rules written in the book of light which is called Truth, from which all other laws are copied' (*De Trinitate*, 14, 15, 21)). For others yet, the form of discovery is of this latter style, but what is apprehended is simply the ungrounded will of God expressed in commands to act or to refrain from action, and not guidance offered in accord with a law of nature.

So much for the developing complexity of pre-scholastic thought about the source of morality. There was also a variety of views concerning the objects of moral assesment, i.e. those features which are properly judged to be right or wrong. St Augustine had claimed that merit only attaches to actions which conform to God's moral law if they are performed with the appropriate motive, i.e. a love of God and a wish to perfect oneself so as to draw closer to him. As he puts it: 'To live well is nothing other than to love God with all one's heart, soul and mind' (*De Moribus Ecclesiae Catholicae*, I, 25, 46). This introduces a focus on the state of mind of the agent, rather than on the performance as such, and introduces the possibility that while two people could perform actions of the same type, e.g. nursing the sick, only one would do something creditable, inasmuch as his motive was *love* whereas that of the other was *Pharisaism*, i.e. the self-righteous desire to be thought well of.

Other authors, drawing upon the parable(s) of the talents (Matt. 25) or pounds (Luke 19), tended to regard merit as appropriate to the achievements or consequences of conduct. The most wide-ranging and exacting account of moral assessment, however, held that for an action to be good, everything about it – its type, its motive and its outcome – must be good, and that should just one of these be bad, then the action is bad and the agent culpable. This strict doctrine seems to have originated in a work written in the fourth or fifth century by Dionysius the Areopagite entitled *On the Divine Names* (*De divinis nominibus*). This author's writings, known collectively as the *Corpus Dionysiacum*, were of great influence from the sixth century onwards into the Renaissance. Indeed, he was the main channel through which Platonic and Neoplatonic ideas passed from the Greek into the Christian worlds. Besides being one of the main sources of the 'flight of the soul' theological psychology and of the strict doctrine of moral assessment mentioned above, he advanced the view (as did Augustine) that evil is nothing other than the privation of good, just as sickness may be thought of not as a distinct independent condition but merely as the absence of health. This idea, and the doctrine about what is required for an action to be good, were endorsed and elaborated by Aquinas in the thirteenth century and have remained as part of the general body of Thomist teaching. The considerable respect accorded the *Corpus Dionysiacum* throughout the Middle Ages and the Renaissance was due in part to its value as a source of Platonic philosophy but also because of a mistaken belief about its authorship. The writer claims to have been a witness to events recorded in the New Testament and uses the pseudonym 'Dionysius the Presbyter', from which he came to be identified with an Athenian converted by St Paul. However, from internal evidence, it has long been generally agreed that these writings were produced around the year 500.

Before proceeding to consider the central period of scholasticism, it is appropriate to give some rough idea of relevant historical developments within the preceding centuries. This history is in effect that of the fall and re-establishment, as a Christian institution, of the Roman Empire. In the fifth century the Western Roman Empire succumbed to Teutonic invasions from the north, and when the Eastern Roman Empire, based on Byzantium, succeeded in the sixth century in re-establishing an hegemony in the Mediterranean, it was in turn attacked by the Arabs in the east and the south. Among the damage wrought by these invasions was the destruction of the Roman educational system which, through schools located in the main cities, had provided administrators for the Empire. As has been the case in Britain in this century, an education suited to the staffing needs of a civil service also produced men of wide culture with something of a philosophical cast of mind. Following the invasions, however, such centres of education as remained or were created were attached to monasteries situated in isolated rural areas. In the very changed circumstances, the aim of these monastic schools became the more limited one of preserving the culture of the past.

In the year 800, Charlemagne was crowned first Holy Roman Emperor, and for a period following this there was something of a revival of the imperial idea and associated with it a cultural renaissance. Indeed the only original Western philosopher writing between Boethius (475–525) and St Anselm (1033–1109), namely Eriugena, was head of the Palace school founded at Charlemagne's court. A series of wars, political conflicts and disputes beween the Church and the Empire led by stages to the recovery of Christendom and the victory of the Papacy over the Emperor, marked by Pope Gregory VII's reforms of the Church, begun in 1073, and by the Emperor Henry IV doing penance before the Pope at Canossa in 1077.

iii The golden age of scholasticism

During the patristic and early medieval periods, educated discussion of morality was of an entirely theological sort. It was concerned either with *normative* questions (like those discussed in Part IV of this volume) about which virtues to cultivate, what actions to avoid and what goals to aim for, or else it set out the *general structure* of morality, indicating, for example, its relation to natural processes or to revealed doctrine. By and large, however, it was neither systematic nor interested in what are now characterized as *meta-ethical* issues; that is, issues about the content and logical character of moral concepts. (Part VI of this volume deals with meta-ethics.) In the eleventh and twelfth centuries this began to change, as there evolved the scholastic method of enquiry.

The 'father' of scholasticism was St Anselm, Archbishop of Canterbury and now best known as the originator of the 'ontological proof' of the existence of God. In the sixth century, Boethius had held that some propositions, including some moral principles, are intuitively self-evident. He also favoured a more rigorous style of reasoning than was then common. In Anselm's writings these two factors come togeher to yield a logically ordered discussion proceeding from 'axioms' to implied conclusions. He applied this method of systematic and discursive reasoning to a range of theological issues, and in citing authority (*auctoritas*), in the form of quotations from scripture or patristic writings, was concerned to use it as a means of proceeding towards additional conclusions. This innovative attitude is expressed in a passage, the concluding words of which compose the motto of scholasticism. He writes: 'It seems to me to show negligence if after we have become established in the Faith we do not strive *to understand what we believe*' (*Cur Deus Homo*, i, 2).

In his moral theory Anselm is influenced by Augustine's psychology, and adopts the view that grace induces in the soul a disposition to move towards the good (*affectio justitiae*) by conforming its actions to the will of God. The importance of the will is also emphasized by Abelard (1079–1142). The Augustinian tendency to voluntarism (from the Latin: *voluntas*, meaning 'will') is pursued in relation to both the subject and the criterion of goodness. As regards the latter the standard is, as mentioned, conformity to the divine will. In regard to the former, Abelard insists that in themselves actions are morally neutral. Moreover, he suggests that desires or inclinations are likewise not good or bad as such. The appropriate object of moral assessment is the agent's *intention*. Vice is nothing other than knowledgeable consent to sin, that is to action performed in the knowledge of its disobedience to God's commands. As he writes: 'Defect, then, is whereby we are ... inclined to consent to what we ought not to do ... What is that consent but to despise God and to violate His laws?' And later in the same work he illustrates how vice lies not in desire but in consent. The example is of a man who in seeing a woman has his 'concupiscence aroused; his mind enticed by fleshly lust and stirred to base desire but who yet bridles this lascivious longing by the power of temperance' (*Scito Teipsum*, Ch. 2), and so reaps the reward of obeying God's commandment (presumably the ninth: Thou shalt not covet thy neighbour's wife).

This view, shared by Anselm and Abelard (and later adopted in part or in whole by Henry of Ghent (1217–93), Duns Scotus (1266–1308), William of Ockham (1290–1350) and in the Renaissance by Francisco Suarez (1548–1617)) has certain potentially troublesome implications. If virtue consists in rightness of intention, and this in turn is analysed in terms of consent to God's commandments, (conceived of under *that* description, i.e. as 'conduct commanded by God') then a problem arises if the agent does not know what God commands, or that he commands anything, or indeed that there is even a God to issue commands. Certainly if one lacks this knowledge then one cannot be sinful or vicious (i.e. vice-filled), since in that circumstance one cannot knowingly intend to breach a divine commandment. By the same token, however, neither can one be virtuous, not knowing to what to give consent. And if virtue is necessary for salvation then the ignorant are in trouble, albeit perhaps a less damnable predicament than that facing those who know God's law and intend to contravene it. As regards the first of these implications, Abelard took it to show that those who (in ignorance) persecuted and crucified Christ committed no sin – an opinion apparently not shared by his contemporaries, for it was condemned at the Council of Sens in 1141. In connection with the second implication, he offers an unconvincing version of the suggestion discussed earlier, that those existing outside the scope of the Christian revelation might yet be virtuous inasmuch as they conform their intentions to the content of the moral law as this is revealed to reason.

The second problem facing the ʾAnselm/Abelard view arises from the location of moral character in the agent's intentions rather than in the type of actions he performs. If one believes that it is publicly determinable what kind of action each of several people has performed but that it is not determinable what intention each has, then, if intention is the locus of moral quality, one is not in a position to say whether they have all acted virtuously even if one somehow knows that one of them has. For Abelard this problem is overcome by the claim that God can 'see' into the hearts of men, though they are unobservable to others. That possibility, however, will be of little comfort to those mortals who may have a responsibility to assess moral character, which in any event we do often take to be manifest in publicly observable events. This latter presumption suggests a different solution: to deny that agent's intentions are necessarily private objects and to allow that they are sometimes open to assessment.

The greatest of medieval and scholastic philosophers, St Thomas Aquinas, was born eighty years after the death of Abelard. Only those who have made the effort to comprehend the philosophy of Aquinas can properly appreciate the extent of his system and the power of his mind. Albertus Magnus (1206–80) – St Albert the Great – his sometime teacher and patron, said of the young St Thomas, who had acquired the nickname 'the dumb ox' on account of his taciturnity and stout figure, that 'he will eventually bellow so loudly in his teaching that it will resound throughout the whole world'. At least by the standard this suggests, viz. renown, there can be no doubt that Aquinas is the greatest of the scholastics and perhaps of all philosophers born between Aristotle and Descartes.

The Thomistic genius lay in the capacity to see how Greek thought and Catholic doctrine might be synthesized into a Christian philosophy. So far as this vision concerned ethics, it took the form of showing that the previously noted parallels between ideas of virtue originating in the philosophy of classical antiquity and those recurrent within Christian thought could be developed so as to give a rational foundation to ethics and thereby demonstrate an account of true virtue which could be compelling to any intelligent human being. The scale of St Thomas's synthesis of ethics and moral theology is vast. It covers both theoretical and normative issues and is spread through many texts. Fifteen volumes of the current Blackfriars edition of the *Summa Theologiae* and many other independent commentaries and treatises are concerned with ethics and value in one form or another. Given the extent of this corpus, therefore, it would be absurd to do other than identify the essence of the theory.

Something of Aquinas' views has already been indicated, including the fact that he held a rationalistic account of moral thinking – regarding the 'natural law' as discoverable by the exercise of 'right reason'. In arguing for this he was greatly assisted by the recent availability in the Christian West of the ethical writings of Aristotle. Drawing on these he was able to develop a form of consequentialist eudaimonism, according to which right action is conduct that either tends to promote or actually realizes human flourishing. On this view there is a distinctive and essential human nature, and associated with it a set of values constituting excellence in the conduct of life. Hence, virtues are those habits of action which are conducive to the fulfilment of an agent's rational nature.

To speak of the 'natural law' is thus to refer to that part of the general order of things which involves human kind and its progress to perfection. This law is embodied in natural human tendencies, such as the inclinations to preserve one's life, to mate and rear children, to co-operate with others in society, and so on. In addition to this empirical source of moral values and requirements there is the 'law of God' promulgated to mankind via the Mosaic law and other parts of the divine revelation. However, for Aquinas this is not a source of alternative or additional commandments, but rather a supplementary source of those prescriptions conformity with which is necessary for achieving well-being. What Christian theology adds to the basically Aristotelian moral theory is first, supernatural assistance, through revelation and grace, and second, a supernatural transformation of the goal of virtue, from the state conceived of by Aristotle as flourishing (*eudaimonia*) to that of blessedness (*beatitudo*) consisting of eternal union with God.

In giving due place to the religious dimension of morality while combining it with a broadly rationalist theory, Aquinas trod a path between two groups of contemporary philosophers: the Latin Averroists and the Franciscan voluntarists. The former, of whom the most important was Siger of Brabant (1240–84), maintained an unqualifiedly naturalistic version of Aristotelian eudaimonism. The latter, by contrast, challenged the idea that divine law is in effect a 'users' guide' to human life, and maintained that it is an independent source of obligation rooted in God's legislative will. This revival of Augustinian thought began in St Thomas's lifetime in works of a mystical inclination by St Bonaventure (1217–74), Ramón Lull (1235–1315) and Meister Eckhardt (1260–1327) which emphasized divine illumination and the turning of the soul's will to God. More philosophically significant, however, were the writings of the two greatest Franciscan thinkers of this period, namely, Duns Scotus and William of Ockham.

Until recently it was common to regard both men (but especially Ockham) as espousing straightforward versions of theistic voluntarism, i.e. the view that an action is good if and only if God commands or approves of it. However, the situation is not so simple. Scotus holds much in common with the 'right reason' theory of Aquinas but he accords two special roles to the will. On the one hand, the object of moral assessment is always an act of will, and on the other, God is able to invest moral prescriptions with the additional status of absolute obligations by willing that they be obeyed (*Opus Oxoniense* III).

Ockham moves further towards locating the source of morality in the divine will by arguing that since God is omnipotent he can do anything save the logically impossible. The criterion of logical impossibility is contradiction. So, if a statement is not a contradiction, then the situation it describes is at least logically possible and hence is such as can be brought about by God. But a moral statement such as 'theft is permissible' is not contradictory – even if it is false. Accordingly, if God is omnipotent then it must be possible for him to make it the case that theft is permissible without this being achieved by changing any other logically independent fact of the matter. One, and perhaps the only, way in which this could be achieved would be if permissibility, requirement and prohibition are constituted simply by God's attitudes. That is, if the moral character of an action is an immediate logical consequence of God's allowing, commanding or prohibiting it. In fact, Ockham was willing to allow that much of what we hold to be right and wrong is so for reasons presented by natural law theory. But he also saw, like

Scotus, that such a theory has some difficulty accounting for the legalistic character of some moral requirements, and he further held that belief in the absolute
omnipotence of God must imply that the moral order could be reversed by nothing
other than God's willing it to be so (*Reportatio*, IV, q9).

iv Renaissance pluralism and the decline of scholasticism

Ockham was the last philosopher of the golden age of medieval scholasticism. In
the century following his death the intellectual and political worlds were transformed by the rise of science and the decline of the Church of Rome. Once again
Western Europe became subject to political and religious warfare, but in regard
to the latter the source of attack was not, as before, an alien faith; rather it came
from within the Christian Church, from scandalized or disaffected clergy and other
members of the religious orders. It is not altogether surprising, therefore, that the
leaders of the Reformation and those of the new natural science were both apt to
set aside a philosophical tradition which had by then come to be closely associated
with the old order.

This said, the movement to develop Aristotle's ethical theory did not come to
a halt. Rather, it split into two directions and proceeded onwards for some while
longer. The division corresponded to secular and religious interests and was also
largely geographical. In Italy a group of writers and natural scientists located in
and around Padua looked back to the Latin Averroists of two hundred years
before, and beyond them to Aristotle himself, as sources for a wholly naturalistic
ethical theory consonant with their wider scientific world view. The most
renowned of this otherwise little-known group was Pietro Pomponazzi (1462–
1525), who, given his philosophical materialism, sceptical epistemology and quasi-
utilitarian ethical theory, would no doubt find the contemporary philosophical
environment rather congenial.

Meanwhile in the Iberian peninsula the Thomist tradition persisted among a
group of Catholic neo-scholastics. Much of their word consisted of expounding
and commenting upon the writings of Aquinas and Aristotle, but they also
contributed something to the tradition by attempting to relate it to the changed
circumstances. The Dominican, Francisco de Vitoria (1480–1546), for example,
considered the legitimacy of using violence in defence of society, and thereby
advanced the development of 'just war' doctrine. The same issue also formed part
of the normative ethics proposed by the Jesuit, Francisco Suarez. He was probably
the most distinguished of all the Iberian Thomists, though while he was a major
commentator on Aquinas his ambitions went far beyond re-presenting the 'Angelic
Doctor's' teachings. His own synthesis of scholasticism also drew from the metaphysical ideas of Ockham, and this led to his espousing a view in which the will
of the agent and that of God play a large part in determining the moral value of
conduct. Perhaps the main historical significance of Suarez's writings, however,
is as the channel through which Thomist moral philosophy was made available
throughout Europe to those who had not been educated in the scholastic tradition,

including those who, like Hugo Grotius (1583–1645), were deeply hostile to its particular religious associations but who nonetheless, often unknowingly, developed moral views similar of those of the Catholic scholastics. Much closer in theological outlook to Suarez, but living in isolation from Thomist circles, was his English contemporary Richard Hooker (1553–1600) who drew upon the natural law theory presented by Aquinas to develop an account of the relation between natural and revealed law. So great, indeed, was the influence of Thomist ideas upon Hooker in his writing of *The Laws of Ecclesiastical Polity* that he came to be known as the 'Anglican Aquinas'.

Several factors contributed to the post-medieval reaction against scholasticism. Besides the rise of empirical science and the fragmentation of the Universal Church, there was a movement within philosophy against Aristotelianism and in favour of a return to Platonic doctrines. The latter trend was due in part to the rediscovery of the authors of classical antiquity and to the increased availability of their works through translation. This encouraged a somewhat uncritical eclecticism, there being less interest in determining the internal consistency of compilations of ideas than in admiring the aesthetic qualities of both parts and wholes. Early on in this development Nicholas of Cusa (1401–64) had drawn upon Pythagorean and Platonic metaphysics and Christian mysticism to construct an account of reality according to which there is a general movement of all humanity towards God, directed under the guidance of mystical love.

Such ideas were to the fore in the writings of those associated with the Neoplatonic Academy founded in Florence in the fifteenth century under the patronage of Cosimo de' Medici. The two main figures in this circle were Marsilio Ficino (1433–99) and Giovanni Pico della Mirandola. Like Nicholas of Cusa, Ficino blends pre-Socratic and Augustinian ideas about the causal efficacy of love as a universal principle, but then manages to identify this with a generalized concept of man, thereby giving rise to the idea of humanity (*humanitas*) as the primary moral value.

More important, perhaps, than the intoxication resulting from such rhapsodic associations of ideas were the numerous translations of classical texts produced by members of the Florentine Academy. Besides introducing new notions into Renaissance thinking, these texts encouraged the development of a different form in which to cast moral and social thought, namely, lyrical fables of past or future gold ages. While the Renaissance scholastics sought to extend the philosophical methodology of the *Summa Theologiae* by drawing in yet more material for logical analysis and subsequent systematization, the Renaissance humanists looked back to the *Republic*, finding in it the perfect model for the literary expression of ideas. Thus it was that during the long eve of the modern period Vitoria was writing his *Commentary on the Second Part of the Summa Theologiae*, while Sir Thomas More (1478–1535) penned *Utopia*; and Suarez wrote *De Legibus* as Tommaso Campanella (1568–1639) was composing his *City of the Sun*. (Some small degree of essayist's licence should be allowed in relation to the chronological pairings of these works). Of interest also is the fact that whereas Vitoria and Suarez preserve the theocentrism of medieval ethical theory, More and Campanella offer homocentric views presented through visions of secularized political futures. Such was the state of moral thought at the end of the Renaissance.

References

i Works by individual authors

Abelard: *Peter Abelard's Ethics*; ed. D. E. Luscombe (Oxford: Clarendon Press, 1971).

Anselm: *Basic Writings*; trans. S. N. Deane (La Salle: Open Court, 1962).

Aquinas, Thomas: *Summa Theologiae*; ed. T. Gilby et al. (London: Blackfriars and Eyre & Spottiswoode, 1963–75).

——: *Summa Contra Gentiles*; ed. A. C. Pegis et al. (Notre Dame, Ind.: University of Notre Dame Press, 1975).

Augustine: *The Essential Augustine*; ed. V. J. Bourke (New York: Mentor-Omega, 1964).

——: *The Confessions*; ed. E. B. Pusey (London: Dent, 1962).

Campanella, T.: *Città del Sole*; trans. D. J. Donno, *City of the Sun* (Berkeley: University of California Press, 1981).

Dionysius the Areopagite: *On the Divine Names*; trans. C. E. Rolt (London: SPCK, 1950).

Duns Scotus: *God and Creatures: The Quodlibetal Questions*; ed. F. Alluntis and A. Walter (Princeton: Princeton University Press, 1975).

Hooker, R.: *The Laws of Ecclesiastical Polity* (1594); ed. R. Church (Oxford: Clarendon Press, 1876).

More, T.: *Utopia* (1513); ed. G. M. Logan and R. M. Adams (Cambridge: Cambridge University Press, 1989).

Plato: *Timaeus*.

——: *The Republic*.

Pomponazzi, P.: *The Philosophy of Pomponazzi*; ed. Douglas et al. (Hildesheim: Olms, 1962).

Suarez, F.: *De Legibus*; trans. (Oxford: Clarendon Press, 1944).

William of Ockham: *Philosophical Writings*, ed. P. Boehner (Indianapolis: Bobbs-Merrill, 1977).

ii Collections

The most easily available sources of original medieval and Renaissance writings are edited collections of extracts such as:

Hyman, A., and Walsh, J., eds.: *Philosophy in the Middle Ages* (Indianapolis: Hackett, 1973).

McKeon, R., ed.: *Selections from Medieval Philosophers*, 2 vols. (New York: Scribner's, 1958).

Cambridge University Press is currently preparing a series of collections of texts to accompany the volumes on the history of medieval and Renaissance philosophy listed above. The first relevant one of these is:

The Cambridge Translations of Medieval Philosophical Texts. Vol. 3, *Philosophical Psychology, Ethics, Politics and Aesthetics* (Cambridge: Cambridge University Press, forthcoming).

Further reading

i General background

The best general account of the philosophy of the medieval and Renaissance periods is that given in:

Copleston, F.C.: *A History of Philosophy*, Vols. 2 and 3 (London: Burns, Oates & Washbourne, 1946–75).

See also:

Copleston, F.C.: *A History of Medieval Philosophy* (London: Methuen, 1972).

For scholarly essays on particular figures and topics see:

Kretzman, N., Kenny, A. and Pinborg, J., eds.: *The Cambridge History of Later Medieval Philosophy* (Cambridge: Cambridge University Press, 1982); and
Schmitt, C. and Skinner, Q., eds.: *The Cambridge History of Renaissance Philosophy* (Cambridge: Cambridge University Press, 1988).

ii Additional works on particular figures and topics

Bourke, V.J.: *Wisdom from St Augustine* (Houston: Center for Thomistic Studies, 1984).
Haldane, J.: 'Voluntarism and realism in medieval ethics', *Journal of Medical Ethics*, 15, (1989), 39–44.
Kristeller, P.O.: 'Humanism and moral philosophy', *Renaissance Humanism, Foundations, Forms and Legacy*, ed. A. Rabil, Jr., Vol. 3 (Philadelphia: University of Pennsylvania Press, 1988).
McCord Adams, M.: 'William Ockham: voluntarist or naturalist?', *Studies in Medieval Philosophy*, ed. J.F. Wippel (Washington: Catholic University of America Press, 1987).
McInerny, R.: *Ethica Thomistica* (Washington: Catholic University of America Press, 1982).
——: 'Aquinas' moral theory', *Journal of Medical Ethics*, 13 (1987), 31–33.

12

Modern moral philosophy

J. B. SCHNEEWIND

ANCIENT Western philosophical thought about how to live centred on the question of the highest good: what life is most fully and lastingly satisfying? While virtue was meant to govern one's relations with others, it was first of all the condition of attaining the good for oneself. Christianity taught that the highest good was attainable only through salvation, and complicated the pursuit of it by insisting on obedience to God's commands. The distinctive enterprise of modern philosophical ethics grew as ideas of the highest good and of the will of the Christian deity came to seem less and less able to provide practical guidance. Since many people today do not believe, as the ancients did, that there is just one definite way of living which is best for everyone, and since many think we cannot resolve our practical problems on a religious basis, the questions of modern Western ethics are unavoidably still our own questions.

If there is no highest good determined by nature or God, how are we to know whether our desires are misguided or sound? If there are no divinely ordained laws, what can tell us when we should refuse to do what our desires urge us to do, and when we may proceed? Modern moral philosophy emerged from consideration of these problems. There is no standard way of organizing its history, but it is useful to think of it as having three stages.

(1) The first stage is one of gradual emergence from the traditional assumption that morality must come from some authoritative source outside of human nature, into the belief that morality might arise from resources within human nature itself. It was a movement from the view that morality must be imposed on human beings towards the belief that morality could be understood as human self-governance or autonomy. This stage begins with the *Essays* of Michel de Montaigne (1595) and culminates in the work of Kant (1785), Reid (1788) and Bentham (1789).

(2) During the second stage moral philosophy was largely occupied with the elaboration and defence of the view that we are individually self-governing, and with new objections and alternatives to it. The period extends from the assimilation of the work of Reid, Bentham, and Kant to the last third of the present century.

(3) Since then, the attention of moral philosophers has begun to shift away from the problem of the autonomous individual toward new issues concerning public morality.

i Toward autonomy

Montaigne (1533–92) tried to show that the ideas of the good life proposed by classical antiquity fail as guides because most people cannot live as they direct. Though himself a believing Catholic, he also thought most people could not live up to Christian standards. He offered nothing in place of these ideals. He held that there are no clear norms governing social and political life beyond the laws of our own country, which, he held, are always to be obeyed. Positively, he suggested only that each of us might personally find a way of life which our own nature makes necessary for us.

Montaigne's radical challenges to accepted ideas about authoritative morality spoke to the condition of an increasingly diversified, self-reliant and literate European population, but the public life of the time called for principles of a kind he did not present. Endless ferocious wars made evident the deep need for peaceful ways of settling political disputes. Christianity could no longer help, because Protestantism had split Europe so deeply that there could be no agreement on what the historical religion required. Although everyone took religious belief to be essential somehow to morality, it was plainly necessary to go beyond sectarian principles. The universities continued to teach watered-down versions of Aristotelian ethics, but these hardly spoke to the pressing needs of the time. Innovators drew on other sources.

The most durable tradition of thought about the norms governing human conduct was the Thomistic natural law tradition. It claimed to show what principles for public life are available to human reason, independent of revelation and without specifically Christian bias. Accepted by many Protestants as well as by Catholics, it taught that God's laws require us to act in certain ways which, whether we know it or not, are for the benefit of everyone. It held that the laws could be known at least by the wise, who could instruct the rest; and it showed what rewards and punishments God connects with obedience and disobedience. The moral thought of the seventeenth century started from classical natural law theory, but altered it drastically.

Classical natural law saw humans as created to play a part in a divinely ordained community expressing God's glory, and morality as teaching what that part is. Modern natural law began with the assertion that individuals are entitled to determine their own purposes, and that morality comprises the conditions under which these can best be pursued. Hugo Grotius (1583–1645), the acknowledged originator of the new outlook, was the first theorist to claim that rights are a natural attribute of the individual independently of any contribution the individual makes to the community. In his *Law of War and Peace* (1625) he insisted that we are sociable by nature; but when we form political societies, he said, we do so on condition that our individual rights be respected. Though our rights may be traded for political security, we begin, Grotius taught, as naturally entitled to determine our own lives within the space our rights create.

Thomas Hobbes's masterpiece, *Leviathan* (1651), denied natural sociability, and stressed our self-interested aims. There is, for him, no ultimate good: we restlessly seek 'power after power' to protect ourselves from death. Since we are basically equal in natural ability, this would cause a war of all against all if we did not agree to be ruled by a sovereign capable of enforcing peace while we each pursue our private goals. The laws of nature or morality are ultimately no more than indicators of the most essential steps we must take so that an orderly society may exist. Our limitless desires thus create a problem that can only be solved by setting up a ruler who is above any legal control; but it is our desires themselves that move us to solve that problem.

The theory that political society emerges from a social contract makes man and not God the creator of the secular powers that govern him. Many natural lawyers in the seventeenth century accepted this view. While Hobbes aroused almost universal opposition for his assertion that morality serves human selfishness, the natural lawyers nonetheless agreed that humans are unruly beings, needing strong governmental control. John Locke (1632–1704) was opposing Grotius as well as Hobbes when he claimed that some of our rights are inalienable, and hence that there are moral limits to what the government may do. But even Locke held, with his contemporaries, that most people cannot know without instruction what morality requires and that threats of punishment are needed to get the majority to behave decently. Even though the laws of nature are meant to guide us to individual as well as common well-being, and even though we are competent to set up our own political order, we are still to be viewed, according to most seventeenth-century thinkers, as needing to have morality imposed on us.

Late in the seventeenth century criticism of this outlook became vocal; and during the eighteenth century a number of thinkers developed views in which morality was taken, to one degree or another, not simply as suitably imposed on our nature but as an expression of it.

One major step was taken when Pierre Bayle argued in 1681 for the then shocking claim that a group of atheists could form a perfectly decent society. A more systematic effort to sketch a new picture of human nature and morality came from the third Earl of Shaftesbury. In his *Inquiry concerning Virtue* (1711) he argued that we have a moral faculty which enables us to judge our own motives. We are virtuous when we act only on those we approve; and we approve only our benevolent or sociable motives. Shaftesbury thought that our moral sense must even be our guide in determining whether allegedly divine commands came from God or from some demon. Morality thus became an outgrowth of human feelings.

There was much debate in the eighteenth century about the respective roles of benevolence and self-interest in human psychology, and about whether either of them could be the sole explanation for our moral behaviour. Similarly there was considerable discussion of whether our moral convictions result from feeling, as Shaftesbury had suggested, or from reason, as the natural lawyers had believed. Both debates involve the question of the extent to which humans can be autonomous.

It was agreed on all sides that virtue requires us to work for the good of others.

Some argued that this is shown us by moral feelings of approval and disapproval, others that it is learned by intuition or direct moral insight. In either case it might be argued that everyone could be aware of the requirements of morality, since brilliance and education are not required in order to have feelings or to intuit what is self-evident. Some criticized Hobbes's psychology, arguing that we naturally desire the good of others. Then external sanctions are not needed to motivate us; and as we can readily see what brings good to others, we can also direct our own actions without instruction. Those who held with Hobbes that self-interest is all that ever moves anyone tried to show that nature is so constituted that if we act for our own best interests, we will in fact be helping others. Some claimed that nothing is more enjoyable than virtue; others argued that virtue pays because without it we cannot get assistance in pursuing our own projects. In either case, the aim was to show that self-interest – traditionally maligned as the source of evil-doing – would naturally lead us to virtuous behaviour. Even a selfish human nature could then be seen as expressing itself through morality. (See Article 16, EGOISM.)

In all these debates no-one seemed able or willing to say more about the good than that it is whatever gives happiness or pleasure. Still, it was assumed that what we ought to do is always a function of what it would be good to bring about: action can only be right because it produces good. The two most original eighteenth-century moral philosophers, David Hume (1711–76) and Immanuel Kant (1724–1804) challenged this deeply rooted idea, Hume indirectly and in part, Kant frontally.

Hume rejected natural law models of morality and sought to show that a virtue-centred theory could best account for our moral convictions. Morality, he argued, must be rooted in our feelings, since morality moves us to action, and reason alone can never do so. (Michael Smith expounds this position in Article 35, REALISM.) Approval and disapproval are the moral feelings. They are directed at the basic desires and aversions that move us to action. We approve, Hume argued, of those that move us to do what is generally beneficial, and disapprove of those that cause harm. Though we are often self-interested, we also have desires for the good of others, and regular action arising from them constitutes virtue. This is at least the case with virtues such as parental affection and kindness to the needy, which express our natural concern for the well-being of others. The question was whether all the virtues can be explained in this way.

The problem case, Hume thought, was justice. One of his immediate predecessors, Bishop Butler (1692–1752) had noted that following the rules of justice does not always bring about a favourable balance of good either to the agent or to others – as when, for instance, a virtuous impoverished parent returns lost money to a miserly millionaire. If what is right is always determined by what is good, how can we account for the virtue of justice? Hume argued that what benefits society is having an accepted practice of following known rules of justice, even if the practice causes hardship in some cases. He also argued that a disinterested desire to observe these rules grows naturally within us, out of sympathetic appreciation of the feelings of others. On Hume's view we can see how even the virtue of obeying laws can arise entirely from our own feelings and desires.

Kant held a more radical version of the view that morality arises from human nature. He took the central point about morality to be that it imposes absolute duties on us, showing us what we have to do no matter what. But he held that this special kind of moral necessity could only arise from a law we impose on ourselves. The clue to Kant's view is freedom. When we know we morally must do something, we know we can do it; and this can only be true if we are free. Freedom in action excludes determination by anything outside ourselves, and it is not merely undetermined, or random, behaviour. The sole way in which we can be free, for Kant, is if our actions are determined by something within our own nature. This means that in free action we cannot be pursuing natural goods, or conforming to eternal laws or laws God imposes, because in all those cases we would be determined by something external to ourselves. Our moral obligations must arise from a law which we ourselves legislate.

The moral law, Kant holds, is not a requirement to do good to others. It tells us rather to act only in ways which we could rationally agree to have everyone act. The law thus sets a formal requirement, and its function in our thinking is to serve as a test for our plans. Each of us, Kant holds, can methodically think out whether a planned action is allowable or not by asking: can I without self-contradiction will this plan to be a law according to which everyone always acts? Only if I can am I permitted to act on it. The Kantian position is thus a far more thorough alternative than Hume's to the view that good consequences always determine what is right. For Kant we must always settle what is right before we can know what is good.

Kand also holds that a special motive is involved in morality. Our awareness of our activity in legislating for ourselves generates a special respect for the law we have imposed. Since it is always possible for us to be dutiful out of respect, we need not depend on external sources for motivation any more than for guidance. We are fully autonomous. (For a more detailed account see Article 14, KANTIAN ETHICS.)

Kant held an extreme form of the view that morality is an expression of human nature. But one central part at least of his revolutionary view was advocated, quite independently, by both Thomas Reid (1710–96), founder of the important nineteenth-century Scottish 'common sense' school, and Jeremy Bentham (1748–1832), the originator of modern utilitarianism. This was the belief that ordinary people can get adequate guidance for action by consciously applying abstract moral principles. Earlier thinkers had appealed to such principles to explain moral decisions, but did not think that everyone possessed a methodical way of consciously using them. After the work of Kant, Reid, and Bentham, it became widely accepted that a basic principle of morality had to be one which could actually be used by everyone alike.

Thomas Reid, the most conservative of the three, held that common-sense morality embodies principles whose truth everyone can see intuitively and can readily apply. We just know we are required to help others, act fairly, tell the truth, and so on. No further systematization of these principles is possible, or needed. Thus common sense and with it the moral competence of the individual are vindicated against theoretical doubts and simplifications. From this position Reid argued against the secularistic hedonism he saw in Hume. He aimed to defend Christianity, now built into common sense, against its detractors. Bentham, by contrast, thought that appeals to intuition simply hid the dangerous self-interest of those who made them. He claimed that his utilitarian principle – that we are to act so as to bring about the greatest happiness of the greatest number – was rational on the face of it, and provided a rational method of making moral decisions. And he held that no other principle did so. If producing the general happiness and producing our own do not always call for the same action, then, he said, we should change society so that they do: otherwise people will not be reliably moved to act as morality requires. It is no accident that Bentham and his philosophy were the centre of an active group of political reformers.

ii Autonomy and theory: pro and con

In its second period, after Kant, Reid, and Bentham, the enterprise of moral philosophy became more fragmented by nationalities than it had earlier been, and grew increasingly into a technical subject for university study rather than a topic of concern for the whole of educated society. At the cost of ignoring much of its ever more sophisticated development, I will discuss only three aspects of the work done during the period: (1) the continuation of efforts to vindicate and explain moral autonomy; (2) efforts to assert the primacy of the community over the individual; (3) the rise of nihilism and relativism, and the increased significance of questions about the epistemology of morals.

(1) Bentham's utilitarian theory led to some new questions. The principle seemed to yield moral conclusions strongly at odds with common-sense convictions; and despite Bentham's claim that it could be used for decision making, it seemed to call for calculations ordinary people could not make. John Stuart Mill (1806–73) worked out replies in his *Utilitarianism* (1863). Common-sense morality, he said, which we all learn as children, represents the accumulated wisdom of mankind about the desirable and undesirable consequences of actions. Hence we can and must live by it, except in usual or new cases, when direct appeal to the principle of utility is appropriate. But in those cases, common sense is itself apt to be undecided. Utilitarianism so interpreted will not lead to conclusions common sense finds unacceptable. So no appeal to intuitively grasped non-utilitarian principles is needed to explain our ordinary morality. Mill also proposed a new theory of moral motivation. We can come to be directly attached to our moral principles, he argued, just as a miser becomes attached to his money, even if we start by viewing them as instrumental to our own happiness. We can thus have inner motivation to act morally, and so be fully autonomous. (Issues underlying utilitarianism receive more detailed discussion elsewhere in this volume, especially in Article 19; CONSEQUENTIALISM and Article 20, UTILITY AND THE GOOD. See also Article 40, UNIVERSAL PRESCRIPTIVISM.)

Utilitarians continued the attempt to derive principles of right action entirely from consideration of the good that right acts bring about. Though Mill argued for a more complex understanding of human happiness than Bentham allowed, he still held the good to be essentially a matter of satisfying preferences which differ, often drastically, from person to person. Intuitionists, in opposition, held that principles of right action could not simply be derived from consideration of what people actually want. You cannot, they held, even draw a valid conclusion about what is good simply from premises about what people actually want. The premise 'whatever people want is good' must be added. Otherwise the basic principle of utilitarianism has no foundation. But only intuition, it was argued, can supply the missing premise. And in fact, the intuitionists held, not everything people want is good. As Reid had claimed, there are self-evident principles requiring justice and veracity as well as benevolence, and sometimes in conflict with it. So guidance about right action cannot be obtained solely from considering the good.

The nineteenth-century British intuitionists, of whom William Whewell (1794–1866) was the most distinguished, were trying to defend a Christian ethic against the utilitarian claim that the point of morality is to produce worldly happiness for all. But their intuitionism allowed that each person had the ability to know what morality requires. In *The Methods of Ethics* (1874), Henry Sidgwick tried to show that the intuitionist view about the foundations of morality could serve the utilitarian view about its point. Utilitarianism, he allowed, needed an intuition as its foundation; but without the utilitarian method, intuitionism would be useless in settling moral disputes. He argued in detail for the view that utilitarianism gives the best theoretical account of common-sense convictions.

Other varieties of intuitionism were also developed. The German-speaking philosophers Franz Brentano (1838–1917), Max Scheler (1874–1928) and Nicolai Hartmann (1882–1950) worked out different theories of the general nature of value, with moral value as one species. In opposition to Kant, they argued that through feeling we have access to a realm of real values; and they spelled out the structures or hierarchies of objectively existing values thus given to us. These values show the content of the good, and ultimately set the direction for right action. This enables us to move beyond the view, shared by Kant and the utilitarians, that the good for man can only be defined in terms of satisfaction of desires. A similar view of the objectivity and multiplicity of values was defended in England by G. E. Moore, who argued in *Principia Ethica* (1903) that knowledge of values could not be derived from knowledge of facts, but only from intuition of the goodness of kinds of states of affairs, such as beauty, pleasure, friendship, and knowledge. Right acts are those producing the most good, he held, thus advocating a form of utilitarianism going beyond the hedonistic version. But unlike Kantianism and classical utilitarianism, which both claim to provide a rational procedure for settling moral disputes, the intuitional views all rely ultimately on claims to insight, and offer no method for settling disagreements.

(2) The view that moral community depends on decisions made separately by individuals capable of seeing for themselves what morality requires occupied a major place in nineteenth and early twentieth-century Western thought. But

there has also been a constant stream of thinkers rejecting it. Among the early reactions to Kant, the criticisms by G. W. F. Hegel (1770–1831) are most significant. Hegel pointed out that Kant's purely formal principle requires content, and argued that the content can only come from the institutions, vocabularies, and orientations with which society provides its members. The moral personality, Hegel argued, is and must be formed by the community in which the person lives. The claim to have a critical standpoint wholly beyond it is unsustainable; and the community has a structure and an impetus of its own that goes far beyond anything individual choice could deliberately construct. In France Auguste Comte (1798–1857) developed a philosophy of the historical evolution of society that ignored individual moral judgement in favour of policies to be derived from an ever-improving scientific sociology. The stress placed by Karl Marx (1818–83) on inevitable historical development generated by economic forces also attributes little importance to the choices and principles of the individual.

It is often said that although these writers have strong moral views, they have no moral philosophy; but their refusal to give a central place to individual morality as Kant and Mill saw it is itself a philosophical position about how we are to view the ethics of the self-directing agent.

American pragmatism has had less to say about morality than about other subjects, but John Dewey (1859–1952), influenced by Hegelian claims about the primacy of the community in structuring the moral personality, was a notable exception. In *Human Nature and Conduct* (1922) and other works he tried to show that a liberal society need not presuppose, as Hegel had claimed, either a standpoint outside history or a single abstract principle as its basis. Though individuals are shaped by their community, they can through rational inquiry devise new solutions to social problems, working consciously together to reform their community and their own moral outlooks.

(3) Sceptical and relativistic doubts about the existence of an eternal universally binding morality, arising from awareness of the variety of codes and practices throughout the world, had been voiced by Montaigne and debated during the seventeenth and eighteenth centuries. The issue was revived with great force and depth by the brilliant and unsettling attacks which Friedrich Nietzsche (1844–1900) directed against all pretensions of societies or theorists to deliver principles properly binding on everyone. In *The Genealogy of Morals* (1887) and other works Nietzsche did not try to refute Kantian and utilitarian theories. Instead he exposed what he took to be the psychological forces leading people to assert such views. The struggle for mastery, and envy and resentment of those who achieved it, were the roots of modern morality. Not even abstract claims to rationality escaped Nietzsche's unmasking: they too, he held, are fronts behind which nothing but the struggle for power is hidden. There is no impersonal guide to action: all one can do is decide what sort of person one proposes to be, and strive to be so.

The rise of modern anthropology encouraged philosophers like Edward Westermarck (1862–1939) to reopen the old relativistic question of whether there is such a thing as moral knowledge. The debate continues, as Article 39, RELA-TIVISM, indicates. More generally, science-oriented logical positivists such as

Moritz Schlick (1881–1936) held that any alleged beliefs not meeting the tests that scientific beliefs can meet are not simply false: they are meaningless. Moore and others had convinced many people that claims about morality cannot be derived from statements of fact. If that is so, the positivists held, then moral beliefs cannot be empirically tested in the way that scientific beliefs can. Hence moral beliefs are really just expressions of feeling, not cognitive claims at all. The debate thus initiated about the meaning of moral language and the possibility of moral reasoning began in the 1930s and lasted for several decades. (See Article 38, SUBJECTIVISM.)

Unlike earlier discussions of morality, this controversy seemed to be wholly indifferent to the substantive issues of what principles or values should be sustained. It was often said that these were 'meta-ethical' issues, and that philosophers should and could say nothing about actual moral problems and specific principles. But the whole debate was structured by the assumption that what matters about morality is that individuals should be able to make their own moral decisions and live accordingly. The question concerned the status of individual decision-making: is it an outcome of knowledge, or a matter of feeling or custom? In an oddly similar vein the continental writers who, like Jean-Paul Sartre (1905–80) developed existentialist thought, reached back to Nietzschean views to argue that morality rests on nothing but the totally untrammelled free decision of each individual. Nothing general could be said about morality, Sartre held, because each person must make a purely personal decision about it – and then, to be in good faith, live accordingly.

If the existentialists expressed their moral outlooks rather through literature than through formal studies of ethics, this is hardly surprising. The philosophers interested in meta-ethical issues moved back to the study of moral principles, sometimes by means of arguments to the effect that morality can have its own kind of non-scientific rationality and that certain specific principles are required if morality is to be rational. R. M. Hare, Kurt Baier, and Richard Brandt are among the many philosophers working on these lines. (See Article 40, UNIVERSAL PRESCRIPTIVISM, written by Hare, for an example.) They all see the ultimate point of morality as increasing human happiness by providing rational methods for resolving disputes. Though other positions were voiced, it would be fair to say that broadly utilitarian views dominated Anglo-American ethics through the nineteen-sixties.

iii New directions

In opposition to the long tradition of utilitarian thought, Kantian views have more recently been revitalized. Here the work of John Rawls is central. His *A Theory of Justice* (1971) attempts to show how principles of right action, at least in the domain of justice, are justifiable independently of the amount of good that just action brings about. And he has argued powerfully that no utilitarian account of justice can as adequately incorporate our strong common-sense convictions as can his Kantian view that the right is prior to the good.

Rawls's work indicates not only a new rejection of utilitarian thinking. It signals a turn away from the preoccupation with seeing morality as structured around the self-governing individual and taking moral philosophy to have the task of explaining how such an individual can operate. Rawls holds that the problems of justice cannot be resolved by decisions individuals make separately. The issues are simply too complex. Justice can only be achieved through something like a social contract, in which we all autonomously agree on how the basic institutions of our society must be structured so as to be just. Rawls thus tries to combine an Hegelian recognition of the priority of community with a reinterpretation of the Kantian insistence on autonomy.

Three further concerns have marked recent developments in moral philosophy. (1) Much work is being done on actual social and political problems. As the essays in Part V of this volume indicate, questions concerning abortion, environmental ethics, just war, medical treatment, business practices, the rights of animals, and the position of women and children occupy a considerable part of the literature and teaching considered to be moral philosophy or ethics. (2) There has been a return to the Aristotelian vision of morality as centrally a matter of virtue, rather than abstract principles. Alasdair MacIntyre and Bernard Williams, among others, attempt to develop a communitarian view of moral personality and of the functioning of morality. (See Article 21, VIRTUE THEORY.) (3) Finally, there has been a rapid growth of interest in the problems posed by the need to co-ordinate the behaviour of many individuals if effective action is to be taken. If too many people use a lake for a rural retreat, no-one will get the solitude each desires; but one person's decision to stay away may do no good: how are we to decide what is to be done? Many issues, including preservation of resources and the environment, population control, and the prevention of nuclear war seem to have similar structure, and moral philosophers along with economists, mathematicians, and others are being drawn to them.

Issues like these, affecting groups or communities of autonomous individuals, may be coming to have more importance for modern moral philosophy than the historically central problem of explaining and validating the morally autonomous individual as such.

References

Baier, K.: *The Moral Point of View* (Ithaca, NY: Cornell University Press, 1958).

Bentham, J.: *Introduction to the Principles of Morals and Legislation* (1789); (Oxford: Basil Blackwell, 1948).

Brandt, R. B.: *A Theory of the Good and the Right* (Oxford: Clarendon Press, 1979).

Brentano, F.: *The Origin of our Knowledge of Right and Wrong* (1889); trans. Chisholm and Schneewind (London: Routledge and Kegan Paul, 1969).

Butler, Bishop J.: *Fifteen Sermons* (1726); in *Works*, ed. J. H. Bernard, Vol. I (London: Macmillan, 1990).

Comte, A.: *The Essential Writings*; ed. G. Lenzer (New York: Harper and Row, 1975).

Dewey, J.: *Human Nature and Conduct* (1922); (New York: The Modern Library, 1929).

Grotius, H.: *The Law of War and Peace* (1625); trans. Kelsey et al. (Oxford: Clarendon Press, 1925).

Hare, R. M.: *The Language of Morals* (Oxford: Clarendon Press, 1952).

Hartmann, N.: *Ethics* (1926); trans. Coit (London: George Allen and Unwin, 1932).

Hegel, G. W. F.: *Philosophy of Right* (1821); trans. Knox (Oxford: Clarendon Press, 1942).

Hobbes, T.: *Leviathan* (1651); (Oxford: Basil Blackwell, 1946).

Hume, D.: *Treatise of Human Nature* (1738); ed. L. A. Selby-Bigge and P. H. Nidditch (Oxford: Clarendon Press, 1978).

Kant, I.: *Groundwork of the Metaphysics of Morals* (1785); trans. Paton (London: Hutchinson, 1948).

Locke, J.: *Two Treatises of Government* (1690); ed. Peter Laslett (Cambridge: Cambridge University Press, 1988).

MacIntyre, A.: *After Virtue* (1981); 2nd edn (Notre Dame, Ind.: University of Notre Dame Press, 1984).

Marx, K.: *The Marx-Engels Reader*, ed. Robert C. Tucker (New York: Norton, 1972).

Mill, J. S.: *Utilitarianism* (1863); in J. S. Mill, *Collected Works*, Vol. 10, ed. J. M. Robson (Toronto: University of Toronto Press, 1969).

Montaigne, M. de: *Essays* (1595); trans. Frame (Stanford: Stanford University Press, 1965).

Moore, G. E.: *Principia Ethica* (Cambridge: Cambridge University Press, 1903).

Nietzsche, F.: *On the Genealogy of Morals* (1887); trans. Kaufman and Hollingdale (New York: Random House, 1967).

Rawls, J.: *A Theory of Justice* (Cambridge, Mass: Harvard University Press, 1971).

Reid, T.: *Essays on the Active Powers of the Human Mind* (1788); (Cambridge: MIT Press, 1969).

Sartre, Jean-Paul: *Existentialism is a Humanism* (1946); trans. P. Mairet (London: Methuen, 1950).

Scheler, M.: *Formalism in Ethics and Non-formal Ethics of Value* (1916); trans. M. S. Frings and R. L. Funk (Evanston: Northwestern University Press, 1973).

Schneewind, J. B., ed.: *Moral Philosophy from Montaigne to Kant*, 2 vols. (Cambridge: Cambridge University Press, 1990).

Shaftesbury, Lord (A. A. Cooper): *Inquiry concerning Virtue or Merit* (1711); in *Characteristics*, ed. J. M. Robertson (Indianapolis: Bobbs-Merrill, 1968).

Sidgwick, H.: *The Methods of Ethics* (1874); (Indianapolis: Hackett, 1981).

Westermarck, E.: *Ethical Relativity* (London: Routledge and Kegan Paul, 1930).

Whewell, W.: *System of Morality including Polity* (London: 1844).

Williams, B.: *Ethics and the Limits of Philosophy* (Cambridge: Harvard University Press, 1985).

Further reading

d'Entreves, A. P.: *Natural Law* (London: Hutchinson, 1970).

Findlay, J. N.: *Axiological Ethics* (London: Macmillan, 1970).

MacIntyre, A.: *A Short History of Ethics* (New York: Macmillan, 1966).

Halevy, E.: *The Growth of Philosophic Radicalism*; trans. Mary Morris (London: Faber & Faber, 1928).

Schneewind, J. B.: *Sidgwick's Ethics and Victorian Moral Philosophy* (Oxford: Clarendon Press, 1977).

Tuck, R.: *Natural Rights Theories* (Cambridge: Cambridge University Press, 1979).

Walsh, W. H.: *Hegelian Ethics* (London: Macmillan, 1969).

PART IV

HOW OUGHT I TO LIVE?

I 3

Natural law

STEPHEN BUCKLE

i Introduction

THE idea of natural law in ethics has had a long and varied history – so much so, in fact, that it is difficult to pick out the essential ingredients in a natural law ethic. For the same reason, some attempts at exposition are very misleading, typically because they oversimplify: it is tempting to pick out one version of natural law and generalize from its particular features, in the hope that it is representative. The hope will probably be vain, however, partly because the idea of a natural law ethics has itself changed over time. In fact, such change was inevitable because, as this paper will show, from the beginning natural law theories drew on disparate elements, which, waxing and waning at different times, shaped and reshaped the doctrine accordingly.

In order to bring out some of this variation, and also to show what remained relatively constant, the most helpful approach will be to sketch the early development of the idea of natural law, and then turn to consider some distinctive modern aspects. In this way it will be possible to bring out both the plurality of the natural law tradition, and also how abstract and general the idea of natural law must be kept in order to focus on its more stable features. An important implication of recognizing the necessary generality of the idea of natural law is its limited value as a practical ethic, in the sense of providing specific maxims to govern human conduct. The idea of natural law provides no shortcuts for moral reasoning.

It is very important to emphasize this point, because the idea of natural law is so commonly taken by contemporary moralists, especially by its nominal defenders, to provide just such a shortcut. Thus it is not uncommon to find many Roman Catholic moralists, for example, who argue that contraception, or homosexuality, or masturbation (to name just three popular subjects for this kind of treatment), are immoral because they are 'unnatural'. This issue will be considered below. First it is necessary to explain the central thrust of natural law, and this is most economically achieved by tracing its history.

ii A thumbnail history

The seeds of natural law ethics are normally attributed to Aristotle, but they are also evident in the ethical and political dialogues of Plato, which, in their turn,

161

reflect a more widespread debate in ancient Greece, a debate to which Plato and Aristotle came to be the major contributors. The focus of the debate was the contrast between two concepts thought to be crucial to an adequate understanding of human affairs: *nomos* and *phusis*. *Nomos*, from which we have such English words as 'autonomy' (self-rule), referred to the practices established in a society, whether customs or positive laws (i.e. those laws which depend for their existence entirely on the legislative actions of human beings). Since these vary from society to society, and even, within a single society, change over time, what was *nomos* was changeable. In contrast, *phusis*, from which we get our word 'physics', referred to what was unchangeable: nature, or reality. The contrast between the two notions was employed by the Sophists in order to distinguish the human world from the unchanging natural order. For the Sophists, the human world – human society and its institutions, including its moral beliefs – was a world of change, variety, convention: of *nomos* rather than *phusis*.

Plato's dialogues show the different interpretations placed on this conclusion by different Sophists: Callicles maintains that human laws are a device of the weak to frustrate the natural order, which shows the strong to be naturally superior to the weak; while Protagoras holds that, although law and morals are human creations which vary from society to society, they are nevertheless binding for human beings. For Plato, however, even Protagoras' non-sceptical form of conventionalism is inadequate. He holds instead that there is an unchanging moral reality, but one of which human societies, with their great variety of conventional practices, are largely ignorant. Like all knowledge, knowledge of goodness depends on being able to penetrate beyond the veil of appearances to the hidden, unchanging reality of the Forms. Plato thus rejects the idea that morals and law are purely conventional. Against its ancient background, his theory can be understood as an attempt to show that human behaviour is subject not only to established social rules, but first and foremost to an 'unwritten law' – whether understood to be imposed by the gods, as it is put by Sophocles in the tragedy *Antigone*, or a rule to which the gods themselves are subject.

The idea of natural law is sometimes described as the view that there is an unchanging normative order that is a part of the natural world. If this is accepted, then Plato has provided a natural law view in everything but name. This would be a little surprising, since it is more common to attribute the origins of natural law thinking to Aristotle – and an examination of the Aristotelian position shows that it does not equate the natural with the unchangeable.

In the *Nicomachean Ethics*, Aristotle distinguishes between two kinds of justice: legal, or conventional, justice, and natural justice, 'which everywhere has the same force and does not exist by people's thinking this or that' (v. 7). Natural justice is therefore independent of particular positive laws, and applies to all people everywhere. Contrary to what might be expected, however, Aristotle does not distinguish the two kinds of justice in terms of their changeability. He does not do this because, although positive laws (legal justice) are indeed changeable, it is not the case that the natural is entirely free of change. He puts the point somewhat awkwardly:

Now some think that all justice is [conventional], because that which is by nature is unchangeable and has everywhere the same force (as fire burns both here and in Persia), while they see change in the things recognized as just. This, however, is not true in this unqualified way, but is true in a sense; or rather, with the gods it is perhaps not true at all, while with us there is something that is just even by nature, yet all of it is changeable; but still some is by nature, some not by nature. It is evident which sort of thing, among things capable of being otherwise, is by nature; and which is not but is legal and conventional, assuming that both are equally changeable. And in all other things the same distinction will apply; by nature the right hand is stronger, yet it is possible that all men should come to be ambidextrous. (*Nicomachean Ethics*, v. 7)

This passage is rather murky, but it becomes clearer once Aristotle's general account of nature and change (in the *Physics*) is brought into the picture. To understand that account itself, it is necessary to recognize his primary concern with biological phenomena, which leads him to adopt a biological model for explaining all kinds of natural processes. So, for Aristotle, a thing's nature is its inner principle of change, and a change will be natural if it is the work of this inner principle. Consider the case of organic growth: a plant changes over time from seed to seedling to mature plant before eventually dying. These changes are natural because they are due to the work of inner principles which govern its development and eventual decay. They are to be distinguished from other changes which result from external factors, whether these factors are beneficial or detrimental – for example, the many possible effects of human intervention. So, in sharp contrast to Plato's view, Aristotle's account does not imply that the natural (or real) is unchangeable; it requires only that changes occur as the result of the natural inner workings of a being.

Like other biological beings, human beings also grow and mature over time; but more importantly, they are also active beings, and can order their actions in the light of rational understanding. For Aristotle this further feature is the distinguishing mark of human beings: his definition of humans as rational animals is meant to pick out rationality as the most fully human characteristic. Thus if we are to determine what is human nature, what we seek is the inner principle governing distinctively human life; and this is reason. In this way Aristotle provided the raw materials from which the Stoics – and in particular their Roman descendant, Cicero – formulated the first explicit principles of natural law.

The Stoics rejected Aristotle's biologically-flavoured account of natural processes. They developed an explicitly deterministic account of the cosmos, in which the unity – and thus the interconnectedness – of all things was a central theme. This theme resulted in a distinctive approach: in contrast to Aristotle, who had sought out the distinctive element of human or other natures in order to characterize them – a method which emphasized the differences between things – the Stoics understood human nature as one part of the natural order. Nevertheless, they preserved Aristotle's stress on the importance of reason in human beings, because their cosmology placed rational order at the heart of things. Human reason was thus a spark of the creative fire, the *logos*, which ordered and unified the cosmos. Through this connection they were able to formulate the distinctive claim of natural law ethics: the natural law, the law of nature, is the law of *human* nature, and this law is reason. Since reason could be corrupted into serving special interests rather than its own ends, this formula came to be stipulated more narrowly: the natural law is the law of *right* or *sane* reason.

This is the form in which the idea of natural law received its classic formulation in the writings of the eclectic Roman lawyer, Cicero. In perhaps the most famous account of the natural law, in his *Republic*, Cicero describes it as follows:

True law is right reason in agreement with nature; it is of universal application, unchanging and everlasting; it summons to duty by its commands, and averts from wrongdoing by its prohibitions. And it does not lay its commands or prohibitions upon good men in vain, though neither have any effect on the wicked – We cannot be freed from its obligations by senate or people, and we need not look outside ourselves for an expounder or interpreter of it. And there will not be different laws at Rome and at Athens, or different laws now and in the future, but one eternal and unchangeable law will be valid for all nations and all times, and there will be one master and ruler, that is, God, over us all, for he is the author of this law, its promulgator, and its enforcing judge. Whoever is disobedient is fleeing from himself and denying his human nature, and by reason of this very fact he will suffer the worst penalties, even if he escapes what is commonly considered punishment ... (*De Re Publica*, III, xxii)

In order to explain just what this passage implies, it is necessary to remember that, for the practically-minded Roman, the requirement that laws governing human conduct were founded in nature could be accepted without the trappings of Stoic metaphysics. All that was needed was to recognize that human nature provides the elements essential to such a scheme, and that they are (as a rule) shared equally by all. Cicero spells out these features as follows: upright posture (which is necessary for a broad and far-sighted view of things), speech and expressive features (for communication), a natural sense of fellow-feeling (to support social life), and of course rational thought (*Laws*, I. vii–xiii). The more-or-less universal and equal possession of these features by human beings shows the sense in which, for Cicero and his intellectual inheritors, the natural law was understood to be natural.

Once we add to this the sense in which for them the natural law was understood to be *law*, we are in a position to remove a common misconception. Cicero contrasts the correct view of law with the view held by the crowd. For the crowd, law is 'that which in written form decrees whatever it wishes, either by command or prohibition' but for the learned man, 'Law is intelligence, whose natural function it is to command right conduct and forbid wrongdoing – it is the mind and reason of the intelligent man, the standard by which Justice and Injustice are measured' (*Laws*, I. vi).

If this is the core of Ciceronian natural law, then it is free of any substantial commitment to either Stoic or Platonic metaphysics; and therefore it involves no substantial commitment to the existence of a 'normative natural order', at least in any sense that implies more than the facts of human nature already identified. This conclusion contrasts quite sharply with some interpretations of natural law, which see it as the wistful belief that there is a moral code inscribed somewhere in the heavens. The problem with such views is that they have misunderstood the central meaning of the claim that human law and morals are 'founded in nature' – not a surprising error, since, for a modern reader, the expression is a curious one. However, Cicero is quite clear that the belief in natural law is the belief that, on both an individual and a social level, human affairs are properly governed by reason, and that such government gives clear, compelling answers for organizing the lives of rational social beings.

Despite disagreements about the content of natural law, the standard formulations of the basic idea of natural law in medieval Europe were of a piece with the Ciceronian. The theory of Thomas Aquinas (contained in his massive *Summa Theologiae*, and often identified as *the* theory of natural law) is no exception: although Aquinas' largest concerns are metaphysical and religious, his account of natural law appeals to neither metaphysical nor religious doctrines. Rather, he explains both the naturalness and law-like character of natural law in terms of reason.

For Aquinas, the natural law is natural because it is in accordance with human nature, and this nature is a rational nature:

Whatever is contrary to the order of reason is contrary to the nature of human beings as such; and what is reasonable is in accordance with human nature as such. The good of the human being is being in accord with reason, and human evil is being outside the order of reasonableness ... So human virtue, which makes good both the human person and his works, is in accordance with human nature just in so far as it is in accordance with reason; and vice is contrary to human nature just in so far as it is contrary to the order of reasonableness. (*ST*, I–II, q.71, a.2c)

Similarly, the law-like character of natural law is a function of its rationality: Law, he says, is 'an ordinance of reason for the common good'; it is a 'rule and measure of acts, whereby man is induced to act or is restrained from acting', and 'the rule and measure of human acts is the reason'. (*ST*, I–II, q.90, a.1, 4) He also adds that, to be a law, a rule must be promulgated, because only known rules can be a measure of action. This addition appears to indicate a greater concern for the situation of the 'crowd' than does Cicero's aristocratic dismissal of mere popular beliefs; but in other respects Aquinas' view is faithful to the spirit of the Ciceronian formulation.

Aquinas goes well beyond Cicero, however, by offering an account of the relationship between natural law and eternal (divine) law on the one hand, and ordinary human laws on the other. Throughout, his governing concern is to show that, although these are distinct forms of law, they do not come into conflict. Since Aquinas shares the common medieval view that there is an eternal law, and that it is unchanging, whereas human law is manifestly changeable, his attempt at harmonization may appear doomed from the start. His solution is to divide the natural law into primary and secondary principles, of which the latter, but not the former, are changeable. Thus abstractly stated, this may look more like shifting the problem than solving it, but for our purposes two points are important: in the first place, the solution depends on reviving the Aristotelian conception of natural changes; and in the second, the subsequent success of Thomas's views in later medieval Europe meant that the capacity of the natural law to incorporate change became widely accepted. Despite a widespread modern belief to the contrary, then, natural law was not generally understood to be a fixed, unalterable set of rules which could be simply applied to human conduct or society irrespective of the circumstances.

The flexibility thus gained is not, however, entirely an advantage: it avoids one kind of problem by exacerbating another. A common problem for natural law theories is how to translate abstract claims about the existence of natural, rational solutions to questions of the proper governance of human conduct into usefully specific practical rules or maxims. Increasing the flexibility of the idea of natural law exacerbates this problem because it loosens the connection between the general principles and the actual practical maxims. It prevents a straightforward answer to the question, what does natural law imply in practice?

The problem need not be taken to be too serious, provided one keeps in mind the initial point of natural law theories. It is not uncommon for modern critics of natural law to take it as one among many competing theories intended to explain the foundation and nature of our moral duties. In its classic formulations, however, natural law is understood as the alternative to moral scepticism: the alternative, that is, to the view (variously expressed) that there are no right answers to moral questions – only *accepted* answers, mere conventions. In this sense, 'moral scepticism' refers to both strong theses like nihilism, and also weaker ones, such as relativism. All such positions deny that moral beliefs have any objective or (eternally) real foundations, that there are moral conclusions to be discerned *sub specie aeternitatis*. (They are discussed in Article 35, REALISM, Article 38, SUBJECTIVISM, and Article 39, RELATIVISM.) So, when understood as the denial of moral scepticism, the irreducible abstractness of natural law doctrine is not surprising.

iii A theory of human rights

Early modern natural law, like its ancient and medieval forebears, was also pre-eminently concerned to rebut scepticism. It thus also tended to be very general in its conclusions, and so not always very helpful as a practical guide. However, the modern variant has provided the basis for the secular theory of human rights. The basic elements of such a theory are stated clearly in the writings of Hugo Grotius, so Grotius has come to be known as the father of modern natural law.

In his major work, *On the Law of War and Peace* (published in 1625, in the middle of the Thirty Years' War), Grotius adjudicates in detail on the common sources of dispute that led nations into conflict. His hope was to provide a moral framework for nations that could thereby serve to secure peace. In the Prolegomena and opening chapter of that work, he also gives a brief account of the general principles that should govern any such enquiry. These principles provide the basis of modern natural law.

Given that in international relations, moral scepticism – in the form of the belief that there are no moral rules to govern the conduct of conflict between nations, or in the even stronger view that 'reasons of state' override ordinary moral considerations – is accorded more credence than in the conduct of individual lives, and also has a considerably greater capacity for harm, Grotius's concern to rebut scepticism is readily comprehensible. His approach to the task, however, is shaped by his natural law predecessors. Like Cicero, he addresses the sceptical views of Carneades, the most famous ancient critic of natural law; the answers he offers are also recognizably Ciceronian. Carneades had argued that human laws and morals were not 'founded in nature', but were mere conventions, adopted simply because they were useful. Like Cicero before him, Grotius denies the opposition between human nature and utility, arguing that only by framing laws in accordance with human nature could utility be served. (This general argument – that utility cannot stand alone as a measure of human conduct, because it depends on a prior knowledge of the constitution of human nature – is a standard feature of natural law arguments. It appears to put natural law theory at odds with modern utilitarianism. However, the truth is somewhat more complicated than the initial appearances would suggest: the issue will be discussed below.)

In both ancient and medieval accounts, it was held that the law of nature was, in some sense, implanted in us by God (or the gods). Since it was also held, however, that this law was the law of our nature, and consisted in the capacity of (right) reason, it is clear that belief in God was not an essential part of the doctrine. Aquinas' distinction between natural law and the eternal law of God implicitly recognized this, and the autonomy of the natural law was further affirmed by the rationalistic Spanish Jesuits (particularly Francisco Suarez). Grotius's statement of the point was therefore not new, but it was sufficiently direct to catch the attention of a wider audience: 'What we have been saying [i.e. about the foundation of natural law] would have a degree of validity even if we should concede that which cannot be conceded without the utmost wickedness, that there is no God, or that the affairs of men are of no concern to Him' (Grotius, 1625, Prolegomena, 11).

Grotius was not an atheist, so his insistence on the point is all the more significant. Although a clear specification of how extensive he took the 'degree of validity' to be is lacking, his conservative interpreters took the view that, while our knowledge of the law of nature is not dependent on God, our reasons for obeying it are. This is an instructive view, since many contemporary philosophers could be regarded as having come to a comparable conclusion: there is considerably more agreement amongst contemporary moral philosophers about our ability to discern right and wrong than about the source, or even reality, of a sufficient reason to act accordingly.

Grotius's most distinctive contribution, however, was to translate natural law into a theory of human rights. Again, he was not the first to make the connection, nor did subsequent defenders of natural law all follow him down this path. (Samuel

Pufendorf's influential revision of Grotius, *On the Law of Nature and Nations* (1672), retained a theory of rights, but considerably reduced its importance.) What he provided was a clear statement of the idea that the moral domain could be construed as a body of individual rights, and which therefore came to enjoy considerable fame. *On the Law of War and Peace* says that the law can be understood as 'a body of rights … which has reference to the person. In this sense a right becomes a moral quality of a person, making it possible to have or to do something lawfully' (Grotius, 1625, I. I. iv). Since it makes moral action possible, this 'moral quality' is best understood as a sort of moral power or capacity; and as such it invests the individual with an independent moral significance. Consequently, this account implies a dramatic shift in the common understanding of the relationship between the individual and society. Whereas morality had previously been more commonly understood as the cluster of obligations generated by the patterns of interdependence of human social life, it could subsequently be understood as the result of voluntary transactions between independent moral agents, with the further implication so characteristic of modern rights theories (in particular): the moral significance of the separateness of persons. The success of this conception of social relations can be gauged by considering the predominance of the theories which presuppose it: contract theories of political legitimacy, and comparable consensual moral theories, most notably rational choice theories.

Intriguingly, such right-based theories are weak precisely at the point where Grotius's secularism was perceived to be problematic: they seem unable to provide an adequate notion of obligation. If my moral duties depend on my having freely accepted them, why cannot I renege on them when I find it convenient to do so? Of course, if everybody freely adopted this attitude, the social order could well collapse. But recognizing this commits one only to caution in acting on the principle, not to abandon it entirely. Put crudely, the question remains: why not renege on my obligations when it is advantageous, all things considered – including knowing that I can get away with it? So the two most distinctive features of Grotius's modernized natural law, its secularism and its individualist theory of rights, are vulnerable at the same point, thus making the question of obligation perhaps the most persistent problem for the contemporary moral philosopher.

iv Natural law and its modern rivals

Grotius's remarks on method are also instructive, since they help to illuminate the relationship between modern natural law and its principal competitor, modern utilitarianism. He distinguishes between two kinds of method for establishing what is in accord with the law of nature. The a priori method consists of 'demonstrating the necessary agreement or disagreement of anything with a rational and social nature', whereas the a posteriori method follows the more fallible course of 'concluding, if not with absolute assurance, at least with every probability, that that is according to the law of nature which is believed to be such among all nations, or among all those that are more advanced in civilization'. Although the latter method is fraught with difficulties, Grotius employs it in an attempt to discover what is natural to human life: 'an effect that is universal demands a universal cause; and the cause of such an opinion can hardly be anything else than the feeling which is called the common sense of mankind' (Grotius, 1625, I. I. xii. 1).

Suppose we adopt the a posteriori method, only to find prior expectations frustrated: rather than discovering universal or at least generally acknowledged beliefs, as Grotius clearly expected, we instead find that human diversity is so deeply-rooted that it cannot be comprehended by general principles of human nature, nor explained by invoking regulative beliefs (such as 'level of civilization'). If forced to this conclusion, we would also be encouraged, by the a posteriori method, to adopt another. The irreducible diversity of human beliefs, together with the commitment to accepting patterns of those beliefs as a guide to what is natural to humans, would incline us towards a pluralistic view of human goods (or, in an alternative terminology, towards pluralism about human ends); and, if our pluralism was sufficiently whole-hearted, we would be led to the view that there was no criterion for human goods above and beyond the preferences of actual human individuals.

At this point the idea of natural law is in danger of breaking down completely. The issue is sharply expressed by asking the question: If human diversity is so great, and the realm of human value so fragmented, how is society possible? Two quite different kinds of answer are possible. On the one hand, we could insist on the moral significance of the separateness of persons (and their preferences), a view which, in a situation of such diversity, would allow room for recognizing the moral significance of very little else, at least beyond those procedural principles thought to be necessary to preserve the desired separateness. To follow this path would be to move towards an extreme version of natural rights theory, a version which separated the possession and justification of rights from any overarching human good. (The clearest representative of this sort of position is that of Robert Nozick in *Anarchy, State, and Utopia*.) Alternatively, a method could be proposed for harmonizing conflicting preferences. One attractively simple way of doing this would be to allocate an equal weighting to the preferences of individuals, and then to fit them into an outcome that provided the greatest degree of preference-satisfaction. This would be to adopt preference utilitarianism. (If we were to commit ourselves to a hedonistic psychology of action, we would then have adopted classical utilitarianism. Further discussion of these forms of utilitarianism can be found in this volume in Article 20, UTILITY AND THE GOOD.)

This short sketch helps to pick out the principal difference between natural law and its major modern competitors: whether human diversity can be accommodated within a unified system of distinctively human goods, or not. In answering that such a system is possible, natural law is at odds not only with standard forms of utilitarianism, but also with contemporary theories of rights similar to the one mentioned above. So, although modern natural law helped to establish modern rights theories, it would be a mistake to class all rights theories as species of natural law.

Equally, it would be a mistake to class natural law and utilitarianism as simple opposites. If the divide between the two rests, first and foremost, on the degree of diversity thought to exist between different human beings, it will frequently be more illuminating to think of them as differing more in degree than kind. Natural law theories depend, for their distinctiveness, on the assumption that human values, whatever their surface diversity, display underlying uniformities that can provide content for the idea of natural (or true) human goods. But this is a belief which utilitarianism need not reject. In fact, any form of utilitarianism which seeks to identify a rational order in human preferences, rather than simply accepting the preferences anyone happens to have at any given time, proceeds in a manner no natural law theory need oppose. (The 'objective utilitarianism' espoused in David Brink, *Moral Realism and the Foundations of Ethics*, is a good recent example of such a form of utilitarianism.) However, should the assumption of underlying uniformity fail, simpler, less structured forms of utilitarianism – forms not compatible with natural law – would then be difficult to resist.

This conclusion derives implicit support from the general formulations of the natural lawyers themselves, since they standardly insist that, although the natural law is not founded on utility, it nevertheless is reinforced by, or in harmony with, or the only sure guide to, utility. To dissolve or fragment the natural foundation would thus be to leave nothing but (diverse) utilities, and the practical problem of how to regulate or harmonize them. Of course, as already noted, one possible response to this problem is that of rights theories like Nozick's; but since such theories appear to be very unattractive from the standpoint of overall utility, they have in this respect departed further from the spirit of the natural lawyers than the utilitarians.

These brief remarks do not, of course, provide anything like a complete account of the relationship between natural law theories and utilitarianism. Putting the issue in these terms is useful, however, because it helps to avoid an important possible misunderstanding. It is all too easy to think that natural law and modern utilitarianism are simple opposites, especially when one is confronted by modern debates on contentious issues like abortion and euthanasia. On one central point the two theories are agreed. Natural law is, first and foremost, the affirmation that there is a natural foundation to moral beliefs, that morals can be rationally justified. The modern utilitarian agrees. Although typically a revisionist about traditional moral beliefs, the utilitarian is not a moral sceptic, since to embrace utilitarianism is to accept that there are genuine moral goods. The differences between the two positions will then typically reduce to the extent to which underlying facts of human nature (if such there are) are thought to shape or constrain moral conclusions.

v A theory of human goods

One reason for contrasting natural law theories with other contemporary moral theories in such terms is to show that a natural law theory can be expressed as a theory of (a limited number of) genuine human goods. This is the form in which the most recent sophisticated natural law theory has been presented. John Finnis's *Natural Law and Natural Rights* defends the following set of basic human goods: life, knowledge, play, aesthetic experience, sociability (friendship), practical reasonableness, and 'religion'. The last of these categories is not meant to pick out a specific set of beliefs, but all those beliefs that can be called matters of ultimate concern; questions about the point of human existence.

This is at least a plausible list of candidates for the status of basic human goods, but Finnis's account becomes more controversial when he goes on to specify the basic requirements of practical reasonableness. The most contentious of these requirements is that practical reason requires 'respect for every basic value in every act). It is intended to serve a double (and doubly Catholic) role: not merely to rule out all forms of consequentialist reasoning, but also to enshrine the moral viewpoint of the Roman Catholic Church on a range of contentious issues, such as contraception and masturbation. To include this among the basic requirements of practical reasonableness, and even to rank it alongside such irreproachable requirements as concern for the common good and the unjustifiability of arbitrary preferences amongst values or persons, is to bring the theory into line with Roman Catholic orthodoxy at the expense of its general plausibility. The point is not that Catholic moral orthodoxy could not possibly be correct, but that it cannot be established, to the exclusion of all else, simply by enunciating the most general principles of morality and practical rationality.

Nevertheless, natural law *is* commonly understood to be steadfastly deontological. (See Article 17, CONTEMPORARY DEONTOLOGY, for more on deontological ethics.) To attempt to challenge this feature, in the manner of this essay, may be thought quite implausible, and so it may also be thought that Finnis's requirement of practical reason, for all its excess, is the lesser evil. To this charge it is possible to answer as follows. It has certainly not been argued here that all forms of utilitarianism are compatible with natural law, only that some are – and that these are all of a very sophisticated kind, bearing little resemblance to classical act-utilitarianism. Secondly, since natural law is standardly described as the law of reason, everything will depend on the account of rationality. Unless all forms of instrumental rationality are rigidly excluded (itself an implausible hypothesis if the theory is to be genuinely practical), it is very difficult to see why consequences will not, at least on occasions, play a decisive role in selecting or shaping the principles to be followed. In fact, the limited relativity commonly incorporated in natural law theories – such as the acknowledgment that different societies legitimately follow different rules – may be explained along just such lines. Thirdly, the rigidly deontological public image of natural law owes a good deal to the fact that many of its nominal defenders adhere to a version which is insupportable even from a natural law standpoint. Finnis himself sharply criticizes this version. It depends on what he calls the 'perverted faculty argument', an argument which he says is absurd (Finnis, 1980, p. 48). It is nonetheless a popular view, and is also frequently taken to be the very soul of natural law thinking, so it is necessary to outline its nature and failings.

The type of view in question classes certain actions to be wrong simply because they are unnatural. Although there are different versions of this view, they all depend on the idea that unnaturalness consists in the violation of basic principles of human biological functioning. It is most commonly applied to aspects of sexual behaviour, especially to homosexuality, masturbation, and contraception. As a thesis about sexual behaviour, it can be put as follows. Although sexual activity may *give* pleasure, it is not *for* pleasure: pleasure is part of the means to the end, but the end of sexual activity is human procreation. However, the weakness of this style of thought (at least in its simpler forms) is readily apparent. It amounts to the view that an action is wrong if it is at odds with a relevant biological function, and thus implies that even innocuous behaviours like kissing and writing (or typing) are also wrong. Mouths are designed for eating and (perhaps) talking, not kissing; and although the human hand is possibly the most adaptable mechanism in nature, nevertheless writing and typing are no part of its biological function. If this seems a little too quick, it might be thought necessary to distinguish between those non-functional activities which *frustrate* biological functions, and those which do not: kissing does not prevent eating, whereas homosexuality does prevent procreation. But this strategy will not work, since it is only *exclusive* homosexuality, not individual homosexual acts, which prevents procreation, but the immorality is alleged to pertain to the individual acts.

Why does this view, which has seemed to many to be morally compelling, go so wildly astray? The basic problem is its totally inadequate conception of the nature of human beings. The only role it can allow for human rationality is the pinched and narrow role of discovering, and then conforming to, biological functions. This is ironic, since from the beginning the theory of natural law emphasized that its foundation lay in the rational nature of the human being. (There are, of course, sophisticated versions of this view which appeal to a more adequate conception of rationality. However, even these versions appear to be infected by an excessive concern with biological functions, since it is difficult to see how else the conclusions which distinguish these views can be maintained. For this reason it is also hard not to suspect that, despite his objections to the argument, Finnis himself is not entirely immune from its effect.)

One final point: it is sometimes observed that words like 'nature', 'natural', etc., are dangerously ambiguous, since they may have either descriptive or normative meanings, and that the basic failing of natural law is its trade in this ambiguity. The ambiguity is real enough, and certainly it is true that many attempts at natural law theorizing are manifestly guilty. Nevertheless the conclusion is not justified, even though it also cannot be shown to be false. The objection depends on uncritically accepting that a moral position must depend on distinctively moral (rather than, most importantly, prudent) reasons. The most general formulations of natural law, however, are built on precisely the opposite view. They assume that the task of a theory of right human conduct is to know how to live successfully (in the broadest sense). The essential justificatory argument for living in accordance with (one's) nature, reiterated in countless defences of natural law, is that to fail to do so is self-destructive.

This is a large claim, and may seem beyond all hope of justification. There is little doubt that the single most powerful historic support for it has been the Christian doctrine of rewards and punishments in the next life. a doctrine which is able to cast even the most self-denying of modes of life as the very soul of prudence. However, the view does not entirely stand or fall with that doctrine. For example, the belief that one has a determinate nature makes the injunction to live in accordance with it imperative, at least if that nature can be specified in some detail. The problem is thus not merely whether one has a nature of this kind, but whether it can be known in sufficient detail. The shortcoming of natural law theory is therefore its typical failure to go beyond the insistence that human nature is rational nature. If the essential justificatory argument simply defines irrationality as self-destructiveness, and without further specifying the latter, then justification has been bought at the cost of content. If so, there is no sound basis for many of the standard claims of the classical natural lawyers. To take just one example: it cannot be maintained that there is an intimate connection between the requirements of nature and the general observance of established norms of behaviour.

vi Conclusion

Natural law is a very general moral outlook developed, in the first place, to rebut moral scepticism. Its basic premise is that human moral beliefs have a rational foundation, in the form of general principles of right conduct that reflect a determinate and rational human nature. Its weakness has been the difficulty of showing how these most general claims can be translated into reliable and specific practical maxims. In the environment of contemporary ethical theories, natural law differs from its competitors by resisting the tendency to accept that human flourishing admits of an immense variety of forms, achievable by equally diverse ways of living. It need feel no embarrassment about this, but its present task is to provide a plausible account of basic human goods and their implications, and thereby to provide a challenge to the easy pluralism of so much contemporary moral thought.

References

i Historical works

Aquinas, Thomas: *Summa Theologiae.*
Aristotle: *Physics.*
——: *Nicomachean Ethics.*
——: *Politics.*
Cicero: *De Legibus* and *De Re Publica,* Loeb Classical Library (London: Heinemann, 1928).
Grotius, H.: *De Jure Belli ac Pacis* (1625); trans. as *On The Law of War and Peace* (New York: Wildy and Sons, 1964).
Plato: *Gorgias.*
——: *Protagoras.*
——: *The Republic.*

Plato: *The Laws.*

Pufendorf, S.: *De Jure Naturae et Gentium* (1672); trans. as *On the Law of Nature and Nations* (New York: Wildy and Sons, 1964).

Sophocles: *Antigone.*

Suarez, F.: *De Legibus ac Deo Legislatore*, trans. as *Of Laws and God the Lawgiver* (New York: Wildy and Sons, 1964).

ii Contemporary Thomistic work

Finnis, J.: *Natural Law and Natural Rights* (Oxford: Oxford University Press, 1980).

iii Others

Brink, D. O.: *Moral Realism and the Foundations of Ethics* (Cambridge: Cambridge University Press, 1989).

Nozick, R.: *Anarchy, State and Utopia* (Oxford: Basil Blackwell, 1974).

Further reading

i General works

d'Entreves, A. P.: *Natural Law* (London: Hutchinson, 1967).

Hegel, G. W. F.: *Natural Law* (Philadelphia: University of Pennsylvania Press, 1975).

Hittinger, R.: *A Critique of the New Natural Law Theory* (Notre Dame, Ind.: University of Notre Dame Press, 1984).

Locke, J.: *Essays on the Law of Nature* (1690); (Oxford: Oxford University Press, 1954).

Ritchie, D. G.: *Natural Rights* (London: Allen and Unwin, 1894).

Tuck, R.: *Natural Rights Theories* (Cambridge: Cambridge University Press, 1979).

Weinreb, L.: *Natural Law and Justice* (Cambridge, Mass.: Harvard University Press, 1987).

ii Nature and human nature in ancient philosophy

Inwood, B.: *Ethics and Human Action in Early Stoicism* (Oxford: Oxford University Press, 1985).

Lear, J.: *Aristotle: The Desire to Understand* (Cambridge: Cambridge University Press, 1988).

Waterlow, S.: *Nature, Change, and Agency in Aristotle's Physics* (Oxford: Oxford University Press, 1982).

iii Two articles on Aquinas and natural law

Bourke, V. J.: 'Is Thomas Aquinas a natural law ethicist?' *Monist*, 58 (1974), 52–66.

Ross, J. F.: 'Justice is reasonableness: Aquinas on human law and morality', *Monist*, 58 (1974), 86–103.

iv Further contemporary Thomistic works

Finnis, J.: *Fundamentals of Ethics* (Oxford: Oxford University Press, 1983).

Finnis, J., Boyle, J. and Grisez, G.: *Nuclear Deterrence, Morality and Realism* (Oxford: Oxford University Press, 1987).

Grisez, G.: *Life and Death with Liberty and Justice* (Notre Dame: University of Notre Dame Press, 1979).

——: *The Way of the Lord Jesus.* Vol. 1, *Christian Moral Principles* (New York: Franciscan Herald Press, 1983).

14

Kantian ethics

ONORA O'NEILL

i Introduction

IMMANUEL KANT (1724–1804) was one of the most important European philosophers since antiquity; many would say simply that he is the most important. He lived a notoriously uneventful life in the remote Prussian town of Königsberg (now Kaliningrad in the USSR), and published an array of significant works in his later years. His writings on ethics are marked by an unswerving commitment to human freedom, to the dignity of man, and to the view that moral obligation derives neither from God, nor from human authorities and communities, nor from the preferences or desires of human agents, but from reason.

His writings are difficult and systematic; to understand them it helps to keep the following three things separate. First, there is Kant's ethics, contained in his writings of the 1780s and 1790s. Secondly, there is 'Kant's ethics', a (mainly unfavourable) account of Kant's ethics developed by his early and influential critics and still often attributed to Kant. This position has an independent life in current debates. Thirdly, there is 'Kantian ethics', a much broader term which covers both Kant's ethics and 'Kant's ethics' and is also used as a (mainly admiring) label for a range of contemporary ethical positions which claim descent from Kant's ethics, but which diverge from Kant in many ways.

ii Kant's ethics: the critical background

Kant's ethics is to be found in his *Groundwork of the Metaphysic of Morals* (1785), *Critique of Practical Reason* (1787), *The Metaphysics of Morals* (1797), (whose two parts, *The Metaphysical Elements of Justice* and *The Doctrine of Virtue* are often published separately), as well as in his *Religion within the Limits of Reason Alone* (1793) and a large number of essays on political, historical and religious themes. However, the fundamental moves that determine the shape of this work are most fully discussed in Kant's masterpiece, *The Critique of Pure Reason* (1781), and an account of his ethics has to be set in the wider context of the 'critical philosophy' which he develops there.

This philosophy is in the first place critical in a negative sense. Kant argues against most of the metaphysical claims of his rationalist predecessors, and in particular against their supposed proofs of the existence of God. On his account our thinking has to be undertaken from a human standpoint, and we can vindicate no claims about any transcendent reality to which we have no access. The knowledge claims that we can vindicate must therefore be about a reality that meets the condition of being experienceable by us. Hence an inquiry into the structure of our cognitive capacities yields a guide to the aspects of that empirical reality which we can know without referring to particular experiences. Kant argues that we can know a priori that we inhabit a natural world of spatially and temporally extended objects that are causally connected.

Kant is distinctive for insisting that this causal order and our claims to knowledge are restricted to the natural world, but that we have no reason to think that the knowable natural world is all there is. On the contrary, we have and cannot do without a conception of ourselves as agents and as moral beings which makes sense only on the assumption that we have free will. Kant argues that free will and natural causality are compatible, provided that human freedom – the capacity to act autonomously – is not taken to be an aspect of the natural world. Causality and freedom apply in separate domains; knowledge is restricted to the former and morality to the latter. Kant's resolution of the problem of freedom and determinism is the most controversial and fundamental feature of his moral philosophy, and the one that creates the greatest difference between his thought and that of nearly all twentieth-century writing on ethics, including most that is classified as 'Kantian ethics'.

The central question around which Kant arranges his discussion of ethics is 'What ought I do?'. He tries to identify the maxims, or fundamental principles of action, that we ought to adopt. His answer is developed without reference to any supposedly objective account of the good for man, such as those proposed by the perfectionist positions that we associate with Plato, Aristotle and much Christian ethics. Nor does he base his position on claims about whatever subjective conceptions of the good, desires, preferences, or commonly shared moral beliefs we may happen to have, in the way that utilitarians and communitarians do. As in his metaphysics, so in his ethics, he neither introduces claims about a moral reality that transcends our experience nor assigns moral weight to actual beliefs. He repudiates both the realist and theological framework within which natural law theory and accounts of the virtues had been developed, and the appeal to a contingent consensus of feeling or belief on which many eighteenth (and twentieth!) century writers rely.

iii   Kant's ethics: universal law and the construction of duty

Kant's central move is to construct the principles of ethics according to rational procedures. Although he begins his *Groundwork* (which is short, famous and difficult) by identifying a *good will* as the only unconditional good, he denies that the principles of good willing can be fixed by reference to an objective good or *telos* at which they aim. Rather than assuming a determinate account of the good, and using this as the basis for determing what we ought to do, he uses an account of the principles of ethics to determine what it is to have a good will. He asks only one rather minimal question: what maxims or fundamental principles could be adopted by a plurality of agents without assuming *anything* specific about the agents' desires or their social relations? Principles that cannot serve for a plurality of agents are to be rejected: the thought is that nothing could be a moral principle which cannot be a principle for all. Morality begins with the rejection of non-universalizable principles. This idea is formulated as a demand, which Kant calls 'the Categorical Imperative', or more generally the Moral Law. In its best known version it runs: 'Act only on the maxim through which you can at the same time will that it be a universal law'. This is the keystone of Kant's ethics, and is used to classify the maxims agents may adopt.

An example of the use of the Categorical Imperative would be this: an agent who adopts a maxim of promising falsely could not 'will it as a universal law'. For if she were (hypothetically) to do so she would be committed to the predictable result that trust would break down so that she could not act on her initial maxim of promising falsely. This thought experiment reveals that a maxim of false promising is not universalizable, hence cannot be included among the shared principles of any plurality of beings. The maxim of rejecting false promising is morally required; the maxim of promising falsely morally forbidden. It is important to note that Kant does not think false promising wrong because of its presumed unpleasant effects (as utilitarians would) but because it cannot be willed as a universal principle.

The rejection of a maxim of false promising, or of any other non-universalizable maxim, is compatible with a wide variety of courses of action. Kant distinguishes two modes of ethical assessment. In the first place we might evaluate the maxims that agents adopt. If we could discern these we would be able to pick out those who reject non-universalizable principles (so have morally worthy principles) and those who adopt non-universalizable principles, (so have morally unworthy principles). Kant speaks of those who hold morally worthy principles as acting 'out of duty'. However, Kant also holds that we do not have certain knowledge either of our own or of others' maxims. We normally infer agents' maxims or underlying principles from the pattern of their action, yet no pattern will pick out a unique maxim. For example, the activity of the genuinely honest shopkeeper may not differ from that of the reluctantly honest shopkeeper, who deals fairly only out of desire for a good business reputation and would cheat if a safe opportunity arose. Hence for ordinary purposes we can often do no more than concern ourselves with outward conformity to maxims of duty, rather than with claims that an act was done out of such a maxim. Kant speaks of action that would have to be done by anyone who had a morally worthy maxim as action 'in accordance with duty'. Such action is obligatory and its omission forbidden. Evidently, many acts accord with duty although they were not done out of maxims of duty. However, even this notion of outward duty has been defined by reference to being indispensable in a given situation for one who holds underlying principles of acting out of duty. This is in sharp contrast with contemporary accounts of duty which identify it with patterns of outward action. Kant's question 'What ought I do?' therefore receives a double answer. I ought at best to base my life and action on the rejection of non-universalizable maxims, and so lead a morally worthy life whose acts are done out of duty; but even if I fail to do this I ought at least to make sure to do any acts that would be indispensable if I had such a morally worthy maxim.

Kant's more detailed account of duty introduces (versions of) certain traditional distinctions. He contrasts duties to self and others, and under each of these distinguishes perfect and imperfect duties. *Perfect* duties are complete, in the sense that they hold for all agents in all their actions with all possible others. In addition to refraining from false promising, refraining from coercion and violence are examples of principles of perfect duties to others; they are obligations which can be met for all others, (to which negative liberty rights may correspond). Kant derives principles of *imperfect* obligation by introducing one further assumption: he takes it that we not only have to deal with a plurality of rational agents who share a world, but that these agents are not self-sufficient, hence are mutually vulnerable. Such agents, he argues, could not rationally will that a principle of refusing to help others or of neglecting to develop one's own potential be universally adopted: since they know that they are not self-sufficient, they know that to will such a world would be (irrationally) to will away indispensable means to at least some of their own ends. The principles of not neglecting to help those in need or to develop one's own potential are, however, less complete (hence imperfect) principles of obligation. For we cannot help all others in all needed ways, nor can we develop all possible talents in ourselves. Hence these obligations are necessarily selective as well as indeterminate. They lack counterpart rights and are the basis for imperfect duties. The implications of this account of duties are most fully developed in the *Metaphysics of Morals*, whose first part deals with the principles of justice that are matters of perfect obligation and whose second part deals with the principles of virtue that are matters of imperfect obligation.

iv Kant's ethics: respect for persons

Kant develops his basic lines of thought along a number of parallel (he claims equivalent) tracks. The Categorical Imperative is formulated in a number of strikingly different versions. The formulation discussed above is known as 'The Formula of Universal Law', and is said to be the 'strictest'. The one that has had the greatest cultural impact is the so-called 'Formula of the End in Itself', which demands that we treat 'humanity in your own person or in the person of any other never simply as a means but always at the same time as an end'. This second-order principle is once again a constraint on the maxims we adopt; it is a highly articulated version of a demand for respect for persons. Instead of demanding that we check that all could adopt the same maxims, it demands less directly that we act in ways that respect, so leave intact, others' capacities to act (and so, in effect, leave them able to act on the maxims we ourselves adopt). The Formula of the End in Itself is also used to distinguish two sorts of moral failure. To use another is to treat him or her as a thing or tool and not as an agent. On Kant's account to use another is not merely a matter of doing something the other does not actually want or consent to, but of doing something to which the other *cannot* consent. For example, deceivers make it *impossible* for their victims to consent to the deceiver's project. Unlike most other appeals to consent as a criterion of legitimate (or just) action, Kant (in keeping with his basic philosophical position) appeals neither to the hypothetical consent of ideally rational beings, nor to the historically contingent consent of actual others. He asks what is needed to make it possible for others either to dissent or consent. This does not mean that actual dissent may be coercively overridden on the grounds that consent has at least been made possible – for the very act of overriding actual dissent will itself coerce, hence make consent impossible. Kant's contention is that the principles we must adopt if we are not to use others will be the very principles of justice that were identified by considering which principles are universalizable for rational beings.

Correspondingly, Kant interprets the moral failure of not treating others as 'ends' as an alternative basis for an account of the virtues. To treat others who are specifically human in their finitude – hence vulnerable and needy – as 'ends' requires that we support one another's (fragile) capacities to act, to adopt maxims and to pursue their particular ends. Hence it requires at least some support for others' projects and purposes. Kant holds that this will require at least a limited beneficence. Although he does not establish an unrestricted obligation of beneficence, such as utilitarians hold to, he does argue for an obligation to reject a policy of refusing needed help. He also argues that systematic failure to develop one's own potential amounts to disrespect for humanity and its capacities for rational agency 'in one's own person'. Failure to treat others or oneself as ends is once again seen as a failure of virtue or imperfect obligation. Imperfect obligations cannot prescribe universal performance: we can neither help all in need, nor develop all possible talents. We can, however, refuse to make indifference of either sort basic to our lives – and may find that rejecting principled indifference demands a lot. Even a commitment of this nature, taken seriously, will demand much. If we honour it, we have on Kant's account shown respect for persons and specifically for human dignity.

The remaining formulations of the Categorical Imperative bring together the perspectives of one who seeks to act on principles that all others could share, and one who seeks to act on principles that respect all others' capacities to act. Kant makes use of traditional Christian rhetoric and of Rousseau's conception of the social contract to formulate the image of a 'Kingdom of Ends' where each is simultaneously legislator and bound by law, where each is autonomous (literally: self-legislating) on condition that what is legislated is respect for others' like status as 'legislators'. For Kant, as for Rousseau, to be autonomous is no mere matter of wilfulness or independence from others or from social conventions; it is to have the mode of self-control that takes account of others' like moral status. To be Kantianly autonomous is to act morally.

v Kant's ethics: the problems of freedom, religion and history

This basic structure of thought is developed in many different directions. Kant presents arguments to suggest why we should think of the Categorical Imperative as a principle of reason that is binding on us. He explores what is involved in moving from a principle to its concrete application to actual situations. He discusses the relationship between moral principles and our actual desires and inclinations. He develops the political implications of the Categorical Imperative, which include a republican constitution and respect for freedom, especially of religion and speech. He sketches a still influential programme for seeking international peace. He explores how his system of moral thought is connected to traditional religious claims. Many objections of principle and of detail have been raised. Some of the less fundamental objections can be conveniently discussed under the heading of 'Kant's ethics'. However, the most central objection demands independent discussion.

This objection is that Kant's basic framework is incoherent. His account of human knowledge leads to a conception of human beings as parts of nature, whose desires, inclinations and actions are susceptible of ordinary causal explanation. Yet his account of human freedom demands that we view human agents as capable of self-determination, and specifically of determination in accordance with the principles of duty. Kant is apparently driven to a dual view of man: we are both *phenomenal* (natural, causally determined) beings and *noumenal* (non-natural, self-determining) beings. Many of Kant's critics have held that this dual-aspect view of human beings is ultimately incoherent.

In the *Critique of Practical Reason* Kant tackles the difficulty by proposing that provided we accept certain 'postulates' we can make sense of the idea of beings who are part both of the natural and of the moral order. The idea is that if we postulate a benevolent God, then the moral virtue at which free agents aim can be compatible with, indeed proportioned to, the happiness at which natural beings aim. Kant speaks of such perfect co-ordination of moral virtue and happiness as the highest good. Producing the highest good will take a long time: so we have to postulate immortal souls as well as divine providence. This picture has been lampooned time and again. Heine depicted Kant as a bold revolutionary who killed deism: then timidly conceded that practical reason could 'prove' God after all. Nietzsche less kindly likens him to a fox who escapes – then slinks back into the cage of theism.

In later writings Kant dropped both the idea of a guaranteed co-ordination of virtue and rewarding happiness (he thought this might undermine true virtue) and the demand that we postulate immortality, understood as everlasting life (see *The End of All Things*). He offers a variety of historized versions of the thought that we can make sense of our status as free beings who are part of nature only if we adopt certain postulates. For example, he suggests that we must at least *hope* for the possibility of moral improvement in human history, and so for a *this-worldly* co-ordination of the moral and natural ends of mankind. The various historicized accounts he offers of the postulates of practical reason are aspects and precursors of a this-worldly account of human destiny that we associate with the revolutionary tradition, and specially with Marx. However, Kant did not renounce a religious interpretation of claims about human origins and destiny. In his late work *Religion within the Limits of Reasons Alone* he depicts Christian scriptures as a temporal narrative which can be understood as a 'symbol of morality'. The interpretation of this work, which got Kant into trouble with the Prussian censors, presents many problems. However, it is at least clear that he does not reintroduce theological claims to serve as a *foundation* for morality, but rather uses his moral theory as a lens for reading scripture.

If Kant did not go back on his original repudiation of theological foundations, an understanding of the connection he sees between nature and morality remains problematic. One way of understanding it may be by relying on the idea, which he uses in *Groundwork*, that nature and freedom do not belong in two independent worlds, or metaphysical realities, but rather constitute two 'standpoints'. We must see ourselves both as parts of the natural world and as free agents. We cannot without incoherence do without either of these standpoints, although we cannot integrate them, and can do no more than understand *that* thay are compatible. On such a reading, we can have no insight into the 'mechanics' of human freedom, but can understand that without freedom in the activity of cognition, which lies behind our very claims to know, a causally ordered world would be unknown to us. Hence it is impossible for us to think freedom away. For practical purposes this may be enough: for these we do not need to *prove* human freedom. However, we are left trying to conceptualize the hiatus between the natural order and human freedom, and must also commit ourselves to some version of the 'postulates' or 'hopes' that connect the two. At the very least a commitment to acting morally in the world depends on assuming (postulating, hoping) that the natural order is not wholly incompatible with moral intentions.

vi 'Kant's ethics'

Many other criticisms of Kant's ethics recur so often that they have acquired an independent life as elements of 'Kant's ethics'. Some hold that these criticisms do not apply to Kant's ethics, others that they are decisive reasons for rejecting Kant's position.

(1) *Formalism.* The commonest charge against Kant's ethics is the allegation that the Categorical Imperative is empty, trivial or purely formal and identifies no principles of duty. The charge has been widely made by Hegel, by J. S. Mill and in many contemporary works. On Kant's own view the demand for universalizable maxims is a demand that our fundamental principles be fit for adoption by all. This condition can seem pointless: for cannot *any* well-formed act-description be prescribed by a universal principle? Are principles such as 'steal when you can' or 'kill when it isn't risky' universalizable? This *reductio ad absurdum* of universalizability is achieved by replacing Kant's Categorical Imperative with a different principle. The Formula of Universal Law demands not just that we formulate a universal principle incorporating some act-description that applies to a given act. It demands that an agent's maxim, or fundamental principle, be such that the

agent can 'will it as universal law'. The test requires commitment to the normal, predictable consequences of principles to which the agent is committed and to normal standards of instrumental rationality. When maxims are non-universalizable this is typically because commitment to the consequences of their universal adoption would be incompatible with commitment to the means of acting on them (e.g. we cannot be committed both to the results of universal false promising, and to preserving the means to promising, hence to false promising).

Kant's account of universalizability differs from related principles (universal prescriptivism, Golden Rules) in two major respects. First, it does not refer to what is desired or preferred, not even to what it is desired or preferred should be universally done. Second, it is a procedure only for picking out the maxims that must be rejected if the fundamental principles of a life or a society are to be universalizable. Non-universalizable principles are identified in order to discover the side constraints on the more specific principles agents may adopt. These side constraints enable us to identify more specific but still indeterminate principles of obligation. (For a different account of universalizability, see Article 40, UNIVERSAL PRESCRIPTIVISM.)

(2) *Rigorism.* This is the claim that Kant's ethics, far from being empty and formalistic, leads to rigidly insensitive rules, and so cannot take account of differences between cases. However, universal principles need not mandate uniform treatment; indeed they may mandate differentiated treatment. Principles such as 'taxation should be proportionate to ability to pay' or 'the punishment must fit the crime' are universal in scope but demand differentiated treatment. Even principles that do not specifically mandate differentiated treatment will be indeterminate, so leave room for differentiated application.

(3) *Abstraction.* Those who concede that Kant's arguments identify some principles of duty, but do not impose rigid uniformity, often advance a further version of the formalism charge. They will say that Kant identifies ethical principles, but that these principles are 'too abstract' to guide action, hence his theory is not action-guiding. Kant's principles of duty certainly are abstract, and he does not provide a detailed set of instructions for following them. There is no moral algorithm of the sort utilitarianism might provide if we had sufficiently full information about all options. Kant emphasizes that the application of principles to cases involves judgement and deliberation. He also maintains that principles are and must be abstract: they are side-constraints (not algorithms) and can only guide (not make) decisions. The moral life is a matter of finding ways of acting that meet all obligations and violate no moral prohibitions. There is no automatic procedure for identifying such actions, or all such actions. However, for moral practice we begin by making sure that the specific acts we have in mind are not incompatible with acts on maxims of duty.

(4) *Conflicting grounds of obligation.* This criticism points out that Kant's ethics identifies a set of principles which may come into conflict. The demands of fidelity

and of helpfulness, for example, may clash. This criticism is true of Kant's ethics, as for any ethic of principles. Since 'trade-offs' between differing obligations are not part of the theory, there is no routine procedure for dealing with conflicts. On the other hand, since the theory is only a set of side constraints on action, the central demand is to find some action that falls within all constraints. Only when no such action can be found does the problem of multiple grounds of obligation arise. Kant has nothing very illuminating to say about these cases; the charge made by advocates of virtue ethics (e.g. Bernard Williams, Martha Nussbaum), that he does not say enough about the regret that may be appropriate when some moral commitment has unavoidably to be violated or neglected, is apposite.

(5) *Place of the inclinations.* A group of serious criticisms of Kant's moral psychology occurs throughout the secondary literature. In particular it is said that Kant requires that we act 'out of the motive of duty', hence not out of inclination, and so is driven to the claim that action which we enjoy cannot be morally worthy. This grim interpretation, perhaps first suggested by Schiller, involves a tangle of difficult issues. By acting 'out of the motive of duty', Kant means only that we act on a maxim of duty and so experience a feeling of 'reverence for the law'. This reverence is a *response* to and not the *source* of moral worth. It is compatible with action being in line with our natural inclinations and so enjoyed. On one view the apparent conflict between duty and inclination is only epistemological; we can know for sure that we act out of duty only if inclination is lacking. On other views, the issue runs deeper, and leads to a more serious charge that Kant cannot account for wrongdoing.

(6) *No account of wrongdoing.* This charge is that Kant can allow only for free action which is fully autonomous – i.e. done on a principle that meets the constraint that all others can do likewise – and for action which reflects only natural desires and inclinations. Hence he cannot allow for free, imputable but wrong action. Clearly Kant thinks he can give an account of wrong doing, for he frequently gives examples of imputable wrongdoing. This charge probably reflects a failure to keep separate the claim that free agents must be capable of acting autonomously (in the distinctive Rousseauian or Kantian sense which links autonomy with morality) with the claim that free agents always act autonomously. Imputability requires the capacity to act autonomously but this capacity may not always be exercised. Wrongful acts are indeed not autonomous, but they are chosen rather than inflicted mechanically by our desires or inclinations.

vii Kantian ethics

Kant's ethics and the image of his ethics which often replaces it in modern debates do not exhaust Kantian ethics. This term is now often used to cover any of a range of quasi-Kantian positions or commitments in ethics. Sometimes the usage is very broad. Certain writers will talk of Kantian ethics when they have in mind theories of rights, or more generally action-based rather than result-based moral thinking, or any position that treats the right as prior to the good. In these cases the points of resemblance to Kant's ethics are fairly general – for example, concern with universal principles and respect for persons, or more specifically for human rights. In other cases a more structural resemblance may be indicated – for example, a commitment to a single non-utilitarian supreme moral principle, or to the view that ethics is based on reason. The specific understanding of Kantian ethics varies very much from context to context.

The most definite Kantian programme in ethics recently has been that of John Rawls, who has labelled one stage in the development of his theory 'Kantian constructivism'. Many features of Rawls's work are clearly Kantian, above all his conception of ethical principles as determined by constraints on principles chosen by rational agents. However, Rawls's constructivism assumes a quite different account of rationality from Kant's. Rawls identifies the principles that *would* be chosen by instrumentally rational beings to whom he ascribes certain sparsely specified ends – not the principles that *could* consistently be chosen regardless of particular ends. This produces far-ranging differences between Rawls's work, even at its most Kantian, and Kant's ethics. Others who use the label 'Kantian' in ethics are even more loosely related to Kant – for example, many of them offer no account of the virtues, or even deny that an account is possible; many treat rights rather than obligations as fundamental; nearly all rely on a preference-based theory of action and an instrumental account of rationality, all of which are incompatible with Kant's ethics.

viii   The Kantian legacy

Kant's ethics remains the paradigmatic and most influential attempt to vindicate universal moral principles without reference to preferences or to a theological framework. The hope of identifying universal principles, which is so apparent in discussions of justice and in the human rights movement, is constantly challenged by communitarian and historicist insistence that we cannot appeal beyond the discourse and traditions of particular societies, and by utilitarian insistence that principles derive from preferences. For those who find neither of these routes compelling, the neo-Kantian slogan 'Back to Kant' remains a challenge which they must explore or refute.

References

Works by Kant

Groundwork of the Metaphysic of Morals; trans. H. J. Paton, as *The Moral Law* (London: Hutchinson, 1953).

Critique of Practical Reason; trans. L. W. Beck (Indianapolis: Bobbs-Merrill, 1977).

Religion Within the Limits of Reason Alone; trans. T. M. Greene, and H. H. Hudson (New York: Harper and Row, 1960).

The Metaphysic of Morals. There is no English translation of the entire work. The first part appears as *The Metaphysical Elements of Justice,* trans. J. Ladd (Indianapolis: Bobbs-Merrill, 1965), and the second as *The Doctrine of Virtue,* trans. M. Gregor (New York: Harper and Row, 1964). Both translations contain the introduction to the *Metaphysic of Morals.*

Also two anthologies of his shorter writings – H. Reiss, ed.: *Kant's Political Writings* (Cambridge: Cambridge University Press, 1970) and L. W. Beck, ed.: *On History,* Library of Liberal Arts (Indianapolis: Bobbs-Merrill, 1963).

Other references

Nussbaum, M.: *The Fragility of Goodness: Luck and Ethics in Greek Tragedy and Philosophy* (Cambridge: Cambridge University Press, 1986).

Rawls, J.: *A Theory of Justice* (Cambridge, Mass.: Harvard University Press, 1971).

——: 'Kantian constructivism and moral theory', *Journal of Philosophy,* LXXVII (1980), 515–72.

Williams, B.: *Ethics and the Limits of Philosophy* (London: Fontana, 1985).

Further reading

Works on Kant's ethics

Beck, L. W.: *A Commentary on Kant's Critique of Practical Reason* (Chicago: University of Chicago Press, 1960).

H. Paton, *The Categorical Imperative* (London: Hutchinson & Co., 1947).

O'Neill, O.: *Constructions of Reason: Explorations of Kant's Practical Philosophy* (Cambridge: Cambridge University Press, 1989).

For discussion of 'Kant's ethics'

MacIntyre, A.: *After Virtue* (London: Duckworth, 1981).

For recent Kantian ethics

Nozick, R.: *Anarchy, State and Utopia* (Oxford: Blackwell, 1974).

Gewirth, A.: *Human Rights: Essays on Justifications and Applications* (Chicago: University of Chicago Press, 1982).

15

The social contract tradition

WILL KYMLICKA

EVERY moral theory must answer two questions: what are the demands that morality makes of us, and why should we feel obliged to obey those demands? Much of the attractiveness of the social contract approach to ethics is that it seems to provide simple and related answers to these two questions: the demands of morality are fixed by the agreements that humans make to regulate their social interaction, and we should obey these demands because we have agreed to them. What could be simpler?

The appearance of simplicity is deceptive, however, for different theories give widely divergent accounts of the content and normative force of the supposed 'agreement'. Contractarian morality requires that we 'join others in acting in ways that each, together with others, can reasonably and freely subscribe to as a common moral standard' (Diggs, 1982, p. 104). But unless we put limits on what counts as a reasonable and free agreement, then almost any theory can be described as contractarian, since almost any theory claims to provide a common moral standard that people can reasonably and freely subscribe to. To argue for a theory is, in part, to attempt to show that its demands are reasonable, and that people should freely accept them. If we are to put boundaries on contractarian ethics, we need to put limits on the kinds of reasons that can be appealed to in making agreements, and the kinds of conditions under which they are made. But which sort of reasons and conditions make a moral theory a distinctively contractarian theory? I will approach that question historically, to see where and why a distinctive contractarian tradition arose.

i The historical background

While contractarian thinking in ethics goes back to the ancient Greeks, the approach first achieved prominence during the Enlightenment. In the teleological and religious systems which dominated pre-Enlightenment thought, moral obligations were thought to derive from a larger natural or divine order. Each person has a naturally or divinely-ordained place or function in the world, from which their duties follow. As the Enlightenment called into question the various elements of these older ethical systems, philosophers turned to social contract theories to fill the vacuum. One of the first elements to be undermined was the divine-right-of-kings doctrine. Even those who accepted the institution of kingship could no longer accept that the particular person who occupied the throne did so by divine grant. Monarchs were ordinary men and women who happened to inherit or usurp an extraordinary position. But how is it legitimate that some people rule over others, when all are by nature equals?

The first social contract theories were concerned with this limited question – what explains our political obligation to these ordinary men and women? And the heart of their answer is this: while there is no natural or divine duty to obey particular rulers, we can put ourselves under such a duty by promising to obey, for that brings into play our personal obligation to keep promises (a personal obligation which was simply taken for granted as part of natural law or Christian duty).

Why would people agree to be governed? Since political relations lack any natural basis, the natural state of humanity is pre-political. By nature, all people are free and equal, in that there is no higher authority with the power to command their obedience, or the responsibility of protecting their interests. However, this 'state of nature' breeds insecurity – without any government, social norms go unenforced, and transgressors are not fairly punished. People would therefore agree to institute government, and cede certain powers to it, if the governors agreed to use these powers to ensure security. In this way, some people could legitimately come to govern others, despite their natural equality, for the rulers held their power *in trust*, to protect the interests of the ruled. For classical contract theorists, then, the question of political obligation is answered by determining what kind of contract individuals in the state of nature would agree to concerning the establishment of political authority. Once we know the terms of that contract, we know what the government is obliged to do, and what citizens are obliged to obey. But while contract theorists defended political obligation in terms of contractual promises, this approach was embedded within a larger non-contractarian moral theory. The idea of a social contract was used to constrain political rulers, but the content and justificatory force of this contract rests on a pre-existing theory of natural rights and duties, of which the duty to keep promises was just one element. (See Article 13, NATURAL LAW.)

This sort of political contractarianism died out during the nineteenth century. Its death was inevitable, for it suffers from two overwhelming flaws. Firstly, there never was such a contract, and without an actual contract, neither citizens nor government are bound by promises. As a result, all existing governments, however good and just, lack legitimacy according to social contract theory. But this is implausible. The legitimacy of government is determined (we normally think) by the justice of its actions, not by the contractual nature of its historical origins. Contract theorists wanted their theory to endorse just governments (just rulers are the ones that keep their contractual promises), but the insistence on an actual contract strikes down just and unjust governments alike. It may be that people *would have* signed a contract to obey just rulers, if asked, and if so then we can speak of a 'hypothetical contract' between rulers and the ruled. But a hypothetical promise is no promise at all, for no-one has undertaken an obligation. I am obliged to keep my promises, not my hypothetical promises. Thus the idea of a social contract seems either historically absurd, if it is intended to identify actual promises, or morally insignificant, if it is intended to point out purely hypothetical promises. And even if the original creation of government was based on agreement, what serves to bind future generations who are simply born under a government and automatically subjected to its laws?

Secondly, contract theorists say we should obey government because we should keep our word, but, as Hume noted, they 'find [themselves] embarrassed when it is asked, *Why we are bound to keep our word?*' (Barker, 1960, p. 229). The very considerations which put people in doubt about the naturalness of their political obligation to obey rulers soon put them in doubt about the naturalness of their personal obligation to keep promises. Social contract theory, therefore, was a kind of stop-gap response to the dissolution of pre-Enlightenment ethics – it simply replaced one questionable natural duty with another.

Despite these flaws, classical contract theory contained resources which have attracted modern-day moral theorists. Indeed, contract theory has experienced a remarkable rebirth in recent years. This contemporary contract theory is more ambitious than its historical predecessor, for it hopes to provide a contractual justification not only for political obligation, but also for the personal obligations that classical contract theorists simply took for granted. It might seem that a contractual defence of personal obligation is even less plausible than one of political obligation. A contractual defence of political obligation faces many practical problems, but there is a logical problem in grounding personal obligations in contract. It makes no sense to say that people could sign a contract agreeing to keep contractual promises. However, the emphasis on promising is not what contemporary contract theorists draw from the earlier tradition. They draw on two other elements: (1) obligations are conventional, not divine, arising from the interactions of people who are naturally equal; (2) conventional obligations secure important human interests. Combining these two elements, it is possible to (re)-interpret social contracts not primarily as promises, but as devices for identifying social conventions that promote the interests of the members of society.

ii Current social contract theories of ethics

There are two basic forms of contemporary social contract theory. While both accept the classic contract view that people are by nature equals, they have different conceptions of our natural equality. One approach stresses a natural equality of physical power, which makes it mutually advantageous for people to accept conventions that recognize and protect each other's interests and possessions. The other approach stresses a natural equality of moral status, which makes each person's interests a matter of common or impartial concern. This impartial concern is expressed in agreements that recognize each person's interests and moral status. I will call proponents of the mutual advantage theory 'Hobbesian contractarians', and proponents of the impartial theory 'Kantian contractarians', for Hobbes and Kant inspired and foreshadowed these two forms of contract theory.

1   Hobbesian contractarianism: morality as mutual advantage

According to Hobbesian contractarians, the modern world-view rules out earlier notions of divine rights or natural duties. Whenever we try to find objective moral values what we find instead are the subjective preferences of individuals. So there is nothing inherently right or wrong about the goals one chooses to pursue, or the means by which one pursues those goals – even if this involves harming others. However, while there is nothing inherently wrong in harming you, I would be better off by refraining from doing so if every other person refrains from harming me. Such a convention against injury is mutually advantageous – we do not have to waste resources defending our own person and property, and it enables us to enter into stable co-operation. While injury is not inherently wrong, each person gains by accepting conventions that define it as 'wrong'.

The content of such conventions will be the subject of bargaining – each person will want the resulting agreement to protect their own interests as much as possible while restricting them as little as possible. While social conventions are not really *contracts*, we can view this bargaining over mutually advantageous conventions as the process by which a community establishes its 'social contract'. And while this social contract is not intended as a defence of traditional notions of moral obligation, it will include some of the constraints which earlier theorists took to be natural duties – e.g. the duty not to steal, or the duty to share the benefits of co-operation fairly amongst the contributors. Mutually advantageous conventions occupy some of the place of traditional morality, and for that reason can be seen as providing a 'moral' code, even though it is 'generated as a rational constraint from the non-moral premises of rational choice' (Gauthier, 1986, p. 4). Gauthier aptly calls this 'moral artifice', for it artificially constrains what people are naturally entitled to do. But while the resulting constraints partially overlap with traditional moral duties, the overlap is far from complete. Whether it is advantageous to follow a particular convention depends on one's bargaining power, and the strong and talented have greater power than the weak and infirm. The infirm produce little of value, and what little they do produce may be simply expropriated by others without fear of retaliation. Since there is little to gain from co-operation with the infirm, and nothing to fear from retaliation, the strong have little reason to accept conventions which help the infirm.

The resulting conventions will accord rights to various people, but since these rights depend on one's bargaining power, Hobbesian contractarianism does not view individuals as having any inherent moral rights or status. Indeed, the theory allows some people to be killed or enslaved, for 'if personal differences are sufficiently great', then the strong will have the capacity to 'eliminate' the weak or to seize any goods produced by the weak, and thereby set up 'something similar to the slave contract' (Buchanan, 1975, pp. 59–60). This is not simply an abstract possibility. Personal differences *are* that great for defenceless or 'defective' humans beings like babies and the congenitally handicapped, who therefore 'fall beyond the pale' of morality (Gauthier, 1986, p. 268).

I mentioned that Hobbesian contractarianism accepts the classical contract view that humans are by nature equal. What sort of equality underlies a theory which is prepared to contemplate the enslaving of the defenceless? Because the theory recognizes no inherent moral status, any equality of rights between people presupposes a prior physical equality between them. Hobbesians claim that since I am equal to others in physical abilities and vulnerabilities – equal in the ability to harm others and the vulnerability to being harmed – then I must show an equal concern for others, for I must secure an arrangement which gives each person grounds for refraining from exercising that power to harm me. Of course, Hobbesians know that this assumption of a natural equality in physical power is often false. Their claim is not that people are in fact equals by nature, but rather that *morality is only possible insofar as this is so.* By nature, everyone is entitled to use whatever means are available to them, and moral constraints will only arise if people are roughly equal in power. For only then does each person gain more from the protection of their own person and property than they lose by refraining from using other people's bodies or resources. Natural equality is not sufficient, however, for artificial inequalities can also undermine the required basis for moral constraint. People of similar physical capacities may find themselves with radically unequal technological capacities, and those with the more advanced technology can often dictate the terms of social interaction. Indeed, technology may get us to the point where, as Hobbes put it, there is a 'power irresistible' on earth, and for Hobbes and his contemporary followers, such power 'justifieth all actions really and properly, in whomsoever it is found'. Moral constraint would have no place in such a world.

What are we to make of Hobbesian contractarianism as a moral theory? It does not fit our everyday understanding of morality. Hobbesians say that rights flow from the constraints necessary for mutually beneficial co-operation, even when the activity in which people co-operate is the exploitation of other individuals. Everyday morality, however, tells us that mutually beneficial activities must first respect the rights of others, including the rights of those too weak to defend their interests. It may be advantageous for the strong to enslave the weak, but the weak have prior claims of justice against the strong. Indeed, we normally think our moral obligations are strengthened, not diminished, by people's vulnerability. Mutual advantage cannot be the foundation of morality as we normally understand it, for there are moral claims prior to the pursuit of mutual advantage.

Of course, this appeal to everyday morality begs the question. The whole point of the Hobbesian approach is that there are no natural duties to others – it challenges those who believe there is 'a real moral difference between right and wrong which all men [have] a duty to respect' (Gough, 1957, p. 118). To claim that Hobbesian contractarianism ignores our duty to protect the vulnerable is not to give an argument against the theory, for the existence of such moral duties is precisely what is in question. But if Hobbesian contractarianism denies that there is a real moral difference between right and wrong that all people should respect, then it is not so much an alternative account of morality as an alternative to morality. While it may lead to justice wherever people have equal power, it also leads to exploitation wherever 'personal differences are sufficiently great', and there are no grounds within the theory to prefer justice to exploitation. If people act justly, it is not because morality is a value, but only because they lack irresistible power and so must settle for morality. A theory which denies that morality is a value may be a useful analysis of rational egoism (see Article 16, EGOISM) or *realpolitik*, but it is not an account of moral justification.

Again, this is not a refutation of the theory. The fact that Hobbesian contractarianism does not conform to standard views of morality will not worry anyone who thinks that those views are untenable. If standard views of morality are untenable, and if Hobbesian contractarianism cannot yield morality, then so much the worse for morality. Hobbesian morality may be the best we can hope for in a world without natural duties or objective values.

2 Kantian contractarianism: morality as impartiality

The second strand of contemporary contract theory is in many ways the opposite of the first. It uses the device of a social contract in order to develop, rather than replace, traditional notions of moral obligation; it uses the idea of the contract to express the inherent moral standing of persons, rather than to generate an artificial moral standing; and it uses the device of the contract to negate, rather than reflect, unequal bargaining power. In both premises and conclusions, this strand of contract theory is, morally speaking, a world apart from the first.

The best-known exponent of Kantian contractarianism is John Rawls. On his view, people are 'self-originating sources of valid claims' – that is, people matter, from the moral point of view, not because they can harm or benefit others (as in Hobbesian theory), but because they are 'ends in themselves'. Implicit in this Kantian phrase is a concept of moral equality – each person matters and matters equally, each person is entitled to equal consideration. This notion of equal consideration gives rise at the social level to a 'natural duty of justice'. We have a duty to promote just institutions, a duty not derived from consent or mutual advantage, but simply owed to persons as such. What is the content of our natural duty of justice? We have intuitions about what it means to treat people with equal consideration, but they are vague and we need some procedure to help us determine the precise meaning of justice. The idea of a social contract is one such procedure, according to Rawls, for it embodies a basic principle of impartial deliberation – i.e. that each person take into account the needs of others 'as free and equal beings'.

But as we've seen, contracts are not always between free and equal beings, and they may not attend to the needs of the weak. Many people take this to be an unavoidable result of any contract theory, for contracts in the everyday legal sense are agreements between people each of whom is trying to do as well as they can for themselves, rather than trying to do well for everyone equally. Rawls, however, believes that the problem is not with the idea of an agreement between self-interested contractors, but with the conditions under which the contract is determined. A contract can give equal consideration to each of the contractors, but only *if it is negotiated from a position of equality*, which in Rawls's theory is called the 'original position'.

What is this original position of equality? Rawls says that it 'corresponds to the state of nature in the traditional theory of the social contract' (1971, p. 12). But the traditional state of nature allows the strong to exercise greater bargaining power, so it is not a position of genuine equality. Rawls hopes to ensure genuine equality by depriving people in the original position of the knowledge of their ultimate position in society. People must agree on principles of justice under a 'veil of ignorance' – without knowing their natural talents or infirmities, and without knowing what position they will occupy in society. Each contractor is still assumed to be trying to do the best they can for themselves. But since no-one knows what position they will occupy in society, asking people to decide what is best for themselves has the same consequence as asking them to decide what is best for everyone considered impartially. In order to decide from behind a veil of ignorance which principles will promote my good, I must put myself in the shoes of every person in society and see what promotes his or her good, since I may end up being any one of those people. *When combined with the veil of ignorance*, the assumption of self-interest is no different from an assumption of benevolence, for I must sympathetically identify with every person in society and take their good into account as if it were my own. In this way, agreements made on the original position give equal consideration to each person. The original position 'represents equality between human beings as moral persons' (Rawls, 1971, p. 190), and it is only in such a position of equality that contract is a useful device for determining the content of our natural duty of justice.

This, then, is the role of Rawls's social contract from an original position of equality (it is more a generalization of the Golden Rule than a generalization of the traditional state of nature doctrine). Not all Kantian contractarians use Rawls's original position, but, like Rawls, they all replace the traditional state of nature with contracting positions that instruct each contractor to give impartial consideration to the interests of every individual in society. And while they do not agree about which principles would be selected by impartial contractors, they all gravitate towards some sort of equality in rights and resources. Inequalities are not prohibited, but the demand for impartial justification suggests that inequalities must be justified to those made worse off, and perhaps even subject to their veto. As with the Hobbesian version, Kantian contractarianism offers an account of the idea that we are, by nature, equals. But for Kantians, this natural equality refers to a substantive moral equality – indeed, the whole point of Kantian contractarian reasoning is that it 'substitutes a moral equality for a physical inequality' (Diggs, 1981, p. 282).

What are we to make of Kantian contractarian theories of morality? They will be intuitively attractive to those people (the majority, I suspect) who endorse the underlying notions of moral equality and justice. Kantian contractarianism expresses a widely-held belief that impartiality is definitive of the moral point of view – the moral point of view just is the point of view from which each person matters equally. This belief is found not only in Kantian ethics, but throughout the ethical tradition of the West, both Christian (we are all God's children), and secular (utilitarianism provides its own non-contractual interpretation of the requirement of equal consideration for persons; see Article 40, UNIVERSAL PRE-SCRIPTIVISM, for another non-contractual interpretation.) Unlike the Hobbesian version, Kantian contractarianism fits in with these basic elements of our everyday moral understanding.

What is not clear is whether the contract device does any work defending or developing these ideas. Consider Rawls's claim that impartial contractors would agree to distribute resources equally, unless the inequality is to the benefit of the least well-off. This principle is chosen because impartial contractors are (according to Rawls) unwilling to risk being one of the undeserving losers in an inegalitarian society, even if that risk is small compared to the likelihood of being one of the winners. But, as Rawls admits, other assumptions about the dispositions of contractors are possible, in which case other principles would be chosen. If contractors are disposed to gamble, they might choose utilitarian principles which maximize the utility each contractor is likely to have in society, but which create the risk that they may end up being one of the people who is sacrificed for the greater good of others. In fact there are many possible variations in the description of the original position, so that 'for each traditional conception of justice there exists an interpretation of the initial situation in which its principles are the preferred solution' (Rawls, 1971, p. 121). How then do we know which interpretation is the most suitable? According to Rawls we decide by seeing which interpretation yields principles that match our convictions of justice. If the principles chosen in one interpretation of the original position do not match our considered judgements, then we move to another interpretation which yields principles more in line with our convictions.

But if each theory of justice has its own account of the contracting situation, then we have to decide *beforehand* which theory of justice we accept, in order to know which description of the original position is suitable. Rawls's opposition to gambling away one life for the benefit of others, or to penalizing those with undeserved natural handicaps, leads him to describe the original position in one way; those who disagree with Rawls on these issues will describe it in another way. This dispute cannot be resolved by appeal to contractual agreement. It would beg the question for either side to invoke its account of the contracting situation in defence of its theory of justice, since the contracting situation presupposes the theory of justice. All the major issues of justice, therefore, have to be decided beforehand, in order to decide which description of the original position to accept. But then the contract is redundant.

While the idea of contracting from an original position cannot *justify* our basic moral judgements, since it presupposes them, it does serve some useful purposes. It can render our judgements more determinate (contractual agreements must be explicitly and publicly formulated), render them more vivid (the veil of ignorance is a vivid way of expressing the moral requirement of putting ourselves in other people's shoes), and can dramatize our commitment to them (the veil of ignorance dramatizes the claim that we would accept a certain principle however it affected us). In these and other ways, the contract device illuminates the basic ideas of morality as impartiality, even if it cannot help defend those ideas. On the other hand, the contract device is not *required* to express these basic moral judgements. Impartial consideration has also been expressed through the use of ideal sympathizers, rather than impartial contractors. Both theories instruct the moral agent to adopt the impartial point of view, but whereas impartial contractors view each person in society as one of the possible future locations of their own good, ideal sympathizers view each person in society as one of the components of their own good, since they sympathize with and so share each person's fate. The two theories use different devices, but this difference is relatively superficial, for the key move in both theories is to force agents to adopt a perspective which denies them any knowledge of, or any ability to promote, their own particular good. Indeed, it is often difficult to distinguish impartial contractors from ideal sympathizers.

Impartial consideration can also be generated without any special devices at all, just by asking agents to give equal consideration to others notwithstanding their knowledge of, and ability to promote, their own good. We ask each agent to respect the interests of others, not because doing so promotes his or her good, but because it promotes their good, and they are ends in themselves whose well-being is as morally important as the agent's. As we've seen, this understanding of impartiality has been affirmed in many non-contractarian ethical theories, and special devices are not needed to express it. Indeed, there is a curious sort of perversity in using the Kantian contractarian (or ideal sympathizer) device in order to express the idea of moral equality. The concept of a veil of ignorance attempts to render vivid the idea that other people matter in and of themselves, not simply as a component of our own good. But it does so by imposing a perspective from which the good of others is simply a component of our own (actual or possible) good! Rawls tries to downplay the extent to which people in the original position view the various individual lives in society as just so many possible outcomes of a self-interested choice, but the contract device encourages that view, and so obscures the true meaning of impartial concern.

So the contract device may not help to express the idea of moral equality. But whether it helps or not, it is simply an expression of prior moral commitments. It may be, in Whewell's words, 'a convenient form for the expression of Moral Truths' (1845, p. 218), but it neither defends nor generates these truths. The ultimate evaluation of Kantian contractarianism depends, therefore, on one's commitment to the ideals of moral equality and natural duty that underlie it. To the Hobbesian, these ideals have no foundation. Kantian contractarianism claims to express Moral Truths, but Hobbesians deny there are any moral truths to express. Talk of natural moral duties is 'queer', for these alleged moral values are not visible or testable. There is no such thing as a natural moral equality underlying our natural physical (in)equality, and so Kantianism is without foundation.

This objection explains much of the attraction of Hobbesian contractarianism, for it seems to offer a secure answer to the moral sceptic (although it does so by sacrificing any pretence of being a genuine morality). However, Kantian contractarianism is no more vulnerable to this charge than any other genuinely moral theory. Kantians employ a distinctive approach to determining our moral claims, but almost all moral philosophy in the Western tradition shares the assumption that there are obligation-generating claims which all persons have a duty to respect. And, in my view, this assumption is legitimate. Moral values are not physically observable, but different kinds of objectivity apply to different areas of knowledge, and there is no reason to expect morality to have the same kind of objectivity as biology. (See Article 35, REALISM.)

But, as I said earlier, moral theory must not only identify moral norms, it must also explain why we feel obliged to obey them. Why should I care about what I morally ought to do? Hobbesians argue that I only have a reason to do something if the action satisfies some desire of mine. If moral actions do not satisfy any desires, I have no reason to perform them. This theory of rationality may be true even if there are objective moral norms. Kantian contractarianism may give a true account of morality, and yet be only an intellectual perspective that has no motivational effect. In contrast, Hobbesian theories give the agent a clear reason to care about the 'moral' duties they affirm – namely, they increase his or her long-term desire-satisfaction.

Why should people who possess unequal power refrain from using it in their own interests? Buchanan argues that the powerful will treat others as moral equals only if they are 'artificially' made to do so 'through general adherence to internal ethical norms' (1975, pp. 175–6). And indeed Rawls does invoke 'adherence to internal ethical norms', such as our sense of justice, in explaining the reasonableness of obeying moral duties. In saying that such appeals to ethical norms are 'artificial', Buchanan implies that Kantians have failed to find a 'real' motivation for acting morally. But why shouldn't our motivation for acting morally be a moral motivation? To Kant and his contemporary followers, the search for a non-moral motivation for moral action is unnecessary – people can be motivated to act morally simply by coming to understand the moral reasons for doing so. This may seem 'artificial' to those who accept a Hobbesian view of rationality, but the acceptability of that view is presisely what is at issue. Just as the objectivity of morality needn't meet empirical standards of objectivity, so its rationality needn't meet desire-based standards of rationality.

iii Conclusion

What unites the contract tradition as a whole? It is often said that all contract theories ground morality in agreement. But only the classical theorists actually grounded obligation in agreement. For modern theorists, agreement is just a device for identifying the requirements of impartiality or mutual advantage, which are the real grounds of obligation. The idea of social agreement is used to weigh people's interests according to the criteria of impartiality or mutual advantage, but if some other device applied these criteria more accurately, then contract could be dropped out of the theory entirely. It is often said that contract theories are committed to atomistic individualism, viewing society as an artificial product of agreement between pre-social individuals. This is indeed suggested by an excessively literal reading of the term 'social contract'. But only the classical theorists talked about people leaving their natural state in order to create artificial relationships (and even then it was *political* not social relations that were seen as artificial). There is no inherent reason for modern contract theories to be individualistic. Since they are simply devices for weighing interests, they can be used with any account of our interests, including those which affirm our natural sociability. In the end, there is very little that unites the tradition as a whole. We cannot evaluate contract theories simply *as contract theories*, for that label does not explain either their premises or conclusions. We must evaluate the tradition's three component theories as distinct theories, grounded respectively in natural law, mutual advantage, and impartiality. In a sense, there is no contract tradition in ethics, only a contract *device* which many different traditions have used for many different reasons.

References

Barker, E.: *Social Contract: Essays by Locke, Hume and Rousseau* (London: Oxford University Press, 1960).

Buchanan, J.: *The Limits of Liberty: Between Anarchy and Leviathan* (Chicago: University of Chicago Press, 1975).

Diggs, B. J.: 'A contractarian view of respect for persons', *American Philosophical Quarterly*, 18 (1981).

——: 'Utilitarianism and contractarianism', *The Limits of Utilitarianism*, ed. H. B. Miller and W. H. Williams (Minneapolis: University of Minnesota Press, 1982).

Gauthier, D.: *Morals by Agreement* (Oxford: Oxford University Press, 1986).

Gough, J. W.: *The Social Contract*, 2nd edn (London: Oxford University Press, 1957).

Rawls, J.: *A Theory of Justice* (London: Oxford University Press, 1971).

Whewell, W.: *The Elements of Morality* (New York: Harper and Bros., 1845).

Further reading

Hampton, J.: *Hobbes and the Social Contract Tradition* (Cambridge: Cambridge University Press, 1986).

Held, V.: 'The non-contractual society', *Science, Morality and Feminist Theory*, ed. M. Hanen and K. Nielsen (Calgary: University of Calgary Press, 1988).

Lessnoff, M.: *Social Contract* (London: Macmillan, 1986).

Pateman, C.: *The Sexual Contract* (Oxford: Polity Press, 1988).

Riley, P.: *Will and Political Legitimacy: A Critical Exposition of Social Contract Theory in Hobbes, Locke, Rousseau, Kant, and Hegel* (Cambridge, Mass.: Harvard University Press, 1982).

Scanlon, T. M.: 'Contractualism and utilitarianism', *Utilitarianism and Beyond*, ed. A. Sen and B. Williams (Cambridge: Cambridge University Press, 1982).

Vallentyne, P., ed.: *Contractarianism and Rational Choice: Essays on Gauthier* (New York: Cambridge University Press, 1990).

16

Egoism

KURT BAIER

i Introduction

TYPICAL egoists, one might say, are self-centred, inconsiderate, unfeeling, unprincipled, ruthless self-aggrandizers, pursuers of the good things in life whatever the cost to others, people who think only about themselves or, if about others, then merely as means to their own ends.

Perhaps this characterization fits only very crass and ruthless egoists but, whatever its level or degree, egoism involves putting one's own good, interest, and concern above that of others. But this does not seem to be the whole story: surely, I am not an egoist just because I care more about my own health than yours. Nor does my egoism wax and wane precisely in proportion to the number of instances in which I favour myself over others. Rather, what makes me an egoist seems to depend on some special feature of the cases in which I do so.

That feature emerges if we attend to the moral overtones of 'egoism': to call you an egoist is to ascribe to you a moral flaw, namely, a determination to promote your own good or interest even beyond the morally permissible. You behave egoistically if you fail to restrain the pursuit of your own good in situations when it conflicts with mine, and it is morally required or desirable that I observe that restraint. And you are an egoist in this everyday sense if the proportion of your behaviour that is egoistic exceeds a given measure, typically the average.

ii Psychological egoism

Those who think of egoism (and its corresponding opposite, altruism) in this morally loaded way, and believe that excessive egoism and insufficient altruism are among the main causes of most of our social problems, are likely to be surprised, perhaps bewildered or even shocked, if they read books on ethics. For in many of them the view is seriously entertained that everybody is an egoist, and egoism is not always regarded as a bad thing. In the main, they will find two such theories. The first, psychological egoism, to be discussed in this section, is an explanatory theory to the effect that we are all egoists in the sense that all our actions are always motivated by concern for our own best interest or greatest good. The second, to be discussed in subsequent sections, conceives of egoism as an ideal requiring one to act egoistically.

Adherents of psychological egoism can admit that we may not always actually promote or even protect our greatest good, for we may be mistaken about what it is, or how to get it, or we may be too weak-willed to do what is needed to obtain it. Thus, strictly speaking, psychological egoism claims to explain not all human behaviour, but only behaviour explainable in terms of the agent's beliefs and desires, or the considerations and reasons that weighed with the agent.

The 'egoism' meant by the psychological egoist is not, of course, the kind defined in section (i). It is incapable of degrees and is not restricted to what is morally objectionable. It is the motivational pattern of people whose motivated behaviour is in accordance with a principle, namely, that of doing whatever and only what protects and promotes their own welfare, well-being, best interest, happiness, flourishing, or greatest good, either because they are indifferent about that of others or because they always care more about their own than that of others when the two conflict. (There are important differences between these ends, but they can here be ignored.) To be such an 'egoist', one need not consciously apply this principle every time one acts; it is sufficient that one's voluntary behaviour conform to this pattern.

However, the available empirical evidence seems to refute even this psychological egoism of merely motivated behaviour. Many normal people appear quite frequently to be concerned not with their own greatest good but with the attainment of something the pursuit of which they know or believe to be to their own detriment. One may woo one's boss's spouse, though one knows or believes with good reason, that the pursuit, and even more the attainment, of this end will cost one one's livelihood, destroy one's marriage, alienate one's children and friends, and will in other ways ruin one's life.

To dispose of these apparent counter-examples, psychological egoism would have to make it plausible that they are illusory. To that end, it can, of course, point to the fact that many non-egoistic explanations of someone's behaviour are suspect. Since egoistic behaviour is morally disapproved of, people may wish to conceal their real, egoistic, motivation and to persuade us that their behaviour really was non-egoistically motivated. Not infrequently, we are able to unmask such non-egoistic explanations as hypocritical or at least as due to self-deception. But this does not justify us in generalizing to all cases, for quite often we not only cannot unmask someone's seemingly non-egoistic behaviour in this way, but we have no reason to suspect the existence of hidden egoistic motives. Most of us are acquainted with cases of people knowingly endangering their health, risking their worldly fortune, or even their life, in the hope of attaining some end, such as satisfying the (perhaps extravagant) desires of one with whom they are infatuated or the needs of another whom they love or to whom they feel committed for other reasons, as when someone donates a kidney to her sister with whom she had not been on speaking terms for some years, or blood to someone whom she does not even know.

Psychological egoists should not attempt to dispose of these prima facie cases of non-egoistic behaviour, as some tend to do, by insisting that there *must* be an egoistic explanation. Admittedly, a clever psychological egoist can often invent a plausible underlying egoistic explanation of the apparently non-egoistic behaviour in question, just as a dissembling egoist can substitute an invented, nobler explanation for the real egoistic one. But insisting that there must be such an egoistic motive, and inventing a possible one, does not make it the operative one.

Some of us may find any substituted egoistic explanations more plausible than a non-egoistic one, because we already believe that deep down we are all egoists. But, despite the many 'unmasking' explanations to which Marx and Freud have accustomed us, to think the egoistic explanations are as such deeper, more complete, more persuasive, and so more satisfactory than non-egoistic ones – and therefore to find the egoistic explanation more plausible – is simply to assume what needs to be proven. If psychological egoism is based on this assumption, it is not the surprising and disillusioning 'discovery' about human nature it purports to be, but at best an unsubstantiated claim that we have not found the 'real' explanation of someone's behaviour until we have 'unearthed' suitable egoistic motivation. But then to use this 'real' explanation in support of the more general claim is to argue in a circle.

At this point, a psychological egoist may object that all supposedly non-egoistic behaviour is in reality egoistic. For after all, the objection goes, in examples like those given above, the person did what *she really most wanted* to do.

But this objection emasculates psychological egoism. Instead of being a surprising, indeed shocking, empirical theory to the effect that we are all always egoistically motivated in the ordinary sense of 'egoistic', it merely gives a new and rather misleading meaning to 'egoistic motivation'. On this new interpretation, one is egoistically motivated, not if and only if one is motivated to do whatever one takes to be for one's own greatest good even if it harms others, but if one does whatever one most wants to do, whether or not that is what one takes to be for one's greatest good, and even if one's aim is to benefit others in ways costly to oneself. Ordinarily, an egoist is someone who most wants something much more specific, namely, to promote his own good, to promote only interests in his self, to promote his own best interest, to satisfy only self-regarding wants or aims. The non-egoist, by contrast, does not want this most, at least not when it is morally impermissible. Thus, ordinarily, egoists are characterized by the uniformly overriding strength of their self-regarding, non-egoists by an 'adequate' strength of their other-regarding, desires or motivations.

The present version of psychological egoism is, therefore, empty since 'what one "most wants" to do' here must mean, whatever one is finally, all things considered, motivated to do, for instance, to make a large contribution to Oxfam (even if one's *most strongly felt* inclination is to replenish one's wine cellar). Thus, on this last construal, psychological egoism holds that we are all egoists simply because we are all motivated by *our own* motivation, not someone else's; but in this sense the motivation could not conceivably be anyone else's: it is mine, not my sister's, even if, hating it, I regularly light a candle at our father's grave, only because she wants me to.

iii Egoism as a means to the common good

Adam Smith's *An Inquiry into the Nature and Causes of the Wealth of Nations* (published in 1776), presents an argument for egoism as a practical ideal, at least in the economic sphere. He advocated the freedom of entrepreneurs to promote their own interest, that is, their profits, by suitable (as they saw it) methods of production, hiring, sales and so forth, on the grounds that such a general arrangement would best promote the good of the whole community. On Smith's view, the promotion by each entrepreneur of his or her own good, unimpeded by legal or self-imposed moral constraint to protect the good of others, would at the same time be the most efficient promotion of the common good. This would happen, Smith believed, because there is an 'invisible hand' (the pervasive effects of the free enterprise system itself) which co-ordinates these many otherwise unco-ordinated individual economic activities.

This idea, that the removal of legal or self-imposed moral constraints on the pursuit of one's own interest is generally beneficial, has often been extended beyond the narrowly economic sphere. It then becomes the doctrine that, if each pursues her own interest as she conceives of it, then the interest of everyone is promoted. This theory, if advanced without the support of an 'invisible hand', becomes the fallacy, often ascribed to John Stuart Mill, that if each promotes her own interest, then the interest of everyone is thereby necessarily promoted. Clearly, this is a fallacy, for the interests of different individuals or classes may, and under certain conditions (of which the scarcity of necessities is the most obvious), do conflict. Then the interest of one is the detriment of the other.

We can think of the theories just described as extolling egoism, not in opposition to morality, but rather as the best way to attain its legitimate end, the common good. It is doubtful whether this is a form of egoism at all, since it does not embrace egoism for its own sake, but only as – and to the extent that it really is – the best strategy to attain the common good.

It should be plain that this practical ideal – whether genuinely egoistic or not – rests on a dubious factual claim. For the removal of legal or self-imposed moral constraints on the individual pursuit of self-interest is likely to promote the common good only if these individual interests do not conflict, or if something like a 'hidden hand' takes the place of these constraints. If we all rush to get out of the burning theatre, many or all may get trampled to death or perish in the flames. To avoid or minimize mutual interference, we need some suitable co-ordination of our individual activities. Of course, that may not be enough. Even if we form orderly lines, though no-one will then get trampled to death, the last ones in the line may be caught in the fire. Thus, our system of co-ordination may not be able to prevent all harm, and then the contentious problem arises of how the unavoidable harm is to be allocated. So far as egoism as a means to the common good is concerned, the essential point is that the pursuit of individual good does not necessarily promote, and may in fact be disastrous for, the common good.

iv Rational and ethical egoism

I turn, last, to two versions of egoism as a practical ideal, usually called rational and ethical egoism, respectively. In contrast to the previously considered doctrine of egoism as a means to the common good, they do not rest on any factual claims about the social or economic consequences of each of us promoting our own greatest good. They hold, as if this were self-evident or were something for people to decide simply as they saw fit, that promoting one's own greatest good is always in accordance with reason and morality.

Both ideals have a stronger and a weaker version. The stronger maintains that it is always rational (wise, reasonable, reason-backed), always right, (moral, praiseworthy, virtuous) to aim at one's own greatest good, and never rational etc., never right etc., not to do so. The weaker version maintains that it is always rational, always right to do so, but not necessarily never rational or right not to do so.

Rational egoism is highly plausible. We tend to think that when doing something seems not to be in our interest, doing it calls for justification and showing that it actually is in our interest after all provides that justification. In a famous remark, Bishop Butler claimed that 'when we sit down in a cool hour, we can neither justify to ourselves this or any other pursuit till we are convinced that it will be for our happiness, or at least not contrary to it' (Butler, 1726, Sermon 11, Para. 20.) Although Butler says, 'our happiness' rather than 'our greatest good', he really means the same thing, since he believes that our happiness does constitute our greatest good.

Together with another highly plausible premise, rational egoism implies ethical egoism. That other premise is ethical rationalism, the doctrine that if a moral requirement or recommendation is to be sound or acceptable, complying with it must be in accordance with reason. In the two emphasized sentences of the following splendid passage from *Leviathan*, Hobbes suggests both rational egoism and ethical rationalism: 'The kingdom of God is gotten by violence but what if it could be gotten by unjust violence? *Were it against reason so to get it when it is impossible to receive hurt by it? And if it be not against reason, it is not against justice, or else justice is not to be approved for good*' (Hobbes, 1651, Ch. 15). Thus, if we accept the weak version of ethical rationalism – that moral requirements are sound and may be accepted if complying with them is in accordance with reason – and also accept the weak version of rational egoism – that behaving in a certain way is in accordance with reason if by behaving in this way the agent aims at his own greatest good –, then we must in consistency also accept the weak version of ethical egoism – that moral requirements are sound and may be accepted if, by complying with them, the agent aims at his own greatest good. And similarly for the strong versions.

Unfortunately, however, ethical egoism is in direct conflict with another highly plausible conviction, namely, that moral requirements must be capable of authoritatively regulating interpersonal conflicts of interest. Let us call this the doctrine of 'ethical conflict-regulation'. It implies an element of impartiality or universality in ethics; arguments for this are presented elsewhere in this volume, for instance Article 14 KANTIAN ETHICS, and Article 40, UNIVERSAL PRE-SCRIPTIVISM. An example: can it be morally wrong for me to kill my grandfather so that he cannot change his will and disinherit me? Assuming that my killing him will be in my best interest but detrimental to my grandfather, while refraining from killing him will be to my detriment but in my grandfather's interest, then if ethical conflict-regulation is sound, there can be a sound moral guideline regulating this conflict (presumably by forbidding this killing). But then ethical egoism cannot be sound, for it precludes the interpersonally authoritative regulation of interpersonal conflicts of interest, since such a regulation implies that conduct contrary to one's interest is sometimes morally required of one, and conduct in one's best interest sometimes morally forbidden to one. Thus, ethical egoism is incompatible with ethical conflict-regulation. It allows only personally authoritative principles or precepts; they can tell me to kill my grandfather and tell my grandfather not to allow himself to be killed, perhaps preventively to kill me in self-defence, but they cannot, 'regulatively', tell both of us whose interest must give way. But it is precisely this interpersonally regulative function we ascribe to *moral* principles.

Well, then should we accept ethical egoism and so reject ethical conflict-regulation, or should we reject ethical egoism and therefore also reject at least one of ethical rationalism or rational egoism? Most people (including philosophers), have not found it difficult to choose between ethical egoism and ethical conflict-regulation, since most have rejected ethical egoism for other reasons anyway. Similarly, few people (including philosophers), have wanted to give up ethical conflict-regulation. However, as we noted, retaining ethical conflict-regulation and rejecting ethical egoism involves giving up either ethical rationalism or rational egoism, and many have found that choice very difficult. Some utilitarians, following Henry Sidgwick (see his *The Methods of Ethics*, 1874, 7th edn., final chapter) have retained ethical conflict-regulation, ethical rationalism, and rational egoism. (But they can retain rational egoism only in its weak version, since ethical conflict-regulation and ethical rationalism together are incompatible with rational egoism in its strong version. For these two, together with rational egoism in its strong version, would imply that it is sometimes contrary to reason to do what is in one's best interest and also contrary to reason not to do it.) They maintain, in other words, that it is never contrary to reason to do what is in one's best interest nor contrary to reason to do what is morally required or desirable, and that, when the two conflict, doing either is in accordance with reason. Sidgwick was, understandably, unhappy about this 'bifurcation' of practical reason, and equally unhappy about the only 'solution' he could think of: a deity who, in cases of conflict between the right and the advantageous, attaches adequate rewards to the right and punishments to the advantageous, thereby making it rational for people to do what is morally right rather than what but for the rewards and punishments would have been in their best interest. But why should a deity, presumably itself a rational being, attach such exorbitant rewards to choosing what is morally required and such shocking penalties to choosing one's own good, when both ways of acting are supposed to be equally in accordance with reason?

Another possibility is to retain rational egoism in its strong version but abandon ethical rationalism, thereby toppling reason, the monarch among justifiers, from its long-held throne. On this sort of view, the fact that doing the right thing may be detrimental to one's interest and therefore contrary to reason, does not imply that one may, let alone should or ought to, do what is in one's interest rather than what is morally required; accordance with reason constitutes only one type of justification, and 'decent' people will ignore it when it conflicts with moral justification. Taken at face value, this would seem to imply that the choice between the rational and the moral is a matter of taste, a choice comparable to that between being a farmer or a businessman, a choice that is solely the chooser's own business. But many are convinced there is more to being irrational than indulging a personal (perhaps idiosyncratic) taste.

v Conclusion

We have distinguished five versions of egoism. The common-sense version treats it as a vice, the promotion of one's own good beyond the morally permissible. The second, psychological egoism, is the theory that if not on the surface, at least deep down we are all egoists in the sense that as far as our behaviour explainable by our beliefs and desires is concerned, it always is aimed at what we believe to be for our own greatest good. The third, illustrated by the views of Adam Smith, is the theory that under certain conditions the promotion of one's own good is the best means of attaining the legitimate aim of morality, namely, the common good. If there are no moral objections to bringing about or maintaining these conditions, then it would seem to be desirable both from the moral and the egoistic point of view to bring about or maintain these conditions if under them we can attain the moral aim by promoting our own greatest good. The fourth and fifth versions, ethical and rational egoism, present it as practical ideals, to wit as the ideals of morality and reason.

Concerning the second version, psychological egoism, which, because of its purported unmasking of human nature as less than admirable, has had considerable appeal for the disillusioned, we are convinced of its untenability. Concerning the third version, egoism as a means to the common good, we think it fairly clear that no-one has yet found those conditions under which a group of such unconstrained egoists would attain the common good. Certainly, the most promising candidate for these conditions, the actual existence, if it were possible, of a perfectly competitive market as defined by neo-classical economists, could not guarantee the attainment even of their economic version of the common good, efficiency. There is not even initial plausibility in the fourth version, ethical egoism, because it requires the abandonment either of morality as a regulator of conflicts of interest or of the almost certainly true belief that such conflicts are an inescapable fact of life. If ethical and psychological egoism are false, then there is no good reason to reject our first, common-sense, version of egoism as a widespread moral failing. This leaves only rational egoism, the most deeply entrenched normative theory of egoism. But the jury on this case is still in disarray.

References

Butler, J.: *Fifteen Sermons preached in the Rolls Chapel* (1726); ed. J. H. Bernard (London: SPCK, 1970).
Foot, P.: 'Morality as a system of hypothetical imperatives', *Philosophical Review*, (1972).
Hobbes, T.: *Leviathan* (1651); ed. J. P. Plamenatz (London: Collins, 1962).
Sidgwick, H.: *The Methods of Ethics* (1874); 7th edn (London: Macmillan, 1911).
Smith, A. *An Inquiry into the Nature and Causes of the Wealth of Nations* (1776); 6th edn (London: Methuen, 1950).

Further reading

Gauthier, D.: *Morals by Agreement* (Oxford: Clarendon Press, 1986).
Hampton, J.: *Hobbes and the Social Contract Tradition* (Cambridge: Cambridge University Press, 1986).
Harsanyi, J.: 'Morality and the theory of rational behaviour'. *Utilitarianism and Beyond*, ed. A. Sen and B. Williams (Cambridge: Cambridge University Press, 1982).
Laclos, C. de: *Les Liaisons Dangereuses* (1782); (Paris: Editions Garnier Frères, 1961).
Meredith, G.: *The Egoist* (Harmondsworth: Penguin, 1968).
Parfit, D.: 'Prudence, morality and the prisoner's dilemma', *Proceedings of the British Academy*, 65 (1979).
Plato: *The Republic*, Loeb Classical Library (Cambridge, Mass.: Harvard University Press, 1982).
Stirner, M. *The Ego and Its Own* (Leipzig: Phillipp Reclam. jun., 1893).

17

Contemporary deontology

NANCY (ANN) DAVIS

> Ordinary moral understanding, as well as many major traditions of
> Western moral theory, recognize that there are some things which a
> moral man will not do, no matter what. ...
>
> It is part of the idea that lying or murder are wrong, not just bad,
> that these are things you must not do – no matter what. They are not
> mere negatives that enter into a calculus to be outweighed by the
> good you might do or the greater harm you might avoid. Thus the
> norms which express deontological judgments – for example, Do not
> commit murder – may be said to be absolute. They do not say: 'Avoid
> lying, other things being equal', but 'Do not lie, period'.
>
> (FRIED, 1978, p. 7, p. 9)

MANY people profess to believe that acting morally, or as we ought to act, involves
the self-conscious acceptance of some (quite specific) constraints or rules that
place limits both on the pursuit of our own interests and on our pursuit of the
general good. Though these people do not regard the furtherance of our own
interests or the pursuit of the general good as ignoble ends, or ones that we are
morally required to eschew, they believe that neither can be regarded as providing
us with morally sufficient reason to take action. Those who hold such a view
believe that there are certain sorts of acts that are wrong in themselves, and thus
morally unacceptable means to the pursuit of any ends, even ends that are
morally admirable, or morally obligatory. (How strong the prohibition is against
performing such acts is a matter that will be taken up later.) Philosophers call
such ethical views 'deontological' (from the Greek *deon*, 'duty'), and contrast them
to views that are 'teleological' in structure (from *telos*, Greek for 'goal'). Those
who hold teleological views reject the view that there are special kinds of acts that
are right or wrong in themselves. For teleologists, the rightness or wrongness
of our acts is determined by a comparative assessment of their consequences.
Teleological views are discussed in this volume in Article 19, CON-
SEQUENTIALISM, and Article 20, UTILITY AND THE GOOD. The focus of this essay
is on deontological theories.

Fried and other contemporary deontologists often present their views as a
response to, and corrective of, the consequentialist moral theories that were
widely discussed mid-century. Though many of their objections to consequentialist
views have been primarily normative, deontologists' normative dissatisfactions
have often formed the basis for claims that consequentialist views are structurally

or conceptually deficient. Any theory that would allow us to treat other human beings in the ways that consequentialist theories appeared to allow, or enjoin, is, by many contemporary deontologists' lights, a moral theory that has an untenable understanding of what it is to be a person, or what it is for an action to be wrong.

Because the characterization of deontological views is often a contrastive one, it is easiest to begin understanding deontological views by drawing attention to some specific points of contrast between deontological and consequentialist theories.

i Teleological vs. deontological theories

Many philosophers follow John Rawls in supposing that two categories, teleological and deontological, exhaust the possibilities regarding theories of right action. According to Rawls

The two main concepts of ethics are those of the right and the good ... The structure of an ethical theory is, then, largely determined by how it defines and connects these two basic notions ... The simplest way of relating them is taken by teleological theories: the good is defined independently from the right, and the right is defined as that which maximizes the good. (Rawls, 1971, p. 24)

A deontological theory is defined by contrast with teleological theories as

one that either does not specify the good independently from the right, or does not interpret the right as maximizing the good. (p. 30)

Deontologists believe that the right is not to be defined in terms of the good, and they reject the idea that the good is prior to the right. In fact, they believe that there is no clear specifiable relation between doing right and doing good (in the consequentialists' sense, i.e. producing a good outcome). As Fried puts it

The goodness of the ultimate consequences does not guarantee the rightness of the actions which produced them. The two realms are not only distinct for the deontologist, but the right is prior to the good. (Fried, 1978, p. 9)

To act rightly, agents must first of all refrain from doing the things that can be said (and known) to be, before the fact, wrong. The particular requirements to refrain from doing the various things-that-can-be-known-before-the-fact-to-be-wrong are variously called rules, laws, deontological constraints, prohibitions, limitations, proscriptions, or norms, and I shall generally refer to them simply as 'deontological constraints'. Deontological views require agents to refrain from doing the sorts of things that are wrong even when they foresee that their refusal to do such things will clearly result in greater harm (or less good).

From this it is easy to see that deontological views are non-consequentialist, and that they are neither maximizing nor comparative. By a deontologist's lights, it is not the badness of the consequences of a particular lie, or of lying in general, that makes it wrong to lie; rather, lies are wrong because of the sorts of things they are, and are thus wrong even when they foreseeably produce good consequences.

Nor are deontological views based on impartial consideration of the interests or welfare of others, as consequentialist theories are. If we are enjoined to refrain from harming one innocent person even when our harming the one would prevent the deaths of five other innocent people, then it is obvious that the interests of the six do not count, or do not count equally: if they did, then it would be permissible – if not outright obligatory – for us to do the thing that saves the five (and harms the one). Moreover, even if we resist the suggestion that interests can be agglomerated in this way, deontological views are not based on impartial consideration of interests. For that would seem to allow – if not require – that each one of the five's interests be weighed against those of the one; it would seem to allow – if not require – us to (for example) toss a coin five times, in order for each of the five's interests to receive the same consideration that the one's interests are accorded.

And there is yet another respect in which deontological views depart from consequentialist impartiality. Deontologists maintain that we are not permitted to do something that violates a deontological constraint even when our doing so would obviate the necessity of five other agents being faced with the decision either to violate a deontological constraint or allow even more serious harm to occur. Not only are we forbidden to harm an innocent person to decrease the number of deaths, we are also forbidden to harm the one to decrease the number of (wrongful) killings by agents whose motivations and character are no worse, morally, than ours. Many critics have objected to consequentialism's impartialist stance on the grounds that it attacks, or leaves no room for, personal autonomy. If we are to have lives worth living by our own lights, then we cannot regard our own interests, projects, and concerns neutrally – as consequentialists are widely supposed to regard them – as merely one among other equally worthy candidates. Instead, we must be able to assign more weight to them simply because they are ours.

But deontologists go beyond tolerance for such favouritism. Considerations of autonomy might allow us, in non-extreme circumstances, to assign more weight to our own concerns, projects, or values, than to the interests of others. But deontological views not only assign more weight to our own avoidance of wrong-doing – where wrongdoing is narrowly understood as involving the violation of the rules – than to the interests (and even lives) of other agents, they also require that we assign more weight to our own avoidance of wrongdoing than we do to the avoidance of wrongdoing *tout court*, or the prevention of wrongdoing by others. Deontologists' recognition of the importance of avoiding wrongdoing does not translate into an obligation, or even a permission, to minimize the wrongdoing of others. In effect, then, the preservation of our own virtue outweighs not only the preservation of others' lives, it also outweighs the preservation of others' virtue. We may not save a life with a lie even when the lie would prevent the loss of life by deceiving an evil agent who credibly intends to kill several innocent victims.

207

ii The nature and structure of deontological constraints

It is time to look more closely at the nature and structure of deontological constraints – that is, the system of rules or prohibitions which form the basis of deontological views – for doing so may help us get a clearer idea of the nature and structure of deontological views themselves. Three features of deontological constraints are especially noteworthy.

Deontological constraints are usually (1) *negatively formulated* as 'Thou shalt nots' or prohibitions. Though it would seem to be theoretically possible to transform deontological constraints that are formulated as prohibitions into ostensibly 'positive' prescriptions – for example, 'Don't lie' into 'Tell the truth', and 'Do not harm the innocent' into 'Render assistance to those who need it' – deontologists do not think that the positive formulations are equivalent to (or entailed by) the negative ones.

According to the deontologist, though it is evident that lying and failing to tell the truth, or harming and failing to benefit, may well result in the same untoward consequences, and issue from the same sorts of motivations, 'lying' and 'failing to tell the truth' are not the same kinds of acts, nor are 'harming' and 'failing to benefit'. Since it is kinds of acts that are deemed wrong, a deontological constraint may forbid lying and be silent on a (putatively) different but quite closely related kind of act, namely, failures to tell the truth. Says Fried

> In every case the [deontological] norm has boundaries and what lies outside those boundaries is not forbidden at all. Thus lying is wrong, while withholding a truth which another needs may be perfectly permissible – but that is because withholding a truth is not lying. (Fried, 1978, pp. 9–10)

Deontological constraints are thus not only negatively formulated (as prohibitions), they are also (2) *narrowly framed*, and *bounded*. This is critical, for different understandings of the scope of deontological constraints – or different views about what constitute different kinds of acts – will obviously yield very different understandings of agents' obligations and responsibilities.

Finally, (3) deontological constraints are *narrowly directed*: they attach narrowly to agents' decisions and actions rather than to the full range of projected consequences of their choice and action. As Nagel puts the point, 'Deontological reasons have their full force against your doing something – not just against its happening' (1986, p. 177).

The narrow-directedness of deontological constraints is often explained in terms of an interpretation of the notion of agency, and explicated by an appeal to the distinction between intention and foresight. Thus it is held that we violate the deontological constraint against harming the innocent only if we intentionally harm another. If we merely choose not to take action to prevent harm from befalling others, or if the harm that befalls them is seen as a consequence of our (prima facie permissible) action, but not as a chosen means or chosen end, then, though our action may be open to criticism on other grounds, it is not a violation of the deontological constraint against harming the innocent. By deontologists' lights, we are not as responsible for (or not fully agent of) the foreseen consequences of our actions, as we are for the things that we intend.

Though most deontologists believe that we have some 'positive' obligations, most of the moral rules that they take to govern our behaviour are formulated 'negatively' as prohibitions or impermissions. This is not fortuitous or accidental. Deontological views treat the category of the forbidden or impermissible as fundamental in several respects.

For the deontologist, the most important moral distinction is between the permissible and the impermissible, and it is the notion of the impermissible that forms the basis of the definition of the obligatory: what is obligatory is what it is impermissible to omit. Though deontologists differ on the question of just what, apart from avoiding transgression of the rules, agents are obliged to do, they agree in thinking that the largest portion of moral space, and certainly the largest portion of an agent's time and energy, ought to be taken up with the permissible. As Fried expresses the point,

One cannot live one's life by the demands of the domain of the right. After having avoided wrong and doing one's duty, an infinity of choices is left to be made. (1978, p. 13)

The contrast with consequentialist moral theories is here quite a stark one. While deontologists take the notion of the right to be a weak (or exclusionary) one, consequentialists employ a strong (or inclusionary) notion: an agent acts rightly only when his or her actions maximize utility, and wrongly otherwise. Consequentialist theories achieve (what might be called) *moral closure*: every course of action is either right or wrong (and actions are permissible only if they are right).

For the deontologist, an act may be permissible without being the best (or even a good) option. For the consequentialist, however, a course of action is permissible when and only when it is the best (or equal best) option open to an agent: it is never permissible to do less good (or prevent less harm) than one can. This aspect of consequentialism has been much criticized, and many people have objected to consequentialist views on the ground that they leave agents with insufficient moral breathing room. Those of a deontological bent have often taken the strenuousness of consequentialist theories to derive from their (mis)understanding of the notions of permission and obligation. (We shall return to this below.)

The narrow-directedness and the narrow framing of deontological constraints are closely connected. Though a number of philosophers and legal theorists have questioned the tenability of the distinction between intention and mere foresight, and expressed doubts about the wisdom of placing moral weight on that distinction, many deontologists appeal to the distinction between intention and mere foresight to explain what narrow-directedness means. Both Fried and Thomas Nagel speak approvingly of what Nagel calls 'the traditional principle of double effect', which he construes as stating that

to violate deontological constraints one must maltreat someone else intentionally. The maltreatment must be something that one does or chooses, either as an end or as a means, rather than something one's actions merely cause or fail to prevent but that one doesn't aim at. (Nagel, 1986, p. 179)

To violate a deontological constraint, one must do something wrong: but if the thing in question was not something that one intended to do – it was not one's chosen means or end – then one may be said not to have done anything ('in the relevant sense') at all. One is not said to have done something wrong if one did not *intend* to do the thing in question.

The nature of the connection between narrow-directedness and narrow framing is not hard to understand. If the prohibitory force of deontological constraints attaches only to what we intend, then a lie is a different sort of act from a failure to tell the truth. For lies are necessarily intentional (as attempted deceptions), but failures to disclose the truth are not, for they do not necessarily have deception as their object. More broadly, if the notion of intention is explicated in terms of the notions of choice as a means to an end – for example, something is an intentional harming of the innocent only if the harm to the innocent was chosen as an end in itself, or as a means to an end – then harms that are merely foreseen – for example, as a result of the failure to prevent a natural disaster or to pre-empt the action of a wicked tyrant – are different in kind from the harms that are chosen as a means to preventing other harms. If an agent harms one person in order to prevent five others from being killed in a rockslide, what he or she does is an intentional harming, and thus violates a deontological constraint. But if the agent refuses to kill the one to save the five, then, since the deaths of the five are not the agent's chosen means or the agent's chosen end, there is no violation of a deontological constraint.

iii   Unanswered questions and potential problems

Both the overall structure and some of the motivation behind deontological views should by now be clear. But there are some unanswered questions and potential problems that deserve further attention.

1   What are the sorts of things that are wrong, and why are they wrong?
Theories like consequentialism offer a theoretical explanation of what makes wrong acts wrong that is both simple and intuitively appealing: to do the wrong thing is to choose to act in a way that brings more harm (or less good) into the world than one had to. Since it may be difficult to determine what consequences will follow upon one's chosen course of action, and impossible to foresee all of the consequences of all of one's deeds, consequentialism has been criticized as unrealistic or impracticable. Commentators disagree about the force of such criticism, and many consequentialists think that it does not pose a serious objection. But it may appear that deontologists can avoid this practical problem altogether. Since deontologists think that acts are wrong because of the sorts of acts they are, we need not speculate about the projected consequences of our act, or attempt to calculate their value. It is easy enough to say in advance what acts

are wrong, namely those that violate any of the deontological constraints. The list that Nagel offers is representative:

Common moral intuition recognizes several types of deontological reasons – limits on what one may do to people or how one may treat them. There are special obligations created by promises and agreements; the restrictions against lying and betrayal; the prohibitions against violating various individual rights, rights not to be killed, injured, imprisoned, threatened, tortured, coerced, robbed; the restrictions against imposing certain sacrifices on someone simply as a means to an end; and perhaps the special claim of immediacy, which makes distress at a distance so different from distress in the same room. There may also be a deontological requirement of fairness, of even-handedness or equality in one's treatment of people. (Nagel, 1986, p. 176)

Deontologists may appear to do better in the practical domain than consequentialists, but it is evident that they face some serious theoretical problems. And, once we have reflected on those theoretical problems, we will see that the appearance of practical superiority may be largely illusory.

Deontologists reject the view that an act's being wrong has a necessary connection to, and is explicable in terms of, its having bad consequences, or producing more harm than good in the world. But the question must then arise: just what is it about a wrong act that makes it wrong? Why are the things on the deontologist's list (and no others) on that list?

Sometimes deontologists appeal to common moral intuitions, seasoned with a bit of tradition. The things that appear on Nagel's list are the sorts of things that many people think are wrong, and have thought wrong for a long time, based on hundreds of years of Hebrew-Christian teachings. Sometimes deontologists maintain that deontological constraints can be derived from, or be seen to be the expression of, a more fundamental principle. The candidate principle is usually one that owes its origin (perhaps rather foggily) to Immanuel Kant, and is taken to state (something like) 'It is morally obligatory to respect every person as a rational agent'. (Alan Donagan's formulation more closely follows deontologist format: 'It is impermissible not to respect every human being, oneself or any other, as a rational creature' (1977, p. 66).) It is taken to be a requirement (or expression) of respecting others as rational creatures that we not subject them to the sorts of treatment proscribed by deontological constraints. This is roughly the line taken by Donagan and Fried.

Sometimes this approach is supplemented with the claim that it is part of what it means for something to be wrong or evil that we see it as proscribed in deontological terms, as something we must not do (no matter what). According to Nagel, if we identify certain sorts of conduct as evil – for example, hurting a child in order to extract some needed piece of life-saving information from the child's frightened or irrational babysitter – then we have identified our conduct as something we must not do:

our actions should be guided, if they are guided at all, toward [the] elimination [of evil] rather than toward its maintenance. That is what evil *means*. (Nagel, 1986, p. 182)

When we choose to do something like lie, harm the innocent, or violate someone's rights, then we are thereby aiming at evil, and so 'swimming head-on against the normative current' (Nagel, 1986, p. 182) even when that choice is guided by the desire to prevent greater harm or realize greater good thereby. By Nagel's and Fried's lights, consequentialists who allow that it may be right to lie or harm the innocent do not have a satisfactory understanding of what it is for something to be evil, or wrong.

But none of these approaches – the appeal to people's moral intuitions, buttressed (or not) by respectful reference to the teachings of venerated moral theologians; the appeal to a fundamental principle as the basis from which highly specific deontological prohibitions are to be derived; or the assertion that deontological normative judgements are built into the fabric of the concept of wrong (and right?) – is satisfactory.

Appeals to 'ordinary moral understanding' or 'common morality' or 'moral common sense' cannot plausibly be thought to provide a valid theoretical or normative litmus test for a moral theory, even if the theory has a long and distinguished pedigree. Most educated individuals now reject the picture of the universe and its workings held by the Church Fathers. And many aspects of the views of the monks, priests, and clerics that dominated early religious morality (and still influence orthodox Hebrew-Christian morality) are widely rejected as reflecting views of human nature – and men's and women's different roles and abilities – that are prejudiced, parochial and punitive. If traditional common morality can easily be seen to have such weak parts, it is wise to be sceptical, or at least cautious, about other parts, and about the foundation that holds all the parts together. (See Article 42, METHOD AND MORAL THEORY).

Nor are appeals to a fundamental principle more effective. Even if one grants that the violation of any of the items identified as deontological constraints involves a failure of respect, important questions remain unanswered (and often, unasked). Several are especially pressing.

Recall that deontological constraints are narrowly framed and bounded: we act wrongly in misleading another person only if our act is classified as a lie, but the withholding of truth, and the 'dup[ing of] children, madmen, and those whose minds have been impaired by age or illness' for 'benevolent purposes' (Donagan, 1977, p. 89) are not classified as lies, and hence may be permissible, presumably on the ground that they do not constitute the relevant sort of failure of respect. But the notion of respect that is being employed here is by no means a transparent one, nor does talk of respecting others (or oneself) as a rational creature render the notion more perspicuous. The question must arise: why should respect be so narrowly – and technically, or legalistically – understood as requiring us to refrain from lies while tolerating the sort of deception that rational creatures can perpetrate by silence and other allegedly permissible forms of 'withholding the truth'? The question is an especially pointed one, for it is not only true that the consequences of lying and withholding the truth may be the same, it is also true that the person who lies and the person who withholds the truth may both have the same motivation in so doing, whether benevolent or malign. If a lie is a wrongful act that denies to its victim 'the status of freely choosing, rationally valuing, specially efficacious person, the special status of moral personality' (Fried, 1978, p. 29) whatever motivation underlies it, then why isn't the same thing true of deliberate withholding of the truth?

It is also unclear why the requirement of respect should be thought to stop short of (or not include) respect for other beings as possessors of welfare, and thus unclear why consequentialist attempts to maximize well-being (or minimize harm) must be deemed incompatible with respecting other persons. Without minimum conditions of well-being – which surely include the possession of life itself – it is not possible to act as a rational creature. When, as deontological theories decree, we allow five people to be killed by a rockslide (or an evil agent) rather than harm one person ourself, why are we not guilty of failing to respect the five persons?

And, finally, even if it is possible to provide a plausible defence of regarding deontological constraints as narrowly framed and bounded, as well as some plausible account of the narrowness of respect, the question remains: why should respect be seen as something that morally outweighs the requirement to further others' well-being? Donagan tells us that

Common morality is outraged by the consequentialist position that, as long as human beings can remain alive, the lesser of two evils is always to be chosen. Its defenders maintain, on the contrary, that there are minimum conditions for a life worthy of a human being, and that nobody may purchase anything – not even the lives of a whole community – by sacrificing these conditions. (1977, p. 183)

There are problems with this characterization of the consequentialist position. But if we are to justify allowing the whole community to be lost rather than violate the deontological constraint that would prevent this, it is essential to be very clear on just what 'the minimum conditions for a life worthy of a human being' are, and what it is about a proposed effort to save hundreds of lives by (for example) killing one innocent person that constitutes a failure of respect so great that it is worth sacrificing all of those lives.

2   Though deontologists tell us that deontological constraints are absolute, that we are obliged to refrain from violating deontological constraints even when we know that our refusal to do so will have very bad consequences, the sort of absoluteness they have in mind is really both qualified and restricted. As we have seen, significant narrowing of the scope of deontological constraints' absolute force is achieved by the supposition that deontological constraints are narrowly framed and bounded. And further narrowing is achieved through the narrow-directedness of deontological constraints, the insistence that deontological constraints must be understood as applying only to the things that we do as chosen means or ends, and not to untoward consequences or results that we merely foresee as resulting from our action.

It is crucial for deontologists to be able to employ some sort of device to narrow the scope of deontological constraints, and crucial, in particular, for them to be able to distinguish the (permissible) causing of bad consequences from the (impermissible) performance of wrongful action. For unless they can do so, deon-

213

tological views threaten to degenerate into incoherence over the question of serious and irreconcilable conflicts of duty. If we are deemed to have violated the deontological constraint against harming the innocent when we refuse to lie to one person in order to prevent harm from befalling five other people, then we act wrongly whatever we do (nor is the coming about of such a bind necessarily a consequence of our – or anyone's – previous wrongful action). If deontological constraints are absolute (or categorical) – we are never justified in violating them – then we often act wrongly whatever we do. Some philosophers believe that there can be exceptional circumstances in which we act wrongly whatever we do, and they do not take this possibility to undermine an otherwise plausible moral theory. But such an option is not open to the deontologist, for unless there is a way of narrowing the scope of deontological constraints, conflicts of duty will be the norm, not the exception. And the notion of 'wrong' could not intelligibly be regarded as possessing absolute or categorical force; faced with the prospect of doing wrong by lying or doing wrong by causing harm, the unfortunate agent would have to consider which action would be more wrong. And from here it is but a short step to a view that looks much more like some form of consequentialism than deontology.

3   Though, as we have seen, it is essential for deontologists to be able to narrow the scope of deontological constraints, and to be able to distinguish the (permissible) causing of bad consequences from the (impermissible) performance of wrong acts, it is not at all clear that they can successfully do so. A number of philosophers have expressed scepticism about the possibility of producing any clear, principled, and non-question-begging way of distinguishing (wrongful) harming from the (mere) causing of harm. Though their reasoning is too complex to discuss here, its upshot can be briefly indicated. It is often true that our views about what sorts of things are right and wrong, and what sorts of bounds and limits there are on agents' responsibility for their deeds, determine our views about whether an act that causes harm is to be viewed as a case of wrongful harming or as the mere (permissible) causing of harm, rather than – as the deontologists suppose – vice versa. People with different normative moral views thus often have different beliefs about whether their acts merely (permissibly) caused harm or were (wrongfully) harmful. Someone who is initially inclined to believe that we are often obliged to take action to prevent bad consequences from occurring may see a knowing failure to prevent harm as a case of wrongful harming, while someone who (like the deontologist) has a more restricted view of our moral obligations will see it as a case of merely permissibly allowing harm to occur. For example, someone with consequentialist leanings will see a refusal to lie to one person in order to prevent serious harm from befalling five other people as a case of wrongfully harming the five, while someone with less consequentialist leanings might not. But if this is so, then even when people make a good faith effort to do what deontological views decree (e.g. avoid wrongful harming), they will interpret those views as giving rather different advice, and may thus act quite differently in their attempts to follow them.

Nor does the other favourite device of deontologists for attempting to narrow the scope of deontological constraints – reliance on 'the traditional principle of double effect' and the distinction between intended harm and merely foreseen harm – fare much better. As we have noted, both philosphers and legal theorists have criticized the principle of double effect, and raised questions about the tenability of the distinction between intention and mere foresight.

If – as I believe – there is merit in these criticisms, they may pose serious problems for contemporary deontological theories. For they force deontologists either to expand the scope of deontological prohibitions, or to retract the claim that those prohibitions have absolute or categorical force. As we have seen, the first horn of the dilemma lands deontologists with serious problems about conflicts of duty, as well as a view that is normatively implausible. And the second threatens to undermine the very structure of deontological views. If deontological constraints do not possess absolute or categorical force, then what sort of force do they possess, and how can an agent determine when a forbidden act really is forbidden and when it is not? If deontological constraints do not possess the sort of absolute or categorical force that their advocates have maintained they do, then deontological views threaten to collapse into a form of moral pluralism, and one that is deeply intuitionist at that. Agents are told that a whole raft of different things are wrong, but it is left to them to sort out how much force a particular prohibition should have in the particular circumstances, how wrong a putatively wrongful act actually is. There are, of course, philosophers who have held such views. (In this volume, such a position is discussed by Jonathan Dancy in Article 18, AN ETHIC OF PRIMA FACIE DUTIES.) But these views are a far cry from deontology, at least as its contemporary advocates present it.

In fact, though many of their statements suggest that their view is uncompromisingly absolute, deontologists do not think that we are justified in refusing to violate deontological constraints when the consequences of our refusal would be dire. It is worth looking more closely at deontologists' reasoning on this point.

According to Fried,

we can imagine extreme cases where killing an innocent person may save a whole nation. In such cases it seems fanatical to maintain the absoluteness of the judgment, to do right even if the heavens will in fact fall. And so the catastrophic may cause the absoluteness of right and wrong to yield, but even then it would be a non sequitur to argue (as consequentialists are fond of doing) that this proves that judgments of right and wrong are always a matter of degree, depending on the relative goods to be attained and harms to be avoided. I believe, on the contrary, that the concept of the catastophic is a distinct concept just because it identifies the extreme situations in which the usual categories of judgment (including the category of right and wrong) no longer apply. (Fried, 1976, p. 10)

Donagan expresses a similar view in discussing consequentialism (1977, pp. 206–7).

Though allowing that we may violate deontological constraints in dire circumstances saves deontological views from the appearance of fanaticism, and thus confers greater normative plausibility on them, it may well undermine them as theories. The addition of a 'catastrophe clause' is particularly problematic. Why do the effects of our acts on others' weal and woe acquire relevance only at the 'catastrophic' level? And to what (clear and practicable) features can agents appeal to distinguish a 'catastrophic' situation in which 'right' and 'wrong' do not apply from a merely dreadful one in which they do?

It is hard to see how one can justify the view that a decision about whether or not to take the action that is necessary to save the nation (an action that would, in less extreme circumstances, be counted by Fried as being wrongful) is not a *moral* decision. Such a view carries the suggestion that terrible circumstances somehow relieve us of the obligation (though surely not the need!) to act morally. When 'traditional morality' was first formulated and advocated, both the scope and the threat of catastrophe, and people's ability to respond to it, were severely limited. But we now live in a world in which the threat of global 'catastrophe' is a real possibility, and our perceptions of human moral capacity and responsibility must expand to reflect our awareness of this. There are courses of action that might be taken in the face of an impending nuclear or environmental disaster (be it 'natural', 'accidental' or contrived) that would not only be foolish or mad, but wrong. The view that the concepts of right and wrong do not apply in extreme situations is one that encourages complacency, if not actual passivity. It is one that any responsible moral agent ought to reject.

iv Concluding remarks

At the heart of deontologists' insistence on the importance of moral rules or constraints lies the belief that the avoidance of wrongdoing is the principal – if not the only – task of a moral agent *qua* moral agent, and the conviction that, as moral agents, we have it in our power to aim at the avoidance of wrongdoing and achieve this aim, provided only that we make a reasonable and sincere effort. We can be assured of success if we avoid doing certain sorts of things, things which are narrowly and clearly specifiable, and specifiable beforehand, prior to involvement in the often overwhelming circumstances of deliberation and action.

Consider the deontological constraint against lying. What it requires of us is clear and simple, for lies are datable, locatable, and narrowly specifiable bits of conduct. (Similar things can be said about enslaving, torturing, and so forth.) If acting rightly consists mostly in avoiding wrongdoing – in the sense of avoiding the transgression of deontological constraints, or rules – and if the rules are relatively few in number, and clearly and narrowly specified, then the require- ments of morality are dischargeable (at least most of the time, for most agents). Even if it is acknowledged that agents may have some positive duties – they must keep the promises and contracts that they voluntarily make, and look after the children that they chose to have, for example – the requirements of morality are things that it is not difficult to get out of the way. (Recall Fried: 'After having avoided wrong and doing one's duty, an infinity of choices is left to be made' (1978, p. 13).)

That this conception of morality is legalistic is obvious, and the conception of law that it is modelled on is not hard to construct. On such a view, what is required of us by law is that we refrain from violating the statutes, and such a requirement is one that is clear, and usually easily dischargeable, for it is one which usually intrudes only minimally into the private lives of ordinary decent citizens, and obedience to it is generally not difficult. Obedience is understood simply as compliance: whether we refrain from cheating on our taxes, stealing others' goods or harming our neighbours out of fear of the consequences of our transgression, out of Lockean respect for the property of others, or out of Kantian respect for their rational wills, is immaterial. It is our compliance with the law, and that alone, that establishes us as persons of rectitude.

The sort of compliance that is required by this legalistic conception of morality is not only straightforward and simple, it is also – quite speciously, I believe – strict. We are bound to obey carefully formulated laws, but obedience is understood in very narrow terms. We are bound only to comply with the letter of the law; we are not obliged to go beyond that and seek to embody its spirit in our deeds. If we can find loopholes in the law, we cannot be legally chastised if we choose to take advantage of them.

Compliance is also a relatively easy matter. Citizens can ascertain just what the law is, and just what is required of them, if they make a reasonable, but hardly strenuous, effort to find out. And if they cannot find it out, then they are generally not faulted for whatever transgressions they may then go on to (inadvertently) commit.

Whatever merits or problems may attend this interpretation of positive law and its requirements, it is quite unsatisfactory as a framework for understanding moral requirements, or a model for the construction of a moral theory. Some of the reasons are obvious. Without an easily identifiable and authoritative moral law-giver, we cannot be sure of knowing just what moral laws (deontological constraints) must constrain our conduct. And without a clear set of procedures that explain how disputes regarding the content of proposed moral laws are to be settled, there is no way of adjudicating or resolving serious disagreements on that issue. But there are also less obvious reasons for rejecting this legalistic picture of morality.

The belief that the requirements of morality are things that we can or should aim to get out of the way so that we can go about the really important (and presumably, morally neutral) business of living our lives as we choose is one that seems, upon reflection, both normatively and psychologically unsound. For we are members of a moral community, not just discrete rational wills or guardians of our own virtue, and we care about other individuals in that community, as well as about the community itself. And the proper expression of such concern is not just the credo of non-interference that gets reflected in the minimal deontological notion of respect, and the narrow deontological constraints that are taken to express or follow from it (for example, not lying, cheating, or otherwise impeding people from getting on with their own lives), but one that involves, and requires, people's active interest in promoting others' well-being. We must thus reject any picture of morality that views it simply (or primarily) as a burden externally imposed on our lives. If we cannot 'live our life by the demands of the domain of the right', (Fried, 1978, p. 13), we must at least acknowledge that that domain is wider than contemporary deontologists have supposed.

References

Donagan, A.: *The Theory of Morality* (Chicago: University of Chicago Press, 1977).
Fried, C.: *Right and Wrong* (Cambridge, Mass.: Harvard University Press, 1978).
Nagel, T.: *The View from Nowhere* (New York: Oxford University Press, 1986), Chapter IX.
Rawls, J.: *A Theory of Justice* (Cambridge, Mass.: Harvard University Press, 1971).

Further reading

Anscombe, G. E. M.: 'Modern moral philosophy', *Philosophy*, 33 (1958) 1–19; reprinted in J. Thomson and G. Dworkin, eds., *Ethics* (New York: Harper & Row, 1968), pp. 186–210.
Davis, N.: 'The priority of avoiding harm', in Steinbock, B., ed., *Killing and Letting Die* (Englewood Cliffs, NJ., 1980), pp. 172–214.
——: 'The doctrine of double effect: problems of interpretation', *Pacific Philosophical Quarterly*, 65 (1984), 107–23.
Devine, P. E.: *The Ethics of Homicide* (Ithaca, NY: Cornell University Press, 1978).
Mackie, J. L.: *Ethics* (New York: Penguin, 1977). Chapter 7.
Scheffler, S.: *The Rejection of Consequentialism* (Oxford: Oxford University Press, 1982).

18

An ethic of prima facie duties

JONATHAN DANCY

A CLASSIC conception of a moral theory is that it should contain a list of basic moral principles, a justification for each item on the list, and some account of how to derive more ordinary principles from the ones we started with. The obvious example is classical utilitarianism, which offers us a single basic principle, tells us some story about why we should accept this principle (this bit is often missed out, but it shouldn't be), and then shows how to derive from it principles like 'Do not lie', and 'Care for your parents' (an example to which I am becoming increasingly attached). If our theory offers more than one basic principle, it needs also to show how the ones it does offer fit together as a group. This can be done in various ways. We could argue directly that no one of them should be accepted unless the rest were, or more indirectly that together they embody a coherent and attractive conception of a moral agent – and there are other ways too, of course.

The theory of prima facie duties does not look much like this. First, it does not suppose that some moral principles are more basic than others. Second, it does not suggest that there is any coherence in the list of principles it does offer. It is a contribution to moral philosophy, certainly, but it is not a moral theory in the classical sense; it holds that in ethics everything is pretty messy and there is not much room for that sort of theory at all. This is rather like holding that we can say something about the physical nature of the world but that what we can say does not amount to the sort of theory that physicists have come to expect. We may not find this very exciting but it might nonetheless be the only sort of theory we are going to get, since the world (moral or physical) fails to fit the desires of theorists.

To see why that might be so we need to look at how W. D. Ross, the creator of the theory of prima facie duties, argued for it. (He would not have claimed to have been the theory's only parent – rather he was working on ideas at least partly due to H. A. Prichard.)

Ross, who did his main work at the University of Oxford in the 1920s and 30s, started out by arguing that all forms of monism (the view that there is only one basic moral principle) are false. He only knew of two forms of monism – Kantianism and utilitarianism; so he tackled them in turn. His argument against Kant was that Kant's basic principle is incoherent. The principle is something like this: 'Only acts done from the motive of duty are right'. Ross thought that this amounted to saying that we ought to act from a certain motive. But he urged that the only things which one can say we ought to do are things which it is in our power either to do or not to do. We cannot choose what motives we will act from; our motives are not up to us. We can choose what we will do but not why we will do it. So we cannot be required to act from a particular motive. Kant does require this of us, and hence his theory must be rejected. In Article 14, KANTIAN ETHICS, Onora O'Neill denies that Kant holds the view that Ross attributes to him; See p. 183 above.)

Utilitarianism was rejected for rather different reasons. Ross knew that utilitarianism was only one version of the more general approach called consequentialism. He did not suppose that all forms of consequentialism must be monistic, since he was aware that G. E. Moore's ideal utilitarianism was pluralistic. (Moore held that the right action is the one that maximizes the good, but also held that there are just various different sorts of things that are good, such as knowledge and aesthetic experience.) But he argued against consequentialism knowing that if he succeeded here he would also have refuted utilitarianism. The argument starts from a straightforward claim, supported by an example. The claim is that 'ordinary people' think they ought to do what they promised to do, not because of the (probable) consequences of breaking their promises, but simply because they promised. But in thinking this way, they are not considering their moral duties in terms of consequences at all. The consequences of their actions lie in the *future*, but they are thinking more about the *past* (about the promises they made). The example goes as follows: suppose that you have promised to perform some undemanding task – your neighbour's car has broken down and you promised to take him out shopping with you this morning. But now an opportunity arises for you to do something a bit more valuable instead – perhaps just take two other similarly stranded neighbours to meet their daughter at the airport. Ross suggests that viewing the matter solely in terms of the consequences, you would have to agree that what you ought to do was to break your promise, for the dismay of neighbour 1 at being let down would be overbalanced by the pleasure of neighbours 2 and 3 at not having to make three bus changes to get to the airport. But still, he argues, against this balance of the consequences is to be put the fact that you promised, and in a case like this this fact might win the day. You might feel that, in spite of the potential gain in the consequences, what you ought to do is to keep your original promise. Of course, you would not feel this in a case where the benefit gained by breaking your promise was much greater, but that doesn't do anything to show that in *this* case the right course is to break your promise.

What this shows is that though it matters what the consequences of one's actions will be, other things can matter as well. Consequentialism simply fails to capture the whole story. (Philip Pettit indicates how the consequentialist would respond in section (iii) of Article 19, CONSEQUENTIALISM.) Ross's general view is that there are all sorts of things that matter, so that no very neat list of morally significant features can be made. Among the things that matter are that you should be beneficent (help others where you can), that you should foster your own talents, and that you should treat others fairly. Perhaps all these things do have an importance which can be understood in terms of the difference acting in that sort of way can make to the world (i.e. in terms of consequences). But what you ought to do can be affected by other things as well, for instance by earlier actions of your own in various ways (as, in our example, by your earlier promise) or by earlier actions of others, as when you owe a debt of gratitude to someone for a past act of kindness.

Ross expresses this position using the notion of a prima facie duty. He says that we have a prima facie duty to help others, another to keep our promises, another to repay past acts of kindness and another not to let down people who are relying on us. What he means by this is just that these things matter morally; they make a difference to what we should do and to whether we acted rightly in what we chose to do. If we choose to keep a promise, our action is right to that extent – as far as that goes it is right – it's being a promise-keeping counts in favour of it. This is what Ross means when he says that our action is a prima facie duty in virtue of being an act of promise-keeping. Of course whether it is a promise-keeping or not is not the only relevant consideration. Other things matter too, as we have seen; we express this by saying that we have other prima facie duties as well, for instance the prima facie duty to increase the welfare of others (the prima facie duty of beneficence). And these other prima facie duties may matter more in the case we are considering. We cannot tell in advance which relevant prima facie duty will turn out to matter most in the situation we are faced with. All we can do is to consider the circumstances and try to decide whether it is more important here to keep our promise or to drive neighbours 2 and 3 to the airport. No rule or set of rules can help us in this.

So a given action can be a prima facie duty in virtue of one feature (promise-keeping, perhaps), a prima facie duty in virtue of another (it will be a great help to neighbour 1), and prima facie wrong in virtue of some third feature (it means that neighbours 2 and 3 are going to have a hard time getting to the airport). Put in ordinary English, this just means that some features of the action count in its favour and others count against. Once we have established which features count which way, we make an attempt to decide where the balance lies. This is inescapably a matter for judgement, according to Ross, and theory cannot help at all. Theory could only help if we could rank our different prima facie duties in order of importance, so that we knew in advance that, say, it is always more important to help others than to keep one's promises. But no such ranking fits the facts. The plain fact is that sometimes one ought to keep one's promises even at an overall cost to others, and sometimes the cost of keeping one's promise means that here it would be better to break it, for once. Ross would say that this sort of thing is just a feature of our moral predicament. It would no doubt be nice if the world was neat and orderly, so that our different prima facie duties could be ranked once and for all. But 'it is more important that our theory fit the facts than that it be simple' (Ross, 1930, p. 19). There is no general ranking of the different types of prima facie duty, and since different moral principles express different prima facie duties, there is no general ranking of moral principles. There is just a shapeless list of them, which is no more than a list of the things that make a moral difference, a difference to what we should do.

What do these different moral principles tell us? An obvious suggestion is that the principle 'Do not steal' tells us that all actions of theft are actually wrong. If this is what the principle tells us, the principle is false if there is a single act of stealing which is not in fact wrong. This makes it appear that a counter-example to a purported moral principle would consist just of a right action which the principle forbids, or of a wrong action which the principle requires. But in that case probably all moral principles are false. I suspect that for each principle you mention it will be possible to dream up a situation in which one ought to break it. For instance, one ought not to steal, perhaps, but someone whose only method of feeding his family is to steal *ought* to steal, especially if he is going to steal from wealthy people living in great luxury. He would be wrong not to; we would hardly approve his watching his family die of malnutrition while repeating to himself 'I could feed them by stealing, but stealing is wrong'. Similarly, on this account of what moral principles tell us no two principles could both survive a conflict. If I believe that only fish breathe water and that no fish have legs, and I then come across a creature which breathes water and has legs, one of my 'principles' has to be scrapped. In the same vein, suppose I believe that one ought to tell the truth and that one ought to help those in need. What is to happen when I am sheltering a runaway slave in the deep South and the owner comes asking if I know where his 'property' has got to? A case like this would show that one of my principles must be rejected. But this is surely wrong. Principles can survive conflict like this, even though one of them has to give (it is not right *here* to tell the truth). Ross, with his notion of a prima facie duty, can give an account of what principles tell us which shows how this is so. Our two principles say that we have a prima facie duty to tell the truth and a prima facie duty to help those in need. It is true that here I have to choose between telling the truth and helping the needy. But this does nothing to show that either principle should be abandoned. In fact it just shows that we should retain them both, since the very existence of a conflict is evidence that it does matter whether one tells the truth (i.e. that we have a prima facie duty to do so) and it does matter whether we are helping the needy when we can (i.e. we have a prima facie duty to do that too). The conflict is between two things that do matter, and it is resolved not by abandoning either principle but just by coming to a decision about which matters more in this situation.

This gives a different picture of what a counter-example to a moral principle would look like. Instead of being an example where the principle tells us to do one thing and we think we ought to do the opposite ('Do not steal'), it would be an example where, though the principle tells us that some feature counts in favour of any action that has it, we think it either makes no difference at all here or else that it does make a difference, but counts in the opposite direction. To give an example of each: my daughter trod on a sea-urchin on holiday last year, and we caused her great pain (not entirely with her consent) in extracting the spines from her heel. Is this a counter-example to the purported principle 'Do not cause pain to others'? Your answer will depend on whether you think that our actions were morally speaking the worse to the extent that they caused her pain, or whether you think that the pain we caused her made no moral difference or was not a moral reason for not doing what we did. An example of a feature counting in the opposite direction might be the thought that in general it is indeed a point in favour of an action that it is the cause of pleasure both for the agent and for the onlookers. But sometimes it is a point against; consider the suggestion that we have more reason to have public executions of convicted rapists if the event would give pleasure both to the executioner and to the crowds that would no doubt attend. If we reject that suggestion, we have here a counter-example to the purported principle 'It is right to act so as to cause pleasure for yourself and others'.

So Ross gives a distinctive account of what it is that moral principles tell us; they express prima facie duties – duties to act or to avoid acting. Ross contrasts prima facie duties with what he calls duties proper. An action is a prima facie duty in virtue of having a certain property (e.g. being the return of a favour); this property (maybe along with others) counts *for* its being done, while yet further properties may count against. The action is a duty proper if it is one which we ought *overall* to do – if all things considered we should do it. In deciding whether this is so we try to balance against each other the various prima facie duties we have in the case, deciding which matter more here, which side the balance comes down on. There is a clear contrast here between duty proper and prima facie duty.

But there is more to this contrast. Ross wants to say that we often know for certain what our prima facie duties are, but we can never *know* what our duty proper is. Put another way, this means that we have certain knowledge of moral principles, but no knowledge of what we ought overall to do in any actual situation. This is an interesting combination of general moral certainty with a sort of diffidence about particular cases. Ross takes a distinctive position in what is called moral epistemology (the theory of moral knowledge and the justification of moral belief).

First, how do we come to know the truth of any moral principle? Some philosophers hold that we know the truth of such principles directly (it was sometimes said that we know them by a sort of moral intuition). For instance, it has been held that the principle 'One should treat all people equally' is self-evident, in the sense that you only have to consider it with an open mind and its truth will simply strike you. Ross does not believe any such thing. For him, the only way to come to know a principle is to discover its truth in moral experience. It happens like this: first we are faced with a case in which we have to make a decision what to do. My wife and I are going out to dinner with some people that I know but she doesn't know. I am keen not to offend these people and generally to make a good impression. My wife knows this. However, time is getting on and we are already a bit late. My wife emerges, all ready for the fray, and asks me whether she is suitably dressed for the occasion. It is immediately clear to me that she is not. What am I to say? I have three choices. The first is to lie, and hope that the truth will not be apparent to her as soon as we walk into our hosts' house. The second is to tell the truth, so that she goes and puts on something else (making us even later). The third is to say that what she is wearing is not right but that it is too late to change it now because we are already late. This has the advantage of minimizing our lateness but only at the cost of completely poisoning

223

the evening for her and generally causing her distress. Now what Ross wants to say about this is that I can see already three sorts of consideration that are mattering or making a difference here. The first is that it is better if we are not late. The second is that it is better not to lie about the dress. The third is that it is better not to distress one's nearest and dearest. These things are all in the story here; they all matter and I have just got to sort out which is more important than the others. So far everything I have noticed is restricted in its relevance to the case before me. But I can immediately move beyond that, for I can see that what matters here must matter wherever it occurs. It is important not to be late here, and this tells me that it is generally important not to be late. What has happened is that I have learnt the truth of a moral principle (which expresses a prima facie duty) in what I have noticed in a particular case. I did this by generalizing, using a process called 'intuitive induction'. It is the same process as the one by which logical principles are taught (to oneself or to others). I get you to see the validity of some particular argument, such as 'All cows are brown: all heifers are cows: so all heifers are brown'. Then I call on you to generalize from the case before you to this general principle: 'All Bs are Cs: all As are Bs: so all As are Cs'. The idea is that if you are sufficiently alert and intelligent you will just be able to see the general truth that lay in the particular case you started from. It is the same idea in ethics.

Ross held that as our life goes on we come across features that matter to some choice we have to make, and that we learn from this that these features matter generally – matter wherever they occur. In this way experience reveals to us the truth of general principles of prima facie duty. These principles are self-evident, not in the sense that one only has to ask oneself whether they are true to know that they are, but in the weaker sense that they are evident in what the particular case shows us. The act of generalization adds nothing significant to what we already knew. So what happens is that we start from something about which there is no significant doubt, for instance that it is better if we are not late tonight. We move from that by a process which adds nothing contentious to the recognition that it is generally better not to be late, and we have emerged with a grasp of a self-evident moral principle.

We reached that principle from what we noticed about the case before us – that it matters here whether we are late or not, that it matters whether I tell the truth, and so on. But what I notice about the case has to serve another role; it has to help me decide what I should actually do (my duty proper). This is a completely different enterprise, in Ross's view. Here I am engaged in trying to decide not what matters (I already know this) but how much each of the principles matters and which of them matters most here. Questions of balance like this are inherently so difficult that my eventual judgement could never be called *knowledge*, but can at best count as probable opinion. So it emerges that we know many moral principles but can never be said to know which choice we should actually make. We can know our prima facie duties but never our duties proper.

I have told this part of the story in terms of what we can know and what we cannot know. These are terms that Ross himself would have been happy to use, since he held that there are facts about what is right and wrong which we can sometimes get to know. (This is what makes him an intuitionist; see Article 36, INTUITIONISM.) But I could have told the same story in non-cognitivist terms (see Article 38, SUBJECTIVISM) by saying simply that though one may strongly disapprove in general of such things as lying and upsetting one's nearest and dearest, still we should never be too confident that the attitude we are tempted to adopt in a given situation is the right one. Firmness of commitment at the general level can and should go with recognition of the complexity inherent in any difficult moral choice. And we might move from this to the thought that we should be tolerant of those whose attitude here differs from ours, since we should never lose our sense of how unstable such decisions are.

One further feature of the relation between prima facie duties and duties proper is worth mentioning. We have distinguished three elements in the story. First was my recognition of properties which made a difference here. Second was my resulting recognition of general prima facie duties. Third was my judgement about my duty proper. One might suppose that just as we move to the second element from the first, we move to the third from the second. But that is not Ross's view. He holds that I move to the overall judgement directly from the first element, my recognition of the properties that matter here. I don't work through my knowledge of any moral principles. I don't make my decision in the light of any general principles of prima facie duty. He says 'I never seem to be in the position of not seeing directly the rightness of a particular act of kindness, for instance, and of having to read this off from a general principle – "all acts of kindness are right, and therefore this must be, though I cannot see its rightness directly"' (Ross, 1930, p. 171). The only occasions when I might need to do that are ones where I have it on good authority that some property is important when I haven't been able to see this for myself, or where I am so overcome by lust or another strong passion that I need to remind myself of a relevant feature of the situation which I would not be likely to notice otherwise ('Married people ought not to sleep with people they are not married to, and I am not married to this person'). This might restore my lost sense of the relevance of a relevant feature. But normally I don't work through the prima facie principles at all.

This must raise the question what use the principles are, and why, if they are really of no use, Ross sees them as an important element in the story. We have admitted that knowledge of the principles can be of some use occasionally. But this would hardly satisfy those who think that a grip on principles is central to what it is to be a respectable moral agent. There is a very general view that to be a moral agent is just to accept and act on a set of principles which one applies to oneself and others equally. Ross does not accept this picture. For him, respectable agents are ones who are sensitive to the morally relevant features of the situations they find themselves in, not in a general way but just case by case. There is a stress on perception here; moral agents see as relevant the features that are relevant, and see as most relevant the ones that in fact are most relevant. They do not *work out* that these features matter by bringing a packet of moral principles to bear on the situation. They see them as relevant in their own right, without help from the list of moral principles which they admittedly know.

There is one way in which a good list of moral principles might help, and that would be to reassure oneself that one has not missed the relevance of anything. With a complete checklist, one could get this benefit. But of course there is no suggestion in Ross's theory that there will be such a thing as a complete list of prima facie duties – of properties that make a moral difference. There may be a reasonably short list of *types* of prime facie duty, and Ross gives such a list himself, though he is careful not to claim that it is complete; but this does not mean that one could complete an explicit list of the actual prima facie duties we have.

So it does not look as if our moral principles are much use to us, on Ross's theory. And it is not clear to me that there could easily be a different version of the theory, which held that the principles do play a significant role. After all, the main argument for the theory consists in an appeal to the sorts of things people find important in cases that confront them, the point being that not everything that seems to matter can be accounted for by consequentialists. Given this appeal to what we find in particular cases, and the resulting account of how we extract moral principles from what we find, it is very hard to see how we could ascribe a greater role to those principles in future decisions than the one which Ross allows.

Why then is he so convinced that there are any moral principles? The answer is that it just seems obvious to him that if a feature makes a moral difference in one case, it must make the same difference everywhere. It is impossible for a feature to matter in this case alone; mattering must be general mattering. This can be disputed; I will shortly give some reasons for doubting it. Ross believes it, and it is his only reason for allowing that there are such things as moral principles at all. He believes it because it offers him some sense in which as we make moral choices through life we can be said to be choosing *consistently*; we choose consistently because our choices reflect the attempt to allot the same weight to every feature that matters wherever it occurs. So though Ross holds that in moral decision we are responding to the rich particularity of the case before us, he can say that we make each choice in the light of what our moral experience has taught us.

I end with two criticisms of the theory of prima facie duties. The first is that it leaves no real room for thoughts about rights. Although Ross is antagonistic to utilitarianism, his theory shares one feature with it. This is the thought that in every case of moral decision-making, we are in the business of balancing the prima facie duties on the one side against those on the other. But one standard attack on utilitarianism has been that this sort of approach completely fails to capture something we think of as important. In the vexed issue of abortion, we might think it quite unsuitable to decide the fate of the fetus solely on the question whether the world overall will be a happier place with or without it. We may feel that the fetus has a right to its life which is independent of and should stand before any question of balancing the advantages and disadvantages of getting rid of it.

The fetus's right is here viewed as a 'trump'; what this means is that where there are no such rights at issue, other considerations such as those of the overall consequences of our actions come into play and properly decide what we ought to do, but where there are rights (as in the case of abortion) the rights decide the issue, rendering thoughts of consequences null and void. We might even say that to treat rights as lying in the balance with other considerations is deep evidence of immorality. Any such approach as this is in opposition to the theory of prima facie duties, for on that approach all duties are (and are nothing more than) prima facie; there is nothing stronger than that, which can reasonably claim to be a trump.

Ross could offer something in his own defence here. He could remind us that there are many cases where people mistakenly take as trumps considerations which should not be allowed to play that role. For instance, a lawyer who discovers the guilt of his client may feel that he is bound by a duty of confidentiality, a duty which derives from the joint roles of lawyer and client, and suppose that this duty is a trump, i.e. that it precedes and quashes all thoughts of the harm that may be done by remaining silent. There are many similar cases where people feel that they are bound by absolute duties deriving from their role or status, which prevent them from doing acts which in themselves would have enormously good consequences or prevent terribly bad ones. Ross could fairly argue that this is all bad faith. We are using our professional duties as an excuse, hiding behind them to avoid having to face the problem for what it is. But one might agree that *some* appeal to rights and duties is bad faith, without admitting that all such appeals are. And the fact is that many people find morally distasteful the thought that all our moral decisions should be made by balancing pros and cons in the way Ross recommends.

The best defence of Ross now is to argue that the importance of rights is exaggerated if we think of them as trumps. Rights are indeed important, and this fact can itself be captured within the theory of prima facie duties by awarding rights great weight when we come to balance reasons for and against. But there will always come a point where an individual's rights should be infringed; for instance, it would not be right to refuse to imprison an innocent person if by doing so one could prevent a nuclear holocaust.

Opponents of Ross would now argue that even if this is what should be done in such a case, still the action would be intrinsically evil in a way that Ross cannot capture. For Ross, any reasons against doing the action have already been used up in the assessment of the balance of *pros* and *cons*. Defeated reasons do not remain in the story making the action somehow both right (maybe even required) and also evil. A right action, for Ross, cannot be evil. But many philosophers think that in tragic cases such as the one above we can be required to do evil. (See, for instance, Nagel's essay 'War and massacre', 1979.)

The second criticism comes from the opposite direction, and concerns the role of moral principles in the theory. I have already said that these play a minimal role, but the question is why, if we start from the place where Ross starts, we should accept that there are any such principles at all. What Ross supposes, without argument, is that a feature which counts in favour of this action must count in the same way in favour of any action which has it. Now he can be fairly flexible about this. He could say, for example, that though this feature is always a *pro* rather than a *con*, the extent to which it is a *pro* here can be affected by what else is true in this case. So the same feature need not be thought of as always adding just the same amount to the balance, but if it once counts as a *pro* it will always be a *pro*. It is this last point that I think one can reasonably challenge. First, its presence in the theory makes the theory unstable, since Ross has to show somehow that what we notice as mattering in a particular case we immediately see must matter in the same way on every recurrence. But it is hard to see how this is possible, for it supposes implausibly that the ability of a feature to make a difference in a particular case is entirely independent of the other features it is there present with. So the theory allows too small a role to context; it is too atomistic. I prefer a theory which allows the contribution of a feature to be entirely sensitive to the context in which it is here present, so that what here counts in favour may elsewhere count against. To take the example I used before: that an action causes great pleasure to large numbers of people including its agent is surely often a reason for doing it, one might think. But where the action is a public hanging, we might suppose that the pleasure it would cause is a reason *against* doing it. This is only a schematic example, but the qustion is why we should resist it. And if we do not resist it and others like it, we have effectively abandoned the claim that there are such things as moral principles. Ross already admits that they are no *use*. I suggest that he would have done better to do without them altogether.

Ross's reply to this would have been that without principles of any sort there is no possibility of achieving a consistent moral position; to be morally consistent just is to allow the same weight every time to something that matters, independently of its context. My response would be to offer a new account of consistency, which grants context a larger role than Ross allows, in a way that I think fits our actual moral practice better. But this is not the place for that account.

References

Nagel, T.: 'War and massacre', in his *Mortal Questions* (Cambridge: Cambridge University Press, 1979), pp. 53–74.

Prichard, H. A.: 'Does moral philosophy rest on a mistake?', in his *Moral Obligation* (Oxford: Clarendon Press, 1949), pp. 1–17.

Ross, W. D.: *The Right and The Good* (Oxford: Clarendon Press, 1930), especially Chapters 1–2.

——: *Foundations of Ethics* (Oxford: Clarendon Press, 1939).

Further reading

Dancy, J.: 'Ethical particularism and morally relevant properties', *Mind*, XCII (1983), 530–
    47.
Searle, J. R.: 'Prima facie reasons', *Philosophical Subjects*, ed. Z. van Straaten (Oxford: Oxford
    University Press, 1980) pp. 238–59.

19

Consequentialism

PHILIP PETTIT

i The definition of consequentialism

MORAL theories, theories about what individual or institutional agents ought to do, all involve at least two different components. First, they each put forward a view about what is good or valuable, though they do not all make this explicit and may even resist talk of the good: they each put forward a view about which properties we ought to want realized in our actions or in the world more generally. A theory like classical utilitarianism holds that the only property that matters is how far sentient beings enjoy happiness. A natural law theory holds that the property which matters is compliance with the law of nature. Various other theories propose that what matters is human freedom, social solidarity, the autonomous development of nature, or a combination of such features. The possibilities are endless, since about the only commonly recognized constraint is that in order to be valuable a property must not involve a particular individual or setting essentially; it must be a universal feature, capable of being realized here or there, with this individual or that.

This first component in a moral theory is sometimes described as a theory of value or a theory of the good. (This component is discussed by Robert Goodin in Article 20, UTILITY AND THE GOOD.) The second component which every moral theory involves is often described in parallel as a theory of the right. It is a view, not about which properties are valuable, but about what individual and institutional agents should do by way of responding to valuable properties. Depending on the view adopted on this question, moral theories are usually divided into two kinds, consequentialist and non-consequentialist or, to use an older terminology, teleological and non-teleological: the non-teleological is sometimes identified with, and sometimes taken just to include, the deontological. This essay is concerned with consequentialist theories, as theories of the right, but not with any particular theory of value or of the good.

Suppose I decide, in a moment of intellectualist enthusiasm, that what matters above all in human life is that people understand the history of their species and their universe. How ought I to respond to this perceived value? Is my primary responsibility to honour it in my own life, bearing witness to the importance of such understanding by devoting myself to it? Or is my primary responsibility rather to promote such understanding generally, say by spending most of my time on proselytizing and politics, giving only the hours I cannot better spend to the development of my own understanding? Is the proper response to the value one of promoting its general realization, honouring it in my own actions only when there is nothing better I can do to promote it?

Again, suppose I decide that what is of importance in life is nothing so abstract as intellectual understanding but rather the enjoyment of personal loyalties, whether the loyalties of family or friendship. Here too there is a question about how I should respond to such a value. Should I honour the value in my own life, devoting myself to developing the bonds of kith and kin? Or should I only permit myself such devotion so far as that is part of the more general project of promoting the enjoyment of personal loyalties? Should I be prepared to use my time in the manner most effective for that project even if the cost of doing so – say, the cost of spending so much time on journalism and politics – is that my own personal loyalties are put under severe strain?

These two examples are from the sphere of personal morality but the same question arises in the institutional area. Suppose that a liberal government comes to power, a government which is primarily concerned with people's enjoying liberty. Should such a government honour people's liberty punctiliously in its own conduct, avoiding any interference that offends against liberty? Or should it pursue all measures, including offences against liberty, that make for a greater degree of liberty overall? Imagine that a group forms which begins agitating for a return to authoritarian rule: say, a rule associated with an influential religious tradition. Imagine, to make things harder, that the group has a real chance of success. Should the government permit the group to conduct its activities, on the grounds of honouring people's liberty to form whatever associations they choose? Or should it ban the group, on the grounds that while the ban interferes with people's liberty, it makes for the enjoyment of a greater degree of liberty overall; it means that there will not be a return to an illiberal society.

Consequentialism is the view that whatever values an individual or institutional agent adopts, the proper response to those values is to promote them. The agent should honour the values only so far as honouring them is part of promoting them, or is necessary in order to promote them. Opponents of consequentialism, on the other hand, hold that at least some values call to be honoured whether or not they are thereby promoted. Consequentialists see the relation between values and agents as an instrumental one: agents are required to produce whatever actions have the property of promoting a designated value, even actions that fail intuitively to honour it. Opponents of consequentialism see the relation between values and agents as a non-instrumental one: agents are required or at least allowed to let their actions exemplify a designated value, even if this makes for a lesser realization of the value overall.

This way of introducing the distinction between consequentialism and non-consequentialism, by reference just to agents and values, is unusual but, I hope, intuitively appealing. One drawback it involves is that the notion of promoting a value, and even more so the notion of honouring a value, is not carefully defined. In the next section this fault is remedied in some measure. (The section will be too philosophical for many tastes but it can be read lightly without great loss.)

ii Once more, with some formality

In order to introduce our more formal approach, it will be useful to define two notions: that of an option and that of a prognosis associated with an option. An option may be a directly behavioural option such as that expressed by a proposition like 'I do A' but equally it may be only indirectly behavioural, as with options such as 'I commit myself to being faithful to this principle of benevolence' or 'I endorse this trait of competitiveness in myself: I shall do nothing to change it'. The defining feature of an option is that it is a possibility which the agent is in a position to realize or not. He can make it the case – or not – that he does A, that he lets the principle of benevolence dictate his actions, or that he remains complacently competitive.

Although an option is a possibility that can be realized, the agent will almost never be able to determine how exactly the possibility works out; that will depend on other agents and on other things in the world. I may do A and it rains or not, I may do A and there is a third world war or not: the list is open. Given the differences in how such conditions can work out, any option has different prognoses. If an option is a possibility that can be realized, its prognoses are the different possible ways in which the possibility can come to be realised. The notion of a prognosis picks up one version of the familar notion of a consequence.

Returning now to the definition of consequentialism, we can identify two propositions which consequentialists generally defend.

1   Every prognosis for an option, every way the world may be as the result of a choice of option, has a value that is determined, though perhaps not up to uniqueness, by the valuable properties realized there: determined by how far it is a happy world, a world in which liberty is respected, a world where nature thrives, and so on for different valuable properties; the value determined will not be unique, so far as the weightings between such properties are not uniquely fixed.

2   Every option, every possibility which an agent can realize or not, has its value fixed by the values of its prognoses: its value is a function of the values of its different prognoses, a function of the values associated with the different ways it may lead the world to be.

The motivation for going into this level of detail was to give clearer content to the notion of promoting a value. An agent promotes certain values in his or her choices, we can now say, if – and indeed only if – the agent ranks the prognoses of options in terms of these values (proposition 1) and ranks the options – where the ranking determines his choice – in terms of their prognoses (proposition 2). There is an indeterminacy in proposition 2, since it has been left open how exactly the value of an option is fixed by the values of its prognoses. The usual approach among consequentialists, though not the only possible one, is to cast an option as a gamble among the different possible prognoses and borrow a procedure from decision theory to compute its value. On this approach you find the value of the option by adding up the values of the different prognoses – and we assume these are uniquely determined – discounting each such value by the probability the prognosis has – say, a quarter or a half – of being the correct one; I leave open the question of whether the appropriate probability to use is objective chance, subjective credence, 'rational' credence, or whatever. Suppose that the agent's concern is to save life and that in some dire circumstances two options present themselves: one gives a fifty per cent probability of saving one hundred lives, the other a certainty of saving forty. Other things being equal – which they will rarely be – the approach would favour the first option.

We now have a better grasp of what it is the consequentialist says. The consequentialist holds that the proper way for an agent to respond to any values recognized is to promote them: that is, in every choice to select the option with prognoses that mean it is the best gamble with those values. But we can now also be somewhat more specific about what the non-consequentialist says. There are two varieties of non-consequentialism, two ways of holding that certain values should be honoured, not promoted. One variety insists that while there are respectful or loyal options, there is no sense to the notion of promoting the abstract value of loyalty or respect. This is to deny the consequentialist's first proposition, holding that values like loyalty and respect do not determine abstract scores for the different prognoses of an option; the values are irrelevant to prognoses, failing even to determine non-unique scores. The other position which the non-consequentialist may take is to admit the first proposition, acknowledging that the notion of an agent promoting values at least makes sense, but to deny the second: that is, deny that the best option is necessarily determined by the values of its prognoses. The important thing is not to produce the goods but to keep your hands clean.

One last thought, while we are being more formal, on non-consequentialism. This is that non-consequentialists assume with the properties they think should be honoured rather than promoted, that the agent will always be in a position to know for certain whether an option will or will not have one of those properties. Faced with a value like that of respect or loyalty, the idea is that I will never be uncertain whether or not a given option will be respectful or loyal. The assumption of certainty may be reasonable with such examples but it will not generally be so. And that means that with some valuable properties, the non-consequentialist strategy will often be undefined. Take a property like that of happiness. This value can lend itself to being honoured as well as being promoted: honouring it might require concern for the happiness of those you deal with directly, regardless of indirect effects. But it will not always be clear in practice what a non-consequentialist attachment to happiness requires. Non-consequentialists do not tell us how to choose when none of the available options is going to display the relevant value for sure. And there will often be cases of this kind with a value like that of happiness. There will often be cases where none of the options offers a certainty of doing well by the happiness of those you are dealing with directly: cases where one option offers a certain chance of that result and a second option offers the best prospect for happiness overall. The non-consequentialist response in such cases is simply not defined.

iii   The main argument against consequentialism

It is usually said against consequentialism that it would lead an agent to do horrendous deeds, so long as they promised the best consequences. It would forbid nothing absolutely: not rape, not torture, not even murder. This charge is on target but it is only relevant of course in horrendous circumstances. Thus if someone of ordinary values condoned torture, that would only be in circumstances where there was a great potential gain – the saving of innocent lives, the prevention of a catastrophe – and where there were not the bad consequences involved, say, in state authorities claiming the right to torture. Once it is clear that the charge is relevant only in horrendous circumstances, it ceases to be clearly damaging. After all the non-consequentialist will often have to defend an equally unattractive response in such circumstances. It may be awful to think of torturing someone but it must be equally awful to think of not doing so and consequently allowing, say, a massive bomb to go off in some public place.

Probably in view of this stand-off, the charge against consequentialism usually reduces to the associated claim that not only would it allow horrendous deeds in exceptional circumstances, it would allow and indeed encourage the general habit of contemplating such deeds: or if not of actively contemplating the deeds, at least of countenancing the possibility that they may be necessary. Consequentialism, it is said, would make nothing unthinkable. It would not allow agents to admit any constraints on what they can do, whether constraints associated with the rights of other people as independent agents or constraints associated with the claims of those who relate to them as intimates or dependants.

The idea behind this charge is that any consequentialist moral theory requires agents to change their deliberative habits in an objectionable fashion. They will have to calculate about every choice, it is said, identifying the different prognoses for every option, the value associated with each prognosis and the upshot of those various values for the value of the option. Doing this, they will be unable to recognize the rights of others as considerations that ought to constrain them without further thought to consequences; they will be unable to acknowledge the special claims of those near and dear to them, claims that ought normally to brook no calculation; and they will be unable to mark distinctions between permissible options, obligatory options and options of supererogatory virtue. They will become moralistic computers, insensitive to all such nuances. F. H. Bradley made the point nicely in the last century, in *Ethical Studies* (p. 107). 'So far as my lights go, this is to make possible, to justify, and even to encourage, an incessant practical casuistry; and that, it need scarcely be added, is the death of morality.'

But if this sort of charge was made in the last century, so it was also rebutted then, particularly by writers like John Austin and Henry Sidgwick. Such writers defended classical utilitarianism, the consequentialist moral theory according to which the only value is the happiness of human, or at least sentient beings. Austin picked a nice example when arguing in *The Province of Jurisprudence* (p. 108) that the utilitarian does not require agents to be incessant casuists. 'Though he approves of love because it accords with his principle, he is far from maintaining that the general good ought to be the motive of the lover. It was never contended or conceived by a sound, orthodox utilitarian, that the lover should kiss his mistress with an eye to a common weal.'

The point which Austin is making in this passage is that a consequentialist theory like utilitarianism is an account of what justifies an option over alternatives – the fact that it promotes the relevant value – not an account of how agents ought to deliberate in selecting the option. The lover's act may be justified by its promotion of human happiness, in which case the utilitarian will applaud. But that does not mean that the utilitarian expects lovers to select and monitor their overtures by reference to that abstract goal.

The line which non-consequentialists generally run against this response is to deny that it is available to their opponents. They say that if a consequentialist thinks that an agent's choices are justified or not by whether they promote certain values, then the consequentialist is committed to saying that the moral agent – the agent who seeks to be justified – should deliberate over how far in any setting the different options promote those values. In saying this, they assume that such deliberation is the best way for an agent to guarantee that the choice made promotes the values espoused.

This non-consequentialist rejoinder is unpersuasive, however, because that assumption is clearly false. Consider again the lover and his mistress. If the lover calculates his every embrace, fine-tuning it to the demands of the general happiness, there will probably be little pleasure in it for either party. A condition of the embrace's producing pleasure, and therefore of its contributing to the general happiness, is that it is relatively spontaneous, coming of natural and unreflective affections. The point hardly needs labouring.

But though the point is clear, and though it clearly applies in a variety of cases, it raises a question which consequentialists have been too slow to tackle, at least until recently. The question is this. Granted that consequentialism is a theory of justification, not a theory of deliberation, what practical difference – what difference in deliberative policy – is made by being a consequentialist? Suppose the lover in Austin's example were to become himself a utilitarian. What sort of policy could he then adopt, granted he would not tie himself to considering the utilitarian pros and cons of his every action?

The answer usually offered by consequentialists nowadays is motivated by the observation in the last section that the options that call for assessment in consequentialist terms – the possibilities over which an agent is decisive – include options which are only indirectly behavioural as well as alternative actions he may take in any context. They include options such as whether or not to endorse a certain motive or trait of character, letting it have its untrammelled way in some settings, and options such as whether or not to make a commitment to a certain principle – say, the principle of respecting a particular right in others – giving it the status of an automatic behavioural pilot in suitable circumstances.

The fact that the option-sets faced by agents include many of this kind means that if they become consequentialists, their conversion to that doctrine can have a practical effect on how they behave without having the clearly undesirable effect of turning them into incessant calculators. It may have the effect of leading an agent to endorse certain traits or principles, traits or principles that lead him or her in suitable contexts to act in a spontaneous, uncalculating way. It will have this effect, in particular, if choosing to go in thrall to such pre-emptors of calculation is the best way to promote the values that the agent cherishes.

But won't it always be best if agents keep their calculative wits sharpened, having an eye in every case as to whether following the automatic pilot of trait or principle really does best promote their values? And in that case shouldn't the consequentialist agent still remain, in a sense, an incessant calculator?

This is a question at the forefront of contemporary consequentialist discussions. The answers canvassed among consequentialists are various. One answer is that agents are so fallible, at least in the heat of decision-making, that the calculative monitoring envisaged here would probably do more harm than good. Another is that some of the relevant pre-emptors of calculation, for example certain traits that the agent may nurture – say, the trait of being obsessional about completing tasks – are such that once in play they are incapable of being controlled via monitoring. Yet another answer, one particularly favoured by the present writer, is that many values are such that their promotion is undermined if habits of deliberation – pre-emptors of calculation – which are designed to promote them are subjected to calculative monitoring. Suppose I commit myself to the principle of saying what first comes to mind in conversation in order to promote my spontaneity. I will undermine the promotion of that value if I attempt to monitor and control my remarks. Or suppose I commit myself to the principle of letting my teenage daughter have her way in a certain sphere – say, in her choice of clothes – in order to promote her sense of independence and self. Again I will subvert the promotion of that value, at least assuming that I am relatively scrutable, if I try to monitor and moderate the tolerance I offer. In each case, within suitable contexts, I must put myself more or less blindly on automatic pilot if I am to promote the value in question.

The brand of consequentialism which is explicit about the possibility that being a consequentialist may motivate an agent to restrict calculation over consequences is sometimes described as indirect, sometimes as strategic, sometimes as restrictive. Such restrictive consequentialism promises to be capable of answering the various challenges associated with the main argument against consequentialism, but that claim can hardly be documented here. In concluding our discussion of that argument the only point that calls to be made is that restrictive consequentialism in this sense should not be confused with what is called restricted or rule-consequentialism, as distinct from extreme or act-consequentialism. That doctrine, no longer much in vogue, claims that rules of behaviour are justified by whether compliance or attempted compliance best promotes the relevant values, but that behavioural options are justified in other terms: specifically, by whether they comply or attempt to comply with the optimal rules. The restrictive consequentialism to which we have been introduced is not half-hearted in this way; it is a form of extreme or act-consequentialism. It holds that the test for whether any option is justified is consequentialist, whether the option be directly or indirectly behavioural: the best option is that which best promotes the agent's values. What makes it restrictive is simply the recognition that agents may best promote their values in behavioural choices, if they restrict the tendency to calculate, abjuring the right to consider all relevant consequences.

iv The main argument for consequentialism

The key to the main argument for consequentialism is a proposition which we have so far taken for granted, that every moral theory invokes values such that it can make sense to recommend in consequentialist fashion that they be promoted or in non-consequentialist that they be honoured. The proposition is fairly compelling. Every moral theory designates certain choices as the right ones for an agent to make. In any such case, however, what the theory is committed to recommending is not just this or that choice by this or that agent but the choice of this type of option by that sort of agent in these kinds of circumstances; this is a commitment, as it is sometimes said, of universalizability. (See Article 40, UNIVERSAL PRESCRIPTIVISM, for more on this aspect of moral judgement.) The commitment means that every moral theory invokes values, for the fact that such and such choices are made is now seen as a desirable property to have realized.

The other aspect of our key proposition is that with any value at all, with any property that is hailed as desirable, we can identify a consequentialist and a non-consequentialist response. We can make sense of the notion of promoting or honouring the value. I hope that this claim can be supported by the sorts of examples introduced at the beginning. We saw there that an agent might think of honouring or promoting values to do with intellectual understanding, personal loyalty and political liberty. It should be clear by analogy that the same possibilities arise with all desirable properties. As we also saw, I can think of honouring a value traditionally associated with consequentialism such as that of people's enjoying happiness, though uncertainty about options may sometimes leave the strategy undefined; to honour this will be to try not to cause anyone unhappiness directly, even if doing so would increase happiness overall. And I can think of promoting a value as intimately linked with non-consequentialist theories as that of respect for persons; to promote this will be to try to ensure that people respect one another as much as possible, even if this requires disrespecting some.

Our key proposition motivates an argument for consequentialism, because it shows that the non-consequentialist is committed to a theory which is seriously defective in regard to the methodological virtue of simplicity. It is common practice in the sciences and in intellectual disciplines generally to prefer the more simple hypothesis to the less, when otherwise they are equally satisfactory. Consequentialism, it turns out, is indisputably a simpler hypothesis than any form of non-consequentialism and that means that, failing objections such as those rejected in the last section, it ought to be preferred to it. If non-consequentialists have not seen how much their view loses on the side of simplicity, that may be because they do not generally assent to our key proposition. They imagine that there are certain values which are susceptible only to being promoted, others that are susceptible only to being honoured.

There are at least three respects in which consequentialism scores on simplicity. The first is that whereas consequentialists endorse only one way of responding to values, non-consequentialists endorse two. Non-consequentialists all commit themselves to the view that certain values should be honoured rather than promoted: say, values like those associated with loyalty and respect. But they all agree, whether or not in their role as moral theorists, that certain other values should be promoted: values as various as economic prosperity, personal hygiene, and the safety of nuclear installations. Thus where consequentialists introduce a single axiom on how values justify choices, non-consequentialists must introduce two.

But not only is non-consequentialism less simple for losing the numbers game. It is also less simple for playing the game in an *ad hoc* way. Non-consequentialists all identify certain values as suitable for honouring rather than promoting. But they do not generally explain what it is about the values identified which means that justification comes from their being honoured rather than promoted. And indeed it is not clear what satisfactory explanation can be provided. It is one thing to make a list of the values which allegedly require honouring: values, say, like personal loyalty, respect for others, and punishment for wrongdoing. It is another to say why these values are so very different from the ordinary run of desirable properties. There may be features that mark them off from other values, but why do those features matter so much? That question typically goes unconsidered by non-consequentialists. Not only do they have a duality then where consequentialists have a unity; they also have an unexplained duality.

The third respect in which consequentialism scores on the simplicity count is that it fits nicely with our standard views of what rationality requires, whereas non-consequentialism is in tension with such views. The agent concerned with a value is in a parallel position to that of an agent concerned with some personal good: say, health or income or status. In thinking about how an agent should act on the concern for a personal good, we unhesitatingly say that of course the rational thing to do, the rationally justified action, is to act so that the good is promoted. That means then that whereas the consequentialist line on how values justify choices is continuous with the standard line on rationality in the pursuit of personal goods, the non-consequentialist line is not. The non-consequentialist has the embarrassment of having to defend a position on what certain values require which is without analogue in the non-moral area of practical rationality.

If these considerations of simplicity are not sufficient to motivate a consequentialist outlook, the only recourse for a consequentialist is probably to draw attention to the detail of what the non-consequentialist says, inviting reflection on whether this really is plausible. In the second section above we saw that non-consequentialists have to deny either that the values they espouse determine values for the prognoses of an option or that the value of an option is a function of the values associated with those different prognoses. The consequentialist can reasonably argue that either claim is implausible. If one prognosis realizes my values more than another then that surely fixes its value. And if one option has prognoses such that it represents a better gamble than another with those values, then that surely suggests that it is the best option for me to take. So how can the non-consequentialist think otherwise?

Of course, the consequentialist should ideally have an answer to that question. The consequentialist should be able to offer some explanation of how non-consequentialists come mistakenly to think the things they believe. It may be useful to say a word on this in conclusion.

There are at least two observations which ought to figure in a consequentialist explanation of how non-consequentialists come to hold their views. The first has already been suggested in this essay. It is that non-consequentialists probably focus on deliberation rather than justification and, noticing that it will often be counter-productive to deliberate about the promotion of a value involved in action – a value like loyalty or respect – conclude that in such cases choices are justified by honouring the values, not by promoting them. Here there is a mistake but at least it is an intelligible mistake. Thus it may help the consequentialist to make sense of the commitments of opponents.

The second observation is one that we have not made explicitly before and it offers a good ending note. This is that many deontological theories come from acknowledging the force of the consequentialist point about justification but then containing it in some way. One example is the rule-consequentialist who restricts his consequentialism to choices between rules, arguing that behavioural choices are justified by reference to the rules so chosen. Another example, more significantly, is the non-consequentialist who holds that each agent ought to choose in such a way that were everyone to make that sort of choice then the value or values in question would be promoted. Here the thought is that consequentialism is suitable for assessing the choices of the collectivity but not of its members. The collectivity ought to choose so that the values are promoted, the individual ought to choose, not necessarily in the way that actually promotes the values, but in the way that would promote them if everybody else made a similar choice. Here as in the other case the non-consequentialist position is motivated by the consequentialist thought. That will not make it congenial to the consequentialist, who will think that the thought is not systematically enough applied: the consequentialist will say that it is as relevant to the individual agent as to the collectivity. But the observation may help consequentialists to make sense of their opponents and thereby reinforce their own position. They can argue that they are not overlooking any consideration that non-consequentialists find persuasive. What non-consequentialists find persuasive is something which consequentialists are able to understand, and to undermine.

References

Austin, J.: *The Province of Jurisprudence Determined* (1832); ed. H. L. A. Hart (London: Weidenfeld, 1954).

Bradley, F. H.: *Ethical Studies* (1876); (Oxford: Clarendon Press, 1962).
Sidgwick, H.: *The Methods of Ethics* (New York: Don Press, 1966).

Further reading

Adams, R. M.: 'Motive utilitarianism', *Journal of Philosophy*, 73 (1976).
Hare, R. M.: *Moral Thinking* (Oxford: Clarendon Press, 1981).
Lyons, D.: *Forms and Limits of Utilitarianism* (Oxford: Clarendon Press, 1965).
Parfit, D.: *Reasons and Persons* (Oxford: Clarendon Press, 1984).
Pettit, P.: 'The consequentialist can recognise rights', *Philosophical Quarterly*, 35 (1988).
Pettit, P. and Brennan, G.: 'Restrictive consequentialism', *Australasian Journal of Philosophy*, 64 (1986).
Railton, P: 'Alienation, consequentialism and morality', *Philosophy and Public Affairs*, 13 (1984).
Regan, D. H.: *Utilitarianism and Cooperation* (Oxford: Clarendon Press, 1980).
Scheffler, S.: *The Rejection of Consequentialism* (Oxford: Clarendon Press, 1982).
—— ed.: *Consequentialism and its Critics* (Oxford: Clarendon Press, 1988).
Slote, M.: *Common-Sense Morality and Consequentialism* (London: Routledge and Kegan Paul, 1985).
Smart, J. J. C. and Williams, B.: *Utilitarianism: For and Against* (Cambridge: Cambridge University Press, 1973).
Stocker, M.: 'The schizophrenia of modern ethical theories', *Journal of Philosophy*, 73 (1976).

20

Utility and the good

ROBERT E. GOODIN

THEORIES of ethics are standardly partitioned into theories of the right and theories of the good. The latter style of ethical theory, insisting as it does that good consequences be promoted, clearly needs a theory of the good in order to say which consequences are good and to be promoted and which are not. But even the former style of ethical theory often finds itself needing some theory of the good, if only to flesh out the 'duty of beneficence' that is standardly included among the 'right things' to be done: obviously, we will need a theory of the good to tell us how, exactly, to go about discharging that duty to do good for others. So a theory of the good seems pretty well indispensable, whatever your fundamental ethical stance.

Naturally, however, there is much less agreement on the content and the source of a theory of the good than there is on our need for some such theory in the first place. Even a thoroughly ugly world, some would say, might display excellence of a sort. Still, beneath it all, most theories of the good seem ultimately to appeal to broadly similar standards of goodness. Most ultimately have recourse to a broadly Aristotelian principle which analyses excellence in terms of a rich complexity that has been somehow successfully integrated. The good, it is standardly said, consists essentially in the organic unity of a complex whole.

That broad agreement, though, comes basically in the realm of aesthetics. The crucial question is whether any such theory really can do the work cut out for it in our ethical theories. Where our ethics require a theory of the good, is that the sort of thing that can plausibly be plugged in to fill the gap?

Arguably it is not. Ethics is not aesthetics, and no more. We may well have a duty, among our many other duties, to promote truth and beauty, as ends in themselves and even if that quest does no good for anyone. The last person on earth may well have a duty not to destroy it all as he or she dies, even though by so doing no-one's good will have suffered. But promoting things that are good in themselves, without being good *for* anyone, is not what ethics is principally about.

Ethics is a theory of social relations. The injunctions of ethics are principally injunctions to do good for people, and for sentient beings more generally perhaps. Henry Sidgwick may have exaggerated when asking rhetorically in his *Methods of Ethics* whether anything can really be good if it has no effect – direct or indirect, actual or potential – on any being's state of consciousness. Perhaps we can contrive contorted examples to show some such things to be good, in that more abstract sense. But our duty to promote that good would be severely attenuated by such contortions and contrivances. Forced to choose between a good that is good for someone and a good that is good for no-one, morality would almost invariably lead us to prefer the former to the latter.

Therein lies the great appeal of utilitarianism, as the theory of the good most standardly used to fill out the larger consequentialist framework. There is a sense of 'utilitarianism', associated with architects and cabinet-makers, which equates it to the 'functional' and makes it the enemy of the excellent and the beautiful. Yet therein lies one of the great advantages of utilitarianism as a theory of the good: by running everything through people's preferences and interests more generally, it is non-committal as between various more specific theories of the good that people might embrace, and it is equally open to all of them.

Where the utilitarian theory does draw the line is in insisting that to be good something must be good, somehow, *for* someone. 'Utility', in its most general sense, means merely 'useful'. Why, it quite reasonably asks, should we ever require gestures that are of no earthly use to anyone, anyway? Yet any moral theory or religious dogma or aesthetic principle that refused to put considerations of utility and usefulness squarely at its centre must necessarily run the risk of requiring just such empty gestures, from time to time. It is no accident that precisely that attack on 'principles adverse to that of utility' comes right up front in Jeremy Bentham's *Introduction to the Principles of Morals and Legislation*, following hard on the heels of the introduction of the 'principle of utility' itself (Bentham, 1823). It was in Bentham's day, and remains in our own, the very best argument for a utility-based moral theory.

In one obvious respect, though, that argument raises as many problems as it solves. It is well and good to equate utility with usefulness. But that leaves the further glaring question, 'Useful for what?' A very large part of the later history of utilitarian doctrine can be read as an attempt to answer that one very simple taunt.

The initial answer – Bentham's own, borrowed in turn from the proto-utilitarians Hobbes and Hume – was to equate utility with usefulness in promoting pleasure and avoiding pain. That is 'hedonic' (or 'hedonistic') utilitarianism. That is the version that most readily invited caricature by the sophisticated and high-minded. The vision of a mad assembly of pleasure hogs constantly out for a buzz is not a pretty picture.

Such caricatures would have most bite, philosophically, if hedonic utilitarians actually claimed – and still more if, by the logic of their theory, they were somehow committed to claiming – that people should be hedonists. Like all good caricatures, though, that is an exaggeration. Hedonic utilitarianism needs make no such claim. At most, writers like Bentham would merely assert as a baldly empirical proposition that people are in fact hedonists, driven by pleasures and pains, and that our moral theories must respect that fact about them. Ethical hedonism is in that way derived only very loosely from a hypothesis, of an essentially contingent sort, of psychological hedonism.

Benthamite utilitarianism can thus be characterized as an exercise in inferring exceptionable moral conclusions from exceptionable psychological premises. The error is well worth caricaturing. The caricature, however, is principally of Benthamite psychology, not of the structure of Benthamite ethics as such. In principle, any other more credible theory about the true sources of personal satisfaction or indeed of the good for human beings can be fitted into the basic structure of Benthamite ethics. Once that is done, the substance of the ethical conclusions may well have altered, but the structure of the ethic will not.

The most standard modern substitution replaces Bentham's own hedonistic psychology with a notion of 'preference satisfaction'. The idea here is that what is – and, to give the idea ethical bite, preference utilitarians must add 'and should be' – maximized is not the balance of pleasures over pains, but rather the satisfaction of preferences more generally. The latter subsumes the former, for the great majority of cases where Bentham's hedonistic psychology-cum-ethic was indeed on broadly the right track. But it also leaves room to account for those cases in which it was not.

We sometimes engage in acts of self-sacrifice, donating hard-earned dollars to charity, or standing aside so other more deserving claimants can secure their just rewards, or throwing ourselves on live hand grenades to save comrades from certain death. It might cynically be said that, in the end, we perform all such acts of kindness towards others for our own ulterior purposes – if only to ease our own consciences. Still, whatever satisfaction we get out of those acts is not readily described in crassly hedonistic terms. Likewise, when a marathon runner endures great agony to turn in a personal best time or when Republican prisoners undergo torture instead of betraying their comrades, the satisfaction they derive is again ill described in hedonistic terms.

The way to describe these cases, for the modern utility theorist under the spell of the modern micro-economist, is in terms of 'preference satisfaction'. Insofar as a person happens to have preferences that go beyond (or even counter to) that person's hedonistic pleasures, satisfying those preferences is nonetheless a source of utility for that person. For the preference utilitarian, just as for the hedonic utilitarian, there is nothing in the theory that says that people should have those sorts of preferences. It is just a theory about what follows, morally, if they happen to do so. It is good – good for them – to have their preferences satisfied, whatever those preferences might be.

Now, highbrows may still say that that is a pretty impoverished theory of the good. And in many way it is. It makes the good equivalent to the desired, reducing everything to a question of consumer demand. Even in his essay entitled *Utilitarianism*, John Stuart Mill could not help chafing at that conclusion. Surely there are some things – truth, beauty, love, friendship – that are good, whether or not people happen to desire them.

There is a band of self-styled 'ideal utilitarians', taking their lead from G. E. Moore's *Principia Ethica*, making precisely that claim the centrepiece of an ostensibly utilitarian philosophy. But the further this theory distances itself from classic hedonic utilitarianism, and the closer it comes to embracing an aesthetic ideal regardles of whether or not that is good for any living being, the less credible this analysis is as an ethical theory.

243

A more convincing response to broadly the same challenge comes from 'welfare utilitarians', who would have us talk in terms of the satisfaction of interests rather than of mere preferences. Here again, those two standards broadly converge: the former model subsumes the latter for that great majority of cases in which people see their interests clearly and prefer them to be satisfied. Where, through some defect of cognition or of will, the two standards diverge, welfare utilitarianism would suppress short-sighted preference satisfaction in favour of protecting people's long-term welfare interests.

That model must be stated fairly carefully. We must not construe 'welfare interests' so narrowly, and give them such strong priority, that people are never allowed to spend their savings – not even for that thing for which they had been saving. Considered consumption acts might promote a person's welfare, too. So much emphasis here must fall upon the demonstration of defects of cognition or will, in allowing us to suppress preference-based standards in favour of interest-based standards of utility. We must talk in terms of what the person would have chosen in some 'ideal choice situation', characterized by perfect information, strong will, settled preferences, and such like.

But such ideal choice situations are rarely actualized. When they are not, there is at least a case to be made for focusing on interests rather than just preferences as the right standard of utility. Welfare interests need not be all that far removed from preferences, though. The most credible characterization depicts them as simply being abstracted from actual and possible preferences. Welfare interests consist just in that set of generalized resources that will be necessary for people to have before pursuing any of the more particular preferences that they might happen to have. Health, money, shelter, sustenance, and such like are all demonstrably welfare interests of this sort, useful resources whatever people's particular projects and plans.

This move does not address the full range of concerns that motivated the ideal utilitarians, to be sure. By welfarist standards, truth and beauty and such like will qualify for protection and promotion only insofar as they can be construed to be in people's welfare interests. No doubt they can, at least to some extent. But no doubt Moore and his followers would want that endorsement to be far less qualified.

Still, the welfare-utilitarian move has gone far toward meeting the larger style of challenge posed by the ideal utilitarians. What made their objection particularly forceful was the proposition – surely undeniable – that there must be more to utility than what people happen to want, at any particular moment. Welfare utilitarians, by abstracting from people's actual wants to their more generalized welfare interests, has given that intuitively appealing broader notion of utility some practical content.

The path that has led us to the characterization of utility as welfare maximization may seem a long and circuitous one. But however winding the path, notice that that ultimate conclusion chimes nicely with the basic insight with which we began. Utility is essentially a matter of usefulness; and the whole point of the generalized resources that welfare utilitarians strive to protect is that they are so very useful to such a wide range of life plans.

Utilitarianism of whatever stripe is, first and foremost, a standard for judging public action – action which, whether performed by private individuals or public officials, affects various other people besides just yourself. True, utilitarianism may have some implications for purely private affairs. It may lay upon us a duty (a duty to ourselves) to maximize our own utility, even if no-one else's is affected. In the case of preference utilitarianism, that duty would seem pretty vacuous: it would amount to no more than a duty to do what we want to do, anyway. But in the case of welfare utilitarianism it might have more bite, paternalistically laying upon us a duty to look out for our own welfare interests, even if we were not so inclined.

Whatever its application to the purely private case, though, the utilitarian doctrine really comes into its own in public settings. When our actions will affect various people in various different ways, it is the characteristically utilitarian conclusion that the right action is that which maximizes utility (however construed) summed impersonally across all those affected by that action. That is the standard that we are to use, individually, in choosing our own actions. That is, more importantly, the standard that public policy-makers are to use when making collective choices impinging on the community as a whole.

One step in that procedure – summing utilities – has been the subject of much discussion. Aggregating individual utilities into some overall measure of social utility is an obviously tricky business, presupposing comparability of several sorts. It presupposes, first, comparability across goods, so that everyone can compare for themselves the utility that they derive from apples versus oranges. It presupposes, second, comparability across people, so we can say whether what I have lost is more or less than you have gained in consequence of some particular action. Both comparability claims have been queried from time to time, but the latter has proven particularly contentious.

Basically, the problem is that we do not have utility meters implanted into our foreheads that can be read like electricity meters by anyone who wants to see what sort of a charge is flowing through at any particular moment. Instead, every mind is inscrutable to every other mind. Insofar as utility refers essentially to a state of mind (and hedonic or preference-based standards of utility clearly do: even 'satisfying the preferences of my dead friend' requires me to judge, counter-factually, 'what he would have thought'), taking a utility reading requires me to get inside someone else's head. Only in that way can I calibrate his utility scale and mine so they are measuring in comparable units. Clearly, I can say whether a pinprick is or is not worse for me than a broken arm. But there is no Archimedean point from which I can say, unequivocally, whether my broken arm is worse for me than your pinprick is for you. That is what we mean when we talk about the 'impossibility of interpersonal utility comparisons'.

Were we to refuse to engage in such interpersonal utility comparisons, the practical consequences would be dire. We would be left with nothing but weak orderings of alternatives, of the sort recommended by Pareto and myriad economists following him. Without interpersonal utility comparisons, the most we could say would be that one alternative is better than another if everyone is at least as well off and at least one person better off, in their own terms, under it. One disadvantage of that formula is that it is rarely satisfied, and hence it simply leaves most alternatives unranked. Another disadvantage is that it builds a deeply conservative bias into our decision rule, since without some mechanism for making interpersonal comparisons we can never justify redistributions by saying that the gainers gained more than the losers lost.

There is no need to rush headlong into the economist's camp at this point, though. There are available various genuine solutions, and not mere Paretian evasions, to the problem of interpersonal utility comparisons. Many turn on technical tricks, of one sort or another. The simplest and most interesting, however, is merely to point out that the problem is a problem only for hedonic or preference utilitarians. They are the ones asking us to get inside someone else's head. Welfare utilitarians, by abstracting from people's actual preferences, definitely are not. We can know what is in people's interests, in this most general sense, without knowing what in particular is inside their heads. Furthermore, at some suitably general level at least, one person's list of necessary basic resources reads much like anyone else's. Whereas preferences, pleasures and pains are highly idiosyncratic, welfare interests are highly standardized. All that goes a very long way toward helping to solve the problem of making interpersonal utility comparisons.

The basic utilitarian formula, as I have said, asks us to sum utilities impersonally across everyone affected. Historically, most criticism has focused on the problem of comparing those utilities that are to be summed. Recently, criticism has come to focus on the impersonality of such summation itself. In the utilitarian formula, a utile is a utile is a utile – whether it is your own, your daughter's, your neighbour's or some starving Eritrean's. What we ought to do, individually and collectively, is for the utilitarian therefore independent of any consideration of who we are or of any special duties that might arise from that fact. According to the standard caricature, everyone in a utilitarian scheme is in principle interchangeable for anyone else. Such impersonality is widely thought to rankle.

Impersonality has an attractive side, too, though. Putting your thumb on the scales on your own behalf, or on behalf of those of whom you are fond, is not a particularly pretty picture, morally. So opponents of impersonality must first show that, rankle though it may and unnaturally though it may come to us, impersonality is not the morally right stance, nonetheless. They would be wrong to assume that leading the moral life is always going to be easy, or that it will always come naturally.

Having laid that challenge, utilitarians can go on to say, perfectly properly, that as a purely pragmatic matter their calculations will often lead us to show some apparent favouritism toward those near and dear to us. It is easier to know what people nearby need, and how best we can help; it is easier to get the necessary aid to them efficiently, without losing too much in the process; and so on. Those are purely contingent, pragmatic considerations, to be sure. In the ideal world, they may be absent. But in the real world, they are powerfully present. Given those facts, it makes a good deal of utilitarian sense to assign particular responsibilities for particular people and projects to other people near to hand. The utilitarian's point here is simply that those special responsibilities are not moral primitives but rather that they are derived from broader utilitarian considerations.

In similar fashion, it has often been said in criticism of utilitarianism that its impersonal summation of utilities renders it insensitive to the distribution of utilities across people. A distribution that gives everything to one person and nothing to another would, by that standard, be better than one that gives both equal shares, just so long as the utility sum in the former case turns out to be higher than that in the latter case. That is the objection from the left. Analogously, the objection from the right is that utilitarianism would license radical redistribution of people's property (even their body parts – gruesome stories of mandatory redistributions of corneas and kidneys have been conjured up here) just depending upon the utility sums. Both left and right think that we need a notion of rights, constraining utilitarian maximizing, to protect us against outcomes of one sort or the other.

Here again, the utilitarian response appeals pragmatically to utterly contingent and baldly empirical facts. The crucial one in reassuring the left is that most goods (food, money, whatever) yield 'diminishing marginal utility' – i.e. the utility that you derive from the first unit is higher than that you derive from the second, and so on. After a half dozen ice cream cones, you start to feel distinctly ill. After a few million dollars, another dollar would be little more than litter to you. The consequence of diminishing marginal utility (combined with certain other plausible assumptions) is that a poor person – one who does not already have many units of the good – would derive more utility from any given unit of the good than would a rich person. That, in turn, provides a utilitarian rationale for more rather than less egalitarian distributions of goods and resources. It makes the value of equality derivative (and in a pragmatic, empirically contingent way, at that) from the value of utility. But it produces egalitarian conclusions of the sort leftists demand, at least.

Whether we should achieve equality by radical redistribution of present holdings, violating property rights in ways feared by the right, is perhaps another matter. Utilitarians would recognize the value of stability and security in planning our own lives and in anticipating the ways that others' life plans will affect our own. So, for reasons first given by Bentham and Hume and reiterated frequently since, we may be reluctant – again, for purely derivative, empirically contingent reasons – to redistribute property radically, even if we are utilitarians.

These two implications of utilitarianism obviously pull in opposite directions. But it is no contradiction to say that there are utilitarian considerations both for and against any particular policy. Furthermore, there is considerable advantage in being able to say that there is one common standard – utilitarianism – underlying arguments both for and against, and hence capable of adjudicating the conflict. Utilitarianism in that way provides some rational basis for making what all too often seem to be no more than arbitrary value trade-offs, in such situations.

It is right that my discussion of the utility principle should end on the topic of public policies. For it is principally as a guide to public policymakers that utilitarianism was originally – and still is most persuasively – proposed. Bentham's introduction was, after all, to the principles of morals and *legislation*; and judging from his voluminous subsequent works, it is clear that it was always legislators and judges and other public officials for whom Bentham was principally writing. 'What should we do, collectively?' is much more the characteristically utilitarian question than is 'How should I live, personally?'

Seen as a standard for public rather than private choice, the utility principle evades a great many of the hackneyed objections often posed against it. Utilitarian calculations may well require us to violate people's rights, in certain extreme cases; and individuals might find themselves in just such an extreme case, from time to time. But governments, which by their nature must make general policies to cover standardized cases, will not find themselves responding to those rare and extreme cases. In legislating for the more common, standard sort of case, public policymakers will very much more often than not find that the requirements of the utility principle and those of Ten Commandment deontologists will dovetail nicely.

References

Bentham, J.: *An Introduction to the Principles of Morals and Legislation* (London: 1823); ed. J. H. Burns and H. L. A. Hart (London: Athlone Press, 1970).

Mill, J. S.: *Utilitarianism* (London: 1863); in M. Warnock, ed., *Mill: Utilitarianism and Other Writings* (Glasgow: Collins, 1962).

Moore, G. E.: *Principia Ethica* (Cambridge: Cambridge University Press, 1903).

Sidgwick, H.: *The Methods of Ethics* (London: 1874); 7th edn (London: Macmillan, 1907).

Further reading

Brandt, R. B.: *A Theory of the Good and the Right* (Oxford: Clarendon Press, 1979).

Griffin, J.: *Well-Being* (Oxford: Clarendon Press, 1986).

Hardin, R.: *Morality Within the Limits of Reason* (Chicago: University of Chicago Press, 1988).

Hare, R. M.: *Moral Thinking* (Oxford: Clarendon Press, 1981).

Sen, A. and Williams, B., eds.: *Utilitarianism and Beyond* (Cambridge: Cambridge University Press, 1982).

Smart, J. J. C. and Williams, B.: *Utilitarianism, For and Against* (Cambridge: Cambridge University Press, 1973).

21

Virtue theory

GREG PENCE

i Introduction

GEORGE ELIOT in *Middlemarch* writes of her heroine Dorothea Brooke that 'Her mind was theoretic, and yearned by its nature after some lofty conception of the world which might frankly include the parish of Tipton and her own rule of conduct there; she was enamoured of intensity and greatness, and rash in embracing whatever seemed to her to have those aspects.' Dorothea marries Reverend Casaubon, whom she soon discovers to be dull and insecure. Casaubon becomes so dependent on Dorothea that if she revealed her real opinion, he might commit suicide. Locked in a bad marriage of her own choosing, Dorothea resigns herself to small, private moments of happiness. When she meets Will Ladislaw and finds love, she considers abandoning her husband. For most of the novel, Dorothea struggles with herself and agonizes over questions like, 'What kind of person would I be if I leave him? If I stay?'

It is just such questions of how one ought to live in shaping one's own character that have recently engaged moral philosophy. Some moral philosophers have become frustrated with the narrow, impersonal form of the hitherto dominant moral theories of utilitarianism and Kantianism and have revived the neglected tradition of 'virtue theory'. Previously, ethical theory had two concerns. First, it tended to focus on internecine warfare between utilitarianism and deontology. Second, it often abandoned ethical theory altogether. This occurred either by a 'descent' to ethical issues without mention of any theoretical base or by an 'ascent' to descriptions of words and concepts without regard to implications for action. In such theories, considerations of character were notably absent. As Lawrence Blum says, 'It is especially striking that utilitarianism, which seems to advocate that each person devote his or her entire life to the achievement of the greatest possible good or happiness of all people, has barely attempted to provide a convincing description of what it would be like to live that sort of life.' (Blum, 1988.) It is just this goal, describing types of character which we might admire, that virtue theory seeks.

Although 'virtue' sounds antiquated (non-philosophers would use words such as 'integrity' or 'character'), questions about personal character clearly occupy a central place in ethics. Such questions concern what a 'good person' would do in real-life situations. Champions of virtue, while not necessarily rejecting utilitarianism or rights-based theories, believe that those traditions ignore those central features of ordinary moral life involving character. Dorothea's answer to the question of what she ought to do, they say, has nothing to do with calculations of utility, balancing interests, or resolving conflicts of rights. Her problem concerns the kind of person she is.

Utilitarians often defensively reply that their theory implies that one should strive for good character because the possession of good moral traits by most people maximizes general utility. Such a reply misses the point. Take almost anyone regarded as having admirable moral character. Next ask about the explanation of why this person's approach to life should be a model for others. The answer is never that the person has a personal goal of maximizing utility. If the utilitarian agrees, the question then arises: how *is* utility relevant to forming character? Considerations of utility rarely enter into the thinking of 'saints' or 'heroes'. Although utilitarianism has important answers to questions, say, of public health or medical triage, it doesn't explain the 'data' of the life of character and its issues of courage, compassion, personal loyalty, and vice.

Dorothea's situation illustrates two other aspects of virtue theory. First, one might concentrate on the general question of the nature of virtue. Is there some core quality which Dorothea shares with other good people? Some master virtue? Christianity often held that humility was such a master virtue (and pride the master vice).

Second, one might look at specific virtues or traits, especially as they conflict. Dorothea is pulled in one direction by what was called 'fidelity' in the Middle Ages, 'steadfastness' in Victorian times, and might be called 'loyalty' today. This virtue conflicts with something pulling Dorothea the other way, her desire for autonomy. Considered in isolation, both traits are good: loyalty can get Dorothea through the inevitable rough spots in her marriage, autonomy can prevent her from being a doormat.

Questions of this sort would ask whether a good person can ever divorce simply because of incompatibility, especially in a marriage without cruelty or abuse. Moreover, Dorothea's situation is complicated (as is usual in the dilemmas of moral life) because her husband will be irremediably, perhaps fatally, hurt if Dorothea defects. More commonly, children will be harmed. Resolution of her dilemma partly depends on how she answers the question of how a good person in her situation should rank the virtues of loyalty and autonomy.

ii Anscombe and MacIntyre

The revival of interest in virtue in the 1980s was sparked by the earlier work of two philosophers, Elizabeth Anscombe and Alasdair MacIntyre. In 1958, Anscombe argued that historical notions of morality – of moral duty and obligation, of 'ought' in general – were unintelligible today. The world-views within which such notions formerly made sense no longer held sway, but their ethical progeny persisted regardless. Such anchorless 'children' have become contorted into doctrines such as 'Act not to satisfy any want of yours but simply because it's morally right to do so'. For Anscombe, such doctrines are not only not good, they are actually harmful. Virtue perniciously becomes an end in itself, unattached to human needs or desires.

Alasdair MacIntyre agreed with Anscombe and carried her analysis further. In his view, modern societies have inherited no single ethical tradition from the past, but fragments of conflicting traditions: we are Platonic perfectionists in saluting gold medallists in the Olympics; utilitarians in applying the principle of triage to the wounded in war; Lockeans in affirming rights over property; Christians in idealizing charity, compassion and equal moral worth; and followers of Kant and Mill in affirming personal autonomy. No wonder that intuitions conflict in moral philosophy. No wonder people feel confused.

Instead of this hodgepodge, MacIntyre would revive a neo-Aristotelian account of human good which would ground and sustain a set of virtues. Such an account would also provide a conception of a meaningful life. The common question, 'What is the meaning of life?' is almost always a question about how those asking the questions can feel they have a place in life in which they are emotionally committed to those around them, in which their work expresses their natures, and in which individual good connects to some larger project which began before a life and which continues after it. MacIntyre's answer is that such meaning comes – as do the excellences which are the virtues and which sustain the prospering of rational societies – when a person belongs to a *moral tradition* which allows for a *narrative order of a single life* and which depends for its existence on standards of excellence in certain *practices*.

For example, medicine has a moral tradition dating back at least to Hippocrates and Galen. This tradition sets out what a physician is supposed to do when a patient comes bleeding into the emergency room or a plague begins. Within this tradition, physicians' lives can achieve a certain unity or 'narrative'. They can look backwards (and forward) and see how their lives made (make) a difference. Moreover, medicine has its internal 'practices' which allow for intrinsic pleasure beyond its extrinsic rewards: the deft surgical hand, the perspicacious diagnosis of the esoteric disease, the esteem of a great teacher by students. Contrast this life with that of a worker on an assembly line making plastic bolts, who has suddenly seen his factory close. MacIntyre contends that only in certain kinds of societies, just as in only certain kind of jobs, can the virtues prosper.

iii   The historical foundation of virtue theory

It is impossible to understand modern virtue theory without some understanding of the history of ethics. The ancient Greeks (mainly Socrates, Plato, and Aristotle) made three kinds of contributions. First, they focused on virtues (traits of character) as the subject of ethics. For example, Plato's *Republic* described the virtues encouraged by democracy, oligarchy, tyranny, and meritocracy. Second, they analysed specific virtues such as the 'cardinal' (major) ones of courage, temperance, wisdom, and justice (we will discuss ancient views of courage later). Third, they ranked types of character, e.g. Aristotle classified human character into five types, ranging from the great-souled man to the moral monster.

In the thirteenth century, Thomas Aquinas synthesized Aristotelianism and Christian theology. Aquinas added the 'theological virtues' of faith, hope, and charity to the cardinal virtues. Ancient Greek ethics, however, was secular, whereas Aquinas ultimately gave a theological justification of virtues. He is a half-way point between the naturalistic view of character of the ancient Greeks and the hostility to naturalism of Kant.

During the Enlightenment, Kant tried to derive morality from pure reason itself. Although Aquinas claimed that truths of morality could be known by reason alone, he sometimes was forced to appeal to God's existence and nature. Kant later tried to avoid such appeals and to discover an essence of moral character – of virtue or good character – which transcended any particular set of virtues or any particular historical society.

Kant decided that virtuous people act precisely from, and because of, respect for a moral law which is 'universalizable' (see Article 14, KANTIAN ETHICS). When they are acting in their highest capacity as pure rational agents, Kant thought – at least on one interpretation – that people emphatically do *not* act on ordinary desires, even desires to be known as a good person, or because it makes them feel good to ease suffering. On this view, Kant wanted an account of moral character above and beyond the contingent desires fostered by particular societies at specific times in history. Thus, he was left with a very abstract, but also very hollow, position.

Modern virtue theorists think Kant went wrong here and that modern moral philosophy has followed listlessly in his wake. Rather than seeing Kant as a *beginning* of an ethical tradition, they see him as its *reductio ad absurdum*. Utilitarianism commits a spill-over mistake, identifying Kant's abstract duty with the greatest good for the greatest number, and ignoring the problem of how acting on such a duty relates to problems of character, such as being deficient in compassionate feelings. As Joel Kupperman says, 'Despite the opposition between Kantians and consequentialists, it is easy for someone who is reading some of the works of either school to get the picture of an essentially faceless ethical agent who is equipped by theory to make moral choices that lack psychological connection with either the agent's past or future.' (Kupperman, 1988.)

In an influential paper, Susan Wolf argued for a stronger point than that utilitarianism merely omits reference to character. She argued that it actually entails an ideal character at which it would be neither good nor rational to aim. A utilitarian saint, who devoted maximal time and money to saving the starving, would be a boring, one-dimensional person who missed out on the non-moral goods of life such as participation in sports or reading history. In striving to maximize aid to humanity, such saints would devote all their spare time to altruistic acts, leaving no time for the many self-enhancing acts which normally make life rich and satisfying.

iv Eliminatism

Anscombe and MacIntyre sometimes talked as if principle-based ethics had to be abandoned altogether and that a correct account of virtue could accomplish this. Such 'eliminatism' still holds the allegiance of those who would believe they can resurrect in modern life the virtues of the Aristotelian *polis* or the code of the eighteenth-century aristocrat.

This way of thinking often ignores, among many other problems, the fact that the Aristotelian and aristocratic societies were not democracies. Indeed, the accounts of virtues given by aristocrats such as Aristotle and Hume were idealizations of the behaviour of their times, not descriptions. Those who wish for a 'return' to the *polis* or Scottish Enlightenment are not returning to real societies, but to ancient books.

Still, it is argued by some that an account of virtues is possible which is compatible with democracy and which can still dispense with talk of rights and principles in ethics. Instead we would only talk about what is noble, good, honourable, 'appropriate', and in taste. Is this not possible?

To show that it is not possible, we will discuss courage as an example.

v Courage

Any discussion of how one ought to live needs to consider at some point the importance of courage in a life. Here two interesting questions appear. First, can one try to be courageous without knowing what courage is? Second, how is courage connected to other things, such as other virtues and knowledge?

Philosophical discussion of courage can be traced to Plato's dialogue *Laches*, in which Socrates debates the Athenian generals Laches and Nicias over the correct definition of courage. Courage was certainly esteemed as a virtue before Socrates, e.g. among Homer's warriors, but in the fifth century BCE its nature had become a *problem*. When the Athenian navy brought home strange ideas and customs from the world, the Sophists begin to teach that standards of courage varied from society to society, century to century.

Against them, Socrates, Plato and Aristotle argue that courage is a timeless value trait. In the *Laches*, Socrates embarrassed the Athenian generals, who first incorrectly identify it with stereotypic behaviour associated with courage (rescuing babies from burning houses), and who then fail to appreciate the difference between facing any fear and facing *worthy* fears. For Socrates, courage requires wisdom and hence cannot serve evil goals.

Socrates also defends the controversial claim that courage serves an individual's self-interest. As John Mackie has argued in his book, *Ethics: Inventing Right and Wrong*, if one developed the disposition to calculate when courage served one's interest and when it did not, the disposition would neither be real courage nor one which would serve one's real interests (This problem of calculation is also discussed by Philip Pettit in Article 19, CONSEQUENTIALISM.)

Notice that the question here is not between courage and daring. The difference between these two is precisely that courage involves acting to further an ethical ideal, whereas the daring of the clever jewel thief does not. The controversial question about courage and worthy ideals is really about whether courage is courage when serving the 'wrong' ideals.

vi Eliminatism, again

So now we return to the question of eliminatism, i.e. to whether an ethical theory based entirely on character can do all the work of ethics. Let us approach this question by asking whether an officer in the Confederacy could be courageous during the American Civil War. On an ideal-neutral analysis of courage, he can. Courage here is simply facing risks for *some* ideal, not necessarily the right one.

Most people would regard the officer as fighting for the wrong ideal because the Confederacy depended on slavery. So then, presumably, Socrates would say that the Confederate officer wasn't truly courageous. But, alas, this is precisely what Socrates would *not* say. For all the great ancient philosophers thought slavery was natural and correct. Indeed, the lifestyle of the virtues of the aristocrats in the *polis* in part depended on the existence of it. The ancient Greeks had the wrong moral *principle* about relations between humans, and there seems no easy way in which their theory of character can be developed to do the work of this principle.

When we read the ancient Greeks, we are impressed by their sense of developing themselves according to ideals of beauty, courage, and nobility. Ancient Greek ethics was perfectionistic in stressing the perfection of the *polis*, the individual, and the future of man. Such perfectionism scorns the equality of democracies. There is simply no way fully to emulate ancient Greek ideals of character and also to act on principles of moral equality between humans (much less humans and animals).

The German philosopher Frederich Nietzsche also wrote about trying to shape our character with pride and style. Here again we find a perfectionistic ideal of character which is incompatible with moral equality. Indeed, Nietzsche's ideal is more notable for what it rejected (Judeo-Christian ethics) than what it posited. But even Nietzsche seemed unaware of just how a thoroughgoing anti-Christian ideal of character would look. He is aware that his *Übermensch* ('Superman') would lack what Hume called 'the monkish virtues' such as humility and chastity, but he seems not to appreciate that compassion is a virtue historically indebted to 'monkish' traditions such as Judaism, Christianity, and Buddhism. From his Zarathustran heights, the great-souled man *may* at times help the insignificant poor out of his power and magnaminity simply because he feels like doing so. But more likely he will think that their ways of feeling and thinking do not count morally and will find them expendable. Thus ideals of character alone cannot do all the work of ethics.

On the other hand, if one were willing to define courage in a non-Socratic fashion, as capable of serving any ideal or goal, then the problem vanishes. This problem arises only if such virtues as courage and wisdom must do all the work of ethics.

The point could also be made by thinking about the role of rights to privacy and liberty in modern societies. Some rights of non-interference and some liberties are necessary to the minimally smooth functioning of modern society as we know it. The reason it is wrong to steal property or force hysterectomies on unsuspecting women cannot be totally explained by discussing the vices of criminals. Something must be said about why such actions violate the rights of victims. So eliminatism fails in virtue theory, although this leaves quite a lot of room for virtue theory to operate.

vii Essentialism

A related question concerns whether all virtues are excellences because of their connection to a single dominant *telos* (goal) of humankind. This question arises from attempts to revive neo-Aristotelian accounts of virtues which posit one true aim of a perfectly good life. One way to address this issue is to ask, as did Socrates and Aristotle, whether all virtues share a 'master virtue'. Alternatively, all virtues might share not necessarily a virtue, but some common *essence*, such as common sense. Aristotle thought a stupid man could truly have no virtue, and this point shows his difference with Christian accounts.

In recent times, Edmund Pincoffs has argued for a 'functionalist' account of virtues. In his account, the real virtues are those necessary to living well in any of several forms of 'common life'. On his view, a core of virtues exist which are necessary for the flourishing of any form of society at any time in history.

Nevertheless, there seems no more plausible reason why all virtues must share some quality than that all goods must share some quality. Virtues may be seen as skilled excellences and there are myriad things at which one can excel. The idea that there 'must' be a core of all virtue is really the assumption in disguise that there is only one good way to live or one correct way for society to develop. But there are many possible worlds for the future: each would have different mixes of institutions and practices, each would need different kinds of virtues for its ideal development.

For example, in frontier societies, great heroes were often highly intelligent people who functioned beautifully outside the tight bounds of civilized cities with their churches, weddings, schools, lawyers, stores, police, and factories. Such frontier heroes lived by a simple hard code (horse thieves must be caught and killed, 'savages' are the enemy, each person pulls his own weight). When the frontiers became civilized, such heroes often found that their characters did not fit the society they had helped create. Society had required their types, and then moved on.

viii Moral feelings, desires, wants

Virtue theorists often examine the motivation of moral actions in kinds of desires and feelings. In a seminal essay, Jonathan Bennett discusses the role of feelings or empathy in ethical life. He discusses the conflict between compassion and moral duty of Huckleberry Finn and Nazi SS leader Heinrich Himmler. The morality of Huck's time compelled him to turn in the runaway slave Jim, with whom Huck had become friends. In contrast, Himmler urged SS generals to overrule their human revulsion at killing Jews for their higher duty to the Fatherland. Bennett argues for the anti-Kantian conclusion that Huck rightfully heeded his affection for Jim, not his morality, whereas Himmler's generals should have heeded their feelings more. A moral theory which only explains this problem as a cognitive mistake (Huck should have transcended his time and just 'seen' that slavery was evil) does not address the issue which Bennett presses home.

Bennett also discusses the American fire-and-brimstone theologian Jonathan Edwards, who wrote that part of the special pleasures of the saved in heaven will be watching the torments of the damned below ('the seeing of the calamities of others tends to heighten the sense of our own enjoyments'.) Bennett writes that Edwards seems to have had absolutely no sympathy for the eternal suffering of the damned. For Bennett, Edwards is inferior to Himmler because at least Himmler *felt* something.

This theme leads to a common defect in non-virtue theories. On theories of duty or principle, it is theoretically possible that a person could, robot-like, obey every moral rule and lead the perfectly moral life. In this scenario, one would be like a perfectly programmed computer (perhaps such people do exist, and are products of perfect moral educations). In contrast, in virtue theory, we need to know much more than the outer shell of behaviour to make such judgements, i.e. we need to know what kind of a person is involved, how the person thinks of other people, how he or she thinks of his or her own character, how the person feels about past actions, and also how the person feels about actions not done.

For example, almost everyone goes through life without becoming a murderer ('the outer shell'), yet types of character of non-murderers differ significantly. The person who is frequently tempted to murder because of a hot temper, but refrains from doing so for moral reasons, does not seem like a higher moral type. It is far superior never to want, simply because of minor slights, to kill people at all. Better still is the person who would not kill and who mourns innocent lives when murdered.

ix Character, self, and society

Action does not occur in a political vacuum. Virtue theory also studies how different kinds of societies encourage different virtues and vices. One could approach Dorothea's dilemma much more globally by asking whether the limited choices offered her in Victorian society were just. Some modern feminist philosophers pursue similar themes in discussing whether the traditional virtues and vices of women are praiseworthy. Past feminists have advocated androgynous ideals and promoted only human virtues, not male or female virtues. More recently, some feminists have rejected androgynous ideals and returned to the idea that some virtues (nurturing, compassion) may be more open to women than men (See Article 43, THE IDEA OF A FEMALE ETHIC.)

256

In looking at character, one may both be 'philosophical' in looking globally at societies or 'philosophical' in being personal and looking at character from 'within'. How much can a person shape his or her own character?

It is clear that this discussion presupposes that some people have *some* capacity to shape their own character. Some philosophers dispute this, arguing that while individual acts may be free, character is a fixed aspect of humans. In reply, it can be agreed that not everyone has the ability to change, or even to modify, character. However, so long as the critic admits that one act can be free, then the possibility remains open that this act could initiate change in character.

Moreover, our systems of moral praise and blame, our development of manners, and our assumptions about free will, all assume that people can deliberately shape or corrupt their own characters. How much people can change their traits and characters is a subject beyond the scope of this essay, but a sketch of an answer is that situations of crisis often force people to re-examine their basic values, as Miss Brooke must do in her bad marriage when she falls in love with Will. When lucky, people sometimes obtain insight into their problems and are supported by resources for change (this is one value of psychotherapy). And it is a fact that people *do* change – they stop drinking, become more compassionate, or become mean. So it seems that change is possible. (See also Article 47, THE IMPLICATIONS OF DETERMINISM.)

It is a deep fault of non-virtue theories that they pay little or no attention to the areas of life which form character. Perhaps the most important decisions in such areas involve whether to marry, have children, be friends, and where to work. Writers working in ethical traditions based on rights, utility, or Kantian universalization have largely regarded such areas as involving *non-moral* choices. But since ethics is about how we ought to live, and since such areas occupy so much of how we live, is this not a colossal defect?

Modern philosophers are pursuing many questions about virtue, such as the degree to which one is responsible for one's own character, connections between character and manners, connections between character and friendship, and analysis of specific traits such as forgiveness, loyalty, shame, guilt, and remorse. They are even returning to analysis of traditional vices such as inordinate desires for drugs, money, food, and sexual conquest, i.e. the traditional vices of intemperance, greed, gluttony, and lust. The next decade will see many important works on virtue.

References

Anscombe, G. E. M.: 'Modern moral philosophy', *Philosophy*, 33 (1958), 1–19.
Aquinas, Thomas: *Summa Theologiae*.
Bennett, J.: 'The conscience of Huckleberry Finn', *Philosophy*, 49 (1974), 323–33.
Blum, L.: 'Moral exemplars: reflections on Schindler, the Trocmes, and others', *Midwest Studies in Philosophy*, 13 (1988), 196–221.
Eliot, G.: *Middlemarch* (London: 1871–2).

Kupperman, J.: 'Character and ethical theory', *Midwest Studies in Philosophy*, 13 (1988), 115–25.

MacIntyre, A.: *After Virtue* (South Bend, Ind.: University of Notre Dame Press, 1981).

Mackie, J.: *Ethics: Inventing Right and Wrong* (Harmondsworth: Penguin, 1971).

Pincoffs, E.: *Quandaries and Virtues* (Lawrence, Kans.: University of Kansas Press, 1986).

Plato: *The Republic*.

——: *Laches*.

Wolf, S.: 'Moral saints', *Journal of Philosophy*, 79 (1982), 419–39.

Further reading

An excellent bibliography, listing hundreds of articles and books and broken down by sub-areas, follows articles in *The Virtues: Contemporary Essays on Moral Character*, ed. R. Kruschwitz and R. Roberts (Belmont, Cal.: Wadsworth, 1987), pp. 237–63.

French, P., Uehling, T. and Wettstein, H., eds., *Ethical Theory: Character and Virtue – Volume XIII, Midwest Studies in Philosophy* (South Bend, Ind.: University of Notre Dame Press, 1988).

Murdoch, I.: *The Sovereignty of Good* (New York: Schocken Books, 1970).

Pence, G.: 'Recent work on the virtues', *American Philosophical Quarterly*, 21 (1984), 281–97.

Tong, R.: 'Feminist philosophy: standpoints and differences', *American Philosophy Association: Newsletter on Feminism and Philosophy*, ed. N. Tuana (April, 1988), pp. 8–11.

22

Rights

BRENDA ALMOND

i Historical introduction

THE Second World War involved violations of human rights on an unprecedented scale but its ending saw the dawn of a new era for rights. Following their heyday in the seventeenth century, when the idea of rights was propounded by such writers as Grotius, Pufendorf and Locke, rights played a crucial role in the revolutions of the late eighteenth century. In the nineteenth and early twentieth century, however, appeal to rights was eclipsed by movements such as utilitarianism and Marxism which could not, or would not, accommodate them.

The contemporary period has seen a further shift in their fortunes and today they provide an accepted international currency for moral and political debate. In many parts of the world, irrespective of cultural or religious traditions, when issues of torture or terrorism, poverty or power are debated, the argument is very often conducted in terms of rights and their violation. Within societies, too, rights play an important role in the discussion of contentious moral issues: abortion, euthanasia, legal punishment, our treatment of animals and of the natural world, our obligations to each other and to future generations.

Whilst of comparatively recent vintage linguistically, rights belong to a tradition of ethical reasoning which goes back to antiquity. In relation to this tradition, the overtones of the notion are legal rather than ethical. As shown by Stephen Buckle in Article 13, NATURAL LAW, the roots of the conception of universal human rights lie in the doctrine of natural law. The Greeks, in particular the Stoic philosophers, recognized the possibility that actual human laws might be unjust. They observed that laws varied from place to place, and concluded that such existing laws – laws of convention – might be contrasted with a natural law which was not variable or relative in this way, a law to which everyone had access through the individual conscience, and a law by which actual laws in particular times and places might be judged and sometimes found wanting.

While the Greeks themselves did not make such a transition, in fact this idea of natural law readily generates the notion of natural rights as marking out an area in which man-made laws, the laws of states, are subject to limits imposed by a wider conception of justice. But it is significant that in ancient times it was this concept of an inner person independent of social context that made Stoicism a philosophy of special appeal to slaves – people who were most completely lacking in public or social recognition of their rights.

PART IV · HOW OUGHT I TO LIVE?

Later, the spread of the Roman Empire provided a wider legal and political context in which the Roman *jus gentium* gave practical effect to this notion in a system of law which applied to all, whatever their race, tribe or nationality.

A further element in the development of the conception of a moral law independent of local enforcement was supplied by the respect for the individual and for the individual conscience which was the hallmark of the Christian religion, although Christians have divided on the question of whether that law is independent of God or a result of God's commandment. Either view, however, creates a relationship between a human being and his or her conscience which may even justify the rejection of a ruler by the ruled. This was strikingly illustrated by the trial and execution of King Charles I in 1649, an event which some see as marking the beginning of the modern notion of rights.

It was, however, the British philosopher John Locke who set out the claim to rights to life, liberty and property which the Americans later included in their Declaration of Independence of 1776, substituting for property, however, the pursuit of happiness.

Following the French Revolution of 1789 the French National Assembly issued a Declaration of the Rights of Man and of the Citizen, asserting the rights to liberty and property, but adding security and resistance to oppression. It was in answer to Burke's criticisms of that Revolution that Tom Paine, in 1791, published *The Rights of Man*.

Contemporary declarations of rights have been considerably more detailed and far-reaching, taking the form of international agreements, some given legal force by the states endorsing them, others being no more than statements of aspiration. The European Convention for the Protection of Human Rights and Fundamental Freedoms (1950) is an example of the first sort, with the International Court at the Hague available to judge cases which are presented to it. The United Nations' Declaration of Human Rights (1948) is an example of the second sort, although it was later supported by more specific International Covenants on Economic, Social and Cultural Rights and on Civil and Political Rights (1976).

While the eighteenth-century notion of rights was protective and negative, setting limits to the treatment which governments might mete out to their subjects, the modern conception adds to these a positive element, by including rights to various kinds of welfare goods. But since the provision of such items as education or health requires taxation and an elaborate bureaucracy, this has led to a bifurcation of rights. Where the older negative rights limited government, the newer positive rights justify its expansion in the pursuit of greater social wealth, comfort or economic advance. In practice, however, it was only the addition of this second concept of rights that produced the endorsement necessary for the United Nations and later the European agreements to emerge.

ii The analysis of rights

While some welcome these developments, others see the widespread appeal of rights as an unwelcome proliferation of a notion which is either suspect or redundant. Questions surrounding the issue, then, begin with a challenge to the very meaningfulness of the notion. If this challenge is to be met, it is necessary to offer, first of all, a satisfactory analysis of rights, and secondly a justification for using this vocabulary. For rights are only one element in our moral vocabulary, which includes also such terms as 'duty', 'obligation', 'right' (used as an adjective), 'wrong', 'ought', as well as terms which may be seen either as competitors to 'rights', or as an essential part of their meaning – terms such as 'liberties', 'claims', 'immunities', and 'privileges'. If 'rights' can be translated without residue into any of these terms, then it might seem that talk about rights is redundant.

Before considering these questions, however, it will be useful to make some further distinctions. The practical discussions of rights referred to above are likely to involve what are today called human rights. The justification of rights of this sort is essentially ethical, although the international community, in attempting to enshrine them in law, seeks to convert their justification into a matter of fact and practice.

Within sovereign states, many rights are already a matter of legal fact in this way. But not all legal rights are also moral rights, and many moral rights will continue, even in a society which contains much agreement about matters of behaviour, to exist only as moral rights and not as legal ones. A question about the existence of a legal right is to be answered by establishing whether there are legal rules detailing that right and specifying penalities for the violation of those rules. (As the jurist H. L. A. Hart has pointed out, the validity of the legal rules themselves is a further question, which may need to be settled by seeing whether they are consistent with principles set out in a nation's Constitution or Bill of Rights, or, in countries which do not have a written Constitution, by appealing to case law and precedent (Hart, 1976)).

There are many examples of purely legal rights, often merely matters of technical qualification, but also including an important category of rights to do things that morally one ought not to do. They may also include rights to do things which are bad for one, so that a right cannot be defined as something to one's advantage. The existence of moral rights is disputed by some for reasons which will be discussed below, but if there are moral rights, then these include rights which no-one would ever think of converting into legal rights – such things, for example, as a right to gratitude from a beneficiary, or a right to one's own opinion on some uncontentious matter of fact.

There are, then, three broad categories for discussion: universal human rights (which are claimed as moral rights but also aspired to as legal rights); specific legal rights; and specific moral rights. Within this framework, some further questions can be identified:

1   What or who can be the subject of a right? Are there limitations on the kind of being that may be said to have a right?
2   What kind of things can there be a right to? What is the content or object of a right?

3   What can be a ground for, or justification of, a rights? Or are rights *self-justifying*, perhaps in a way that makes them ethically stronger than anything from which they might be derived? If so, does this mean that there is a possibility of grounding morality itself on rights?
4   Are rights inalienable?
5   Are rights ever absolute?

It will be clear that the answers to these questions may vary depending on which of the three categories of rights is involved. A right is not a *thing* except in the sense in which duties, obligations and promises are things. These are all abstract nouns, better understood in terms of what they assert about human relationships and human action. Some writers (for example, A. R. White) argue that sentences including the word 'right' are factual, and may therefore be judged true or false. Others, however, including the Scandinavian realists Axel Hagerström and Karl Olivecrona argue for an emotivist analysis. That is to say, they believe that to assert a right is to take up a position rather than to state a fact. In contrast to both, the American philosopher Ronald Dworkin proposes that they be interpreted as special kinds of fact – moral facts – which, in analogy with card-games, may be regarded as trumps in moral disputes. (Compare the discussion of 'moral trumps' in Article 18, AN ETHIC OF PRIMA FACIE DUTIES.) For example, much good might be achieved by deflecting an inheritance, but the right of an heir prevents this being placed on the moral agenda. A similar point is made by Robert Nozick when he describes rights as side-constraints. Libertarians in general regard rights as setting important limits to the actions of government.

Rights are not, however, all of the same kind. To begin with, there are both active and passive rights: rights to do things, and rights to have things done for or to one. But the term covers rather more variety than this. It is usually agreed that the differences include rights as claims, as powers, as liberties or as immunities. The dominant meaning may well be 'claim' and in this, which is also its narrowest sense, it is the correlative of 'duty'. These distinctions are best displayed in examples:

(i)   *Claims*: a right to have a loan repaid is a claim by a creditor which generates a corresponding duty on the part of the debtor to make the repayment.
(ii)   *Powers*: a right to distribute property by will is an example of a right which is a power, carrying with it the ability to affect the rights of other people.
(iii)   *Liberties*: the law may confer a liberty or privilege on individuals by not imposing upon them a potentially burdensome requirement – for example, giving evidence in a court of law against a spouse.
(iv)   *Immunities*: a person may be protected from the actions of another: for example, in the case of a trade unionist, a right to join a union is a guarantee of immunity from the action of an employer who might seek to forbid this.

The most celebrated taxonomy of rights was provided by the jurist Wesley N.

Hohfeld who set out the following table of jural correlatives and opposites:

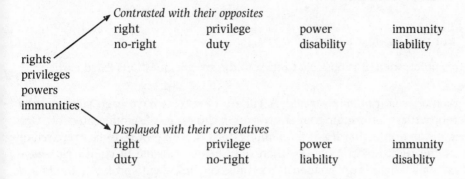

Contrasted with their opposites			
right	privilege	power	immunity
no-right	duty	disability	liability

rights
privileges
powers
immunities

Displayed with their correlatives			
right	privilege	power	immunity
duty	no-right	liability	disablity

iii   Justifying a rights-vocabulary

All the distinctions so far mentioned have been distinctions within the field of rights. They contribute to the analysis of rights, although they do not settle the fundamental issue of whether a rights-assertion is, on the one hand, a description of a state of affairs or, on the other, some kind of decision, proposal or rhetorical utterance. But the question of the deep analysis of rights does not affect their use or usefulness, and this means that justifying the use of a rights-vocabulary is a separate issue, to be approached in a different way.

Nevertheless, the analysis of rights does have implications for this further question. First of all, the analysis of rights reveals a richness and complexity of meaning that cannot be fully conveyed by any of the other moral terms available. And secondly, it shows by implication that there is no reason to regard rights as any more suspect logically than other moral terms such as 'duty' or 'obligation'.

But in addition to these considerations, there are strong pragmatic reasons for favouring a rights-vocabulary. Advocates of rights, for example, see it as an important advantage that rights focus on an issue from the point of view of the victim or the oppressed, rather than from the perspective of those with power. As the black abolitionist leader Frederick Douglass said:

the man who has *suffered the wrong* is the man to *demand redress* ... the man STRUCK is the man to CRY OUT – and ... *he who has endured the cruel pangs of slavery* is the man to advocate Liberty. (Quoted in Melden, 1974.)

Not unconnected with this point is the fact that rights have legal overtones and appear to carry with them at least some implication that the use of force is justified in securing them.

A second pragmatic justification is provided by the recent history of the notion of rights. Appeal to rights is widely understood and accepted everywhere in the world under all types of political regime. It is no small advantage to a moral notion that it should be regarded as valid across many nations and cultures, and that it should have at least the potential of binding governments to the observation of important moral constraints.

iv For and against rights

At this point, then, it is possible to turn to the specific questions listed earlier:

1 *Who or what can have a right?* A variety of criteria have been suggested by different writers for bringing an entity within the range of rights protection. One broad distinction is that if a right is understood to be a power, to be exercised or not at the right-holder's option, then only beings capable of choice can have rights. But if a right is understood as a permission, linked with prohibitions against interference by others, rights may be taken as benefits which are open to any kind of entity capable of being benefited.

Some of the specific criteria suggested under this framework are more restrictive than others. The *capacity to suffer* brings the animal world into the domain of rights but excludes, for example, an irreversibly comatose human being (a consideration of importance in deciding who or what has a right not to be the subject of painful but important scientific experimentation). *Having interests* is a criterion which could include, in addition to animals, the human fetus or embryo; perhaps, too, aspects of the natural world such as trees and plants. *Possessing reason* and the *capacity for choice* may seem to confine rights to humans, but some animals have both these capacities in a limited way. And finally, the requirement of *being a person* provides no solution to the question of criteria for potentially having rights, for these criteria are themselves often proposed as definitions of what it is to be a person, itself a contentious moral issue, as well as a complex legal matter.

In sum, it would seem that there is no agreed a priori solution to the question of who or what may have rights. It seems to be a matter of the generosity or empathy of the person making the judgement to narrow or extend the circle. Nevertheless, if the criterion adopted is too wide, the assertion of rights will tend to lose its unique force; if too narrow, it will weaken the important intuitive strength of the notion by omitting the categories people regard as most fundamental. Some of these issues are taken up elsewhere in this volume, e.g. in Article 24, ENVIRONMENTAL ETHICS, Article 25, EUTHANASIA, Article 26, ABORTION, and Article 30, ANIMALS.

2 *What can be the content or object of a right?* To some extent the answer to this question will depend on the answer to the preceding one. If having interests is an essential qualification for having rights, then rights will consist of anything necessary to protect or further those interests. If the capacity to suffer is singled out, this suggests that rights are passive claims against the infliction of pain by others. If the possession of reason and the capacity for choice are offered as criteria, then rights will be rights to act in certain ways, and to have freedom of action protected from interference by others. A broad condition, however, is that the

behaviour of other people should be relevant to securing the right; a right to clean air, for example, makes sense only in relation to pollution caused by human agency, and would be a meaningless claim in the face of meteorological change beyond the control of human beings.

3   *How can rights be justified?* In the past, as has been indicated above, this question has been answered in terms of the social contract theory as variously put forward by Hobbes, Locke and Rousseau. A contemporary justification in these terms is offered by the American philosopher John Rawls in his book *A Theory of Justice*. Rawls's theory is based on a thought-experiment in which people ('rational contractors') separated by a 'veil of ignorance' from knowledge of their particular lot in life (wealth, social status, abilities, etc.) reflect upon the rules for social life that they would make in advance to bind themselves, whatever their later position in life. Like Locke, Rawls argues that they would commit themselves to basic conditions of liberty and a qualified equality.

Social contract justifications, however, seem to require a prior commitment to the rights they seek to justify. This objection is avoided by theories which ground rights on utility. J. S. Mill offered a justification of this sort in his essay *Utilitarianism*, where he argued that principles such as liberty and justice contribute in the long run to human happiness, and it is the substantial position of his essay *On Liberty*. The contemporary British philosopher R. M. Hare also grounds rights in utility but, unlike Mill, acknowledges that in consequence circumstances could arise in which rights might be sacrificed – in particular, if the sum of human preferences favoured this.

A utilitarian justification, then, cannot give *priority* to rights. If this is what is required of a defence of rights, this purpose is better served by linking the question of justification to the two questions just considered: those concerned with (i) the subjects and (ii) the content of rights. Such a justification is offered by the American philosopher, Alan Gewirth, who argues that rights are necessary for humans to be able to function as moral agents, displaying autonomy in the exercise of choice.

Some philosophers, however, would regard rights as requiring no further justification, but as being morally exigent in themselves. If this is so, then a rights-based morality might be a possibility. The view that rights are self-justifying can be defended, however, without necessarily going on to make the claim that they are the fundamental or primary elements in moral discourse. One reason for taking a more limited view is that the language of rights alone may be insufficient to cover important areas of morality. For example, vitally important environmental considerations may be difficult to express in terms of rights. Against this particular objection, however, it could be argued that enviromental claims may be made just as effectively without attributing rights to inanimate objects – the rights of future generations could have the same implications for practice as far as maintaining the integrity of the planet is concerned.

4   *Are rights inalienable?* Whether a right is alienable or not is a matter of whether it can be handed over or transferred to another person. So-called 'marital rights'

provide a good example of rights which are inalienable in this sense. But there is also another contrast to be drawn here: while some rights may be waived or set aside, others may be thought too important ever to be relinquished even by a willing right-holder. Such fundamental rights would be those to life and liberty. But while it would usually be agreed that this principle invalidates a willingness to sell oneself into slavery, whether it would invalidate the rational decision of a sick person to request euthanasia is more problematic.

5 *Are there absolute rights?* The most difficult problem for anyone wishing to maintain that certain rights are absolute is that some of these rights may be in conflict with each other. This means that it may be impossible to respect one right without violating another. For example, an author's right to publish what he or she chooses without censorship may conflict with a claimed right of a religious group not to be offended in respect of their deepest convictions. Or a policeman may commandeer a private car in order to give chase to a criminal. If the rights in question are rights to goods, then it is even clearer that it may not be possible for everyone in the world to have, for example, modern medical treatment, or an uncrowded habitation.

If there are absolute rights, then, there will be very few such rights – perhaps to life and liberty alone. Even here, however, one person's right to life may need to be set against another's, or against that of several others. And it is an accepted principle of law, not seen as a violation of rights, that a person's liberty is forfeit if that liberty is used to threaten the rights of others. In practice, the UN declarations of rights leave only one right unqualified – the right not to be tortured. All other rights are qualified and made subject to the needs of states.

Rights, then, while they may be self-justifying, cannot stand alone. They are only one element in a universal morality, but an important element in that they form, together with other key moral notions, part of a conception of the primacy of the ethical in human affairs. It is a distinctive feature of this kind of perspective that it is based on what human beings have in common, their common needs and capacities, and on a belief that what they have in common is more important than their differences.

Even in this limited role, however, they have been subjected to attack from a number of directions. To begin with, they would, on the face of it, appear to be unacceptable to utilitarians since they impede the unfettered pursuit of the social good. Indeed the notion of *natural* rights was dismissed as nonsense by the utilitarian Jeremy Bentham who, in a famous phrase, also dismissed absolute natural rights as 'nonsense upon stilts'. It is important to remember, however, that the suppression of such fundamental rights as free speech, freedom of association, free publication and freedom from arbitrary arrest, imprisonment and execution has very frequently seemed to would-be social and political reformers an essential step on the road to the millennium. This would provide a utilitarian justification of rights, but in the light of the human capacity for self-deceit, it may be better seen as providing rights with a direct and independent justification.

(Nevertheless, this very claim – that it is better for rights to be *seen* as justified independently of utility – is something the utilitarian may (privately) accept on utilitarian grounds.)

Rights have also been attacked by Marxists, not only because the rights of individuals may stand in the way of social progress, but also because they do not fit in with the cultural and historical relativism which is a central ingredient in Marxist theory. Because they transcend social and economic context, they are incompatible with a theory that displays human affairs and human society as the product of such factors. Nevertheless, Marxists have recently reinterpreted and reinstated the notion of rights, and made use of it in various popular and revolutionary movements. (Marxist ethics are discussed in Article 45, MARX AGAINST MORALITY.)

However, universal rights do not only provide problems for the political left. They are also criticized by conservative thinkers in the tradition stemming from the writings of the eighteenth-century political philosopher Edmund Burke. The conservative objection is that a doctrine of rights undermines the integrity of culture and custom as these exist in particular times and particular places. It is for reasons such as this that contemporary cultures based on religions such as Islam may reject the liberal focus on rights. Beyond the liberal democracies, pressure for rights may, in addition, be seen as cultural imperialism on the part of Western liberal nations.

In general, contemporary writers in the conservative tradition object to the individualism implicit in assertions of rights. They see the individual of Western liberalism as rootless and want to replace the idea of the individual as a social atom with the idea of individuals in their social roles within an organic community. A general critique of Western liberalism in these terms has recently been offered by Alasdair MacIntyre.

Liberal individualism, then, to which the theory of rights belongs, is attacked from both left and right, and from both inside and outside the liberal democracies. Against such criticisms it may be said that an attempt to formulate a limited list of classic political liberties is bound to be resisted by strong political movements with potentially totalitarian goals. However, it is important in evaluating this opposition to remember that the notion of universal rights provides a moral framework for law under any political regime. Rights are not incompatible with social responsibility. Indeed they presuppose it, in that the assertion of rights necessarily involves recognition of the rights of others as well as one's own. They contribute to overall utility – the general or public good – by being recognized independently rather than being viewed as tools to secure that good. Politically and ethically, they are themselves a part of that good. Their ultimate justification is not that they are in fact universally accepted, but rather that, on the basis of the contribution they can make to the realization of human hopes and aspiration (human 'flourishing'), they have the *potential* for securing widespread agreement and acceptance. In the end, achieving this acceptance is a task of persuasion and argument, and not of establishing any matter of fact, whether legal, political or scientific.

The liberal moral ideal finds its most coherent expression in the doctrine of universal rights, and it can only be fully realized in a political context in which these rights are respected and recognized.

References

Bentham, J.: 'Anarchical fallacies' (1824) in *Works*, ed. J. Bowring, Vol. 2.

Brownlie, I. (ed.): *Basic Documents on Human Rights* (revised edition) (Oxford: Oxford University Press, 1981).

Burke, E.: *Reflections on the Revolution in France* (1790).

Dworkin, R. M.: *Taking Rights Seriously* (London: Duckworth, 1978).

Gewirth, A.: *Human Rights: Essays on Justification and Applications* (Chicago: University of Chicago Press, 1983).

Grotius, H.: *De Jure Belli ac Pacis* (1625); trans. F. W. Kelsey, *The Law of War and Peace* (Oxford: Clarendon Press, 1925).

Hagerström, A.: *Inquiries into the Nature of Law and Morals*, trans. C. D. Broad, ed. K. Olivecrona (Stockholm: Almqvist und Wiksell, 1953).

Hare, R. M.: *Moral Thinking: Its Levels, Methods and Point* (London: Oxford University Press, 1981).

Hart, H. L. A.: *The Concept of Law* (London: Oxford University Press, 1976).

Hohfeld, W. N.: *Fundamental Legal Conceptions* (1919); (London and New Haven: Greenwood Press, 1964).

Locke, J.: *Two Treatises of Government* (1690); ed. C. B. Macpherson (Harmondsworth: Penguin, 1968).

MacIntyre, A.: *After Virtue* (London: Duckworth, 1981).:

——: *Whose Justice? Which Rationality?* (London: Duckworth, 1988).

Marx, K.: *On the Jewish Question* (1843).

Melden, A. I.: *Rights and Persons* (Oxford: Basil Blackwell, 1974).

Mill, J. S.: *Utilitarianism* and *On Liberty* (1863); in *Collected Works*. Vol. 10, ed. J. M. Robson (Toronto: University of Toronto Press, 1969).

Nozick, R.: *Anarchy, State and Utopia* (Oxford: Basil Blackwell, 1974).

Olivecrona, K.: *Law as Fact* (1939); 2nd edn (London: Stevens and Sons, 1971).

Paine, T.: *The Rights of Man* (Part 1, 1791; Part 2, 1792).

Pufendorf, S.: *De Jure Naturae et Gentium* (1672)(2nd edn 1684); trans. C. H. and W. A. Oldfather (Oxford: Clarendon Press, 1934).

Rawls, J.: *A Theory of Justice* (Oxford: Oxford University Press, 1971).

Further reading

Cranston, M.: *What are Human Rights?* (London: Bodley Head, 1973).

d'Entreves, A. P.: *Natural Law* (London: Hutchinson, 1977).

Finnis, J.: *Natural Law and Natural Rights* (Oxford: Clarendon Press, 1980).

Hobbes, T.: *Leviathan* (1651); ed. C. B. Macpherson (Harmondsworth: Penguin, 1968).

Kamenka, E. and Tay A. E.-S., eds., *Human Rights* (London: E. Arnold, 1978).

Mackie, J.: *Ethics: Inventing Right and Wrong* (Harmondsworth: Penguin, 1977).

Raphael, D. D., ed.: *Political Theory and the Rights of Man* (London: Macmillan, 1967).

Raz, J.: *The Morality of Freedom* (Oxford: Clarendon Press, 1986).

Sumner, L. W.: *The Moral Foundations of Rights* (Oxford: Clarendon Press, 1987).

Rousseau, J. J.: *The Social Contract* (1762); trans. M. Cranston (Harmondsworth: Penguin, 1984).

Tuck, R.: *Natural Rights Theories: Their Origin and Development* (Cambridge: Cambridge University Press, 1979).

Waldron, J., ed.: *Theories of Rights* (Oxford: Oxford University Press, 1984).

Waldron, J.: *Nonsense upon stilts: Bentham, Burke and Marx on the Rights of Man* (London: Methuen, 1987).

Wellman, C.: *A Theory of Rights: Persons under Laws, Institutions and Morals* (Totowa, NJ: Rowman and Allanheld, 1985).

White, A. R.: *Rights* (Oxford: Oxford University Press, 1984).

PART V
APPLICATIONS

23

World poverty

NIGEL DOWER

i   The challenge

CONSIDER the following two facts: first, a thousand million human beings – a fifth of the world's population – live in absolute poverty: hunger, malnutrition, widespread disease, high infant mortality, squalid living conditions, fear and insecurity. Most of these people live in the poorer countries of the world, often referred to as 'developing countries'. Second, there are many rich individuals living in the 'rich' countries with the wealth and resources to help reduce that absolute poverty; and many governments in rich countries who similarly have the capacity to transfer resources and expertise to reduce that poverty.

The question is: ought those of us who are well off help to alleviate poverty in developing countries? Some say that we have no duty to do so, and some say that we have a very extensive duty to do all we can. This essay examines these arguments.

ii   What is helping?

The phrase 'help to alleviate poverty' already contains several ambiguities which need to be brought out. On the one hand there are disasters of various kinds, like earthquakes, droughts or floods. Emergency assistance is given, people write cheques, and for a moment, there is a strong sense of human solidarity.

On the other hand, there is the steady grinding poverty which grips hundreds of millions of people and does not attract media attention. In response to this there are various kinds of programmes, some organized by governments (with or without foreign aid), some organized by private charities. These programmes aim to help the very poor escape from their poverty, or to ensure that people do not get into situations of extreme poverty in the first place. These programmes are less glamorous than emergency aid, but their impact is far greater. My main concern is with such 'development assistance'.

Archbishop Helda Camara once remarked 'When I help the poor I am called a saint, but when I ask why they are poor I am called a communist'. What this really shows is that true helping is not merely the palliative response of immediate compassion, but the search for the causes of poverty and then the removal of those causes which can be removed by human action. One need not be a communist to recognize that amongst the causes may be injustices, economic policies, and so on.

What kind of helping is involved here? I am not just thinking here of the variety of ways in which individuals can, of their own initiative, take action with the aim of reducing distant poverty. In addition, there are many things that governments can do, both through official aid and through appropriate trading policies. The perspective which I shall assume is that the normal arguments for assistance apply equally at both levels.

The word 'help' may also signal the idea that assistance is an expression of benevolence, kindness or a desire to do good, and it is often linked with the idea of 'charity'. Whilst terms like 'benevolence', and 'charity', are acceptable if they are carefully interpreted, they can give rise to a false impression. What is done out of kindness or charity is often seen as something lying beyond duty or beyond what is morally required. That is, if we do something to help, we can feel positively good about it. The issue of this essay is whether helping is a duty, and in some sense required of us.

iii   Justice not charity

Sometimes in development circles the point is made by saying that the issue is about 'justice, not charity, for the world's poor'. One of the points made by this important phrase is that justice is something required of us, whereas charity is not. This point is misleading, since appeals to kindness, charity or compassion, can all be seen as ways of stating an important duty, and as such they may require quite as much action – if not more – than appeals to justice. Indeed 'caring' is the term which I prefer to use, both because it brings out what helping is an expression of, and because it can readily be seen as a 'duty' – and indeed a duty which incorporates claims of justice.

The phrase 'justice not charity' is also used to indicate two further important points. First, we tend to think of charity very much in terms of the responses of individuals, whereas the idea of justice does not simply cover what individuals do to one another but also covers the general structures and relationships which exist, or ought to exist, in a society. For instance many people would accept it as part of 'social justice' that a society should be so organized, with progressive taxation to finance it, to ensure that the basic needs of all people are met. If this is accepted for individual societies, why not accept it for the world as a whole? International institutions and agreements should then reflect this goal. 'A fair distribution of the world's resources' requires at the very least that all should have enough to meet basic needs.

But for many people a fair distribution of the world's resources requires a lot more than this. It requires that many things which are done in the world of international trade and economic activity should be changed because they are in themselves unjust. What is done in and to developing countries may be seen as unjust, because of the exploitation of resources and of cheap labour. So the demand for justice is not merely a forward-looking demand that the world be so organized as to meet basic needs. It is the demand that we stop active injustice as well, and also make recompense for what has been done. Of course most of 'us' are not directly involved in all this; but we are all part of, and beneficiaries of, the system that does this.

This type of appeal to justice depends upon a rather more controversial interpretation of what governments, banks and transnational companies are doing. Whilst I have much sympathy with it, I think it is important not to base the moral argument for aid too firmly on it. To do so would be to incur the consequence of accepting that the very poor in a country which we were not exploiting would not be entitled to our concern. Caring is primarily forward-looking in orientation. Alleviating suffering, meeting basic needs, realizing basic rights, implementing the principle of social justice, these are all aspects of the good we can do. Stopping or rectifying injustices done by others 'on our behalf' is only a part of that good.

iv   What is development?

I mentioned earlier that our real focus is with 'development assistance'. But what is 'development'? Many people are put off by this word precisely because it suggests the idea of economic growth. There are at least three kinds of difficulty with thinking of development in terms of economic growth. First, growth as such may not benefit the very poor, and indeed may be coupled with processes that actually make things worse for the poor. Entrepreneurial use of the land or new agricultural techniques may simply exclude poor peasants from the economic process. Second, there is a danger that growth models reflect inappropriate Western models of the changes which should be taking place, and that their implementation is part of a global economy essentially controlled by the West. Third, even if the model of growth which is advocated is designed to put priority on 'growth for the poor', the assumption that *general* growth is necessary for the latter to happen may be questioned. It needs in any case to be set in the context of environmental constraints such as pollution and land degradation.

It has to be said that some, perhaps much, of the aid that is given is directed to overall economic development in poorer countries and is not particularly targeted upon the reduction of absolute poverty. Official aid is of course constrained by the fact that it is a bilateral government-to-government transfer, or a multi-lateral government-to-UN-agency-to-government transfer. It has to some extent to respect the wishes of the recipient government which may not itself have poverty reduction at the top of its development agenda. On the other hand this is not true of all government aid, nor is it true generally of the development assistance funded by voluntary agencies which are explicitly concerned with the very poor. (See R. Riddell, *Foreign Aid Reconsidered*, 1987, for a full and candid survey.)

The cynics who say that they would give generously or support government aid but for the fact that aid does not work, must recognize that whilst some aid certainly does not work, some does work, particularly that of voluntary agencies. If one is committed to the goal of reducing poverty, one will take the necessary means, and if that involves being selective about what agencies one supports, or involves campaigning to change the priorities in government aid policy, then one will do that. One will not just give up being concerned. The fact that aid or assistance sometimes fails, either because the goals are wrong or because things just do not succeed, is rarely a reason for not supporting it, unless there are other deeper reasons lying behind one's refraining from supporting it.

It is necessary then to distinguish what may be called 'real' development from conventional conceptions of development. Broadly one can see development as a process of socio-economic change which *ought to take place*. This says very little until one fills out what ought to happen, but it does show that at root the definition of development is an evaluative matter which presupposes one's value system. If one thinks the general spread of economic and material prosperity, or the just distribution of such growth, is what a country ought to be going for, one will settle for conventional 'growth', or 'growth with equity' models. If we think that other things are important, like processes which enable more and more to achieve 'non-materialistic' well-being, or processes which meet the basic needs of the poor, or processes which are in harmony with the natural environment, then we will present other models accordingly (Dower, 1988). Since aid is a 'means' to the 'end' of development, we need to be clear what the end is!

v World population trends

A further argument casting doubt on the long-term value of aid comes from pointing to population growth. This factor is sometimes used to justify one of two conclusions. First, aid simply fuels the population explosion, which will simply produce more problems in the future, so what is the point? Second, since the world cannot carry vastly increasing populations without producing ecological catastrophes which will pull everyone down, nations that are well off are entitled to look after their own interests and ignore the rest.

The challenges here are great, but, briefly, it is by no means clear that 'real' development fuels population growth. Much evidence suggests that once basic development is achieved – adequate food supplies, basic health, security in old age, etc. – there is a 'demographic transition' to much lower levels of fertility (e.g. Rich, 1973). 'Development is the best pill', as has been said.

Second, if the world is heading for ecological catastrophe it is more because of the damage done by rich nations through 'overdevelopment' and the consequences of the affluent consumer society, than because of the effects of underdevelopment, such as soil erosion and desertification. No doubt there is an upper limit to what the world can carry sustainably in the way of human population. But the general empirical assumption made by many is that *if* rich nations take serious measures to reduce consumption and environmental damage and *if* poor nations can achieve the kinds of basic development which give poor people the confidence to reduce sizes of families and make sustainable use of the land, then the world's consumption and population could stabilize at a level which would allow 'sustainable development' for all countries. Whilst the conditions indicated by those 'ifs' may not come to be realized, we are still in a position to act in a globally co-operative way, both to further development and to protect the environment, as the Brundt-land Commission Report *Our Common Future* (1987) assumes. The questions is: ought we to do so?

vi   The duty to alleviate poverty

Why then do we have a duty to help alleviate poverty in other countries? It is not being suggested that we do not have a duty to help alleviate poverty in our own society. On the other hand, we would not suppose that one normally had a duty to help alleviate poverty in another rich country like France or the United States.

The basic background assumption is this. A so-called rich country has the resources to alleviate poverty and other forms of serious suffering within its own borders and has further resources which it can use to help alleviate poverty in other countries which lack the resources to alleviate extreme suffering. The general force of this argument is not weakened if one accepts that in practice public services and private caring do not in fact adequately meet all the needs of people in rich countries, and that governments and rich people within poor countries do not do all they can either. The argument is concerned with resources and what could be done, not with what is done.

A further point is relevant. Whilst we should certainly care for those less fortunate within our own societies or support publicly funded education, health-care and other services, the poverty in poorer countries is on the whole far greater than the poverty and problems that face people in rich countries. That greater degree of poverty gives it a certain moral urgency or seriousness which, if one thinks one has a duty to care at all, will weigh in deciding what to support. I say 'urgency' rather than 'priority' because the idea of priority suggests that one could put evils into some kind of order of degree or kind and then say: 'Alleviate these first, then when that is done these, and so on'. But this is not how we either do, or should, determine the ways in which to express our caring. There are many complicating factors.

One of these has to do with cost effectiveness. Clearly one may be able to make more difference with a unit of resource helping to alleviate a lesser evil in one's own society than helping to alleviate a greater evil elsewhere. This is one of the sources of the commonly-stated resistance to overseas assistance, namely 'charity begins at home'. Here 'home' means 'our own society' and the implication is that charity ends here too. However, it is clear that this is not always so: £10 to an overseas aid organization may actually do more good than £10 to a domestic charity. In any case it overlooks the fact that, as I said, there is a special moral urgency or seriousness attached to absolute poverty. Should we say: the more evil something is, the greater moral reason there is, other things being equal, to reduce it?

We can in fact identify three aspects of extreme poverty which make it a serious evil. First, it is significantly life-shortening. Second, it involves great suffering and pain (from disease and hunger). Third, it undermines an essential

277

dignity and decency to life. Although all three aspects usually go together, none is essential to what makes extreme poverty a very bad state to be in. Great suffering and humiliation may not shorten life, but still make life terrible. Early deaths which rob lives of their potential fullness over time strike us as terrible for this reason, even if there is little suffering or loss of dignity – consider the way infant mortality is regarded. Sometimes great suffering and early deaths can be endured with great dignity.

Can the special moral significance of extreme poverty be somehow registered by invoking the idea of human rights? It is certainly the case that many who advocate concern for world poverty would wish to couch their position in terms of a right to subsistence, a right to basic needs, or a right to life (meaning a right not just not to be attacked but to have the conditions necessary for a satisfactory life). Does asserting such rights help the argument?

Unless one claimed that the only rights people had were these basic rights to subsistence – and it would seem strange so to restrict the range of rights – the problem re-emerges as to why some rights take precedence over other rights, such as liberty-rights. One therefore needs a normative principle other than appeal to rights themselves to establish what rights have priority or special moral seriousness.

If we turn to the perspective of the agent who as a caring person needs to decide how to express that caring, the factors which determine those decisions are complex. Much has to do with circumstances, with temperament and ability, and with occasion or opportunity. If someone put her energies into say prison reform within her own country but did little about poverty elsewhere, it would be a mistake to say that she ought to do that less and proportion her commitment to overseas aid according to some objective ordering principle. Indeed it seems equally clear that some people who are well off may find themselves committed to caring for some particular individual, a friend in serious trouble, a handicapped child, a dependent elderly relative, and this commitment may absorb virtually all their time, energy and resources. Sometimes this would rightly do so.

Nevertheless we can recognize that, within the general duty of caring, the reduction of extreme poverty has a special status, and that in normal circumstances, a caring person would have reason to contribute to the alleviation of extreme poverty, amongst the things he cares about. But why should one care at all?

Whilst many may share the moral intuition that we have a duty to care for others, there are a variety of ways in which that intuition can be supported or interpreted. Some would see it as a specific duty to alleviate suffering; other as an important application of a more general duty of beneficence – a duty to promote good, of which reducing evil is an important part. Again, as we noted earlier in the essay, the duty may be based on an appeal to justice; either to the realization of rights or to some principle of 'social justice' which requires that we all have a responsibility to ensure that everyone's basic needs are met. One recent and well known theory of the latter kind is John Rawls's *A Theory of Justice* (1971), discussed in Article 15, THE SOCIAL CONTRACT TRADITION.

Rather than explore these alternative ways of defending the duty of caring, I shall consider two major objections to the whole idea that we have a duty to care about distant poverty. The first objection claims that, whilst we may have a duty to care for others, that duty does not extend beyond our own country's borders. The second denies that we have a general duty of caring at all, either within our own country or outside it.

vii Beyond the domain of our responsibility

The claim that 'charity begins at home' often stands for a more general objection to assistance for other countries, namely a refusal to see what happens in the rest of the world as being morally relevant at all. Suffering outside one's country just is not something one has a duty to help alleviate, because those suffering belong to a different *society*, and hence a different moral community. Duties arise between members of single communities, bound by ties of mutual co-operation and reciprocity. Whether we stress the duty to relieve suffering, the duty of beneficence, the duty to realize rights or the duty to implement social justice, all these duties are bounded by their social context. They are duties we have because of the social relationships we have towards one another within our society.

Here two related claims are being made; first, a claim about what a society is, second a claim that the domain of morality is restricted to a society so defined. Thus one way of thinking of morality is to think of it as a set of rules governing the interrelations between moral agents who live in an established community with common traditions under a common legal authority, each playing his or her part in a scheme of social co-operation for mutual benefit. One can see morality so conceived as based on convention, consent, implicit agreement or contract. (See Article 15, THE SOCIAL CONTRACT TRADITION.)

A crucial issue about the nature of morality is being raised here. A quite different view can be taken, if we deny one or both of the claims above. Another way then of thinking of morality is to think of it in terms of individuals who as moral agents recognize that they have the capacity by their choices to affect the well-being of others and that therefore they have a duty to take into account the effects of their actions on the well-being of others who are affected by their choices.

On this view it is irrelevant whether the 'others' whose well-being may be affected are themselves reciprocating members of the same established, ongoing moral community, or even that they are moral agents at all. What is important is that they are beings who have a good or well-being which can be affected and which makes them 'morally considerable', i.e. relevant to moral deliberation.

Whatever the origins of moral consciousness in the setting of particular societies, reflection on the rationale of moral rules shows that it is arbitrary to restrict the scope of the good promoted by these rules. This rationale does not just include distant peoples, it also includes future generations whose environmental well-being may be crucially affected by our decisions. It may also include animals, life in general, species, the biosphere – indeed anything which is taken to have value.

In any case, even if we were to think it right to restrict the scope of moral obligation to one's own society, the relevant sense of 'society' to invoke would not be what those who take the 'anti-global' approach assume. The relevant sense has to do with the fact that there are extensive interactions and transactions between people, interdependencies, shared institutions etc., not with the more stringent conditions of shared traditions, common authority or a widespread *sense* that one belongs to the same society. In the relevant sense there already is a global society: we need only look at world trade, global institutions and environmental interdependence. The world is therefore actually, and not just potentially, a moral community, even if the sense of it is poorly developed in most people. We are global citizens even if we have not yet acquired our global souls.

If then we accept that the world is one moral domain across which responsibilities may in principle extend, we can go on to argue that aid should be seen as an expression of such moral responsibility. So indeed should the general conduct of international relations by governments, transnational corporations and other 'international actors'.

viii   Not harming people and the value of liberty

We now come to the most basic objection to the idea that we have significant duties to help the poor. This boldly challenges the underlying premise, namely that we have a general duty to help – anywhere! Morality is more to be seen as a set of rules which if followed prevents us from *harming* others or restricting their liberty unduly, than as a requirement to prevent or reduce harm or suffering in others. To be sure, people may have specific duties of care, as a parent has to a child, or a doctor to a patient. But these are based on special relations, which are often contractual in nature. No generalized duty of caring need be recognized.

This approach puts a high value on economic liberty and claims that so long as possessions or 'holdings' are acquired through a succession of legitimate 'voluntary' transfers, the person is entitled to them (Nozick, 1974). At one level this is seen as a way of showing that people are morally entitled to what they possess and therefore have no duty to give it away. At another level it is seen as a way of showing that the role of the 'minimal state' is to ensure that such free transactions occur properly. The state's role otherwise is to keep out of the process, e.g. by not taxing wealth at progressive rates in order to finance 'welfare' programmes or overseas aid programmes. Taxation is the coercive taking of wealth and therefore, beyond the minimum needed for maintaining social order, wrong.

In considering this approach, the question must first be asked: do we have a clear and neat conception of what constitutes 'harming' anyway? Where does, in the competing of interests, a legitimate infringement of another person's liberty end and an undue infringement start? More specifically, we can see that much of the 'harm' which we do is not done directly, or even consciously, but is an unwanted consequence of what we do. Often it is the cumulative effects of many individual acts that cause the harm. Environmental damage is usually like that, and so is much of the poverty in the world, being the unwanted but natural result of unrestricted free market transactions.

A more radical objection to those who deny a duty of caring is the 'negative actions' thesis which some have put forward (e.g. Harris, 1980). This depends upon questioning the moral significance of the distinction often drawn between 'doing' and 'letting happen'. If killing a person is wrong, i.e. causing a person to die, then what is so different about letting someone die, i.e. not acting to prevent the death where one could have intervened (e.g. by sending a cheque to an agency which uses it to save lives)? Is not one's failure to act part of the causal chain that led to the person's death? If we accepted such an approach, (also discussed in Article 17, CONTEMPORARY DEONTOLOGY, and Article 25, EUTHANASIA) clearly letting people suffer would seem morally equivalent to, if not a form of, 'harming' them. Our failure to act reflects our priorities, e.g. our preference to spend money on other things or to save it. So ultimately it is our lifestyles which are a (negative) cause of continuing poverty.

Whilst this collapsing of the act/omission distinction is, I believe, liable to be overdone (I return to the point below), it does usefully bring out the general idea of 'negative responsibility', the idea that we are responsible at least to a degree for the evils we can prevent, as well as for the evils we actively cause. Part of the general disquiet often felt about high military spending, in rich countries and in poor countries, is that if less were spent on armaments, then the resources released both could and *should* be spent on welfare and development programmes. Indeed, from this perspective, one of the significant causes of world poverty is excessive commitment to military spending everywhere.

ix How much caring?

A final question has to be faced: how much should we care? One answer that can be given is: as much as we can. The 'negative actions' thesis mentioned earlier, has this implication, as indeed does its positive counterpart, namely that we ought to prevent all preventable evils, at least so long as we do not sacrifice anything of comparable moral significance, as we would by breaking promises, stealing etc. (Singer, 1979). So too does the utilitarian interpretation of beneficence, namely that we always ought to promote the greatest balance of good over bad. So too indeed could any theory which said that we ought to promote justice as much as possible. Since promoting justice is quite different from acting justly in our own personal interactions (see Philip Pettit's distinction between promoting and honouring values, in Article 19, CONSEQUENTIALISM), what may be done in combatting injustices and the failures of others to realize or protect rights is in principle only limited by one's capacity.

And yet there is something deeply counter-intuitive about this general suggestion – as counter-intuitive as the idea that we have no general duty of caring. Virtually no-one, even amongst those who would be regarded as generous people, actually acts on such a principle of unrelenting caring. Some exceptions – Mother Theresa for instance – come to mind, but what is perhaps significant is that in such cases what for most people would be seen as a major sacrifice to their own quality of life is not seen as such by those who live in that way. And there lies a key to understanding the problem.

We all of us seek quality of life and think we do so legitimately. We do so for ourselves, for those close to us, and we do so for our future selves, when we make provision for our retirement, etc. Typically we form major goals and projects, commit ourselves (if we can) to satisfying careers, all of which may absorb great amounts of our time and energy. It is also a feature of quality of life, at least for most people, that one has a degree of 'moral space' in the sense that, within the constraints of what we must do and must not do morally, there is a significant area of decision in which we can decide what to do – with our time and our resources – *just as we want*, not as we think we ought. The measures we take for our own well-being and the things we do within the space which we allow ourselves – these are all things we choose. We could do otherwise. So if we do so legitimately it is not true that we ought to care for others as much as we can.

Perhaps then we should say: we ought to care for others as much as we can consistent with a reasonable concern for the quality of our own lives. Such a modification, which would clearly be more realistic, would still constitute a challenge to most of us. Few, at least of those reasonably well off, can honestly claim that their quality of life is threatened if they are generous in their giving, spend some time working for social change or writing letters to their elected representatives, take more care over what they buy and consume, and so on. Most would recognize that such activities may actually contribute to quality of life. Nobody who is at all affected by the concerns explored in this essay is likely, once the question is asked 'What does your quality of life consist in?', to return the answer: 'Having and consuming as many material goods as one can.' Greed has nothing to do with quality of life.

My argument then has been for a significant obligation to help alleviate world poverty, not a relentless, overburdening one. But you may ask: how much is 'significant'? My answer will seem like no answer: there is no percentage of wealth or amount of time to be pulled out of a magic moral box. Caring is an unquantifiable dimension to moral responsibility. But if we have a proper appreciation of the facts of·world poverty, of our global moral identities, of the moral seriousness of responding to extreme suffering, of what quality of life really consists in, and of the duty of caring as much as we can consistent with our quality of life, then we will care as we ought.

References

Dower, N.: *What is Development? A Philosopher's Answer* (Glasgow University Centre for Development Studies: Occasional Paper Series No. 3, 1988).
Harris, J.: *Violence and Responsibility* (London: Routledge and Kegan Paul, 1980).
Nozick, R.: *Anarchy, State and Utopia* (Oxford: Basil Blackwell, 1974).
Rawls, J.: *A Theory of Justice* (Princeton: Princeton University Press, 1971).

Rich, W.: *Smaller Families Through Social and Economic Progress* (Overseas Development Council Monograph No. 7, 1973).

Riddell, R.: *Foreign Aid Reconsidered* (London: James Currey Ltd; Baltimore: Johns Hopkins University Press, 1987).

Singer, P.: *Practical Ethics* (Cambridge: Cambridge University Press, 1979), Chapter 8.

World Commission on Environment and Development: *Our Common Future* ('The Brundtland Report') (Oxford: Oxford University Press, 1987).

Further reading

Aiken, W. and LaFollette, H., eds.: *World Hunger and Moral Obligation* (Englewood Cliffs, NJ: Prentice-Hall, Inc., 1977).

Beitz, C.R.: *Political Theory and International Relations* (Princeton: Princeton University Press, 1979), especially Part III.

Dower, N.: *World Poverty Challenge and Response* (York: Ebor Press, 1983).

Fromm, E.: *To Have or to Be?* (London: Jonathan Cape, 1978; London: Abacus, Sphere Books, 1979).

Gasper, D.: 'Distribution and development ethics', in R. Apthorpe and A. Krahl, eds., *Development Studies: Critique and Renewal* (Leiden: E.J. Brill, 1986).

Goulet, D.: 'Obstacles to world development – an ethical reflection', *World Development*, 11, No. 7 (1983) (and other writings).

Hayter, T.: *The Creation of World Poverty: An Alternative View to the Brandt Report* (London: Pluto, 1981).

Honderich, T.: *Violence for Equality* (London: Penguin Books, 1976).

Independent Commission on International Development Issues: *North-South: A Programme for Survival* ('The Brandt Report') (London: Pan Books, 1980).

McCuen, G.E., ed.: *World Hunger and Social Justice* (Ideas in Conflict Series: Wisconsin: G.E. McCuen Publications Ltd, 1986).

Madeley, J.: *Human Rights Begin with Breakfast* (Oxford: Pergamon Press, 1982).

O'Neill, O.: *Faces of Hunger* (London: Allen & Unwin, 1986).

Shue, H.: *Basic Rights: Subsistence, Affluence and US Foreign Policy* (Princeton: Princeton University Press, 1980).

Sider, R.: *Rich Christians in an Age of Hunger* (London: Hodder and Stoughton, 1978).

Vincent, R.J.: *Human Rights and International Relations* (Cambridge: Cambridge University Press, 1986).

24

Environmental ethics

ROBERT ELLIOT

i What is an environmental ethic?

KAKADU NATIONAL PARK in Australia's Northern Territory, contains rugged woodlands, swamps and waterways supporting a rich variety of life; it contains species found nowhere else, including some, such as the Hooded Parrot and the Pig-nosed Turtle, which are endangered. Kakadu affords aesthetic enjoyment and recreational and research opportunities. Many think it is a place of immense beauty and ecological significance. It is of spiritual significance to the Jawoyn aboriginals. Kakadu is also rich in gold, platinum, palladium and uranium, which some think should be mined. If this happens then, environmentalists claim, aesthetic, recreational and research opportunities will be reduced, the beauty of Kakadu will be lessened, species will disappear, ecological richness will decrease, the naturalness of the place will be compromised and the spiritual values of the Jawoyn discounted. Mining already goes on in the Kakadu area and there is pressure to allow more. Should more mining be allowed? Should any mining at all be allowed? How exactly might we reach answers to these ethical questions?

Empirical or factual evidence certainly plays a role. For example, opponents of mining claim that it is likely to pollute rivers, poison wildlife, endanger species and disrupt ecosystems. This opposition to mining relies on empirical claims; that is, claims about what does and will in fact happen. Many supporters dispute these empirical claims and there are some who think that even if the claims are true it is better to go ahead with mining. Settling the facts does not ensure that the issue is settled. Arguments about such facts only have point, only make sense, against a certain kind of background, and differences in this background give rise to different assessments of what should be done. What constitutes this background are such things as desires, preferences, aims, goals and principles, including moral principles. An environmentalist might want to know whether mining is a threat to wildlife because he or she desires that wildlife be protected or, more seriously, because he or she thinks it is morally wrong to cause the death of wildlife. The evaluative background need not include moral principles; some people might be amoral. (They might be the kind of rational egoists described in Article 16, EGOISM.) However, many people do want their own actions and the actions of others, including corporations and governments, to conform to moral principles. For such people the resolution of the Kakadu controversy requires an appeal to principles which offer moral guidance in our treatment of wild nature and which enable us to answer questions like: would it matter if our actions caused a species to become extinct? Would it matter if our actions caused the death of individual animals? Would it matter if we caused widespread erosion in Kakadu? Would it matter if we turned the South Alligator River into a watercourse devoid of life? Is it better to protect Kakadu or to generate increased material wealth which might improve the lives of a number of people? Is the extinction of a species an acceptable price to pay for increased employment opportunities? Such sets of principles, which would guide our treatment of wild nature, constitute an environmental ethic in the most general sense. There is a variety of competing, including partly overlapping, environmental ethics.

People who have views of a moral kind about environmental issues are committed to an environmental ethic consisting of at least one, but usually a number of principles. Consider environmentalists who say that the extinction of species as a result of human actions is a bad thing, maybe even a bad thing no matter what the cause. This might be a basic principle in an environmental ethic. Without having explicitly represented it as such, an environmentalist might nevertheless be committed to the view that the extinction of species etc. is bad considered in itself, quite apart from any consequences it might have. Another possibility is that the principle is not itself basic but rests on a principle enjoining concern for human welfare, combined with the belief that humans are harmed by the extinction of species. Making the ethical commitment explicit is a first step in subjecting it to critical appraisal or justification. Justification is necessary if we are to adjudicate between the various competing environmental ethics we encounter. It is not enough that an environmental policy conform to the principles of some or other environmental ethic, it should conform to the correct, or best justified, one. We have two questions: how might an environmental ethic be fleshed out? How might putative environmental ethics be justified?

1   Human-centred ethics

Some think that environmental policies should be evaluated solely on the basis of how they affect humans (see Baxter, 1974, and Norton, 1988). This entails a human-centred environmental ethic. Although the classical utilitarians include animal suffering in their ethical calculation, a variant of utilitarianism, which enjoins us to maximize the surplus of human happiness over human unhappiness, is one example of a human-centred ethic. Taking this ethic seriously obliges us to calculate the varying effects of the Kakadu options on human happiness and unhappiness. We might discover that mining would reduce the ecological richness of the wetlands and that if this happened then some people would be made unhappy; for instance, some might be moved by the plight of individual animals, some might be saddened by the loss of species, some, including members of future generations, might miss out on the chance of particular recreational or aesthetic enjoyments, some might be adversely affected by resultant climatic changes, changes in flood patterns and so on, some might be psychologically harmed by the despoliation of areas to which they have a spiritual attachment. These negative effects would have to be subtracted from any increases in happiness which resulted from mining in Kakadu. A human-centred ethic could lead to substantial agreement with environmentalists about policy. This would depend on the facts about the effects on humans of changes to the natural environment. However, this decision would have been reached by considering the interests of humans alone. A helpful way of putting this is to say that this ethic treats only humans as morally considerable. Something is morally considerable if it enters into ethical evaluation in its own right, independently of its usefulness as a means to other ends. Consider the Pig-nosed Turtle. On the human-centred ethic just now described neither the species as a whole nor the individual members of it are morally considerable: it is only the happiness and unhappiness of humans which is morally considerable and this might or might not be affected by what happens to the turtles.

2 Animal-centred ethics

There is a view of ethics which counts not only humans as morally considerable but non-human animals as well; it includes all animals in its scope. Many of the things which we do to the natural environment do affect non-humans adversely and this, it is suggested, must be taken into account. For example, if we thought that cyanide pollution in the South Alligator River would cause non-humans to suffer then this is a moral minus which must be taken into account independently of how things will be for humans. The example is not fanciful: consider the effect on non-humans caused by clear-cutting forests, damming river valleys, quarrying mountains, constructing pipelines and so on. An animal-centred ethic enjoins the moral consideration of individual animals not of species: what happens to species is only of indirect concern insofar as it affects individual animals.

While an animal-centred ethic counts all animals as morally considerable it does not necessarily rank them equally. A useful way of putting this is to say that some animal-centred ethics will accord different moral significance to animals of different kinds. One form this differentiation might take involves the arbitrary, and many would say unjustified, discounting of the interests of non-humans simply because they are the interests of non-humans. Just how this will affect judgements about policy will depend on the degree of the discounting. It could be such as to make human interests always count for more than non-human interests no matter what the intensity or strength of the interests and no matter what the numbers involved. It could be such as to allow stronger or more numerous non-human interests to prevail over weaker or fewer human interests. Avoiding arbitrariness seems to require that equal interests be treated equally. This would leave scope for differentiation, which might still be made on the basis of interests which not all animals have. For example, humans have a capacity for developing theoretical knowledge or for rational autonomous action, which are arguably not capacities of kangaroos. These capacities might underpin certain interests which, because they lack them, kangaroos could not have. Such additional interests might swing a decision in favour of humans and against kangaroos. This is particularly likely in, although not restricted to, cases in which their common interests are equally threatened or equally protected: the appeal to the additional, unshared interest acts as a tie-breaker. Imagine that some important medical breakthrough depended on confining either humans or kangaroos. Keeping kangaroos in a very large enclosure in order to study them may be morally preferable if it threatens no interests of theirs; if they are not treated cruelly, if they are fed, if they are able to behave according to their nature. Confining humans in the same way is not morally acceptable because of the additional interests of humans. This mode of differentiation treats equal interests equally regardless of species and it also allows that unshared interests leave room for degrees of moral significance. (See Article 30, ANIMALS, for further discussion of animal-centred ethics.)

3 Life-centred ethics

The class of living things includes more than humans and non-human animals; it includes plants, algae, single-celled organisms, perhaps viruses and, it is sometimes suggested, ecosystems and even the whole biosphere itself (See Attfield, 1983, Goodpaster, 1978, and Taylor, 1986). The complexity of a life-centred ethic will depend on how the question 'What is living?' is answered. However this question is settled it will make much of the idea of a self-regulating system which strives, not necessarily consciously, towards certain goals. Moreover, it is this feature which is typically supposed to confer moral considerability on living things. A life-centred ethic counts all living things as morally considerable, although not necessarily of equal moral significance. So, it might be better to save a Pig-nosed Turtle than a waratah shrub, even though both are morally considerable. The former, however, might be more morally significant because it is a more complex living thing. Here complexity acts as an intensifier: if living, then the more complex, the more morally significant. To take a different kind of case, it morally might be preferable to save some plant rather than to save the Pig-nosed Turtle, because only that plant can fill its particular ecological niche, whereas the Pig-nosed Turtle fills a niche that perhaps could be filled by similar turtles of a different species. Here the differentiation is based on a moral assessment of the respective consequences of the plant ceasing to exist and the Pig-nosed Turtle ceasing to exist, and not on internal characteristics of the living things themselves.

A life-centred ethic requires that in deciding how we should act we need to take account of the impact of our actions on every living thing affected by them. For example, if mining goes on in Kakadu, it will involve cutting down trees and destroying other plants; it will cause the death of some animals and impair, if not destroy, wetland ecosystems. These facts and others count against mining and collectively must be weighed against the good things that might result if mining does go ahead. Since the good things would seem to include only material benefits for some humans, it would be difficult to do the evaluation sum in such a way that it sanctioned mining. This is not so say that it is never morally permissible to fell trees, to flatten dunes, to kill animals, to modify ecosystems and so on. Whether it is permissible depends on what the outcomes are and on differences in moral significance within the class of the morally considerable. A life-centred ethic, incidentally, might take a radical form: it might claim that not only are all

287

living things morally considerable but also that they are of equal moral significance. (See Naess, 1979.) This biotic egalitarianism, if it could be justified, would make it very difficult indeed to defend morally human interventions in the natural environment. It would allow only quantitative judgements; for example, that two living things count for more than one. Most proposed life-centred ethics allow for differential significance within the class of living things, although humans might not be counted the most significant. The preservation of the biosphere and of large ecosystems might be thought more significant than the preservation of large numbers of humans.

4 Rights for rocks?

The ethics so far considered each evaluate actions by considering consequences for individuals and adding them. What distinguishes these ethics are the kinds of individuals within their scope; moreover, the later ones include all individuals included by earlier ones in the list. It could be argued that we are drawn inexorably to a life-centred ethic; that there is no non-arbitrary way of stopping the drift from the ethic of narrowest scope to the ethic of widest scope. Why not take the argument another step and count non-living things too as morally considerable? There is no attempt here to attribute a mental life or a point of view to non-living things; that would be to enter into an entirely different dispute. The claim is that non-living things, which, like many living things, lack consciousness and which also lack even rudimentary biological organization, are morally considerable. Call this ethic the 'everything ethic'.

Take rocks for example. Mining will involve smashing up rocks, disturbing geological structures, spoiling fossils and the like. Is there anything wrong in doing these things? Here we must take care to forget for a moment the consequential damage which would be done to plants, animals and ecosystems; we must ask whether these things would be wrong considered in themselves. Another example might highlight the issue. Imagine a plan to test a missile by firing it at some distant and completely lifeless celestial body which will be thereby destroyed. Would this be wrong considered in itself? On the ethic which attributes 'rights' to rocks, so to speak, it would be. All things considered it might not be wrong, but according to this ethic that is a case which must be made. Like the life-centred ethic, this one can be fleshed out in a variety of ways. It may allow degrees of moral significance and attribute comparatively minimal moral significance to non-living things. It may mirror biological egalitarianism and deny that there are gradations of moral significance, or it may fall somewhere in between.

5 Ecological holism

It was earlier said that any ethic which would guide us in our treatment of the natural environment is, in the most general sense, an environmental ethic. The term 'environmental ethic' sometin.es has narrower uses. It is sometimes used to indicate an ethic which counts as morally considerable individuals other than humans and which provides some solid purchase for the moral demands of environmentalists. A life-centred ethic is an environmental ethic in this sense, an animal-centred ethic less clearly so. However, some reserve the term for a specific ethic, ecological holism, presumably because they think that only such an ethic provides morally satisfactory protection for the natural environment. (See Callicott, 1979.) Ecological holism counts two kinds of things as morally considerable; the biosphere as a whole and the large ecosystems which constitute it. Individual animals, including humans, as well as the plants, rocks, molecules etc. which constitute these large systems are not morally considerable; they matter only insofar as they contribute to the maintenance of the significant whole to which they belong. Why should we worry if some species is caused to become extinct? We should worry not because of what this implies for its individual members or even for the species itself but because the extinction runs counter to the goal of maintaining the biosphere or ecosystems. It is a moot point whether ecological holism should be thought to differ structurally from the other ethics. They had as their focus individuals, and 'holism' might be thought to signal a different focus. However, it is possible to view the biosphere and ecosystems as individuals, albeit extremely complex ones. If so, the holism amounts to the view that individuals many have hitherto regarded as morally considerable are not. Note that, although the principles of ecological holism differ from those of the other ethics, this does not entail that it differs from all of them in its policy implications. The life-centred ethic and the everything ethic are likely to sanction similar environmental policies as a result of the nature of the mechanisms which maintain ecosystems and the biosphere. Also, it is possible to combine ecological holism with any of the other ethics described. If, for instance, it was combined with the animal-centred ethic we would be enjoined to consider the interests of animals and the goal of biospheric maintenance. Where these conflict, for example in some odd case where animals can only be saved by simplifying an ecosystem, then some kind of trade-off or balancing would be required.

ii Justifying an environmental ethic

It is not too difficult to appreciate what is compelling about the claim that humans are morally considerable. Most obviously they are considerable because they have interests which can be harmed or advanced. These interests are based on capacities which humans have; for example, the capacity to experience pain and pleasure, the capacity for rational choice, the capacity for free action. Less obviously, they are considerable because of properties or characteristics which they possess which do not give rise to interests, to things in which they themselves have a stake. For example, it might be argued that anything which has the property of being a complex living thing is, to that extent, intrinsically valuable, which is to say that there is a moral reason for preserving it for its own sake independently of whatever uses it serves.

What is compelling about a human-centred ethic pushes us toward an animal-centred ethic, possibly further. (This argument is developed by Lori Gruen in Article 30, ANIMALS.) Consistency and the avoidance of arbitrary moral distinctions fuel the shift from a human-centred ethic to an animal-centred ethic. Also, in thinking about non-humans we might notice new reasons for moral considerability; for example, non-humans might have aesthetic properties such as beauty, which we might think make them morally considerable. This, too, is a case where they are morally considerable not because they have interests but because they possess some property which gives them intrinsic value.

Do the reasons advanced in support of animal-centred ethics also support life-centred ethics? If plants (and ecosystems or the biosphere) can be said to have interests, such as an interest in continued existence, then perhaps they do. The concept of *interest* is often explained in terms of a thing having a good of its own which can be harmed or promoted. Some claim that plants have a good of their own; for example, that the good of a tree is promoted by sufficient nutrients for its continued flourishing and harmed when it is deprived of nutrients. A plant's good is determined by the kind of thing it is, by the type of biological organization it exemplifies, by what it is for it to be a flourishing member of its kind. Plants have a good in this sense but this is obviously not enough to ground the claim that they have interests in any morally relevant sense. Plants do not have a point of view from which they experience the world. It doesn't matter to the tree that it withers and dies from want of water; it would matter to a kangaroo. While plants have natural goals, they have no attitude to those goals and progress towards them is not something which they experience. Similar points can be made about the biosphere and about ecosystems. It is this difference which is thought by some to stop the drift, by providing a non-arbitrary cut-off, from an animal-centred to a life-centred ethic.

Even if it is denied that plants have interests, however, it does not follow that they are not morally considerable. Recall that there were reasons suggested, which did not have to do with interests, in virtue of which humans and non-humans are morally considerable. These concerned the property of being a complex living thing and the property of being beautiful. Plants can possess these properties and if animals are morally considerable in virtue of possessing them, then so too are plants. The key to defending thus a life-centred ethic is to establish that the properties appealed to are intrinsically valuable.

Is there anything that might be said in defence of a life-centred ethic which pushes us toward an everything ethic? The property of being a complex living thing cannot be exemplified by rocks etc. but a related property, namely that of being a complex system, can be exemplified by collections of non-living things exhibiting certain relationships with one another. If it is organizational complexity *per se* that makes something morally considerable, then some non-living things will be morally considerable; for example, the bodies which make up the solar system, patterns of weathering on a cliff and a snowflake. The relevance of this suggestion to the Kakadu case depends, among other things, on whether ecosystems count as living things. If they do not then they are non-living things which exhibit complexity and which, given the suggestion, are morally considerable. The fact that they are morally considerable would provide an ethical reason for opposing mining. Or again, we might judge that one reason we think that living things are morally considerable is because they exemplify beauty. In some cases beauty might be exemplified by a thing's more general, external features, as in the case of tigers, whales, orchids and proteas. In addition, beauty might be exemplified in the more specific detail of a thing's biological functioning. Now some non-living things such as boulders, dunes, lifeless moons and icebergs can be beautiful, so, if exemplification of beauty is a basis for attributing moral considerability to living things, then at least some non-living things are morally considerable. The claim that exemplifying beauty is a basis for moral considerability is contentious; however, it is strongly supported by some, for example Rolston, 1988. Those who oppose it typically urge that it is the appreciation of beauty rather than beauty itself which is morally significant.

So, one way in which the move from one ethic to the next is accomplished is by finding a determinant of moral considerability in that ethic and showing that a rigorous application of it leads us to the next kind of ethic. Another way is by showing that there are new morally relevant features which the more restrictive ethics unjustifiably ignore. One such feature might be the property of being a natural object; that is, an object which is not the product of human technology and culture. Rocks are natural objects and so on this view it would be wrong, although perhaps not all things considered wrong, to destroy them. There are other candidate properties: for example, the property of exhibiting diversity of parts, the property of functional integration of parts, the property of exhibiting harmony and the property of being a self-regulating system. This last group of properties, if deemed determinants of moral considerability, move us in the direction of ecological holism or in the direction of a mixed ethic. This is because they are properties quintessentially exemplified by ecosystems and the biosphere. If we accept that they are determinants of moral considerability, then we are provided with a reason, in addition to any we might derive from the other ethics we have considered, for resisting policies which would lead to disruption of ecosystems.

How do we decide whether candidate determinants of moral considerability are in fact such? Consider naturalness and exhibiting diversity of parts. Imagine that a certain mine requires the destruction of a group of trees on a rocky outcrop and of the outcrop itself. Environmentalists protest that this involves an uncompensated loss of value. The mining company promises to reconstruct the outcrop from synthetic parts and to replace the trees with plastic models. This bit of artificial environment will be indistinguishable, except by laboratory analysis, from what was originally there. It will be exactly as appealing to look at, no animals will be harmed as a consequence and no ecosystem will be disrupted. Neither the human-centred ethic nor the animal-centred ethic provides space for an environmentalist rejoinder. The life-centred ethic does to the extent that it permits a complaint about the killing of living trees. However, this does not seem to some to be the only thing morally amiss with the mining company's proposal. Isn't it also morally suspect because it replaces the natural with the artificial? Imagine a modified case in which only a rock outcrop, devoid of life, is removed and later replaced with synthetic rock. Not even the life-centred ethic allows for a complaint about the morality of this. Some people think that even in the modified case the mining company does something to which a moral minus attaches. If this thought is persistent it provides support for a variant of an everything ethic which includes within its scope all natural items. (See Elliot, in VanDeVeer and Pierce, 1986, 142–50.) It is difficult to be entirely sure about the source of the belief, if we have it, that naturalness is a determinant of moral considerability. It is possible that we think that there is something dubious about the artificial outcrop because we cannot distance ourselves from the thought that it will be detectably different or from the belief that it will harm animal interests or that it will result in ecosystemic disruption. If these are the sources of our belief, then we have no basis for the view that naturalness is a determinant of moral considerability. There is another possibility to which we should be alert. Naturalness might be a conditional determinant; that is, it might require the presence of some other property, for instance complexity. So, it isn't natural items which are morally considerable but things which are both natural and complex.

Consider the property of having a diversity of parts. Is this a determinant of moral considerability? Here we might compare an area which is covered with rainforest with an area which has been cleared of rainforest and is under cultivation. Which is more valuable in itself? Again we must distance ourselves from certain thoughts; for example, the thought that clearing rainforests is contrary to long-term human interests, the thought that wild animals would have suffered during the clearing or the thought that aboriginal peoples were displaced. Having attempted this, many would say that the rainforest is of more value. Imagine, then, that only one of these areas could be saved from massive devastation. Many would say that, considering them just in themselves, the rainforest should be saved. Moreover, one reason that will be given is that the rainforest exhibits more diversity; it is constituted in a more complex, richer fashion. There are other reasons that might also be given; for example, that there are aesthetic properties possessed by the rainforest but not possessed by the cultivated area. Our preparedness, by the way, to attribute aesthetic properties, such as beauty, to the rainforest, may well depend on whether we have an understanding of it as an ecological system: knowing how the parts work in concert to maintain the whole might assist us in seeing it as a thing of beauty. Counting these kinds of reasons as reasons for avoiding environmental despoliation provides the basis for an environmental ethic which reaches beyond either a human or animal-centred one and possibly beyond a life-centred one as well.

Even if we accept, for example, that the ecosystems of Kakadu are morally considerable, how do we weigh this against human (or other) interests? A first step is to ask whether there are alternative ways of satisfying human interests. Often there are. Moreover, the modification of ecosystems is often contrary to long-term human interests. Sometimes there will be cases of genuine conflict where the different moral considerations pull in different directions. Here we must carefully enumerate the relevant moral considerations, ask ourselves how important they are and then make an all-things-considered judgement. There is no decisive calculus available to assist us in these judgements. It is not correct to say that humans should always come first nor is it correct to say that preserving an ecosystem is always more important than protecting any set of human interests. Nevertheless there will be cases, such as Kakadu, where the morally appropriate policy is clear enough.

References

Attfield, R.: *The Ethics of Environmental Concern* (Oxford: Blackwell, 1983).

Baxter, W.F.: *People or Penguins: the Case for Optimal Pollution* (New York: Columbia University Press, 1974).

Callicott, J.B.: 'Elements of an environmental ethic: moral considerability and the biotic community', *Environmental Ethics*, 1 (1979), 71–81.

Goodpaster, K.: 'On being morally considerable', *Journal of Philosophy*, 75 (1978), 308–25.

Naess, A.: 'Self-realisation in mixed communities of humans, bears, sheep and wolves', *Inquiry*, 22 (1979), 231–42.

Norton, B.: *Why Preserve Natural Variety?* (Princeton: Princeton University Press, 1988).

Rolston III, H.: *Environmental Ethics: Duties to and Values in the Natural World* (Philadelphia: Temple University Press, 1988).

Taylor, P.: *Respect for Nature* (Princeton: Princeton University Press, 1986).

VanDeVeer, D. and Pierce, C., eds.: *People, Penguins and Plastic Trees: Basic Issues in Environmental Ethics* (Belmont, Cal.: Wadsworth, 1986).

Further reading

Elliot, R. and Arran, G., eds.: *Environmental Philosophy: A Collection of Readings* (St Lucia: University of Queensland Press, 1983).

Mannison, D., McRobbie, M. and Routley, R. eds.: *Environmental Philosophy* (Canberra: Research School of Social Sciences, Australian National University, 1980).

Partridge, E., ed.: *Obligations to Future Generations* (Buffalo: Prometheus, 1981).

Regan, T., ed.: *Earthbound: New Introductory Essays in Environmental Ethics* (New York: Random House, 1984).

Sylvan, R.: *A Critique of Deep Ecology* (Canberra: Research School of Social Sciences, Australian National University, 1985).

25

Euthanasia

HELGA KUHSE

i Introduction

'EUTHANASIA' is a compound of two Greek words – *eu* and *thanatos* – meaning, literally, 'a good death'. Today, 'euthanasia' is generally understood to mean the bringing about of a good death – 'mercy killing', where one person, A, ends the life of another person, B, for the sake of B. This understanding of euthanasia emphasizes two important features of acts of euthanasia. First, that euthanasia involves the deliberate taking of a person's life; and, second, that life is taken for the sake of the person whose life it is – typically because she or he is suffering from an incurable or terminal disease. This distinguishes euthanasia from most other forms of taking life.

Every society known to us subscribes to some principle or principles prohibiting the taking of life. But there are great variations between cultural traditions as to when the taking of life is considered wrong. If we turn to the roots of our Western tradition, we find that in Greek and Roman times such practices as infanticide, suicide and euthanasia were widely accepted. Most historians of Western morals agree that Judaism and the rise of Christianity contributed greatly to the general feeling that human life has sanctity and must not deliberately be taken. To take an innocent human life is, in these traditions, to usurp the right of God to give and take life. It has also been seen by influential Christian writers as a violation of natural law. This view of the absolute inviolability of innocent human life remained virtually unchallenged until the sixteenth century when Sir Thomas More published his *Utopia*. In this book, More portrays euthanasia for the desperately ill as one of the important institutions of an imaginary ideal community. In subsequent centuries, British philosophers (notably David Hume, Jeremy Bentham and John Stuart Mill) challenged the religious basis of morality and the absolute prohibition of suicide, euthanasia and infanticide. The great eighteenth-century German philosopher Immanuel Kant, on the other hand, whilst believing that moral truths were founded on reason rather than religion, nonetheless thought that 'man cannot have the power to dispose of his life' (Kant, 1986, p. 148).

Mercy for a hopelessly ill and suffering patient and, in the case of voluntary euthanasia, respect for autonomy, have been the primary reasons given by those who have argued for the moral permissibility of euthanasia. Today, there is widespread popular support for some forms of euthanasia and many contemporary philosophers have argued that euthanasia is morally defensible. Official religious opposition (for example, from the Roman Catholic Church) does, however, remain unchanged, and active euthanasia remains a crime in every nation other than the Netherlands. There, a series of court cases, beginning in 1973, have established the conditions under which doctors, and only doctors, may practise euthanasia: the decision to die must be the voluntary and considered decision of an informed patient; there must be physical or mental suffering which the sufferer finds unbearable; there is no other reasonable (i.e. acceptable to the patient) solution to improve the situation; the doctor must consult another senior professional.

Before looking more closely at the arguments for and against euthanasia, it will be necessary to draw some distinctions. Euthanasia can take three forms: it can be voluntary, non-voluntary and involuntary.

ii Voluntary, non-voluntary and involuntary euthanasia

The following case is an example of *voluntary* euthanasia:

Mary F. was dying from a progressively debilitating disease. She had reached the stage where she was almost totally paralysed and, periodically, needed a respirator to keep her alive. She was suffering considerable distress. Knowing that there was no hope and that things would get worse, Mary F. wanted to die. She asked her doctor to give her a lethal injection to end her life. After consultation with her family and members of the health-care team, Dr H. administered the asked-for lethal injection, and Mary F. died.

The case of Mary F. is a clear case of voluntary euthanasia; that is, euthanasia carried out by A *at the request of* B, for the sake of B. There is a close connection between voluntary euthanasia and assisted suicide, where one person will assist another to end her life – for example, when A obtains the drugs that will allow B to suicide.

Euthanasia can be voluntary even if the person is no longer competent to assert her wish to die when her life is ended. You might wish to have your life ended should you ever find yourself in a situation where, whilst suffering from a distressing and incurable condition, illness or accident have robbed you of all your rational faculties, and you are no longer able to decide between life and death. If, whilst still competent, you expressed the considered wish to die when in a situation such as this, then the person who ends your life in the appropriate circumstances acts upon your request and performs an act of voluntary euthanasia.

Euthanasia is *non-voluntary* when the person whose life is ended cannot choose between life and death for herself – for example, because she is a hopelessly ill or handicapped newborn infant, or because illness or accident have rendered a formerly competent person permanently incompetent, without that person having previously indicated whether she would or would not like euthanasia under certain circumstances.

Euthanasia is *involuntary* when it is performed on a person who would have been able to give or withhold consent to her own death, but has not given consent – either because she was not asked, or because she was asked but withheld consent, wanting to go on living. Whilst clear cases of involuntary euthanasia would be relatively rare (for example, where A shoots B without B's consent to save her from falling into the hands of a sadistic torturer), it has been argued that some widely accepted medical practices (such as the administration of increasingly large doses of pain-killing drugs that will eventually cause the patient's death, or the unconsented-to withholding of life-sustaining treatment) amount to involuntary euthanasia.

iii   Active and passive euthanasia

So far, we have defined 'euthanasia' loosely as 'mercy-killing', where A brings about the death of B, for the sake of B. There are, however, two different ways in which A can bring B's death about: A can kill B by, say, administering a lethal injection; or A can allow B to die by withholding or withdrawing life-sustaining treatment. Cases of the first kind are typically referred to as 'active' or 'positive' euthanasia, whereas cases of the second kind are often referred to as 'passive' or 'negative' euthanasia. All three kinds of euthanasia listed previously – voluntary, non-voluntary and involuntary euthanasia – can either be passive or active.

If we change the above case of Mary F. but slightly, it becomes one of passive voluntary euthanasia:

Mary F. was dying from a progressively debilitating disease. She had reached the stage where she was almost totally paralysed and periodically needed a respirator to keep her alive. She was suffering considerable distress. Knowing that there was no hope and that things would get worse, Mary F. wanted to die. She asked her doctor to ensure that she would not be put on a respirator when her breathing would fail next. The doctor agreed with Mary's wishes, instructed the nursing staff accordingly, and Mary died eight hours later, from respiratory failure.

There is widespread agreement that omissions as well as actions can constitute euthanasia. The Roman Catholic Church, in its *Declaration on Euthanasia*, for example, defines euthanasia as 'an action or omission which of itself or by intention causes death' (1980, p. 6). Philosophical disagreement does, however, arise over *which* actions and omissions amount to euthanasia. Thus it is sometimes denied that a doctor practises (non-voluntary passive) euthanasia when she refrains from resuscitating a severely handicapped newborn infant, or that a doctor engages in euthanasia of any kind when she administers increasingly large doses of a painkilling drug that she knows will eventually result in the patient's death. Other writers hold that *whenever* an agent deliberately and knowingly engages in an action or an omission that results in the patient's foreseen death, she has performed active or passive euthanasia.

In spite of the great diversity of views on this matter, debates on euthanasia have time and again focused on certain themes:

1   Does it make a moral difference whether death is actively (or positively) brought about, rather than occurring because life-sustaining treatment is withheld or withdrawn?

2   Must all available life-sustaining means always be used, or are there certain

'extraordinary' or 'disproportionate' means that need not be employed?

3   Does it make a moral difference whether the patient's death is directly intended, or whether it comes about as a merely foreseen consequence of the agent's action or omission?

The following is a brief sketch of these debates.

iv   Actions and omissions/killing and letting die

To shoot someone is an action: to fail to help the victim of a shooting is an omission. If A shoots B and B dies, A has killed B. If C does nothing to save B's life, C lets B die. But not all actions or omissions that result in a person's death are of central interest in the euthanasia debate. The euthanasia debate is concerned with *intentional* actions and omissions – that is, with deaths that are deliberately and knowingly brought about in a situation where the agent could have done otherwise – that is, where A could have refrained from killing B, and where C could have saved B's life.

There are some problems in distinguishing between killing and letting die, or between active and passive euthanasia. If the killing/letting die distinction were to rest simply on the distinction between actions and omissions, then the agent who, say, turns off the machine that sustains B's life, kills B, whereas the agent who refrains from putting C onto a life-sustaining machine in the first place, merely allows C to die. That killing and letting die should be distinguished in this way has struck many writers as implausible, and attempts have been made to draw the distinction in some other way. One plausible suggestion is that we understand killing as initiating a course of events that leads to death; and allowing to die as not intervening in a course of events that leads to death. According to this scheme, the administration of a lethal injection would be a case of killing; whereas not putting a patient on a respirator, or taking her off, would be an instance of letting die. In the first case, the patient dies because of events set in train by the agent. In the second case, the patient dies because the agent does not intervene in a course of events (e.g. a life-threatening disease) already in train that is not of the agent's making.

Is the distinction between killing and letting die, or between active and passive euthanasia, morally significant? Is killing a person always morally worse than letting a person die? Various reasons have been proposed why this should be so. One of the more plausible ones is that an agent who kills causes death, whereas an agent who lets die merely allows nature to take its course. This distinction between 'making happen' and 'letting happen', it has been argued, is a morally important one insofar as it sets limits to an agent's duties and responsibilities to save lives. Whilst it requires little or no effort to refrain from killing anyone, it usually requires effort to save a person. If killing and letting die were morally on a par, so the argument goes, then we would be just as responsible for the deaths of those whom we fail to save as we are for the deaths of those whom we kill – and failing to aid starving Africans would be the moral equivalent of sending

297

them poisoned food. (See Foot, 1980, p. 161–2.) This, the argument continues, is absurd: we are more, or differently, responsible for the deaths of those whom we kill than we are for the deaths of those whom we fail to save. Thus, to kill a person is, other things being equal, worse than allowing a person to die.

But even if a morally relevant distinction can sometimes be drawn between killing and letting die, this does not, of course, mean that such a distinction always prevails. Sometimes at least we are as responsible for our omissions as we are for our actions. A parent who does not feed her infant, or a doctor who refrains from giving insulin to an otherwise healthy diabetic, will not be absolved of moral responsibility by merely pointing out that the person in her charge died as a consequence of what she omitted to do.

Moreover, when the argument about the moral significance of the killing/letting die distinction is raised in the context of the euthanasia debate, an additional factor needs to be considered. To kill someone, or deliberately to let someone die, is generally a bad thing because it deprives that person of her life. Under normal circumstances persons value their lives, and to continue to live is in their best interest. This is different when questions of euthanasia are at issue. In cases of euthanasia, death – not continued life – is in the person's best interest. This means that an agent who kills, or an agent who lets die, is not harming but benefiting the person whose life it is. This has led writers in the field to suggest: if we are, indeed, more responsible for our actions than for our omissions, then A who kills C in the context of euthanasia will, other things being equal, be acting morally better than B who lets C die – for A positively benefits C, whereas B merely allows benefits to befall C.

v Ordinary and extraordinary means

Powerful medical technologies allow doctors to sustain the lives of many patients who, only a decade or two ago, would have died because the means were not available to avert death. With this an old question is raised with renewed urgency: must doctors always do everything possible to try to save a patient's life? Must they engage in 'heroic' efforts to add another few weeks, days, or hours to the life of a terminally ill and suffering cancer patient? Must active treatment always be instigated with regard to babies born so defective that their short life will be filled with little more than continuous suffering?

Most writers in the field agree that there are times when life-sustaining treatment should be withheld and a patient allowed to die. This view is shared even by those who regard euthanasia or the intentional termination of life as always wrong. It raises the pressing need for criteria to distinguish between permissible and impermissible omissions of life-sustaining means.

Traditionally, this distinction has been drawn in terms of so-called ordinary and extraordinary means of treatment. The distinction has a long history and was employed by the Roman Catholic Church to deal with the problem of surgery prior to the development of antisepsis and anaesthesia. If a patient refused ordinary means – for example, food – such refusal was regarded as suicide, or the intentional termination of life. Refusal of extraordinary means (painful or risky surgery, for example), on the other hand, was not regarded as the intentional termination of life.

Today, the distinction between life-sustaining means that are regarded as ordinary and obligatory and those that are not is often expressed in terms of 'proportionate' and 'disproportionate' means of treatment. A means is 'proportionate' if it offers a reasonable hope of benefit to the patient; it is 'disproportionate' if it does not. (See Sacred Congregation for the Doctrine of the Faith, 1980, pp. 9–10.)

Understood in this way, the distinction between proportionate and disproportionate means is clearly morally significant. But it is not, of course, a distinction between means of treatment, considered simply as means of treatment. Rather, it is a distinction between the proportionate or disproportionate benefits different patients are likely to derive from a particular treatment. The same treatment can thus be proportionate or disproportionate, depending on the patient's medical condition and on the quality and quantity of life the patient is likely to gain from its employment. A painful and invasive operation, for example, might be an 'ordinary' or 'proportionate' means if performed on an otherwise healthy 20-year-old who is likely to gain a lifetime; it might well be considered 'extraordinary' or 'disproportionate' if performed on an elderly patient, who is also suffering from some other serious debilitating disease. Even a treatment as simple as a course of antibiotics or physiotherapy is sometimes judged to be extraordinary and non-obligatory treatment. (See Linacre Centre Working Party, 1982, pp. 46–8.)

This understanding of ordinary and extraordinary means suggests that an agent who refrains from using extraordinary means of treatment engages in passive euthanasia: A withholds potentially life-sustaining treatment from B, for the sake of B.

Not everyone agrees, however, that the discontinuation of extraordinary or disproportionate treatment is a case of passive euthanasia. 'Euthanasia', it is often argued, involves the deliberate or intentional termination of life. Administering a lethal injection, or withholding ordinary life-sustaining means, are cases of the intentional termination of life; withholding extraordinary means and allowing the patient to die, is not. The question then becomes: what does the doctor 'do' when she withholds disproportionate life-sustaining treatment from B, foreseeing that B will die as a consequence? And how can this mode of bringing the patient's death about (or of allowing the patient's death to occur) be distinguished, in terms of the agent's intention, from the withholding of ordinary care on the one hand, and the administration of a lethal injection on the other?

This brings us to the third major theme on which the debate about euthanasia has focused: the distinction between deaths that are directly intended and deaths that are merely foreseen.

vi   Intending death and foreseeing that death will occur

If A administers a lethal injection to B to end B's suffering, A has intentionally terminated B's life. This case is uncontroversial. But has A also intentionally terminated B's life when she seeks to alleviate B's pain by increasingly large doses of drugs ('pyramid pain-killing') that she knows will eventually bring about B's death? And has A terminated B's life intentionally when she turns off the respirator that sustains B's life, knowing that B will die as a consequence? Those who want to hold that the first case is, but the second and third case is not, a case of euthanasia or the intentional termination of life have sought to draw a distinction between these cases in terms of directly intended results, and foreseen but non-intended consequences. Reflecting on the administration of increasingly large and potentially lethal doses of pain-killing drugs, the Vatican's *Declaration on Euthanasia* thus holds that 'pyramid pain-killing' is acceptable because, in this case, 'death is in no way intended or sought, even if the risk of it is reasonably taken' (p. 9). In other words, even if A foresees that B will die as a consequence of what A does, B's death is only foreseen and not directly intended. The direct intention is to kill the pain, not the patient.

This distinction between intended results and foreseen but non-intended further consequences is formalized in the Principle of Double Effect (PDE). The PDE lists a number of conditions under which an agent may 'allow' or 'permit' a consequence (such as a person's death) to occur, although that consequence must not be intended by the agent. Thomas Aquinas, with whom the PDE is said to have its origin, applied the distinction between directly intended and merely foreseen consequences to actions of self-defence. If a person is attacked and kills the attacker, her intention is to defend herself, not to kill the attacker (*Summa Theologiae*, II, ii).

Two main questions have been raised regarding the intention/foresight distinction:

– Can a clear distinction always be drawn between those consequences that an agent directly intends and those that she merely foresees?
– Is the distinction, to the extent that it can be drawn, morally relevant in itself?

Consider the first point in the light of the following frequently cited example:

A party of explorers is trapped in a cave, in whose narrow opening a rather fat member of the party is lodged, and the waters are rising. If a member of the party explodes a charge of dynamite next to the fat man, should we say that he intended the fat man's death or that he merely foresaw it as a consequence of either freeing the party, removing the fat man's body from the opening, or blowing him to atoms?

If one wants to hold that the fat man's death was clearly intended, in what way, then, is this case different from the one where a doctor can administer increasingly large doses of a pain-killing drug that will forseeably bring about the patient's death, without that doctor being said to have intended the patient's death?

There are serious philosophical problems in any systematic application of the intention/foresight distinction, and the literature is replete with criticisms and refutations. Nancy Davis discusses some of this literature in the context of deon-tological ethics (where the distinction is crucial) in Article 17, CONTEMPORARY DEONTOLOGY. Assuming that the difficulties can be overcome, the next question presents itself: is the distinction between directly intended results and merely foreseen consequences morally relevant in itself? Does it matter, morally, whether a doctor when administering what she believes to be a lethal drug merely intends to relieve the patient's pain, or whether she directly intends to end the patient's life?

Here a distinction is sometimes drawn between the goodness and badness of agents: that it is the mark of a good agent that she not directly intend the death of another person. But even if a distinction between the goodness and badness of agents can sometimes be drawn in this way, it is of course not clear that it can be applied to euthanasia cases. In all euthanasia cases, A seeks to benefit B, thus acting as a good agent would. Only if it is assumed that there is a rule which says 'A good agent must never directly intend the death of an innocent', does the attempt to draw the distinction make sense – and that rule then lacks a rationale.

vii Conclusion

The above distinctions represent deeply felt differences. Whether or not these differences are morally relevant, and if so on what grounds, is a debate that is still continuing.

There is, however, one other aspect of the euthanasia debate that has not yet been touched on. People frequently agree that there may be no intrinsic moral difference between active and passive euthanasia, between ordinary and extra-ordinary means, and between deaths that are directly intended and deaths that are merely foreseen. Nonetheless, the argument is sometimes put that distinctions such as these represent important lines of demarcation as far as public policy is concerned. Public policy requires the drawing of lines, and those drawn to safe-guard us against unjustified killings are among the most universal. Whilst it is true that such lines may appear arbitrary and philosophically troubling, they are nonetheless necessary to protect vulnerable members of society against abuse. The question is, of course, whether this kind of reasoning has a sound basis: whether societies that openly allow the intentional termination of life under some circumstances will inevitably move onto a dangerous 'slippery slope' that will lead from justified to unjustified practices.

In its *logical* version, the 'slippery slope' argument is unconvincing. There are no logical grounds why the reasons that justify euthanasia – mercy and respect for autonomy – should logically also justify killings that are neither merciful nor show respect for autonomy. In its *empirical* version, the slippery slope argument asserts that justified killings will, as a matter of fact, lead to unjustified killings. There is little empirical evidence to back up this claim. Whilst the Nazi 'euthanasia' programme is often cited as an example of what can happen when a society acknowledges that some lives are not worthy to be lived, the motivation behind these killings was neither mercy nor respect for autonomy; it was, rather, racial prejudice and the belief that the racial purity of the *Volk* required the elimination of certain individuals and groups. As already noted, in the Netherlands a 'social experiment' with active voluntary euthanasia is currently in progress. As yet there is no evidence that this has sent Dutch society down a slippery slope.

References

Aquinas, T.: *Summa Theologiae*, II, ii, question 64, articles 5 and 7.

Foot, P.: 'The problem of abortion and the doctrine of double effect', *Killing and Letting Die*, ed. B. Steinbock (Englewood Cliffs, NJ: Prentice-Hall, 1980).

Kant, I.: 'Duties towards the body in regard to life', *Lectures on Ethics*, trans. Louis Infield (New York: Harper and Row, 1986).

Linacre Centre Working Party: *Euthanasia and Clinical Practice: Trends, Principles and Alternatives* (London: The Linacre Centre, 1982).

More, T.: *Utopia* (1518); (Harmondsworth: Penguin, 1951).

Sacred Congregation for the Doctrine of the Faith: *Declaration on Euthanasia* (Vatican City: 1980).

Further reading

Bennett, J.: 'Whatever the consequences', *Killing and Letting Die*, ed. B. Steinbock (Englewood Cliffs, NJ: Prentice-Hall, 1980), pp. 109–27.

Capron, A. M.: 'The right to die: progress and peril', *Euthanasia Review*, 2, Nos. 1 and 2, (1987), 41–59.

Davis, N.: 'The priority of avoiding harm', *Killing and Letting Die*, ed. B. Steinbock (Englewood Cliffs, NJ: Prentice-Hall, 1980), pp. 173–215.

Glover, J.: *Causing Death and Saving Lives* (Harmondsworth: Penguin, 1987).

Goldman, H.: 'Killing, letting die and euthanasia', *Analysis*, 40 (1980), 224.

Kuhse, H.: *The Sanctity-of-Life Doctrine in Medicine – A Critique* (Oxford: Oxford University Press, 1987).

Humphry, D. and Wickett, A.: *The Right to Die – Understanding Euthanasia* (New York: Harper and Row, 1986).

Morillo, C. R.: 'Doing, refraining, and the strenuousness of morality', *American Philosophical Quarterly*, 14 (1977), 29–39.

Rachels, J.: 'Active and passive euthanasia', *Killing and Letting Die*, ed. B. Steinbock (Englewood Cliffs, NJ: Prentice-Hall, 1980).

——: *The End of Life: Euthanasia and Morality* (Oxford: Oxford University Press, 1987).

26

Abortion

MARY ANNE WARREN

i Introduction

Do WOMEN have the right to abort unwanted pregnancies? Or is the state entitled (or perhaps ethically required) to prohibit deliberate abortion? Should some abortions be permitted and others not? Does the proper legal status of abortion follow directly from its moral status? Or should abortion be legal, even if it is sometimes or always morally wrong?

Such questions have aroused intense debate during the past two decades. Interestingly enough, in most of the industrialized world abortion was not a criminal offence until a series of anti-abortion laws were passed during the second half of the nineteenth century. At that time, proponents of the prohibition of abortion generally stressed the medical dangers of abortion. It was also sometimes argued that fetuses are human beings from conception onward, and that deliberate abortion is therefore a form of homicide. Now that improved techniques have made properly performed abortions much safer than childbirth, the medical argument has lost whatever force it may once have had. Consequently, the focus of anti-abortion arguments has shifted from the physical safety of women to the moral value of fetal life.

Advocates of women's right to choose abortion have responded to the anti-abortion argument in several ways. I shall examine three lines of argument for the pro-choice view: (1) that abortion should be permitted, because the prohibition of abortion leads to highly undesirable consequences; (2) that women have a moral right to choose abortion; and (3) that fetuses are not yet persons and thus do not yet have a substantial right to life.

ii Consequentialist arguments for abortion

If actions are to be morally evaluated by their consequences, then a strong case can be made that the prohibition of abortion is wrong. Throughout history women have paid a terrible price for the absence of safe and legal contraception and abortion. Forced to bear many children, at excessively short intervals, they were often physically debilitated and died young – a common fate in most pre-twentieth-century societies and much of the Third World today. Involuntary childbearing aggravates poverty, increases infant and child death rates, and places severe strains upon the resources of families and states.

Improved methods of contraception have somewhat alleviated these problems. Yet no form of contraception is 100 per cent effective. Moreover, many women lack access to contraception, e.g. because they cannot afford it, or it is unavailable where they live, or unavailable to minors without parental permission. In most of the world, paid work has become an economic necessity for many women, married or single. Women who must earn have an acute need to control their fertility. Without that control, they often find it impossible to obtain the education necessary for any but the most marginal employment, or impossible to combine the responsibilities of childrearing and paid labour. This is as true in socialist as in capitalist economies, since in both economic systems women must contend with the double responsibility of paid and domestic work.

Contraception and abortion do not guarantee reproductive autonomy, because many people cannot afford to have (and properly raise) any children, or as many children as they would like; and others are involuntarily infertile. However, both contraception and abortion are essential if women are to have the modest degree of reproductive autonomy which is possible in the world as it is presently constructed.

In the long run, access to abortion is essential for the health and survival not just of individual women and families, but also that of the larger social and biological systems on which all our lives depend. Given the inadequacy of present methods of contraception and the lack of universal access to contraception, the avoidance of rapid population growth generally requires some use of abortion. Unless population growth rates are reduced in those impoverished societies where they remain high, malnutrition and starvation will become even more widespread than at present. There might still be enough food to feed all the people of the world, if only it were more equitably distributed. However, this cannot remain true indefinitely. Soil erosion and climatic changes brought about by the destruction of forests and the burning of fossil fuels threaten to reduce the earth's capacity for food production – perhaps drastically – within the next generation.

Yet opponents of abortion deny that abortion is necessary for the avoidance of such undesirable consequences. Some pregnancies are the result of rape or involuntary incest, but most result from apparently voluntary sexual behaviour. Thus, anti-abortionists often claim that women who seek abortions are 'refusing to take responsibility for their own actions'. In their view, women ought to avoid heterosexual intercourse unless they are prepared to complete any resulting pregnancy. But is this demand a reasonable one?

Heterosexual intercourse is not *biologically* necessary for women's – or men's – individual survival or physical health. On the contrary, women who are celibate or homosexual are less vulnerable to cervical cancer, AIDS, and other sexually transmitted diseases. Nor is it obvious that sex is necessary for the psychological health of either women or men, although the contrary belief is widespread. It is, however, something that many women find intensely pleasurable – a fact which is morally significant on most consequentialist theories. Furthermore, it is part of the form of life which the majority of women everywhere appear to prefer. In some places, lesbian women are creating alternative forms of life which may better serve their needs. But for most heterosexual women, the choice of permanent celibacy is very difficult. In much of the world, it is very difficult for single women to support themselves (let alone support a family); and sexual intercourse is usually one of the 'duties' of married women.

In short, permanent celibacy is not a reasonable option to impose upon most women. And since all women are potentially vulnerable to rape, even those who are homosexual or celibate may face unwanted pregnancies. Hence, until there is a fully reliable and safe form of contraception, available to all women, the consequentialist arguments for abortion will remain strong. But these arguments will not persuade those who reject consequentialist moral theories. If abortion is inherently wrong, as many believe, then it cannot be justified as a means of avoiding undesirable consequences. Thus, we must also consider whether women have a moral right to seek abortion.

iii Abortion and women's rights

Not all moral philosophers believe that there are such things as moral rights. Thus, it is important to say a bit here about what moral rights are; in section (viii) I will say more about why they are important. (See also Article 22, RIGHTS.) Rights are not mysterious entities that we discover in nature; they are not, in fact, entities at all. To say that people have a right to life is to say, roughly, that they should never deliberately be killed or deprived of the necessities of life, unless the only alternative is some much greater evil. Rights are not absolute, but neither are they to be overridden for just any apparently greater good. For instance, one may kill in self-defence when there is no other way to protect oneself from death or serious harm unjustly inflicted; but one may not kill another person merely because others may gain a great deal from the victim's death.

Basic moral rights are those which all persons have, in contrast to those rights which depend upon particular circumstances, e.g. promises or legal contracts. The basic moral rights of persons are usually held to include the rights to life, liberty, self-determination, and freedom from the infliction of bodily harm. The prohibition of abortion appears to infringe upon all of these basic rights. Women's lives are endangered in at least two ways. Where abortion is illegal, women often seek unsafe illegal abortions; the World Health Organization estimates that over 200,000 women die from this cause each year. Many others die from involuntary childbirth, when abortion is unavailable, or when they are pressured not to use it. Of course, voluntary childbirth also involves some risk of death; but in the absence of coercion, there is no violation of the woman's right to life.

The denial of abortion also infringes upon women's rights to liberty, self-determination, and physical integrity. To be forced to bear a child is not just an 'inconvenience', as opponents of abortion often claim. To carry a pregnancy to term is an arduous and risky undertaking, even when voluntary. To be sure, many women enjoy (much of) their pregnancies; but for those who remain pregnant against their will the experience is apt to be thoroughly miserable. And involuntary pregnancy and childbirth are only the beginning of the hardships caused by the denial of abortion. The woman must either keep the child or surrender it for adoption. To keep the child may make it impossible to continue her chosen life work, or to meet her other family obligations. To surrender the child means that she must live with the unhappy knowledge that she has a daughter or son for whom she cannot care, often cannot even know to be alive and well. Studies of women who have surrendered infants for adoption show that, for most, the separation from their child is a great and lasting grief.

Even if we accept the view that fetuses have a right to life, it is difficult to justify the imposition of such hardships upon unwilling individuals for the sake of fetal lives. As Judith Thomson pointed out in her much-discussed 1971 article, 'A defense of abortion', there is no other case in which the law requires individuals (who have been convicted of no crime) to sacrifice liberty, self-determination, and bodily integrity in order to preserve the lives of others. Perhaps one analogy to involuntary childbirth is military conscription. However, that comparison can lend only moderate support to the anti-abortion position, since the justifiability of compulsory military service is itself debatable.

In popular rhetoric, especially in the United States, the abortion issue is often seen as purely and simply one of 'women's right to control their bodies'. If women have the moral right to abort unwanted pregnancies, then the law should not prohibit abortion. But the arguments for this right do not entirely solve the moral issue of abortion. For it is one thing to have a right, and another to be morally justified in exercising that right in a particular case. If fetuses have a full and equal right to life, then perhaps women's right to abort should be exercised only in extreme circumstances. And perhaps we should question further whether fertile human beings – of either sex – are entitled to engage in heterosexual intercourse when they are not willing to have a child and assume the responsibility for it. If popular heterosexual activities are costing the lives of millions of innocent 'persons' (i.e. aborted fetuses), then should we not at least try to give up these activities? On the other hand, if fetuses do not yet have a substantial right to life, then abortion is not nearly so difficult to justify.

iv Questions about the moral status of fetuses

When in the development of a human individual does she or he begin to have a full and equal right to life? Most contemporary legal systems treat birth as the point at which a new legal person comes into existence. Thus, infanticide is generally classified as a form of homicide, whereas abortion – even where pro-hibited – generally is not. But, at first glance, birth seems to be an entirely arbitrary criterion of moral status. Why should human beings attain full and equal basic moral rights at birth, rather than at some earlier or later point?

Many theorists have sought to establish some universal criterion of moral status, by which to distinguish between those entities that have full moral rights and those that have no moral rights, or different and lesser rights. Even those who prefer not to speak of moral rights may feel the need for a universally applicable criterion of moral status. For instance, utilitarians need to know which entities have interests that must be considered in calculations of moral utility, while Kantian deontologists need to know which things are to be treated as ends in themselves, and not merely means to the ends of others. Many criteria of moral status have been proposed. The most common include life, sentience (the capacity to have experiences, including that of pain), genetic humanity (biological identification as belonging to the species *Homo sapiens*), and personhood (which will be defined later).

How are we to choose among these conflicting criteria of moral status? Two things are clear. First, we may not treat the selection of a criterion of moral status as a mere matter of personal preference. Racists, for instance, are not entitled to recognize the moral rights only of members of their own racial group, since they have never been able to prove that members of 'inferior' races lack any property that can reasonably be held to be relevant to moral status. Second, a theory of moral status must provide a plausible account of the moral status not only of human beings, but also of non-human animals, plants, computers, possible extra-terrestrial life forms, and anything else that might come along. I will argue that life, sentience and personhood are all relevant to moral status, though not in the same ways. Let us consider these criteria in turn, beginning with the most basic, i.e. biological life.

v The ethic of 'reverence for life'

Albert Schweitzer argued for an ethic of reverence for all living things. He held that all organisms, from microbes to human beings, have a 'will to live'. Thus, he says, anyone who has 'an unblunted moral sensibility will find it natural to share concern with the fate of all living creatures'. Schweitzer may have been wrong to claim that all living things have a *will* to live. Will is most naturally construed as a faculty which requires at least some capacity for thought, and is thus unlikely to be found in simple organisms that lack central nervous systems. Perhaps the claim that all living things share a will to live is a metaphorical statement of the fact that organisms are teleologically organized, such that they generally function in ways that promote their own survival or that of their species. But why should this fact lead us to feel a reverence for all life?

I suggest that the ethic of reverence for life draws strength from ecological and aesthetic concerns. The destruction of living things often damages what Aldo Leopold has called the 'integrity, stability and beauty of the biotic community'. Protecting the biotic community from needless damage is a moral imperative, not just for the good of humanity, but because the unspoiled natural world is worth valuing for its own sake.

Reverence for life suggests that, other things being equal, it is always better to avoid killing a living thing. But Schweitzer was aware that not all killing can be avoided. His view was that one should never kill without good reason, and certainly not for sport or amusement. Thus, it does not follow from an ethic of reverence for all life that abortion is morally wrong. Human fetuses are living things, as are unfertilized ova and spermatazoa. However, many abortions may be defended as killing 'under the compulsion of necessity'.

vi   Genetic humanity

Opponents of abortion will reply that abortion is wrong, not simply because human fetuses are *alive*, but because they are *human*. But why should we believe that the destruction of a living human organism is always morally worse than the destruction of an organism of some other species? Membership in a particular biological species does not appear to be, in itself, any more relevant to moral status than membership in a particular race or sex.

It is an accident of evolution and history that everyone whom we currently recognize as having full and equal basic moral rights belongs to a single biological species. The 'people' of the earth might just as well have belonged to many different species – and indeed perhaps they do. It is quite possible that some non-human animals, such as dolphins and whales and the great apes, have enough so-called 'human' capacities to be properly regarded as persons – i.e. beings capable of reason, self-awareness, social involvement, and moral reciprocity. Some contemporary philosophers have argued that (some) non-human animals have essentially the same basic moral rights as human persons. Whether or not they are right, it is certainly true that any superior moral status accorded to members of our own species must be justified in terms of morally significant differences between humans and other living things. To hold that species alone provides a basis for superior moral status is arbitrary and unhelpful.

vii   The sentience criterion

Some philosophers hold that sentience is the primary criterion of moral status. Sentience is the capacity to have experiences – for instance, visual, auditory, olfactory, or other perceptual experiences. However, the capacity to have pleasurable and painful experiences seems particularly relevant to moral status. It is a plausible postulate of utilitarian ethics that pleasure is an intrinsic good and pain an intrinsic evil. True, the capacity to feel pain is often valuable to an organism, enabling it to avoid harm or destruction. Conversely, some pleasures can be harmful to the organism's long-term well-being. Nevertheless, sentient beings may be said to have a basic interest in pleasure and the avoidance of pain. Respect for this basic interest is central to utilitarian ethics.

The sentience criterion suggests that, other things being equal, it is morally worse to kill a sentient than a non-sentient organism. The death of a sentient being, even when painless, deprives it of whatever pleasurable experiences it might have enjoyed in the future. Thus, death is apt to be a misfortune for that being, in a way that the death of a non-sentient organism is not.

But how can we know which living organisms are sentient? For that matter, how can we know that non-living things, such as rocks and rivers, are not sentient? If knowledge requires the absolute impossibility of error, then we probably cannot know this. But what we do know strongly suggests that sentience requires a functioning central nervous system – which is absent in rocks, plants, and simple micro-organisms. It is also absent in the early human fetus. Many neurophysiologists believe that normal human fetuses begin to have some rudimentary capacity for sentience at some stage in the second trimester of pregnancy. Prior to that stage, their brains and sensory organs are too undeveloped to permit the occurrence of sensations. The behavioural evidence points in the same direction. By the end of the first trimester, a fetus may have some unconscious reflexes, but it does not yet respond to its environment in a way suggestive of sentience. By the third trimester, however, some parts of the fetal brain are functional, and the fetus may respond to noise, light, pressure, motion and other sensory stimuli.

The sentience criterion lends support to the common belief that late abortion is more difficult to justify than early abortion. Unlike the presentient fetus, a third-trimester fetus is already a *being* – already, that is, a centre of experience. If killed, it may experience pain. Moreover, its death (like that of any sentient being) will mean the termination of a stream of experiences, some of which may have been pleasurable. Indeed, the use of this criterion suggests that early abortion poses no very serious moral issue, at least with respect to the impact upon the fetus. As a living but non-sentient organism, the first-trimester fetus is not yet a being with an interest in continued life. Like the unfertilized ovum, it may have the potential to *become* a sentient being. But this means only that it has the potential to become a being with an interest in continued life, not that it already has such an interest.

While the sentience criterion implies that late abortion is more difficult to justify than early abortion, it does not imply that late abortion is as difficult to justify as homicide. The principle of respect for the interests of sentient beings does not imply that all sentient beings have an *equal* right to life. To see why this is so, we need to give further thought to the scope of that principle.

Most normal mature vertebrate animals (mammals, birds, reptiles, amphibians and fish) are obviously sentient. It is also quite likely that many invertebrate animals, such as arthropods (e.g. insects, spiders, and crabs), are sentient. For they too have sense organs and nervous systems, and often behave as if they could see, hear, and feel quite well. If sentience is the criterion of moral status then not even a fly should be killed without some good reason.

But what counts as a good enough reason for the destruction of a living thing whose primary claim to moral status is its probable sentience? Utilitarians generally hold that acts are morally wrong if they increase the total amount of pain or suffering in the world (without some compensatory increase in the total amount of pleasure or happiness), or vice versa. But the killing of a sentient being does not always have such adverse consequences. There is room in any environment for only a finite number of organisms of any given species. When a rabbit is killed (in some more or less painless fashion), another rabbit is likely to take its place, so that the total amount of rabbit-happiness is not decreased. Moreover, rabbits, like many other rapidly reproducing species, must be preyed upon by some other species if the health of the larger biological system is to be maintained.

Thus, the killing of sentient beings is not always an evil in utilitarian terms. However, it would be morally offensive to suggest that people can be killed just because they are too numerous, and are upsetting the natural ecology. If killing people is harder to justify than killing rabbits – as even most animal liberationists believe – it must be because people have some moral status that is not based upon sentience alone. In the next section, we consider some possible arguments for this view.

viii   Personhood and moral rights

Once they are past infancy, human beings typically possess not only a capacity for sentience, but also such 'higher' mental capacities as self-awareness and rationality. They are also highly social beings, capable – except in pathological cases – of love, nurturance, co-operation, and moral responsibility (which involves the capacity to guide their actions through moral principles and ideals). Perhaps these mental and social capacities can provide sound reasons for ascribing a stronger right to life to persons than to other sentient beings.

One argument for that conclusion is that the distinctive capacities persons have enable them to value their own lives and those of other members of their communities more than other animals do. People are the only beings who can plan years into the future, and who are often haunted by the fear of premature death. Perhaps this means that the lives of persons are worth more to their possessors than those of sentient non-persons. If so, then killing a person is a greater moral wrong than killing a sentient being which is not a person. But it is also possible that the absence of fear for the future tends to make the lives of sentient non-persons more pleasant, and more valuable to them, than ours are to us. Thus, we need to look elsewhere for a rationale for the superior moral status that most (human) persons accord to one another.

Moral rights are a way of talking about how we should behave. That it is evidently only persons who understand the idea of a moral right does not make us 'better' than other sentient beings. However, it does give us compelling reasons for treating one another as moral equals, with basic rights that cannot be over-ridden for narrowly utilitarian reasons. If we could never trust other persons not to kill us whenever they judged that some net good might result, social relationships would become immeasurably more difficult, and the lives of all but the most powerful persons would be greatly impoverished.

A morally sensitive person will respect all life-forms, and will be careful to avoid needlessly inflicting pain or death upon sentient beings. However, she will respect the basic moral rights of other persons *as equal to her own*, not just because they are alive and sentient, but also because she can reasonably hope and demand that they will show her the same respect. Mice and mosquitoes are not capable of this kind of moral reciprocity – as least not in their interactions with human beings. When their interests come into conflict with ours, we cannot hope to use moral argument to persuade them to accept some reasonable compromise. Thus, it is often impossible to accord them fully equal moral status. Even the Jain religion of India, which regards the killing of any being as an obstacle to spiritual enlightenment, does not require the total avoidance of such killing, except in the case of those who have taken special religious vows. (For further information see Article 9, INDIAN ETHICS.)

If the capacity for moral reciprocity is essential to personhood, and if personhood is the criterion for moral equality, then human fetuses do not satisfy that criterion. Sentient fetuses are closer to being persons than are fertilized ova or early fetuses, and may gain some moral status on that account. However, they are not yet reasoning, self-aware beings, capable of love, nurturance, and moral reciprocity. These facts lend support to the view that even late abortion is not quite the equivalent of homicide. On this basis, we may resonably conclude that the abortion of sentient fetuses can sometimes be justified for reasons that could not justify the killing of a person. For instance, late abortion may sometimes be justified because the fetus has been found to be severely abnormal, or because the continuation of the pregnancy threatens the woman's health, or creates other personal hardships.

Unfortunately, the discussion cannot end at this point. Personhood is important as an *inclusion* criterion for moral equality: any theory which denies equal moral status to certain persons must be rejected. But personhood seems somewhat less plausible as an *exclusion* criterion, since it appears to exclude infants and mentally handicapped individuals who may lack the mental and social capacities typical of persons. Furthermore – as opponents of abortion point out – history proves that it is all too easy for dominant groups to rationalize oppression by claiming, in effect, that the oppressed persons are not really persons at all, because of some alleged mental or moral deficiency.

In view of these points it may seem wise to adopt the theory that all *sentient* human beings have full and equal basic moral rights. (To avoid 'speciesism', we could grant the same moral status to sentient members of any other species whose normal, mature members we believe to be persons.) On this theory, so long as an individual is both human and capable of sentience, his or her moral equality cannot be questioned. But there is an objection to the extension of equal moral status even to *sentient* fetuses: it is impossible in practice to grant equal moral rights to fetuses without denying those same rights to women.

ix Why birth matters morally

There are many instances in which the moral rights of different human individuals come into apparent conflict. Such conflicts cannot, as a rule, be solved justly by denying equal moral status to one of the parties. But pregnancy is a special case. Because of the unique biological relationship between the woman and the fetus, the extension of equal moral and legal status to fetuses has ominous consequences for women's basic rights.

One consequence is that abortion 'on request' would not be permitted. If sentience is the criterion, then abortion might be permitted only in the first trimester. Some argue that this is a reasonable compromise, since it would allow most women time enough to discover that they are pregnant, and decide whether or not to abort. But problems involving fetal abnormality, the woman's health, or her personal or economic situation, sometimes arise or become severe only at a later stage. If fetuses are presumed to have the same moral rights as already-born human beings, then women will often be compelled to remain pregnant at great risk to their own lives, health, or personal well-being. They may also be compelled to submit, against their will, to dangerous and invasive medical procedures such as Caesarean section, when others judge that this would be beneficial to the fetus. (A number of such cases have already occurred in the United States.) Thus, the extension of full and equal basic moral rights to fetuses endangers the basic rights of women.

But, given these apparent conflicts between fetal rights and women's rights, one may still wonder why it is women's rights that should prevail. Why not favour fetuses instead, e.g. because they are more helpless, or have a longer life expectancy? Or why not seek a compromise between fetal and maternal rights, with equal concessions on each side? If fetuses were already persons, in the sense I have described, then it would be arbitrary to favour the rights of woman over theirs. But it is difficult to argue that either fetuses or newborn infants are persons in this sense, since the capacities for reason, self-awareness, and social and moral reciprocity seem to develop only after birth.

Why, then, should we treat birth, rather than some later point, as the threshold of moral equality? A major reason is that birth makes it possible for the infant to be granted equal basic rights without violating anyone else's basic rights. It is possible in many countries to find good homes for most infants whose biological parents are unable or unwilling to raise them. Since most of us strongly desire to protect infants, and since we can now do so without imposing excessive hardships upon women and families, there is no evident reason why we should not. But fetuses are different: their equality would mean women's inequality. Other things being equal, it is worse to deny the basic moral rights to beings that are clearly not yet full persons. Since women are persons and fetuses are not, we should come down on the side of respecting women's rights in cases of apparent conflict.

x Potential personhood

Some philosophers argue that, although fetuses may not be persons, their potential to *become* persons gives them the same basic moral rights. This argument is implausible, since in no other case do we treat the potential to achieve some status entailing certain rights as itself entailing those same rights. For instance, every child born in the United States is a potential voter, but no-one under the age of 18 has the right to vote in that country. Besides, the argument from potential proves too much. If a fetus is a potential person, then so is an unfertilized human ovum, together with enough viable spermatazoa to achieve fertilization; yet few would seriously suggest that *these* living human entities should have full and equal moral status.

Yet the argument from fetal potential refuses to go away. Perhaps this is because the potential which fetuses have is often a sound reason for valuing and protecting them. Once a pregnant woman has committed herself to the continued nurturance of the fetus, she and those close to her are likely to think of it as an 'unborn baby', and to value it for its potential. The fetus's potential lies not just in its DNA, but in that maternal (and paternal) commitment. Once the woman has committed herself to the pregnancy, it is appropriate for her to value the fetus and protect its potential – as most women do, without any legal coercion. But it is wrong to demand that a woman complete a pregnancy when she is unable or unwilling to undertake that enormous commitment.

xi Summary and conclusion

Abortion is often approached as if it were *only* an issue of fetal rights; and often as if it were *only* an issue of women's rights. The denial of safe and legal abortion infringes upon women's rights to life, liberty, and physical integrity. Yet if the fetus had the same right to life as a person, abortion would still be a tragic event, and difficult to justify except in the most extreme cases. Thus, even those who argue for women's rights must be concerned with the moral status of fetuses.

Even an ethic of reverence for all life does not, however, preclude all intentional killing. All killing requires justification, and it is somewhat more difficult to justify the deliberate destruction of a sentient being than of a living thing which is not (yet) a centre of experience; but sentient beings do not all have equal rights. The extension of equal moral status to fetuses threatens women's most basic rights. Unlike fetuses, women are already persons. They should not be treated as something less when they happen to be pregnant. That is why abortion should not be prohibited, and why birth, rather than some earlier point, marks the beginning of full moral status.

References

Jaini, P.: *The Jaina Path of Purification* (Berkeley: University of California Press, 1979).
Leopold, A.: *A Sand County Almanac* (New York: Ballantine Books, 1970).
Schweitzer, A.: *The Teaching of Reverence for Life*, trans. R. and C. Winston (New York: Holt, Rinehart and Winston, 1965).
Thomson, J. J.: 'A defense of abortion', *Philosophy and Public Affairs* 1:1 (Fall 1971), 47–66.

Further reading

Feinberg, J., ed.: *The Problem of Abortion* (Belmont, Cal.: Wadsworth Publishing Company, 1984).
Goldstein, R. D.: *Mother-Love and Abortion: A Legal Interpretation* (Berkeley: University of California Press, 1988).
Harrison, B. W.: *Our Right to Choose: Toward a New Ethic of Abortion* (Boston: Beacon Press, 1983).

Mohr, J.C.: *Abortion in America: The Origins and Evolution of National Policy, 1800–1900* (Oxford: Oxford University Press, 1978).

Regan, T.: *The Case for Animal Rights* (Berkeley: University of California Press, 1983).

Singer, P.: *Animal Liberation: A New Ethics for Our Treatment of Animals* (New York: Avon Books, 1975).

Sumner, L.W.: *Abortion and Moral Theory* (Princeton, NJ: Princeton University Press, 1981).

Tooley, M.: *Abortion and Infanticide* (Oxford: Oxford University Press, 1983).

27

Sex

RAYMOND A. BELLIOTTI

i Introduction

QUESTIONS about the proper role of sex in the pursuit of the good life were central in classical philosophy. But there came a time when sexual questions, although still contested hotly by poets and libertines, assumed diminished significance among philosophers. With the surge of contemporary interest in applied ethics, however, discussion of sex is once again perceived as a legitimate and important philosophical topic. We can only speculate whether the libidos of philosophers are (happily) becoming more active or whether philosophers are merely confronting and responding to more open societal attitudes about sex.

This essay addresses some of the major sexual issues about which philosophers puzzle: are gender and reproductive roles natural or are they socially constructed? Must morally permissible sex have only one function? Must it be heterosexual? Must it occur within the confines of the institution of marriage? Which kinds of sexual activity are morally permissible under what sort of circumstances?

Two cautions: the phrase 'morally permissible' means 'not morally prohibited'. Thus, to label an act morally permissible does not necessarily imply that the act is 'laudatory' or 'morally required' or the 'best available action' or 'in one's best long-term interests'. Furthermore, the essay addresses the moral permissibility of various kinds of sex from the standpoint of the actions themselves, not from the standpoint of the widest conceivable consequences they produce. Thus, the essay ignores extraordinary cases where the sexual acts seem of themselves morally permissible but because of accompanying circumstances they produce extremely harmful consequences for third parties.

ii Traditional Western morality

1 Dualism in ancient Greece

More than five centuries before the birth of Christ, the Pythagoreans taught a sharp dualism between mortal human bodies and immortal human souls. Animated by a belief in the unity of all life, they taught that individual souls were fragments of the divine, universal soul. Pythagoreans contended that the proper quest of persons on earth should be spiritual purity which prepared human souls for their return to the universal soul. They argued that purification was gained through silence, contemplation, and abstention from animal flesh. Until individual souls

315

return to the universal soul, Phythagoreans claimed that souls are imprisoned in bodies and endure transmigration: death dissolves the union of an individual soul with a particular body, and that soul transmigrates into a new body of a human or animal.

The Pythagoreans had significant influence on Plato's doctrines of the immortality of the soul, the existence of Universals in a world of higher Truth and Reason, and philosophy as preparation for human assimilation with the divine. Later, Stoics posited the ideal of inner tranquillity based on self-discipline and freedom from passion, an ideal accomplished in part by withdrawing from the material world and its physical preoccupations in deference to ascetic, spiritual concerns; while Epicureans aspired to a peace of mind forged in part by suppressing raging physical desires.

Thus the seeds of dualism were firmly in place well before the birth of Christ, and one strain of Western sexuality emerged: an asceticism that counsels detachment and freedom from sexual passion, or at least advises the subordination of sexual desire to reason; that regards the body as a prison of the immortal human soul; and is often accompanied by the view that our world is an ersatz version of Truth and Reality.

2 Judeo-Christian thought

The predominant view of the Old Testament emphasized the joy of sex, counselled fecundity, and assumed that marriage and parenthood were natural. Motivated in part by a concern for reproduction of family lines, the patriarchs and kings of Israel practised polygamy; newly married males were excused from military service for one year in order that couples might enjoy wedded sexual bliss; and levirate marriages, in which the childless widow of a man could be impregnated by his brother and the resulting child regarded as the offspring of the deceased, were permitted. In contrast to Greek dualism and asceticism, the Old Testaments's attitudes toward sex and the material world were overwhelmingly positive.

In the few recorded gospel verses in which Jesus addressed sex he condemned adultery and divorce. But he nowhere stigmatizes erotic impulses as inherently evil. Preaching a law of love and assessing people on the basis of their inner motives and intentions, Jesus castigates sex and the material world as obstacles to eternal salvation only when they assume the role of idols.

It was St Paul who first presented the Christian ideal of celibacy ('It is well for a man not to touch a woman ... I wish that all men were as I myself am' 1 Cor. 7) while advising against long periods of sexual abstinence within marriage for those whose passions precluded celibacy ('If they cannot restrain themselves, let them marry. Better marry than be aflame with passion!'). He cautioned that sex, along with all other things merely of this world, must be subordinate to earning eternal salvation ('The unmarried man is anxious about the affairs of the Lord ... but the married man is anxious about wordly affairs.'). Although St Paul posited an ideal which contrasts with the counsel of the Old Testament, and though he was affected by Greek dualist tendencies, he fell short of suggesting that sex is inherently evil.

As the Church sought converts among the Gentiles, its Jewish heritage tended to diminish while Greek influences increased. With the rise of the Gnostics, virginity became an important virtue and marriage an allowance for the spiritually weak. After renouncing his colourful past, St Augustine in his *Of Holy Virginity* and *On Marriage and Concupiscence* became the chief systematizer and refiner of a tradition that exhorted humans to abrogate bodily pleasures for the higher ideal of contemplation.

According to this line of thought, sex before the fall of Adam and Eve was uncontaminated by raging passion and was controlled and restrained by the mind. With original sin came burning sexual desire and much loss of control over the body. Accordingly, all sexual desire was thought to be tainted with evil because of its source. Moreover, original sin itself was thought to be transmitted generationally through sexual intercourse. Thus, the requirement of the virgin birth: Jesus could be free from original sin only if he was not begotten through the sexual act. Celibacy was reaffirmed as the highest ideal, and sex within marriage was regarded as an evil necessary for the continuation of the species: morally permissible only if it was motivated by a desire for children, realized by an act which did not by its nature preclude procreation, and engaged in moderately and decorously. Centuries later, St Thomas Aquinas in his *Summa Theologiae* echoed Augustine's account of sex, but ameliorated to some degree Augustine's distrust of bodily pleasure and joy within marriage.

While agreeing with most of the Augustinian-Thomist position on sex, Luther rejected celibacy as an ideal. In his *Letter to the Knights of the Teutonic Order*, Luther observed that few are liberated from erotic impulses, and that God has initiated and demands marriage as a duty for all but a few. Calvin echoed this theme and reaffirmed that sexual activity within marriage must be restrained and decorous. Procreation remained for the Protestant reformers the main positive function of sex.

The Roman Catholic position on sex has been reaffirmed numerous times in papal encyclicals by Pope Leo XIII (1880), Pope Pius XI (1930), Pope Paul VI (1968), and the Vatican's *Declaration on Certain Questions Concerning Sexual Ethics* (1975): sex is morally permissible only if it occurs within the institution of marriage and the act is not deliberately rendered incompatible with human reproduction. Under this view, all sexual activities that occur outside the institution of marriage (e.g. adultery, promiscuity) and all sexual expressions that are deliberately incompatible with human reproduction (e.g. masturbation, homosexuality, oral and anal sex, and even the use of a contraceptive device) are stigmatized as 'unnatural' and thus immoral.

Various modifications can be made on this position. For example, one might hold that sex is morally permissible if it occurs within the institution of marriage, even when of a kind incompatible with reproduction. Thus oral and anal sex may be accepted because pleasure within marriage may be acknowledged as a legitimate goal of sex.

3 Critique of the Christian position

These positions are usually criticized for their underlying presuppositions: an ahistorical conception of human nature; an unchanging and limited perception of the proper place of sex within that nature; a specialized view of the one acceptable form of family; and a narrow perception of the function of human sexual activity. Rather than deriving moral theory from an objective analysis of human nature, those who make claims about what is 'natural' for humans often seem to choose those elements of our nature which correspond to their own preconceptions about how we ought to behave. Why is sex within marriage for the purpose of procreation more in accordance with human nature than sex outside marriage for the purpose of pleasure? (Article 13, NATURAL LAW, shows the fallacy of attempting to use the notion of 'natural law' in this way.)

4 Love and intimacy

One way of developing some of the basic classical positions is to contend that sex is morally permissible only if it occurs within the experience of love and intimacy. Variations of this position are held by Vincent Punzo in his *Reflective Naturalism* and Roger Scruton in his *Sexual Desire*. This position, at least in Punzo's version, removes the restriction of ceremonial marriage but replaces it with a deeper view of the necessity of mutual trust, acceptance, and reciprocal sharing of innermost thoughts. Love and intimacy, although usually a part of successful marriages, are not logically necessary for or confined to marriages.

Such a position is supported by two main allegations: a view of human nature that suggests that sex is a paramount human activity reflective of those aspects of personality closest to our being; and a claim that sex without love debases and ultimately fragments human personality. This approach is animated by the impulse to evade the alleged dehumanizing effects of mechanical, merely promiscuous sex and, instead, to exalt sex as the most intimate physical expression of the human self – an act worthy of special concern because of its unique effects on our existential integrity.

Various modifications occur within this approach. Some proponents would contend that the requisite love and intimacy must be exclusive. Thus, morally permissible sex may occur with only one other person; but even here successive sexual interactions which involve love would be morally permissible. Other proponents argue that sex may be non-exclusive because a person is capable of simultaneously loving more than one other person. Hence, simultaneous love liaisons could be morally permissible.

5 Critique of love and intimacy

Critics charge that the love–intimacy approach overrates and universalizes the importance of sexual activity for existential integrity and psychological flourishing. First, it is clear that many people have not confined themselves to sex only with love, yet such people do not necessarily exhibit the effects of dehumanization and psychological disintegration so feared by proponents of this approach. Second, even where sex without love does lead to existential fragmentation it does not follow that the sexual interactions were *morally* impermissible. Unless we are morally required always to perform only those actions which facilitate existential integrity the most that can follow is that sex without love in such cases is strategically unsound or imprudent. The realm of the 'moral' is not co-extensive with the realm of that which is in my 'best interests'. That is, one is not morally *required* to do all and only actions that facilitate one's best interests. Finally, although love and intimacy are important aspects of human personality it is not clear that they are always primary. We engage in many worthwhile activities that are unaccompanied by love and intimacy. Why must sex be different? If it is claimed that sex is different because it is necessarily and deeply connected to human personality, further questions remain: is that connection an ahistorical fact? Cannot pleasure, without love and intimacy, serve as a legitimate goal of sex for many people? Is the importance of sex for existential integrity a biological fact or merely a social construct of certain sub-groups within society?

Dissatisfaction with traditional Western sexual morality has led to several different approaches. The idea of contract has often provided an alternative to traditional moralities, not only in regard to political obligation and justice, but also in regard to sexual morality.

iii Contractarian approaches

Contractarian approaches contend that sexual activity must be morally assessed by the same criteria as any other human activity. Hence they underscore the importance of mutual, voluntary informed consent and highlight the appropriateness of tolerating sexual diversity as a recognition of human freedom and autonomy. Some contractualists, such as Russell Vannoy in his *Sex Without Love*, are influenced by a strain of Western thought which depicts sex as a valuable gift to be exercised boldly and frequently (e.g. Rabelais, Boccaccio, Kazantzakis); while other contractarians subscribe to an ancient view that sex should be savoured in proper moderation (e.g. Homer, Aristotle, Montaigne).

1 *Libertarian view*

A libertarian position often gains much initial acceptance because it is invariably proposed in those cultures that regard the right of contract as necessary for the sanctity of human freedom. Applying libertarian philosophy to sexual relations results in the view that sex is morally permissible if and only if it is consummated with mutual and voluntary informed consent. Rather than focusing on a particular conception of the marriage institution or a specialized understanding of the 'proper' function of sex or a natural law perception of the necessary link between sex and human personality, this view highlights the importance of human autonomy as reflected in the agreements we choose to undertake. Proponents insist that the paramount values are individual freedom and autonomy. Thus it is tyranny to insist on a particular kind of sexual interaction or to prescribe a specific domain for acceptable sex. The test of morally permissible sex is simple: have the parties, possessing the basic capacities necessary for autonomous choice, voluntarily agreed to a particular sexual interaction without force, fraud, and explicit duress? Accordingly, sex is impermissible where one or both parties lack the capacities for informed consent (e.g. under-age, or significantly mentally impaired, or non-human); or where there is explicit duress (e.g. threats or extortion), force (e.g. coercion), or fraud (e.g. one party deceives the other as to the nature of the act or the extent of his or her feelings as a way of luring the other to 'accepting' the liaison).

2 Critique of libertarianism

The most glaring weakness of this position is that it ignores numerous moral distortions that occur in the realm of contract: parties to a contract may have radically unequal bargaining power, prominent differences in vulnerability, one of the parties may bargain under the oppression of destitute circumstances, or the contract may treat important attributes constitutive of human personality as if they were mere commodities subject to market bartering. Such distortions call into question whether a particular contract is truly morally permissible. The existence of a contract is not morally self-validating. That is, once we know that a contract, arrived at through 'voluntary consent', exists, there is still the further question: are the terms of that contract morally permissible? The libertarian position can succeed only if voluntary contractual interaction comprises the totality of morality. The following illustration is designed to call that assumption into question.

Rocco is a poor but honest barber's son whose family is in desperate need of the basic requirements of life. He tries a variety of ways to secure the money he needs but is unsuccessful. Finally, Rocco learns of the strange proclivities of his neighbour, Vito. Vito, a wealthy and sadistic chap, has a standing offer of $5,000 plus medical expenses to all who will allow him to chop off the middle finger of their right hand. In fact, Vito displays a handsome collection of various human digits mounted tastefully on the wall of his den. Rocco approaches Vito and asks him if the offer still stands. Vito brandishes $5,000 and exclaims, 'Let's make a deal!' After negotiating minor aspects such as the type of axe to be used, whether or not Rocco's hospital room should be private, and Rocco's share of the proceeds Vito will realize from the admission fees he charges those who view his den, the contract is finalized and its terms consummated. Rocco is $5,000 richer and one finger poorer!

Even though the contract imagined was voluntarily agreed to in the absence of force, fraud, or duress, many would insist that such a contract is immoral because Vito has exploited the dire circumstances, vulnerability, and outright desperation that characterized Rocco's situation. Moreover, both parties treated part of Rocco's body as if it were a mere commodity subject to market forces. It might be objected that the libertarian can avoid such a counter-example because Vito did *harm* Rocco: he cut off his finger. But this objection is not persuasive because a libertarian seems to be committed to allowing Rocco to judge whether the loss of a finger, combined with a gain of $5,000, amounts to a 'harm'. For libertarians, consent vitiates harm, and thus they cannot claim that Vito violated Rocco's negative right not to be harmed. While libertarians have identified important *aspects* of morality – notions of individual freedom and autonomy – they may be seen as having exaggerated them to the point where these aspects constitute the whole of morality.

3 Kantian modifications

It is possible to meet the above objection by modifying the libertarian view. One way of doing this is to incorporate the Kantian principle that 'it is morally wrong for persons to treat others merely as a means to their own ends'. (See Article 14, KANTIAN ETHICS, for discussion of this principle and its basis in Kant's ethics.) Such an approach is taken by Raymond Belliotti in 'A philosophical analysis of sexual ethics' (1979). Kant's maxim suggests that individuals are culpable if they objectify their victims: if they treat others as mere objects or tools to be manipulated and used for the users' own purposes. One of the worst acts that one person can inflict upon another is to recognize and treat the other as something less than the other really is: to recognize the other not as an end, not as an equal subject of experience. Arguably, treating important attributes constitutive of human personality as if they are mere commodities susceptible to market transactions is one example of exploitation in this broad sense. Here we acknowledge the important insight that eluded libertarians: contracts are not morally self-validating. Accordingly, such an approach maintains that sex is immoral if and only if it involves deception, promise-breaking, illicit force, or exploitation.

This approach concedes that the nature of sexual interactions is contractual and involves the notion of reciprocity. When two people voluntarily consent to a sexual liaison they create mutual obligations based on their respective need and expectations. We interact with others sexually in order to fulfil certain desires which we cannot fulfil by ourselves (e.g. reproductive urges, desire for pleasure, yearning for love and intimacy, and longing for validation by others, as well as less laudatory drives such as aggression, submission and domination). This position acknowledges explicitly that sexual activities are evaluated morally by the same rules and principles generally relevant for assessing human actions. There is no attempt here to conflate the domains of the 'moral' and 'prudent': to claim that an act is morally acceptable does not imply that it is advisable to pursue. That is, the morality of an action is not the only criterion we should use when deciding whether to pursue it. An act may be morally permissible but stragegically unsound and ill-advised because it is not in a person's best long-term interests, or because it is offensive to our tastes, or because it distracts us from more worthy endeavours.

4 Critique of the Kantian modification

Critics of this approach concentrate on a number of possible weaknesses: Does not this view reduce sex to the same cold, bottom-line calculation endemic to corporate transactions? Why is the realm of contract applicable to such an intimate area? Unlike business contracts, sexual 'contracts' are rarely spelled out or subject to protracted negotiations. How do we know when a contract is in place and what reasonable expectations can be formed? How can sex be morally permissible yet contrary to our best long-term interests and happiness? Is not the notion of 'exploitation' malleable and indeterminate? Are not the indeterminate slogans 'it is wrong to use another' and 'it is wrong to commodify constitutive attributes' worthless as guides to moral assessment?

iv Challenges from the political left

Marxist and feminist perspectives criticize other approaches on the basis of an analysis of the nature of personal relationships, and deny the possibilities of genuinely equal sexual relationships in the kind of society prevalent in the West.

1 Classical Marxism

In his *The Origin of the Family, Private Property, and the State*, Engels observed that in bourgeois families wives provided cheap domestic labour and socially necessary tasks (e.g. care of children and the elderly) and were expected to produce identifiable and legitimate heirs for the orderly transfer of capitalist property, while husbands provided lodging and board in return. This exchange presumably explained the need for conjugal fidelity on the part of women and provided, in predictable Marxist fashion, an economic basis for the existence of male prerogatives within the family. The bourgeois family was conceived on the unremitting foundation of capitalism: private gain. Because bourgeois women in a capitalist society were excluded from the public workplace, they were forced to tie themselves financially to men. The emotional and personal attachments seemingly at play in marital sex reduce in fact to a series of commercial interactions where purportedly reciprocal contractual benefits are exchanged. Accordingly, the rhetoric of commodities pervades even the inner, private sanctum of capitalist life.

Here Engels turns the Christian argument on its head: sex *within* the bourgeois family is a form of prostitution (in a pejorative sense) and is thus immoral, because its genesis is the economic exploitation of the deprived by the powerful and its result is the commodification of the attributes constitutive of women's innermost selves. The solution to the maladies of the bourgeois family is the socialization of housework, the full inclusion of women in the public arena, and, most important, the dismantling of the capitalist framework which nurtures class division and economic exploitation.

Classical Marxism protests that in a capitalist society the notion of 'informed consent' is contaminated by the underlying need for economic survival. Reports of 'mutual agreement' and 'reciprocal benefit' may be illusions emanating from the false consciousness of capitalist materialism. Sex is morally permissible only if the parties share a measure of equality, are not motivated by (conscious or subconscious) economic needs, and do not treat their constitutive attributes as mere commodities – all of which in turn require the elimination of capitalism.

2   Critique of Marxism

Criticisms of the classical Marxist account of sex focus on more general complaints about the persuasiveness of Marxism's explanations of false consciousness, its historical rendering of the origins of exploitation, its understanding of capitalist economics, and its portrayal of the relationships of the various social classes. The fuller presentation and analyses of these criticisms, however, must remain outside the scope of this essay. A detailed account of Marxism and ethics can be found in Article 45, MARX AGAINST MORALITY.

3   Feminist perspectives

Speaking from a socialist-feminist perspective in her *Feminist Politics and Human Nature*, Alison Jaggar insists that Marxism underscores the economic basis of women's oppression, but fails to highlight the true source of that oppression: the aggression and domination of men. She points out that the elimination of the capitalist economic system has not substantially transformed women in socialist nations; distinguishes the kind of exploitation suffered by capitalist workers from the oppression which suffocates wives; and thereby denies that gender inequality can be explained adequately by economic causes.

Theological and contractual accounts fare no better at the hands of feminists. Catharine MacKinnon, in her *Feminism Unmodified*, argues that the notions of 'natural law' and 'autonomous choice' which underlie those traditional accounts are fatally flawed. Radical feminists such as MacKinnon contend that socially constructed sexual roles make it extraordinarily difficult for women to identify and nurture their own sexual desires and needs. Women are socialized to meet male sexual wants and needs in order to prove their own value and fulfil their socially created duties. Male dominance and female submission are the accepted norms of sexual behaviour, and broadly define the respective roles of the sexes generally. The Christian reliance on natural law is misplaced because our sexual needs and desires are mainly a matter of social conditioning, while the con-tractarian faith in informed consent is a sham because that same social con-ditioning limits the range of women's real opportunities and choices and nurtures a false consciousness about women's place in the world and in relationship to men.

Feminists such as MacKinnon claim to unmask the political implications of sexual activity and conclude that women will always remain subordinate to men unless sexuality is re-imagined and remade. Because they connect perceptions of the proper kinds of sexual activity with wider views of the proper forms of politics, the most radical feminists (e.g. lesbian separatists) tend to be suspicious of the kinds of sexual activity commended in centrist regimes: married, heterosexual, monogamous, reproductive, private, in a well-defined relationship, and so forth. Many feminists suspect that such carefully defined sexual activity facilitates in a direct fashion the general political subjugation of women. In her *Lesbian Nation*, Jill Johnston champions the separatist position and endorses sex among women only as a way of making a political statement and transcending male oppression.

Under this view, women must undermine the domination and power of men in all relevant contests, one of the most important of which is sexual activity.

What, then, do feminists view as morally permissible sex? Although there is much internal disagreement, a few things do seem clear. Sex is morally permissible only if the traditional roles of male dominance and female submission are absent, women are not politically victimized by their sexuality, and women have the power and capacity to control access to and define themselves. What events can ensure that such conditions pertain? Here intramural disagreements intensify. The range of answers includes: the total separation of women from men, including a female boycott of heterosexual relations; the decommodification of the female body; a biological revolution (e.g. artificial reproduction) to liberate women from the fundamentally unequal tasks of child-bearing and rearing; economic independence of women from men; pay for those women who provide domestic and socially necessary services which is comparable to the wages earned by men in the public sphere; obliteration of the distinction between 'men's work' and 'women's work'; and full access for women into the public spheres, particularly those prestigious positions which define political and social power.

4 Critique of feminism

Criticisms of feminism are often highly specific. For example, lesbian separatists would contend that only total separation from men can allow women to exercise power and control over their bodies. Less radical feminists and non-feminists, on the other hand, insist that such a posture is unnecessary and also limits women's choices and denies even the theoretical possibility of engaging in non-exploitative, consensual heterosexual activity. It portrays men as incapable by nature of anything other than oppression and exploitation. The separatist view seems flawed because while it begins in a general disparagement of the idea of an ahistorical human nature, it ends in reliance upon just such a notion.

More general criticisms of feminism focus on its conception of 'free consent' and its invocation of 'false consciousness'. Taken literally, some feminists suggest that virtually all women are incapable of informed consent because they have been victimized by extended conditioning by male-dominated society. This concession, however, seems too broad and could be used as a justification for paternalism: if women are truly incapable of informed consent then why should they not be subject to the same paternalistic treatment that is afforded other groups, such as children, who lack that capacity? Moreover, if a woman does report satisfaction and fulfilment from her heterosexual relations, should her report automatically be stigmatized as arising from false consciousness just because it differs from the fundamental doctrine of certain feminists?

Furthermore, why should we assume that sexuality is so essential to personhood or womanhood? One of the assumptions feminists have made is that sexual activity implicates a woman's innermost being and most important constitutive attributes. But is *that* fact a biological necessity or merely a social artefact of male-dominated society? In what principled way can we distinguish the constitutive attributes implicated in ordinary wage-labour from those animated in sexual activity? If we cannot, then perhaps Marxists are correct in thinking that both wage-labour and sex must be decommodified; or perhaps certain contractualists are correct in thinking that both wage-labour and sex may be commodified under certain circumstances. Finally, political liberals would argue that the public sphere is increasingly open to women, public consciousness has been raised concerning the equitable allocation of domestic work and child-rearing, day care centers abound, early education and socialization is much more compatible with sexual equality, and women enjoy more opportunities for social and political power. For a liberal this shows that heterosexual activity is not necessarily accompanied by exploitation, commodification, and lack of informed consent.

v Epilogue

Perhaps the most persuasive position on sexual morality is one based on the libertarian model as modified by the Kantian maxim, but which pays special heed when defining 'exploitation' to classical Marxism's sensitivity to economic coercion and feminism's concern with the vestiges of male oppression.

This approach can reply to some of the criticisms raised earlier. The contractual basis of sexual interaction stems from voluntary agreement founded on the expectations of fulfilment of reciprocal needs and desires. While important feelings of intimacy, which distinguish sex from normal business transactions, are often at stake, and these feelings invoke special emotional vulnerabilities, that does not prove sex is not contractual; rather, it shows that sexual contracts are often the most important agreements we undertake. Moreover, while it is true that sexual encounters are usually not as explicit as business pacts, the notion of reasonable expectation based on specific context should guide us. This guide could be supplemented by a principle of caution: when in doubt do not overestimate what the other party has offered and seek a more explicit overture if appropriate.

Furthermore, under this position the concepts of 'morality' and 'happiness' are not co-extensive. We would assume that if we performed only actions that are morally permissible then a measure of happiness would ensure, but that cannot be guaranteed. Achieving happiness is, among other things, hostage to a variety of physical and material items (e.g. health and fulfilment of certain biological needs) that moral action does not of itself provide.

But there is much that remains contestable and controversial. First, it must be admitted that 'exploitation' is not a self-executing concept. The content of expressions such as 'use another as a mere means', 'commodify illegitimately constitutive attributes of self', and 'objectify another' must be supplied by a more general social and political theory. Critics are correct in thinking that Kantians use such phrases too often as talismanic incantations whose magical meanings are intuitively obvious to all. Certainly, the position advocated here considers the following cases illustrative of exploitation: taking advantage of another's limited alternatives, desperate situation, or dire needs; manipulating another into consent through use of an inequality of power; and undermining the voluntary or informed consent of another through deception or various forms of physical or economic coercion. But even these explanations of 'exploitation' are in need of further specification. If they go too far when explicating these notions, proponents of this approach will find themselves in the uncomfortable Marxist position of ruling most ordinary wage-labour contracts illegitimate because employees often have limited alternatives and they work in part to fulfil basic needs, whereas employers often enjoy an advantage in bargaining power.

Moreover, when arguing that one party has taken advantage of another, advocates of this approach must make fine distinctions between 'justified persuasion', 'unjustified manipulation', and 'implicit economic coercion'. Arguably, any two parties will always be unequal in rhetorical skill, argumentative technique, and personal charisma. Are these attributes the source of inherent domination and ideological distortion, or merely the legitimate instruments of rational persuasion? In this way questions about sexual morality lead to more general issues about social relationships.

References

Aquinas, Thomas: *On the Truth of the Catholic Faith*, trans. V. J. Bourke (New York: Doubleday, 1956), Book 3, *Providence*, Part 2.

Augustine: *Of Holy Virginity* and *On Marriage and Concupiscence*. In *Fathers of the Church*, ed. R. Deferrari et al. (New York: 1948–).

Belliotti, R. A.: 'A philosophical analysis of sexual ethics', *Journal of Social Philosophy*, 10 (1979), 8–11.

Engels, F.: *The Origin of the Family, Private Property, and the State* (New York: International Publishers, 1972).

Johnston, J.: *Lesbian Nation: The Feminist Solution* (New York: Simon and Schuster, 1974).

Luther, M.: *Letter to the Knights of the Teutonic Order*. In *Luther's Works*, ed. J. J. Pelikan and H. T. Lehmann (St Louis: 1955).

MacKinnon, C. A.: *Feminism Unmodified: Discourses on Life and the Law* (Cambridge, Mass.: Harvard University Press, 1977).

Punzo, V. C.: *Reflective Naturalism* (New York: Macmillan, 1969).

Sacred Congregation for the Doctrine of the Faith: *Declaration on Sexual Ethics* (Vatican City: 1975).

Scruton, R.: *Sexual Desire: A Moral Philosophy of the Erotic* (New York: Free Press, 1986).

Vannoy, R.: *Sex Without Love: A Philosophical Exploration* (Buffalo: Prometheus, 1980).

Further reading

Baker, R. and Elliston, F., eds.: *Philosophy and Sex* (Buffalo: Prometheus, 1984).

Cole, W. G.: *Sex in Christianity and Psychoanalysis* (New York: Oxford University Press, 1955).

Hunter, J. F. M.: *Thinking About Sex and Love: A Philosophical Inquiry* (New York: St Martin's Press, 1980).

Jaggar, A. M.: *Feminist Politics and Human Nature* (Totowa, NJ: Rowman and Littlefield, 1983).

Soble, A., ed.: *Philosophy of Sex* (Totowa, NJ: Rowman and Littlefield, 1980).

28

Personal relationships

HUGH LAFOLLETTE

i Morality and personal relationships: Do they conflict?

MORALITY and personal relationships appear to conflict. Morality, as typically conceived, requires impartiality: we must treat all humans (creatures?) alike unless there is some general and morally relevant difference which justifies a difference in treatment. A teacher should give equal grades to students who perform equally; unequal grades are justified only if there is some general and relevant reason which justifies that difference. For example, it is legitimate to give a better grade to a student who does superior work; it is illegitimate to give her a better grade because she is pretty, wears pink, or is named 'Judith'.

On the other hand, personal relationships are partial to the core. We behave toward intimates in ways we would never behave toward strangers; we allow intimates to treat us in ways we wouldn't tolerate from strangers. We give preferential care; we expect it in return. Hence, the conflict. How can it be resolved? Should we presume that morality is always more important? Could the demands of personal relationships supersede those of morality? Or is there a way to show that the conflict is more apparent than real?

The standard move is to deny that there is a conflict, to assume that the apparent partiality of personal relationships is straightforwardly explicable by impartial moral principles. Let me explain. The principle of equal consideration of interests is not a substantive moral principle: it does not specify exactly how anyone is to be treated. Rather it is a formal principle which requires that we treat people the same unless there is some general and relevant reason which justifies our treating them differently. It does not specify what counts as a general and relevant reason, and thus does not specify how people should be treated.

Those taking this tack will then go on to claim that *one* general and relevant reason why I should treat Eva (my wife) better than I treat Phyllis (a stranger) is simply that she is my wife. All spouses, friends, lovers, etc. should treat their intimates better than they treat others – after all, they have a personal relationship and personal relationships are, by definition, partial. The moral rule which justifies partiality is impartial: it allows (requires?) *everyone* to treat intimates better than they treat strangers. The demands of morality and of personal relationships are not at odds.

Does this strategy succeed? Well, intimacy *is* a general characteristic, but differentiating characteristics must also be morally relevant. Is it? It is not difficult to see why we might think it is. Intimacy promotes honesty, caring, loyalty, self-knowledge, patience, empathy, etc. These are significant moral values by anyone's lights – values which arguably are best promoted by intimate relationships. So by this line of reasoning impartial moral principles dictate that we pursue intimacy. Since intimacy requires partiality, it is legitimate to treat intimates preferentially.

There is some force to this response, though it is not apparent that it is entirely adequate as it stands. Even if this manoeuvre resolves the apparent tension between morality and self-interest at this level, a parallel problem emerges at a lower level. The previous considerations allegedly show that it is legitimate to treat intimates better than we treat strangers. They thereby imply that we should treat all intimates the same unless there is some general and relevant reason that justifies a difference in treatment. However, we assume it is legitimate to treat different friends differently. It is not clear that we can provide general and relevant reasons which would justify *this* variation in treatment.

Perhaps we should conclude, instead, that the requirement of impartiality undermines personal relationships as we presently understand them. That is, relationships may be partial only in limited ways consistent with the principle of the equal consideration of interests. As Rachels (1989, p. 48) puts it: '[U]niversal love is a higher ideal than family loyalty, and the obligation within families can be properly understood only as particular instances of obligations to all mankind.'

Thus, people might still have special duties to others, but these would be more limited than on our present view. For instance, we might decide that some people should give preferential care for children in the same sort of way that we decide that people in certain institutional roles (police-officers, judges, doctors, or lifeguards) should give preferential consideration to people under their care. These role-specific duties are, in important respects, stronger than general impersonal obligations. Your doctor should look after your health in ways that she does not have to look after mine. Her duty to her patients will take precedence over the medical needs of strangers.

We can similarly explain why parents have special responsibilities for their children. They have special assigned roles which legitimate limited preferential treatment of them. But not so preferential, Rachels claims, that they can justifiably ignore the needs of other less well-off children. Hence, the conflict is resolved by denying that *fundamentally* partial personal relationships are morally permissible, let alone obligatory. We *thought* personal relationships as we conceived them were compatible with morality, but we were wrong. The only legitimate personal relationships are derivative from impartial duties, and therefore, are distant kin to intimacy as we conceive it. The demands of morality are always superior.

This view will likely strike most readers as wrong and undesirable. To an extent I agree. In its raw form it is wrong. Wrong, but not nonsense. It has significant insights we should not ignore. Impartiality is vital to our understanding of morality, 'something deeply important, that we should be reluctant to give up. It is useful, for example, in explaining why egoism, racism, and sexism are morally odious, and if we abandon this conception we lose our most natural and persuasive means of combatting these doctrines' (Rachels, 1989, p. 48).

Moreover, though it is appealing to be able to lavish attention on those for whom we care, such attention seems at least tacky and probably cosmically unfair given that other people, through no fault of their own, are so poorly off. These other people's lives could be improved if we would spread our attention beyond our close friends and family. For instance, it seems unfair that Sarah can legitimately buy her child an expensive new toy or treat her husband to an exorbitant gourmet meal, while the people living next door starve. Luck plays an inordinately large role in determining a person's lot in life. Morality should attempt to diminish, if not eradicate, the undesirable effects of luck.

Despite these insights, if we completely embrace Rachels's suggestion, there are some undesirable consequences. It is not just that friends will be unable to share the same depth and range of relationships they presently do – though that most assuredly will be so. It appears it might completely undermine the very possibility of personal relationships. On his view parents would care for children because the impartial generalized rules of morality require it, not because they love their children. Likewise, I would assume, for friends or spouses. We could still establish quasi-intimate relationships, but these would be founded on general moral rules, not on personal attraction or personal choice.

That would eliminate some of the primary benefits of personal relationships; for instance, that they heighten our sense of self-worth. Close relationships are those in which people like us because of who we are, because of our specific personality traits. Thus, when someone loves you it makes you feel better about yourself; they have *chosen* to love you because of who you are.

In contrast, on Rachels's proposal others would befriend you because some moral rule requires it. Duties of friendship would be just like other role-specific duties. We think lawyers should work to promote their clients' interests and that physicians should be concerned with their patients' medical needs – that is their job. Likewise, parents would care for their children, and friends would care for each other as prescribed by general moral rules.

But friends don't want that sort of impersonal care; they want to be loved for who they are. A complete commitment to an impartial moral theory seems to preclude the love for which humans yearn.

This problem has led philosophers such as Bernard Williams, Susan Wolf, and Thomas Nagel to argue that personal relationships and morality inevitably conflict, and, at least on some occasions, morality loses. Suppose, Williams says, two people are drowning and a rescuer can save only one of them. One is the rescuer's wife. Should he be impartial between them and decide, for example, by flipping a coin? No, says Williams, he should straightforwardly save his wife. He doesn't need to argue for or justify his decision; nor need he make any reference to impartial moral principles. In fact, to attempt to justify the action in that way would be completely inappropriate.

The consideration that it was his wife is certainly, for instance, an explanation which should silence comment. But something more ambitious than this is usually intended [in someone's saying that he was justified in his action], essentially involving the idea that moral principle can legitimate his preference, yielding the conclusion that in situations of this kind it is at least all right (morally permissible) to save one's wife ... But this construction provides the agent with one question too many: it might have been hoped by some (for instance, his wife) that his motivating thought, fully spelled out, would be the thought that it was his wife, not that it was his wife and that in situations of this kind it is permissible to save one's wife. (Williams, 1981, p. 18)

When close personal relationships are at stake it is inappropriate to assume all of our actions must be guided by impartial moral standards. Moral standards will occasionally be trumped by our personal projects – especially our commitments to friends and family. Without such relationships or projects, Williams asserts, 'there will not be enough substance or conviction in a man's life to compel allegiance to life itself', (p. 18). Put differently, if life is to be meaningful, we cannot guide our lives by impartial moral principles.

ii The interplay of morality and personal relationships

It seems we have reached an impasse. There is something appealing about both views. Sometimes when moral concern for strangers conflicts with concern for those we love, we assume concern for our intimates should take precedence. Yet that appears to conflict with the principle of impartiality, and that principle lies at the heart of our ordinary moral understanding; moreover, it seems cosmically unfair that someone's life chances are significantly affected by an accident of birth. I cannot completely resolve this conflict in this brief essay, but I offer the following suggestions.

The problem arises if we assume the demands of morality and the concerns of personal relationships unavoidably conflict. I acknowledge that they occasionally conflict; however, we should focus instead on the important ways in which they are mutually supportive. If we could identify these, then perhaps we might have a clue about how to deal with apparent (or real) conflicts.

Here are two ways in which they are supportive: (1) close personal relationships empower us to develop an impersonal morality; and (2) intimacy flourishes in an environment which recognizes the impersonal demands of all. If this is right, then the tensions between impersonal moral demands and close personal relationships may not evaporate, but they will be more amenable to resolution.

Close personal relationships are grist for the moral mill. Different ethical theorists disagree about the extent of the concern we must have for everyone, but all agree that morality requires that we consider (even promote) the interests of others. But how do we learn to do that? And how do we become motivated to do it?

We can develop neither the moral knowledge nor empathy crucial for an impartial morality unless we have been in intimate relationships. Someone reared by uncaring parents, who never established close personal ties with others, will simply not know how to look after or promote the interests of either intimates or strangers. No-one knows how to do mathematics or to play football without acquaintance with the discipline or the game. Likewise, no-one knows how to consider the interests of others unless they have been in an intimate relationship.

Consider the following situation: suppose you are standing next to someone who has an epileptic seizure, but you have never heard of epilepsy, let alone witnessed a seizure. Or suppose you are stranded on an elevator with someone having a heart attack, but you didn't know people had hearts, let alone that they could malfunction. In short, try to imagine that you were in one of these circumstances when you were seven years old. You would do nothing. Or if you tried, it would very likely do more harm than good; success would surely be serendipitous.

The same would be true generally of efforts to promote the interests of others. We cannot promote interests we cannot identify. And the way we learn to identify the interests of others is through interaction with others. Most of us learn how to discern the needs of others within our families: our parents comforted us when we were hurt; they laughed with us when we were happy. Eventually, we came to recognize *their* pain and happiness, and subsequently learned to be concerned about them.

But without that experience, not only would we not have the knowledge to promote other's interests, we wouldn't have the inclination either. Though I expect we may have *some* biologically inherited sympathetic tendencies, these will not be developed adequately unless others have cared for us and we have cared for them. If we are not motivated to promote the needs of our families or friends, how can we be motivated to promote the needs of a stranger?

On the other hand, if we develop empathy toward our friends, we will be inclined to generalize it to others. We become so vividly aware of our intimate's needs that we are willing to help them even when it is difficult to do so. But since empathy is often non-specific, we will be likewise inclined to 'feel' pain in acquaintances and strangers. Having felt it, we are more likely to do something about it.

That is not to say that those who develop close relationships always come to care for the impersonal other, although most do. My point is simply that a person must have some exposure to personal relationships to be motivated to be moral or to know how to be moral. Put differently, people cannot be just or moral in a vacuum; they can become just only within an environment which countenances personal relationships.

Correspondingly, relationships between non-moral people are at risk. Intimates must be honest with one another; any dishonesty will chip away at the foundations of the relationship. Yet people cannot be as honest as they need to be if they are immersed in a subculture built on dishonesty and deceit. Dishonesty, like all traits, is not something someone can turn on and off. If people are dishonest with large numbers of people at work, they will be similarly inclined at home.

Likewise, close relationships are possible only inasmuch as each party trusts the other. But trust cannot survive, let alone flourish, in an environment of distrust and hate. And, to tie these issues together, you cannot be completely honest with me unless you trust me. Mistrust squelches honesty.

In short, the possibility of genuine personal relationships is limited, if not eliminated, in an immoral environment. If people are uninterested in the welfare of other people – that is, if they are amoral or immoral – then when they enter seemingly personal relationships, they will enter them for their own personal gain; thus, the relationships will not be personal in the relevant sense. Since they are not at all inclined to see the legitimate needs of other people, they will not be inclined to see these needs in people they presumably befriend.

Consequently, personal relationships and morality are not at odds in the ways many philosophers have supposed. Rather, they are mutually supportive. Experience and involvement in close relationships will enhance one's interest in and sympathy for the plight of others. Concern about the plight of the stranger will help her develop the traits necessary for close personal relationships.

Given these observations it appears we should seek a hybrid view to resolve the conflict between morality and personal relationships. I have argued that (1) only those who have experienced intimacy can have the knowledge and motivation which undergirds an impartial morality, and (2) intimacy can flourish only in a society which recognizes the demands of the impersonal other. Consequently, these two points must be part of some larger moral picture.

Perhaps that picture can be sketched like this: if an impartial morality required that we treat everyone impartially all of the time, then we couldn't develop the knowledge or motivation which enables us to act morally. So impartiality can't require *that*. It must allow at least some personal relationships – relationships where people can justifiably treat intimates partially. Otherwise it is self-defeating.

Exactly how much partiality does it allow? Enough to permit people to develop genuinely intimate relationships. How much is that? I don't know. It seems evident, however, that this would not justify unlimited partiality toward our intimates. Partiality which regularly disregards strangers while heaping trivial benefits on intimates is not justified. To that extent Rachels's position is vindicated.

Of course conflicts will arise, but when they do, they will arise in the same way that any moral conflicts arise; duties to two friends may conflict as may duties to two strangers. But such conflicts don't show that morality is impossible; they only show that it is difficult to achieve. But then, we already knew that.

References

Nagel, T.: *Mortal Questions* (Cambridge: Cambridge University Press, 1979).
——: *The View from Nowhere* (Oxford: Oxford University Press, 1986).
Rachels, J.: 'Morality, parents, and children', *Person to Person*; eds. G. Graham and H. LaFollette (Philadelphia; Temple University Press, 1989).
Williams, B.: 'Persons, character, and morality', *Moral Luck* (Cambridge: Cambridge University Press, 1981).
Wolf, S.: 'Moral saints', *Journal of Philosophy*, 69 (1982), 419–39.
——: 'Above and below and line of duty', *Philosophical Topics*, 14 (1986), 131–48.

29

Equality, discrimination and preferential treatment

BERNARD R. BOXILL

i Introduction

LOOKING back on the United States Supreme Court's 1954 decision against segregated schools, and the civil rights revolution it started, many people in the late twentieth century began to hope that America's sense of fair play had finally gained the upper hand over prejudice and racism. They were therefore bitterly disappointed when, more than thirty years after that historic decision, a wave of racial incidents swept major American universities. They were aware, of course, that racism persisted; they would have been saddened, but not surprised to hear of comparable or even worse incidents in some rural backwater in the deep South. But these incidents had happened in the North, and in traditional bastions of enlightenment and liberalism like the universities of Massachussetts, Michigan, Wisconsin, as well as Dartmouth, Stanford and Yale. What had caused the setback?

According to some pundits, the blame should be placed on preferential treatment. Writing in *Commentary*, for example, Charles Murray maintained that preferential treatment promotes racism because it maximizes the likelihood that blacks hired for a job, or admitted to a university, will be less capable than the whites besides them; and, he warned ominously that the recent racial incidents were only a 'thin leading edge of what we may expect in the coming years'.

The advocates of preferential treatment reply that although preferential treatment may provoke immediate animosity it will in the long run lead to a racially and sexually harmonious society. Many also maintain that it is justified because it helps to compensate those who have been wrongly harmed by racist and sexist practices and attitudes. This essay is an attempt to evaluate these claims.

As the preceding paragraph suggests, there are two main kinds of argument for preferential treatment. The first, forward-looking argument, justifies preferential treatment because of its supposed good consequences. The second, backward-looking argument, justifies preferential treatment as compensation for past wrongful injuries. In this section I will briefly describe these arguments and the egalitarian principles they rely on. Let us begin with the backward-looking argument.

The most plausible version of the backward-looking argument relies on the principle of equal opportunity. The controlling idea of this principle is that the positions in a society should be distributed on the basis of a fair competition among individuals. It has two parts, both necessary to capture that idea. The first is that positions should be awarded to individuals with the qualities and abilities enabling them best to perform the functions expected of those filling the positions. Thus it requires that individuals be evaluated for positions strictly on the basis of their qualifications for those positions. The second is that individuals should have the same chances to acquire the qualifications for desirable positions. At a minimum this requires that elementary and secondary schools provide everyone with the same advantages whether they are rich or poor, black or white, male of female, handicapped or whole.

Most societies routinely violate both parts of the equal opportunity principle. In most societies, for example, people are frequently ruled out of consideration for positions simply because they are handicapped, or aged, or female, or members of a racial minority. And in most societies these violations of the first part of the equal opportunity principle are compounded by violations of the second part of the equal opportunity principle. Schools for the rich are usually better than schools for the poor; schools for whites are usually better than schools for blacks; talented girls are steered away from careers in engineering architecture and the physical sciences; and the handicapped are more or less generally ignored.

Advocates of the backward-looking argument for preferential treatment maintain that violations of the equal opportunity principle are seriously unjust, and that those who have been harmed by these violations normally deserve compensation. In particular, they argue that preferential treatment is justified as a convenient means of compensating people who have been systematically denied equal opportunities on the basis of highly visible characteristics like being female or black.

Let us now consider the forward-looking argument. Advocates of this argument believe that preferential treatment will not only help to equalize opportunities by breaking down racial and sexual stereotypes, but will also have deeper and more important egalitarian consequences. To understand what these consequences are it is necessary to see that the equal opportunity principle has limitations as an egalitarian principle.

If we relied exclusively on the equal opportunity principle to distribute positions, we would tend to put the more talented in the more desirable positions. Since these positions usually involve work which is intrinsically more satisfying than the work other positions involve, our practice would tend to do more to satisfy the interests of the more talented in having satisfying work than to satisfy the like interests of the less talented. Further, because the more desirable positions generally pay better than the less desirable positions, use of the equal opportunity principle to distribute positions would also enable the more talented more fully to satisfy their other interests than the less talented, insofar at least as satisfying these other interests costs money.

In general then, exclusive reliance on the equal opportunity to distribute positions would tend to give greater weight to satisfying the interests of the more talented than to satisfying the like interest of the less talented. This violates the principle of equal consideration of interests which forbids giving any person's interests greater or lesser weight than the like interests of any other person. This principle does not presuppose any factual equality among individuals, for example, that they are equal in intelligence or rationality or moral personality. Consequently it is not contradicted by the fact that some people are more talented than others, and it does not have to be withdrawn because of that fact. It is a fundamental moral principle. It says that whatever the differences between people are, equal weight ought to be given to their like interests.

The principle of equal consideration of interests is the moral basis of the principle of equal opportunity. That principle has a limited place in egalitarian theories because it helps to implement the principle of equal consideration of interests. For, although it tends to give greater weight to the interests of the more talented in having satisfying work, it also tends to get talent into positions where it can better serve everyone's interests. This defence of the equal opportunity principle is, however, only partial. Although it justifies some reliance on the equal opportunity principle to match talent and occupational position, it does not justify the higher incomes which normally go with the more desirable positions. Admirers of the market often argue, of course, that such incomes are necessary to encourage the talented to acquire the qualifications required for the more desirable positions; but this is not very compelling given that these positions are already usually the most intrinsically satisfying in the society.

Advocates of the forward-looking argument for preferential treatment believe that it will help implement the principle of equal consideration of interests in addition to helping to equalize opportunities. Most societies don't come close to implementing either principle. They deny equal opportunities to certain individuals and give far less weight to satisfying the interests of those individuals than to satisfying the exactly similar interests of other individuals. For example, the interests of the aged in finding rewarding employment are routinely treated as being intrinsically less important than the similar interests of younger people, and for this reason they are often denied rewarding employment, even when they are the best qualified. The interests of the handicapped are more often downgraded in violations of the second part of the equal opportunity principle, as are the interests of women and the members of racial minorities. Such individuals are normally not given the same chance to acquire qualifications for desirable positions as men or those in the dominant racial group. If those favouring the forward-looking argument are right, preferential treatment will gradually abolish these violations of the equal opportunity principle, and help to usher in a society in which equal consideration is given to the like interests of all.

We have now sketched the two main arguments for preferential treatment and the egalitarian principles which are supposed to justify them. We must now see how these arguments are worked out in detail, and whether they can stand up to criticism. I will examine them mainly as they apply to preferential treatment for women and black people, but they can be applied to other cases where preferential treatment seems justified. In section (ii) I will examine the backward-looking argument, in section (iii) the forward-looking argument.

335

ii The backward-looking argument

Perhaps the most common objection made against preferential treatment is that distinctions based on race or sex are invidious. Especially in America, critics tend to brandish Justice Harlan's dictum, 'Our Constitution is colour-blind . . .'.

Justice Harlan's point was that the American Constitution forbids denying a citizen any of the rights and privileges normally accorded to other citizens on account of his or her colour or race. The critics argue that the colour-blind principle Justice Harlan's dictum appeals to, and the similar sex-blind principle follow from the equal opportunity principle if we assume that citizens have rights to be evaluated for desirable positions solely on the basis of their qualifications for these positions, and that neither colour, nor sex is normally a qualification for a position. If they are right, preferential treatment violates the equal opportunity principle because it violates the colour-blind and sex-blind principles.

Preferential treatment certainly seems to violate the first part of the equal opportunity principle. It may, for example, require that a law school refuse admission to a white male and admit instead a woman or black who on most standards seems less qualified. But we must not forget the second part of the equal opportunity principle that everyone must have an equal chance to acquire qualifications. Unless it is satisfied, the competition for places will not be fair. And in the case under discussion the second part of the equal opportunity principle may very well not be satisfied. Whites generally go to better schools than blacks, and society supports a complex system of expectations and stereotyping which benefits white males at the expense of blacks and women. So preferential treatment need not make the competition for desirable places and positions unfair. On the contrary, by compensating women and blacks for being denied equal chances to acquire qualifications, it may make that competition more fair.

In America the objection is often made that if blacks deserve compensation for being unjustly discriminated against, so also do Italians, Jews, Irish, Serbo-Croatians, Asians, and practically every ethnic group in America, since these groups too have been unjustly discriminated against. The implication is that since the society obviously cannot meet all these claims for compensation, it has no good reason to meet black claims for compensation.

I find no merit in this objection. In America, at least, discrimination against blacks has historically been far more severe than discrimination against other racial and ethnic groups. Further, while various European ethnic groups were certainly discriminated against, they also profited from the severer discrimination against blacks since they immigrated to America to take the jobs native blacks were denied because of their race. So, the claim that many other ethnic groups besides blacks have been discriminated against falls short of its goal. If society can only meet some claims for compensation, it should meet the most pressing claims, and blacks appear to have the most pressing claims.

This argument is compelling if we focus our attention on certain segments of the black population, especially the black underclass. The black underclass is characterized by alarming and unprecedented rates of joblessness, welfare dependence, teenage pregnancies, out-of-wedlock births, female-headed families, drug abuse and violent crime. But most blacks are not in the underclass. In particular, many if not most of the blacks who benefit from preferential treatment have middle-class origins. To be preferentially admitted to law school or medical school, a black or woman must usually have attended a good college, and earned good grades, and this gives those from the middle and upper classes a decided advantage over those from the lower socio-economic classes. This fact has raised many eyebrows.

Some critics complained that it showed that the typical beneficiaries of preferential treatment have no valid claim for compensation. They evidently assumed that middle and upper-class blacks and women are unscathed by racist or sexist attitudes. This assumption is unjustified. Because of the civil rights victories, most forms of racial and sexual discrimination are illegal, and potential discriminators are likely to be wary of indulging their prejudices against blacks and women who have the money and education to make they pay for their illegality. But it does not follow that middle-class blacks and women are unscathed by racist and sexist attitudes. These attitudes do not support only discrimination. As I noted earlier, they support an elaborate system of expectations and stereotyping which subtly but definitely reduces the chances of women and blacks to acquire qualifications for desirable positions.

A somewhat more serious objection, stemming from the facts about the middle-class origins of the beneficiaries of preferential treatment, is that preferential treatment does not compensate those who most deserve compensation. The objection itself can be easily dismissed. As long as preferential treatment compensates those who deserve compensation, the fact that it does not compensate those who most deserve compensation is hardly an argument against it. The objection does, however, raise a serious difficulty since the society may not be able to compensate all those who deserve compensation. In that case present programmes of preferential treatment which benefit mainly middle-class blacks and women may have to be scrapped to make way for other programmes which compensate those who more deserve it. Besides the underclass, the main candidate is the 'working poor'.

Recent commentators have complained that in the hullabaloo about the underclass, society has forgotten the 'working poor'. The schools their children attend may be only slightly better than the schools black children in the underclass attend. If so, present programmes of preferential treatment may be particularly unfair. Because they compensate for the disadvantages of race and sex, but tend to ignore the disadvantages of class, they are apt to discriminate against white males from the 'working poor' and in favour of middle or even upper-class blacks or women whose opportunities are already much better.

Fortunately, blacks, women and the 'working poor' need not quarrel among themselves over who most deserves compensation. Although each of these groups has probably profited from discrimination against the other two, preferential treatment need not compensate one of them at the expense of the others. Conceivably, it can compensate all of them at the expense of white middle-class males.

337

The members of this group have profited from discrimination against the members of the other groups, but have escaped all systematic discrimination, as well as the disadvantages of a lower-class education.

There is, however, a serious difficulty with viewing preferential treatment as compensation. Insofar as its beneficiaries have been denied equal opportunities, they deserve compensation; but it is not clear what compensation they deserve. Perhaps this will be clear for specific violations of the first part of the equal opportunity principle. If a firm denies a woman a job because of her sex, she deserves that job as compensation whenever it becomes available, even if others are at that time better qualified. In violations of the second part of the equal opportunity principle, it will be more difficult to determine what compensation those who have been wronged deserve. In particular it is far from clear that the compensation they deserve is desirable places and positions.

Let us consider this difficulty as it applies to the middle class beneficiaries of preferential treatment. In that case the stock answer to the difficulty is that, were it not for racial and sexual discrimination and stereotyping, the middle-class blacks and women who receive preferential treatment for desirable places and positions would have been the best qualified candidates for these places and positions. Unfortunately, however, it must contend with the equally stock objection that were it not for the past history of racial and sexual discrimination and stereotyping, the middle-class blacks and women who receive preferential treatment for desirable places and positions would probably not even exist, let alone be best qualified for any places and positions.

The point this objection makes cannot be gainsaid. Racial and sexual discrimination and stereotyping have radically changed the face of society. Had they never existed, the ancestors of middle-class blacks and women receiving preferential treatment would almost certainly never have met, which implies that the middle-class blacks and women receiving preferential treatment would almost certainly never have existed. But the objection may be irrelevant. The proposal is not to imagine a world without a history of racial and sexual discrimination and stereotyping; it is to imagine a world without racial and sexual discrimination and stereotyping in the present generation. In such a world, most of the middle-class blacks and women receiving preferential treatment would certainly exist; and the argument is that they would be the most qualified for the places and positions they receive in the present world because of preferential treatment.

Unfortunately, this won't quite do. In the alternative world we are asked to imagine, most of the middle-class blacks and women who receive preferential treatment would probably be much better qualified than they are in our present world, for they would not have to contend with any racial or sexual discrimination and stereotyping. It does not follow, however, that they would be the *most* qualified for the places and positions they receive because of preferential treatment. Present programmes of preferential treatment have forward-looking aims. They try to break down racial and sexual stereotypes by hastening the day when the races and sexes are represented in desirable positions in proportion to their numbers. This aim may not be consistent with a policy of benefiting only those who would be the most qualified for the places and positions they receive were there no racial or sexual discrimination and stereotyping.

It may seem that this difficulty can be met if we assume that the races and sexes are equally talented. Given this assumption it may seem to follow that in a world without racial or sexual discrimination, the races and sexes will be represented in desirable positions in proportion to their numbers, and accordingly that the blacks amd women who receive preferential treatment for desirable places and positions would be the most qualified for these places and positions were there no racial or sexual discrimination. Both inferences, however, forget the complication of class.

Take first this complication as it applies to race. The black middle class is much smaller relative to the total black population than is the white middle class relative to the total white population. Those who compete for the desirable positions in society are drawn overwhelmingly from the middle classes; many in the lower socio-economic classes are excluded by their relatively poor education. Consequently, even if the races are equally talented, and there were no racial discrimination, the numbers of blacks in desirable positions would still be disproportionately small, and less than the number benefited by programmes of preferential treatment.

A weaker, but still significant version of this difficulty affects the argument for women. Since women are half the middle class, and half the population, perhaps we can argue that preferential treatment benefits women who would have been the most qualified for the positions it awards them, were there no sexual discrimination. It does not follow, however, that they deserve preferential treatment. The force of the appeal to a world without sexual discrimination and stereotyping is that, as far as possible, compensation should give people what they would have received in a world without injustice. Sexual discrimination is not, however, the only injustice. It is also an injustice that poor children are badly educated compared to rich children. In the absence of that injustice it is far from clear that were there no sexual discrimination and stereotyping the middle-class white women receiving preferential treatment would have been the most qualified for the positions it awards them.

I conclude that the forward-looking aims of preferential treatment outstrip its backward-looking justification. Present programmes of preferential treatment with their forward-looking aims cannot be justified solely on the backward-looking ground that they are compensation for violations of the equal opportunity principle.

iii The forward-looking argument

As we saw earlier, the forward-looking aims of preferential treatment are to help make opportunities more equal, and ultimately, to enable society to give more equal consideration to the like interests of its members. A plausible case can be made for the claim that preferential treatment can help to make opportunities more equal. Suppose, for example, that the culture and traditions of a society lead its members to the firm conviction that women cannot be engineers. Since engineering is a rewarding and well-paid profession, and many women have the talent to excel at it, preferential treatment to encourage more women to become engineers may help to break the stereotype and equalize opportunities.

These possible consequences of preferential treatment may not be enough to justify it if, as some critics object, it violates the rights of white males to be evaluated for positions solely on the basis of their qualifications. This objection follows from the colour-blind and sex-blind principles, which in turn follow from the equal opportunity principle if we assume that the qualifications for positions can never include colour or sex, but must be things like scores on aptitude tests, and grades and university diplomas. I will argue, however, that this assumption is false, and consequently that the colour-blind and sex-blind principles must sometimes be relaxed. The crucial premise in my argument is the point made earlier that applications of the equal opportunity principle must be framed so as to serve the principle of equal consideration of interests.

Suppose that a state establishes a medical school, but most of the school's graduates practise in cities, so that people in rural areas do not get adequate medical care. And suppose it was found that applicants for medical school from rural areas are more likely upon graduation to practise in these areas than applicants from urban areas. If the state gave equal weight to the interests of rural and urban people in receiving medical treatment, it seems that it could justifiably require the medical school to begin considering rural origins as one of the qualifications for admission. This could cause some applicants from urban areas to be denied admission to medical school who would otherwise have been admitted; but I do not see how they could validly complain that this violated their rights; after all, the medical school was not established in order to make them doctors, but in order to provide medical services for the community.

A similar example shows how race could conceivably be among the qualifications for admission to medical school. Thus suppose that people in the black ghettos do not get adequate medical care because not enough doctors choose to practise there; and suppose it was found that black doctors are more likely than white doctors to practise in black ghettos; as in the previous case, if the state gave equal weight to the interests of black and white people in receiving medical treatment, it could easily be justified in requiring medical schools to begin considering being black as a qualification for admission.

Critics sometimes object that some white doctors are more likely to practise in black ghettos than some black doctors. Although what they say is undeniable, it does not invalidate the case for considering race a qualification for admission to medical school. Practically all policies awarding places and positions must rely on generalizations which everyone knows are not true in every case. For example, no reasonable person suggests that universities should abandon their policy of awarding places partly on the basis of test scores, although these scores do not, of course, infallibly predict success and failure in university.

The implication of this discussion is that what counts as qualification for a position is ultimately determined by the principle of equal consideration of interests. In particular, the qualifications for a position are the qualities and abilities a person needs in order to perform adequately the functions expected of anyone filling the position, and thereby to enable society to give more equal weight to the like interests of all. So conceived, colour and sex may be among the qualifications for positions. Although this implies that the colour-blind and sex-blind principles are not always acceptable, it does not challenge the equal opportunity principle. It allows that people have rights to be evaluated for positions strictly on the basis of their qualifications for these positions. What it denies is that preferential treatment necessarily violates these rights of white males.

Although preferential treatment need not violate anyone's rights, the forward-looking argument may be open to other sorts of objection. In particular, it depends on factual claims about the consequences of preferential treatment. Sceptics challenge these claims. They claim, for example, that preferential treatment powerfully encourages the belief that women and blacks cannot compete against white males without special help. This was the point of Charles Murray's criticism of preferential treatment cited in the beginning of this essay. But even if the sceptics are mistaken, and preferential treatment is justifiable on purely forward-looking grounds, the backward-looking considerations favouring it remain significant. People have like interests in being acknowledged to have equal moral standing. When, as in the US, a society has systematically excluded the members of a racial minority from the moral and political community, and in word and deed denied their equal moral standing, it does not acknowledge that equality simply by awarding them benefits, even if the benefits are generous. It must admit that they are owed these benefits because of their past treatment. In such cases especially, programmes based on preferential treatment are an important means to achieving an egalitarian society.

References

Harlan: Justice Harlan's comment may be found in: Bell, D. A., Jr., ed.: *Civil Rights: Leading Cases* (Boston: Little, Brown and Co., 1980). See *Plessy v. Ferguson*, 1986.
Murray, C.: 'The coming of custodial democracy', *Commentary*, 86 (1988), 20–26.

Further reading

i Books

Boxill, B. R.: *Blacks and Social Justice* (Totowa, NJ: Rowman and Allenheld, 1984).
Clark, K.: *Dark Ghetto* (New York: Harper and Row, 1965).
Fishkin, J. S.: *Justice, Equal Opportunity, and the Family* (New Haven: Yale University Press, 1983).
Fullinwider, R. K.: *The Reverse Discrimination Controversy* (Totowa, NJ: Rowman and Little-field, 1980).
Goldman, A. H.: *Justice and Reverse Discrimination* (Princeton: Princeton University Press, 1979).
Singer, P.: *Practical Ethics* (Cambridge: Cambridge University Press, 1979).
Wilson, W. J.: *The Truly Disadvantaged* (Chicago: University of Chicago Press, 1988).

ii Articles

Blackstone, W.: 'Reverse discrimination and compensatory justice', *Social Theory and Practice*, 3 (1975), 258–71.

Boxill, B. R.: 'The morality of reparations', *Social Theory and Practice*, 2 (1972), 113–24.

——: 'The morality of preferential hiring', *Philosophy and Public Affairs*, 7 (1978), 246–68.

McGary, H., Jr.: 'Justice and reparations', *Philosophical Forum*, 9 (1977–78), 250–63.

——: 'Reparations, self-respect and public policy', *Ethical Theories and Social Issues*, ed. David Goldberg (New York: Holt, Rinehart and Winston, Inc. 1989).

Nagel, T.: 'Equal treatment and compensatory discrimination', *Philosophy and Public Affairs*, 2 (1973), 348–63.

Wasserstrom, R. A.: 'Racism. sexism, and preferential treatment: an approach to the topics', *UCLA Law Review*, 24 (1977), 581–622.

——: 'The university and the case for preferential treatment', *American Philosophical Quarterly*, 13 (1976), 165–70.

30

Animals

LORI GRUEN

i Introduction

IN ORDER to satisfy the human taste for flesh, over five billion animals are slaughtered every year in the United States alone. Most chickens, pigs and calves raised for food never see the light of day. These animals are often so intensively confined that they are rarely able to turn around or spread a wing. An estimated 200 million animals are used routinely in laboratory experiments around the world annually. A large portion of the research causes the animals pain and discomfort while providing absolutely no benefit to human beings. An estimated 250 million wild animals are shot and killed each year by hunters in the United States. Over 650 different species of animals now threatened may be extinct by the turn of the century. These realities have caused many people to question our relationship to non-human animals.

The conditions under which animals are kept and the ways in which they are used by factory farmers, experimenters, furriers, commercial developers and others, tend to disregard the fact that animals are living, feeling creatures. Peter Singer's 1975 publication, *Animal Liberation*, challenged the attitude that animals are ours to use in whatever way we see fit and offered a 'new ethics for our treatment of animals'. This book also provided the moral foundation for a budding and boisterous animal liberation movement, and at the same time forced philosophers to begin addressing the moral status of animals. The ensuing discussion led to a general agreement that animals are not mere automata, that they are capable of suffering, and are due some moral consideration. The burden of proof shifted from those who want to protect animals from harm to those who believe that animals do not matter at all. The latter are now forced to defend their view against the widely accepted position that, at least, gratuitous animal suffering and death is not morally acceptable.

A few defences have been attempted. In his book, *The Case for Animal Experimentation* (1986a), Canadian philosopher Michael A. Fox set out to prove that animals are not members of the moral community and therefore humans have no moral obligation to them. He argued that 'a moral community is a social group composed of interacting autonomous beings where moral concepts and precepts can evolve and be understood. It is also a social group in which the mutual recognition of autonomy and personhood exist' (Fox, 1986a, p. 50). An autonomous person, according to Fox, is one who is critically self-aware, able to manipulate complex concepts, capable of using sophisticated language, and has the capacity to plan, choose, and accept responsibility for actions. Members of the moral community as described are morally superior. Animals, not having valuable lives of their own to lead, cannot function as members of the moral community. He concludes that 'full members of the moral community may use less valuable species, which lack some or all of these traits as means to their ends for the simple reason that they have no obligation not to do so' (p. 88).

Picking out one or more characteristics that are thought to differentiate non-humans from humans has been a constant theme in discussions regarding our relationship to animals. In the Christian tradition the line was drawn at possession of a soul; only creatures who had a soul mattered. When leaps of faith became unacceptable grounds for argument, the focus shifted to other 'measurable' differences such as tool use or brain size, but these did not prove particularly helpful in maintaining the desired distinction. The line-drawing concepts that Fox relied on, i.e. language use and autonomy, are more commonly used.

Some philosophers, most notably Donald Davidson in *Inquiries into Truth and Interpretation* and R. G. Frey in *Interests and Rights*, have argued that beings cannot have thoughts unless they can understand the speech of another. Language, according to this view, is necessarily linked to propositional attitudes, such as 'desires', 'beliefs', or 'intentions'. A being cannot be excited or disappointed without language. While a being's ability to conceptualize and thus be aware of its role in directing the course of its life may indeed grant that being different moral status, the desired exclusion of all animals and no humans by virtue of their alleged lack of these abilities fails. It would be nonsensical to hold a lion morally responsible for the death of a gnu. As far as we know, lions aren't the sort of creatures that can engage in deliberations about the morality of such behaviour. Similarly, however, an infant cannot be held responsible for destroying an original sculpture, or a child held culpable for accidentally shooting her sister. Animals are not moral agents. While they may have choices, their choices are not the sort we would call value choices – choices which underlie ethical decisions. Infants, young children, developmentally impaired people, those in comas, victims of Alzheimer's disease, and other disabled human beings are also incapable of making moral decisions. All of these being cannot be considered members of the moral community, as Fox would have it. Therefore, according to Fox's own logic, animals are not the only beings whom moral community members can use as we wish: the 'marginal' humans are also fair game.

Recognizing this problem, Fox attempts to bring humans, of whatever capability, into the protective moral community by arguing that their condition could very well have been our own. I might have been born without a brain, autistic or otherwise mentally impaired and if I had been, I would not want to be treated as if my suffering did not matter. Thus, 'charity, benevolence, humaneness, and prudence require' that we extend the moral community to include 'under-developed, deficient or seriously impaired human being' (Fox, 1986a, pp. 61–63). One could argue, however, that I can no more imagine what it would be like to be autistic than I could imagine what it would be like to be an aardvark.

Simply being part of the same species doesn't grant me a particularly special insight into another human's perspective, especially one who has a severe disability; My autonomous awareness doesn't necessarily provide me with a sensitivity toward deficient humans that I don't also have, or could not cultivate, towards animals. Fox's readiness to include the former but not the latter is arbitrary.

Recognizing this, and other mistakes in his work, Fox radically changed his views (Fox, 1986b; 1987). Less than a year after his book was published, Fox rejected the main thesis of his book, stating: 'I eventually came to believe that our basic moral obligations to avoid causing harm to other people should be extended to animals. and since I could not see any justification for our benefiting from harm caused other humans, I inferred that it would likewise be wrong for us to benefit from the suffering of animals.' Yet there is another conclusion that could have been drawn after recognizing that one couldn't find a moral basis for drawing the line around the human species while excluding non-humans. This is a position that is maintained by R. G. Frey. Frey recognizes that animals and 'marginal' humans deserve certain moral considerations and includes them within the moral community because they are beings who can suffer. However, he believes that their lives are not of comparable value to those of normal adult human beings, beings who are autonomous persons. Because he bases his argument on quality of life and assumes that the quality of life of an normal adult human is always greater than that of an animal or a deficient human, he concludes that one cannot invariably use animals in preference to 'marginal' humans. He writes 'the only way we could justifiably do this is if we could cite something that always, no matter what, cedes human life greater value than animal life. I know of no such things' (Frey, 1988, p. 197).

Others have tried to argue that species membership is enough. Animals are not ethical beings and since they are not we owe them no moral considerations. They insist that this cannot be refuted by the argument for marginal humans because marginal humans are still humans and our obligations to them are derived from the essential nature of human beings, not from borderline cases. Frey, himself a proponent of a limited use of both animals and 'marginal' humans, has a compelling response to those who hold this human supremacist view. 'I cannot see that species membership is a ground for holding that we stand in a special moral relationship to our fellow humans ... how, through merely being born, does one come to stand in a special moral relationship to humans generally?' (Frey, 1980, p. 199).

Frey's position also has its problems. One might question his claim that normal adult humans necessarily have lives more worth living than normal adult animals. Yet Frey's evolving position, unlike those attempts to maintain a total rejection of the claim that animals matter, has benefited tremendously from the arguments presented by the defenders of animals, arguments to which I will now turn. While there are a number of them, I will discuss two of the most common ethical positions, the rights argument and utilitarianism. I will point out some of the problems with these views and attempt to clarify common misunderstandings. I will then propose a less common way of looking at the question and suggest that this alternative may be worthy of further exploration.

ii Rights

The view that animals deserve moral consideration is often labelled with the words 'animal rights'. Journalists and activists alike have taken this slogan to refer to a wide range of positions. While 'animal rights' serves as a catchy way to draw attention to the plight of animals, much the way 'women's rights' did a couple of decades ago, it really refers to a very specific philosophical position. The view that animals have rights was most eloquently articulated by Tom Regan in *The Case for Animal Rights*.

Regan's view, greatly abbreviated, goes like this: only beings with inherent value have rights. Inherent value is the value that individuals have independent of their goodness or usefulness to others and rights are the things that protect this value. Only subjects-of-a-life have inherent value. Only self-conscious beings, capable of having beliefs and desires, only deliberate actors who can conceive of the future and entertain goals, are subjects-of-a-life. Regan believes that basically all mentally normal mammals of a year or more are subjects-of-a-life and thus have inherent value which allows them to have rights.

The rights which all subjects-of-a-life hold are moral rights, not to be confused with legal rights. Legal rights are the products of laws, which can vary from society to society. (See Article 22, RIGHTS.) Moral rights, on the other hand, are said to belong to all subjects-of-a-life regardless of their colour, nationality, sex, and as Regan argues, species. When people speak of animal rights then, they are not speaking of a cow's right to vote, a guinea pig's right to a fair trial, or a cat's right to religious freedom (three examples of legal right that adults have in the US), but about the right an animal has to be treated with respect as an individual with inherent value.

According to Regan, all beings who have inherent value have it equally. Inherent value cannot be gained by acting virtuously or lost by acting evilly. Florence Nightingale and Adolf Hitler, by virtue of the fact that they were subjects-of-a-life, and that fact alone, had equal inherent value. Inherent value is not something that can grow or diminish based on fads or fashion, popularity or privilege.

While this position is egalitarian and respects the value of individuals, it does not provide any guiding principle for action in cases where values conflict. Consider the following example, which Regan mentions: 'Imagine five survivors are on a lifeboat. Because of limits of size, the boat can only support four. All weigh approximately the same and would take up approximately the same amount of space. Four of the five are normal adult human beings. The fifth is a dog. One must be thrown overboard or else all will perish. Whom should it be?' (Regan, 1983, p. 285). Regan argues that we should kill the dog, because he says 'no reasonable person would deny that the death of any of the four humans would be a greater prima facie loss, and thus a greater prima facie harm, than would be true in the case of the dog. Death for the dog, in short, though a harm, is not comparable to the harm that death would be for any of the humans. To throw any one of the humans overboard, to face certain death, would be to make that individual worse off (i.e. would cause *that* individual a greater harm) than the harm that would be done to the dog if the animal was thrown overboard.' He goes further and suggests that this would be true if the choice had to be made between the four humans and any number of dogs. He writes 'the rights view still implies that, special considerations apart, the million dogs should be thrown overboard and the four humans saved' (pp. 324–5).

Regan argues that a human being is made worse off by being killed than a dog is, no matter who the dog or the human is. While it is true that humans can aspire to things that animals can't, such as finding a cure for AIDS or retarding the greenhouse effect, it is not obvious that the value of these aspirations play any morally significant part in determining the severity of the harm that death is. For example, if I am thrown overboard before I get home to write the play I so often dream of writing or a dog is killed before he gets to go for one more run by the river, we both are having our desires thwarted and thwarted to the same degree – totally. One can only say that I am worse off because one thinks writing a play is more important than running by the river. But it surely isn't more important to the dog. The desire that a person has to accomplish their goals is presumably just as great for a dog, even if the goals are very different. As Dale Jamieson has put it, 'Death is the great equalizer ... Black or white, male or female, rich or poor, human or animal, death reduces us all to nothing' (Jamieson, 1985).

Regan's rights view does have problems. It is a view that must either leave one paralysed when making tough decisions or force one to contradict oneself by maintaining that all are equal but in certain cases some beings are more equal than others. His view is one that tries to preserve the value of the individual apart from any consideration of that individual's worthiness or usefulness to others. However, in his attempt to minimize the impact on the individual of claims to promote 'the greater good' or 'welfare', Regan fails to provide a consistent prescription for action.

iii Utilitarianism

A utilitarian position does not focus on the equal value of all beings and therefore does not leave one unable to choose in conflict situations. Utilitarianism is, nonetheless, an egalitarian position. A utilitarian holds that in any situation the equal interests of all beings affected by an action must be considered equally. The equality that is important for this view is not the equal treatment of individuals, *per se*, but the equal consideration of their abilities to experience the world, most fundamental of which is the ability to suffer. (See Article 20. UTILITY AND THE GOOD.)

The founding father of utilitarianism, Jeremy Bentham, writing in the late eighteenth century, stated the positions thus:

The day may come when the rest of the animal creation may acquire those rights which never could have been withholden from them but by the hand of tyranny. The French have already discovered that the blackness of the skin is no reason why a human being should be abandoned without redress to the caprice of a tormentor. It may one day come to be recognized that the number of the legs, the villosity of the skin, or the termination of the os sacrum are reasons equally insufficient for abandoning a sensitive being to the same fate. What else is it that should trace the insuperable line? Is it the faculty of reason, or perhaps the faculty of discourse? But a full-grown horse or dog is beyond comparison a more rational, as well as a more conversable animal, than an infant of a day or a week, or even a month, old. But suppose they were otherwise, what would it avail? The question is not, Can they reason? nor Can they talk? but Can they suffer? (*Introduction to the Principles of Morals and Legislation*, Chapter 17, footnote.)

Like the rights view, a utilitarian position is one which does not allow arbitrary or prejudicial attitudes to influence moral judgements. All like interests are counted, regardless of the skin colour, sex, or species of the interest holder. As Peter Singer has stated. 'If a being suffers, there can be no moral justification for refusing to take that suffering into consideration. No matter what the nature of the being, the principle of equality requires that its suffering be counted equally with the like suffering – in so far as rough comparisons can be made – of any other being.' (Singer, 1979, p. 50)

The utilitarian position works very well when the moral issue at hand involves making a decision that will cause pain or bring about pleasure. If an evil tyrant forces you to decide whether to slap your mother or have your cat's eye put out, a utilitarian would slap her mother and thus bring about the least amount of suffering, all else being equal. It should be pointed out that the principle of minimizing pain and maximizing pleasure does not apply only to physical suffering, but should also be looked to when psychological pain or pleasure is at stake, although, admittedly, that is harder to determine. But the utilitarian does run into problems when killing is involved. Let's return to Regan's lifeboat, only this time let's fill it with utilitarians and see what happens.

For a utilitarian, the lifeboat case becomes very complex. Because decisions must be based on a range of considerations, the example must be clarified before proceeding. Throwing any one of the passengers overboard may have effects on others who are not immediately present, such as their families and friends. Since a utilitarian must take into account the pain or suffering of everyone affected, not just those immediately present, we will have to assume that the survivors on the lifeboat lost all of their friends and family in the catastrophe which brought them to their current situation. This way, the only being affected by the act is the being who gets thrown overboard. We will also have to assume that whoever is thrown overboard will be painlessly killed by a lethal injection before being dumped in the ocean. No being's death will be longer, or more painful, than any other.

For a classical utilitarian, the answer is now fairly straightforward. The being who should be thrown overboard is that being who is the least happy now and is not likely to be particularly happy throughout his life. Since dogs are generally easily satisfied, this could mean that one of the humans should be thrown overboard. What matters to the utilitarian is not the species of those beings capable of contributing to the overall happiness of the moral universe, but the amount they contribute. In this situation, one is forced to reduce the total pleasure in the universe by removing one of the passengers in the lifeboat. In order to minimize the overall loss of happiness, the being who is the most likely to lead an unhappy life will be the one to go.

Most people, even those who consider themselves utilitarians, can't easily swallow this decision. Indeed, it is exactly this sort of analysis that has spawned such theories as that held by Regan. Singer, however, defends a more sophisticated version of utilitarianism, namely preference utilitarianism, which attempts to side-step this unsavoury conclusion. Singer argues that self-conscious, rational human beings are capable of having a specific preference for continued existence. Killing the humans on the lifeboat would clearly be in direct conflict with this preference. It is not clear that dogs have distinct preferences for continued existence, although they may have other preferences which would require continued existence in order to be satisfied. The conclusion that an 'enlightened' utilitarian might reach is similar to that reached by Regan, but the reasons are very different.

This agreement in practice is not uncommon. Those who agree with the rights argument as well as those who adhere to utilitarianism will not eat animals, but for different reasons. The former will be vegetarians, and perhaps vegans (those who avoid all animal products, including milk and eggs), because to use animals in such a way is not consistent with treating them as beings with inherent worth. To a person who holds the rights view, using an animal as a means to an end, in this case as food for the dinner table, is a violation of that being's right to be treated with respect. A utilitarian will abstain from eating animal products as long as the process that is used to raise them involves a net balance of suffering. If the animals live happy, stress-free, natural lives before they are painlessly killed, the utilitarian may not object to their use as food.

In the case of using animals in experimentation, the conclusions reached again differ more sharply in theory than in practice. According to Regan, 'the rights view is categorically abolitionist ... This is just as true when they [animals] are used in trivial, duplicative, unnecessary or unwise research as it is when they are used in studies that hold out real promise of human benefits ... The best we can do when it comes to using animals in science is – not to use them' (Regan, 1985, p. 24). Singer's position is very different. He would not advocate abolitionism in theory because 'in extreme circumstances, absolutist answers always break down ... if a single experiment could cure a major disease, that experiment would be justifiable. But in actual life the benefits are always much, much more remote, and more often than not they are nonexistent ... an experiment cannot be justifiable unless the experiment is so important that the use of a retarded human being would also be justifiable' (Singer, 1975, pp. 77–78).

Singer is not advocating that mentally retarded humans be used in experimentation, although some have accused him of holding this view. The point
being made is that it is wrong to decide to experiment on animals rather than on
humans with similar abilities to comprehend their situation if the readiness to
experiment is based only on the fact that the animal is a different species. This
bias in favour of one's own species has been called 'speciesism' and is considered
morally on par with sexism and racism.

As the animal liberation issue has become more popular, species-based discrimination has become synonymous with bigotry. This is a dangerous sim-
plification. Discrimination is not always unjust, and in fact, in some cases it may
be crucial. As Mary Midgley has pointed out, 'It is never true that, in order to
know how to treat a human being, you must first find out what race he belongs
to ... But with an animal, to know the species is absolutely essential' (Midgley,
1983, p. 98). The difference between an African and a cheetah is not the same as
the difference between an African and an Eskimo. We do animals a great disservice
if by including them in our sphere of moral concern we overlook their vast,
marvellous differences from us, some of which may be relevant in moral deliberations.

iv Sympathy

Regan and Singer argue that giving greater weight to the interests of members of
one's own species is indefensible. They suggest that animals and humans share
the same morally relevant characteristics which provide each with equal claims.
In a very simple world, this suggestion would not be problematic. But animals
are not just animals – they are Lassie the dog and the family's companion cat;
bald eagles and bunnies; snakes and skunks. Similarly, humans are not just
humans – they are friends and lovers, family and foe. Kinship or closeness is a
very important element in thinking about virtually every feature of our daily lives.
To deny the reality of the influence this factor has on our decision-making in
favour of some abstraction, like absolute equality, may be considered saintly, but
probably is not possible for most mortals faced with complex decisions. (Compare
Article 28, PERSONAL RELATIONSHIPS.)

This focus on abstraction is not unique in moral theorizing. Philosophers long
before Regan and Singer postulated that in order for a decision to be ethical it
must go beyond our own preferences or partiality. Ethics, it has been said,
must be universal, and universality can only be accomplished through abstract
reasoning. (See Article 40, UNIVERSAL PRESCRIPTIVISM.) If one values the life
of a being who can enjoy life, then one must value every life of like beings in the
same way. As Regan says, 'We know that many – literally, billions and billions –
of these animals are subjects-of-a-life in the sense explained and so have inherent
value if we do. And since, in order to arrive at the best theory of our duties to one
another, we must recognize our equal inherent value as individuals, reason – not
sentiment, not emotion – reason compels us to recognize the equal inherent value

of these animals and, with this, their equal right to be treated with respect' (Regan, 1985, pp. 23–24).

In the preface to *Animal Liberation*, Singer describes the justification of opposition to the Nazi experiments and animal experiments as 'an appeal to basic moral principles which we all accept, and the application of these principles to the victims of both kinds of experiments is demanded by reason, not emotion'. Obviously, reason has played a tremendous role in discussions of morality in general and particularly in discussions pertaining to the way moral principles apply to animals. If reason were the sole motivator of ethical behaviour, one might wonder why there are people who are familiar with the reasoning of Singer's work, for example, but who nonetheless continue to eat animals. While many have suggested that to act rationally entails acting morally, reason is only one element in decision-making. Emotion, though often dismissed, plays a crucial role as well. Feelings of outrage or revulsion, sympathy or compassion are important to the development of complete moral sensibilities. As Mary Midgley has said, 'Real scruples, and eventually moral principles, are developed out of this kind of raw material. They would not exist without it.' (Midgley, 1983, p. 43). (See also the discussions of the role of reason in morality in Article 14, KANTIAN ETHICS, and Article 35, REALISM.)

Recognizing that appeals to sympathy are avoided by other proponents of animal liberation, John Fisher suggests that the very project of including animals in the moral community may be undermined by neglecting the powerful role sympathy plays. He argues that sympathy is fundamental to moral theory because it helps to determine who the proper recipients of moral concern are. Fisher suggests that those beings with whom we can sympathize must be morally considered. Presumably, how we treat those beings would be a function of our ability to sympathize with them (Fisher, 1987.)

By arguing for the inclusion of animals in the moral sphere on the basis of reason, not emotion, philosophers are perpetuating an unnecessary dichotomy between the two. Certainly it is possible that a decision based on emotion alone may be morally indefensible, but it is also possible that a decision based on reason alone may be objectionable as well. One way to overcome the false dualism between reason and emotion is by moving out of the realm of abstraction and getting closer to the effects of our everyday actions. Much of the problem with the attitude many have towards animals stems from a removal from them. Our responsibility for our own actions has been mediated. Who are these animals who suffer and die so that I can eat pot roast? I do not deprive them of movement and comfort; I do not take their young from them; I do not have to look into their eyes as I cut their throats. Most people are shielded from the consequences of their actions. Factory-farms and laboratories are not places where many people go. The sympathy that people might naturally feel towards a being who is suffering, coupled with reasoned moral principles, would probably cause most to object to these institutions. While it is not possible for everyone directly to experience the effect of each and every one of their actions, that is no reason not to try. As feminist theorist Marti Kheel suggests, 'in our complex, modern society we may never be able to fully experience the impact of our moral decisions, we can, nonetheless, attempt as far as possible to experience emotionally the knowledge of this fact' (Kheel, 1985).

While there are different philosophical principles that may help in deciding how we ought to treat animals, one strand runs through all those that withstand critical scrutiny: we ought not to treat animals the way we, as a society, are treating them now. We are very rarely faced with lifeboat decisions; our moral choices are not usually ones that exist in extremes. It simply isn't the case that I will suffer great harm without a fur coat or a leg of lamb. The choice between our baby and our dog is one that virtually none of us will be forced to make. The hypothetical realm is one where we can clarify and refine our moral intuitions and principles, but our choices and the suffering of billions of animals are not hypothetical. However the lines are drawn, there are no defensible grounds for treating animals in any way other than as beings worthy of moral consideration.

References

Bentham, J.: *The Principles of Morals and Legislation* (1789); (New York: Hafner Press, 1948).

Davidson, D.: *Inquiries into Truth and Interpretation*, (Oxford: Oxford University Press, 1984).

Fisher, J.: 'Taking sympathy seriously', *Environmental Ethics*, 9, no. 3 (Fall 1987), 197–215.

Fox, M.: *The Case for Animal Experimentation* (Berkeley: University of California Press, 1986a).

——: Letter in *The Scientist* (15 December 1986b).

——: 'Animal experimentation: A philosopher's changing views', *Between the Species*, 3 (1987), 55–60.

Frey, R. G.: *Interests and Rights: The Case Against Animals* (Oxford: Clarendon Press, 1980).

——: 'Moral standing, the value of lives, and speciesism', *Between the Species*, 4, no. 3 (Summer 1988), 191–201.

Jamieson, D.: 'Two problems with Regan's theory of rights'; paper presented to Pacific Division, American Philosophical Association (Spring 1985).

Kheel, M.: 'The liberation of nature: a circular affair', *Environmental Ethics*, 7, no. 2 (Summer 1985), 135–49.

Midgley, M.: *Animals and Why They Matter* (Harmondsworth: Penguin Books, 1983).

Regan, T.: *The Case for Animal Rights* (Berkeley: University of California Press, 1983).

——: 'The case for animal rights', *In Defence of Animals*, ed. P. Singer (Oxford: Basil Blackwell, 1985).

Regan, T. and Singer, P., eds.: *Animal Rights and Human Obligations*; 2nd edn (Englewood Cliffs, NJ: Prentice-Hall, 1989).

Singer, P.: *Animal Liberation* (1975); 2nd edn (New York: New York Review/Random House, 1990).

——: *Practical Ethics* (Cambridge: Cambridge University Press, 1979).

Further reading

Frey, R. G.: *Rights, Killing and Suffering* (Oxford: Basil Blackwell, 1983).
Rollin, B.: *Animal Rights and Human Morality* (Buffalo: Prometheus Books, 1981).
Sapontzis, S. F.: *Morals, Reasons, and Animals* (Philadelphia: Temple University Press, 1987).
Singer, P.: 'Animals and the value of life', *Matters of Life and Death* (New York: Random House, 1980).

31

Business ethics

ROBERT C. SOLOMON

The public be damned. I'm working for my stockholders.

WILLIAM VANDERBILT

i Introduction

BUSINESS ethics occupies a peculiar position in the field of 'applied' ethics. Like its kin in such professions as medicine and law, it consists of an uneasy application of some very general ethical principles (of 'duty' or 'utility' for example) to rather specific and often unique situations and crises. But unlike them, business ethics is concerned with an area of human enterprise whose practitioners do not for the most part enjoy professional status and whose motives, to put it mildly, are often thought (and said) to be less than noble. 'Greed' (formerly 'avarice') is often cited as the sole engine of business life, and much of the history of business ethics, accordingly, is not very flattering to business. In one sense, one can trace that history back into medieval and ancient times, where, in addition to the attacks on business in philosophy and religion, such practical thinkers as Cicero gave careful attention to the question of fairness in ordinary business transactions. But for much of this history, too, the focus of attention was almost entirely on such particular transactions, surrounding the field with a strong sense of the *ad hoc*, an allegedly non-philosophical practice which was more often than not dismissed as 'casuistry'.

Accordingly, the subject of business ethics as currently practised is not much over a decade old. Only ten years ago, the subject was still an awkward amalgam of a routine review of ethical theories, a few general considerations about the fairness of capitalism, and a number of already-standard business cases – most of them disgraces, scandals and disasters displaying the corporate world at its worst and its most irresponsible. Business ethics was a topic without credentials in 'mainstream' philosophy, without conceptual subject matter of its own. It was too practical-minded even for 'applied ethics' and, in a philosophical world enamoured with unworldly ideas and merely 'possible' worlds, business ethics was far too concerned with the vulgar currency of everyday exchange – money.

But philosophy itself has tilted again toward the 'real world', and business ethics has found or made its place in the junction between the two. New applications and renewed sophistication in game theory and social choice theory have allowed the introduction of more formal analysis in business ethics, and, much more important, the interaction with and the submersion of business ethics

354

practitioners in the working world of corporate executives, labour unions and small business owners has consolidated the once awkwardly amalgamated elements of business ethics into a subject matter, attracted the interest and attention of business leaders and turned once 'academic' practitioners into active participants in the business world. Sometimes, one might add, they even get listened to.

ii   A brief history of business ethics

In a broad sense, business has been around at least since the ancient Sumerians who (according to Samuel Noah Kramer) carried out extensive trading and record-keeping nearly six thousand years ago. But business has not always been the central and respectable enterprise that it is in modern society, and the ethical view of business for most of history has been almost wholly negative. Aristotle, who deserves recognition as the first economist (two thousand years before Adam Smith) distinguished two different senses of what we call economics; one of them, *oikonomikos* or household trading, which he approved of and thought essential to the working of any even modestly complex society, and *chrematisike* which is trade for profit. Aristotle declared such activity wholly devoid of virtue and called those who engaged in such purely selfish practices 'parasites'. Aristotle's attack on the unsavoury and unproductive practice of 'usury' held force virtually until the seventeenth century. Only outsiders at the fringe of society, not respectable citizens, engaged in such practices. (Shakespeare's Shylock, in *The Merchant of Venice*, was an outsider and a usurer.) This, on a large historical canvas, is the history of business ethics – the wholesale attack on business and its practices. Jesus chased the money-changers from the temple, and Christian moralists from Paul to Thomas Aquinas and Martin Luther followed his example, roundly condemning most of what we today honour as 'the business world'.

But if business ethics as condemnation was led by philosophy and religion, so too was the dramatic turn-around towards business in early modern times. John Calvin and then the English Puritans taught the virtues of thrift and enterprise, and Adam Smith canonized the new faith in 1776 in his masterwork, *The Wealth of Nations*. Of course, the new attitude to business was not an overnight transformation and was built on traditions with a long history. The medieval guilds, for example, had established their own industry-specific codes of 'business ethics' long before business became the central institution of society, but the general acceptance of business and the recognition of economics as a central structure of society depended on a very new way of thinking about society that required not only a change in religious and philosophical sensibilities but, underlying them, a new sense of society and even of human nature. This transformation can be partly explained in terms of urbanization, larger more centralized societies, the privatization of family groups as consumers, rapidly advancing technology, the growth of industry and the accompanying development of social structures, needs and desires. With Adam Smith's classic work, *chrematisike* became the central institution and primary virtue of modern society. But the degraded popular ('greed is good') version of Smith's thesis was hardly conducive to the subject of business ethics ('isn't that a contradiction in terms?'), and moralizing about business retained its ancient and medieval bias against business. Businessmen like Mellon and Carnegie gave public lectures on the virtues of success and the *noblesse oblige* of the rich, but business ethics as such was for the most part developed by socialists, as a continued diatribe against the amorality of business thinking. It is only very recently that a more moral and more honourable way of viewing business has begun to dominate business talk, and with it has come the idea of studying the underlying values and ideals of business. We can readily understand how freedom of the market will always be a threat to traditional values and antagonistic to government control, but we no longer so glibly conclude that the market itself is without values or that governments better serve the public good than markets.

iii The myth of the profit motive

Business ethics is no longer concerned solely or primarily with the criticism of business and business practice. Profits are no longer condemned along with 'avarice' in moralizing sermons, and corporations are no longer envisioned as faceless, souless, amoral monoliths. The new concern is just how profit should be thought of in the larger context of productivity and social responsibility and how corporations as complex communities can best serve both their own employees and the surrounding society. Business ethics has evolved from a wholly critical attack on capitalism and 'the profit motive' to a more productive and constructive examination of the underlying rules and practices of business. But the old paradigm – what Richard DeGeorge has called 'the myth of amoral business' – persists, not only among the suspicious public and some socialist-minded philosophers but among many businesspeople themselves. The first task in business ethics, accordingly, is to clear the way through some highly incriminating myths and metaphors, which obscure rather than clarify the underlying ethos that makes business possible.

Every discipline has its own self-glorifying vocabulary. Politicians bask in the concepts of 'public service' while they pursue personal power, lawyers defend our 'rights' on the basis of handsome fees – and professors describe what they do in the noble language of 'truth and knowledge' while they spend most of their time and energy in campus politics. But in the case of business the self-glorifying language is often especially unflattering. For example, executives still talk about what they do in terms of 'the profit motive', not realizing that the phrase was invented by the last century's socialists as an *attack* on business and its narrow-minded pursuit of money to the exclusion of all other considerations and obligations. To be sure, a business does aim to make a profit, but it does so only by supplying quality goods and services, by providing jobs and by 'fitting in' to the community. To single out profits rather than productivity or public service as the central aim of business activity is just asking for trouble. Profits are not as such the end or goal of business activity: profits get distributed and reinvested. Profits are a means to building the business and rewarding employees, executives and investors. For some people, profits may be a means of 'keeping score', but even in those cases, it is the status and satisfaction of 'winning' that is the goal, not profits as such.

A more sophisticated but not dissimilar executive self-image states that the managers of a business are bound above all by one and only one obligation, to maximize the profits for their stockholders. We need not inquire whether this is the actual motive behind most upper management decisions in order to point out that, while managers do recognize that their own business roles are defined primarily by obligations rather than the 'profit motive', that unflattering image has simply been transferred to the stockholders (i.e. the owners). Is it true that investors/owners care *only* about the maximization of their profits? Is it the stockholder, finally, who is the incarnation of that inhuman *homo economicus* who is utterly devoid of civic responsibility and pride, who has no concern for the virtues of the company he or she (or it?) owns, apart from those liabilities that might render one vulnerable to expensive law suits? And if some four-month 'in and out' investors do indeed care only about increasing their investments by 30 per cent or so, why are we so certain that the managers of the firm have *any* obligation to them other than not to intentionally fritter away or waste their money? The pursuit of profits is not the ultimate, much less the only goal of business. It is rather one of many goals and then by way of a means and not an end-in-itself.

This is how we misunderstand business: we adopt a too narrow vision of what business is, e.g. the pursuit of profits, and then derive unethical or amoral conclusions. It is this inexcusably limited focus on the 'rights of the stockholders', for example, that has been used to defend some of the very destructive and certainly unproductive 'hostile takeovers' of major corporations in the last few years. To say this is not to deny the rights of stockholders to a fair return, of course, nor is it to deny the 'fiduciary responsibilities' of the managers of a company. It is only to say that these rights and responsibilities make sense only in a larger social context and that the very idea of 'the profit motive' as an end in itself – as opposed to profits as a means of encouraging and rewarding hard work and investment, building a better business and serving society better – is a serious obstacle to understanding the rich tapestry of motives and activities that make up the business world.

iv Other business myths and metaphors

Among the most damaging myths and metaphors in business talk are those macho 'Darwinian' concepts of 'survival of the fittest' and 'it's a jungle out there'. (For the origin of these concepts, see Article 44, THE SIGNIFICANCE OF EVOLUTION.) The underlying idea, of course, is that life in business is competitive, and it isn't always fair. But that obvious pair of points is very different from the 'dog-eat-dog', 'every [man] for [him]self' imagery that is routine in the business world. It is true that business is and must be competitive, but it is not true that it is cut-throat or cannibalistic or that 'one does whatever it takes to survive'. However competitive a particularly industry may be, it always rests on a foundation of shared interests and mutually agreed-upon rules of conduct, and the competition takes place not in a jungle but in a community which it presumably both serves and depends upon. Business life is first of all fundamentally *co-operative*. It is only within the bounds of mutually shared concerns that competition is possible. And quite the contrary of the 'every animal for itself' jungle metaphor, business almost always involves large co-operative and mutually trusting groups, not only corporations themselves but networks of suppliers, service people, customers and investors. Competition is essential to capitalism, but to misunderstand this as 'unbridled' competition is to undermine ethics and misunderstand the nature of competition too. (So, too, we should look with suspicion upon the familiar 'war' metaphor that is popular in so many boardrooms and the current 'game' metaphor and the emphasis of 'winning' that tends to turn the serious business of 'making a living' into something of a self-enclosed sport.)

The most persistent metaphor, which seems to endure no matter how much evidence is amassed against it, is atomistic individualism. the idea that business life consists wholly of mutually agreed-upon transactions between individual citizens (avoiding government interference) can be traced back to Adam Smith and the philosophy which dominated eighteenth-century Britain. But most of business life today consists of roles and responsibilities in co-operative enterprises, whether they be small family businesses or gigantic multi-national corporations. Government and business are as often partners as opponents (however frustrating the labyrinth of 'regulation' may sometimes seem), whether by way of subsidies, tariffs and tax breaks or as an intimate co-operative enterprise ('Japan, Inc.' and such grand projects as the National Aeronautics and Space Administration space shuttle.) But atomistic individualism is not only inaccurate in the face of the corporate complexity of today's business world; it is naïve in its supposition that no institutional rules and practices underlie even the simplest promise, contract or exchange. Business is a social practice, not an activity of isolated individuals. It is possible only because it takes place in a culture with an established set of procedures and expectations, and these are not (except in the details) open to individual tinkering.

Accordingly, it is a sign of considerable progress that one of the dominant models of today's corporate thinking is the idea of a 'corporate culture'. As with any analogy, there are, of course, disanalogies, but it is important to appreciate the virtue of this metaphor. It is social, and rejects atomistic individualism. It recognizes the place of people in the organization as the fundamental structure of business life. It openly embraces the idea of ethics. It recognizes that shared values hold a culture together. There is still room for that individualistic maverick, the 'entrepreneur', but he or she too is possible only insofar as there is a role (an important one) for eccentricity and innovation. But the problem with the 'culture' metaphor, too, is that it tends to be too self-enclosed. A corporation is not like an isolated tribe in the Trobriand Islands. A corporate culture is an inseparable part of a larger culture, at most a sub-culture (or a sub-sub-culture), a specialized organelle in an organ in an organism. Indeed, it is the tendency to see business as an isolated and insulated endeavour, with values different from the values of the surrounding society, that characterizes all of these myths and metaphors. Breaking down this sense of isolation is the first task of business ethics.

v Micro-, macro- and molar ethics

We might well distinguish between three (or more) levels of business and business ethics, from the *micro* – the rules for fair exchange between two individuals, to the *macro* – the institutional or cultural rules of commerce for an entire society ('the business world'). We should also carve out an area which we can call the *molar* level of business ethics, concerning the basic unit of commerce today – the corporation. Micro-ethics in business, of course, is very much part and parcel of much of traditional ethics – the nature of promises and other obligations, the intentions, consequences and other implications of an individual's actions, the grounding and nature of various individual rights. What is peculiar to business micro-ethics is the idea of a fair exchange and, along with it, the notion of a fair wage, fair treatment, what counts as a 'bargain' and what instead is a 'steal'. Aristotle's notion of 'commutative' justice is particularly at home here, and even the ancients used to worry, from time to time, whether, for example, the seller of a house was obliged to tell a potential buyer that the roof had had its day and might start to leak at the first heavy rains.

Macro-ethics, in turn, becomes part and parcel of those large questions about justice, legitimacy and the nature of society that constitute social and political philosophy. What is the purpose of the 'free market' – or is it in some sense a good of its own, with its own *telos*? Are private property rights primary, in some sense preceding social convention (as John Locke and more recently Robert Nozick have argued), or is the market too to be conceived as a complex social practice in which rights are but one ingredient? Is the free market system 'fair'? Is it the most efficient way to distribute goods and services throughout society? Does it pay enough attention to cases of desperate need (where a 'fair exchange' is not part of the question)? Does it pay enough attention to merit, where it is by no means guaranteed that virtue will be in sufficient demand so as to be rewarded? What are the legitimate (and illegitimate) roles of government in business life, and what is the role of government regulation? Macro-ethics, in other words, is an attempt to take in the 'big picture', to understand the nature of the business world and its functions as such.

The definitive 'molar' unit of modern business, however, is the corporation, and the central questions of business ethics tend to be unabashedly aimed at the directors and employees of those few thousand or so companies that rule so much of commercial life around the world. In particular, they are questions that concern the role of the corporation in society and the role of the individual in the corporation. Not surprisingly, many of the most challenging issues are found in the interstices of the three levels of ethical discourse, for instance, the question of

359

corporate social responsibility – the role of the corporation in the larger society, and questions of job-defined responsibilities – the role of the individual in the corporation.

vi   The corporation in society: the idea of social responsibility

The central concept of much of recent business ethics is the idea of social responsibility. It is also a concept that has irritated many traditional free market enthusiasts and prompted a number of bad or misleading arguments. Perhaps the most famous of these is the diatribe by Nobel-winning economist Milton Friedman in *The New York Times* (13 September 1970) entitled 'The social responsibility of business is to increase its profits'. In this article, he called businessmen who defended the idea of corporate social responsibility 'unwitting puppets of the intellectual forces that have been undermining the basis of a free society' and accused them of 'preaching pure and unadulterated socialism'. Friedman's argument is, in essence, that managers of a corporation are the employees of the stockholders and, as such, have a 'fiduciary responsibility' to maximize their profits. Giving money to charity or other social causes (except as public relations aimed at increasing business) and getting involved in community projects (which do not increase the company's business) is akin to stealing from the stockholders. Furthermore, there is no reason to suppose that a corporation or its officers have any special skill or knowledge in the realm of public policy, and so they are over-extending their competence as well as violating their obligations when they get involved in community activities (that is, as managers of the company, not as individual citizens acting on their own).

Some of the fallacies involved in such reasoning are consequent to the narrow 'profit-minded' view of business and the extremely unflattering and unrealistic one-dimensional portrait of the stockholder that we mentioned earlier; others ('pure unadulterated socialism' and 'stealing') are rather excesses of rhetoric. The 'competence' argument (also defended by Peter Drucker in his influential book on *Management*) makes sense only insofar as corporations undertake social engineering projects that are indeed beyond their abilities; but does it require special skills or advanced knowledge to be concerned about discriminatory hiring or promotion practices within your own company or the devastating effects of your waste products on the surrounding countryside? The overall rejoinder to Friedmanesque arguments of this sort that has recently become popular in business ethics can be summarized in a modest pun: instead of the 'stockholder' the beneficiaries of corporate social responsibilities are the *stakeholders*, of whom the stockholders are but a single sub-class. The stakeholders in a company are all of those who are affected and have legitimate expectations and rights regarding the actions of the company, and these include the employees, the consumers and the suppliers as well as the surrounding community and the society at large. The virtue of this concept is that it greatly expands the focus of corporate concern, without losing sight of the particular virtues and capacities of the corporation itself. Social responsibility, so considered, is not an additional burden on the corporation but part and parcel of its essential concerns, to serve the needs and be fair to not only its investors/owners but those who work for, buy from, sell to, live near or are otherwise affected by the activities that are demanded and rewarded by the free market system.

vii   Obligations to stakeholders: consumers and community

The managers of corporations have obligations to their shareholders, but they have obligations to other stakeholders as well. In particular, they have obligations to consumers and the surrounding community as well as to their own employees (see section (viii)). The purpose of the corporation, after all, is to serve the public, both by way of providing desired and desirable products and services and by not harming the community and its citizens. For example, a corporation is hardly serving its public purpose if it is polluting the air or the water supply, if it is snarling traffic or hogging communal resources, if it is (even indirectly) promoting racism or prejudice, if it is destroying the natural beauty of the environment or threatening the financial or social well-being of the local citizens. To consumers, the corporation has the obligation to provide quality products and services. It has the obligation to make sure that these are safe, through research and through appropriate instructions and, where appropriate, warnings against possible misuse. Manufacturers are and should be liable for dangerous effects and pre-dictable abuse of their products, e.g. the likelihood of a young child swallowing a small, readily detachable piece of a toy made specially for that age group, and it is now suggested by some consumer advocate groups that such liability should not be excessively qualified by the excuse that 'these were mature adults and knew or should have known the risks of what they were doing'. This last demand, however, points to a number of currently problematic concerns, notably, the general presumption of maturity, intelligence and responsibility on the part of the consumer and the question of reasonable limits of liability on the part of the producer. (Special considerations obviously apply to children.) To what extent should the manufacturer take precautions against clearly idiosyncratic or even idiotic uses of their products'? What restrictions should there be on manufacturers who sell and distribute provably dangerous products, e.g. cigarettes and firearms – even if there is considerable consumer demand for such items – and should the producer be liable for what is clearly a foreseeable risk on the part of the consumer? Indeed, it is increasingly being asked whether and to what extent we should reinstate that now ancient caveat, 'Buyer beware', to counteract the runaway trend toward consumer irresponsibility and unqualified corporate liability.

Consumer intelligence and responsibility are also at issue in the much-debated topic of advertising, against which some of the most serious criticisms of current business practices have been directed. The classic defence of the free market system is that it supplies and satisfies existing demands. But if manufacturers actually *create* the demand for the products they produce, then this classic defence is clearly undermined. Indeed, it has even been charged that advertising is itself coercive in that it interferes with the free choice of the consumer, who is no longer in a position to decide how best to satisfy his or her needs but has instead been subjected to a barrage of influences which may well be quite irrelevant or even opposed to those needs. And even where the desirability of the product is not in question, there are very real questions about the advertising of particular brand names and the artificial creation of 'product differentiation'. And then there are those familiar questions of taste – on the borderline (and sometimes over) between ethics and aesthetics. There is the use of sex – often seductive and sometimes quite undisguised – to enhance the appeal of products from chewing gum to automobiles; there are the implied but obviously false promises of social success and acceptability if only one buys this soap or toothpaste; and there are the offensive portrayals of women and minorities and often of human nature as such, just in order to sell products that most of us could perfectly well do without. But is such superfluous consumption and the taste (or lack of it) that sells it an ethical issue? Is anyone actually expected to believe that his or her life will change with an added hint of mint or a waxless, yellow-free kitchen floor?

Much more serious, of course, is outright lying in advertising. But what counts as a 'lie' is by no means straightforward in this world of seduction, kitsch and hyperbole. No-one, perhaps, will actually believe that a certain toothpaste or pair of designer jeans will guarantee your success with the lover of your dreams (though millions are willing to take the chance, just in case), but when a product has effects that may well be fatal, the accuracy of advertising is put under much closer scrutiny. When a medical product is advertised on the basis of misleading, incomplete or simply untrue technical information, when an over-the-counter 'cold remedy' is sold with the promise but without any hard evidence that it can relieve symptoms and prevent complications, when known and dangerous side-effects are hidden behind a generic 'with this as with all medicines, check with your doctor', then seemingly simple 'truth in advertising' becomes a moral imperative and ethical principles (if not the law) have been violated.

It has often been argued that in an ideally functioning free market the only advertising that should be either necessary or permitted is pure information regarding the use and qualities of the product. But in certain circumstances, the average consumer may neither have nor be able to understand the relevant information concerning the product in question. In a great many cases, however, consumers take too little responsibility for their own decisions, and one cannot properly blame advertising for their irresponsibility or irrationality. Corporations have responsibilities to their customers, but consumers have responsibilities too. As so often, business ethics is not a question of corporate responsibility alone but an interlocking set of mutual responsibilities.

viii   The individual in the corporation: responsibilities and expectations

Perhaps the most abused stakeholder in the pattern of corporate responsibilities is the company employee. In traditional free market theory, the employee's labour is itself just one more commodity, subject to the laws of supply and demand. But whereas one can sell at 'firesale' prices or simply dispose of pins or parts of machinery that are no longer in demand, the employee is a human being, with very real needs and rights quite apart from his or her role in production or in the market. Cramped uncomfortable working space or long, gruelling hours for employees may reduce overhead or increase productivity, and paying sub-subsistence wages to employees who for one reason or another cannot, dare not or do not know how to complain may increase profits, but such conditions and practices are now recognized by all but the most unreconstructed 'Darwinian' to be highly unethical and legally inexcusable. And yet, the 'commodity' model of labour still holds powerful sway over much business thinking, concerning managers and executives as well as workers both skilled and unskilled. It is for this reason that much of recent business ethics has focused on such notions as employees' rights and, from a very different angle, it is for this reason too that the old notion of 'company loyalty' had come back into focus. After all, if a company treats its employees as nothing but disposable parts, no-one should be surprised if the employees start treating the company as nothing but a transient source of wages and benefits.

The other side of this disturbing picture, however, is the equally renewed emphasis on the notion of employee roles and responsibilities, one of which is loyalty to the company. It cannot be over-emphasized that 'loyalty' here is a two-way concern; the employee may by virtue of his or her employment have special obligations to the company but the company has its obligations to the employee in turn. But there is a danger in stressing such concepts as 'loyalty' without being very clear that loyalty is tied not just to employment in general but to one's particular role and responsibilities as well. A role, according to R. S. Downie, is 'a cluster of rights and duties with some sort of social function' – in this case, a function in the corporation. (*Roles and Values*, p. 128.) Certain aspects of one's role and responsibilities may be specified in an employment contract and in the law, but many of them – for example, the local customs, patterns of deference and other aspects of what we earlier called 'the corporate culture' – may become evident only with time on the job and continued contact with other employees. Moreover, it is not just a matter of 'doing one's job' but, as a matter of ethics as well as economics, doing one's job as well as possible. Norman Bowie says in this regard, I think rightly, 'A job is never just a job'. It also has a moral dimension: pride in one's product, co-operation with one's colleagues and concern for the well-being of the company. But, of course, such role-defined obligations have their limits (however conveniently some managers tend to deny this). Business is not an end in itself but is embedded in and supported by a society that has other, overriding concerns, norms and expectations.

We sometimes hear employees (and even high level executives) complain that their 'corporate values conflict with their personal values'. What this usually means, I suggest, is that certain demands made by their companies are unethical or immoral. What most people call their 'personal values' are in fact the deepest and broadest values of their culture. And it is in this context that we should understand that now-familiar tragic figure of contemporary corporate life – the 'whistle-blower'. The whistle-blower is not just some eccentric who cannot 'fit'

363

into the organization he or she threatens with disclosure. The whistle-blower recognizes that he or she cannot tolerate the violation of morality or the public trust and feels obliged actually to do something about it. The biographies of most whistle-blowers do not make happy reading, but their very existence and occasional success is ample testimony to the interlocking obligations of the corporation, the individual and society. Indeed, perhaps the most singularly important result of the emergence of business ethics in the public forum has been to highlight such individuals and give renewed respectability to what their employers wrongly perceive as nothing but a breach of loyalty. But when the demands of doing business conflict with the morality or well-being of society, it is business that has to yield, and this, perhaps, is the ultimate point of business ethics.

References

Aristotle: *Politics*, Loeb Classical Library (Cambridge, Mass.: Harvard University Press), Book I, chapters 8–11.

Bowie, N.: *Business Ethics* (Englewood Cliffs, NJ.: Prentice-Hall, 1982).

Calvin, J.: *Institutes of the Christian Religion* (Philadelphia: Library of Christian Classics, 1954).

DeGeorge, R.: *Business Ethics* (New York: Macmillan, 1982).

——: *Ethics, Free Enterprise and Public Policy* (New York: Oxford University Press, 1978).

Downie, R. S.: *Roles and Values: An Introduction to Social Ethics* (London: Methuen, 1971).

Drucker, P.: *Management* (London: Pan, 1979).

——: 'Ethical chic', *Forbes*, 14 September 1981, pp. 160–173.

Friedman, M.: 'The social responsibility of business is to increase its profits', *The New York Times* (13 September 1970).

Kramer, S. N.: *History Begins at Sumer* (New York: Doubleday, 1959).

Locke, J.: *Second Treatise of Government* (1690); ed. P. Laslett (Cambridge: Cambridge University Press, 1988).

Nozick, R.: *Anarchy, State and Utopia* (New York: Basic Books, 1974).

Solomon, R. (with Hanson, K.): *Above the Bottom Line* (San Diego: Harcourt Brace Jovanovich, 1983).

Smith, A.: *The Wealth of Nations* (1776); 6th edn (London: Methuen, 1950).

Further reading

Beauchamp, T. and Bowie, N., eds.: *Ethical Theory and Business* (Englewood Cliffs, NJ: Prentice-Hall, 1979).

Ciulla, J.: 'Casuistry and the case for business ethics', *Business and the Humanities* (1989 Ruffin Lectures), ed. E. Freeman (New York: Oxford University Press, 1990).

Freeman, R. E. and Gilbert, D.: *Corporate Strategy and the Search for Ethics* (Englewood Cliffs, NJ.: Prentice-Hall, 1988).

French, P.: *Collective and Corporate Responsibility* (New York: Columbia University Press, 1984).

Goodpaster, K. and Mathews, J.: 'Can a corporation have a conscience?' *Harvard Business Review*, 60, No. 1, 132–41.

Pastin, M.: *The Hard Problems of Management* (San Francisco: Jossey-Bass, 1986).

Solomon, R. (with Hanson, K.): *It's Good Business* (New York: Atheneum, 1985; Harper and Row, 1987).

Velasquez, M.: *Business Ethics* (Englewood Cliffs, NJ.: Prentice-Hall, 1982).

32

Crime and punishment

C. L. TEN

THE criminal law prohibits certain forms of conduct such as murder, assault, rape and burglary. Offenders are liable to be punished, often with imprisonment. What justifies the punishment? Punishment is a deprivation, taking away from offenders what they value – their freedom, or some of their money when they are fined. We are normally not justified in depriving people of these things. Even if we are justified in punishing convicted offenders, there are limits to the extent of the punishment. If a petty thief were sentenced to ten years' imprisonment, this would be considered excessive. On the other hand, if a cold-blooded murderer were released after only one week in jail, this would be condemned as excessively lenient punishment. But how do we determine the appropriate amount of punishment for various offenders?

Theories of punishment seek to answer these and related questions. The aim of these theories is not to explain the prevalence of certain kinds of crime in terms of social conditions such as poverty. They do not tell us why crimes are committed. They are normative theories, telling us how criminals ought to be treated. They state the conditions under which punishment is justified, and provide the basis for assessing the correct punishment.

There are two main types of theories of punishment. The utilitarian theory justifies punishment solely in terms of its good consequences. Punishment is not considered as good in itself. On the contrary, since punishment deprives offenders of something they value, it is, taken on its own in isolation from its consequences, bad. The utilitarian regards every kind of suffering as bad in itself, and to be justified only if it prevents even greater suffering, or if it brings about greater good. So if by punishing offenders you prevent them from repeating their crimes, or you deter potential offenders from committing similar crimes, then the punishment produces desirable consequences which outweigh the harm to the offender. The chief function of punishment is to reduce crime.

The second type of theory is the retributive theory. There are many different versions of this theory, but the central contention is that punishment is justified because the offender has voluntarily committed a wrong act. Wrongdoers deserve to suffer for what they have done, whether or not the suffering produces any good consequences. Unlike utilitarians, retributivists do not regard the suffering through punishment of wrongdoers as bad in itself. Whereas the suffering of the innocent is bad, the deserved suffering of the guilty is just.

Various objections have been raised against both theories. The main problem for the utilitarian is to explain why punishment should be confined to the guilty and not be extended to the innocent under appropriate circumstances. On the other hand, retributivists have difficulty in explaining why the guilty should be punished at all if punishment fails to produce any good consequences.

In most legal systems only those who have broken the criminal law are punishable. But utilitarians are committed to punishing the innocent if by so doing the best consequences are produced. For example, suppose that a particularly horrific crime has been committed by a member of one racial or religious group against a member of a different group, and unless an innocent member of the first group is framed for the crime, the people in the second group will take the law into their own hands and attack other innocent members of the first group. Swift punishment is needed to restore the harmonious relationship between the two groups, but the guilty person cannot be found, whereas it is quite easy to fabricate evidence against an innocent person.

Utilitarians would respond to this objection by pointing out that in the long run the bad consequences of framing and punishing an innocent person will outweigh whatever good consequences are produced in the short run. The truth will out, and confidence in the administration of justice will be destroyed. Innocent people will be generally apprehensive that they too will, on future occasions, be sacrificed for the social good.

However, this utilitarian calculation of the undesirable consequences of punishing the innocent, even if correct, does not capture the full force of the objection to such punishment. We do not punish the innocent for the crimes committed by others, because we think it unfair or unjust to use them as means for the benefit of society. This would be the major reason why, for example, we do not punish families of criminals even if we are convinced that such punishment would be most effective in reducing the rates of serious crimes.

It also seems unfair to punish offenders who could not reasonably have avoided committing acts prohibited by the criminal law. Thus offenders who cause harm accidentally, under duress, or because they were suffering from some serious mental illness, should be excused from punishment. The utilitarian would try to justify the recognition of excuses on the grounds that the punishment of these offenders would be quite unnecessary in inducing compliance with the law. For example, the fear of punishment could not have prevented a person from accidentally breaking the law in the way that one who deliberately flouted the law could have been stopped by the likelihood of being punished. My accidental acts are not the product of my conscious choices, and I have no control over them.

The utilitarian justification of legal excuses is not wholly satisfactory. The recognition of excuses makes it possible for those who voluntarily break the law to fake excuses. The costs (in terms of increased crime) of accepting excuses could be significant, and it might be quite unclear whether these costs are outweighed by the benefits.

Finally, the utilitarian account of punishment permits punishment which is disproportionate to the gravity of the offences. Utilitarians would not of course inflict a form of punishment that causes worse consequences than the consequences of not punishing the crime, but this restriction on the amount of punishment to be imposed does not rule out the infliction of exemplary punishment to deter many potential offenders from committing relatively minor crimes. The harm caused by each offence is small, but the total harm of many offences is quite great, and might be greater than the suffering inflicted on one offender. The punishment is disproportionate to the actual harm done by the particular offender, even though it is proportionate to the total harm that can be prevented by deterring numerous offenders. But since the offender is only responsible for what he himself has done, and not for acts committed by others, there is again unfairness in imposing an exemplary punishment.

The retributive theory, on the other hand, restricts punishment to those who voluntarily broke the law, for only they are guilty of moral wrongdoing. The innocent may not be punished. Even those who broke the law with some relevant excuse are not to be blamed for what they did. I am not morally responsible for acts committed accidentally, and I do not deserve to be punished for them. Again, since the retributivist justifies punishment on the basis of a person's past wrongdoing, the degree of punishment should vary with the extent of the wrongdoing. A person who deliberately kills someone is obviously guilty of a far more seriously wrong act than one who simply steals a shirt, and so the murderer should be punished severely whereas the petty thief should not. In all these respects the retributive theory seems to be superior to the utilitarian theory. However, if we accept the retributive theory the case for punishing the guilty becomes unclear, because the purpose of punishment is not to reduce crime.

Suppose we accept the claim that wrongdoers deserve to suffer for their past acts. This in itself does not justify the imposition of punishment by the state in order to make them suffer. Why is it the function of the state to see that wrongdoers are given their deserts? Of course the state has the function of protecting its citizens and punishment, if it deters crime, can be an instrument for such protection. But the retributive theory does not rely on the effects of punishment to justify it, and hence it cannot appeal to this protective function of the state to vindicate its interest in making wrongdoers suffer. Again, some wrongdoers already suffer either as a result of their crime or independently of it. A burglar breaks her leg in the course of committing her crime; an incompetent armed robber shoots his foot; an assailant suffers from an illness unrelated to the crime. None of them suffers through punishment. Should the state make them suffer more by inflicting punishment?

In an attempt to get round these difficulties, some retributivists have moved away from the bald assertion that wrongdoers deserve to suffer. They try to justify punishment by claiming that criminals have taken an unfair advantage of law-abiding citizens, thereby upsetting the just balance of benefits and burdens in social life. Punishment, by taking away the unfair benefits of criminals, restores the correct balance. The criminal law prohibits certain forms of conduct and confers benefits on all who live in a society by providing an area of freedom for them to carry out their plans secure from interference by others. But these benefits can only be obtained if people accept the burdens of self-restraint by refraining from engaging in forbidden acts. Law-abiding citizens accept the burdens, but criminals accept only the benefits. For example, assailants enjoy the protection of the criminal law just as much as law-abiding citizens, but they fail to exercise the self-restraint which law-abiding citizens show in obeying the law.

The theory locates the wrongness of the criminal's act in the taking of an unfair advantage of law-abiding citizens. But this is often misleading. The wrong done by the murderer is mainly to his or her victim, and not to third parties. We punish murder not just to remove the unfair advantage that the murderer has taken of law-abiding citizens, but primarily to prevent more people from being killed. Moreover, the claim that law-abiding citizens have accepted the burden of self-restraint, which criminals renounce, presupposes that law-abiding citizens have a desire to break the law. But many law-abiding citizens have no desire to kill, assault, or steal. So in many cases the law does not impose any burden of self-restraint on them. It is doubtful that the benefits and burdens are equally distributed. The social circumstances of some people make them more likely to be victims of crime. Again, the poor and deprived have to exercise greater restraint in not stealing than the rich and privileged.

The retributive theory allows criminals to be punished without reference to the social consequences of punishment. But suppose that, for a variety of reasons, punishment significantly increases the crime rate rather than reduces it. Mentally unstable persons might be attracted by the prospect of punishment. Punishment might embitter and alienate criminals from society and increase their criminal activities. If punishment had these and other bad effects, utilitarians would renounce punishment in favour of some other more effective approach for dealing with offenders. But retributivists are still committed to punishing criminals. The effect of retributive punishment in such a situation is that there will be an increase in the number of innocent victims of crime. For whose benefit is punishment to be instituted? Surely not for the benefit of law-abiding citizens who run an increased risk of being victims of crime. Why should innocent people suffer for the sake of dispensing retributive justice?

Attempts have been made to remedy the defects of utilitarian and retributive theories by putting forward mixed theories which combine elements from both. One such mixed theory maintains that the justifying aim of punishment is the utilitarian goal of preventing or reducing crime, but insists that the pursuit of this aim must be constrained by the requirement that only those who have voluntarily broken the law may be punished, and that their punishment should be pro-portionate to the gravity of their offences (Hart, 1968). These restrictions on who may be punished and on the extent of the punishment are dictated by requirements of fairness to individuals which insist that they should not be used for the benefit of society unless they had the capacity and fair opportunity to conform to the law. On the other hand if we punish those who voluntarily breached the law in order to prevent them from repeating their offences, or to deter potential offenders, we are not using them unfairly. The failure to punish in these cases would result in there being additional innocent victims of crime. These victims could not reason-ably have avoided being harmed by criminal acts in the way that those who

369

voluntarily broke the law could have refrained from criminal acts and therefore avoided the resultant punishment.

Theories of punishment have a significant role to play in the ongoing debate on capital punishment, especially for murder. Some retributivists appeal to the *lex talionis*, the law of retaliation, to determine the appropriate amount of punishment. This principle specifies that the punishment should inflict on offenders what they have done to their victims: 'an eye for an eye, a tooth for a tooth', and 'a life for a life'. Capital punishment is therefore the only appropriate punishment for murder. But the *lex talionis* is deeply flawed. It focuses on the harm done by offenders without regard to their mental states. A life may be taken intentionally or accidentally; a person may be killed for personal gain or in order to relieve him or her of the agony of a terminal illness. Even if we restrict the scope of the *lex talionis* to cases in which the wrongdoing is fully intentional, there is still the problem about the level at which the punishment should imitate the crime. Should murderers be killed in exactly the manner that they killed their victims? In any case it is impossible to apply the *lex talionis* to many offenders: the penniless thief, the toothless assailant who knocks out his victim's teeth, the tax evader, etc.

If, conscious of the defects of the *lex talionis*, retributivists merely insist that the punishment should be proportionate to the moral gravity of the offence, then this requirement can be satisfied so long as the murderer is punished more severely than less serious offenders. There is no need for capital punishment.

From the utilitarian point of view, capital punishment can only be justified if it produces better consequences than less severe forms of punishment. This condition would be satisfied if capital punishment is a superior deterrent to alternative forms of punishment such as long periods of imprisonment. So utilitarians will try to settle the issue on the basis of the evidence about the effects of capital punishment. The statistical evidence is based on comparisons of murder rates in countries where there is capital punishment with those in socially similar countries where there is no capital punishment, and on comparisons of the murder rates in one and the same country at different times when it had capital punishment and when it later abolished it, or when it restored capital punishment after a period of abolition. The evidence does not show that capital punishment is a superior deterrent.

However, the utilitarian approach is rejected by those who wish to place greater value on the lives of the innocent victims of murder than on the lives of convicted murderers. It is suggested that the evidence does not conclusively rule out the superior deterrence of capital punishment, and in the presence of such uncertainty, it is better to have capital punishment. If there is capital punishment, and it turns out that capital punishment is not a superior deterrent, then convicted murderers have been unnecessarily executed. If, on the other hand, we abolish capital punishment, and it turns out that it is a superior deterrent, then there would be additional innocent victims of murder. But this argument is unacceptable because where there is capital punishment, it is certain that convicted murderers will die, but in the absence of capital punishment and in the light of the available evidence there is only a remote probability that there would be more innocent victims of murder (Conway, 1974). In any case, there is a risk of a few innocent people being wrongly convicted of murder and executed if there is capital punishment. This has to put on the scales against capital punishment.

In recent years attempts have been made to replace punishment by alternative methods of crime control. Insofar as these attempts reflect dissatisfaction with particular forms of punishment they are to be welcomed. The indiscriminate use of imprisonment has resulted in overcrowded jails. There is a need to search for new and more imaginative forms of punishment for some offences. But so far we are referring to changes within the institution of punishment itself. More radical critics wish to replace the whole institution of punishment by some system of social hygiene which, it is claimed, is more effective in reducing socially harmful acts. To these critics there is something distinctly odd in, for example, punishing severely those who intentionally killed, but in exempting from punishment those who killed accidentally or with some other excuse. More social harm is caused by non-voluntary killings, for example in traffic accidents, than by deliberate murders. If the function of the criminal law is to prevent social harm rather than to punish moral wickedness, it should ignore the mental state of offenders, and make all offenders subject to possible treatment with a view to preventing them from repeating their offences. It is sufficient for criminal conviction that a person has committed an act forbidden by the law. It is not necessary that those who are convicted should be at fault for what they have done. After conviction offenders come up for sentencing. At this later stage some account may be taken of the offender's state of mind at the time of the crime, not with a view to determining the degree of his or her fault, but as a guide to discovering the appropriate form of treatment. The treatment is aimed at preventing a recurrence of the offence (Wootton, 1981).

But the case for a system of social hygiene is not convincing. The criminal law is not morally justified in adopting any means solely because it will most effectively achieve its aim of preventing or reducing harmful conduct. For example, it might be possible to reduce crime significantly by widespread telephone tapping and by monitoring people's conduct through massive invasions of their privacy. But the cost is unacceptably high. So too it would be unjust to convict people and subject them to compulsory treatment for non-voluntary conduct that they could not reasonably have avoided. Individuals will lose control over their lives if they may be interfered with by the law for conduct which does not reflect their free choices. I do not know when I will accidentally cause harm to others, whereas my deliberate acts are the results of choices I have made. Again, at the sentencing stage, there is a danger that offenders who are treated as social nuisances, and whose treatment need not be proportionate to their degree of moral culpability, will be detained for indeterminate periods of treatment without adequate safeguards.

Winston Churchill said that democracy is the worst system of government, except for all the others! Attempts to justify punishment face a similar situation. No ethical theory appears to justify the institution of punishment in its present form. Contending theories of punishment identify different flaws in the institution and suggest different and incompatible changes. Meanwhile, since our present practice of punishment appears to serve an essential social purpose in a manner broadly compatible with widely held ethical views, the institution of punishment survives, and shows every sign of doing so for a long time to come.

References

Conway, D. A.: 'Capital punishment and deterrence: some considerations in dialogue form', *Philosophy and Public Affairs*, 3 (1974), 431–43.
Hart, H. L. A.: *Punishment and Responsibility* (Oxford: Clarendon Press, 1968).
Wootton, B.: *Crime and the Criminal Law* (London: Steven and Sons, 1981).

Further reading

Burgh, R. W.: 'Do the guilty deserve punishment?', *Journal of Philosophy*, 79 (1982), 193–210.
Duff, R. A.: *Trials and Punishments* (Cambridge: Cambridge University Press, 1986).
Honderich, T.: *Punishment: The Supposed Justifications*, (Harmondsworth: Penguin, 1984).
Kleinig, J.: *Punishment and Desert* (The Hague: Nijhoff, 1973).
Lacey, N.: *State Punishment: Political Principles and Community Values* (London: Routledge, 1988).
McCloskey, H. J.: 'A non-utilitarian approach to punishment', *Contemporary Utilitarianism*, ed. M. D. Bayles (New York: Doubleday, 1968).
Morris, H.: 'Persons and punishment', *Punishment and Rehabilitation*, ed. J. G. Murphy (Belmont, Cal.: Wadsworth, 1973).
Murphy, J. G.: *Retribution, Justice, and Therapy* (Dordrecht: Reidel, 1979).
Primoratz, I.: *Justifying Legal Punishment* (Atlantic Highlands: Humanities Press, 1989).
Sprigge, T. L. S.: 'A utilitarian reply to Dr McCloskey' *Contemporary Utilitarianism*, ed. M. D. Bayles (New York: Doubleday, 1968).
Ten, C. L.: *Crime, Guilt, and Punishment: A Philosophical Introduction* (Oxford: Clarendon Press, 1987).

33

Politics and the problem of dirty hands

C. A. J. COADY

i Introduction

POLITICS has always posed threatening questions about the scope and authority of common understandings of morality. It is politics that Thrasymachus has foremost in mind, in Plato's *Republic*, when he challenges Socrates to refute his startling definition of justice as 'the interest of the stronger'.

In a similarly deflationary spirit, some modern political theorists and advisers seem to think that political realism implies that moral considerations have no place at all in politics. One of President Kennedy's advisers in the Cuban missile crisis of 1962, Dean Acheson, proudly records that, when the deaths of hundreds of thousands of innocent people and much else stood in the balance, 'those involved ... will remember the irrelevance of the supposed moral considerations brought out in the discussions ... moral talk did not bear on the problem' (Acheson, 1971, p. 13). This seems to have been largely true of Acheson's own contributions to the crucial debates, but his view did not prevail and some of the other arguments put to the President had a moral flavour, such as Robert Kennedy's belief that the aerial attack upon the Cuban missile bases, a course favoured by Acheson, would be a Pearl Harbor in reverse. Characteristically, Acheson thought this a mere obfuscation and part of an 'emotional or intuitive' response (Acheson, 1965, pp. 197–198). Nonetheless, if moral considerations were not irrelevant, they were surprisingly lacking in weight when compared to other factors of a more obviously political or even personal kind, such as the need for President Kennedy to regain prestige, demonstrate his courage, and eliminate the prospect of impeachment, as well as the necessity to avoid Democratic Party defeats in upcoming Congressional elections.

Kennedy thought that political necessity justified what he himself counted as a very high risk (between 1/3 and 1/2) of nuclear holocaust. (A more detailed account of risk-taking in nuclear weapons policies can be found in Article 34, WAR AND PEACE.) Those who refer to the necessities of politics have, at least since Machiavelli, often thereby signified not only necessary risks of an apparently immoral kind but necessary lies, cruelties and even murders. Taking their lead from Sartre's play of the same name, modern philosophers tend to talk of the necessity for 'dirty hands' in politics, meaning that the vocation of politics somehow rightly requires its practitioners to violate important moral standards which prevail outside politics.

373

There is much that is puzzling about the idea that politics has some special exemption from the moral order, not least the fact that the historical record gives abundant reasons for wanting particularly close moral scrutiny to be directed upon the activities of politicians. Nor do writers in this area always make clear what they mean by morality or politics or 'dirty hands'. I think that we best interpret Machiavelli as insisting that political necessity sometimes rationally requires the overriding of genuine moral reasons that would otherwise be decisive. But modern discussions sometimes approach what is recognizably the same problem by suggesting that there is a specific morality appropriate to political activity and that its deliverances outweigh considerations of 'ordinary' or 'private' morality. Often this is bolstered by appeals to the notion of role morality, with some implication that the political role exclusively or predominantly generates the need for dirty hands. My own view, put too simply, is that insofar as there is an issue about overriding the claims of morality (whether 'real' or merely 'ordinary') in the face of some overwhelming necessity, then it is an issue which can arise in any area of life. It is not special to politics, though there are some aspects of politics which perhaps raise the issue more acutely or dramatically.

ii The Machiavellian challenge

It is not clear that Machiavelli would have disagreed. He is writing for and about rulers and their advisers, and so his emphasis is heavily political; but, at least sometimes, he writes as though the need for 'dirty hands' is part of the human rather than the political condition. More recent philosophical writing, though sometimes visited by this suspicion, has usually made a rather sharp division between the political or public, on the one hand, and the private, personal or ordinary, on the other. A book devoted in part to the issue of 'dirty hands' is revealingly entitled *Public and Private Morality* and its editor, Stuart Hampshire, speaks of 'a conflict between two ways of life' (p. 45). Michael Walzer, in his seminal paper on the topic, proceeds for the most part as if the problem is quite special to politics, though he says that he doesn't want to argue that 'it is only a political dilemma' but merely that 'it is easy to get one's hands dirty in politics and it is often right to do so' (Walzer, 1973, p. 174). This is presumably not meant to be true of what Walzer calls 'private life', though Walzer and other contemporary writers on this theme do little to elucidate the basis for distinguishing private and public. Public life is indeed so diffused and pluralistic (ranging from politicians to clergymen, bankers to nurses, academics to town planners, parliaments to local suburban associations) that it can come to seem that there is very little left to contrast it with, other than drastic domesticity. The idea that traditional morality speaks only to the familial or, perhaps, the amicable, is a very strong but surely implausible one. There are serious problems lurking here: but we shall not delay at this point with them, but shall proceed on the assumption of some intuitively grasped contrast between the strongly political and the obviously non-political.

Notoriously, there is a great deal of controversy about the interpretation of

Machiavelli's own views. I believe that his advocacy of 'necessary immorality' is perfectly serious (rather than, as some hold, ironic), and that, although he has in mind the need to override Christian morality, the point has wider application to moral codes and virtues that are recognized in secular and other contexts beyond Christianity. When Machiavelli says, 'a man who wishes to profess goodness at all times will come to ruin among so many who are not so good. Hence it is necessary for a prince who wishes to maintain his position to learn how not to be good, and to use this knowledge or not to use it according to necessity' (*The Prince*, 1513, p. 52) he is genuinely challenging a very deep and compelling picture of morality. According to this picture, we can understand what it is to lead a good life in terms of virtue and/or the duties of a moral code, and such an understanding provides us with final, authoritative guidance on how to act. Moral reason may not always have something to say to us about our choices and decisions (though some have implausibly thought that it speaks to us ceaselessly) but when it does intervene seriously and relevantly, it must carry the day against all competing considerations.

This picture is challenged by Machiavelli because he thinks that there are powerful reasons which can and should overrule the moral reasons. One could anaesthetize the shock of his position (as he sometimes shows a tendency to do himself) by incorporating these powerful reasons within morality. The utilitarian reconstruction of morality does precisely this: it makes any reason for acting which is 'rationally' strong enough to carry the day a moral reason. Other moral stances can do something similar by treating the 'learning how not to be good' as simply acquiring distinctively political virtues or carrying out distinctively political duties, but if they take both moral experience and Machiavelli's challenge seriously, they will inevitably put pressure on the classical idea that the virtues form a unity. Machiavelli explicitly casts doubt upon the unity of the virtues, at one point, when he insists that it is not possible (especially for a prince) to observe all the virtues 'because the human condition does not permit it' (1513, p. 52). Hence, doing 'the right thing' in politics will really sometimes mean cultivating what is a genuine human vice. (Though Machiavelli sometimes backslides from the severity of this position by talking of what 'seems to be a vice' as on p. 53 of *The Prince*.) Similar considerations apply, perhaps even more stringently, to the treatment of our problem area in terms of the morality of roles. No-one's life is exhausted by any one role and we seem to have no guarantee that the imperatives of various roles must be in harmony. A serious clash between the demands of significant roles is certain to require resolution in terms that transcend resort to role morality. If role-morality is all there is to morality then the resolution will be achieved by non-moral considerations. For a monistic utilitarian, by contrast, whatever settles the matter rationally or satisfactorily will, *ipso facto*, be a moral consideration.

Let us see what contemporary philosophers urge in favour of their view that there is something special about politics that licenses Machiavellian conclusions. We shall then return to Machiavelli, whose own arguments have a somewhat different flavour. The modern Machiavellians urge or assume several consider-

375

ations. There is something in most of the points they make but they do not generally go deep enough. Here are a few considerations gathered from their writings. The 'necessity' to manipulate, lie, betray, steal or kill may arise in private life occasionally but it is much more *frequent* in politics. The political arena involves choices and consequences of much greater *weight* than does private life. Actors in political life are *representatives* and so need to be morally assessed in a different way. This point is often underpinned by some appeal to role morality. Relatedly, much is made by some writers (Thomas Nagel comes particularly to mind) of the dominance of considerations of *impartiality* in the morality appropriate to politics. Nagel thinks that this fact underpins the legitimacy we accord to the state's resort to violence in contrast to the way we frown upon such resort by the individual citizen.

iii   The contemporary debate examined

I cannot treat these arguments at length; a few comments will have to suffice. To begin with, one may readily concede that some areas of life lead to more frequent clashes between moral and non-moral values but we need to recall both that precisely which areas these are is a matter of historical contingency, and that frequency of confrontation need not correlate with frequency of justified overriding. Politics may be very bland as, I imagine, in Monaco, and private life can be a maelstrom of agonizing conflicts, as in a black ghetto or an Ethiopian village during famine. Moreover, where politics is more morally perturbing it doesn't follow that decisions against morality will necessarily be legitimate. Some area may be more morally dangerous than another without being less morally constrained. Politics may often be sleazier than housekeeping without this fact licensing fewer moral constraints in politics. On the contrary, the more frequent temptation is, the greater, we might naturally suppose, the need for stern attachment to moral standards and virtue. (This was indeed the view of Machiavelli's famous humanist contemporary, Erasmus, in his *The Education of a Christian Prince*.)

But if frequency itself is not enough perhaps the weight of consequences is. Most of the modern discussions treat the dirty hands decisions as at least partly dictated by the significance or weight of the consequences involved. It is true that political decisions do have wide-ranging effects and often concern important interests, though it is also true that the significance of political decisions and crises can be easily exaggerated and politicians are the first to do so – closely followed by the mass media. There is also the logical point that if political decisions are so weighty, then so are many private decisions to get on with activities which preclude a feasible involvement in politics. We do not want to say that these are political decisions, but the fact that Jones is cultivating his garden or his intellect instead of dealing with national affairs may have momentous consequences. In addition, however, to the significance of outcomes and the numbers affected, there is the question of probability. It is notoriously difficult to be at all confident in the outcome of one's political choices. By contrast some costs and issues in the personal realm are of the greatest weight and frequently of much greater certainty. Consider the necessity of preventing the maiming or perversion of one's own child and compare it with the need to maintain a political career in the interests of national independence.

The claims about representation and neutrality or impartiality raise very large questions about which I can say only a little here. They are related to a certain conception of the political role, and what one says about this will depend a good deal on what one thinks about considerations of role morality. As already suggested, my own view is that the political role is hardly a role at all, in the way that being a doctor or a fireman is. The tasks of politics are so diffuse, so subject to cultural determinations, so morally contestable, that drawing functional norms from the interplay of actual political behaviour makes little sense. When one politician says of another that he is 'a real pro' he is offering an assessment of actual skills, relevant to certain political processes, but he may well be talking of Josef Stalin or Adolf Hitler.

In any case, representation, by itself, does not do much to alter one's moral status; it extends one's powers and capacities, though it also restricts them in various ways, but the question of moral limits and freedoms will be largely a matter for ordinary moral assessment of the institutional purposes for which these powers have been created. The case of violence, the employment of which is cited by Walzer, Hampshire and Nagel as distinctive of the political, may serve as an illustration. It is often suggested that where it would be wrong for citizens to use violence or the threat of it in their dealings with other citizens, it can be right for their political representative to use it on their behalf. If this is meant to imply that private citizens are never entitled to use violence, even lethal violence, to protect their rights, then it is clearly dubious. One of the most plausible routes to the legitimacy of the state's employment of violence is through 'the domestic analogy' of an individual's right to self-defence. But the implication may be weaker; certainly, state agents are entitled to use or authorize violence where an individual isn't. Thomas Nagel puts this forcefully in discussing the issues of taxation and conscription. As he says of taxation: 'If someone with an income of $2,000 a year trains a gun on someone with an income of $100,000 a year and makes him hand over his wallet, that is robbery. If the federal government withholds a portion of the second person's salary (enforcing the laws against tax evasion with threats of imprisonment under armed guard) and gives some of it to the first person in the form of welfare payments, food stamps, or free health care, that is taxation.' (Nagel, 1978, p. 55.) He goes on to say that the former is morally impermissible and the latter morally legitimate, claiming that this is a case in which public morality is not 'derived' from private morality but 'from impersonal consequentialist considerations'. 'There is no way,' he adds, 'of analysing a system of redistributive taxation into the sum of a large number of individual acts all of which satisfy the requirements of private morality' (p. 55).

Leaving aside any doubts about the unjustifiability of an individual's stealing *in extremis,* what is odd about Nagel's treatment of the problem is that the crucial determinants that differentiate the cases of theft and taxation make reference to perfectly ordinary moral considerations. Nagel's general position is that political

377

morality differs from private morality in allowing much more weight to consequentialist thinking whereas private morality is more agent-centred. There are interpretations of this idea which do not involve any 'dirty hands' implications. For instance, public officials should be particularly circumspect about the giving and receiving of gifts, and they have to think a great deal about the consequences of what they do and steel themselves to do the right thing even where it may cause distress. But the example of taxation actually illustrates the strong continuity of public and private morality. The ruler can take money from citizens, by threat of violence if necessary, for such public purposes as the relief of the poor, because this is much *fairer* than such alternatives as individual forays into even 'justifiable' theft. Given that some redistributive goal is morally legitimate, taxation ensures that the burdens are distributed even upon those rich enough to afford bodyguards and secure houses, and the benefits go even to those too timid or upright to steal. It is also better for everyone that citizens not be judges in their own cause on such matters, especially where violence may be invoked. The concepts of fairness, justice and good at work here are surely the very same ones that operate within familial and other intimate contexts. What Nagel says about the impossibility of analysing a tax system into some sum of individual acts satisfying the requirements of 'private' morality may nonetheless be true, but for reasons that have nothing to do with morality in particular, i.e. no institutional system is analysable into a sum of individual acts of whatever kind.

Nagel's claim that political morality puts a much greater emphasis upon the impartiality of the underlying core morality from which both it and private morality supposedly derive is worth some attention. It is true that some political cultures place a premium upon the avoidance of nepotism and patronage, but I doubt that a great deal of mileage can be got from this. To begin with, there are, or have been, many political cultures in which such restrictions on preference to relatives and friends have been less prominent or non-existent; I do not want to argue that the lack of such restrictions creates no problems but merely that it is implausible to make their presence distinctive of political morality. We need to recall that cultures which frown upon family patronage frequently condone or encourage the advancement of political friends or cronies. It is true that the exploitation of political position for personal profit is strongly disapproved of in many cultures (though consistently practised in both direct and indirect ways). Against this must be set the fact that the serious exploitation of *highly personal* relationships for profit is profoundly immoral. Just think of people who sell children or pimp for their sexual partners. Furthermore, there is the recalcitrant fact, for the impartiality thesis, that politicians are widely regarded as being correctly influenced by considerations of partiality that differ only in scale from those of the private citizen. Political leaders are thought to have special obligations to *their* nation, *their* constituency, *their* party, *their* faction and even *their* race. The impartiality thesis is not convincing. (See Article 28, PERSONAL RELATIONSHIPS, for an examination of the impartiality thesis in private morality; and see Article 19, CONSEQUENTIALISM, for a consequentialist approach to impartiality.)

iv The problem of corruption

A more general difficulty confronts all of these arguments insofar as they rely upon common features of political behaviour, and that is the way in which any thesis about 'dirty hands' and the special nature of political morality has to come to terms with the fact that political environments are so often morally corrupt. The Psalmist warns against putting one's trust in princes (Ps. 146: 3) and the prophet Micah speaks for many when he says: 'That they may do evil with both hands earnestly, the prince asketh, and the judge asketh for a reward; and the great man, he uttereth his mischievous desire ...' (Micah 7: 3). The point is not just that 'power tends to corrupt', though it does, but that the values which politicians find themselves driven to promote, and others find themselves driven to endorse, may be the product of degraded social circumstances and arrangements. Both Rousseau and Marx have pertinent things to say here, as well as the prophets of an earlier day.

Nonetheless, the problem posed by corruption is not just that we are likely to draw the wrong norms from political behaviour (though this is important for those who rely so heavily upon appeals to role morality) but that we tend to focus our moral concerns too narrowly. We concentrate upon the particular act that will require dirty hands and ignore the contingency and mutability of the circumstances that have given rise to it. Yet it is precisely these circumstances which often most deserve moral scrutiny and criticism, and the changes which may result from such criticism can eliminate the 'necessity' for those types of dirty hands in the future. This suggests that philosophers and other theorists have in fact been too complacent in their acceptance of the neutrality and immutability of the background circumstances which generate 'dirty hands' choices. Robert Fullinwider once remarked that we need politicians just as we need garbage collectors, and in both cases we should expect them to stink. But, once upon a time, we needed the collectors of what was euphemistically called 'night soil' and, in many parts of the world, human ingenuity has eliminated the need for that very malodorous occupation.

v The relevance of 'moral situations'

We need to focus, as the contemporary debate does not, upon the ways in which specific political predicaments embody quite general features which link the political to the non-political and help to explain why the political arena should pose the perplexities it does. These general features testify to the existence of certain broad types of what I shall call 'moral situations'. There are at least three such moral situations pertinent to our subject: compromise, extrication and moral isolation. In what follows I shall briefly sketch and discuss them. (I have discussed some or all of them more fully in Coady, 1989, 1990a and 1990b.) All three can occur in any area of life but they are specially significant for collaborative activities, either joint enterprises or those which rely more indirectly upon the co-operation of others. Here lies their special relevance to politics, which is pre-eminently collaborative in this sense.

Compromise. A compromise is a sort of bargain in which several agents who see advantages in co-operative efforts of some sort agree to proceed in a way that requires each of them to surrender, perhaps only temporarily, some of their ends, interests or policies, in order to secure others. There is nothing immoral in compromise, as such, but it is not surprising that the word commonly has some negative implications, and that there is an application of it with essentially derogatory meaning. This occurs when we talk of a person or an institution being compromised. Some deals, we seem to think, go beyond the regrettable denial of a worthy goal or abandonment of a significant interest; they require the undermining of self and integrity.

These morally damaging compromises involve the sacrifice of basic principle, where the notion of principle concerned is more to do with depth than universality. Consequently, although it will inevitably have a moral flavour about it, such a principle need not itself be a moral principle such as might be thought binding upon every rational agent. It must nonetheless be sufficiently exalted to rule out such guiding convictions as the Vicar of Bray's axiom ('Whatso'er king may reign I'll still be the Vicar of Bray, sir!'). Clearly, there are difficulties in characterizing such a notion more accurately; here I shall have to rest with an intuitive grasp on the idea, which should anyhow suffice to suggest the way in which principle, in this sense, does much to constitute the core of character and to shape people's fundamental expectations of each other. Hence it is a central criticism of someone that they are unprincipled or lack principle. When compromise reaches to the sacrifice of principle then it ceases to be a normal, if perhaps unfortunate, requirement of collaboration or conflict and becomes morally suspect. The Machiavellian challenge suggests that this is sometimes or often necessary.

Extrication. An extrication problem exists when an agent has embarked on a course of immoral actions or has instituted an abiding immoral state of affairs and now repents of it and seeks to extricate him or herself from the mess. In the political context, an agent may not have initiated the immorality herself, but may be part of a group which did, or, more interesting still, the agent may have inherited responsibility for the situation. Believing her situation to be seriously immoral, she must surely try to change it, but just stopping may sometimes cause greater harm than temporary persistence in the evil with a view to extrication. Whether she stops or persists, the agent will cause harms for which she must take responsibility, since they are not merely evils consequent upon her actions but wrongs that she does. To say as much is not to engage in the wholesale attribution of negative responsibility, characteristic of much utilitarian theory, for in the extrication situation the agent has a quite specific responsibility for the situation which generates harms whatever she does.

Suppose, as a political leader, you were responsible for embroiling your nation in an unjust war, the injustice of which you have come to see or to repent of. You are largely responsible for conditioning people to believe in the justice of the cause and for inculcating devotion to it. Were you to order immediate cessation, there is not only the danger that your orders would be disobeyed and the slaughter continue indefinitely, but also the strong probability that the enemy (whose cause is, perhaps, also unjust, and whose methods certainly are) will respond to your laying down of arms by exacting terrible vengeance against your people, including thousands who are innocent of complicity in the war. Gradual disengagement, however, offers good prospects of avoiding all this, though it means that you continue to direct an unjust war and the unjust killings it entails. In some cases, this may still be the right thing to do, even though, on non-utilitarian premises, it involves acting immorally. Note, however, that it is not a simple case of politics triumphing over morality; the primary moral verdict on the war remains dominant because the agent is guided by it in seeking extrication. This idea is central to the development of a non-consequentialist theory of moral extrication.

Moral isolation. This third situation is one much emphasized by Machiavelli, though often ignored by his commentators, and it is of considerable independent interest for any discussion of collaborative action. It is the problem posed by the demands of virtue in a world or context dominated by evildoers. Machiavelli (and later, Hobbes) thought it folly to behave virtuously in such a situation.

The insight behind the accusation of folly is that there is some fundamental point to morality which is undermined by the widespread non-co-operation of others. For both Machiavelli and Hobbes, it is a kind of survival. The survival of the state and all it stands for (including a sort of glory) is pre-eminent in Machiavelli, whereas the individual's self-preservation is Hobbes's principal focus, though each shares something of the other's concerns.

Compelling as these ideas can seem, they are inadequate to the complex realities of moral life. The accusation of folly makes most sense for those areas of life which are dominated, in one way or another, by convention or other forms of agreement. Indeed, there are some immoralities which cannot exist without conventions: it is not folly to practise marital fidelity in a society without marriage institutions, it is literally impossible. (Though there may be other forms of sexual fidelity that are morally praiseworthy.) Less drastically than this, there may be a widespread breakdown in compliance with a convention which makes it pointless for the few who want to achieve the goal of the convention to continue their compliance. There are obvious advantages in the various informal conventions that dictate waiting in queues (or lines) for the availability of certain goods, and these advantages are sufficiently important for most of us to keep conforming in the face of the occasional queue-jumper. When, however, civilization has so deteriorated that the majority are queue-jumpers then the advantages can no longer be achieved for anyone by continued minority compliance. We must look to other methods, such as law or violence, to protect the ill, the weak, and the non-assertive.

But cases differ. Even where convention is involved, one might still prefer to

381

conform in the face of widespread defection in order to try to halt the defection, or merely to make a point, perhaps to a wider audience, about the values being undermined. Even in the present political climate in democratic countries, one might, in this spirit, make a point of giving few electoral promises and keeping all of them. More broadly, there are important issues of character and integrity, there are significant goals and achievements, that arguably go beyond the concern for success, glory or survival, whether it be individual or national. In the moral chaos of the Nazi death camps, individuals chose moral integrity ahead of survival, and it is not at all clear that grave national dishonour is preferable to the loss of a particular ruler or regime no matter how admirable.

Finally, we should stress that the ways in which politics can be challenging to moral sensitivities are varied, and some do not raise issues as dramatic as those usually invoked in the Machiavellian tradition. It is one thing to hold that politics might require moral crimes, quite another to insist that it involves a lifestyle which closes off certain morally attractive options. The life of politics may mean that the values and pleasures of friendship, of family life and of certain forms of spontaneity or privacy are less available. There is undoubtedly scope for regret here, but any choice of lifestyle involves some closing of value options and some consequent disadvantage to self and others. If this is dirty hands, then it is merely the human condition.

References

Acheson, D.: 'Ethics in international relations today', *The Vietnam Reader*, ed. M. G. Raskin and B. Fall (New York: Random House, 1965).

——: 'Homage to plain dumb luck', *The Cuban Missile Crisis*, ed. R. A. Divine (Chicago: Quadrangle Books, 1971).

Coady, C. A. J.: 'Escaping from the bomb: immoral deterrence and the problem of extrication', *Nuclear Deterrence and Moral Restraint*, ed. H. Shue (New York: Cambridge University Press, 1989).

——: 'Hobbes and "The Beautiful Axiom" ', *Philosophy*, 90, No. 251 (1990a).

——: 'Messy morality and the art of the possible', *Proceedings of the Aristotelian Society*, Supplementary Volume LXIV (1990b).

Erasmus, Desiderius: *The Education of a Christian Prince* (1516); trans. and intro. L. K. Born (New York: 1936).

Hampshire, S.: 'Morality and pessimism', *Public and Private Morality*, ed. S. Hampshire (Cambridge: Cambridge University Press, 1978).

Hobbes, T.: *Leviathan* (1651); ed. C. B. Macpherson (Harmondsworth: Penguin, 1981).

Machiavelli, N.: *The Prince* (1513); ed. P. Bondanella (Oxford: Oxford University Press, 1984).

——: *The Discourses* (1513); trans. and ed. L. J. Walker (Harmondsworth: Penguin, 1950).

Marx, K.: *Writings of the young Marx on Philosophy and Society*, trans. and ed. L. D. Easton and K. H. Guddat (New York: Anchor, 1967).

Nagel, T.: 'Ruthlessness in public life', *Public and Private Morality*, ed. S. Hampshire (Cambridge: Cambridge University Press, 1978).

Plato: *The Republic*, any edition; especially Book I.
Walzer, M.: 'Political action: the problem of dirty hands', *Philosophy and Public Affairs*, 2, No. 2 (1973).

Further reading

Kavka, G. S.: 'Nuclear coercion', *Moral Paradoxes of Nuclear War*, ed. Kavka (Cambridge: Cambridge University Press, 1987).
Oberdiek, H.: 'Clean and dirty hands in politics', *International Journal of Moral and Social Studies*, 1, No. 1 (1986).
Rousseau, J. J.: *The First and Second Discourses, together with the Replies to Critics and Essay on the Origin of Languages* (1754); ed. V. Gourevitch (New York: 1986).
Stocker, M.: *Plurality and Conflicting Values* (Oxford: Oxford University Press, 1990).
Williams, B.: 'Politics and moral character', *Public and Private Morality*, ed. S. Hampshire (Cambridge: Cambridge University Press, 1978).

34

War and peace

JEFF MCMAHAN

i Ethics and the use of violence in war

THE thinking of policy-makers about issues of war and peace, as well as that of the intellectuals whose work is most influential in the policy-making process, is normally structured by a framework of assumptions that is largely amoral. The problems are conceived of as 'practical' in nature: policy options are compared solely in terms of their expected consequences, and consequences are evaluated solely in terms of their impact on the national interest. To the extent that ethical issues are raised at all, they are presented in a crude and oversimplified form best suited to the manipulation of public opinion, which, interestingly, tends to reject the amoralism of the policy-making elites.

In this article we will briefly explore the theory on which most national security policies are founded and then go on to consider several alternative views which insist that ethical principles must have a prominent role in the formulation of these policies. Next we will examine the justification for the resort to violence and killing in warfare, and will explore the grounds for the claim that there are limits to the permissible use of violence in war. In the second half of the article we will discuss the ethical issues raised by the practice of nuclear deterrence.

1 Realism

The theory that generally underlies the formulation of policy is called 'political realism'. It holds that moral norms do not apply to the conduct of states, which should instead be guided exclusively by a concern for the national interest. This position faces an immediate objection. There are limits to what I, as an individual, am permitted to do in order to protect or promote my interests. The same is true of you. So how could it be that, by banding together and declaring ourselves a state, we acquire the right to do things to protect or promote our collective interests which neither of us alone would be entitled to do? The formation of the state may (like the creation of a club) create new rights, but all are derivable from rights which individuals possess independently of their membership in the state. Hence the rights and prerogatives of states can extend no further than those of their individual members taken collectively.

The realist may attempt to meet this challenge in one of three ways. He might embrace moral nihilism, deriving the claim that moral norms do not apply to states from the broader claim that moral norms have no application at all, even to the conduct of individuals. (See the comments on this position in Article 35, REALISM, and Article 38, SUBJECTIVISM.) Or he might argue that the condition of anarchy that structures relations among states is such as to suspend the requirements of morality that would apply in other conditions. Or, finally, he might claim that there is some peculiar alchemy in the formation of the state that makes the state more than just a collective composed of individuals; that the state is a higher and altogether different sort of entity that transcends the constraints that apply to individuals. As I will often have to do in this short article, I can only point towards the arguments rather than present and discuss them in detail; but I am persuaded that none of these replies is defensible and that realism, though influential, is untenable.

Given the fact that national policies tend to be founded on purely prudential reasoning, it should not be surprising that discussions of the ethics of war and nuclear deterrence generally endorse positions and policies quite far removed from the actual practices of states. Careful and conscientious ethical reflection tends to be deeply subversive of established ideas about war, peace, and security.

2 Pacifism

According to the realist view, war is justified when it serves the national interest, unjustified when it is against the national interest. The interests of other states or nations are considered to be largely irrelevant, except instrumentally. But, just as individuals are not normally permitted to ignore the interests of other individuals, so too states are required to give some weight to the interests of other states (or, rather, to the interests of people in other states). It seems implausible, however, to suppose that states are required to be perfectly impartial, giving as much weight to the interests of people in other states as they give to those of their own citizens. In short, neither absolute partiality nor perfect impartiality seems appropriate. It remains an unsolved problem of moral theory to determine in what conditions and to what extent a state is entitled to give priority to its own interests and concerns over those of other states or national groups. (Some forms of partiality seem to us morally justified. For example, parents seem to be not merely permitted but required to be partial, at least in some respects, to their own children. But other forms of partiality, such as favouring the interests of members of one's own race, are morally arbitrary. It seems that nationalism and patriotism are in some respects analogous to familial loyalty, but are in other aspects analogous to racism. A deeper investigation of these analogies might help to illuminate the problem of determining the scope and limits of justified national partiality.)

Most people believe that the justifiability of war depends, not just on considerations of actual or expected consequences, but also on what are often called matters of principle. On this view, the rightness or wrongness of an act may be, at least in part, a function of the inherent nature of the act itself, which is independent of what its consequences are. (See Article 17, CONTEMPORARY DEONTOLOGY, and Article 19, CONSEQUENTIALISM.) Some people (called 'absolutists') even believe that there are certain acts which can never be justified, simply because of the kinds of acts they are. Persons who are absolutists with respect to acts of war are called pacifists. They believe that it is never permissible to engage in war. While virtually everyone believes that there is a strong moral presumption against the violence and killing involved in war, pacifists differ from most of us in their belief that this presumption cannot be overridden, that the challenge to provide a moral justification for war can never be met.

Like realism, however, pacifiscm is a difficult position to sustain. While it is not implausible to hold that the burden of justification falls on the person who claims that it may be permissible to engage in war, the situation is reversed in the case of certain uses of violence at the individual level. If I am the victim of an unjust and potentially lethal attack, the burden of justification falls, not on those who believe that I am entitled to use violence to defend myself, but on those who would deny this. Many pacifists would reply that what they reject is *war* and not all uses of violence; hence individual self-defence may be justified even though war is not. It is doubtful, however, that an *absolute* rejection of war can be coherently grounded on anything other than an absolute prohibition of certain types of act necessarily involved in war – e.g. intentional violence and killing. And any prohibition of certain types of action that will rule out war in all instances will almost certainly rule out the use of violence in individual self-defence. Indeed, the acceptance of individual acts of self-defence may itself imply an acceptance in principle of certain types of war, since certain wars may simply consist, on one side, in the collective exercise of individual rights of self-defence.

3 Just-war theory

Over a number of centuries a tradition of thinking about the ethics of war has developed which attempts to define a defensible middle ground between pacifism and realism. The resulting view – known as the theory of the just war – provides a defence of the use of violence in war that parallels both the common-sense justifications for the use of violence by individuals and, perhaps more to the point, common-sense justifications for the use of violence by the state for the domestic defence of rights. Just as domestic police violence may be legitimate provided both that it is intended to serve just and well-specified goals and that it is governed and constrained by rules, so too the state's use of violence against external threats may be legitimate provided that the ends are just and the means subject to proper limitations.

The theory of the just war, which provides the framework within which most contemporary treatments of the ethics of war are developed, has two components: a theory of ends and a theory of means. The first of these, known as the theory of *jus ad bellum*, defines the conditions under which it is permissible to resort to war. The second theory, that of *jus in bello*, sets the limits of permissible conduct in war.

Both theories are too complex to be rehearsed here, even in outline. We should, nevertheless, consider some of their more important provisions. The principal component of the theory of *jus ad bellum*, for example, is the requirement that war must be fought for a just cause. While just-war theorists are virtually unanimous in the belief that national self-defence may provide a just cause for war, there is little agreement beyond that. Other candidates for just cause include the defence of another state against unjust external aggression, the recovery of rights (that is, the recovery of what may have been lost when earlier unjust aggression was not resisted, or when earlier resistance ended in defeat), the defence of fundamental human rights within another state against abuse by the government, and the punishment of unjust aggressors.

If, as I have claimed, the rights of states are derived from and cannot exceed the rights of the individuals who make up the state, then the right of national self-defence will be compounded out of the rights of individual self-defence of the citizens. The state is simply a vehicle through which its individual members collectively exercise their individual rights to self-defence in a co-ordinated fashion. The limits to what the state may do in national self-defence are therefore set by the limits to what individual citizens may permissibly do to defend themselves.

The theory of *jus in bello* consists of three requirements. (1) *The requirement of minimal force*: The amount of violence used on any occasion must not exceed what is necessary to achieve one's aim. (2) *The requirement of proportionality*: The expected bad consequences of an act of war must not outweigh, or be greater than, its expected good consequences. (3) *The requirement of discrimination*: Force must be directed only against persons who are legitimate targets of attack.

4   The requirement of discrimination

Each of these requirements raises formidable problems of interpretation. Consider, for example, the requirement of discrimination. What determines whether a person is a legitimate or illegitimate target of violence in war? It is often claimed that the distinction between those who are and those who are not legitimate targets coincides with the distinction between combatants and non-combatants, or with the distinction between the morally innocent and the morally guilty. These latter distinctions do, of course, have moral content: moral innocence entails an absence of liability to punishment and, according to certain theories at least, non-combatancy entails an absence of liability to self-defensive violence. But the relevance of these notions to the permissibility of attacking certain types of people needs to be established more directly. What is it about certain types of people that confers on them a moral immunity to attack?

Our beliefs about discrimination are a function primarily of (1) our theory of why violence and killing are normally wrong and (2) our theory of how, on occasion, violence and killing may be justified. The latter tells us not only what sorts of grievance can justify the resort to violence but also how people may be rendered liable to attack through being connected to the relevant grievance in certain ways. In short, it is our theory of how violence can be justified that tells us which people are liable and which are innocent – innocent in the generic sense that they are not connected with the grievance which provides the justification for engaging in war in a way that makes them liable to attack. (For example, if the justification for the use of violence is self-defence, then our theory of self-defence will tell us who is liable and may be attacked.) Our theory of why violence is normally wrong then tells us the precise way in which the distinction between

387

those who are innocent and those who are liable functions to limit permissible violence.

The justification for the violence and killing involved in war is given by the theory of *jus ad bellum*. The requirement of discrimination is thus in part a corollary of the theory of *jus ad bellum*. This contradicts the standard view that *jus ad bellum* and *jus in bello* are logically independent. (Walzer, 1977, p. 21.) According to the standard view, soldiers fighting in a just cause and those fighting in an unjust cause are both permitted to use violence within the same constraints. On the view that I have sketched, this is a mistake. Soldiers fighting in a just cause are justified in using violence within certain limits. But soldiers fighting in an unjust cause are *not* morally justified in using violence, even against enemy combatants, in the service of their country's war aims. For no-one has a right to use violence as a means to the achievement of immoral aims. Of course, if, as is usually the case, a soldier's participation in an unjust war is the result of some combination of deception, indoctrination, and coercion, then his wrongful action may be to some extent excused and his use of violence for the purpose of individual self-defence may even be justified. But it remains the case that the range of legitimate targets is narrower for the soldier fighting in an unjust cause than it is for the soldier fighting in a just cause. (McMahan, 1991.)

The requirement of discrimination has been challenged in a variety of ways. It is sometimes claimed, for example, that, once a state of war exists, all moral requirements are suspended, at least for the belligerent whose cause is just. (This is an extreme variant of the view that *jus ad belum* and *jus in bello* are logically related.) If, however, the rights of states are derived from and thus cannot exceed the rights of individuals, then this view must be false; for there are always limits to what individuals are morally entitled to do even in pursuit of ends which are morally just. Apart from doctrines of collective responsibility which hold that wars are fought between states as wholes, so that no-one within a belligerent state may claim a right of immunity to attack, the main challenge to the requirement of discrimination comes from the view that, in somes cases at least, considerations of consequences are more important than matters of principle. According to one such view, while attacking the innocent (in our generic sense) is normally wrong, it may be permissible in circumstances in which the probable consequences of refraining from attacking would be considerably worse than the consequences of attacking. (Walzer, 1977, Ch. 16.) A more radical view is that the conduct of war should be entirely governed by considerations of consequences. On this view there simply is no class of people who enjoy a general moral immunity to attack in war.

Those who hold that only consequences matter need not, however, consider the issue of innocence irrelevant. They may distinguish between innocence and non-innocence in terms of whether or not a person has done anything which renders him or her liable to attack. And they may coherently believe that, other things being equal, it is a worse outcome when an innocent person is killed than it is when a non-innocent person is killed. But they are nevertheless committed to the view that there may be cases in which it is permissible or even morally required to attack and kill the innocent – for example, when this is necessary to prevent an even greater number of killings of the innocent.

These people – to whom we will refer, somewhat misleadingly, as 'consequentialists' – might argue as follows: 'The wrongness of killing is to be explained in terms of the effects of killing on the victim. It is a function of both the harm involved in the victim's loss of the future goods of life and the harm involved in the violation of the victim's autonomy. But the requirement of discrimination, as it has been traditionally understood, presupposes that the wrongness of killing cannot be explained in this way. According to the requirement of discrimination, the wrongness of killing is at least in part inherent in the nature of the act itself. This does not mean, however, that the requirement of discrimination holds that the *act* of killing is itself a bad *event* or *occurrence*. A killing need not be regarded as more horrible *as an event* than an accidental death. (Thus one may believe that one's reason to prevent the killing of an innocent person is no stronger than one's reason to prevent the accidental death of an innocent person.) But, if it is wrong to kill because of the nature of the act, but not because of the nature of the act considered as an event, then the wrongness of killing must have something to do with the nature of the relations between the agent, his or her action, and the consequences of the action. This, however, shifts the focus of moral concern away from the victim of killing and towards the agent, thereby distorting our understanding of the ethics of killing. Killing is wrong because of what it does to the victim, not because of some fact about the way in which the agent is related through his or her action to the death of the victim.' (Compare Philip Pettit's defence of promoting, rather than honouring, values, in Article 19, CONSEQUENTIALISM.)

The defender of the requirement of discrimination may reply that our moral intuitions favour the agent-centred rather than the victim-centred account of the wrongness of killing. Consider the following example drawn from the area of ethics and war. Most people distinguish between terrorism, which is wrong, and legitimate acts of war. But what is terrorism? Insofar as the term retains any descriptive meaning, it refers to the intentional use of violence, for political purposes, against persons who are innocent in our generic sense, normally as a means of influencing the behaviour of some other person or group of persons. Terrorism, in short, consists in the violation of the requirement of discrimination. Thus, if we are to uphold our unequivocal condemnation of terrorism, we will have to accept an agent-centred explanation of the wrongness of killing. For what we find particularly repugnant about terrorism is not simply that it involves harming the innocent. Many legitimate acts of war also foreseeably harm the innocent. What distinguishes terrorism from legitimate acts of war is rather that terrorism *aims* to harm or kill the innocent, whereas legitimate acts of war, when they do harm the innocent, do so *unintentionally*. Thus the difference between terrorism and legitimate acts of war is not a difference of expected consequences. It is, rather, a difference in the inherent natures of the two types of act, as defined by their respective intentions. (The intention/foresight distinction is discussed in Article 17, CONTEMPORARY DEONTOLOGY, and Article 25, EUTHANASIA.)

The question whether only consequences matter is among the deepest problems of ethical theory. It is considered elsewhere in this volume, in the articles referred to above, and cannot be resolved here. It is perhaps worth noting, however, that consequentialists are not necessarily committed to the view that terrorism is no worse than ordinary acts of war that foreseeably harm the innocent are generally thought to be. For an alternative view, equally compatible with consequentialism, is that ordinary acts of war that harm the innocent are just as objectionable as terrorism is ordinarily thought to be.

ii Ethics and nuclear weapons

The ethical questions raised by nuclear weapons may be divided into two groups: questions concerning the actual use of nuclear weapons in war and questions concerning the possession of nuclear weapons for purposes of deterrence. Questions of the first sort are normally answered by reference to the requirements of *jus in bello*. Could the use of nuclear weapons satisfy the requirements of discrimination and proportionality? It has seemed to most (though by no means all) moral theorists that there are some *possible* uses of nuclear weapons that would not violate either requirement. As it has actually been practised, however, deterrence has always involved threats to use nuclear weapons for the intentional destruction of civilian populations, and this would clearly violate the requirement of discrimination and almost certainly that of proportionality as well. (Finnis et al., 1987, Ch. I.) This fact raises fundamental questions for the morality of nuclear deterrence: does deterrence depend on threats to use nuclear weapons in ways that would be immoral? If so, what does this imply about the morality of deterrence?

There are both moral and strategic issues here. Suppose we knew which possible uses of nuclear weapons would be morally acceptable. We would then need to ask whether those uses are sufficiently extensive that the threat to use nuclear weapons *in those ways only* could effectively deter whatever threats we think it necessary to deter. This is a question of strategic theory. Given the fact that all actual deterrent policies have involved explicit threats to destroy civilian populations, together with the fact that there has been no significant challenge within the strategic community to the idea that these threats are necessary, it is reasonable to conclude that there is a broad consensus among strategists that viable and effective deterrence requires threats to use nuclear weapons in ways that would be condemned by the requirements of *jus in bello*.

1 The wrongful intentions argument

If we assume that deterrence depends on threats to use nuclear weapons in ways that would be morally wrong, then we confront a problem that has generated considerable discussion in the literature on the ethics of deterrence. For it seems that, to be credible, nuclear deterrent threats must be sincere – that is, they must be backed by an intention (given institutional expression in the elaborate plans and preparations for the firing of nuclear weapons) to fulfil them in the event that they are defied; hence deterrence involves a conditional intention to use nuclear weapons in ways that would be immoral. If, further, we accept the principle that it is wrong to intend to do that which it would be wrong to do (usually referred to as the 'Wrongful Intentions Principle'), then it follows that deterrence is wrong.

This argument, which we may call the Wrongful Intentions Argument, has been enormously influential, especially in theological circles where it is widely accepted that the moral character of an act is principally determined by the intention which defines its inherent nature. (It is defended, for example, in Finnis et al., 1987.) Critics, however, have assailed all three of the argument's premises. Some have sought to establish the claim that deterrence could be adequately based on sincere threats to use nuclear weapons in morally permissible ways only. These critics have, for example, proposed deterrent strategies which renounce any intention to harm the innocent and instead threaten the destruction of military assets only. (See, for example, Ramsey, 1968.) These proposals often appeal to the idea that deterrence would in part be guaranteed by the fact that potential adversaries could never be entirely confident that one's renunciation of immoral uses was sincere. (Kenny, 1985.) These sanitized strategies have, however, been forcefully criticized on the ground that even most uses of nuclear weapons against purely military targets would violate the requirement of proportionality, either directly through their immediate incidental effects on civilian populations or indirectly through the risk of escalation to levels of violence that would be directly disproportionate. Other critics of the Wrongful Intentions Argument have claimed, rather lamely, that deterrence is or could be based on threats which are in fact bluffs, so that deterrence need not involve wrongful intentions. (See Hare in Cohen and Lee, 1986.) Still others have either rejected the Wrongful Intentions Principle or else claimed that it fails to apply or is overridden in cases in which the formation of a putatively wrongful intention would be likely to prevent the occurrence of disastrous consequences, as many claim is true of the intentions required by the practice of deterrence. (Kavka, 1987, Chs. 1 and 2.)

This latter view seems to have the endorsement of common-sense morality. If there is a moral objection to deterrence that is not based entirely on considerations of consequences, it is not that deterrence involves people having wrongful intentions (which, in any case, are not *our* intentions, since we, as ordinary citizens, cannot control the use of nuclear weapons and hence can have no intentions regarding their use). The objection to deterrence is, rather, that it involves a serious risk that we will, through the agency of those whom we hire to implement the policy, someday engage in terrorist violence on an unprecedented scale by fulfilling our deterrent threats. Futhermore, in risking this future wrongdoing, we now deliberately impose a risk of death and injury on millions of innocent people as a means of reducing the risks that we ourselves face. If we believe that consequences are not all that matter (and even perhaps if we believe that they are), then these related facts about deterrence establish a strong moral presumption against it.

Some people believe that the presumption against deterrence is absolute – that is, that it cannot be overridden by countervailing considerations. These people often seek to defend their position by appealing to the traditional Christian principle that one may not do evil that good may come – for example, in order to prevent greater evil from being done by others. Most of us, however, believe that the objection to deterrence can in principle be overridden by considerations of consequences (or perhaps by some other countervailing duty, such as the duty of the state to protect its citizens). The presumption against deterrence could be overridden if the expected consequences of abandoning deterrence would be very much worse than those of continuing to practice it. Therefore even if we believe that consequences are not all that matter, we will not, unless we are absolutists, be able to avoid examining deterrence in the light of its expected consequences.

2   Deterrence and consequences

The conventional wisdom is that the expected consequences of abandoning deterrence would be in fact considerably worse than those of continuing to practice it. This view is, however, far from obviously true. To see why this is so, it will be helpful to introduce a technical sense of the term 'war'. As the term is ordinarily used, an attack to which there is no military response may count as a war. But, for the purposes of our discussion, let us stipulate that a *war* must involve attacks by each of two sides against one another. The term 'conflict' can refer to either an attack or a war in our sense.

The principal aim of a policy of nuclear deterrence is to prevent the loss or compromise of a state's political sovereignty and independence, primarily through the prevention of attacks against the state (since it is through being attacked that a state is most likely to have its independence compromised). But deterrence is only one means of reducing the risk of attack. What the best means of preventing attack are depends on what the likely causes of attack are. For prevention of an attack requires suppressing the cause, and there are various possible causes of attack. For example, if the threat of attack derives from the possibility of a calculated act of aggression intended to achieve some political aim, then one must aim to *deter* attack, either by driving up the costs and risks to the attacker or by demonstrating a defensive capacity so robust as to convince potential aggressors that an attack would be futile. (Here and elsewhere I am assuming that the attack would be unjust.) If, on the other hand, the threat of attack arises because a potential adversary appears likely to strike pre-emptively as a result of a fear of being attacked first, then seeking to strengthen deterrence may be counterproductive. For it may be one's own deterrent posture that is the problem. What is necessary is instead to take action to reassure the potential adversary that one's intentions are not aggressive. (The recognition that military preparations may provoke an attack rather than deterring it has led to proposals, primarily in Western Europe, for a restructuring of a non-nuclear forces in such a way that they physically could not be used for offensive operations.) There are other possible causes of attack which a policy of deterrence may be largely powerless to eliminate – for example, attack by accident, or inadvertence, or as a result of some other form of misunderstanding. As in the case of pre-emptive attack, the practice of deterrence may even exacerbate the risk of attack arising from these sources.

Not only is deterrence not the only means of attempting to prevent war, but the prevention of war is not the only goal of a security policy. Another important goal, for example, is to reduce the expected costs (including the costs to people outside of one's own state) of any conflict that might occur. There is, however, an antagonism between this goal and the goal of deterring attack. Deterrence works by driving up a potential attacker's expected costs from the attack. For the more likely it is that an attack would lead to a war that would be costly to the attacker, the more reluctant (other things being equal) it will be to attack; while the lower the expected costs of attacking are, the safer and more rational it will seem for a state to resort to attack as a means of achieving its ends. But a state that practises deterrence cannot drive up the costs of aggression to an attacker without driving up the costs to all parties. So there is a trade-off to be made between the two goals of reducing the likelihood of attack and reducing the magnitude of the damage that both sides are likely to suffer in the event of a conflict. Deterrence resolves this trade-off by giving more weight to the goal of preventing attack.

The common view that deterrence reduces the risk of nuclear war is therefore misleading, unless what is meant by nuclear war is simply a one-sided nuclear attack. The practice of deterrence by a state in fact *increases* the probability of large-scale nuclear war relative to what it would otherwise be. By threatening nuclear war as the penalty for an attack, a state manipulates the risk of nuclear war *as a means of preventing attack*.

It is important to bear in mind that the trade-off between the likelihood of attack and the costs of conflict is not to be made on the basis of prudential or self-interested criteria alone. Should war occur between major powers, the effects would be suffered by people the world over. Consider, for example, the situation in Europe. The West European defence establishment is concerned to link the fate of the US to that of Europe by arranging matters so that any attack on Western Europe will have a high probability of escalating to global nuclear war. These theorists want the Soviets to believe that they could not fight a war confined to European territory, but would instead become embroiled in a strategic nuclear war with the US should they ever initiate a war in Europe. It is, they believe, this prospect of large-scale nuclear war involving the Soviet Union itself that will provide the most effective deterrence of Soviet aggression. But notice that what increases the deterrence of conventional aggression is the deliberate creation of a large-scale nuclear war. (Thus the risk of conventional attack is greater the more stable relations of mutual nuclear deterrence are; while the risk of conventional attack is lower the greater the risk of escalation to nuclear war is. The choice between a lower risk of conventional attack and lower expected costs in the event of an attack is an instance of the type of trade-off identified earlier.)

The important point here is that the practice of deterrence in Europe puts the entire world at risk for the sake of West European security. Admittedly, the risks to innocent people outside the Soviet bloc are not intended. So in this respect they are unlike the risks the US imposes on innocent people within the Soviet Union. Nevertheless the voluntary creation of these risks is profoundly unjust. To see this we need only consult our own beliefs about the problem of nuclear proliferation. Consider the conflict between Israel and the various Arab nations. The outcome of this conflict is of tremendous importance to both groups. It cannot be considered a trivial affair. Yet we would regard it as monstrous if the various states within the region were to acquire major nuclear arsenals, thereby imperilling the lives of people everywhere, and putting at risk the very existence of future generations, for the sake of their interests and parochial concerns. But, if our indignation at being put at risk in this way would be justified, then the people of the world who are endangered by the policies of the present nuclear powers are equally entitled to condemn the practices that unjustly expose them to risk.

Let us now return to the question whether deterrence can be justified on the basis of its expected consequences. While the conventional view is that any moral presumption against deterrence can be defeated by the overwhelming value of deterrence in preventing catastrophe, it seems that, on the contrary, a consideration of expected consequences establishes yet a further presumption against deterrence. The argument for this claim may be stated in greatly oversimplified terms as follows. Suppose we consider two broadly defined possible policies of the US and its allies – namely, deterrence and non-nuclear defence – and the two most salient of their possible disastrous outcomes – namely, Soviet domination and large-scale nuclear war. It seems clear that nuclear war would be a worse outcome than Soviet domination, even if we take into account only the interests of the US and its allies, leaving aside those of the Soviet bloc, neutral countries, and future generations. It is also the case that deterrence involves a greater risk of large-scale nuclear war than non-nuclear defence does. It follows that deterrence involves a *greater risk of the worse outcome*. Thus the onus is on the defender of deterrence to show that this fact is outweighed by other considerations.

Some defenders of deterrence have sought to do this by arguing that non-nuclear defence has a greater overall risk of disaster. The argument is that the probability of domination under a policy of non-nuclear defence is *considerably* higher than the probability of large-scale nuclear war under deterrence, while the probability of domination under deterrence is either lower than or roughly equal to that of large-scale nuclear war under a policy of non-nuclear defence. Let us suppose that these claims are true, as they may well be. A dilemma remains. Should we opt for a *lower* probability of *some* disaster at the cost of a *higher* probability of the *worst* disaster, or should we aim to minimize the probability of the worst disaster at the cost of accepting a higher overall probability of some disaster? In short, we face the sort of trade-off identified earlier between minimizing the *likelihood* of disaster and minimizing the likely *magnitude* of disaster. (Kavka, 1987, Chs. 3 and 6; and McMahan, 1989.)

Given the nature of states and international society, no policy concerned with problems of war, peace, and security is without grave risks. It may, however, make a moral difference whether the risks associated with our policies are primarily ones we choose to accept or whether they are primarily ones that we impose on others. If we believe that there is a principled objection to imposing risks on the innocent in order to reduce the risks to ourselves, then there will be a moral presumption against deterrence. And, if there is such a presumption, it will not be easy to overturn. For, as we have seen, not only is it not obvious that abandoning deterrence would have consequences that would be considerably worse than those of continuing to practise it; it is not even clear that the abandonment of deterrence would have worse consequences at all.

References

Cohen, A. and Lee, S., eds.: *Nuclear Weapons and the Future of Humanity* (Totowa, NJ: Rowman & Allanheld, 1986).

Finnis, J. et al.: *Nuclear Deterrence, Morality, and Realism* (Oxford: Oxford University Press, 1987).

Kavka, G.: *Moral Paradoxes of Deterrence* (Cambridge: Cambridge University Press, 1987).

Kenny, A.: *The Logic of Deterrence* (London: Firethorn Press, 1985).

McMahan, J.: 'Is nuclear deterrence paradoxical?' *Ethics* (January 1989).

——: *The Ethics of Killing* (forthcoming, 1991).

Ramsey, P.: *The Just War* (Lanham, Md: University Press of America, 1968).

Walzer, M.: *Just and Unjust Wars* (Harmondsworth: Penguin, 1977).

Further reading

Beitz, C. et al., eds.: *International Ethics* (Princeton: Princeton University Press, 1985).

Blake, N. and Pole, K., eds.: *Objections to Nuclear Defence* (London: Routledge & Kegan Paul, 1984).

Child, J.: *Nuclear War: The Moral Dimension* (Transaction Books, 1986).

Copp, D., ed.: *Nuclear Weapons, Deterrence, and Disarmament* (Calgary: University of Calgary Press, 1986).

Hardin, R. et al., eds.: *Nuclear Deterrence: Ethics and Strategy* (Chicago: University of Chicago Press, 1985).

Holmes, R.: *On War and Morality* (Princeton: Princeton University Press, 1989).

Johnson, J. T.: *Can Modern War Be Just?* (New Haven: Yale University Press, 1984).

Lackey, D.: *Moral Principles and Nuclear Weapons* (Totowa, NJ: Rowman & Allanheld, 1984).

Mack, E. et al.: *Social Philosophy & Policy* 3: special issue, *Nuclear Rights/Nuclear Wrongs* (1985).

MacLean, D., ed.: *The Security Dilemma* (Totowa, NJ: Rowman & Allanheld, 1984).

Shue, H., ed.: *Nuclear Deterrence and Moral Restraint* (Cambridge: Cambridge University Press, 1989).

Teichman, J.: *Pacifism and the Just War* (Oxford: Basil Blackwell, 1986).

PART VI

THE NATURE OF ETHICS

35

Realism

MICHAEL SMITH

IT IS a commonplace that we appraise each other's behaviour and attitudes from the moral point of view. We say, for example, that we did the *wrong* thing when we refused to give to famine relief this year, though perhaps we did the *right* thing when we handed in the wallet we found on the street; that we would be *better* people if we displayed a greater sensitivity to the feelings of others, though perhaps *worse* if in doing so we lost the special concern we have for our family and friends.

Most of us take appraisal of this sort pretty much for granted. To the extent that we worry about moral appraisal, we simply worry about *getting it right*. Philosophers too have been concerned to get the answers to moral questions right. However, traditionally, they have also been worried about the whole business of moral appraisal itself. Their worry can be brought out by focusing on two of the more distinctive features of moral practice; for, surprisingly, these features pull against each other, so threatening to make the very idea of a 'moral' point of view altogether incoherent.

To begin, as we have already seen, it is distinctive of moral practice that we are concerned to get the answers to moral questions *right*. But this concern presupposes that there are correct answers to moral questions to be had. It thus seems to presuppose that there exists a domain of moral facts about which we can form beliefs and about which we may be mistaken. Moreover, these moral facts have a particular character. For we seem to think that the only relevant determinant of the rightness of an act is the circumstances in which the action takes place. Agents whose circumstances are identical face the same moral choice: if they did the same then either they both acted rightly or they both acted wrongly.

Indeed, something like this view of moral practice seems to explain our preoccupation with moral argument. What seems to give moral argument its point and poignancy is the idea that, since we are all in the same boat, a careful mustering and assessment of the reasons for and against our moral opinions is the best way to discover what the moral facts really are. If the participants are open-minded and thinking correctly then, we seem to think, such an argument should result in a *convergence* in moral opinion – a convergence upon the truth. Individual reflection may serve the same purpose, but only when it simulates a real moral argument; for only then can we be certain that we are giving each side of the argument due consideration.

We may summarize this first feature of moral practice in the following terms: we seem to think moral questions have correct answers, that the correct answers are made correct by objective moral facts, that moral facts are determined by circumstances, and that, by moralizing, we can discover what these objective moral facts determined by the circumstances are. The term 'objective' here simply signifies the possibility of a convergence in moral views of the kind just mentioned.

A second and rather different feature of moral practice concerns the practical implications of moral judgement, the way in which moral questions gain in their significance for us because of the special influence our moral opinions are supposed to have upon our actions. The idea is that when, say, we come to think that we did the wrong thing in refusing to give to famine relief, we come to think that we failed to do something for which there was a good reason. And this has motivational implications. For now imagine the situation if we refuse to give to famine relif when next the opportunity arises. Our refusal will occasion serious puzzlement, for we will have refused to do what we are known to think we have a good reason to do. Perhaps we will be able to explain ourselves. Perhaps we thought there was a better reason to do something else, or perhaps we were weak-willed. But, the point remains, an explanation of some sort will need to be forthcoming. An explanation will need to be forthcoming because, we seem to think, other things being equal, to have a moral opinion simply *is* to find yourself with a corresponding motivation to act.

These two distinctive features of moral practice – the *objectivity* and the *practicality* of moral judgement – are widely thought to have both metaphysical and psychological implications. However, and unfortunately, these implications are the exact opposite of each other. In order to see why this is thought to be so, we need to pause for a moment to reflect more generally on the nature of human psychology.

According to the standard picture of human psychology – a picture we owe to David Hume, the famous Scottish philosopher of the eighteenth century – there are two main kinds of psychological state. On the one hand there are beliefs, states that purport to represent the way the world is. Since our beliefs purport to represent the world, they are subject to rational criticism: specifically, they are assessable in terms of truth and falsehood according to whether or not they succeed in representing the world to be the way it really is.

On the other hand, however, there are also desires, states that represent how the world is to be. Desires are unlike beliefs in that they do not even purport to represent the way the world is. They are therefore not assessable in terms of truth and falsehood. Indeed, according to the standard picture, our desires are at bottom not subject to any sort of rational criticism at all. The fact that we have a certain desire is, with a proviso to be mentioned presently, simply a fact about ourselves to be acknowledged. It may be unfortunate that we have certain combinations of desires – perhaps our desires cannot all be satisfied together – but, *in themselves*, our desires are all on a par, rationally neutral.

This is important, for it suggests that though we may make discoveries about the world, and though these discoveries may rightly affect our beliefs, such discoveries should, again with one proviso to be mentioned presently, have no rational impact upon our desires. They may of course, have some *non*-rational impact. Seeing a spider I may be overcome with a morbid fear and desire never to be near one. However, this is not a change in my desires mandated by reason. It is a *non*-rational change in my desires.

Now for the proviso. Suppose, contrary to the example I just gave, that I acquire the desire never to be near a spider because I come to believe, falsely, that spiders give off an unpleasant odour. Then we would certainly ordinarily say that I have an 'irrational desire'. However, the reason we would say this clearly doesn't go against the spirit of what has been said so far. For my desire never to be near a spider is *based on* a further desire and belief: my desire not to smell that unpleasant odour and my belief that that odour is given off by spiders. Since I can be rationally criticized for having the belief, as it is false, I can be rationally criticized for having the desire it helps to produce.

The proviso is thus fairly minor: desires are subject to rational criticism, but only insofar as they are based on beliefs that are subject to rational criticism. Desires that are not related in some such way to beliefs that can be rationally criticized are not subject to rational criticism at all. We will return to this point presently.

According to the standard picture, then, there are two kinds of psychological state – beliefs and desires – utterly distinct and different from each other. The standard picture of human psychology is important because it provides us with a model for understanding human action. Human action is, according to this picture, produced by a combination of the two. Crudely, our beliefs tell us how the world is, and thus how it has to be changed, so as to make it the way our desires tell us it is to be. An action is thus the product of these two forces: a desire representing the way the world is to be and a belief telling us how the world has to be changed so as to make it that way.

Let's now return to consider the two features of moral judgment we discussed earlier. Consider first the objectivity of such judgement: the idea that moral questions have correct answers, that the correct answers are made correct by objective moral facts, that moral facts are determined by circumstances, and that, by moralizing, we can discover what these objective moral facts are. The metaphysical and psychological implications of this may now be summarized as follows. Metaphysically, the implication is that, amongst the various facts there are in the world, there aren't just facts about (say) the consequences of our actions on the well-being of our families and friends, there are also distinctively *moral* facts: facts about the rightness and wrongness of our actions having these consequences. And, psychologically, the implication is thus that when we make a moral judge-ment we thereby express our *beliefs* about the way these moral facts are. In forming moral opinions we acquire beliefs, representations of the way the world is morally.

Given the standard picture of human psychology, there is a further psycho-logical implication. For whether or not people who have a certain moral belief desire to act accordingly must now be seen as a further and entirely separate question. They may happen to have a corresponding desire, they may not. However, either way, they canot be rationally criticized. Having or failing to have a corresponding desire is simply a further fact about a person's psychology.

But now consider the second feature, the practicality of moral judgment. We saw earlier that to have a moral opinion simply *is*, contrary to what has just been said, to find ourselves with a corresponding motivation to act. If we think it right to give to famine relief then, other things being equal, we must be motivated to give to famine relief. The practicality of moral judgement thus seems to have a psychological and a metaphysical implication of its own. Psychologically, since making a moral judgement requires our having a certain desire, and no recognition of a fact about the world could rationally compel us to have one desire rather than another, our judgement must really simply *be* an expression of that desire. And this psychological implication has a metaphysical counterpart. For it seems to follow that, contrary to initial appearance, when we judge it right to give to famine relief we *are not* responding to any moral fact – the rightness of giving to famine relief. Indeed, moral facts are an idle postulate. In judging it right to give to famine relief we are really simply expressing our desire that people give to famine relief. It is as if we were yelling 'Hooray for giving to famine relief!' – no mention of a moral fact there, in fact, no factual claim at all.

We are now in a position to see why philosophers have been worried about the whole business of moral appraisal. The problem is that the *objectivity* and the *practicality* of moral judgement pull in quite opposite directions from each other. The objectivity of moral judgement suggests that there are moral facts, determined by circumstances, and that our moral judgements express our beliefs about what these facts are. This enables us to make good sense of moral argument, and the like, but it leaves it entirely mysterious how or why having a moral view is supposed to have special links with what we are motivated to do. And the practicality of moral judgement suggests just the opposite, that our moral judgements express our desires. While this enables us to make good sense of the link between having a moral view and being motivated, it leaves it entirely mysterious what a moral argument is supposed to be an argument about.

The idea of a moral judgement thus looks like it may well be incoherent, for what is required to make sense of such a judgement is a queer sort of fact about the universe: a fact whose recognition necessarily impacts upon our desires. But the standard picture tells us that there are no such facts. Nothing could be everything a moral judgement purports to be – or so it may now seem.

At long last we are in a position to see what this essay is about. For *moral realism* is simply the metaphysical (or ontological) view that there exist moral facts. The psychological counterpart to realism is called 'cognitivism', the view that moral judgements express our beliefs about what these moral facts are, and that we can come to discover what these facts are by engaging in moral argument and reflection.

Moral realism thus contrasts with two alternative metaphysical views about morality: *irrealism* (sometimes called 'anti-realism') and *moral nihilism*. According to the irrealists, there are no moral facts, but neither are moral facts required to make sense of moral practice. We can happily acknowledge that our moral judgements simply express our desires about how people behave. This, the psychological counterpart to irrealism, is called 'non-cognitivism'. (There are different versions of irrealism: e.g. emotivism, prescriptivism, and projectivism. For a fuller discussion of these theories see Article 36, INTUITIONISM, Article 38, SUBJECTIVISM, and Article 40, UNIVERSAL PRESCRIPTIVISM.)

By contrast, according to the moral nihilists, the irrealists are right that there are no moral facts, but wrong about what is required to make sense of moral practice. The nihilist thinks that without moral facts moral practice is all a sham, much like religious practice without belief in God.

I have taken some time before introducing the ideas of moral realism, irrealism, and nihilism because, as it seems to me, each has much to be said both in its favour and against it. In what follows I will explain in more detail some of the substantive views people have taken in this whole debate. However, I want to emphasize at the outset that nearly every substantive position is fraught with difficulty and controversy. The long introduction will hopefully have given some hint of why this is so. The very idea of moral practice may well be in deep trouble, much as the moral nihilist suggests.

Remember that, according to the irrealist, when we judge it right to give to famine relief we are expressing our desire that people give to famine relief; it is as if we were yelling 'Hooray for giving to famine relief!' Irrealism is certainly an option to be considered. But it seems to me that it is ultimately an unattractive option.

To be sure, irrealists have a perfect explanation of the practicality of moral judgement. But it seems utterly implausible to suppose, as they therefore must, that moral judgements aren't truth-assessable at all. They must say this because they model a moral judgement on a yell of approval or disapproval. But when I yell 'Hooray for giving to famine relief!', though my yell may be sincere or insincere, it can hardly be true or false. My yell reveals something about myself – that I have a certain desire – not about the world.

The problem here isn't just that we *say* that moral judgements can be true or false, though we certainly do do that. The problem is rather that the whole business of moral argument and moral reflection only makes sense on the assumption that moral judgements *are* truth-assessable. When we agonize over our moral opinions, we seem to be agonizing over whether our reasons for our beliefs are good enough reasons for believing what we believe to be true. And no irrealist surrogate seems up to the task of explaining this appearance away. For example, it seems utterly hopeless to suppose that we are agonizing over whether we *really* have the desires we have. Surely *this* question isn't so hard to answer!

Indeed, in this context, it is worthwhile asking what the irrealists' view of moral argument is supposed to be. They presumably imagine that what we are trying to do, when we engage in moral argument, is to get our opponent to have the same desires as we have. But, at bottom, they must also say that we are trying to do this *not* because the opponent rationally should have these desires – remember that, subject to the proviso mentioned, desires aren't supposed to be subject to rational criticism at all – but rather just because these are the desires *we* want him to have. But in that case moral argument begins to look massively self-obsessed, an imposition of *our* wants on others.

Irrealism isn't an attractive option. The irrealist's account of moral judgement as the expression of a desire simply fails to make sense of moral reflection. And the irrealist's account of moral argument makes moral persuasion look like it is itself immoral! What about the alternative, moral realism?

It might be thought that, since the moral realist admits the existence of moral facts, he has therefore no problem explaining the objectivity of moral judgement and the related phenomena of moral reflection and moral argument. It might be thought that the realist's only problem is that, if he is to eschew the existence of 'queer' moral properties whose recognition connects necessarily with the will, then he cannot explain the practicality of moral judgement. But matters are in fact much more complicated.

Certainly the moral realist needs to face up to the fact that the practicality of moral judgement is problematic, from his point of view. But his problem is more than that. His problem is that, *because* he has no explanation of the practicality of moral judgement, he has no plausible story about what *kind* of fact a moral fact is. And if he has no plausible story about the kind of fact a moral fact is, then, despite initial appearance, he has no plausible story about what moral reflection and moral argument are all about.

In order to see this, remember what we said at the outset when we first introduced the idea of the practicality of moral judgement. We said then that the practicality of moral judgement is a consequence of the fact that judgements about right and wrong are judgements about what we have reason to do and reason not to do. This is the subject matter of moral reflection and moral argument, *our reasons for action*. But the moral realist who admits an array of moral facts about which we may be motivationally neutral must reject such a conception of rightness and wrongness. After all, we could hardly remain motivationally neutral about what we think we have reason to do! The challenge such a realist faces is thus to provide us with some alternative account of what *kind* of fact a moral fact is; an alternative account of what moral reflection and moral argument are *about*.

Some moral realists do face up to this challenge. They have claimed, for example, that moral facts are facts that play a certain *explanatory role* in the social world: right acts are those that tend towards social stability, whereas wrong acts are those that tend towards social unrest. An Aristotelian version of this might be: right acts are those in accord with the 'proper function' of human beings – a quasi-biological notion – wrong acts are those that are not in accord with this proper function. Moral reflection and moral argument are thus, they suggest, arguments about which features of actions feed this tendency towards unrest and stability. Or, in the Aristotelian version, they are arguments about which acts are in accord with the proper function of humans (and thus, ultimately, about what the proper function of a human being is). The word 'tendency' is not idle here, for such realists are quick to emphasize that other factors may mitigate the tendency towards stability and unrest, or may stop humans actually having their proper function.

Let's focus for a moment on the suggestion that a moral fact can be characterized in terms of a tendency towards social stability or unrest. This suggestion cannot be dismissed out of hand, for reflection of an armchair-sociological kind does suggest that the acts we are disposed to think of as right – those that provide for a more equitable satisfaction of different people's interests, say – do tend towards social stabilty, and that the acts we are disposed to think of as wrong – those that provide for a less equitable satisfaction of different people's interests, say – do tend towards social unrest. It is thus best to assume that we have here two *competing* conceptions of a moral fact. Which conception seems the more plausible?

On the one hand, we have the idea of a moral fact as a fact about what we have reason to do or not to do. On the other, we have the idea of a moral fact in terms of what tends towards social stability and unrest. If the question is 'Which conception allows us to make the best sense of moral argument?' then the answer must surely be the former. For, to the extent that moral argument does focus on what tends towards social stability, it does so because social stability is deemed morally important, an outcome we have reason to produce.

Indeed, it seems to me that even this kind of moral realist's focus on *explanation* pushes us back in the direction of the idea of a moral fact as a fact about what we have reason to do. For, again, to the extent that we think of right acts as acts that tend towards social stability, we think that they have this tendency *because* they represent the reasonable thing for people to do. It is the tendency people have to do what is reasonable that is doing the explanatory work. But that, too, simply returns us to the original conception of a moral fact in terms of what we have reason to do. (We might say similar things about the idea that we can characterize a moral fact in terms of the proper function of human beings; for insofar as we understand the idea of the 'proper function' of human beings, we think that their proper function is to be reasonable and rational.)

In the end, then, we might object that this kind of moral realist fails to provide us with a real *alternative* to our original conception of a moral fact. The real question, then, is whether the moral realist is forced to reject the idea that rightness and wrongness have to do with what we have reason to do and reason not to do. In the remainder of this essay I want to explore this question.

The devil of the piece is what I have been calling the 'standard picture' of human psychology. For the standard picture gives us a model of what it is to have a reason in terms of a desire/belief pair. If the moral realist is to make headway in combining the objectivity and the practicality of moral judgement without appealing to 'queer' moral facts, he must challenge this standard picture.

The trouble is, however, that the standard picture looks substantially correct as an account of human motivation. After all, it is uncontroversial that the psychological states that motivate actions must be dispositions of some sort, dispositions to produce acts of the relevant kind. And it is also uncontroversial that actions are motivated by psychological states that have content: either they are produced by states that represent the way the world is (beliefs) or by states that represent the way the world is to be (desires), or, as the standard picture has it, they are produced by a pairing of the two (a desire and a belief).

But now reflect for a moment. A disposition to produce acts of some relevant kind, if it has content, must have, as its content, a representation of the way the world is to be, and so it must be a desire. For how else could the psychological state in question *target* the state of affairs to be produced? (And how could it produce what is to be produced without having targeted it?) Moreover, if this state is to produce the targeted state of affairs, it must also be paired with a representation of how the world is, and so it must be paired with a belief. For only so will the relevant *change* in the world be produced so as to bring about the targeted state of affairs.

It therefore seems that the standard picture is right in insisting that desires are required in order to motivate actions. The place to challenge the standard picture, then, is not in its account of what motivates action, but rather in its tacit conflation of *reasons* with *motives*. Seeing why this is a conflation also enables us to see why we may legitimately talk about our *beliefs* about the reasons we have, and why having such beliefs makes it rational to have corresponding desires.

Imagine that you are giving the baby a bath. As you do, it begins to scream uncontrollably. Nothing you do seems to help. As you watch it scream, you are overcome with a desire to drown the baby in the bathwater. Certainly you may now be *motivated* to drown the baby. (You may even actually drown it.) But does the mere fact that you have this desire, and are thus motivated, mean that you have a *reason* to drown the baby?

One commonsensical answer is that, since the desire is not *worth* satisfying, it does not provide you with such a reason; that, in this case, you are motivated to do something you have *no* reason to do. However, the standard picture seems utterly unable to accept this answer. After all, your desire to drown the baby need be based on no false belief. As such, it is entirely beyond rational criticism – or so that standard picture tells us.

The problem, here, is that the standard picture gives no special privilege to what we would want if we were 'cool, calm and collected' (to use a flippant phrase). Yet we seem ordinarily to think that not being cool, calm and collected may lead to all sorts of irrational emotional outbursts. Having those desires that we would have if we were cool, calm and collected thus seems to be an independent rational ideal. When cool, calm and collected, you would wish for the baby not to be drowned, no matter how much it screams, and no matter how overcome you may be, in your uncool, uncalm and uncollected state, with a desire to drown it. This is why you have no reason to drown the baby.

Perhaps we have already said enough to reconcile the objectivity of moral judgement with its practicality. Judgements of right and wrong are judgements about what we have reason to do and reason not to do. But what sort of fact is a fact about what we have reason to do? The preceding discussion suggests an answer. It suggests that facts about what we have reason to do are not facts about what we *do* desire, as the standard picture would have it, but are rather facts about what we *would* desire if we were in certain idealized conditions of reflection: if, say, we were well-informed, cool, calm and collected. According to this account, then, I have a reason to give to famine relief in my particular circumstances just in case, if I were in such idealized conditions of reflection, I would desire that, even when in my particular circumstances, I give to famine relief. And this sort of fact may certainly be the object of a belief.

Moreover, this account of what it is to have a reason makes it plain why the standard picture of human psychology is wrong to insist that beliefs and desires are altogether distinct; why, on the contrary, having certain beliefs, beliefs about what we have reason to do, does make it rational for us to have certain desires, desires to do what we believe we have reason to do.

In order to see this, suppose I believe that I would desire to give to famine relief if I were cool, calm and collected – i.e. more colloquially, I believe I have a reason to give to famine relief – but, being uncool, uncalm and uncollected, I don't desire to give to famine relief. Am I rationally criticizable for not having the desire? I surely am. After all, from my own point of view my beliefs and desires form a more coherent, and thus a rationally preferable, package if I do in fact desire to do what I believe I would desire to do if I were cool, calm and collected. This is because, since it is an independent rational ideal to have the desires I would have if I were cool, calm and collected, so, from my own point of view, if I believe that I would have a certain desire under such conditions and yet fail to have it, then my beliefs and desires fail to meet this ideal. To believe that I would desire to give to famine relief if I were cool, calm and collected, and yet to fail to desire to give to famine relief, is thus to manifest a commonly recognizable species of rational failure.

If this is right, then it follows that, contrary to the standard picture of human psychology, there is in fact no problem at all in supposing that I may have genuine *beliefs* about what I have reason to do, where having those beliefs makes it rational for me to have the corresponding *desires*. And if there is no problem at all in supposing that this may be so, then there is no problem in reconciling the practicality of moral judgement with the claim that moral judgements express our beliefs about the reasons we have.

However, this doesn't yet suffice to solve the problem facing the moral realist. For moral judgements aren't *just* judgements abut the reasons we have. They are judgements about the reasons we have *where those reasons are supposed to be determined entirely by our circumstances*. As I put it earlier, people in the same circumstances face the same moral choice: if they did the same action then either they both acted rightly (they both did what they had reason to do) or they both acted wrongly (they both did what they had reason not to do). Does the account of what it is to have a reason just given entail that this is so?

Suppose our circumstances are identical, and let's ask whether it is right for each of us to give to famine relief: that is, whether we each have a reason to do so. According to the account on offer it is right that I give to famine relief just in case I have a reason to give to famine relief, and I have such a reason just in case, if I were in idealized conditions of reflection – well-informed, cool, calm and collected – I would desire to give to famine relief. And the same is true of you. If our circumstances are the same then, supposedly, we should both have such a reason or both lack such a reason. But do we?

The question is whether, if we were well-informed, cool, calm and collected, we would tend to *converge* in the desires we have. Would we converge or would there always be the possibility of some non-rationally-explicable difference in our desires *even under such conditions?* The standard picture of human psychology now returns to centre-stage. For it tells us that there is *always* the possibility of some non-rationally-explicable difference in our desires even under such idealized conditions of reflection. This is the residue of the standard picture's conception of desire as a psychological state that is beyond rational criticism.

If this is right then the moral realist's attempt to combine the objectivity and the practicality of moral judgement must be deemed a failure. We are forced to accept that there is a *fundamental relativity* in the reasons we have. What we have reason to do is relative to what we would desire under certain idealized conditions of reflection, and this may differ from person to person. It is not wholly determined by our circumstances, as moral facts are supposed to be.

Many philosophers accept the standard picture's pronouncement on this point. But accepting there is such a fundamental relativity in our reasons seems altogether premature to me. It puts the cart before the horse. For surely moral practice is itself the forum in which we will *discover* whether there is a fundamental relativity in our reasons.

After all, in moral practice we attempt to change people's moral beliefs by engaging them in rational argument: i.e. by getting their beliefs to approximate those they would have under more idealized conditions of reflection. And sometimes we succeed. When we succeed, other things being equal, we succeed in changing their desires. But if we accept that there is a fundamental relativity in our reasons then we can say, in advance, that this procedure will never result in a massive *convergence* in moral beliefs; for we know in advance that there will never be a convergence in the desires we have under such idealized conditions of reflection. Or rather, and more accurately, if there is a fundamental relativity in our reasons then it follows that any convergence we find in our moral beliefs, and thus in our desires, must be entirely contingent. It could in no way be explained by, or suggestive of, the fact that the desires that emerge have some *privileged* rational status.

My question is: 'Why accept this?' Why not think, instead, that if such a convergence emerged in moral practice then that would itself suggest that these particular moral beliefs, and the corresponding desires, *do* enjoy a privileged rational status? After all, something like such a convergence in mathematical practice lies behind our conviction that mathematical claims enjoy a privileged rational status. So why not think that a like convergence in moral practice would show that moral judgements enjoy the same privileged rational status? At this point, the standard picture's insistence that there is a fundamental relativity in our reasons begins to sound all too much like a hollow dogma.

The kind of moral realism described here endorses a conception of moral facts that is a far cry from the picture presented at the outset: moral facts as queer facts about the universe whose recognition necessarily impacts upon our desires. Instead, the realist has eschewed queer facts about the universe in favour of a more 'subjectivist' conception of moral facts. This emerged in the realist's analysis of what it is to have a reason. (For a fuller discussion of subjectivist theories see Article 38, SUBJECTIVISM.) The realist's point, however, is that such a conception of moral facts may make them subjective only in the innocuous sense that they are facts about what we would *want* under certain idealized conditions of reflection, where wants are, admittedly, a kind of psychological state enjoyed by subjects. But moral facts remain objective insofar as they are facts about what *we*, not just *you* or *I*, would want under such conditions. The existence of a moral fact – say, the rightness of giving to famine relief in certain circumstances – requires that, under idealized conditions of reflection, rational creatures would *converge* upon a desire to give to famine relief in such circumstances.

Of course, it must be agreed on all sides that moral argument has not yet produced the sort of convergence in our desires that would make the idea of a moral fact – a fact about the reasons we have entirely determined by our circumstances – look plausible. But neither has moral argument had much of a history in times in which we have been able to engage in free reflection unhampered by a false biology (the Aristotelian tradition) or a false belief in God (the Judeo-Christian tradition). It remains to be seen whether sustained moral argument can elicit the requisite convergence in our moral beliefs, and corresponding desires, to make the idea of a moral fact look plausible. The kind of moral realism described here holds out the hope that it will. Only time will tell.

Further reading

Ayer, A. J.: 'Critique of ethics and theology', in his *Language, Truth and Logic* (London: 1936); (London: Gollancz, 1970).
Harman, G.: *The Nature of Morality* (Oxford: Oxford University Press, 1977).
Honderich, T., ed.: *Morality and Objectivity* (London: Routledge and Kegan Paul, 1985), especially the papers by Blackburn and Williams.
Hume, D.: *A Treatise of Human Nature* (1738); ed. L. A. Selby-Bigge (Oxford: Clarendon Press, 1978), especially Book II, Part III, Section III.
Mackie, J.: *Ethics: Inventing Right and Wrong* (Harmondsworth: Penguin, 1977), especially ch. 1.
Nagel, T.: *The View From Nowhere* (Oxford: Oxford University Press, 1986), especially ch. 8.
Sayre-McCord, G., ed.: *Essays on Moral Realism* (Ithaca, NY: Cornell University Press, 1988). This is the best book to read on the topic of moral realism, if you can only manage one, as it collects together papers by many of the leading figures: e.g. Ayer, Blackburn, Harman, Mackie, McDowell, Wiggins, Williams and others. Sayre-McCord's introduction is also well worth reading.
Smith, M., Lewis, D. and Johnston, M.: Symposium on 'Dispositional theories of value', *Proceedings of the Aristotelian Society*, Supplementary Volume (1989).

Williams, B.: 'Internal and external reasons', in his *Moral Luck* (Cambridge: Cambridge University Press, 1981).

——: *Ethics and the Limits of Philosophy* (Cambridge, Mass.: Harvard University Press, 1985), especially the first four chapters.

36

Intuitionism

JONATHAN DANCY

BETWEEN the 1860s and the 1920s the term 'intuitionism' was another name for pluralism, the view that there are a large number of different moral principles which cannot be put into any general order of importance in a way that would help to resolve conflicts between them. Pluralism of this sort would be naturally contrasted with utilitarianism; utilitarians (e.g. J. S. Mill) tried to hold that there was only one Supreme Principle. But nowadays an intuitionist is thought of as someone who holds a particular view about the way in which we come to find out which actions are right and which are wrong. Intuitionists in this sense claim that we grasp basic moral principles by intuition, and one can believe this without thinking that there is more than one such principle. To give one eminent example, Henry Sidgwick was a utilitarian but thought of the basic principles he espoused as grasped by intuition. He held that they were self-evident, meaning by this that one only had to consider them in order to recognize their truth.

It was the work of W. D. Ross and H. A. Prichard in the 1930s which put the two senses of intuitionism together, for they were both pluralists – that is, intuitionists in the old sense – and committed to a special mode of cognition – that is, intuitionistic in the new sense. (In this it resembled the position of the forefather of modern intuitionism, Richard Price, who wrote 200 years earlier.) They held that there are very many true moral principles, all of which we know by intuition (i.e. they held them to be self-evident). Ross's arguments in favour of his pluralism are discussed in Article 18, AN ETHIC OF PRIMA FACIE DUTIES, and I shall not repeat them here. I am more concerned now with the claim that the principles are known by intuition. There are two suggestions here which can be separated, first that moral principles are the sorts of things that can be true and known, second that they are known in a special and unfamiliar way, perhaps even by a special faculty called moral intuition.

These things are contentious. Many thinkers (often called non-cognitivists) hold that moral attitudes are not true or false, since there is nothing for them to get right or wrong. A moral attitude is an expression of the individual's moral position, and as such can be sincere or insincere in itself and consistent or inconsistent with other such, but hardly mistaken or correct. If moral attitudes cannot be true or false, we should not claim that any such attitude amounts to knowledge, since knowledge is only of what is true. So on this view moral principles can be neither true nor known. Ross and Prichard held however that there are facts of the matter about what is morally right and wrong, and that our grasp on some of these facts is firm enough to deserve the title of knowledge. This second claim is even more disputable. If there are these moral facts, how do we come to know them? The claim that they are known by intuition seems to suggest that we have a moral faculty which reveals moral truth to us in much the same sort of way that our eyes reveal truths about our surroundings. There would be a tendency, if we thought this, to accuse those who disagree morally with us of moral blindness; their moral faculty is not in good working order, as we can see since their views are different from ours. But, in the absence of any account of how this faculty is supposed to work, the idea is mysterious; no wonder it became common for philosophers to complain that talk of moral intuition was just an attempt to award an authority to one's own moral opinion that one was not willing to grant to others'.

I will begin with the notion of a moral sense or faculty called intuition. Before criticizing the intuitionists, it is best first to be clear what their views here really were. First, what did Ross think we can know by intuition? As I explained in the essay referred to above, Ross held that moral knowledge arises first when we notice a feature of the situation we are in which makes a moral difference to how we should behave here; that I would have to distress you is a reason for me not to say what I really think about your marriage. This knowledge is knowledge of something that matters *here*; its relevance is at first restricted to the case before us. But we immediately notice that what matters here must matter in the same way wherever it appears; we discover a moral principle by *intuitive induction* from what the initial case contains. Ross held that the principles we come to know are self-evident to us, but for him this means only that no more is needed to reveal their truth to us as general guides to our behaviour than what is in the case before us. It doesn't mean that we can discover whether a principle is true just by thinking about it.

In what way does this story suppose that we have a mysterious faculty of moral intuition? (Ross used the word 'intuition' very sparingly, if at all.) There are two places for this faculty in the story. The second is in the move from what we see as relevant to our action *here* to the thought that the same feature is relevant in the same way everywhere. Ross thinks of this move as similar to the one we make when looking at a particular argument helps us to see that any argument of that form is valid. (Note that it is because this sort of logical move was called 'intuitive induction' that the notion of intuition appears in Ross at all.) Most would find this sort of generalization quite innocuous; it would be hard to suggest that we need a special faculty to do it with. So it must be at the *earlier* stage that intuition proper is supposed to come in, when we notice some feature of the case as one which makes a difference to what we ought to do. The idea is that if what is going on is that we are *deciding* to allow that feature to influence us, there can be no complaint. The trouble only arises when we say that there is a fact of the matter here – this feature's mattering – which we somehow discern and which we or another person might have missed; it is not so much a matter for decision as for discovery. But what do we discover it with? Our eyes? Can one literally *see* that something matters here?

It would have been worse if Ross had held that we discern the truth of moral principles directly, for then he would have had to show what faculty enabled us to do this. A faculty that homes in on the true principles and naturally rejects the false ones is very mysterious indeed (though Sidgwick seems happy enough to suppose that we have one). But Ross doesn't say that. Our knowledge of the principles is not direct but indirect; we reach it via something we know better, namely the nature of the particular case before us.

I said there were two generally contentious views held by the intuitionists. The first is that there are moral truths which can be known, and the second is an account of how we come to know them (by intuition?). Perhaps, in order to understand how we come to know them, we would do better to ask some questions about these so-called truths. Ross never seems to have doubted that there are moral truths, facts of the matter in ethics which we can come to know. But he could have argued for his position in the following way. Consider what it is like to make up your mind how to act in a morally tricky situation. First you try to decide which features here make a difference to how you should behave. It is true we call this 'deciding', but it is no different from deciding that it will probably not rain tomorrow; in both cases we think of what we are doing as the attempt to get things right. We don't suppose that it is up to us what matters, so that any sincere 'decision' is right, any more than that it is up to us what the weather will be. We think that we may well miss the truth, and so that a feature does not count as important because we take it to be important – rather we hope that we take it to be important because it *is* important. Its importance is there for us to recognize, and if we miss it there is a truth which we have failed to notice. This is why there is a sense of thin ice about the whole process. Ross wants to say that this sense is justified; he claims in general that his theory is true to ordinary moral thought, and he would claim that in this case too.

But what sort of facts are these moral facts? And is there any room for facts like these in a world which can be described by science? It would be easy to answer this question if we could *identify* moral facts with natural facts. Naturalism is the claim that moral facts just are natural facts. (See Article 37, NATURALISM.) For instance, some utilitarians are naturalists, holding that the fact that this action generates less happiness than some available alternative is the same fact as the fact that it is wrong. If this were true, there would not be too much trouble finding room for moral facts in a world of science. But the intuitionists rejected naturalism. They did this because of their pluralism. If one thinks that there are lots of different sorts of things that matter to how one should behave, in no very clear order or shape, one is going to think that there are too many different ways in which actions can be right or wrong. Rightness cannot be identified with any one of these ways in preference to the others, and if we put them all together we find that there is no natural similarity between them all – the only common feature is the moral one, that each is a way in which an action gets to be right. The *natural* base for moral facts has no *natural* shape, and hence there is no common natural feature present for us to identify rightness with.

The best approach for an intuitionist is to try to show that though moral 'facts'

413

are not to be identified with natural facts, they are not so very different from other facts as one might initially suppose. If we allow that the world we live in is roughly the one captured by physics, where in that world are the moral facts to be found? The first answer is to say that the world does not contain facts; the facts are facts about the world, not in it. Second, the moral facts are facts about actions and agents, things which clearly exist even though physics does not say a great deal about them. Third, there is a comprehensible relation between moral and non-moral facts; it is not as if the two are completely unrelated. The moral facts *exist in virtue of* the non-moral ones. This 'existing in virtue of' is not well understood, but it is common enough in other areas not to raise special problems in ethics. For instance, the dangerousness of a cliff bears this relation to other features of the cliff, such as its crumbly nature and steepness. Sometimes we express this relation harmlessly using the word 'because'. When we say that this is a house because it has solid walls, doors, rooms and a roof, we are saying that this is what makes it a house. Similarly, what makes an action good will be its generosity, considerateness etc.; it is good because of its generosity or whatever it may be, and generous because it was a substantial personal sacrifice, perhaps. Here we see a moral fact existing in virtue of non-moral ones. So even though the world can be described by physics, it cannot be completely described that way; there remain other facts to mention, including moral facts, which are comprehensibly related to the basic physical facts from which they result.

The question how one notices these facts has still to be answered. I think it is made more difficult by a view which Ross took, and which his critics reasonably fastened upon. He accepted the Humean view that beliefs cannot be an independent source of motivation. Hume argued that our motives (our reasons for action) are our beliefs and our desires. The beliefs are inert representations of the world, and cannot comprehensibly be what drives us to action. What *moves* us is our desires, which are *pushy* states. We have a desire (for an orange, say) which is channelled by a belief that there is one in the larder so as to get us to stir ourselves in that direction. Now for Ross our moral attitudes are beliefs, and so depend on the existence of a suitable desire if they are to motivate us to action. So if our moral opinions are to make any difference to how we act, there must be present also in us something like a general desire to do the good – a desire which we might comprehensibly have lacked. And if we had lacked it, we would still have been able to tell what is right and what is wrong; we would merely have found in the distinction between right and wrong nothing that made any difference to how we felt called on to behave. Morality, being purely factual, is thus deprived of any intrinsic relation to conduct in a way that critics found it easy to ridicule.

What the critics asked, quite fairly, was why, if moral facts are as the intuitionists said, we should *care* about them at all. There is enormous plausibility in the thought that moral attitudes are intrinsically related to behaviour; to adopt an attitude is just to accept a reason for action – to be motivated to do or not to do actions of a certain sort. Of course that motivation can be defeated by stronger motivation on the other side, or even annulled by a fit of severe depression. But, barring these accidents, it can't be right to say that one could be perfectly well aware of the wrongness of what one is doing and not think of this at all as a reason for desisting. We could express this by saying that there is an *internal* relation between moral attitudes and action, against Ross whose view was that the relation is external; moral judgements, for Ross, only make a difference to those who have an independent desire to do what is right, rather as horticultural judgements only make a difference to those who care about that sort of thing. So the critics' view has been called internalism; an internalist holds that to accept that one's action is wrong is itself to be motivated not to do it. By contrast, an externalist holds that moral judgements need the help of an independent desire if they are to motivate us and make a difference to how we act.

So in asking why we should care about the moral facts that the intuitionists talk about, these critics were complaining about Ross's externalism. And I think they were right. It is ludicrous to say that we might accept that an action is outrageously wrong and still think of this as not in itself giving us good reason to hold back. Surely to accept that the action is wrong is just to care about its not being done. But in that case, given Hume's views about motivation and the difference between belief and desire, a moral judgement must be some form of desire (or, more generally, some form of 'pro-attitude') rather than, as the intuitionists thought, a form of belief. For desires are forms of minding or caring, while beliefs are not. It is this argument that led to the dominance of non-cognitivism in the English-speaking world from the 1930s to the 1970s, and the eclipse of intuitionism. (See Article 38, SUBJECTIVISM.) The argument between cognitivists and non-cognitivists is about whether moral attitudes are more like beliefs or like desires; intuitionists come out as cognitivists on this approach, and therefore as externalists (given the Humean picture).

The view that moral facts are inert states of the moral world, which one can notice in a way which bears no direct relation to one's choice of action, made it all the harder for the intuitionists to answer the question how one comes to find out about these funny facts. It was not really plausible to say that we infer them from something else; our moral beliefs are not the product of reason. So they must be the products of the senses, and since they cannot be the products of the normal five senses they must be produced by a further, moral, sense. This is why intuitionism is sometimes called the moral sense theory. And the absence of any account of how this further, unnoticed sense works is what led to G. J. Warnock's well-known charge that here the intuitionists offer nothing better than a confession of bewilderment got up to look like an answer.

I think, however, that the problem lies more in Ross's externalism that in his claim that there are moral facts (which we might call his realism; see Article 35, REALISM). Ross would have done better not to have accepted Hume's account of motivation and the account it gives of the different roles of belief and desire. More recently writers in the intuitionist tradition such as Thomas Nagel and John McDowell have challenged Hume here, claiming that desire is not necessary to get an action going; belief alone is enough to do the job, sometimes. Ordinarily, they admit, the story is as Hume tells it. I want an orange (desire) and my beliefs, which are inert in themselves, channel the desire so that it can drive me in one direction (the larder) rather than another. But things are not always like this. When I am standing on the kerb looking for a gap in the traffic so that I can cross the street safely, I am not doing this because I desire a long and healthy life. I *experience* no desire; I'm just looking for a gap in the traffic before I cross. Why insist that there must have been a desire in there somewhere? All that is happening here is that I take a *fact* (there is a bus coming now) as a reason for me not to step out yet. This is what we call being prudent; prudent people are people whose *beliefs* about safety and danger are enough to motivate them. The same is true in ethics. One's beliefs about right and wrong can be enough to move one to stop what one is doing or change one's intentions, without needing the help of an independent desire. These moral beliefs are able to motivate us (stand as reasons for us) in their own right.

This position is an internalist one, and for that reason generally preferable to Ross's externalism. Externalism was always implausible, and since it emerged as a direct result of applying Hume's views on motivation to Ross's views on ethics, the way to improve Ross's position must be to abandon Humean accounts of belief and desire. And I think this move also offers an easier answer to the question how we come to find out moral facts. When we thought of these facts as inert, in the Humean way, we only had two possible accounts of how we come to know them – by the senses or by reason. But now we are thinking of them rather differently, as reasons for action. Given this, we might claim that their discovery is a matter of practical *judgement*, not of inference nor of perception, and in this way try to avoid the suggestion that we have invented a special faculty or moral sense. After all, we will be claiming that the story in the moral case is not significantly different from the story in the case of prudence, and surely there it is a matter of judgement, not of perception, when we take the fact that a bus is coming as a reason for not stepping out yet.

All this, however, is extremely controversial in the present state of moral philosophy. (For an alternative view, see Article 35, REALISM.) What I have been aiming to do so far is to present the most effective objections that were raised against the intuitionism of Ross and Prichard, and then to see how one might move to escape them, with an eye to what has actually happened in moral philosophy since. The most debatable point is the idea that Hume may have been wrong about motivation, so that a set of beliefs alone can be enough to cause an action. Since the non-cognitivist tradition is driven by Hume's view here, we cannot expect much consensus on the point.

The crucial application of Hume's position is the following argument. No set of beliefs alone is enough to motivate us (get an action going). But when we add to a set of beliefs a moral attitude, we move to a new set which is capable of motivating. So the moral attitude must either be or at the least centrally contain a desire – probably the general altruistic desire for the welfare of others (which Hume called a 'natural sympathy'). It follows from this that there can be no moral facts. Beliefs aim at facts, but desires do not. If moral judgements expressed beliefs, we might suppose that there must be some moral facts for those beliefs to aim at. But since they express desires, there is no such need for moral facts at all. And this is a welcome conclusion, for it removes from us all sorts of unpleasant possibilities such as the idea that there might be accredited moral experts who would somehow be in a position to dictate to the rest of us about which of our actions are morally acceptable and which are not.

Intuitionists who want to escape this argument do best to start early, by denying the first premise.

But even if everything we have so far said is accepted, there still remain some awkward questions about these moral facts. The main difficulty lies in the question whether these facts are objective or not. How can there be facts about the world which are able in their own right to make a difference to how we should act? McDowell asks this question by asking how an objective fact can be intrinsically related to the will. The reason why this question seems worth asking is that there is a very attractive conception of what it is for a fact to be objective, which derives from physical science. An objective fact, on this conception, is just a scientific fact. But scientific facts concern a world which exists independent of us. So objective facts are facts which hold independent of the human mind. How then can there be facts which are both objective and intrinsically related to the human will?

There are two current attempts to answer this hard question in the post-intuitionist tradition. The first, Nagel's, accepts the role of natural science in determining our conception of objectivity. The second, McDowell's, is more sceptical. But both are working with the thought that in some sense or other there are values which are there for us to recognize or miss. The world, as McDowell nicely puts it, is not motivationally inert. One way to express this thought we have already seen; we claim that beliefs alone can be enough to motivate, and are not as Hume held inert. Another is to say that the world is richer than science conceives. The physical world is motivationally inert, but the world for us is not the physical world and our world is not so limited.

For Nagel, objectivity is a matter of degree. A point of view is more objective if it is less coloured by the peculiarities of perspective of those who view the world from that point of view. So, to make our metaphor literal, the colour we see in the world would not appear from the most objective point of view, the point of view with no peculiarities at all. From that point of view, the world is the world of physical science, and that world is a world which lacks the sort of colour we know. However, many of the ways the world seems to us from our present, subjective point of view would persist for a while as we move towards greater objectivity, gradually stripping off those features whose presence is due to peculiarities of our viewpoint. For instance, the fear of heights from which I suffer makes heights seem terrible to me, but I know perfectly well that from even a slightly more objective point of view than mine the heights that terrify me would appear fairly unworrying. I express this by saying that *really* this drop is not the awful chasm it appears to me. But the idea of what is real here is a matter of degree, and we can travel further towards uncovering true (extreme) reality by saying that *really* nothing is terrifying at all. There is no terrifyingness out there, only terrified people. But this recognition does not prevent us from agreeing that some things are really terrifying (King Kong, say, or nuclear war) and other things (spiders) are not. For Nagel, moral values are real enough in this way. They would not be visible from the most objective point of view, but they are more than mere appearance. They are objective, but other things are more objective.

McDowell's way of claiming the objectivity of moral value is to distinguish two conceptions of objectivity (Nagel says there is only one, but it is a matter of degree). The first conception takes the objective to be that which exists independent of human awareness or response, and in this sense physical facts are objective and moral facts are not. The second conception takes the objective to be that which exists independent of any particular human response. This is a much broader conception of the objective. Colours are objective in this sense, since for an apple to be red it is not required that anyone should actually be looking at it. The redness of an apple can persist unseen; it is somehow there waiting for us to notice it. In this weaker sense, then, the colour is objective. It is not objective in the stronger sense, since colour is something essentially to do with *appearance*, and appearance is appearance *to us*; so colour does not exist independent of human awareness and response. McDowell claims that values have the second, weaker form of objectivity, and takes this to show that there can be objective facts about what is right and wrong. If the world contains value in as strong a sense as it contains colour, he would be satisfied.

I have slipped back to talking about moral facts, but intended rather to suggest that these facts are best thought of not as *facts perceived* but as *reasons* recognized in the exercise of practical moral *judgement*. Intuitionists hold that these reasons exist for us to recognize – are there to be recognized. There are truths, facts of the matter, about what reasons there are; and we may miss these truths if we are not careful. What is more, a person whose grasp on the reasons is secure enough can be said to know what ought to be done. So with the availability of moral truth comes the possibility of moral knowledge.

I end by mentioning two main criticsms that are laid at the door of intuitionism. The first is John Mackie's complaint that it involves the gratuitous invention of peculiar properties (rightness, wrongness) which bear little relation to others and have the strange ability to attract us when we recognize them, as if they enjoyed a form of odd magnetism (see Mackie, 1977, Ch. 1). I think this criticism is misplaced. The post-intuitionist theories of Nagel and McDowell do not talk about rightness and wrongness much, but concentrate on the thought that the pain I would cause someone if I do what I intend is a reason for me not to act in that way, and it is a reason whether I recognize it as such or not. There are no peculiar properties here, only the comparatively ordinary suggestion that the pain of others is relevant to one's moral choice.

A different criticism, pressed by Simon Blackburn, asks again how we are supposed to recognize the existence of these reasons. If it is suggested that they are in some way analogous to colours, perhaps our awareness of them is to be like our awareness of colours. But we discover what colours things are by entering into causal relations with them. There is a complex causal story to be told about how the colours of objects can impress themselves on us. But there is no such story to be told about how values or reasons can impress themselves on us. This is because they are unable to enter into causal relations at all; so our awareness of them cannot be seen as any sort of a *response* to what is independently there. Instead we should accept that we *project* moral properties onto a world which in itself has none. (Hence this position has come to be known as projectivism.)

There are two ways of replying to this attack. The first is to argue with McDowell that values do enter into causal relations, though they cannot be said to pull their own weight there. He compares this with the way in which we tell the story of colour-perception. There is a causal story here, but the colours of the objects we see do not pull any weight in that story; the story goes instead straight from the nature of the surfaces we see to our perception of them as having this or that colour. However, we are not tempted in this case to deny that the colours are real (in McDowell's weaker sense), and McDowell would say the same about the values.

The other possibility is to compare intuitionism in ethics with intuitionism in mathematics. In mathematics intuitionists claim that numbers are abstract objects of whose existence and nature we can become aware, not by entering into natural causal relations with them (which is impossible) but by the operation of reason and judgement. The point here is that we can be led to recognize the properties of real, independent objects in ways which are not causal.

These matters are still hotly debated, and I think it would be fair to say that the interestingly new forms of intuitionism at present being worked out have not yet entirely escaped the problems that dogged their predecessors.

References

Blackburn, S.: 'Errors and the phenomenology of value', *Morality and Objectivity*, ed. T. Honderich (London: Routledge and Kegan Paul, 1985), pp. 1–22.

Hume, D.: *A Treatise Of Human Nature* (1738); ed. L. A. Selby-Bigge (Oxford: Clarendon Press, 1978), esp. Book II, Part 3, Section 3.

McDowell, J.: 'Values and secondary qualities', *Morality and Objectivity*, ed. T. Honderich (London: Routledge and Kegan Paul, 1985), pp. 110–29.

Mackie, J. L.: *Ethics: Inventing Right and Wrong* (Harmondsworth: Penguin, 1977), ch. 1.

Mill, J. S.: *Utilitarianism* (1863); ed. A. D. Lindsay (London: Dent, 1910).

Nagel, T.: *The View From Nowhere* (Oxford: Oxford University Press, 1986).

Price, R.: *Review of the Principal Questions and Difficulties in Morals* (1758); ed. D. D. Raphael (Oxford: Oxford University Press, 1948).

Prichard, H. A.: 'Does moral philosophy rest on a mistake?' in his *Moral Obligation* (Oxford: Oxford University Press, 1949), pp. 1–17.

Ross, W. D.: *The Right and The Good* (Oxford: Clarendon Press, 1930).

Sidgwick, H.: *The Methods of Ethics* (1874); (London: Macmillan, 1907).

Warnock, G. J.: *Contemporary Moral Philosophy* (London: Macmillan, 1967), ch. 2.

Further reading

Falk, W.D.: 'Ought and motivation', in his *Ought, Reasons, and Morality* (Ithaca, NY: Cornell University Press, 1986).

Stevenson, C.L.: *Ethics and Language* (New Haven: Yale University Press, 1944), ch. 1.

Strawson, P.: 'Ethical intuitionism', *Philosophy*, 24 (1949), 23–33.

Urmson, J.O.: 'A defence of intuitionism', *Proceedings of the Aristotelian Society*, 75 (1975), 111–19.

Williams, B.A.O.: 'What does intuitionism imply?', *Human Agency: Language, Duty, Value*, eds. J. Dancy et al. (Stanford: Stanford University Press, 1988), pp. 189–98.

37

Naturalism

CHARLES R. PIGDEN

i What naturalism is

IN PHILOSOPHY, not only the doctrines but the definitions of the doctrines are subject to dispute. Thus it is with ethical naturalism. My definition, therefore, is personal but not, I hope, idiosyncratic. By naturalism I mean more or less what other philosphers have in mind – though the more and the less will vary from case to case.

Naturalism, then, is a cognitivist doctrine (or family of doctrines). It states that moral judgements are propositions, capable of truth and falsity. Moral judgements purport to tell it like it is. Naturalism is thus opposed to non-cognitivism, to emotivism and prescriptivism, which represent moral judgements variously as exclamations, psychological prods and quasi-commands. It is also (in a weak sense) a realist doctrine; that is, it takes *some* moral judgements to be true. (More detailed accounts of these positions can be found in Article 35, REALISM, Article 38, SUBJECTIVISM, and Article 40, UNIVERSAL PRESCRIPTIVISM.) It is thus opposed to the error-theory of J. L. Mackie which agrees that moral judgements make claims that are either true or false, but denies that any of them are true. Morality, for the naturalist, is not a fiction, a mistake or a myth but a body of knowledge, or at least, of information. Finally, naturalism is (in a loose sense) a reductive doctrine. Though there are moral truths (i.e. true propositions) there are no peculiarly moral facts or properties (no distinctively moral states of affairs) over and above the facts and properties that can be specified using non-moral terminology. The contrast here is with 'intuitionist' philosophers such as G. E. Moore (1874–1958): 'If I am asked "What is good?", my answer is that good is good and that is the end of the matter. Or if I am asked "How is good to be defined?", my answer is that it cannot be defined and that is all I have to say about it' (Moore, 1903, p. 6). Moore does not mean he cannot tell you what things *are* good. (He thinks for example that friendship and the contemplation of beauty are good.) No, he is making a metaphysical or ontological point: the goodness of good things consists in their possessing the property of goodness, a basic feature of reality which cannot be further analysed or explained. (See Article 36, INTUI-TIONISM.) Naturalists disagree. For them, goodness *can* be further analysed or explained; reduced to something else or identified with some other property. Indeed naturalists think that goodness as Moore conceives it, a unique and *sui generis* property, does not exist. (And the same goes, naturally, for badness, rightness and wrongness.)

But there consensus ends. Naturalists differ as to what good, evil etc. are to be reduced to, and how this reduction is to be carried out. There are hedonistic naturalists who reduce facts about goodness to facts about pleasure and pain. (The goodness of friendship consists in its conduciveness to pleasure.) There are Aristotelian naturalists who prefer (alleged) facts about human nature and human flourishing. (Friendship is good in that it is somehow consonant with human needs or human nature.) There are even theological naturalists, who think the goodness of friendship amounts to its being sanctioned by God. Naturalists, in short, resort to all sorts of supposed facts – sociological, psychological, scientific, even metaphysical and theological – so long as they are not driven back on a realm of irreducibly *moral* facts or properties. Since some of these facts are metaphysical or supernatural, rather than natural in any ordinary sense of the word (facts about the natural world) you may well wonder how such a disparate group of moral theories came to wear the same label. The answer is historical. According to G. E. Moore they all stand accused of the naturalistic fallacy (of which, more later). He called this (supposed) fallacy *naturalistic* because it was more common among philosophers of a narrowly naturalistic stamp – those who wished to base morals on the kinds of facts that science could countenance. But these were only a subclass of those who – according to Moore – commit the fallacy. Nevertheless the name has stuck.

What is the impetus behind naturalism – what makes it attractive as a theoretical option? This is a difficult question to deal with since naturalism is not so much a doctrine as a family of doctrines held together by some shared theses. But a rough answer is this. Naturalists combine a yen for moral truth, that is, a conviction that some things really are right and others wrong, with a distaste for Moore's non-natural qualities of goodness, badness etc. Often this distaste is due to the scientific outlook and the conviction that nothing exists beyond what science licenses us to suppose. But it can be due to religious convictions, e.g. the belief that value springs from God and cannot be separated from what he wills. Either way, Moore's peculiarly moral properties are unwelcome, and a reduction must be sought which bases moral truths on the preferred metaphysic.

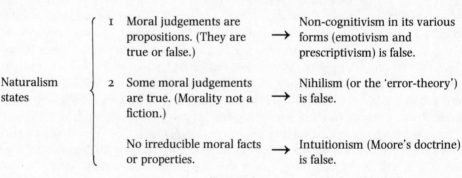

Naturalism states	1	Moral judgements are propositions. (They are true or false.)	→	Non-cognitivism in its various forms (emotivism and prescriptivism) is false.
	2	Some moral judgements are true. (Morality not a fiction.)	→	Nihilism (or the 'error-theory') is false.
		No irreducible moral facts or properties.	→	Intuitionism (Moore's doctrine) is false.

Figure 1

ii No-'ought'-from-'is', or the autonomy of ethics

If morality can be boiled down to truths of some other kind, ethics is not 'auton-omous'. Truth in morals is determined by the goings-on in some other realm. However, when naturalists and anti-naturalists quarrel about the autonomy of ethics, this is not (usually) what they have in mind. By 'the autonomy of ethics' they mean some such thesis as that 'ought' cannot be derived from 'is', or more generally that moral conclusions cannot be derived from non-moral premises, values from facts. This is often mixed up with the idea that moral words do not *mean the same* as non-moral words; that they lack 'naturalistic' synonyms. The issue is thus about inference rather than reduction; about what can be inferred from what. However, it is often assumed that *if* moral judgements can be derived from non-moral propositions, naturalism is true. If not, naturalism is false. This last claim is a mistake as I hope to show.

Anti-naturalists take as their text a famous passage from Hume (1711–1776). Moralists (complains Hume) 'proceed for some time in the ordinary way of reasoning' with proofs 'of the being of God' or 'observations concerning human affairs', 'when of a sudden, I am surprised to find that instead of the usual copulations of propositions *is* and *is not*, I meet with no proposition that is not connected with an *ought*, or an *ought not* ... as this *ought* or *ought not* expresses some new relation or affirmation 'tis necessary that it be observed and explained; and at the same time a reason should be given for what seems altogether incon-ceivable, how this new relation can be a deduction from others which are entirely different from it' (Hume, 1738, Book III, Part 1).

This passage is often summed up in the slogan 'no-"ought"-from-"is"' and deified as 'Hume's Law'. It is alleged to do wonders – to point up a fundamental distinction between facts and values, to prove non-cognitivism and (above all) to refute naturalism. (This last is an odd claim, since Hume himself was a naturalist.) In fact it can do none of these things. For Hume is making a simple logical point. A conclusion containing 'ought' cannot (as a matter of logic) be derived from 'ought'-free premises. (The same, of course, goes for the other moral words.) Logic is conservative; the conclusions of a valid inference are contained within the premises. You don't get out what you haven't put in. Hence if 'ought' appears in the conclusion of an argument but not in the premises, the inference is not logically valid.

Some anti-naturalists (notably R. M. Hare) have taken this 'is'/'ought' gap as a datum and sought to explain it by means of non-cognitivism. The reason you can't derive an 'ought' from an 'is', or, more generally, a moral conclusion from non-moral premises, is because moral judgements differ fundamentally from factual propositions. They don't (primarily) describe how the world *is* but prescribe how it *should be* – they are, in short, akin to orders. But we need not resort to non-cognitivism to explain this logical gulf. For there is a similar gap between conclusions about hedgehogs and premises which make no mention of them. You can't get 'hedgehog' conclusions from hedgehog-free premises (at least, not by logic alone). Yet nobody proposes a fact/hedgehog distinction or alleges that propositions about hedgehogs are not really propositions but a quaint subclass of commands. In both cases it is the conservativeness of logic that creates the gap, not any arcane difference in semantic kind. There is thus no more reason to convert moral judgements into quasi-commands than to subject hedgehog-propositions to the same fate. Ethics may be logically autonomous, but it shares this trait with every other kind of talk.

But even this innocuous thesis has been challenged. A. N. Prior (1914–1969) proposed a number of logically valid inferences in which 'ought' does appear in the conclusion but not in the premises. Here is one

(1)   Tea-drinking is common in England.

Therefore

(2)   Either tea-drinking is common in England or *all New Zealanders ought to be shot*. (Prior, 1976)

There is something very fishy about this inference. You can't help feeling that the conclusion is not genuinely concerned with 'ought' at all. After all, the following is also a consequence of (1):

(2′)   Either tea-drinking is common in England or *all New Zealanders are hedgehogs*.

Here we have apparently hedgehog-conclusions from a hedgehog-free premise. What this shows is that Prior's counter-examples do not just threaten the autonomy of ethics (no 'ought' from 'is') but the conservativeness of logic, the idea that in logic you don't get out what you haven't put in. But it also becomes apparent that the (italicized) last clauses in (2) and (2′) are vacuous in a certain sense. Given the premises they can be filled in anyhow without making the conclusions untrue or affecting the validity of the inference.

We are now in a position to restate both the conservativeness of logic and the autonomy of ethics. First we define inference-relative vacuity. An expression occurs vacuously in the conclusion of a valid inference if it can be (uniformly) switched for any other expression of the same grammatical type without prejudice to the validity of the inference. (The italicized last clauses of (2) and (2′) are vacuous in this sense, since in an inference from (1) each can be switched with the other.) The conservativeness of logic becomes the claim that no (non-logical) expression can occur non-vacuously in the conclusion of a valid inference unless it appears in the premises. This claim is susceptible of proof. The autonomy of ethics is simply the moral incarnation of this claim – no *non-vacuous* 'ought' from 'is'. (See Pigden, 1989.)

Where does all this leave naturalism? In fine fettle. We have already seen that logical autonomy affords no support for non-cognitivism. Nor (despite a widespread philosophical belief) does it endanger naturalism. As we have seen, hedgehog-conclusions cannot be derived non-vacuously from hedgehog-free premises. But this does not entail that there is a realm of irreducible hedgehog-facts. (Hedgehogs are composite creatures whose workings can be explained in terms of their parts.) So why should we posit a realm of irreducible *moral* facts to explain why 'ought' cannot be derived from 'is'?

The mistake is due to a confusion. For there are three forms of the autonomy of ethics, *logical*, *semantic* and *ontological*. These are often confounded. But only the last is incompatible with naturalism. Logical autonomy I have dealt with already. Semantic autonomy (semantic because concerned with meanings) is the thesis that moral words do not *mean the same* as any others, and furthermore that they cannot be paraphrased in a naturalistic (or non-moral) idiom. Ontological autonomy is the thesis that moral judgements, to be true, must answer to a realm of *sui generis* moral facts and properties. (I call it ontological autonomy because it is concerned with the kinds of things there must *be*.) Ontological autonomy is thus the reverse of naturalism, which insists that nothing so queer as Moore's moral properties is required to sustain the truths of morals.

Now logical autonomy is correct. But it is no threat to naturalism unless it entails ontological autonomy. The hedgehog parallel proves that it does not. Does logical autonomy entail semantic autonomy? Again no. Logic alone does not license us to infer conclusions about hedgehogs from premises dealing with *Erinaceus europeus*. Hedgehog-talk is logically autonomous. But this says nothing one way or the other about whether 'hedgehog' and *'Erinaceus europeus'* are synonymous (as in fact they are). So too in morals. Conclusions about good cannot be logically derived from premises about pleasure. But this says nothing one way or the other about whether 'good' and 'pleasant' are synonymous (as in fact they are not).

'But this can't be right,' you may say. 'After all, if "good" *did* mean "pleasant" we could logically derive conclusions about good from premises about pleasure so long as these included the appropriate definition. Ethics would not be logically autonomous after all. So if it *is* logically autonomous, it follows that goodness cannot be defined. Which amounts to semantic autonomy.' (See Prior, 1949, p. 24.) This is a mistake. For a definition, although verbal, and hence, in a sense, insubstantial, still constitutes an extra premise. So if 'good' appears in a conclusion as the result of a definition, this in no way violates logical autonomy. For it had to appear in at least one premise to get there. So too with 'hedgehog'. If hedgehog-conclusions are derived from premises about *Erinaceus europeus* with the aid of a definition (in this case a true one), this in no way violates the logical autonomy of hedgehog-talk. For it had to appear in at least one premise to get there. The truth or otherwise of the definition does not affect the logic of the matter. Now, logical autonomy is about *validity* while semantic autonomy is about *meanings*. It is a doctrine concerned with definitions. And on the truth or otherwise of definitions, logic is not competent to decide. (See Pigden, 1989.)

But is semantic autonomy true? And if so, does this entail ontological autonomy and hence the falsehood of naturalism? This brings us back to –

425

iii   The naturalistic fallacy

In his famous *Principia Ethica*, G. E. Moore contended that most moralists have been naturalists and that all naturalists are guilty of a common fallacy. They have confused the property of goodness with the things that possess that property or with some other property that good things possess. This is what the naturalistic fallacy is; a mixing up of two distinct items.

Moore has two main arguments for this.

(1)   Suppose goodness were identical with some other property such as pleasantness. (Moore's favoured candidate is *what we desire to desire*, but we shall stay with pleasantness for shortness' sake.) Then 'good' and 'pleasant' would be synonymous. This would be known to every competent speaker. Hence the question 'Is what is pleasant, good?' would be unintelligible. Here Moore's choice of words is unfortunate. It is not that the question would be senseless. Rather, to ask it would show a want of sense, or at any rate, of understanding. For the answer would be very obvious – yes. The question would be a mere tautology with a question-mark tacked on the end. It would have the same meaning as 'Is what is pleasant, pleasant?' or 'Is what is good, good?' Now, Moore takes it to be obvious that the question 'Is what is pleasant, good?' is an open question; a question it makes sense to ask. Hence 'good' does not mean 'pleasant'. Hence goodness and pleasantness are distinct. And the same goes for the other properties with which goodness is identified.

A similar argument (dating back to Plato's *Euthyphro*) has been deployed against the theological naturalist. Does 'X is right' mean 'X is commanded by God'? Then 'What God commands is right' means 'What God commands is what God commands', and the moral praise of God degenerates into a fanfare of tautologies. But 'What God commands is right' is not a tautology. Hence the naturalistic definition is false.

(2)   If 'good' meant 'pleasant' then to say 'What is pleasant is good' would provide us with no extra reason for promoting pleasurable states of affairs. (It would amount to the tautology that what is pleasant is pleasant, and a tautology cannot provide a motive for action.) But to call pleasure good is to suggest some *extra* reason for promoting it. Therefore 'good' doesn't mean 'pleasant'. Again the argument can be generalized.

These arguments fail in their intended purpose. They do not establish onto-logical autonomy and hence the falsehood of naturalism. At best they establish semantic autonomy and thus disprove semantic naturalism – the thesis that moral facts can be reduced to non-moral facts, because moral words are synonymous with (combinations of) non-moral words. And there is some doubt even of this.

Argument (1) assumes that if goodness is identical with pleasantness, 'good' and 'pleasant' must be synonymous. This is false. Water and H_2O are identical. Yet 'water' is not synonymous with 'H_2O' even though they stand for the same stuff. 'Water' expresses a pre-scientific concept accessible to children and savages – roughly, the colourless, tasteless fluid that falls from the sky and is found in lakes and rivers. 'H_2O', by contrast, expresses a scientific notion. You can't understand it fully without a modicum of chemistry. People did not find out that water was H_2O by meditating upon meanings. Empirical enquiry did the trick. So too with goodness and pleasantness. 'Good' may not be synonymous with 'pleasant'. But they might both stand for the same property. Semantic naturalism might be false but synthetic naturalism might be true. That is, moral properties might be identified with natural properties by means of empirical research rather than conceptual analysis. Thus semantic autonomy, which says that moral words do not *mean the same* as any others, does not entail ontological autonomy – that moral properties are not *identical* with any others.

But there is more. Argument (1) also assumes that if two words or phrases are synonymous, this is known to every competent speaker. And we can grant that if synonymy is given a strict interpretation, this is so. But our concepts are not transparent to us. The rules they obey, the presuppositions they embody, are not things we are always fully conscious of. Thus it may be possible to give an analysis of a word – a conceptual breakdown – which won't be obvious to competent speakers, although in some sense it expresses the word's meaning. (Otherwise the 'paradox of analysis' would preclude useful conceptual analyses.) So it may be possible to formulate an analysis, X, of 'good' such that 'Are X things good?' is an open question (i.e. one a competent speaker might sensibly ask) even though X articulated the meaning of 'good'. This puts semantic autonomy into question.

Argument (2) likewise supports the conclusion that 'good' is without naturalistic (i.e. non-moral) synonyms or paraphrases. But this is semantic autonomy, not the ontological autonomy that controverts naturalism. Moreover, the argument is suspect. It trades on the idea that 'good' conveys some requirement on action. If someone thinks something good, this usually disposes them to pursue or promote it (in the appropriate circumstances). Fair enough. But perhaps an analysis can be given which spells out this requirement without recourse to non-natural properties. 'Pleasant' may be a poor choice for this role, but this is not to say that a better can't be found. (For example, 'good' could mean *required* where the requirements relate to some goal all rational beings could be expected to share.) Of course, if such an analysis, X, could be constructed, 'What is X, is good' would be a tautology or conceptual truth, bereft of motivating power. But this is irrelevant. For such a proposition would not be designed to commend X-ness, or to indicate that X-ness was somehow required. Rather the purpose would be to articulate the requirements wrapped up in the predicate 'good'; to explain why it is that calling things 'good' usually suggests a reason to promote them.

To sum up. *Logical* autonomy (no-'ought'-from-'is') can be proved in an amended form. But this does not endanger naturalism. *Semantic* autonomy may be true too. Perhaps 'good' and the other moral words lack naturalistic or non-moral synonyms or paraphrases – at least, synonyms or paraphrases with which they are *strictly* synonymous. This disposes of semantic naturalism, but leaves other kinds of naturalism intact. So naturalism could be true, despite Hume and despite G. E. Moore.

Thus there is no need for naturalists to evade the arguments of Moore and

Hume by making out that the moral 'ought' and the predicative 'good' (Hume's 'ought' and Moore's 'good') are senseless. (Something Anscombe in 'Modern moral philosophy' and Geach in 'Good and evil' try to do.) Insofar as they are valid, Hume's arguments, and Moore's too, are compatible with naturalism. Formal attempts to refute naturalism having failed, it remains a live option.

iv Variants of naturalism

I conclude with a survey of the leading brands of naturalism. My purpose is exposition rather than critique, but I won't forswear critical comments.

(A)   The best bet, given our objections to Moore, looks like synthetic naturalism. 'Good' (and the same goes for the other moral words) does not mean the same as any naturalistic 'X'. Nevertheless there is (or could be) some naturalistic predicate 'X' which stands for the same property. (Just as 'water' and 'H$_2$O' don't express the same concept, though they stand for the same stuff.) The identity between goodness and X-ness would not be analytic, holding in virtue of the meanings of words, but synthetic, a matter of (empirical?) fact. R. M. Adams, a theological naturalist, tries to rehabilitate the Divine Command theory of ethics using this idea (Adams, 1981). To say 'X is right' does not *mean* that God commands it. Hence 'What God commands is right' is not tautologous. Nevertheless, rightness and being commanded by God come to much the same thing. We apprehend that certain actions are right and subsequently discover (through revelation or rational theology) that what we were aware of was the Voice of God. But the problems with this approach are best seen in a secular setting. If goodness is to be identified with a naturalistic something by means of empirical enquiry, 'good' must express an empirical concept. That is, 'good' must be defined in such a way that goodness impinges upon us and can figure within an empirical theory. For instance, it might be defined as the cause of certain effects, the 'goodness-phenomena'; which phenomena can (at least sometimes) be sensed by human beings. (Otherwise empirical enquiry could not determine whether goodness and X-ness applied to the same things.) But this, in turn, presupposes that 'good' can be subject to a naturalistic analysis; that in some sense it *means the same as* a paraphrase which relates it to sensory evidence. In other words, Moore must be wrong and 'good' must be analysable – although it need not be strictly synonymous with the paraphrase which constitutes the analysis. The best candidate is the kind of theory that (on some interpretations) was propounded by David Hume. 'Good' is not defined in terms of our ordinary sensations – sight, smell, hearing, touch – but in terms of internal sensations of approval and disapproval. 'Good' is (roughly) what every informed and impartial spectator would approve of (and hence what we *do* tend to approve of, when we rid ourselves of partial passions and try to work out what is right.) Of course, once we have got such an analysis, naturalism is already home and hosed. We don't need to go on to establish a synthetic identity between goodness, so analysed, and some other, natural property. If being good means being approved of by an ideal spectator, we need not determine what the spectator would approve of to know we have moral truths without irreducible moral facts (though what the spectator approves of will be of considerable practical import). Morals boils down to an idealized psychology. Naturalism is vindicated.

The theory is beset by problems. Here are two. (a) It is not clear that all human observers however impartial and well-informed would agree in their reactions. Hence the possibility opens up that no (or very few) actions are good, since none would excite the approbation of every spectator. We revert to the error theory we were trying to avoid (Section i). (b) The analysis looks circular. For to approve of something is to think (or feel) it is good or right. Hence the analysis of 'good' contains the very concept it is designed to explicate.

(B)   (This theory is suggested by the writings of G. E. M. Anscombe, though I am not sure whether she would agree with it. Sabina Lovibond, *Realism and Imagination in Ethics*, believes something of the sort.) Suppose I have ordered some potatoes and the grocer has delivered them and sent me the bill. Then I owe the grocer money. Now, what makes it the case that I am in debt to the grocer? (i) A history of personal transactions between the grocer and me; (ii) some general rules, holding in virtue of social institutions and conventions, about how debts are contracted; and (iii) the absence of special conditions which might cancel or invalidate the debt. In other words, a complex of social facts which boil down to human dispositions and actions. There is nothing more to my being in debt than this; no special non-natural realm of debt-facts – just human actions in the context of human institutions; which institutions are themselves dependent on continued human action.

The naturalist hypothesis, then, is that some moral judgements ('It was wrong of you to tell that lie') are like 'I owe the grocer money' – true in virtue of individual human actions in the context of our institutions or language games. Other, more general, judgements ('It is usually wrong to lie') resemble the propositions stating the rules for contracting a debt – they hold true in virtue of human conventions and institutions, shared social practices. Thus we have moral truths, both general and particular, without peculiarly moral facts. Morals boils down to a sophisticated sociology. Naturalism is vindicated.

The problem here (as Anscombe seems to realize) is relativity. Different societies have different moral institutions sustaining different moral codes. Do we index moral truth to the codes of particular societies, so that there is rightness for the Azande, and rightness for the Aussies, but no such thing as rightness *period*? What about divided societies where different codes and institutions compete (like most Western societies)? And what becomes of moral dissidents? It seems that they are not merely bad (because they disregard the only moral truth there is) but incoherent, since we can give no content to the dissident's thought that the code her society sustains is not really right. (Sabina Lovibond wrestles with this problem for 100 pages. She does not come off the victor.) Finally, this approach has the unfortunate consequence that the moral opinions of Margaret Thatcher and the Ayatollah Khomeini do not really contradict one another, since both are indexed to the institutions of their own society. (For a more sympathetic view of relativism,

429

see Article 39, RELATIVISM.) Suppose we remove the indices and just talk about right or wrong. Then in the absence of cross-cultural institutions determining a super-cultural ethic there is no such thing as moral truth. But a naturalistic basis for moral truth was the object of the enterprise.

(C)   Lastly I turn to a form of neo-Aristotelian naturalism hinted at by P. T. Geach and developed in a rather haphazard way by M. Midgley and others. Rather than worrying about what things are good and what goodness is (a mythical property anyway) we should be concerned about what it is to be a good human being and to perform good human acts. Geach seems to think that these notions carry no metaphysical commitments and can be given a purely natural explication. Man (presumably) has a function, and once we find out what that function is, we will have no trouble finding out what being a good man consists in. Geach's religious beliefs have led him away from this project towards a Divine Command theory of ethics. It has been left to others, principally Midgley, to develop these ideas in a secular and biological context. Drawing on ethological literature, she suggests that, given our natures, there are constraints on the kinds of lives humans will find fulfilling, and hence on human action. Morality (it seems) can be boiled down to a refined biology. Naturalism is vindicated.

I can only record my impression that after thirty years of effort, not a lot of progress has been made with this programme. The writings of Geach, Midgley and their allies are 'suggestive' but nothing more. First, it is far from obvious that 'good human' *can* be given a naturalistic reading without relapsing into the sociologistic naturalism discussed above. Secondly, I doubt whether the Aristotelian concept of a function can be revived within modern biology, at least for such a flexible and acculturated creature as man. And this needs to be done if the programme is to achieve anything concrete. If morals are to be based on biology we must somehow generate a set of requirements out of human nature. These must be (i) reasonably specific; (ii) rationally binding or at least highly persuasive; and (iii) morally credible. So far, no such biologically based requirements have been provided. We live in hope. (Michael Ruse discusses the relationship between biology and ethics in Article 44, THE SIGNIFICANCE OF EVOLUTION.)

This concludes my survey of the leading brands of naturalism. They are not so much wrong in principle as deficient in detail. As we have seen, there is no sweeping argument which condemns the naturalistic enterprise as unworkable. It can't be excluded on formal grounds. Nevertheless the variants currently on offer leave much to be desired. But this doesn't dispose of naturalism either, since there may be other options. So for all the apocalyptic pronouncements of Moore and the non-cognitivists, who dismissed naturalism (almost by definition) as fallacious, naturalism nowadays is very much a going concern. Whether it is right or wrong only time – and further argument – will tell.

References

Adams, R. M.: 'Divine command metaethics as necessary a posteriori', *Divine Commands and Morality*, ed. P. Helm (Oxford: Oxford University Press, 1981).

Anscombe, G. E. M.: 'On brute facts', 'Modern moral philosophy' and 'On the source of the authority of the state', in her *Ethics, Religion and Politics* (*Collected Papers, Vol. 3*), (Oxford: Basil Blackwell, 1981).

Geach, P. T.: 'Good and evil', *Theories of Ethics*, ed. P. Foot (Oxford: Oxford University Press, 1967).

Hare, R. M.: *The Language of Morals* (Oxford: Oxford University Press, 1952).

Hume, D.: *Treatise on Human Nature* (1738); ed. L. A. Selby-Bigge (Oxford: Clarendon Press, 1978).

Lovibond, S.: *Realism and Imagination in Ethics* (Oxford: Basil Blackwell, 1983).

Mackie, J.: *Ethics: Inventing Right and Wrong* (Harmondsworth: Penguin, 1977).

Midgley, M.: *Beast and Man* (Ithaca, NY: Cornell University Press, 1978).

Moore, G. E.: *Principia Ethica* (Cambridge: Cambridge University Press, 1903).

Pigden, C. R.: 'Logic and the autonomy of ethics', *Australasian Journal of Philosophy*, 67 (1989), 127–51.

Plato: *Euthyphro*.

Prior, A. N.: *Logic and the Basis of Ethics* (Oxford: Oxford University Press, 1949).

——: 'The autonomy of ethics', in his *Papers on Logic and Ethics*, (London: Duckworth, 1976).

Further reading

Carson, T. L.: *The Status of Morality* (Dordrecht: Reidel, 1984).

Chisholm, R. M.: *Brentano and Intrinsic Value* (Cambridge: Cambridge University Press, 1986).

Clark, S. R. L.: 'The lack of gap between fact and value', *Proceedings of the Aristotelian Society*, Supplementary Volume 54 (1980) 225–40.

Foot, P.: *Virtues and Vices* (Oxford: Basil Blackwell, 1978).

Geach, P. T.: *The Virtues* (Cambridge: Cambridge University Press, 1977).

Hume, D.: *Moral and Political Philosophy*, ed. D. Aiken (New York: Hafner, 1948).

Lewis, D.: 'Dispositional theories of value', *Proceedings of the Aristotelian Society*, Supplementary Volume 63 (1989), 113–137.

Midgley, M.: 'On the lack of gap between fact and value', *Proceedings of the Aristotelian Society*, Supplementary Volume 54 (1980), 207–23.

Pigden, C. R.: 'Geach on "Good"', *Philosophical Quarterly*, 40 (1990), 1–20.

Putnam, H.: *Reason, Truth and History* (Cambridge: Cambridge University Press, (1981). See especially Chapter 9.

38

Subjectivism

JAMES RACHELS

IN 1973 religious conservatives were stunned by the US Supreme Court decision legalizing abortion. Since then they have worked for the reversal of that decision. They have had powerful allies in the White House, first in Ronald Reagan, who made opposition to *Roe* v. *Wade* a condition for appointment to the federal bench, and subsequently in George Bush, who after his election suggested to the Court that it should reconsider the entire matter.

In President Bush's mind, the question whether abortion should be legal is closely linked to whether it is morally wrong: he opposes legalized abortion, he says, because he believes that abortion is immoral. What should be our reaction to this? One possibility is that we might agree with him, and say that abortion is in fact immoral. Another possibility is that we might disagree, and say that abortion is in fact morally acceptable. But there is a third possibility. We might say something like this:

'Where morality is concerned, there are no "facts" and no one is "right" or "wrong". President Bush is expressing his own personal feelings about abortion, and nothing more. He says it is wrong, but that is merely the way *he* feels about it. Others disagree, and his feelings are no more "correct" than anyone else's. Different people have different feelings, and that's the end of it.'

This is the basic idea of ethical subjectivism. Ethical subjectivism is a theory which says that, in making moral judgements, people are doing nothing more than expressing their personal desires or feelings. On this view, there are no moral 'facts'. It is a fact that there have been over a million abortions performed annually in the United States since 1973, but it is not a fact that this is a good thing or a bad thing. And of course, abortion is only a convenient example; the same thing can be said about any moral issue whatever.

This idea has appealed to a wide range of thinkers, especially those with an empiricist turn of mind. David Hume expressed the essential point in 1738 when he wrote in his great work *A Treatise of Human Nature* that morality is a matter of 'feeling, not reason':

Take any action allow'd to be vicious: Wilful murder, for instance. Examine it in all lights, and see if you can find that matter of fact, or real existence, which you call *vice* ... You can never find it, till you turn your reflexion into your own breast, and find a sentiment of disapprobation, which arises in you, toward this action. Here is a matter of fact; but 'tis the object of feeling, not reason.

432

The function of moral judgement, says Hume, is to guide conduct; but reason alone can never tell us what to do. Reason merely informs us of the nature and consequences of our actions, and of the logical relations between propositions. Thus, reason may tell a woman that if she has an abortion, her life will be easier in some ways, but the fetus will die. However, nothing follows from this about whether she *should* have an abortion. In order to decide what to do, it is necessary for her emotions to come into play – does she *care* whether the fetus dies? How much does she care about the easier life she may have? If she imagines herself having the abortion, is she comfortable with the thought, or is she repelled by it? Hume concludes that, in the final analysis, 'Morality is determined by sentiment'.

People have been attracted to this view for various reasons, some of them good and some not so good. Sometimes people embrace ethical subjectivism because they associate it with an attitude of tolerance. We should be tolerant, they say, of those who disagree with us. Each person has a right to their own opinion, and no-one has the right to dictate to others what moral views they must accept. Ethical subjectivism, which says that morality is nothing but a matter of personal feelings, provides a plausible rationale for this attitude of tolerance. If no-one's feelings are any more 'correct' than anyone else's, then no-one could be justified in forcing their opinions upon others. Where morals affect politics, as it does in the case of abortion, the implication is obvious: no segment of the community has the right to impose its moral view on another.

This line of thought, however, involves a subtle mistake. The idea that we ought to be tolerant is itself a moral judgement, and subjectivism does not mandate the acceptance of any particular moral judgement, including this one. It is not that sort of theory. Someone who accepts the theory will still have moral opinions, of course – they might say that abortion is morally acceptable, or that it is odious. But the theory does not tell us *which* stance to adopt. It only says that, whichever stance we choose, our choice will not represent the 'truth'. Our opinions will represent our own personal feelings, and nothing more.

Exactly the same is true of a value such as tolerance. People who accept ethical subjectivism might affirm the value of tolerance or deny it. But whichever stance they choose, they will not believe their choice represents the 'truth' about how we ought to behave. They will instead recognize that they are only expressing their personal feelings. Moreover, a belief in tolerance is not the exclusive prerogative of the subjectivist. Those who *reject* ethical subjectivism, and believe instead that there are objective moral truths, might nevertheless believe that they should be tolerant, because they might believe that 'We should be tolerant' is one of the objective moral truths. (See Article 39, RELATIVISM, for a discussion of tolerance in the context of cultural or social divergence of moral views.)

Another common misconception is that, if ethical subjectivism is true, then nothing is 'really' right or wrong. This notion might be expressed in different ways: it might be said that 'Everything is permitted' or that 'Nothing really matters'. However it is expressed, many people find it a liberating idea and count it as an argument in favour of subjectivism. Others think it is a pernicious idea which negates all morality, and conclude that subjectivism should be rejected on

433

account of it. Both reactions, however, are misguided, because ethical subjectivism does not really entail that nothing is morally right or wrong.

To see why not, we need only to remember that, according to ethical subjectivism, moral judgements express feelings. Therefore, if you say that 'Nothing is right or wrong' or that 'Nothing matters', you are expressing a truly extraordinary lack of feeling about anything. This hardly seems possible, unless you are suffering from some sort of extreme melancholia. Does it follow, if you accept ethical subjectivism, that you will stop having feelings of the sort associated with moral opinions? Does it even follow that you *should* stop having such feelings, or that it is improper for you to have them? No. Therefore, it does not follow, if you accept ethical subjectivism, that you must conclude that 'Nothing is right or wrong'. You may, in fact, have exactly the same moral views that you would have had if you were not a subjectivist. Being a subjectivist only means that you have a particular philosophical understanding of what such views come to.

We might call the idea that nothing is right or wrong *moral nihilism*. While many philosophers have been attracted to subjectivism, few have been nihilists. There is a simple reason why not. Consider what it would be like for someone actually to believe that nothing is right or wrong. Someone who said this would mean, presumably, that rape is neither right nor wrong; that torture is neither right nor wrong; that murder is neither right nor wrong; and so on for anything else that might be mentioned. If all this were said *seriously*, and not just as part of a philosophical discussion, it would be alarming in the extreme. It would mean that they *were not opposed* to rape, torture, murder, or anything else. Think how strange this would be. Would they not mind if such things were done to them? Would they think nothing of doing as much to others? No-one who was not in the grip of a frightening pathology could endorse such an outlook; on the contrary, it might be suggested that anyone tempted by it – really tempted to adopt it in real life, and not just tempted to defend it in a philosophy seminar – should seek psychiatric help.

This dismissal of moral nihilism may strike some readers as too quick. Surely, they might think, there must be a connection at some deeper level between subjectivism and nihilism. Doesn't subjectivism mean that nothing is *really* right or wrong? The answer just depends on what is meant by '*really* right or wrong'. If by this we mean 'right or wrong independent of how anyone feels', then of course subjectivism denies that anything is right or wrong in *that* sense. Ethical subjectivism denies that there are moral facts independent of our feelings. If this is what one means by moral nihilism, then ethical subjectivism does imply moral nihilism. Nonetheless, it is still worth emphasizing that the subjectivist is not committed to moral nihilism in our original sense: the subjectivist is not compelled to say that nothing matters, or that nothing is right or wrong.

The historical development of ethical subjectivism illustrates a process typical of philosophical theories. It began as a simple idea – in the words of David Hume, that morality is more a matter of feeling than of reason. But, as objections were raised against the theory, and as its defenders tried to answer those objections, the theory became more complicated. So far, we have not attempted to formulate the theory very precisely – we have been content with a rough statement of its basic idea. Now, however, we need to go a bit beyond that.

One way of formulating ethical subjectivism more precisely is this: we take it to be the thesis that *when a person says that something is morally good or bad, this means that he or she approves of that thing, or disapproves of it, and nothing more*. In other words,

'X is morally acceptable' 'X is right' 'X is good' 'X ought to be done'	all mean: 'I (the speaker) approve of X';

and, similarly:

'X is morally unacceptable' 'X is wrong' 'X is bad' 'X ought not to be done'	all mean: 'I (the speaker) disapprove of X'.

We might call this version of the theory *simple subjectivism*. It expresses the basic idea of ethical subjectivism in a plain, uncomplicated form, and many people have found it attractive. However, simple subjectivism is open to several rather obvious objections, because it has implications that are contrary to what we know to be the case (or at least, contrary to what we *think* we know) about the nature of moral evaluation.

For one thing, simple subjectivism contradicts the plain fact that we can sometimes be *wrong* in our moral evaluations. None of us are infallible. We make mistakes, and when we discover that we are mistaken we may want to change our judgements. But, if simple subjectivism were correct, this would be impossible – because simple subjectivism implies that each of us is infallible.

Consider again Mr Bush, who says that abortion is immoral. According to simple subjectivism, what he is really saying is that he, George Bush, disapproves of it. Of course it is possible that he is not speaking sincerely – as recently as 1980 he publicly supported *Roe* v. *Wade*. Either he has changed his mind, or now he is merely playing to his conservative audience. But, *if we assume he is speaking sincerely* – if we assume he really does disapprove of abortion – then it follows that what he says is true. So long as he is honestly representing his own feelings, he cannot be mistaken.

Another serious problem is that simple subjectivism cannot account for the fact that people *disagree* about ethics. George Bush says that abortion is immoral. Betty Friedan, author of *The Feminine Mystique* and a leading feminist thinker, denies this, saying that abortion is not immoral. Plainly, Mr Bush and Ms Friedan disagree. But consider what simple subjectivism implies about this situation.

435

According to simple subjectivism, when Mr Bush says that abortion is immoral, he is merely making a statement about his attitude – he is saying that he, George Bush, disapproves of abortion. Would Ms Friedan disagree with that? No, she would *agree* that Bush disapproves of abortion. At the same time, when she says that abortion is not immoral, she is only saying that she, Betty Friedan, does not disapprove of it. And why should Mr Bush disagree with that? In fact, Mr Bush would certainly acknowledge that Friedan does not disapprove of abortion. Thus, according to simple subjectivism, there is no disagreement between them – each would acknowledge the truth of what the other is saying! Surely, though, there is something wrong here, for surely Bush and Friedan do disagree about whether abortion is immoral.

There is a kind of eternal frustration implied by simple subjectivism: Bush and Friedan are deeply opposed to one another; yet they cannot even state their positions in a way that joins the issue. Friedan may *try* to deny what Bush says, by denying that abortion is immoral, but according to simple subjectivism she only succeeds in changing the subject.

These considerations, and others like them, show that simple subjectivism is a bad theory. In the face of such difficulties, many philosophers have chosen to reject the whole idea of ethical subjectivism. Others, however, have taken a different approach. The problem, they say, is not that the basic idea of ethical subjectivism is wrong. The problem is that 'simple subjectivism' is too simple a way of expressing that idea. Thus, these philosophers have continued to have confidence in the basic idea of ethical subjectivism, and have tried to refine it – to give it a new, improved formulation – so that these difficulties can be overcome.

The improved version was a theory that came to be known as *emotivism*. Developed most fully by the American philosopher Charles L. Stevenson, emotivism has been one of the most influential theories of ethics in the twentieth century. It is a more subtle and sophisticated theory than simple subjectivism because it incorporates a more sophisticated view of language.

Emotivism begins with the observation that language is used in a variety of ways. One of its principal uses is in stating facts, or at least in stating what we believe to be facts. Thus we may say:

> George Bush is President of the United States;
> George Bush opposes abortion;
> There have been over 1,000,000 abortions in the US each year since *Roe* v. *Wade*;

and so on. In each case, we are saying something that is either true or false, and the purpose of saying such things is, typically, to convey information to the listener.

However, there are other purposes for which language may be used. For example, suppose I say to a pregnant woman, who is contemplating an abortion, 'Please don't do it!' This utterance is neither true nor false. It is not a *statement* of any kind; it is a *command* (or a request, or an entreaty), which is something altogether different. Its purpose is not to convey information; rather, its purpose is to prescribe a particular action or course of conduct.

Or, consider utterances such as these, which are neither statements of fact nor commands:

> Hurrah for Betty Friedan!
> Would that abortion were illegal!
> Alas!
> Damn *Roe* v. *Wade!*

These are perfectly familiar, common types of sentences which we understand easily enough. But none of them is true or false. (It would make no sense to say 'It is true that hurrah for Betty Friedan' or 'It is false that alas'.) Again, these sentences are not used to state facts; instead, they are used to express the speaker's attitudes.

We need to note clearly the difference between *reporting* an attitude and *expressing* the same attitude. If I say 'I like Betty Friedan', I am reporting the fact that I have a positive attitude toward her. The statement is a statement of fact, that is either true or false. On the other hand, if I shout 'Hurrah for Friedan!' I am not stating any sort of fact. I am expressing an attitude, but I am not reporting that I have it.

Now, with these points in mind, let us turn our attention to moral language. According to emotivism, moral language is not fact-stating language; it is not typically used to convey information. Its purpose is entirely different. It is used, first, as a means of influencing people's behaviour: if someone says 'You ought not to do that', *they are trying to stop you from doing it.* And, second, moral language is used to express (*not* report) one's attitude. Saying 'Betty Friedan is a good woman' is not like saying 'I approve of Friedan', but it *is* like saying 'Hurrah for Friedan!'

The difference between emotivism and simple subjectivism should now be obvious. Simple subjectivism interpreted ethical sentences as statements of fact, of a special kind – namely, as reports of the speaker's attitude. According to simple subjectivism, when Mr Bush says 'Abortion is immoral', this means the same as 'I (Bush) disapprove of abortion' – a statement of fact about his attitude. Emotivism, on the other hand, would deny that his utterance states any fact at all, even a fact about himself. Instead, emotivism interprets his utterance as equivalent to something like 'Abortion – yecch!' or 'Don't have an abortion!' or 'Would that no-one ever had an abortion'.

This may seem to be a trivial, nit-picky difference that isn't worth bothering about. But, from a theoretical point of view, it is actually a very big and important difference. It means that emotivism will not be vulnerable to the sorts of difficulties that plagued simple subjectivism. Consider the two problems that we mentioned, having to do with infallibility and disagreement. The problem about infallibility arose only because simple subjectivism interprets moral judgements as statements about our feelings. If people sincerely report their feelings, how can they be wrong? Emotivism does not interpret moral judgements as statements about feelings, or as statements that in any sense are true-or-false; and so the same problem will not arise for it. Similarly with moral disagreement. Emotivism deals with this problem by emphasizing that there is more than one way in which people may disagree. If I believe that Lee Harvey Oswald acted alone in the assassination of John Kennedy, and you believe there was a conspiracy, it is a disagreement over the facts – I believe something to be true that you believe to be false. But consider a different type of disagreement. Suppose I favour strict gun-control legislation, and you are opposed to it. Here we disagree, but in a different sense. It is not our beliefs that are in conflict, but our desires. (You and I may agree about all the facts surrounding the gun-control controversy, and yet still take different sides concerning what we want to see happen.) In the first kind of disagreement, we believe different things, both of which cannot be true. In the second, we want different things, both of which cannot happen. Stevenson calls this a disagreement *in* attitude, and contrasts it with disagreement *about* attitudes. Moral disagreements, says Stevenson, are disagreements in attitude. Simple subjectivism could not explain moral disagreement because, once it interpreted moral judgements as statements *about* attitudes, the disagreement vanished.

There is no doubt that emotivism represented an advance over simple subjectivism. This was not, however, the end of the story. Emotivism also had its problems, and they were sufficiently serious that today most philosophers reject the theory. One of the main problems was that emotivism could not account for the place of reason in ethics.

A moral judgement – or, for that matter, *any* kind of value judgement – must be supported by good reasons. If someone tells you that a certain action would be wrong, for example, you may ask *why* it would be wrong, and if there is no satisfactory answer, you may reject that advice as unfounded. In this way, moral judgements are different from mere expressions of personal preference. If someone says 'I like coffee', he does not need to have a reason – he may be making a statement about his personal taste, and nothing more. But moral judgements require backing by reasons, and in the absence of such reasons, they are merely arbitrary. This is a point about the *logic* of moral judgement. It is not merely that it would be a good thing to have reasons for one's moral judgements. The point is stronger than that. One *must* have reasons, or else one is not making a moral judgement at all. Therefore, any adequate theory of the nature of moral judgement should be able to give some account of the connection between moral judgements and the reasons that support them. It is at just this point that emotivism falters.

What can an emotivist say about reasons? Remember that, for the emotivist, a moral judgement is primarily a verbal means of trying to influence peoples' attitudes and conduct. The view of reasons that naturally goes with this idea is that reasons are any considerations that will have the desired effect, that will influence attitudes and conduct in the desired way. Suppose I am trying to persuade you to reject Betty Friedan's view of abortion. Knowing you are anti-Semitic, I say: 'Friedan, after all, is one of those Jews'. That does the trick; your attitude changes, and you agree that her view of abortion ought to be rejected. Therefore, it would seem that, for the emotivist, the fact that Friedan is Jewish is, at least in some contexts, a reason in support of the judgement that abortion is immoral. In fact, Stevenson takes exactly this view. In his classic work *Ethics and Language* he says: '*Any* statement about *any* fact which *any* speaker considers likely to alter attitudes may be adduced as a reason for or against an ethical judgement' (Stevenson, 1944).

Obviously, something had gone wrong. Not just any fact can count as a reason in support of just any judgement. The fact must be relevant to the judgement, and psychological influence does not necessarily bring relevance with it. Emotivism will not do; we need at least one more refinement to produce a theory that will account not only for the connection between moral judgement and emotion, but for the connection between morality and reason as well.

The third and final refinement of ethical subjectivism, which its defenders hope might solve this problem, has been suggested by such thinkers as John Dewey and W. D. Falk. They have argued that, while moral judgements express feelings, not just any feelings will do. The process of 'thinking through' the various facts, arguments, and other considerations surrounding a moral issue can change the way a person feels. It can cause old feelings to weaken, to be modified, or to disappear; and new feelings to form. Or, it might have the effect of strengthening the feelings that one already had. A distinction must be made, therefore, between the feelings one has prior to 'thinking things through', and the feelings one might have afterwards. It is the latter feelings – the ones that are produced or sustained by reason – that are the proper basis of moral judgement. Hume had already made this point in his *Inquiry Concerning the Principles of Morals*, when he wrote:

But in order to pave the way for such a sentiment [i.e. a sentiment that forms the basis of a moral judgement] and give a proper discernment of its object, it is often necessary, we find, that much reasoning should precede, that nice distinctions be made, just conclusions drawn, distant comparisons formed, complicated relations examined, and general facts fixed and ascertained. (Hume, 1752)

A person might have strong feelings about abortion, for example, without ever having thought through the various issues surrounding it. Who, exactly, are the women who have abortions? How are their lives affected by it? How are the lives of women who do *not* have abortions affected? What of the fetus itself? Should it be regarded as a person with a right to life? What characteristics must an individual possess in order to have a right to life? Does a fetus have such characteristics? If a fetus is a person with a right to life, does it follow that abortion is wrong in all circumstances? In any circumstances? What part, if any, should religious arguments play in supporting moral judgements? Is there, in fact, a decent religious argument against abortion, or is the so-called religious argument just a fundamentalist bluff? Obviously there is a lot to think about here. Anyone who wants to have an informed opinion about any of these matters has a great deal of work to do.

But suppose someone *had* thought through all this in a thoroughly intelligent and impartial manner, with their feelings being shaped by this process. Then their feelings would be as much in harmony with reason as is possible. They would have considered the nature and consequences of abortion, along with every possible reason for or against it, in an open-minded way, and every such consideration would have been allowed to have whatever effect on their attitudes it could have. Reason, then, could do no more. Any disagreements that remained between such people would be irresoluble – or at least, not resoluble by rational means. Surely, one might think, there is no further role that reason in ethics could have.

Thus, as our final attempt to formulate an adequate subjectivist understanding of ethical judgement, we might say: something is morally right if it is such that the process of thinking through its nature and consequences would cause or sustain a feeling of approval toward it in a person who was being as reasonable and impartial as is humanly possible. This is just a convoluted way of saying that the morally right thing to do is whatever a completely reasonable person would approve. This may seem to be some distance from the simple idea with which we started, but it is the closest thing to that original idea which has a chance of being true.

It is an encouraging fact that, as we have added qualifications to ethical subjectivism to make it more adequate, it has become less subjectivist and has begun to resemble other theories whose advocates have been working toward the same goal. Our final formulation of ethical subjectivism makes it a close relative to the ideal observer theory, which says that the right thing to do is whatever a perfectly rational, impartial, and benevolent judge would think best. It also has much in common with Richard Brandt's theory – Brandt holds that, in deciding what is right, the key question is 'What would a person (perhaps all persons), if rational in the sense of having made optimal use of all available information, want and choose to do?' And it has many obvious features in common with R. M. Hare's theory (see Article 40, UNIVERSAL PRESCRIPTIVISM.) This is encouraging because, if there is any such thing as truth in moral philosophy, we should expect eventual convergence in those theories which seek after it. Agreement on basic points, while not an absolute guarantee of truth, is at least more reassuring than ceaseless argument.

References

Brandt, R. B.: *A Theory of the Good and the Right* (Oxford: Clarendon Press, 1979).

Dewey, J.: *Theory of Valuation* (Chicago: University of Chicago Press, 1939).

Falk, W. D.: 'Goading and guiding', in *Ought, Reasons, and Morality* (Ithaca, NY: Cornell University Press, 1986), ch. 2.

Hare, R. M.: ' "Nothing matters" ', in *Applications of Moral Philosophy* (Berkeley: University of California Press, 1972), ch. 4.

Hume, D.: *A Treatise of Human Nature* (London: 1740); ed. L. A. Selby-Bigge (Oxford: Clarendon Press, 1978), Book III.

——: *An Inquiry Concerning the Principles of Morals* (London: Cadell, 1752).

Stevenson, C. L.: *Ethics and Language* (New Haven: Yale University Press, 1944).

Further reading

Ayer, A. J.: *Language, Truth and Logic* (London: Gollancz, 1936), ch. 6.

Bambrough, R.: 'A proof of the objectivity of morals', *Understanding Moral Philosophy*, ed. J. Rachels (Encino: Dickenson, 1976).

Blanshard, B.: 'The new subjectivism in ethics', *Philosophy and Phenomenological Research*, 9 (1949), 504–11.

Mackie, J. L.: *Ethics: Inventing Right and Wrong* (Harmondsworth: Penguin, 1977).

Moore, G. E.: *Ethics* (London: Oxford University Press, 1912), ch. 3.

Rachels, J.: 'John Dewey and the truth about ethics', *New Studies in the Philosophy of John Dewey*, ed. S. Cahn (Hanover: University Press of New England, 1977), pp. 149–71.

Stevenson, C. L.: *Facts and Values* (New Haven: Yale University Press, 1963).

Urmson, J. O.: *The Emotive Theory of Ethics* (London: Hutchinson, 1968).

39

Relativism

DAVID WONG

i Introduction

MORAL relativism is a common response to the deepest conflicts we face in our ethical lives. Some of these conflicts are quite public and political, such as the apparently intractable disagreement in the United States over the moral and legal permissibility of abortion. Other conflicts inviting the relativistic response are of a less dramatic but more recurrent nature. This author's experience as a first-generation Chinese American exemplifies a kind of conflict that others have faced: that between inherited values and the values of the adopted country. As a child I had to grapple with the differences between what was expected of me as a good Chinese son and what was expected of my non-Chinese friends. Not only did they seem bound by duties that were much less rigorous in the matter of honouring parents and upholding the family name, but I was supposed to feel superior to them because of that. It added to my confusion that I sometimes felt envy at their freedom.

Moral relativism, as a common response to such conflicts, often takes the form of a denial that any single moral code has universal validity, and an assertion that moral truth and justifiability, if there are any such things, are in some way relative to factors that are culturally and historically contingent. This doctrine is *meta-ethical* relativism, because it is about the relativity of moral truth and justifiability. Another kind of moral relativism, also a common response to deep moral conflict, is a doctrine about how one ought to act toward those who accept values very different from one's own. This *normative* moral relativism holds that it is wrong to pass judgement on others who have substantially different values, or to try to make them conform to one's values, for the reason that their values are as valid as one's own. Another common response to deep moral conflict, however, contradicts moral relativism in its two major forms. It is the universalist or absolutist position that both sides of a moral conflict cannot be equally right, that there can be only one truth about the matter at issue. This position is so common, in fact, that William James was led to call us 'absolutists by instinct' (James, 1948). The term 'universalism' will be used hereafter, because 'absolutism' is used not only to refer to the denial of moral relativism, but also to the view that some moral rules or duties are absolutely without exception.

442

ii Meta-ethical relativism

The debate between moral relativism and universalism accounts for a significant proportion of philosophical reflection in ethics. In ancient Greece at least some of the 'Sophists' defended a version of moral relativism, which Plato attempted to refute. Plato attributes to the first great Sophist, Protagoras, the argument that human custom determines what is fine and ugly, just and unjust. Whatever is communally judged to be the case, the argument goes, actually comes to be the case (*Theaetetus*, 172AB; it is unclear, however, whether the real Protagoras actually argued in this manner). Now the Greeks, through trade, travel, and war, were fully aware of wide variation in customs, and so the argument concludes with the relativity of morality. The question with this argument, however, is whether we can accept that custom determines in a strong sense what is fine and ugly, just and unjust. It may influence what people *think* is fine and just. But it is quite another thing for custom to determine what *is* fine and just. Customs sometimes change under the pressure of moral criticism, and the argument seems to rely on a premise that contradicts this phenomenon.

Another kind of argument given for relativism is premised on the view that the customary ethical beliefs in any given society are functionally necessary for that society. Therefore, the argument concludes, the beliefs are true for that society, but not necessarily in another. The sixteenth-century essayist, Michel de Montaigne, sometimes makes this argument ('Of custom, and not easily changing an accepted law', in Montaigne, 1595), but it has had its greatest acceptance among anthropologists of the twentieth century who emphasize the importance of studying societies as organic wholes of which the parts are functionally inter-dependent. (See Article 2, ETHICS IN SMALL-SCALE SOCIETIES.) The problem with the functional argument, however, is that moral beliefs are not justified merely on the grounds that they are necessary for a society's existence in anything like its present form. Even if a society's institutions and practices crucially depend on the acceptance of certain beliefs, the justifiability of those beliefs depends on the moral acceptability of the institutions and practices. To show that certain beliefs are necessary for maintaining a fascist society, for instance, is not to justify those beliefs.

Despite the weaknesses of these arguments for moral relativism, the doctrine has always had its adherents. Its continuing strength has always been rooted in the impressiveness of the variation in ethical belief to be found across human history and culture. In an ancient text (*Dissoi Logoi* or the *Contrasting Arguments*; Robinson, 1979) associated with the Sophists, it is pointed out that for the Lacedaemonians, it was fine for girls to exercise without tunics, and for children not to learn music and letters, while for the Ionians, these things were foul. Montaigne assembled a catalogue of exotic customs, such as male prostitution, cannibalism, women warriors, killing one's father at a certain age as an act of piety, and recites from the Greek historian Herodotus the experiment of Darius. Darius asked Greeks how much they would have to be paid before they would eat the bodies of their deceased fathers. They replied that no sum of money could get them to do such a thing. He then asked certain Indians who customarily ate the bodies of their deceased fathers what they would have to be paid to burn the bodies of their fathers. Amidst loud exclamations, they bade him not to speak of such a thing (Montaigne's 'Of custom' (1595), and Herodotus, *Persian Wars*, Book III, 38).

But while many have been moved by such examples to adopt moral relativism, the argument from diversity does not support relativism in any simple or direct way. As the Socrates of Plato's dialogues observed, we have reason to listen only to the wise among us (*Crito*, 44CD). The simple fact of diversity in belief is no disproof of the possibility that there are some beliefs better to have than the others because they are truer or more justified than the rest. If half the world still believed that the sun, the moon, and the planets revolved around the earth, that would be no disproof of the possibility of a unique truth about the structure of the universe. Diversity in belief, after all, may result from varying degrees of wisdom. Or it may be that different people have their own limited perspectives of the truth, each perspective being distorted in its own way.

It is sometimes thought that the extent and depth of disagreement in ethics indicates that moral judgements are simply not judgements about facts, that they assert nothing true or false about the world but straightforwardly express our own subjective reactions to certain facts and happenings, whether these be collective or individual reactions (e.g. see C. L. Stevenson, *Ethics and Language* (1944); for further discussion, see Article 38, SUBJECTIVISM). A more complicated view is that moral judgements purport to report objective matters of fact, but that there are no such matters of fact (see J. L. Mackie, *Ethics: Inventing Right and Wrong*, 1977). The success of modern science in producing a remarkable degree of convergence of belief about the basic structure of the physical world probably reinforces these varieties of scepticism about the objectivity of moral judgements. It is hard to deny that there is a significant difference in the degree of convergence of belief in ethics and in science. Yet there are possible explanations for that difference that are compatible with claiming that moral judgements are ultimately about facts in the world. These explanations might stress, for instance, the special difficulties of acquiring knowledge of subjects that pertain to moral knowledge.

An understanding of human nature and human affairs is necessary for formulating an adequate moral code. The enormously difficult and complex task of reaching such an understanding could be a major reason for differences in moral belief. Furthermore, the subject matter of ethics is such that people have the most intense practical interest in what is established as truth about it, and surely this interest engenders the passions that becloud judgement (for a reply in this spirit see Nagel, 1986, pp. 185–88). Universalists could point out that many apparently exotic moral beliefs presuppose certain religious and metaphysical beliefs, and that these beliefs, rather than any difference in fundamental values, explain the apparent strangeness. Consider, for example, the way our view of Darius' Indians would change if we were to attribute to them the belief that eating the body of one's deceased father is a way of preserving his spiritual substance. Finally, some of the striking differences in moral belief across societies may not be rooted in differences in fundamental values but in the fact that these values may have to be implemented in different ways given the varying conditions that obtain across societies. If one society contains many more women than men (say, because men are killing each other off in warfare), it would not be surprising if polygamy were acceptable there, while in another society, where the proportion of women to men is equal, monogamy is required. The difference in accepted marriage practice may come down to that difference in the proportion of women to men, and not to any difference in basic moral ideals of marriage or of the proper relationships between women and men.

The mere existence of deep and wide disagreements in ethics, therefore, does not disprove the possibility that moral judgements can be objectively correct or incorrect judgements about certain facts. Moral relativists must chart some other more complicated path from the existence of diversity to the conclusion that there is no single true or most justified morality. I believe (and have argued, in *Moral Relativity*, 1984) that the relativist argument is best conducted by pointing to particular kinds of differences in moral belief, and then by claiming that these particular differences are best explained under a theory that denies the existence of a single true morality. This would involve denying that the various ways that universalists have for explaining ethical disagreement are sufficient for explaining the particular differences in question. (For another strategy of argument that relies more on an analysis of the meaning of moral judgements, see Harman, 1975.)

One apparent and striking ethical difference that would be a good candidate for this sort of argument concerns the emphasis on individual rights that is embodied in the ethical culture of the modern West and that seems absent in traditional cultures found in Africa, China, Japan and India. The content of duties in such traditional cultures instead seems organized around the central value of a common good that consists in a certain sort of ideal community life, a network of relationships, partially defined by social roles, again, ideal, but imperfectly embodied in ongoing existing practice. The ideal for members is composed of various virtues that enable them, given their place in the network of relationships, to promote and sustain the common good.

Confucianism, for instance, makes the family and kinship groups the models for the common good, with larger social and political units taking on certain of their features, such as benevolent leaders who rule with the aim of cultivating virtue and harmony among their subjects. (See Article 6, CLASSICAL CHINESE ETHICS.) Moralities centred on such values would seem to differ significantly from ones centred on individual rights to liberty and to other goods, if the basis for attributing such rights to persons does not seem to lie in their conduciveness to the common good of a shared life, but in a moral worth independently attributed to each individual. By contrast a theme frequently found in ethics of the common good is that individuals find their realization as human beings in promoting and sustaining the common good. Given this assumption of the fundamental harmony between the highest good of individuals and the common good, one might expect the constraints on freedom to have greater scope and to be more pervasive

445

when compared to a tradition in which no such fundamental harmony between individual and common goods is assumed.

If the contrast between the two types of morality is real, it raises the question of whether one or the other type is truer or more justified than the other. The argument for a relativistic answer may start with the claim that each type focuses on a good that may reasonably occupy the centre of an ethical ideal for human life. On the one hand, there is the good of belonging to and contributing to a community; on the other, there is the good of respect for the individual apart from any potential contribution to community. It would be surprising, the argument goes, if there were just one justifiable way of setting a priority with respect to the two goods. It should not be surprising, after all, if the range of human goods is simply too rich and diverse to be reconciled in just a single moral ideal.

Such an argument could be supplemented by an explanation of why human beings have such a thing as a morality. Morality serves two universal human needs. It regulates conflicts of interest between people, and it regulates conflicts of interest within the individual born of different desires and drives that cannot all be satisfied at the same time. Ways of dealing with those two kinds of conflict develop in anything recognizable as human society. To the extent that these ways crystallize in the form of rules for conduct and ideals for persons, we have the core of a morality. Now in order to perform its practical functions adequately, it may be that a morality will have to possess certain general features. A relatively enduring and stable system for the resolution of conflict between people, for instance, will not permit the torture of persons at whim.

But given this picture of the origin and functions of morality, it would not be surprising if significantly different moralities were to perform the practical functions equally well, at least according to standards of performance that were common to these moralities. Moralities, on this picture, are social creations that evolve to meet certain needs. The needs place conditions on what could be an adequate morality, and if human nature has a definite structure, one would expect further constraining conditions on an adequate morality to derive from our nature. But the complexity of our nature makes it possible for us to prize a variety of goods and to order them in different ways, and this opens the way for a substantial relativism to be true.

The picture sketched above has the advantage of leaving it open as to how strong a version of relativism is true. That is, it holds that there is no single true morality, yet does not deny that some moralities might be false and inadequate for the functions they all must perform. Almost all polemics against moral relativism are directed at its most extreme versions: those holding that all moralities are equally true (or equally false, or equally lacking in cognitive content). Yet a substantial relativism need not be so radically egalitarian. Besides ruling out moralities that would aggravate interpersonal conflict, such as the one described above, relativists could also recognize that adequate moralities must promote the production of persons capable of considering the interests of others. Such persons would need to have received a certain kind of nurturing and care from others. An adequate morality, then, whatever else its content, would have to prescribe and promote the sorts of upbringing and continuing interpersonal relationships that produce such persons.

A moral relativism that would allow for this kind of constraint on what could be a true or most justified morality might not fit the stereotype of relativism, but would be a reasonable position to hold. One reason, in fact, that not much progress has been made in the debate between relativists and universalists is that each side has tended to define the opponent as holding the most extreme position possible. While this makes the debating easier, it does nothing to shed light on the vast middle ground where the truth indeed may lie. Many of the same conclusions could be drawn about the debate over normative moral relativism: much heat, and frequent identification of the opponent with the most extreme position possible.

iii Normative relativism

The most extreme possible position for the normative relativist is that no-one should ever pass judgement on others with substantially different values, or try to make them conform to one's own values. Such a definition of normative relativism is usually given by its opponents, because it is an indefensible position. It requires self-condemnation by those who act according to it. If I pass judgement on those who pass judgement, I must condemn myself. I am trying to impose a value of tolerance on everyone, when not everyone has that value, but this is not what I am supposed to be doing under the most extreme version of normative relativism. Philosophers are usually content with such easy dismissals of the most extreme version of normative relativism, but there is reason to consider whether more moderate versions might be more tenable. The reason is that normative relativism is not just a philosophical doctrine but a stance adopted toward morally troubling situations.

Anthropologists are sometimes identified with this stance, and it is instructive to understand how this identification emerged from a historical and sociological context. The birth of cultural anthropology in the late nineteenth century was in part subsidized by colonizing governments needing to know more about the nature and status of 'primitive' peoples. Influenced by Darwinian theory, early anthropological theory tended to arrange the peoples and social institutions of the world in an evolutionary series, from primordial man to the civilized human being of nineteenth-century Europe. Many anthropologists eventually reacted against the imperialism of their governments and to its rationalization supplied by their predecessors. More importantly, they came to see the peoples they studied as intelligent men and women whose lives had meaning and integrity. And this led to questioning the basis for implicit judgements of the inferiority of their ways of life, especially after the spectacle of the civilized nations in brutal struggle with one another in the First World War (see, for example, Ruth Benedict, *Patterns of Culture*, 1934, and more recently, Melville Herskovits, *Cultural Relativism: Perspectives in Cultural Pluralism*, 1972).

The normative relativism of some of the anthropologists of that period, then, was a response to real moral problems concerning the justifiability of colonization

447

and more generally concerning intervention in another society so as to cause major changes in previously accepted values or in people's ability to act on those values. No simple version of normative relativism is the answer to these problems, as was illustrated by the fact that an ethic of non-judgemental tolerance would self-destruct when used to condemn the intolerant. The inadequacy of the simple versions also is illustrated by the swing in anthropology on the question of normative relativism after the Second World War. That war, many realized, was a battle against enormous evil. Such a realization brought vividly to the forefront the necessity of passing judgement at least sometimes and of acting on one's judgement. And accordingly there was a new trend within cultural anthropology toward finding a basis for making judgements that would depend on criteria to be applied to all moral codes.

A more reasonable version of normative relativism would have to permit us to pass judgement on others with substantially different values. Even if these different values are as justified as our own from some neutral perspective, we still are entitled to call bad or evil or monstrous what contradicts our most important values. What we are entitled to do in the light of such judgements, however, is another matter. Many of us who are likely to read this book would be reluctant to intervene in the affairs of others who have values substantially different from ours, when the reason for intervention is the enforcement of our own values, and when we think that we have no more of an objective case for our moral outlook than the others have for theirs. The source of this reluctance is a feature of our morality. A liberal, contractualist outlook is very much part of our ethical life in the postmodern West, whether we acknowledge it or not. (See Article 15, THE SOCIAL CONTRACT TRADITION.) We want to act toward others in such a way that our actions could be seen as justified by them if they were fully reasonable and informed of all relevant facts. If we hold a meta-ethical moral relativism, however, then we must recognize that there will be occasions when some otherwise desirable course of action toward others with different values will violate this feature of our morality.

At that point, there is no general rule that will tell us what to do. It would seem to depend on what other values of ours are at stake. If a practice performed by others were to involve human sacrifice, for example, then the value of tolerance might indeed be outweighed, and we may decide to intervene to prevent it. The disagreement over the legal permissibility of abortion demonstrates how difficult the weighing can be, however. Consider the position of those who believe that abortion is morally wrong because it is the taking of life that has moral status. Within this group some seem undisturbed by the fact that there is deep disagreement over the moral status of the fetus. They wish to prohibit abortion. But others in this group, while holding that abortion is wrong, admit that reasonable persons could disagree with them and that human reason seems unable to resolve the question. For this reason they oppose legal prohibitions of abortion. The former believe that the latter do not take the value of human life seriously, while the latter believe that the former fail to recognize the depth and seriousness of the disagreement between reasonable persons. (See also Article 26, ABORTION.)

Each position has some force, and clearly normative relativism offers no simple solution to the dilemma. What the doctrine provides, however, is a set of reasons for tolerance and non-intervention that must be weighed against other reasons. The doctrine applies not only to proposed interventions by one society in another, but also, as in the case of abortion, to deep moral disagreements within pluralistic societies containing diverse moral traditions. If meta-ethical relativism is true, even if only with respect to a limited set of moral conflicts such as abortion, then our moral condition is immeasurably complicated. We must strive to find what will be for us the right or the best thing to do, and also deal with the feelings of unease caused by the recognition that there is no single right or best thing to do. This task, no matter how difficult, is not the end of moral reflection. It instead may be the beginning of a different sort of reflection that involves on the one hand an effort to reach an understanding with those who have substantially different values, and on the other the effort to stay true to one's own values. Some of those who believe that abortion is the taking of a life with moral status, for instance, have chosen to oppose it by placing their efforts into organizations that aim to lessen the perceived need for abortion, organizations that aid unwed mothers, for example.

One final issue regarding relativism needs addressing. Relativism has a bad name in some quarters because it is associated with a lack of moral conviction, with a tendency toward nihilism. Part of the reason for the bad name may be the identification of relativism with its most extreme forms. If these forms are true, then everything is permitted, on someone's morality. But another reason for the bad name is the assumption that one's moral confidence, one's commitment to act on one's values, is somehow dependent on maintaining the belief that one's morality is the only true or the most justified one. But surely some reflection will reveal that such a belief alone would not guarantee a commitment to act. The commitment to act involves a conception of what one's morality means to the self, whether it be the only true one or not. It involves making a connection between what one desires, what one aspires to, and the substantive content of one's moral values. It is being able to see morality as important to us in these ways that allows us to avoid nihilism. The belief that our morality is the only true or most justified one does not automatically create this kind of importance, nor is it a necessary condition for this kind of importance, because the values I may see as important and part of what makes life most meaningful to me may not have to be values that all reasonable persons would accept or recognize to be true.

Here, as in other matters concerning relativism, the emotion provoked by the mere name tends to muddle the issues and to polarize unnecessarily. When we get through defending and attacking what most people conceive as relativism or what they associate with it, then most of the real work remains to be done. What is left is a moral reality that is quite messy and immune to neat solutions. But why should we have expected anything else?

References

Benedict, R.: *Patterns of Culture* (New York: Penguin, 1934).

Harman, G.: 'Moral relativism defended', *Philosophical Review* 84 (1975), 3–22.

Herodotus: *The Persian Wars*, trans. George Rawlinson (New York: Modern Library, 1942).

Herskovits, M.: *Cultural Relativism: Perspectives in Cultural Pluralism* (New York: Vintage, 1972).

James, W.: 'The will to believe', *Essays in Pragmatism*, ed. Aubrey Castell (New York: Hafner, 1948).

Mackie, J. L.: *Ethics: Inventing Right and Wrong* (Harmondsworth: Penguin, 1977).

Montaigne, M. de: *Complete Essays* (1595); trans. Donald M. Frame (Stanford: Stanford University Press, 1973).

Nagel, T.: *The View from Nowhere* (New York: Oxford University Press, 1986).

Plato: *Crito* and *Theaetetus*; trans. E. Hamilton and H. Cairns, *Collected Dialogues of Plato* (Princeton: Princeton University Press, 1961).

Robinson, T. M., trans.: *Contrasting Arguments: an edition of the Dissoi Logoi* (New York: Arno Press, 1979).

Stevenson, C. L.: *Ethics and Language* (New Haven: Yale University Press, 1944).

Wong, D. B.: *Moral Relativity* (Berkeley: University of California Press, 1984).

40

Universal prescriptivism

R. M. HARE

UNIVERSAL PRESCRIPTIVISM is best seen as an attempt to locate both the faults and the true insights in other current ethical theories, to remedy the faults while preserving the insights, and so to provide a synthesis between them. The expression 'ethical theory' covers attempts to say what we are asking when we ask moral questions. What do we mean by the words or the sentences that we use in moral discourse; what is the nature of the moral concepts or of morality? If successful, these attempts will have implications for another, epistemological, question which also belongs to ethical theory: how should we set about answering our moral questions rationally? Or can there be no rational way – is it just a matter of how we feel or what the current mores dictate? On the other hand, if there can be rational discussion of moral questions, does it demand that there be a truth about them, or a set of facts, that can be discovered?

The main division is between *descriptivist* and *non-descriptivist* theories. These are distinguished in various more or less misleading ways (Hare, 1985b). It is said that descriptivists hold that moral judgements can be true or false, while non-descriptivists deny this. But since there is a perfectly good sense, as we shall see, in which non-descriptivists can use the term 'true' of moral judgements, this way of speaking obscures the issue. So does the use of the terms 'cognitivism' and 'non-cognitivism', implying that the former does, and the latter does not, allow that we can *know* that some moral judgements are true. For again, there is a perfectly good sense in which non-descriptivists can allow this, as we shall see. Equally misleading is the ontological way of putting the distinction, by saying that descriptivists claim that there are moral qualities or facts existing in the world, whereas non-descriptivists deny this; for as soon as we start asking what it is for a moral quality or fact to exist in the world, we get lost.

Both non-descriptivism in all its varieties, and the descriptivist theories to be discussed, are *semantical*, not ontological theories. So-called ontological theses in ethics (e.g. 'ontological naturalism') may be substantial moral claims about what is or is not right, etc. (e.g. that what maximizes happiness is always, or perhaps even necessarily, right). The question of what they mean, which is our present topic, is a different one. On the futility of ontological disputes in ethics, see Hare, 1985b; for a different view, see Article 37, NATURALISM.

We can avoid these difficulties if we put the distinction in terms of a theory of meaning which has been very popular: the *truth-condition* theory. This is not the same as the old 'verification theory' advocated by some logical positivists; but it shares some of its insights. According to this theory, to understand the meaning of a sentence, as used to make a statement, is to understand the truth-conditions of the statement, i.e. what has to be the case for it to be called true. Those who hold that this is true of all sentences may be called descriptivists *tout court*.

Descriptivism of this sweeping sort is obviously false – Austin even called it 'the descriptive fallacy' (Austin, 1961, p. 234; 1962, p. 3). For there are certainly sentences and utterances whose meaning is not determined by truth-conditions. Imperatives are the obvious example: in order to know what the request 'Shut the door' means, we do not have to know, and cannot know, its truth-conditions, because it does not have any. But maybe one can safely be a descriptivist with regard to large classes of sentences. It can perhaps be said that sentences expressing typical ordinary statements of fact *do* have their meaning determined by the truth-conditions of the statements they express, so perhaps we can happily be descriptivists with regard to such sentences. But since not all sentences are like this, as we have seen, the question arises, for any given class of sentences, whether their meaning is wholly determined by truth-conditions or not – i.e., whether they can be classified as purely descriptive.

The word 'purely' is important. It is possible for part, but not the whole, of the meaning of a sentence to be determined by truth-conditions. We may call such 'mixed' sentences 'descriptive' in a weak sense, but not in the strong sense here being used. In the strong sense a sentence is not descriptive (i.e. not purely descriptive) unless its meaning is wholly determined by truth-conditions. Ethical descriptivism is the view that this is true of sentences expressing moral judgements. Ethical non-descriptivists, including prescriptivists, can readily admit that there is an element in the meaning of moral judgements (the *descriptive meaning*) which *is* determined by truth-conditions; but they differ from descriptivists in thinking that there is a further element in their meaning, the prescriptive or evaluative, or in earlier writers the emotive, which is not so determined, but expresses prescriptions or evaluations or attitudes which we assent to without being constrained by truth-conditions.

Kant was saying the same thing in other words when he spoke of the autonomy of the will: 'the property the will has of being a law to itself (independently of any property belonging to the objects of volition)' (Kant, 1785, BA87 = 440). To adopt an attitude, evaluation or prescription is a function of the autonomous will, constrained only, in Kant's words, 'by the fitness of its maxims for its own making of universal law' (Kant, 1785, BA88 = 441 – see below).

Having distinguished descriptivist from non-descriptivist ethical theories in general, we can now proceed to subdivide each of these, in order to put prescriptivism in its proper slot. Descriptivist theories can be divided broadly into naturalism and intuitionism. Both terms can be misleading, but they will serve. The dispute between these is about whether or not the truth-conditions or moral judgements, which according to descriptivism give them their meaning, are to be determined by definitions (or, more loosely, explanations of meaning) which refer only to non-moral truths or properties. Naturalists think that this is possible; intuitionists, by contrast, think that no such definitions or explanations can capture the meanings of the moral words. Note that the dispute between natu-ralists and their intuitionist opponents is not the same as that between descrip-tivists and non-descriptivists: it is a dispute *within* descriptivism. Non-descriptivists reject naturalism because they reject descriptivism of all kinds. They can use such of the intuitionist arguments against naturalism as are valid; but the main impetus of their attack is independent of these.

The main impetus comes from the recognition that both forms of descriptivism, in different ways, are destined to collapse into relativism. Though relativism has its supporters (among them, we are often told, most of the callower among American students – though this is an exaggeration), it is certainly *not* what most descriptivists are trying to establish. They set out with the aim of showing, rather, that there can be rational moral enquiry, yielding conclusions to which we must all in reason assent. It is the fact that both kinds of descriptivism signally fail, and are bound to fail, to show this that condemns them even by their own standards.

Naturalism collapses into relativism in the following way. If the meanings of moral words are explained in terms of truth-conditions, then what will ultimately determine the truth or falsity of moral judgements will be the particular truth-conditions accepted in a given society as determining the meanings of the moral words. So (to take an over-crude example) if we explain the meaning of 'ought' in the sentence 'Wives ought to obey their husbands in all things' by saying that the statement it expresses is true if and only if some conjunction of non-moral statements is true, we shall then have to specify this set of non-moral statements. Perhaps we shall say that the statement is true if and only if wives obeying their husbands would contribute to the stability of society. Now it may be that in a given society it is generally accepted that one ought to do what would contribute to the stability of society. That, perhaps, is one of the moral principles that the society believes in. But this is a principle which could be rejected by feminists. They might think that although wives obeying their husbands would indeed contribute to the stability of society, they ought not always to obey, because husbands sometimes make demands that wives ought to disobey even at the cost of impairing stability.

What is happening in this example is that a substantial moral principle, that one ought to do what would contribute to the stability of society, has got promoted into an analytic truth, true in virtue of the meaning of 'ought'. But it is not an analytic truth. If it were, then the anti-feminists would win the argument, because the feminists, in contending that wives sometimes ought not to obey although this would destabilize society, would be contradicting themselves, by saying something which the very meaning of 'ought' establishes as false. If 'ought' has its meaning fixed by truth-conditions, and if the truth-conditions are those accepted by native speakers of the language, and if the native speakers of this language (apart from a very few deviants) use 'ought' in such a way that what destabilizes society must be something that one ought not to do, then one cannot in logical consistency say what the feminists are saying. We can see from this over-simple example that the effect of naturalism is to force everybody to embrace the accepted mores on pain of self-contradition; and this is relativism. For a fuller account see Hare, 1985a, 1986; for a defence of a form of relativism, see Article 39, RELATIVISM.

The other variety of descriptivism, *intuitionism*, collapses into relativism in an even simpler way. Intuitionism is the view that the truth-conditions of moral judgements, which give them their meaning, consist in conformity with the data on which we have to base our moral reasoning, and with which its conclusions have to square; and these data are the common moral convictions that all morally educated people have. Since these convictions will vary from one society to another, the effect of intuitionism is, again, to anchor our moral reasoning to something relative to particular societies. True, there are convictions which are common to most societies; but there are others which are not, and no way is given by intuitionists of telling which are the authoritative data. To revert to our example, if it is a universal conviction in a society that wives ought to obey their husbands, then the feminists' case is ruled out of court; but if there were a society, as there may come to be, in which it was a universal conviction that wives have no such duty, then the anti-feminists' case will similarly be ruled out of court. Relativism is again the result.

One further kind of descriptivism may be mentioned here, namely *subjectivism*. This term is used very loosely, but here we shall be using it strictly for that kind of naturalistic descriptivism which holds that the meaning of 'ought' and other moral words is to describe the attitudes or feelings of people – for example to attribute to people in general, or to the speaker of the sentence, an attitude or feeling of approval or disapproval towards a certain kind of act. This is intended to be understood as a statement of non-moral, psychological fact about the speaker or about people in general – a fact which could be discovered by observation or reported introspection. Thus the theory is a naturalistic one. But the fact in question (which establishes the truth of a moral judgement, and is thus its truth-condition) instead of being, as in our previous example, one about what would happen in society if wives disobeyed their husbands, is a *subjective* fact about what people disapprove of. (James Rachels uses the term simple subjectivism to refer to this theory; See Article 38, SUBJECTIVISM.)

The words 'objective' and 'subjective' have a clear use here; we are distinguishing between two kinds of facts: facts about what will actually happen in society if wives disobey, and facts about what people think. The former are objective facts, the latter subjective. To define the moral words in terms of subjective facts would be one kind of naturalistic descriptivism. It is helpful, however, to notice that there is no important distinction between this kind of subjectivism and intuitionism; for intuitions and moral convictions are also subjective facts – facts about what people think; and therefore many of the objections that are commonly accepted against subjectivism apply equally to intuitionism. That explains why intuitionism collapses into relativism; intuitionists are appealing for support to nothing objective, but only to their own and other people's thoughts, and these will vary from one person and society to another.

When used outside this context, the words 'objective' and 'subjective' can be a source of confusion (Hare, 1976). In particular, if various kinds of non-descriptivism are said to be 'subjectivist', this can only be in a quite different sense. They do not make moral judgements equivalent to statements of psychological fact, because they do not make them equivalent to any kind of factual statement. True, they agree with subjectivists in rejecting both objectivistic naturalism, and the objectivist claims of intuitionists; but that is all they have in common. Subjectivism, in the sense used here, and prescriptivism (or for that matter emotivism) fall on opposite sides of the main division of ethical theories into descriptivist and non-descriptivist theories (see above). It therefore risks serious confusion to use the term 'subjectivist' to apply to both.

Non-descriptivism likewise can be subdivided. The earlier versions, mostly forms of emotivism, were essentially irrationalist. Having rejected the view that moral judgements are equivalent to statements of non-moral facts (naturalism) and the view that they are *sui generis* statements about moral facts discernible by intuition or appeal to convictions (intuitionism), they concluded too hastily that one cannot reason about moral questions; moral judgements are the expressions of irrational or at least non-rational attitudes of approval or disapproval. They concluded this because they added an additional premise which is false, namely that the only questions one can reason about are factual ones. A reading of Kant with his 'Practical Reason' (1785, BA101 = 448), or even of Aristotle with his *'phronēsis'* or 'practical wisdom' (which he says is epitactic or prescriptive – *Nicomachean Ethics*, 1143a 8) should have cured them of this mistake.

The genesis of prescriptivism lay in the realization that this premise *is* false. It has been generally recognized that there is something unsatisfactory about emotivism. Those who are beguiled by the false premise just mentioned have reacted by reverting to some form of descriptivism. Prescriptivists, on the other hand, have reacted in a more positive way by looking for a kind of non-descriptivism which would not be open to the charge of irrationality – a charge which most moral philosophers want to escape. They claim to have found it by showing that there are rules of reasoning which govern non-descriptive as well as descriptive speech acts.

The standard example is again imperatives: if (as is certainly the case) there can be logical inconsistency between contradictory prescriptions, someone who wants the totality of the imperatives, or in general prescriptions, that he (or she) accepts to be self-consistent will have to observe the rules which govern consistency. What these rules are should therefore be the main concern of the practical philosopher.

Some emotivists became irrationalists because they both assimilated moral judgements to imperatives and made a mistake about imperatives which is still too common, namely to think that they get their meaning from their causal properties. This may be termed the 'verbal shove' theory of the meaning of imperatives. It involves a failure to distinguish between what Austin calls per-locutionary acts (what one is doing *by* saying things) and illocutionary acts (what one is doing *in* saying them) (Austin, 1962). Verbal shoves and psychological prods are not part of the meaning of either imperatives or moral speech acts (Urmson, 1968, p. 130 ff.; Hare, 1971, s.f.).

455

If one thought that imperatives owed their meaning to their causal properties, one might easily become an irrationalist about imperatives and thus about moral judgements, if these were prescriptive. But if this mistake is avoided, the thesis that moral judgements are a kind of prescriptions (perhaps not identical with the simple imperative kind, and certainly more complex in their logic) is consistent with there being reasoning-rules that govern moral thinking.

Prescriptivists have looked for such rules. They claim to have found them in a combination of the rules that govern ordinary simple imperatives, and a further set of rules that govern 'ought' and other deontic modal words like 'must' in its moral sense, which stands to imperatives in much the same relation as modal indicatives to non-modal ones (Hare, 1981, p. 23). These words are not peculiar to moral discourse, so it may be that further rules are needed for moral discourse in particular. But that can be left open for the present (see Hare, 1981, p. 52ff.).

In any case some differentia is needed to distinguish the rules common to all prescriptions, which govern imperatives as well as 'ought'-statements, from those which are peculiar to 'ought'-statements; otherwise we shall be left making no logical distinction between two classes of speech acts which are clearly different in their meaning, and therefore in their logic.

The most-discussed kind of prescriptivism, known as *universal prescriptivism*, finds this differentia in what has been called the *universalizability* of 'ought'-sentences and other normative or evaluative sentences. Most descriptivists too acknowledge this feature of moral judgements. One cannot with logical consistency, where *a* and *b* are two individuals, say that *a* ought, in a certain situation specified in universal terms without reference to individuals, to act in a certain way, also specified in universal terms, but that *b* ought not to act in a similarly specified way in a similarly specified situation. This is because in any 'ought'-statement there is implicit a principle which says that the statement applies to all precisely similar situations. This means that if I say 'That is what ought to be done; but there could be a situation exactly like this one in its non-moral properties, but in which the corresponding person, who was exactly like the person who ought to do it in this situation, ought not to do it', I contradict myself (Hare, 1963, p. 10ff.). This would become even clearer if I specified my reasons for saying why it ought to be done: 'It ought to be done because it was a promise, and there were no conflicting duties'.

Three warnings are necessary here to avoid confusions which have been too common. First, the 'situation' is to be taken as including the characteristics of the people in it, including their desires and motivations. If, therefore, the speaker says that *a* ought to do something to *c*, but that *b* ought not to do the same thing to *d*, because the desires of *c* and *d* are quite different, he is not offending against universalizability, because the different desires make the situations different. Bernard Shaw said 'Do not do unto others as you would they should do unto you. Their tastes may not be the same' (Shaw, 1903, p. 227); but this is not an objection to universalizability. If I ought to tickle one child's toes because it loves it, it does not follow that I ought to tickle another child's toes, however similar, if the second child hates it.

Secondly, universality must not be confused with generality (Hare, 1972, p. 1ff.) The principle involved in an 'ought'-statement may be a highly specific, complex and detailed one, perhaps too complex for formulation in words. It does not have to be very general and simple. Complaints against universalizability, that it makes us the slaves of very simple general rules, therefore miss their target. To use an example which gave trouble to Kant: my moral principles do not have to be as general as '*Never* tell lies'; they can be more specific, like 'Never tell lies except when it is necessary in order to save an innocent life, and except when ..., and except when ...' (Kant, 1797). In a morally developed person the exceptions may get too complex to be formulated in words. But see below for the value, in our human situation, of general (i.e. not too specific) principles.

Thirdly, there can be universal relations as well as qualities (many-place as well as one-place predicates). Such is the relation *mother of*. The statement that everyone ought to look after his (or her) mother in her old age is therefore a universal statement, and the statement that *a* ought to look after his mother (but has no such duty to look after other people's mothers), is universalizable. The same can be said about the statement that I ought to keep my promises but not other people's. It is therefore no objection to the thesis of universalizability that there can be duties that one owes just to one person, provided that that person can be specified in universal qualititative or relational terms. It is no objection, even, that one can have the relation in question only to one person. 'Mother of' is an example.

This point can be related to the previous one by citing a famous though much misused example given by Jean-Paul Sartre (1946, p. 40). During the Nazi occupation of France, a student came to seek Sartre's advice. The student's dilemma was whether to join the Free French forces to fight against the evil of Nazism, or to stay with his widowed mother, who depended on him. Sartre uses the case to suggest that universal principles are useless in such situations, since each case is unique. Sartre himself seems to confuse universality with objectivity, though they are obviously different concepts.

But apart from that, his student did not have to find for himself any very simple, general principle. Perhaps he was the only person who had ever been in that particular complex situation. But he ought to have been able to form for himself a principle (a highly specific one) which he could accept for situations *just* like his. Perhaps other such situations would never occur. But one can *conceive* of hypothetical situations as like to his as one wishes; and he would be committed, on pain of self-contradiction, to admit that *if* they occurred, the same thing should be done in them. That our moral judgements have to extend to identical situations, hypothetical as well as actual, is an important tool in moral argument (Hare, 1981, p. 112ff.). But none of this implies that Sartre's pupil would be entitled to reproach or interfere with, unasked, someone else in the same situation who acted otherwise; he might think it an impertinence not to keep his thoughts to himself.

Universal prescriptivists hold, then, that 'ought'-judgements are prescriptive like plain imperatives, but differ from them in being universalizable. The task of explaining what prescriptivity is (the feature that 'ought'-statements share with

457

imperatives) can be attempted here only in the sketchiest way. A speech act is prescriptive if to subscribe to it is to be committed, on pain of being accused of insincerity, to doing the action specified in the speech act, or, if it requires someone else to do it, to willing that he do it.

Prescriptivism thus falls within the class of ethical theories known as 'internalist': those which hold that to accept some moral judgement is *eo ipso* to be motivated in a certain way. This must not be confused with the view that for a moral judgement to be *true* is for someone to be motivated in some way; this would be a form of subjectivism in the sense used above. Internalist theories are contrasted with externalist theories, which hold that one can accept a moral judgement independently of one's motivations. So, for example, one may, according to externalists, say without contradiction or even pragmatic inconsistency 'I ought, but I have absolutely no inclination to'. By 'pragmatic inconsistency' is meant the logical fault that we all find in the statement 'He has been here already, but I don't believe it'.

Internalists and prescriptivists have been attacked on the ground that they make it impossible consistently to say 'You ought, but don't', or to think that one ought, but not be at all disposed to. The opposite side of this coin is that, as the 'but' shows, we all feel that there is *something* – even something conceptually and not just morally – wrong with people who say this sort of thing, which there would not be if externalism and descriptivism were correct. If someone were agonizing about what he ought to do, the agony would evaporate if he came to think the answer to his question quite irrelevant to his motivations or to what he actually did. This problem, sometimes called the problem of *akrasia* or weakness of will, is outside the scope of this article (see Hare, forthcoming).

We are now in a position to take up again the question of whether moral judgements can be called true or false. Imperatives clearly cannot. We can most easily sort out the problem by reverting to the notion of descriptive meaning explained earlier. Moral judgements have this because of their universalizability. To make one is, as we have seen, implicitly to invoke some principle, however specific. In any moderately stable society, the principles that people accept and invoke in their moral judgements will be fairly uniform and constant. As a result, when one person says that somebody did what he ought in the circumstances, anybody who knows the circumstances and shares these commonly accepted moral principles will assume that, if he did what he ought, what he did was in accord with them; so he will think he knows what in particular the speaker was saying he did. If, then, it turned out that the person did not do that, he will say that the speaker was speaking falsely. And so he was, according to the commonly accepted descriptive meaning (i.e. truth-conditions) of the word 'ought' in that society.

This is not inconsistent with prescriptivism – which is why the 'true-or-false' characterization of descriptivism is so misleading. For prescriptivists too can give a limited role to truth-conditions in determining the meanings, in a given society, of moral words. If, as descriptivists think, the descriptive meanings of moral judgements, as so determined, were their entire meaning, then relativism would be the consequence. For we can know the descriptive meaning of 'ought' in a given society; but it does not follow that it will have the same meaning in another society. A visitor from Saudi Arabia, hearing an Australian say that Tom's wife did what she ought, might assume that he meant that the wife obeyed. But the Australian might have meant that she disobeyed, because the subjection of women is not one of the principles accepted in Australia; Australians have another principle, that one ought to keep one's own end up.

So, although there is a perfectly good sense in which Saudi Arabians, speaking among themselves, can attribute truth or falsity to each others' moral judgements on the basis of the descriptive meanings of the moral words that they all accept, this attribution will break down when they are talking to Australians. It would break down even if they were speaking in Saudi Arabia to an Australian feminist missionary. The difficulty could be concealed by saying that both mean by 'ought' something rather vague, for example that to do it would make people happy. But if they try to establish the truth-conditions or descriptive meaning of *this*, they will disagree as before, and communication will again break down; for we may suppose that what counts as domestic happiness in Australia and Saudi Arabia is very different. The only way a descriptivist can get out of this difficulty is to say either (if he is a naturalist) that 'ought' and 'happy' have different meanings in the two places, and therefore different truth-conditions, or (if he is an intuitionist) that, because the convictions of people in the two places differ, there is *eo ipso* also a difference in how wives ought to behave; and both these ways of escape lead to relativism (MacIntyre, 1985; Hare, 1986).

The fact that moral judgements have descriptive meaning, and can therefore be said, within the limits just explained, to have truth-conditions and to be true or false, can be used to shed light on the much-disputed question of whether 'ought' can be derived from 'is' (moral judgements from non-moral facts). Given these features of moral judgements, it is easy to see why people should have thought that they can be derived from non-moral descriptive judgements, either deductively with the aid of a naturalistic definition, or by appeal to some substantial synthetic a priori moral principle grasped by intuition. For, as a Saudi Arabian might say, it is *obvious* that if a wife disobeys her husband (fact) she does what she ought not (moral judgement). Either this is true in virtue of the meanings of the words, given that disobedience by wives disrupts society (naturalism), or it is obvious anyway to those who have been properly morally educated (intuitionism).

This obviousness is reinforced if, as will be the case in stable societies, the moral education has instilled not just a certain use of language, nor just consistent behaviour in accord with the current mores, but deeply held convictions and feelings that such behaviour is required – that to depart from it goes against conscience. It is easy to see how people become naturalists or intutionists, and in both cases think that some non-moral factual premises make some 'ought'-conclusions inescapable. Prescriptivists have to deny this, because they hold that moral judgements commit the speaker to motivations and actions, but non-moral facts by themselves do not do this. The moral judgement, therefore, introduces a further element into the thought (the prescriptive or motivative element) which

459

is not there in the bare description of the facts. But the prescriptivist, if he is to win over the opposition, will have to provide an explanation, not merely of why people should *think* that moral judgements are inescapable given the facts, but of how (by what rational process) we can arrive at a prescriptive moral judgement on the basis of the given facts. Is this possible for prescriptivists, who think that moral judgements are prescriptions, and so more than factual? It will not seem possible to those who think that only facts can be discovered by reason; but this is an error, as we have seen.

Kant, who understood that it is an error, gives some hints on how to proceed. He says 'Act only on that maxim through which you can at the same time will that it should become a universal law', applicable, that is, whatever role you yourself occupy in the resulting situations (Kant, 1785, BA 82 = 421). If moral judgements have the features of prescriptivity and universalizability that prescriptivists say they have, this method is imposed on us by the logic of the moral concepts. What maxims we can adopt, or what moral judgements we can accept, will then depend on what we are prepared to prescribe for all like situations (whether, for example, we were the unfaithful husband or his deserted wife).

'Imagining ourselves in others' positions' is a difficult operation which presents both practical and philosophical problems. The practical ones are evidence only that moral thought just is difficult: humans cannot do it at all well. The remedy for this incapacity we shall discuss below. The philosophical difficulties are too big a subject for this short article. They concern the problem of how to compare the strengths of the preferences of different people with each other and with our own preferences; the problem of 'other minds' to which philosophers have devoted so much attention; the problem of whether it makes sense to imagine *myself* being *someone else* (would it still be *me*?), and of what I am constrained to say about that person's situation when I do it (Hare, 1981, Ch. 7 and refs.).

A possible move for one who is looking for the necessary constraints on moral thinking is to say that unless I treat the person, in whose place I am imagining myself being, on equal terms with myself, showing him equal concern, I am not really imagining him as being *me*. This entails treating his preferences as of equal weight with my own present preferences, and thus forming preferences for the hypothetical situation in which I am he, equal in strength to those which he actually has.

This is what is involved in following the Golden Rule, doing to others as we wish others to do to us, and loving our neighbours as ourselves. It is also implicit in Bentham's maxim 'Everybody to count for one, nobody for more than one' (cited in Mill, 1861, Ch. 5 s.f.). The Kantian method we have been outlining is consistent with a form of utilitarianism (though not, we must add, exactly Bentham's form, because that is put in terms of pleasure, whereas Kant's theory is put in terms of will).

It is wrong to think, as many do, that Kantianism and utilitarianism have to be at odds. To treat a person 'never simply as a means but always at the same time as an end' requires, as Kant himself says on the next page, that 'the ends of a subject who is an end in himself must, if this conception is to have its *full* effect in me, be also, as far as possible, *my* ends' (1785, BA 69 = 430 f.). An end is what is willed for its own sake; so we are, according to Kant, to give equal respect to everybody's wills-for-ends, including our own; and this is what utilitarianism also binds us do. This involves, in a harmless sense, treating the ends of many people as if they were the ends of one person (myself). But this does not involve failing to 'take seriously the distinction between persons' (Rawls, 1971, pp. 27, 187) – a distinction of which Kant and the utilitarians are well aware.

Kant, though he may not have realized it, runs up here against the same difficulty that has often been alleged against utilitarianism, that it leads us to moral conclusions which seem counter-intuitive (e.g. that punishment of the innocent would be right, given assumptions which in practice would seldom be satisfied). For this might, on such rare occasions, be what someone would do who was making other people's ends his own and so trying maximally to further them. To punish an innocent man might avert some major disaster to almost everybody's ends. The solution is that actually suggested by many utilitarians, which involves a division of moral thinking into two levels – an idea that reminds us of the distinction made by Plato (*Meno*, 98b) and Aristotle (*Nicomachean Ethics*, especially Book VI) between right opinion or desire and practical understanding or wisdom (*phronēsis*). 'Critical' and 'intuitive' thinking are convenient names for these two levels. If we were perfect moral thinkers we might use the Kantian-utilitarian method, i.e. critical thinking, always. But if humans did this it would lead them astray: they would not have enough time or information, and would be at the mercy of self-deception and special pleading; and as a result they would often pretend to themselves that the conclusion which suited their own interests was the one demanded by the method.

Humans, therefore, would be well advised to school themselves to have the good dispositions or virtues which will lead them, on the whole, to do what an unbiased and otherwise perfect critical moral thinker would bid them do – if necessary without too much thought, if thought is inopportune. In other words, they should cultivate the same intuitions as intuitionists appeal to, coupled with strong inclinations to follow them, and with other morally desirable feelings (love, for example) which will reinforce them. Only when these general dispositions conflict (as they sometimes will) shall we be driven to do some critical thinking, and even then we shall doubt our own powers.

However, if it comes to deciding *what* intuitions and dispositions to cultivate, we cannot rely on the intuitions themselves, as intuitionists do. When we have the leisure and are free from selfish bias, we should think critically about which are the right or the best ones, as judged by the extent to which, in general, their cultivation fulfils people's ends. And over the ages the wise have done this; so there is a presumption that the moral convictions shared by thinking people are the right ones to have. But it is only a presumption: some of them may not be the right ones. Is it right, for example, to think that it is morally quite legitimate to eat non-human animals? If we doubt whether our predecessors are right, we are constrained to do some critical thinking ourselves; but even then it will be as well to be humble and not too self-confident. The 'wisdom of the ages' has some authority simply because it is the result of the thought of a great many people in diverse situations.

Descriptivists draw comfort from this 'wisdom of the ages'; they claim that they *know* that its deliverances are correct. And indeed in a sense they do know; they have learnt, and not forgotten, that certain kinds of act are right and others wrong. But before they draw too much comfort, they should have a conversation with an Afrikaner who knows that it is wrong for blacks to claim equality with whites, or a Muslim fundamentalist who knows that it is right to stone adulteresses.

References

Aristotle: *Nicomachean Ethics*.

Austin, J. L.: *Philosophical Papers* (Oxford: Oxford University Press, 1961).

——: *How to Do Things with Words* (Oxford: Oxford University Press, 1962).

Hare, R. M.: *Freedom and Reason* (Oxford: Oxford University Press, 1963).

——: 'Wanting: some pitfalls', *Agent, Action and Reason*, eds. R. Binkley et al. (Toronto: Toronto University Press and Oxford: Basil Blackwell, 1971). Reprinted in his *Practical Inferences* (London: Macmillan, 1971).

——: 'Principles', *Proceedings of Aristotelian Society*, 73 (1972/3). Reprinted in his *Essays in Ethical Theory* (Oxford: Oxford University Press, 1989).

——: 'Some confusions about subjectivity', *Freedom and Morality*, ed. J. Bricke (Lawrence: University of Kansas, 1976). Reprinted in his *Essays in Ethical Theory* (Oxford: Oxford University Press, 1989).

——: *Moral Thinking* (Oxford: Oxford University Press, 1981).

——: 'How to decide moral questions rationally', in Italian, *Etica e diritto: le vie della giustificazione razionale*, ed. E. Lecaldano (Laterza, Rome, 1985). English version in *Critica* 18 (1987), reprinted in his *Essays in Ethical Theory* (Oxford: Oxford University Press, 1989). (1985a).

——: 'Ontology in ethics', *Morality and Objectivity: Essays in Memory of John Mackie*, ed. T. Honderich (Routledge, London, 1985). Reprinted in his *Essays in Ethical Theory* (Oxford: Oxford University Press, 1989). (1985b).

——: 'A *reductio ad absurdum* of descriptivism', *Philosophy in Britain Today*, ed. S. Shanker (London: Croom Helm, 1986). Reprinted in his *Essays in Ethical Theory* (Oxford: Oxford University Press, 1989).

——: *Essays in Ethical Theory* (Oxford: Oxford University Press, 1989).

——: 'Weakness of will', *Encyclopedia of Ethics*, ed. L. Becker (New York: Garland, forthcoming).

Kant, I.: *Grundlegung zur Metaphysik der Sitten* (1785). Refs. of form BA88 = 441 are, respectively, to pages of earliest editions and of royal Prussian Academy edn, as given in margin of translation by H. J. Paton under title *The Moral Law* (London: Hutchinson, 1948).

——: 'On a supposed right to tell lies from benevolent motives', *Kant's Critique of Practical Reason and Other Works on the Theory of Ethics*, trans. T. K. Abbott, 6th edn (London: Longmans, 1927), p. 361.

MacIntyre, A.: 'Relativism, power and philosophy', *Proceedings of American Philosophical Association* 59 (1985).

Mill, J. S.: *Utilitarianism* (1863); ed. H. B. Acton (London: Dent, 1972).

———: *A System of Logic* (1843); 5th edn (London: Parker, 1862), last chapter of last volume.

Plato: *Meno*.

Rawls, J.: *A Theory of Justice* (Cambridge, Mass.: Harvard University Press, 1971).

Sartre, J.-P.: *L'Existentialisme est un humanisme* (Paris: Nagel, 1946); trans. P. Mairet, *Existentialism and Humanism* (London: Methuen, 1948).

Shaw, Bernard: *Maxims for Revolutionists*, appendix to *Man and Superman* (London: Constable, 1903).

Urmson, J. O.: *The Emotive Theory of Ethics* (London: Hutchinson, 1968).

Further reading

Seanor, D. and Fotion, N.: *Hare and Critics* (Oxford: Oxford University Press, 1988).

41

Morality and psychological development

LAURENCE THOMAS

i Introduction

ARE there universal stages of psychological development? Are there universal stages of moral development? The first question asks whether proper psychological development is the same for all human beings. It asks whether there are beliefs, (other and self-regarding) attitudes, emotions, modes of interaction, motivational orientation, cognitive skills, and so on which should be characteristic of all human beings at different stages of life. An affirmative answer means that the psychological growth of all human beings can be assessed from the same vantage point. The second question asks whether proper moral development is the same for all human beings. It asks whether there are moral beliefs, values, judgements and behaviour which should be characteristic of all human beings at different stages of life. An affirmative answer means that the moral growth of all human beings can be assessed from the same vantage point. Many would like to think that these two questions admit of an affirmative answer.

Now, there is a third question which raises the stakes, so to speak: if the answer to the first two questions is affirmative, then are these two universal forms of development linked in fundamental ways? An affirmative answer to this question would be very significant, indeed. It perhaps seems clear enough that moral development presupposes a considerable measure of psychological development. After all, we do not suppose that a one-year-old can engage in abstract moral reasoning: for example, grasp Kant's categorical imperative or understand the utilitarian edict of the greatest good for the greatest number. But this shows only that moral development is impossible without psychological development – not that if we have psychological development, then we must have moral development. So, the more interesting question is: are psychological and moral development related in such a way that moral development goes hand in hand with psychological development – or at least with some aspects of psychological development?

In recent times, Lawrence Kohlberg stands foremost among those who have offered an affirmative and systematic answer to these questions. He believes that there are definitive stages of moral development and, moreover, that there is a measure of congruence between it and psychological development. Specifically, he believes that in the wake of psychological development, with regard to cognitive skills, comes moral development. Cognitive skills refer to, among other things, the reasoning skills characteristic of logical and abstract thinking, the imaginative capacity, and the ability to engage in significant conceptual categorization – animals and sand fall into different moral categories; merely hurting a person, which can be done accidentally and without negligence, is different from intentionally hurting a person. So, the latter may be understood to include the ability to grasp the ways in which actions (and events, generally) may differ from one another.

While I am very much in sympathy with many aspects of Kohlberg's theory, I believe that there are insuperable difficulties with it. One of these difficulties, concerning gender bias, has been raised by Carol Gilligan (1982). I shall not discuss this concern, since the question of the separateness of a 'female ethic' is discussed by Jean Grimshaw in this volume (Article 43). I voice other concerns in the final section, 'What is moral development?'

ii Kohlberg's account of moral development

Kohlberg maintains that there are three levels of moral development, each having two stages. So, we have six stages in all; and it is claimed that these stages are invariantly followed, meaning each individual moves from one stage to the next without ever skipping any. The claim here is not that all must advance to the highest level – Stage 6. A person may, in fact, plateau at Stage 4 or 5. Rather, the point is simply that in order to reach Stage 6 a person must pass through each of the preceding stages, and do so sequentially. Here is a brief description of each of the stages, grouped according to levels.

Level A. Preconventional
Stage 1   The stage of punishment and obedience. One obeys in order to avoid being punished; consequently, one's only reason for doing what is right is to avoid punishment. The concerns and interests of others are irrelevant to one except insofar as they bear upon one's well-being.
Stage 2   The stage of individual instrumental purpose and exchange. One's objective is to do what one can to advance one's own interests while acknowledging that others have interests. It is deemed right for all individuals to pursue their own interests. The only reason to do what is right is to advance one's own interests. Conflicts are to be resolved through instrumental exchange of services.

Level B. Conventional level
Stage 3   The stage of mutual interpersonal expectations, relationships, and conformity. The expectations of others become important to one. The concerns of one's group can take primacy over one's own interests. One is able to put oneself into the other's position. Doing what is right means living up to the expectations of those who are close to one. One does what is right in order to meet with their approval.
Stage 4   The stage of social system and conscience maintenance. One is loyal to one's social institutions. Doing what is right means fulfilling one's

465

institutional duties and obligations. One does what is right in order
to maintain one's institutions.

Level C. Postconventional and principled level

Stage 5 The stage of prior rights and social contract. One acknowledges that
there is a rational perspective according to which there are values
and rights – such as life and liberty – which do not owe their
importance to social institutions, and which must be upheld in any
society. Otherwise, one is concerned that the laws and duties to society
be based upon the ideal of the greatest good for the greatest number.
So long as life and liberty are protected, doing what is right means
honouring the values of one's society *because* they are widely accepted
and impartially adhered to. One does what is right because as a
rational creature one is obligated to abide by the precepts, which
embrace life and liberty, to which one had otherwise agreed.

Stage 6 The stage of universal ethical principles. There are universal ethical
principles that all should follow, and which take priority over all legal
and other institutional obligations. Doing what is right is acting in
accordance with these principles. One does what is right because as
a rational creature one grasps the validity of these principles and is
committed to following them.

At the very heart of Kohlberg's view is the following most provocative thesis:
we begin life with an egocentric point of view and, through cognitive development
owing both to our endeavour to resolve increasingly more complex conflicts and
to our capacity for sympathy, come to have an increasingly genuine altruistic or
other-regarding moral perspective, the full expression of which is reached at
Stage 6.

Kohlberg maintains that each higher stage represents a form of cognitive
development which in fact constitutes a form of moral development, as well. He
writes:

I present a psychological theory explaining ... *why* movement is always upward and
occurs in an invariant sequence. My psychological theory as to why moral development
is upward and sequential is broadly the same as my *philosophical* justification for claiming
that a higher stage is more adequate or more moral than a lower stage. (Kohlberg, 1981,
p. 131, emphasis in original)

Thus, I have argued for a parallelism between a theory of psychological development and
a formalistic moral theory on the ground that the *formal psychological* development criteria
of differentiation and integration of structural equilibrium map into the *formal moral*
criteria of prescriptiveness and universality. (Kohlberg, 1981, p. 180, emphasis in original)

Cognitive and moral development are said to go hand in hand because (1)
conflicts are an ineliminable part of the fabric of social interactions; (2) appeal to
morality is ultimately the only satisfactory way to resolve conflicts; and (3) since
conflicts will inevitably become increasingly difficult, it is necessary to move to a
higher stage, and so to a more adquate form of moral reasoning in order to resolve

them adequately. The moral reasoning at each higher level is said to be both more morally adequate and cognitively complicated, involving new forms of reasoning as opposed to merely extending the existing forms of reasoning to new circumstances (Kohlberg, 1981, pp. 137, 147). An adult whose cognitive skills were the equivalent of a five-year-old's could, in terms of moral development, never advance to Stage 4 or higher, because the individual would not be capable of the abstract thinking which these stages call for. Nor would the individual ever be able to see the inadequacy of the moral reasoning characteristic of the lower stage.

Kohlberg maintains that the moral stage of persons can be determined by their responses to various moral scenarios presented to them, such as the Heinz dilemma. This dilemma arises from an imaginary case of a woman who is dying from a kind of cancer. A drug exists which might save her, but the druggist wants $2,000 for a small dose of it, which is ten times what the drug costs to make. Being able to procure only about $1,000 and proving unsuccessful in his pleas to the druggist, Heinz in a fit of desperation breaks into the druggist's store and steals the drug for his wife (Kohlberg, 1981, p. 12). According to Kohlberg, Heinz does the right thing, because life is more valuable than property; what is more, Kohlberg claims that only Stage 6 moral reasoning can adequately handle this dilemma. What follows is a brief statement as to why, in Kohlberg's view, each of the earlier stages cannot adequately handle the Heinz dilemma, where this is understood to mean yielding the conclusion that the husband should put his wife's life over the safety of the druggist's property.

Stage 5 moral reasoning cannot adequately do so, although it recognizes that there are values independent of society, because Stage 5 thinkers believe morality to be based essentially upon rational agreement in the endeavour to secure the greatest good for the greatest number, with life and liberty *both* being non-negotiable goods. Thus, this stage does not have the resources to resolve conflicts arising from competing claims between life and liberty. Stage 4 moral reasoning cannot because according to Stage 4 moral thought right and wrong is simply a matter of what the law says it is; and the law may or may not acknowledge the importance of all life. The moral reasoning of Stages 1 through 3 cannot really do justice even to the idea that life should be respected. Individuals at Stage 3 define right and wrong in terms of the expectations of others; those at Stage 2 believe that doing what is right comes second to advancing one's interests; and those at Stage 1 are only concerned with avoiding punishment. It is not a feature of these three stages that even lip service is paid to the importance of life itself.

The most salient feature of Stage 6 individuals is said to be their cognitive capacity for what Kohlberg calls reversibility:

a moral judgment must be reversible ... we must be able to live with our judgements or decisions when we trade places with others in the situation being judged. (Kohlberg, 1981, p. 197)

all Stage 6's can agree *because* their judgements are fully reversible: they have taken everyone's viewpoint in choosing insofar as it is possible to take everyone's viewpoint, where viewpoints conflict. (Kohlberg, 1981, p. 214, emphasis added)

Reversibility, so Kohlberg seems to hold, is our capacity for sympathy given its fullest and most logical expression in the context of social interaction. (See also the concept of universalizability, discussed in this volume in Article 14, KANTIAN ETHICS, and Article 40, UNIVERSAL PRESCRIPTIVISM.) As Kohlberg remarks: 'Anyone who understands the values of life and property recognizes that life is morally more valuable than property' (Kohlberg, 1981, p. 123). A Stage 6 person sees this rather like a person sees that the night follows the day.

Before turning to examine Kohlberg's theory, some final observations are in order. First, Kohlberg does not hold that all persons reach Stage 6. Indeed, he seems to think that most people are at Stage 4. Second, although Kohlberg seems to suggest that moral development comes in the wake of psychological development, he does hold that the parallelism between cognitive and moral stages is not perfect. He claims: 'This is because a person at a given cognitive stage may be one or more stages lower in morality' (138). Of Stage 6 he observes: 'but perhaps those *capable* of reasoning that way [at Stage 6] do not wish to be martyrs like Socrates, Lincoln, or King and *prefer* to reason at a lower level' (p. 139, emphasis in the original). (In due course, I shall offer an explanation of this claim.) Kohlberg invokes these three figures in history as exemplars of Stage 6 thinking.

Finally, Kohlberg's account of moral development is not neutral between moral theories. He tells us that 'Stage 6 is a deontological theory of morality' (169), whereas with Stage 5 we get a utilitarian moral theory (175). (See Article 14, KANTIAN ETHICS, Article 17, CONTEMPORARY DEONTOLOGY, and Article 19, CONSEQUENTIALISM). But since each higher stage is claimed to be more adequate than those below it, then it follows, on Kohlberg's view, that deontological moral theory is more adequate than utilitarian moral theory. This is a very controversial claim, to say the least. Our critical discussion of Kohlberg might well begin here.

iii Kohlberg's theory examined

Many have claimed that utilitarian moral theory is inadequate. Whether or not the criticisms are sound, what seems manifestly false on the face of it is Kohlberg's contention that moral reasoning which embraces utilitarianism is, on that very account alone, cognitively less sophisticated than moral reasoning which embraces a deontological moral theory, such as Kant's. The very idea seems ludicrous when one considers the long line of distinguished thinkers who have embraced some form of utilitarianism: Jeremy Bentham, John Stuart Mill, and Henry Sidgwick.

It is not at all obvious why Kohlberg thinks that he has made a case for the view that deontological moral reasoning is cognitively more sophisticated than utilitarian moral reasoning. Recall that the cognitive skill of reversibility is the most salient feature of the moral reasoning of Stage 6 individuals. Their judgements are said to be fully reversible. Reversibility is the cognitive ability to put oneself imaginatively into another's place, and to stand by a judgement which takes into account as much as possible the other's point of view. A fully reversible moral judgement is a non-egocentric one. But given this characterization of Stage 6 deontological moral reasoning, there is absolutely no reason to think that utilitarian moral reasoning cannot exhibit such cognitive complexity and richness. Indeed, Kohlberg is plainly mistaken here. (See Article 40, UNIVERSAL PRESCRIPTIVISM.)

Now, what Kohlberg wants to claim, of course, is that the cognitive skill of reversibility, coupled with universality, is loaded with substantial moral content – that it comes with a particular set of moral lenses, so to speak. Thus, he maintains that all Stage 6 people just plainly 'see' that life is always more valuable than property – a judgement which utilitarianism allegedly fails to yield. This claim on behalf of cognitive skills with regard to Stages 5 and 6 is at the very heart of Kohlberg's theory. But, alas, Kohlberg seems to say nothing at all in defence of it.

This a good point at which to bring out an important difference between the claims concerning moral reasoning made on behalf of the cognitive skills of Stages 5 and 6, on the one hand, and Stages 1 through 4, on the other. The cognitive skills of 5 and 6 are claimed to have substantive moral content, with the cognitive skills of the latter having more such content than those of the former. With their exercise one 'sees' that certain moral values are to be embraced: society must always respect both life and liberty, in the case of Stage 5; life is always to be valued over property, in the case of Stage 6. By contrast, the cognitive skills of earlier stages are not claimed to have any substantive moral content. There is no identifiable set of values the embracing of which is characteristic of persons at these earlier stages.

Rather, individuals at Stages 1 through 4 are, it seems, identifiable solely by the way in which they arrive at the moral values they embrace. With the Stage 4 person what is right is what society says is right – no more, no less. With the Stage 3 person, what is right is what the group with which one identifies says is right. With Stage 2, what is right is what advances one's own interest – though one acts with an awareness that others have interests, too. And with Stage 1, doing what is right comes to no more nor less than avoiding punishment. From Stages 1 through 4, what we have essentially is a progression along a single dimension, namely that of identifying with the interests and values of others: at each succeeding stage of moral development a person identifies with the interests of a significantly wider circle of people. With these stages, there are no restrictions whatsoever on what the objects of these interests and values can be or how interests and values are to be ranked. So, from a Stage 4 perspective, a society which seeks to preserve its homogeneity at the expense of minority ethnic groups is just as good as a society which endeavours to treat all people equally, regardless of their ethnic background. Accordingly, proper moral development for children in either society would be for them to embrace at Stage 4 the interests and values of their own society because they (the children) sufficiently identify with members of their society. The implications of this point are astounding, and I shall return to it in the following section.

Starting with Stage 5, however, we get a qualitative change in the character of moral development. What we get is not so much a newer or deeper form of identification with others, but instead a judgement about the content and ranking of interests and values. Whereas with lower stages life and liberty are negotiable, so to speak, they become non-negotiable at Stage 5. For the first time, moral development includes a critical component, as an aspect of this development is now the wherewithal to criticize those with whom one identifies. A society which summarily takes the life and restricts the liberty of any of its members is wrong, period. A Stage 5 person would judge the matter in this way – and presumably would do so regardless of how many members of society thought otherwise. Thus, moral courage also enters into the picture; for unlike those at Stage 4, Stage 5 individuals are not so concerned to identify with the interests and values of others that they uncritically adopt the moral perspective of society. And individuals who are prepared to be known for having moral beliefs which are at odds with the majority of their fellow citizens exhibit a measure of moral courage. For example, in the United States some two hundred years ago, anyone who spoke out against chattel slavery, if only in casual conversation, exhibited a measure of moral courage, given the moral climate of the time. To be sure, an abolitionist exhibited even more courage. But then courage is not an all-or-nothing matter.

The difference between Stages 5 and 6 is not only that the cognitive skills characteristic of Stage 6 are said to yield more substantive moral content and thus a wider critical perspective, but also that moral courage is more fully exhibited. Recall Kohlberg's remarks that 'perhaps those *capable* of reasoning that way [at Stage 6] do not wish to be martyrs like Socrates, Lincoln, or King and *prefer* to reason at a lower level'. The natural inference to make here is that Stage 6 persons are prepared to lay down their lives for their moral convictions (since these individuals were killed for what they believe) and that individuals who are not prepared to do so are not fully at Stage 6. This would certainly suggest that courage now has a more central role in moral development. It would seem that in the move from Stage 5 to 6 two things are equally important: the development of the requisite cognitive skills and the acquisition of a certain motivational structure to have the courage of one's convictions though one's life should be at stake. And by his own admission Kohlberg cannot claim that the former entails the latter, since he acknowledges that persons can be capable of reasoning at Stage 6 but prefer to reason at a lower stage. The question that obviously comes to mind then is: how do individuals come to have the courage which is required to be at Stage 6? Kohlberg does not offer an answer to this very important question.

Whether or not one agrees with Kohlberg's explanation for how people progress from Stages 1 through 5, he does address how this is supposed to happen. And even with the qualitative move from Stage 4 to Stage 5, Kohlberg says enough to give us a handle on how the transition might come about. It does seem intuitively acceptable that with sufficient cognitive skills a person comes to see that summarily restricting the liberty of others or depriving them of their life is morally wrong. And it makes sense to suppose that in the normal course of things we come to identify with a wider range of people, at least up to a point. But with cognitive skills in place, what brings it about that individuals become full-fledged Stage 6 individuals – that is, that they come to have in a profound way the courage of their convictions? I attempt an answer in the following section.

iv What is moral development?

Consider what Kohlberg-like moral development up to Stage 4 means in contemporary Canada, on the one hand, and what it means in the case of the Third Reich, on the other. Canada represents an example of a liberal egalitarian society, which with its wide-ranging health care benefits would seem to place the importance of life at the very pinnacle of values. Nazi Germany, on the other hand, is one of a few institutions in modern history (American slavery, Stalinist Russia, and Apartheid are among others) which are unequivocally thought to be deeply evil institutions. If Kohlberg's theory is to be taken literally, then the initial stages of moral development have nothing whatsoever to do with the kinds of values which persons come to embrace, the kind of training that persons receive. Thus, Kohlberg offers a very non-Aristotelian approach to moral development, since Aristotle thought that a person could come to be morally good only by first coming to do morally good things habitually (*Nicomachean Ethics*).

If Kohlberg is to be taken literally, then people who at Stage 4 came to embrace Nazi anti-Semitic ideology were exhibiting as much proper moral development as contemporary Canadians who at Stage 4 come to embrace the egalitarian ideology of Canadian society. For at Stage 4, there are no proper moral values to embrace – only the values of one's society. Now, it seems reasonable enough to hold that the ability to identify increasingly with a wider group of people and, in the end, with society itself, constitutes a form of psychological development. Accordingly, there is no difficulty supposing that we have parallel psychological development in these two cases. But parallel moral development? Well, that seems to be another matter entirely.

The above suggests two things. One is that we cannot talk about moral development completely independent of content. The other is that cognitive and moral development are not as parallel or isomorphic as Kohlberg would like to think (Kohlberg, 1983, p. 136). For if Nazi Germany is any indication, it would seem that people can be at Stage 4 cognitively and yet be downright evil human beings. And Kohlberg has to hold that by and large the people of Nazi Germany were – for all of their cognitive skills – no higher than Stage 4, since he claims that, by Stage 5, a person recognizes life and liberty as non-negotiable values to which all people have a claim.

In defence of Kohlberg, it might be pointed that his theory allows that even Stage 6 people can hold different moral judgements about fundamentally important moral issues, since he acknowledges that 'Socrates was more accepting of slavery than was Lincoln, who was more accepting of it than King' (Kohlberg, 1983, p. 129). Indeed, Kohlberg writes that 'It is easier to develop to Stage 6 in modern America than in fifth-century Athens or first-century Jerusalem' (ibid.). But even if we concede, as I believe we should, that historical contexts should be taken into account (Thomas, 1989, Sect. 1), this thought hardly serves to put Nazi Germany in a better moral light. We can say that Socrates and Lincoln were both in morally admirable ways ahead of their time, although they were accepting of slavery to varying degrees (Thomas, 1989, Sect. 1). No such claim can be made on behalf of Nazi Germany.

471

But supposing historical contexts do matter, does this not vitiate the Kohlbergian enterprise in a fundamental way? If people at Stage 6 can hold different moral values, then what exactly are we to make of the universality of moral judgements that he claims for this stage? Or did he mean by this claim, not the strong thesis that all Stage 6 persons hold the same moral judgements regardless of historical contexts, but instead, only the considerably weaker thesis that all Stage 6 persons in the same historical contexts hold the same moral judgements? If not the strong thesis, then, once again, this would suggest that cognitive and moral development are not as isomorphic as Kohlberg would like to believe – if the isomorphism is taken to mean that cognitive moral development yields the same set of substantive moral judgements, period..

Now, as I remarked, on Aristotle's view, moral training is indispensable to moral development; for he held, among other things, that a firm disposition to do what is right is necessary for having a good moral character; and it seems reasonable enough to hold that in general a firm disposition to do what is right is acquired only with the passing of time. To see that Aristotle's view plainly makes more sense here, consider the implication of Kohlberg's thought with regard to Stage 4 persons in a Nazi society and their moving to Stages 5 and 6.

In terms of so moving, what does it mean to say that Nazi society exhibits proper moral development at Stage 4? One is hard-pressed to think of Nazi ideology as in any way a precursor of better moral thought and attitudes. The point here is that if the move to a higher stage constitutes a form of moral betterment, then it would seem that not anything whatsoever can serve as a touchstone for such betterment. If acquiring the virtue of honesty is an instance of moral betterment, one hardly contributes to this end by teaching individuals how to prevaricate masterfully. Again, if acquiring the virtue of kindness is an instance of moral betterment, one certainly does not contribute to this end by teaching people how to treat others ruthlessly and sadistically. It seems absolutely ludicrous and thoroughly contrary to common sense to say that a Stage 4 Canadian who embraces the ideals of equality and a Stage 4 member of the Third Reich who embraces the ideals of Nazi ideology are both making equally good progress along the road of moral development.

In general, it would seem that there can be no moral development in the absence of some substantive content about right and wrong. It seems true enough that moral development calls for a significant measure of identification with others. However, this does not suffice – even early on. Accordingly, it is not clear that Kohlberg's earlier stages constitute stages of moral development. Moral development would seem to be absolutely impossible in the absence of moral training. Kohlberg's theory is not incompatible with such training. It is just that he presents his theory as if such training were not really central to this kind of development. The claim here is that this is no small omission.

Even if an adequate theory of moral development must give moral training a central role among its tenets, another very important question remains: are the fully developed moral persons those who are prepared to give their lives for their moral convictions? Martin Luther King, Jr., proclaimed that life is not worth living if one is not prepared to die for something. This seems intuitively right. But if it is not on account of the mere recognition of what is right that a person is prepared to die for something, as Kohlberg himself concedes, then on account of what is this so? An answer that very strongly recommends itself is moral self-esteem.

Self-esteem generally is anchored in the conviction that there are activities which *we are capable of performing especially well* and in virtue of which our lives can be judged meritorious by those at least with whom we identify. Our self-esteem can be tied to almost any kind of activity: dancing, boxing, scholarship, housekeeping, parenting; our ability to attract sexual partners (recall Oscar Wilde's Dorian Gray), our mechanical skills, our loyalty, and so on. In particular, our self-esteem can be tied to our moral activities. Self-esteem so anchored is being called moral self-esteem here. Usually more than one activity contributes to a person's general self-esteem: a person is a good spouse and parent, a good (but not exceptional) businessperson, and a highly respected member of the local syna-gogue – not to mention a fairly decent individual. However, it is quite possible that the primary source of a person's self-esteem is a single endeavour. Virtually all of their efforts and energies are devoted to its success, and nothing else much matters to them. Presumably, Mother Teresa is a case in point. In comparison to the success of her charitable efforts no doubt everything else pales in importance to her; and we deeply admire her for being that way. Many professional athletes (on the American scene, at any rate) constitute another example of individuals for whom the primary source of their self-esteem is very largely a single endeavour. In the twilight of their careers this has often proved to be a very poignant matter; accordingly, some often postpone retirement to the point where it becomes embarrassing for virtually everyone. This is significant because it points to the extraordinary difficulty of giving up an end, the successful pursuit of which has been the primary source of our self-esteem.

When the successful pursuit of a singular end is the primary source of a person's self-esteem, virtually no sacrifice is too great to ensure its success. So, I suggest that if the mark of Stage 6 is that individuals at this stage are prepared to be martyrs for the cause of right, then this is because Stage 6 individuals are those for whom leading a moral life is the primary source of their self-esteem. If this statement seems all too innocuous, then think again. First, for most of us who lead meaningful lives, leading a moral life is probably not the primary source of our self-esteem. More often than not, our careers are. This should come as no surprise: most of us generally lead ordinary moral lives; we do not in any significant way stand head and shoulders above others in our moral living. We need not suppose this is simply a matter of our choosing as such. It is probably the case that most of us go through life without ever finding ourselves in a situation which would catapult us into such a position. Secondly, nothing is without a price, including leading a high moral life – or so it seems. Socrates was too concerned with teaching virtue to be much of a father and husband to his family. Gandhi, who made civil disobedience against the British an art form, and whom we greatly admire for it, was far from being a good husband. And Martin Luther King, Jr., had important shortcomings on the home front as well. Having our self-esteem so tied to the pursuit of one aspect of morality can leave us less sensitive to moral claims in other areas.

Being highly successful in most endeavours in life is thought to have its pitfalls, which are not easily avoided. Morality, one might have thought, is surely the exception. These last remarks, however, would suggest otherwise. Our commitment to morality is not independent of the positive effects it will have upon our self-esteem. And when our self-esteem is deeply anchored in any activity, be it moral or otherwise, we tend to experience blind spots in other areas of life – even other areas of the moral life. From the standpoint of moral development, especially in terms of a commitment to morality for which one is prepared to die, this is a very sobering thought, indeed – whether or not in the end there turn out to be Kohlberg-like stages of moral development.

v Conclusion

One of Kohlberg's most interesting claims is that there is a universal parallelism between both psychological and moral development. Another is that up to a point, at any rate, moral development can take place without reference to any substantive moral content. A third is that deontological moral reasoning is superior to utilitarian moral reasoning.

While I have not denied that there are universal stages of moral and psychological development, I have strenuously challenged the thesis that there is a parallelism between the two. If, on any account, we cannot call the attitudes embodied in Nazi ideology a form of moral development, then perhaps there is some universal content to moral development in that, at the very least, there are some universal restrictions on what can be countenanced as a species of such development. And the reference to Artistotle with regard to moral training invites the idea that when it comes to such development there is some universality with respect to procedure: lessons in gratuitous harm are not likely to inspire moral development. These remarks speak to the second claim as well. As to the third, suffice it to say that the debate between utilitarians and deontologists is a longstanding one, which is not likely to be settled by an appeal to cognitive psychology.

References

Aristotle: *Nicomachean Ethics*.
Gilligan, C.: *In a Different Voice: Psychological Theory and Women's Development* (Cambridge, Mass.: Harvard University Press, 1982).
Kohlberg, L.: *Essays on Moral Development*; Vol. 1, *The Philosophy of Moral Development: Moral Stages and the Idea of Justice* (New York: Harper and Row, 1981).
Thomas, L.: *Living Morally: A Psychology of Moral Character* (Philadelphia: Temple University Press, 1989).

474

Further reading

Baier, A.: 'Trust and antitrust', *Ethics*, 96 (1986), 231–60.

——: 'What do women want in moral theory', *Nous*, 19 (1985), 53–63.

Blum, L. A.: 'Gilligan and Kohlberg: implications for moral theory', *Ethics*, 98 (1988), 472–91.

Bowlby, J.: *Child Care and the Growth of Love* (Baltimore: Penguin Books, 1953).

——: *The Making and Breaking of Affectional Bonds* (London: Tavistock Publications, 1979).

Card, C.: 'Women's voices and ethical ideals: must we mean what we say?', *Ethics*, 99 (1988), 125–35.

Coopersmith, S.: *The Antecedents of Self-Esteem* (San Francisco: W. H. Freeman, 1967).

Flanagan, O. and Jackson, K.: 'Justice, care, and gender: the Kohlberg–Gilligan debate revisited', *Ethics*, 97 (1987), 622–37.

Hinde, R. A.: 'Social development: a biological approach', *Human Growth and Development*, eds. J. Bruner and A. Garton (New York: Oxford University Press, 1978).

Kagan, J.: *The Second Year: The Emergence of Self-Awareness* (Cambridge, Mass.: Harvard University Press, 1981).

Piaget, J.: *The Essential Piaget*, eds. Howard Gruber and J. Jacques Voneche (New York: Basic Books, 1977). With a foreword by Piaget.

Pritchard, M. S.: 'Cognition and affect in moral development: a critique of Kohlberg', *Journal of Value Inquiry*, 18 (1984) 35–50.

Rawls, J.: *A Theory of Justice* (Cambridge, Mass.: Harvard University Press, 1971).

Wolf, S.: 'Moral saints', *Journal of Philosophy*, 79 (1982), 419–39.

Ziller, R. C.: 'A helical theory of personal change', *Personality*, ed. Rom Harré (Totowa, NJ: Rowman and Littlefield, 1976), pp. 98–142.

42

Method and moral theory

DALE JAMIESON

i Introduction

CONTEMPORARY moral philosophers have taken up a wide range of questions. These questions include the significance of moral language, the nature of value and obligation, the defensibility of various normative theories, and the duties we may have concerning animals and future generations. Contemporary moral philosophers have been much less interested in questions concerning moral theories themselves: what they are, why we might want to have them, and what methods we should use in constructing them. In this article I will take up some of these questions. I will be mainly concerned with questions *about* moral theory rather than with questions *in* moral theory.

One reason why questions about moral theory have been relatively neglected is because, until recently, there appeared to be widespread agreement about the nature of moral theories and the acceptability of various methodological practices Moral theories were commonly regarded as abstract structures whose role is to supply justification rather than motivation. The proper method was thought by most to be some version of coherentism (see section (iii. 2) for a discussion of this concept). While these remain the dominant views, the intellectual landscape is not as uniform as it once was.

In recent years there has been increasing anxiety about the nature, status, and role of moral theory. For example Bernard Williams has expressed scepticism about the deliverances of theory, Jonathan Dancy and John McDowell see little role for theories to play in practical reasoning, and Susan Wolf has attacked the ideals that she sees as implicit in traditional moral theories. Robert Fullinwider has staked an avowedly anti-theoretical position. Michael Stocker has proffered a diagnosis: the problems of modern moral theory stem from its 'schizophrenic' nature.

While problems of theory have been the main focus of some philosophers, others have primarily been concerned with what they see as a crisis of method. According to Alasdair MacIntyre, modern moral philosophy serves up a cafeteria of conflicting moralities among which it is powerless to decide. Annette Baier claims that this way of teaching moral philosophy breeds scepticism in students.

In this article I cannot hope to resolve or even address all of these disputes. I will discuss some of them, survey the issues that I take to be central, and gesture towards what I take to be the truth. In the next section I will discuss the nature of theories, and in the following section I will discuss some questions of method. In section (iv) I will discuss the role of examples in producing the 'moral intuitions' with which theories work. In the final section I will draw some conclusions.

ii The nature of moral theories

There is a dominant conception of moral theory that is presupposed or endorsed by theorists of many different stripes. Although this conception is currently under vigorous attack, there is surprisingly little explicit defence or even articulation of it. The dominant conception is mainly known through the writings of its opponents and the practices of its adherents. I will try to make explicit some of the imporant features of this conception.

1 The dominant conception

On the dominant conception, moral theories are abstract structures that sort agents, actions, or outcomes into appropriate categories. Proposed categories include virtuous, vicious, right, wrong, permitted, forbidden, good, bad, best, worst, supererogatory, and obligatory. Characteristically outcomes are ranked according to their goodness, actions according to their rightness, and agents according to their virtuousness. Different theories take different categories as primary. For example utilitarianism takes the goodness of outcomes as primary, and from this derives accounts of the rightness of actions and the virtuousness of agents. Deontology, on the other hand, takes the rightness of actions as primary and either derives from this accounts of other categories that it takes to be morally relevant, or supplements it with accounts of the other categories. (See Article 17, CONTEMPORARY DEONTOLOGY, and Article 19, CONSEQUENTIALISM.)

The job of moral theorists, on the dominant conception, is to make particular moral theories explicit, to describe their universality, and to make vivid their coercive power. This is done through examining arguments, assessing evidence, and scrutinizing logical relationships. Moral-theoretic reasoning is often modelled on legal or economic reasoning. The legal model is implicit in the work of Bentham, while the economic model is often identified with Hobbes. The difference between law or economics on the one hand, and morality on the other, is often taken to involve the reasons agents have for conformity to the practices of the respective institutions, or the mechanisms that are available for enforcing conformity.

As I have said, the dominant conception is mainly implicit rather than explicit in contemporary ethical theory. For this reason it is dangerous to name names. However, without suggesting that they would endorse every feature of the dominant conception as I have described it, we can associate the dominant conception with the nineteenth-century philosopher, Henry Sidgwick, and such contemporary philosophers as Richard Brandt, Derek Parfit, John Rawls, and Judith Jarvis Thomson.

477

2 The anti-theorists

Challenges to the dominant conception have become increasingly prominent. One source of these challenges is a feminist sensibility that began to emerge in professional philosophy in the 1970s. Another source is the widespread scepticism about authority that was characteristic of the 1960s. Philosophers whose views were affected by these tendencies have profound differences among them. However, many of these philosophers have emphasized character and motivation rather than consequences and obligations. They have found their inspiration in Aristotle and Hume rather than Kant and Sidgwick. They are inclined to view morality 'from the ground up', as a kind of social practice, rather than 'from the top down', as an expression of theory.

One of the first influential critiques of the dominant conception was G. E. M. Anscombe's 1958 essay, 'Modern moral philosophy'. Here Anscombe objects to the 'law conception of ethics', which she sees as characteristic of English philosophy from Sidgwick on. Anscombe argues that this view is untenable without the notion of a divine lawgiver. Since modern moral philosophy banishes God, regarding him as either dead, non-existent, or irrelevant, its conception of moral theory is ultimately anachronistic.

It is as if the notion 'criminal' were to remain when criminal law and criminal courts had been abolished and forgotten. (Anscombe, 1958, p. 30)

Anscombe's conclusion is that if moral philosophy is to be secular, it had better be more like Aristotle's than Sidgwick's. But if we do return to Aristotle, then moral philosophy 'should be laid aside ... until we have an adequate philosophy of psychology' (p. 26).

According to Alasdair MacIntyre and Bernard Williams, moral theory does not have the authority that it claims for itself. MacIntyre argues generally that there can be no moral authority in pluralistic, liberal societies. He urges us to subvert liberalism by developing common narratives and ways of life. Williams, on the other hand, takes pluralism and liberalism as given in societies like ours, and goes on to reflect on the prospects for living an ethical life in such societies.

Despite their differences, both MacIntyre and Williams find modern moral philosophy to be part of our cultural problem rather than a solution. In *Whose Justice? Which Rationality?* MacIntyre writes that:

[m]odern academic philosophy turns out by and large to provide means for a more accurate and informed definition of disagreement rather than for progress toward its resolution. (1988, p. 3)

In *Ethics and the Limits of Philosophy* Williams tells us that 'philosophy should not try to produce ethical theory' (p. 17), because ethical theory does not have the authority to 'give some compelling reason to accept one intuition rather than another' (p. 99).

Williams has much in common with Anscombe, but there are important differences. Although both advocate the abolition of morality as it is understood by many philosophers, their reasons are quite different. For Anscombe, the belief in a distinctive, authoritative kind of obligation that is moral is a perversion of theistic ethics. The abolition of this kind of morality would clarify our existing beliefs and practices since morality, as many of us understand it, does not exist anyway. Williams distinguishes ethics from morality, and identifies morality with a 'peculiar institution' that is a modern expression of the ethical. Morality focuses on obligations, and makes claims for itself that are so grandiose that fidelity to this harsh master alienates us from our personal relationships and commitments and erodes our integrity. For Anscombe, the law conception of morality is untenable without God. For Williams, the law conception of morality may be tenable, but it is vicious and repressive. We can be free to live our own lives in a truly secular society only when we have overcome the bondage of morality.

Much of the feminist critique of traditional moral theories has been influenced by psychological research, such as Carol Gilligan's, that suggests that women have different patterns of moral response than men. Annette Baier, an influential feminist voice in contemporary philosophy, takes this research to suggest that while traditional male ethics focuses on obligation, female ethics focuses on love. Baier hopes to reconcile these moralities in an ethics of trust. (See also Article 43, THE IDEA OF A FEMALE ETHIC.)

Without endorsing all of their claims, there is much that we can learn from the anti-theorists. Their attacks on the dominant conception challenge us to rethink the relationship between moral theory and moral practice.

3 Reconciling theory and practice

In my view moral theorizing is something that real people do in everyday life. It is not just the domain of professors, expounding in their lecture halls. Moral theorizing can be found on the highways and byways, practiced by everyone from bartenders to politicians.

In everyday life it is common for people to apply role reversal tests, to appeal to possible outcomes of actions or policies, or to point to special responsibilities and obligations. This is the stuff of moral persuasion, reasoning, and education. For example we ask children how they would feel if they were treated as they have treated others. To an acquaintance we point out that it would not cost much to visit a sick parent, and that it would do the parent a world of good. We condemn a friend for not acting as a friend.

When we ask why we should be moved by such considerations, or we test them in order to see whether they hang together with other beliefs and commitments that we have, we are engaging in moral theorizing. However, the result of this theorizing hardly ever leads to the creation of a full-blown moral theory. Generally we are pushed into theorizing by pragmatic considerations rather than by the disinterested search for truth. We are usually pushed out of it by conversational closure – one of us gets our way, or we agree to disagree. Moral theorizing typically emerges when there is a conversational niche for it to fill.

If this is correct, then the distinction between moral theorizing and moral practice is an untenable dualism. Moral theorizing is part of moral practice. It is a way of trying to ensure that the moralizing of ourselves and others is defensible

It is a way in which our 'better self', or at least our more reflective self, sometimes tries to carry the day.

Moral theories, the abstract conceptions that we study in moral philosophy, are derivative of moral theorizing. They are hypostatizations of an activity that is part of everyday moral practice. We use these abstract structures for various purposes: to grade and categorize agents, acts, and outcomes; to relate to various religious beliefs and cultural outlooks; to evaluate, analyse, extend, and so on. As the anti-theorists point out, what we almost never use them for is making moral decisions.

But this overstates the case. Many of us, and not just philosophers, are driven to evaluate systematically our own moral theorizing and that of others. These evaluations often go beyond what would be required by the exigencies of the immediate situation. Some of these systematic evaluations result in theories or theory-fragments. While these theories or theory-fragments may not play a starring role in moral decision-making, they surely have some effect, even if indirectly, on our moral practices.

The anti-theorists remind us that people in their everyday moral practices create theory; that there are limits on what these theories can do; that their job is to help us do what is right rather than to be true. In these ways their attack on the dominant conception is important and helpful. However, what they do not succeed in showing is that we would be better off without moral theory.

iii The methods of theorizing

If what I have said in the previous section is correct, much of our moral theorizing goes on as part of our ordinary moral practices. Rather than being orderly and systematic, it is eclectic and incremental. Despite this, many philosophers have been concerned to discover principles of grand method. Philosophers who are enthralled by the dominant conception of moral theory have wanted to construct theories that are explicit and universal. In order to help them to do this they have wanted to identify the principles that govern theory building. Such philosophers have often looked to epistemology – the study of how we can know things – as providing the models for this enterprise.

The two most influential approaches to theory construction in epistemology are foundationalism and coherentism. Most attempts at theory construction in ethics follow one of these two models. Coherentism is currently in vogue but it suffers from serious difficulties, as does foundationalism.

1 *Foundationalism*

Foundationalism is (roughly) the view that systems of belief are justified in virtue of the logical relations that obtain between beliefs that require justification, and other beliefs that themselves are in no need of justification.

Consider an example. Suppose that John believes that it is wrong to kill his next-door neighbour gratuitously, and takes this to follow from the self-evident principle that it is wrong to kill people gratuitously, and his belief that his next-door neighbour is a person. What has been offered is a foundationalist justification for this fragment of John's belief system.

Traditionally people have been tempted by foundationalist accounts for the following reason. At some point, it seems, justification must end. The beliefs in which a chain of justification terminates must themselves be justified but require no justification. For if they were not justified then the system of beliefs which is justified by reference to them would not itself be justified. If these 'terminating' beliefs themselves required justification then they would not in fact be the beliefs in which the chain of justification terminates.

There are a number of problems with this foundationalist picture. One problem concerns how it could be that some beliefs require no justification. Traditionally such beliefs have been thought either self-justifying or self-evident.

Consider first the idea that some beliefs are self-justifying. My belief that there are such things as beliefs may be an example of a self-justifying belief, for it is true in virtue of my believing it to be true (although some would deny even this). It is a long way from this kind of self-justifying belief, however, to an interesting moral theory. Other candidates for self-justifying beliefs have been suggested. Some philosophers have thought that there are common-sense propositions that we cannot help but believe: for example that we sometimes act freely, that there is an external world, and so on. On this view, since we cannot help but believe these things, these beliefs are self-justifying. But this claim is far from convincing. It seems possible that we are the sort of creatures who cannot help but believe some things that are false. There seems to be no guarantee that our epistemic capacities really give us access to the world.

There are also problems about deriving a moral theory from self-evident truths. There is little controversy about whether logical truths are self-evident (for example that all ravens are ravens), so logical truths are good candidates for self-evident truths. But logical truths are not rich enough to permit the derivation of any interesting moral theory. And once we go beyond logical truths, disagreement breaks out about what other truths, if any, are self-evident.

This leads to a further problem. If there are self-evident or self-justifying truths that are rich enough to permit the derivation of an interesting moral theory, then they must go beyond logical truths and those which are 'pragmatically necessary'. Yet it is far from clear that there are such truths or how we could recognize them if there are.

Foundationalism dominated epistemology for the first half of this century, but it has fallen upon hard times. Attempts to construct the world from the incorrigible deliverances of the senses have largely been abandoned in the wake of attacks by Wittgenstein, Quine and others. Foundationalism in ethics was always more problematical than foundationalism in general epistemology, for it was never clear what was to do the work of sense-data. It is not surprising that in our post-positivist philosophical climate, there are few moral theorists willing to endorse foundationalist methodology.

2 Coherentism

These days some version of coherentism is the dominant view of what constitutes proper method for theory construction in ethics. Coherentism can be roughly characterized as the view that beliefs can be justified only by their relation to other beliefs. This is in clear distinction to foundationalism which holds that some beliefs, those that are foundational, are justified independently of their relations to other beliefs.

The most influential form of coherentism is Rawls's method of reflective equilibrium. According to Rawls, proper method involves beginning with a set of considered beliefs, formulating general principles to account for them, and then revising both principles and beliefs in the light of each other, until an equilibrium is reached.

There are many problems with this methodology. Some philosophers, such as Brandt, Hare, and Singer, have denied that our considered beliefs have probative force. It appears that Nazis or Pharaohs employing the method of reflective equilibrium would arrive at outlooks that are grossly immoral. This is an instance of an old problem for coherence theories: there can be an indefinite number of sets of beliefs in reflective equilibrium, yet there may be no reason to suppose that any of these constitute a true theory.

One response, suggested by Holmgren, is to couple reflective equilibrium with a commitment to objective moral truths. But this only raises the question of how objective moral truths are to be identified. Rawls's own solution is to introduce (tacitly) further considerations for evaluating considered judgements and moral outlooks. This shifts the burden of justification from reflective equilibrium to these reliability tests. The question then arises as to what underwrites these reliability tests. And this seems to put us back in the soup. Is our belief in these tests foundational, or do the beliefs that are sanctioned by these tests gain their credibility from their relations to other beliefs?

Coherentism and foundationalism have resourceful defenders, and this short discussion cannot do justice to the subtle versions of these approaches that have been developed. Moreover, methodological space is not exhausted by foundationalism and coherentism. Many other views are possible. One that seems increasingly popular is derivationism. Philosophers such as Brandt and Gauthier seek to derive a moral theory from what they regard as more fundamental considerations concerning rationality. They do this because they regard questions about rationality as clearer than questions about morality, or because they believe that rationality has motivational force in a way that morality does not. Though Brandt and Gauthier are derivationists, they are not foundationalists. For they do not claim that the beliefs from which their theories are derived are self-evident or self-justifying.

3 Other questions of method

Dramatically contrasting foundationalism and coherentism on the big screen of the philosophical dialectic may obscure the fact that they have much in common.

One important issue in the background of this debate concerns whether and to what extent moral theories can or must be revisionary. On this issue foundationalism and coherentism have more in common than might be imagined.

Some have thought that since coherentist views begin with our considered moral beliefs, they must inevitably sanctify 'common sense morality' – that ragtag collection of moral prejudices, habits, judgements, and behaviours which people of 'our' class and culture exhibit or engage in. Because foundationalist approaches start from the beginning, it has been thought that only they are in a position to challenge those prejudices and promote moral progress. While there may be something to this view, it would be very difficult to say exactly what it is. Even if we are coherentists and believe that our considered moral beliefs are privileged, it is still not clear how we should settle conflicts between those beliefs and the deliverances of a moral theory. The corpus of our beliefs may be privileged, but it does not follow from this that each belief is privileged, or that those beliefs that are privileged are all equally privileged. It thus does not follow (for example) that utilitarianism should be rejected or revised because it makes demands that many people believe are excessive. It is consistent with even conservative views in moral epistemology to suppose that (some of) our everyday moral beliefs should be revised or rejected instead. Nor is it obvious that foundationalism must serve the cause of moral progress. Whether a foundationalist morality is conservative or not depends on what people take for foundational beliefs, not on the fact of its being a foundationalist theory.

There are also some constraints that any moral theory, whether coherentist or foundationalist, must satisfy. One of these is consistency. An inconsistent theory implies anything, and therefore fails to fulfil whatever role we might want theories to play. Theories must also be complete enough to provide a moral perspective. While it may be appropriate for moral theories to be silent over some range of hard cases, too much silence about the wrong cases would vitiate the claims to importance that are made on their behalf.

The goal of both foundationalists and coherentists is also the same: the identification of a defensible set of moral beliefs, convictions, dispositions, and purposes. Sometimes the members of this set are called 'intuitions'.

The search for this set begins in midstream. Even foundationalists must grant that we begin as well as end with moral intuitions. Both foundationalists and coherentists are interested in methods for identifying and assessing the intuitions with which we begin. Since coherentists are in the business of systematizing our 'considered' intuitions, they need methods for identifying them. Since derivations of moral truths from foundational beliefs are notoriously indeterminate (or at least controversial), foundationalists may want to identify our considered intuitions, in order to see how bodies of belief hang together, or how their proposed derivations map on to people's pre-theoretical beliefs.

For these reasons (and others) both coherentists and foundationalists have been interested in mechanisms for identifying and assessing our moral intuitions. Different techniques for eliciting and assessing moral intuitions have been employed. One of the most common is the use of examples. Philosophers present us with various cases – some from literature, some from real life, some from the imagination – and ask what intuitions we have about them. Although the intuitions that are elicited play different roles in foundationalist and coherentist theories, the use of examples is common to both. I believe that the limitations of this approach have not been sufficiently appreciated. In order to see why this approach is problematical, I shall conclude with a brief discussion of the role of examples in moral philosophy.

iv The role of examples

In moral philosophy examples are used for many different purposes. Kant, in the *Groundwork*, uses a series of examples to show us how the several formulations of the categorical imperative may be applied to cases. In 'Existentialism is a humanism' Sartre discusses the young man who is torn between caring for his mother and fighting for the Free French in order to show that there are (many?) moral problems that cannot be solved by appeals to principles. In contemporary moral philosophy examples are often used as 'intuition-pumps'. For example in *Reasons and Persons* Derek Parfit describes a number of worlds with different populations at different levels of welfare in order to elicit our intuitions about different population policies.

Following (but revising) Onora O'Neill, we can distinguish four kinds of examples that are used in moral theorizing: literary, ostensive, hypothetical, and imaginary. Literary examples are commonly used and have various strengths and weaknesses that cannot be explored here. (For an example, see the opening of Article 21, VIRTUE THEORY.) Ostensive examples are those taken from real life. We may discuss the My Lai massacre, for example, as a case in which soldiers had to choose between following orders and obeying moral injunctions.

The distinction beween hypothetical and imaginative examples is important, but difficult to make clear. A hypothetical example may involve a decision between going to the movies or visiting a sick friend. The question of whether or not to enter a teletransporter that will destroy your body at point of entry but create a replica at your destination is an imaginary example. Hypothetical examples involve instances of situations or events that have occurred, or could occur without requiring us to rewrite physics or change our basic conception of how the world works. Imaginary examples involve logical possibilities that could occur only in worlds very different from ours.

Almost all philosophers make appeals to hypothetical cases. It is hard to see how we could go on without doing so. Deciding what to do involves hypothetical reasoning. Appeals to imaginary cases, however, are problematical because such examples are indeterminate with respect to background. In order to be valid, counterfactual reasoning must go on against a fixed background. When we consider whether to visit a sick friend or to go to the movies instead, we have a relatively clear idea about what will be different and what will be the same whatever we do. In imaginary cases we often do not really know what is up for grabs. We have intuitions, but these intuitions may be untrustworthy. For we may have dragged along part of the 'real world' into the counterfactual one. Imaginary examples are often described in a very schematic way. We tacitly supply the background that makes these cases intelligible. But we may simply be wrong about what a world with teletransporters would be like.

A second problem is that imaginary cases are (typically) tendentiously described. This is due to the function that they are supposed to perform. A 'good' imaginary case is one about which we have clear intuitions. The idea is to transfer these clear intuitions to a relevantly similar case about which our intuitions are confused. However, it may be that our intuitions are different about the two cases because they are not relevantly similar. What we may think, on the face of it, is that some important features of the actual case are not present in the imaginary one. One such feature is ambiguity and complexity. As O'Neill points out in 'How can we individuate moral problems?', how we identify and describe cases is already an important part of our response to them. Real life is open to different descriptions and interpretations. It may not even be clear when some situation or circumstance presents a moral problem, or if it does, what kind of moral problem it presents. Imaginary cases come with their own descriptions. The battle for identification and description is suppressed. For this reason our intuitions about them are untrustworthy.

These problems can be seen by considering a series of imaginary examples, presented by Michael Tooley in his book, *Abortion and Infanticide* (pp. 191 ff), in defence of 'the moral symmetry principle' – roughly the view that the wrongness of intervening to stop a causal process is equivalent to the wrongness of failing to initiate the process. Tooley asks us to imagine a chemical that, when injected into the brain of a kitten, causes it to develop into a cat 'possessing a brain of the sort possessed by normal adult human beings'. According to Tooley, killing a kitten that has been injected but has not yet begun to develop 'those properties that would make it a person' is morally equivalent to killing an uninjected kitten. He goes on to apply these results to the issue of abortion, arriving at the conclusion that 'it is prima facie no more seriously wrong to kill a human organism that is a potential person, but not a person, than it is intentionally to refrain from injecting a kitten with the special chemical, and to kill it instead'.

Should we trust our intuitions about these cases? I think not. It is not clear what continuities and differences there are between our world and one in which it is possible to transform kittens into persons. Nor is it clear that we have been presented with all the relevant moral features of these cases. When we imagine cats with language are we also supposed to imagine that they have developed vocalization capacities like ours and now speak English? What do they talk about? Are they burdened with shame and guilt? Do they appreciate art, music, and literature? We might also want to know whether we like them and whether they like us. Only by asking these and other questions can we expose what has been suppressed by the schematic description of the case, and thus even begin to know whether or not we should trust our intuitions.

v Conclusion

The general topic of theory and method in moral philosophy is large, important, and underexplored. In this article I have canvassed various views, and expressed some of my own: that moral theories are derivative of moral theorizing, that moral theorizing is part of everyday moral practice, that both foundationalism and coherentism are problematical, and that appeals to imaginary cases are often misleading and unreliable.

References

Anscombe, G. E. M.: 'Modern moral philosophy', in her *Collected Philosophical Papers; Volume Three, Ethics, Religion and Politics* (Minneapolis: University of Minnesota Press, 1981), pp. 26–42.

Baier, A.: *Postures of the Mind: Essays on Mind and Morals* (Minneapolis: University of Minnesota Press, 1985), Part II.

Brandt, R. B.: *A Theory of the Good and the Right* (Oxford: Oxford University Press, 1979).

Dancy, J.: 'Ethical particularism and morally relevant properties', *Mind*, 92 (1983), 530–47.

——: 'The role of imaginary cases in ethics', *Pacific Philosophical Quarterly*, 66 (1985), 141–53.

Fullinwider, R.: 'Against theory, or: applied philosophy – a cautionary tale', *The Public Turn in Philosophy*, ed. J. Lichtenburg and H. Shue (Cambridge: Cambridge University Press, forthcoming).

Gauthier, D.: *Morals By Agreement* (Oxford: Oxford University Press, 1986).

Gilligan, C.: *In a Different Voice* (Cambridge: Cambridge University Press, 1982).

Hare, R. M.: *Moral Thinking* (Oxford: Oxford University Press, 1981).

Holmgren, M.: 'Wide reflective equilibrium and objective moral truth', *Metaphilosophy*, 18, 2 (1987), 108–24.

Kant, I.: *Groundwork of the Metaphysic of Morals* (1785); (many editions).

McDowell, J.: 'Virtue and reason', *Monist*, 62 (1979), 331–50.

MacIntyre, A.: *Whose Justice? Whose Rationality?* (Notre Dame, Ind.: Notre Dame University Press, 1988).

O'Neill, O.: 'The power of example', *Philosophy*, 61 (1986), 5–29.

——: 'How can we individuate moral problems?', *Applied Ethics and Ethical Theory*, ed. D. M. Rosenthal and F. Shehadi (Salt Lake City: University of Utah Press, 1988), pp. 84–99.

Parfit, D.: *Reasons and Persons* (Oxford: Oxford University Press, 1984), Parts I and IV.

Quine, W. V. O.: 'Two dogmas of empiricism', in his *From a Logical Point of View* (Cambridge, Mass.: Harvard University Press, 1953), pp. 20–46.

Rawls, J.: *A Theory of Justice* (Cambridge, Mass.: Harvard University Press, 1971), Chapter I.

Sartre, J.-P.: 'Existentialism is a humanism', in his *Existentialism and Human Emotions* (New York: The Philosophical Library, 1957).

Sidgwick, H.: *The Methods of Ethics* (1874); 7th edn. 1907 (Indianapolis: Hackett, 1981).

Stocker, M.: 'The schizophrenia of modern ethical theories', *Journal of Philosophy*, 63 (1976), pp. 453–66.

Thomson, J. J.: *Rights, Restitution, and Risk: Essays in Moral Theory* (Cambridge: Harvard University Press, 1986).

Tooley, Michael: *Abortion and Infanticide* (Oxford: Clarendon Press, 1983).

Williiams, B.: *Ethics and the Limits of Philosophy* (Cambridge, Mass.: Harvard University Press, 1985).

Wittgenstein, L.: *Philosophical Investigations*, trans. G. E. M. Anscombe (Oxford: Basil Blackwell, 1967).

Wolf, S.: 'Moral saints', *Journal of Philosophy*, 79 (1982), 419–30.

Further reading

Aristotle: *Nicomachean Ethics* (many editions).

Singer, P.: 'Sidgwick and reflective equilibrium', *Monist*, 58 (1974), 490–517.

Wilkes, K. V.: *Real People: Personal Identity Without Thought Experiment* (Oxford: Clarendon Press, 1988), Chapter 1.

PART VII
CHALLENGE AND CRITIQUE

43

The idea of a female ethic

JEAN GRIMSHAW

QUESTIONS about gender have scarcely been central to mainstream moral philosophy this century. But the idea that virtue is in some way *gendered*, that the standards and criteria of morality are different for women and men, is one that has been central to the ethical thinking of a great many philosophers. It is to the eighteenth century that we can trace the beginnings of those ideas of a 'female ethic', of 'feminine' nature and specifically female forms of virtue, which have formed the essential background to a great deal of feminist thinking about ethics. The eighteenth century, in industrializing societies, saw the emergence of the concern about questions of femininity and female consciousness that was importantly related to changes in the social situation of women. Increasingly, for middle class women, the home was no longer also the workplace. The only route to security (of a sort) for a woman was a marriage in which she was wholly economically dependent, and for the unmarried woman, the prospects were bleak indeed. At the same time, however, as women were becoming increasingly dependent on men in practical and material terms, the eighteenth century saw the beginnings of an idealization of family life and the married state that remained influential throughout the nineteenth century. A sentimental vision of the subordinate but virtuous and idealized wife and mother, whose specifically female virtues both defined and underpinned the 'private' sphere of domestic life, came to dominate a great deal of eighteenth and nineteenth-century thought.

The idea that virtue is gendered is central, for example, to the philosophy of Rousseau. In *Emile*, Rousseau argued that those characteristics which would be faults in men are virtues in women. Rousseau's account of female virtues is closely related to his idealized vision of the rural family and simplicity of life which alone could counteract the evil manners of the city, and it is only, he thought, as wives and mothers that women can become virtuous. But their virtue is also premised on their dependence and subordination within marriage; for a woman to be independent, according to Rousseau, or for her to pursue goals whose aim was not the welfare of her family, was for her to lose those qualities which would make her estimable and desirable.

It was above all Rousseau's notion of virtue as 'gendered' that Mary Wollstonecraft attacked in her *Vindication of the Rights of Woman*. Virtue, she argued, should mean the same thing for a woman as for a man, and she was a bitter critic of the forms of 'femininity' to which women were required to aspire, and which, she thought, undermined their strength and dignity as human beings. Since the time of Wollstonecraft, there has always been an important strand in feminist thinking which has viewed with great suspicion, or rejected entirely, the idea that there are specifically female virtues. There are very good reasons for this suspicion. The idealization of female virtue, which perhaps reached its apogee in the effusions of many nineteenth-century male Victorian writers such as Ruskin, has usually been premised on female subordination. The 'virtues' to which it was thought that women should aspire often reflect this subordination – a classic example is the 'virtue' of selflessness, which was stressed by a great number of Victorian writers.

Despite this well-founded ambivalence about the idea of 'female virtue', however, many women in the nineteenth century, including a large number who were concerned with the question of women's emancipation, remained attracted to the idea, not merely that there were specifically female virtues, but sometimes that women were morally superior to men, and to the belief that society could be morally transformed through the influence of women. What many women envisaged was, as it were, an *extension* throughout society of the 'female values' of the private sphere of home and family. But, unlike many male writers, they used the idea of female virtue as a reason for women's entry into the 'public' sphere rather than as a reason for their being restricted to the 'private' one. And in a context where any sort of female independence was so immensely difficult to achieve, it is easy to see the attraction of any view which sought to re-evaluate and affirm those strengths and virtues conventionally seen as 'feminine'.

The context of contemporary feminist thought is of course very different. Most of the formal barriers to the entry of women into spheres other than the domestic have been removed, and a constant theme of feminist writing in the last twenty years has been a critique of women's restriction to the domestic role or the 'private' sphere. Despite this, however, the idea of 'a female ethic' has remained very important within feminist thinking. A number of concerns underlie the continued interest within feminism in the idea of a 'female ethic'. Perhaps most important is concern about the violent and destructive consequences to human life and to the planet of those fields of activity which have been largely male-dominated, such as war, politics, and capitalist economic domination. The view that the frequently destructive nature of these things is at least in part *due* to the fact that they are male-dominated is not of course new; it was common enough in many arguments for female suffrage at the beginning of the twentieth century. In some contemporary feminist thinking this has been linked to a view that many forms of aggression and destruction are closely linked to the nature of 'masculinity' and the male psyche.

Such beliefs about the nature of masculinity and about the destructive nature of male spheres of activity are sometimes linked to 'essentialist' beliefs about male and female nature. Thus, for example, in the very influential work of Mary Daly, all the havoc wreaked on human life and the planet tends to be seen as an undifferentiated result of the unchanging nature of the male psyche, and of the ways in which women themselves have been 'colonized' by male domination and brutality. And contrasted with this havoc, in Daly's work, is a vision of an uncorrupted female psyche which might rise like a phoenix from the ashes of male-dominated culture and save the world. Not all versions of essentialism are quite as extreme or vivid as that of Daly; but it is not uncommon (among some supporters of the peace movement for example) to find the belief that women are 'naturally' less aggressive, more gentle and nurturing, more co-operative, than men.

Such essentialist views of male and female nature are of course a problem if one believes that the 'nature' of men and women is not something that is monolithic or unchanging, but is, rather, socially and historically constructed. And a great deal of feminist thinking has rejected any form of essentialism. But if one rejects the idea that any differences between male and female values and priorities can be ascribed to a fundamental male and female 'nature', the question then arises as to whether the idea of a 'female ethic' can be spelled out in a way that avoids essentialist assumptions. The attempt to do this is related to a second major concern of feminist thinking. This concern can be explained as follows. Women themselves have constantly tended to be devalued or inferiorized (frequently at the same time as being idealized). But this devaluation has not simply been of women themselves – their nature, abilities and characteristics. The 'spheres' of activity with which they have particularly been associated have also been devalued. Again, paradoxically, they have also been idealized. Thus home, family, the domestic virtues, and women's role in the physical and emotional care of others have constantly been praised to the skies and seen as the bedrock of social life. At the same time, these things are commonly seen as a mere 'backdrop' to the more 'important' spheres of male activity, to which no self-respecting man could allow himself to be restricted; and as generating values which must always take second place if they conflict with values or priorities from elsewhere.

The second sort of approach to the idea of a 'female ethic' results, then, both from a critique of essentialism, and from an attempt to see whether an alternative approach to questions about moral reasoning and ethical priorities can be derived from a consideration of those spheres of life and activity which have been regarded as paradigmatically female. Two things, in particular, have been suggested. The first is that there *are* in fact common or typical differences in the ways in which women and men think or reason about moral issues. This view of course, is not new. It has normally been expressed, however, in terms of a *deficiency* on the part of women; women are incapable of reason, of acting on principles; they are emotional, intuitive, too personal, and so forth. Perhaps, however, we might recognize *difference* without ascribing *deficiency*; and maybe a consideration of female moral reasoning can highlight the problems in the male forms of reasoning which have been seen as the norm?

The second important suggestion can be summarized as follows. It starts from the assumption that specific social practices generate their own vision of what is 'good' or what is to be especially valued, their own concerns and priorities, and their own criteria for what is to be seen as a 'virtue'. Perhaps, then, the social practices, especially those of mothering and caring for others, which have traditionally been regarded as female, can be seen as generating ethical priorities

493

and conceptions of 'virtue' which should not only not be devalued but which can also provide a corrective to the more destructive values and priorities of those spheres of activity which have been dominated by men.

In her influential book *In A Different Voice: Psychological Theory and Women's Development* (1982) Carol Gilligan argued that those who have suggested that women typically reason differently from men about moral issues are right; what is wrong is their assumption of the inferiority or deficiency of female moral reasoning. The starting point for Gilligan's work was an examination of the work of Lawrence Kohlberg on moral development in children. Kohlberg attempted to identify 'stages' in moral development, which could be analysed by a consideration of the responses children gave to questions about how they would resolve a moral dilemma. The 'highest' stage, the stage at which, in fact, Kohlberg wanted to say that a specifically *moral* framework of reasoning was being used, was that at which moral dilemmas were resolved by an appeal to rules and principles, a logical decision about priorities, in the light of the prior acceptance of such rules or principles. (For a general consideration of Kohlberg's work, see Article 41, MORALITY AND PSYCHOLOGICAL DEVELOPMENT.)

A much quoted example of Kohlberg's method, discussed in detail by Gilligan, is the case of two eleven-year-old children, 'Jake' and 'Amy'. Jake and Amy were asked to respond to the following dilemma; a man called Heinz has a wife who is dying, but he cannot afford the drug she needs. Should he steal the drug in order to save his wife's life? Jake is clear that Heinz *should* steal the drug; and his answer revolves around a resolution of the rules governing life and property. Amy, however, responded very differently. She suggested that Heinz should go and talk to the druggist and see if they could not find some solution to the problem. Whereas Jake sees the situation as needing mediation through systems of logic or law, Amy, Gilligan suggests, sees a need for mediation through communication in relationships.

It is clear that Kohlberg's understanding of morality is based on the tradition that derives from Kant and moves through the work of such contemporary philosophers as John Rawls and R. M. Hare. The emphasis in this tradition is indeed on rules and principles, and Gilligan is by no means the only critic to suggest that any such understanding of morality will be bound to misrepresent women's moral reasoning and set up a typically male pattern of moral reasoning as a standard against which to judge women to be deficient. Nel Noddings, for example, in her book *Caring: A Feminine Approach to Ethics and Moral Education* (1984), argues that that a morality based on rules or principles is in itself inadequate, and that it does not capture what is distinctive or typical about female moral thinking. She points out how, in a great deal of moral philosophy, it has been supposed that the moral task is, as it were, to abstract the 'local detail' from a situation and see it as falling under a rule or principle. Beyond that, it is a question of deciding or choosing, in a case of conflict, how to order or rank one's principles in a hierarchy. And to rank as a *moral* one, a principle must be universalizable; that is to say, of the form 'Whenever X, then do Y'. (See Article 40, UNIVERSAL PRESCRIPTIVISM.) Noddings argues that the posing of moral dilemmas in such a way misrepresents the nature of moral decision-making. Posing moral issues in the 'desert-island dilemma' form, in which only the 'bare bones' of a situation are described, usually serves to conceal rather than to reveal the sorts of questions to which only situational and contextual knowledge can provide an answer, and which are essential to moral judgement in the specific context. (See also Dale Jamieson's remarks about the use of examples in moral philosophy in Article 42, METHOD AND MORAL THEORY.)

But Noddings wants to argue, like Gilligan, not merely that this sort of account of morality is inadequate in general, but that women are less likely than men even to attempt to justify their moral decisions in this sort of way. Both of them argue that women do not tend to appeal to rules and principles in the same sort of way as men; that they are more likely to appeal to concrete and detailed knowledge of the situation, and to consider the dilemma in terms of the relationships involved.

Gilligan and Noddings suggest, therefore, that there are, as a matter of fact, differences in the ways in which women and men reason about moral issues. But such views of difference always pose great difficulties. The nature of the evidence involved is inevitably problematic; it would not be difficult to find two eleven-year-old children who reacted quite differently to Heinz's dilemma; and appeals to 'common experience' of how women and men reason about moral issues can always be challenged by pointing to exceptions or by appealing to different experience.

The question, however, is not just one of empirical difficulty. Even if there *were* some common or typical differences between women and men, there is always a problem about how such differences are to be described. For one thing, it is questionable whether the sort of description of moral decision-making given by Kohlberg and others really does adequately represent its nature. Furthermore, the view that women do not act on principle, that they are intuitive and more influenced by 'personal' considerations, has so often been used in contexts where women have been seen as deficient that it is as well to be suspicious of any distinction between women and men which seems to depend on this difference. It might, for example, be the case, not so much that women and men *reason differently* about moral issues, but that their ethical priorities differ, as that what is regarded as an important principle by women (such as maintaining relationships) is commonly seen by men as a *failure* of principle.

At best then, I think that the view that women 'reason differently' over moral issues is difficult to spell out clearly or substantiate; at worst, it runs the risk of recapitulating old and oppressive dichotomies. But perhaps there is some truth in the view that women's ethical *priorities* may commonly differ from those of men? Again, is not easy to see how this could be very clearly established, or what sort of evidence would settle the question; but if it is correct to argue that ethical priorities will emerge from life experiences and from the ways these are socially articulated, then maybe one might assume that, given that the life experiences of women are commonly very different from those of men, their ethical priorities will differ too? Given, for instance, the experience of women in pregnancy, childbirth and the rearing of children, might there be, for example, some difference in the way they will view the 'waste' of those lives in war. (This is not an idea that is unique to contemporary feminism; it was, for example, suggested by Olive Schreiner in her book *Woman and Labour*, which was published in 1911.)

There have been a number of attempts in recent feminist philosophy to suggest that the practices in which women engage, in particular the practices of childcare and the physical and emotional maintenance of other human beings, might be seen as generating social priorities and conceptions of virtue which are different from those which inform other aspects of social life. Sara Ruddick, for example, in an article entitled 'Maternal thinking' (1980) argues that the task of mothering generates a conception of virtue which might provide a resource for a critique of those values and priorities which underpin much contemporary social life – including those of militarism. Ruddick does not want to argue that women can simply enter the public realm 'as mothers' (as some suffragist arguments earlier in the twentieth century suggested) and transform it. She argues, nevertheless, that women's experience as mothers is central to their ethical life, and to the ways in which they might articulate a critique of dominant values and social mores. Rather similarly, Caroline Whitbeck has argued that the practices of caring for others, which have motherhood at their centre, provide an ethical model of the 'mutual realization of people' which is very different from the competitive and individualistic norms of much social life (Whitbeck, 1983).

There are, however, great problems in the idea that female practices can generate an autonomous or coherent set of 'alternative' values. Female practices are always socially situated and inflected by things such as class, race, material poverty or well-being, which have divided women and which they do not all share. Furthermore, practices such as childbirth and the education and rearing of children have been the focus of constant ideological concern and struggle; they have not just been developed by women in isolation from other aspects of the culture. The history of childcare this century, for example, has constantly been shaped by the (frequently contradictory) interventions both of 'experts' in childcare (who have often been male) and by the state. Norms of motherhood have also been used in ways that have reinforced classist and racist assumptions about the 'pathology' of working-class or black families. They have been used, too, by women themselves, in the service of such things as devotion to Hitler's 'Fatherland' or the bitter opposition to feminism and equal rights in the USA. For all these reasons, if there is any usefulness at all in the idea of a 'female ethic', I do not think it can consist in appealing to a supposedly autonomous realm of female values which can provide a simple corrective or alternative to the values of male-dominated spheres of activity.

Nevertheless, it is true that a great deal of the political theory and philosophy of the last two hundred years *has* operated with a distinction between the 'public' and 'private' spheres, and that the 'private' sphere has been seen as the sphere of women. But that which is opposed to the 'world' of the home, of domestic virtue and female self-sacrifice, is not just the 'world' of war, or even of politics, it is also that of the 'market'. The concept of 'the market' defines a realm of 'public' existence which is contrasted with a private realm of domesticity and personal relations. The structure of individuality presupposed by the concept of the market is one which requires an instrumental rationality directed towards the abstract goal of production and profit, and a pervasive self-interest. The concept of 'the market' precludes altruistic behaviour, or the taking of the well-being of another as the goal of one's activity.

The morality which might seem most appropriate to the marketplace is that of utilitarianism, which, in its classic forms, proposed a conception of happiness as distinct from the various activities which lead to this, of instrumental reason, and of an abstract individuality, as in the 'felicific calculus' of Bentham, for example, whereby all subjects of pain or happiness are to be counted as equal and treated impersonally. But, as Ross Poole has argued, in 'Morality, masculinity and the market' (1985), utilitarianism was not really able to provide an adequate morality, mainly because it could never provide convincing reasons why individuals should submit to a duty or obligation that was not in their interests in the short term. It is Kantianism, he suggests, that provides a morality that is more adequate to the market. Others have to figure in one's scheme of things not just as means to an end, but as agents, and the 'individual' required by the market must be assumed to be equipped with a form of rationality that is not purely instrumental, and to be prepared to adhere to obligations and constraints that are experienced as duty rather than inclination. The sphere of the market, however, is contrasted with the 'private' sphere of domestic and familial relations. Although of course men participate in this private sphere, it is the sphere in which female identity is found, and this identity is constructed out of care and nurturance and service for others. Since these others are known and particular, the 'morality' of this sphere cannot be universal or impersonal; it is always 'infected' by excess, partiality and particularity.

The first important thing to note about this contrast between the public sphere of the market and the private sphere of domestic relations is that it does not, and never has, corresponded in any simple way to reality. Thus working-class women have worked outside the home since the earliest days of the Industrial Revolution, and the exclusive association of women with the domestic and private sphere has all but disappeared. Secondly, it is important to note that the morality of the marketplace and of the private sphere exist in a state of tension with each other. The marketplace could not exist without a sphere of domestic and familial relations which 'supported' its own activities; yet the goals of the marketplace may on occasion be incompatible with the demands of the private sphere. The 'proper' complementarity between them can only exist if the private sphere is subordinate to the public sphere, and that subordinacy has often been expressed by the dominance of men in the household as well as in public life. The practical subordinacy of the private sphere is mirrored by the ways in which, in much moral and political philosophy and social thought, the immediate and personal morality of the private sphere is seen as 'inferior' to that which governs the exigencies of public life.

Furthermore, although, ideologically, the public and private spheres are seen as separate and distinct, in practice the private sphere is often governed by constraints and requirements deriving from the public sphere. A clear example of this is the ways in which views on how to bring up children and on what the task of motherhood entailed have so often been derived from broader social imperatives, such as the need to create a 'fit' race for the task of ruling an empire, or the need to create a disciplined and docile industrial workforce.

The distinction between the public and the private has nevertheless helped to shape reality, and to form the experiences of people's lives. It is still commonly true, for example, that the tasks of the physical and emotional maintenance of other people largely devolve upon women, who often bear this responsibility as well as that of labour outside the home. And the differences between male and female experience which follow from these things allow us to understand both why there may well often be differences between women and men in their perception of moral issues or moral priorities, and why these differences can never be summed up in the form of generalizations about women and men. Women and men commonly participate both in domestic and familial relations and in the world of labour and the marketplace. And the constraints and obligations experienced by individuals in their daily lives may lead to acute tensions and contradictions which may be both practically and morally experienced. (A classic example of this would be the woman who faces an acute conflict between the 'impersonal' demands of her situation at work, as well as her own needs for activity outside the home, and the needs or demands of those such as children or aged parents whose care cannot easily be fitted into the requirements of the workplace.)

If ethical concerns and priorities arise from different forms of social life, then those which have emerged from a social system in which women have so often been subordinate to men must be suspect. Supposedly 'female' values are not only the subject of little agreement among women; they are also deeply mired in conceptions of 'the feminine' which depend on the sort of polarization between 'masculine' and 'feminine' which has itself been so closely related to the subordination of women. There is no autonomous realm of female values, or of female activities which can generate 'alternative' values to those of the public sphere; and any conception of a 'female ethic' which depends on these ideas cannot, I think, be a viable one.

But to say this is not necessarily to say that the lives and experiences of women cannot provide a source for a critique of the male-dominated public sphere. Experiences and perspectives which are articulated by gender cannot be sharply demarcated from those which are also articulated along other dimensions, such as race and class; and there is clearly no consensus among women as to how a critique of the priorities of the 'public' world might be developed. Nevertheless taking seriously the experiences and perspectives of women – in childbirth and childcare for example – whilst not immediately generating any consensus about how things might be changed, generates crucial forms of questioning of social and moral priorities. It is often remarked, for example, that if men had the same sort of responsibility for children that women have, or if women had the same

498

sorts of power as men to determine such things as priorities in work, or health care, or town planning, or the organization of domestic labour, many aspects of social life might be very different.

We cannot know in advance exactly what sorts of changes in moral and social priorities might result from radical changes in such things as the sexual division of labour or transformed social provision for the care of others; or from the elimination of the many forms of oppression from which women and men alike suffer. No appeal to current forms of social life can provide a blueprint. Nor should women be seen (as they are in some forms of feminist thinking) as 'naturally' likely to espouse different moral or social priorities from men. Insofar as there are (or might be) differences in female ethical concerns, these can only emerge from, and will need to be painfully constructed out of, changes in social relationships and modes of living; and there is every reason to suppose that the process will be conflictual. But there is every reason, too, to suppose that in a world in which the activities and concerns which have traditionally been regarded as primarily female were given equal value and status, moral and social priorities would be very different from those of the world in which we live now.

References

Daly, M.: *Gyn/Ecology: The Metaethics of Radical Feminism* (Boston: Beacon Press, 1978).
Gilligan, C.: *In a Different Voice: Psychological Theory and Women's Development* (Cambridge, Mass.: Harvard University Press, 1982).
Kohlberg, L.: *The Philosophy of Moral Development* (San Francisco: Harper and Row,1981).
Noddings, N.: *Caring: A Feminine Approach to Ethics and Education* (Berkeley: University of California Press, 1978).
Poole, R.: 'Morality, masculinity and the market', *Radical Philosophy*, 39 (1985).
Rousseau, J. J.: *Emile* (London: Dent, Everyman's Library, 1974).
Ruddick, S.: 'Maternal thinking', *Feminist Studies*, 6, (Summer 1980).
Schreiner, O.: *Woman and Labour* (1911); (London: Virago, 1978).
Whitbeck, C.: 'A different reality; feminist ontology', *Beyond Domination*, ed. C. Gould (Totowa, NJ: Rowman and Allanheld, 1983).
Wollstonecraft, M.: *A Vindication of the Rights of Woman* (Harmondsworth: Pelican, 1975).

Further reading

Grimshaw, J.: *Feminist Philosophers: Women's Perspectives on Philosophical Traditions* (Brighton: Wheatsheaf, 1986).
——: 'Mary Wollstonecraft and the tensions in feminist philosophy', *Radical Philosophy*, 52 (1989).
Mahowald, M.: *Philosophy of Woman: Classical to Current Concepts* (Indianapolis: Hackett, 1978).
Segal, L.: *Is the Future Female: Troubled Thoughts on Contemporary Feminism* (London: Virago, 1987).

44

The significance of evolution

MICHAEL RUSE

i Introduction

EVOLUTIONARY ethics is a subject with a bad reputation, not entirely undeserved.
It is associated with some of the more grotesque moral and political excesses of
the past century, not to mention philosophical fallacies of the most blatant kind.
Yet, thanks particularly to new developments in biological evolutionary theory –
most particularly those associated with social behaviour (so-called 'sociobiology') –
there is a growing feeling that perhaps the last word has not yet been said.

I shall start with a brief review of traditional evolutionary ethicizing: 'social
Darwinism'. Following criticism, I shall look at new directions being taken today.
It will be seen that many of the usual fears are no longer well-grounded, although
it will be seen also that an evolutionary approach does have some fairly serious
implications for our thinking about morality.

ii Social Darwinism

Charles Darwin, the father of modern evolutionary theory, published his major
work, *On the Origin of Species*, in 1859. He argued that all organisms are the end
products of a long, slow natural process of development or evolution. In addition
he proposed a mechanism: natural selection. More organisms are born than can
possibly survive and reproduce. This leads to a 'struggle for existence'. The success
of the successful – the 'fittest' – tends to be a function of their superior features.
Given enough time, this natural process of selection leads to full-blown change,
where the distinguishing mark of organisms is their adaptedness. And, although
Darwin rather downplayed this point in the *Origin*, he made it clear always that
his theory was intended to apply, absolutely and completely, to our own species.

Darwin drew on threads already floating in the air of Victorian Britain. Indeed,
even before he published there were those – dissatisfied with Christianity as a
working philosophy for industrialized societies – who tried to convert biological
ideas into a fully fledged socio-political-economic programme. After the *Origin*,
this movement gathered strength, particularly at the hands of Darwin's fellow
Englishman Herbert Spencer. Thus was born 'social Darwinism'. It came in many
forms; but usually it involved a simple move of Darwinian struggle and selection
from the world of biology to the human social realm. Generally – although there
are interesting exceptions we shall note in a moment – this was believed to yield

500

a fairly straightforward *laissez-faire* social morality. Just as in nature one has competition, struggle, success and failure, so also in society one has competition, struggle, success and failure. Moreover, depending on one's viewpoint, this is either positively a good thing or (more negatively), an inevitable consequence which it would be foolish to ignore.

It is perhaps not surprising that social Darwinism transplanted particularly well to North America. It appealed to the successful businessmen of the day, who found within it justification of their beliefs and practices. In the words of the Yale sociologist and spokesperson for the cause, William Graham Sumner:

Let it be understood that we cannot go outside of this alternative: liberty, inequality, survival of the fittest; not-liberty, equality, survival of the unfittest. The former carries society forward and favors all its best members; the latter carries society downwards and favors all its worst members. (Sumner, 1914, p. 293)

I referred above to variants. In Germany, particularly at the hands of Ernst Haeckel, social Darwinism became more of an ideology glorifying the state. There was less emphasis on the individual and more on the group. More interesting as alternative readings of Darwinism, perhaps, were those strands which tried to justify less harsh, more gentle and caring social policies. One who tried to do just this was the Russian anarchist Prince Peter Kropotkin (1902). He argued that the struggle takes place only between species. Within a group, such as the human race, biology promotes harmony and friendship ('mutual aid') and therefore it is our moral duty to go with this.

By this stage, questions and objections start to rise up. Why should we follow the dictates of evolution? What of foundations? What meta-ethical justification can be offered for the various dictates, admirable or otherwise?

Both biologists and philosophers sense trouble here. The biological worry is that the foundation of the social Darwinian is invariably some kind of biological progress. It is argued that development is an upward process – molecules to men – and to avoid degeneration and fall-back it is therefore our moral duty to aid, to enforce, the processes of evolution. Unfortunately, since Darwin it has been seen that all such hopes of progress are illusory (Midgley, 1985). Natural selection cares only about winners, not about the best. As Darwin's great supporter, T. H. Huxley, said: ' "Fittest" has a connotation of "best"; and about "best" there hangs a moral flavour. In cosmic nature, however, what is "fittest" depends upon the conditions' (Huxley, 1947, p. 298). You cannot avoid the conclusion that evolution is a slow process, going nowhere, which in itself justifies nothing.

The philosophical worry is that the social Darwinian makes an illicit slide from the way that things are to the way that things ought to be. One crashes through the is/ought barrier (on which see Article 37, NATURALISM). In pre-evolutionary times, David Hume pointed to the failure of this as a general strategy (Hume, 1738). Specifically against Herbert Spencer, the British philosopher G. E. Moore showed that it was necessary to smuggle in extra premises (about morality) to get conclusions about the virtue of individualism in the state (Moore, 1903).

In short, whatever the merits or demerits of the social Darwinians' proposals for action, under scrutiny the foundations crumble and decay. No true support is offered.

iii Sociobiology: from 'altruism' to altruism

So much for traditional evolutionary ethics. Have we said all that there is to be said on the subject? Some, myself included, think not. We believe that it simply has to matter that we are modified monkeys rather than the special creation of a good God, in his image, on the Sixth Day. Fortunately, in recent years, advances in biological science enable us to put some flesh on our intuitions. So let us start there.

The new scientific claims are as simple as this. We now know that despite an evolutionary process, centring on a struggle for existence, organisms are not necessarily perpetually at conflict with weapons of attack and defence. In particular, co-operation can be a good biological strategy. We know also that humans are organisms which have pre-eminently taken this route of co-operation and working together. Further, there is good reason to think that a major way in which humans co-operate together is by having an ethical sense. Humans believe that they *should* work together, and – with obvious qualifications – they do so. I emphasize, in connection with this last point, that the claim is not that humans are hypocritically consciously scheming to get as much out of each other as they possibly can whilst perhaps pretending to be nice, but rather that humans do have a genuinely moral sense and awareness of right and wrong. It is this which motivates them.

Now, let us unpack the science. We begin with the general claims about co-operation, or as today's evolutionists dealing with social behaviour (the so-called 'sociobiologists') like to call it, altruism (Wilson, 1975; Dawkins, 1976). I should emphasize at this point there is nothing being said about disinterested giving to others because it is right – that is to say, literal altruism, or what one might call Mother Teresa altruism. Rather, the talk is of co-operating for one's biological ends, which today translates into co-operation to maximize one's units of heredity (the genes) in the next generation (Maynard Smith, 1978). In this sense, therefore, evolutionary altruism is a metaphorical sense of the term and perhaps is best thus marked in quotes: 'altruism'.

Both the theory and the empirical evidence that biological 'altruism' is widespread and promoted by natural selection is very secure and well documented. The simple fact of the matter is that, although winning outright in the struggle for existence is the best of all possible results, such success is often not possible – especially given that every other organism is likewise trying to win. Consequently, one is frequently much better off if one decides to accept a cake shared rather than gambling on the possibility of a whole cake but one which might be lost entirely.

There are various mechanisms which are believed to promote this kind of co-operation. The most striking examples occur in the social insects, where some females devote their whole lives to the well-being of the offspring of their mother, having none of their own (Hamilton, 1964a, b). But in organisms closer to us one likewise sees much evolutionary 'altruism' (Trivers, 1971). The dog family, for instance, relies very heavily on co-operative hunting, with the concern of the whole pack being devoted to the well-being of pregnant or lactating females and their offspring.

The next point is that humans are obviously animals that need biological 'altruism' and are moreover animals which are very skilled at employing it. They are not particularly good as hunters or fighters or even as escapers from danger; but they are good at working together (Isaac, 1983). Of course, our ability to co-operate and our need to co-operate did not just come about by chance. There was a feedback process in evolution, as so frequently occurs. It is now believed by paleoanthropologists that a very important part of human evolution involved scavaging together in bands. Clearly, if one is to be successful at this, one must have the ability to locate dead or dying animals and to warn or frighten off possible competitors – which competitors may or may not have been our fellow humans. By working together humans succeeded, and those that worked together more successfully tended to have more offspring than those who did not. Hence, down through the ages we evolved as highly successful 'altruists'.

Now we start to get more speculative – although I emphasize that this is still intended as claims of empirical fact. The question arises as to how humans have evolved to put their 'altruism' into place. How is it that we work so well together? The key hypothesis is that evolution has made us innately inclined to think in certain ways. In particular, biology has pre-programmed us to think favourably about certain broad patterns of co-operation. This pre-programming is not so stringent as to restrict our actions completely in any particular situation. We are not hardline 'genetically determined' like (say) ants, who go through life like robots. Nor are our patterns of thinking so fixed by our biology that culture has no effect. But, the fact remains that, to make us co-operators, to make us 'altruists', nature has filled us full of thoughts about the need to co-operate. We may not always follow these thoughts, but they are there.

We humans, therefore, are somewhat in the same situation as today's computers which have been programmed to play chess. The early chess-playing computers thought through every option rationally before making a move. Unfortunately, they were virtually useless because, within a move or two, there were so many alternatives to be calculated they could never make up their minds. Today's computers can, in fact, be beaten by the very top masters, but normally they win because, when a particular configuration comes up on the board, they have certain strategies pre-programmed in which are best in those circumstances. Likewise, we humans may sometimes act against our own best interests, but overall we do fairly well because we have thoughts about the need to co-operate. (In biology, as in chess-playing, time and efficiency are valuable commodities. We need to co-operate, but we need to get on with life.)

What is the nature of these thoughts about the need to co-operate? The final move of today's evolutionary biologists is to suggest that these thoughts are none other than beliefs about obligations to help. In other words, to make us 'altruists' nature has made us altruists. At once, I emphasize a point made just above, namely that there is no question that we are scheming to do what is in our own interests and yet pretending to be nice. Rather, as any evolutionist will point out, often we perform better if we are deceived by our biology – and this seems to be the general case with respect to co-operation (Trivers, 1976). We think that we ought to help, that we have obligations to others, because it is in our biological interests to have these thoughts. But, from an evolutionary perspective these thoughts exist because and simply because those of our would-be ancestors who had such thoughts survived and reproduced better than those that did not. In other words, altruism is a human adaptation, just as our hands and eyes and teeth and arms and feet are. We are moral because our genes, as fashioned by natural selection, fill us full of thoughts about being moral.

This is the empirical background to the new evolutionary ethics. I re-emphasize that although much of what has just been presented is speculative it is intended seriously as empirically true. Indeed, today, much evidence is starting to come in support. For instance, detailed studies have and are being done on some of our closest relatives, like the gorillas and chimpanzees (de Waal, 1982; Goodall, 1986). These suggest that such animals rely heavily on altruistic acts (or if you prefer, since they do not have articulate language, proto-altruistic acts). Likewise, there is evidence from human studies pointing to uniformities of moral beliefs beneath all the cultural variations and that these uniformities are innate rather than learned (van den Berghe, 1979). Without putting too great an emphasis on the analogy between language and morality, just as the evidence seems to be hardening that some form of Chomsky's beliefs about the innate nature of language is well-taken (Lieberman, 1984), so likewise cross-cultural and developmental studies suggest that human moral beliefs are rooted in biology as well as in the environment of culture.

iv The biological contract

Let us suppose now, if only for the sake of argument, that the empirical scenario sketched in the last section is correct. We now must ask about implications. With respect to questions about what is expected of us as social beings, questions to do with substantive rules, note that the discussion has been knocked sideways a little. The question is no longer 'What should we do?' but 'What (thanks to our biology) do we think we should do?' With this revision noted (a revision we shall have to pick up again in a moment), the answers come fairly readily. Moreover, if the biology be accepted, even if only for the sake of discussion, then they are probably not as surprising as all that. The kinds of animals whose evolution has just been sketched will be animals which work together, certainly for their own ultimate biological gain, but not necessarily for their own conscious immediate gain. They will rather be animals which, as it were, throw their efforts into the general pool and then draw upon them as needed or as necessary. Animals, furthermore, who think it is right and proper to behave in the way that they do.

In some respects, therefore, this sounds remarkably like animals which have made some sort of social contract. (See Article 15, THE SOCIAL CONTRACT TRADITION.) And, indeed, if one thinks of some of the versions of social contract theory, particularly some of the modern versions like that of John Rawls, then the above-given evolutionary scenario seems to mesh very nicely. In other words, we have a social contract, but it is not one which involved our ancestors deciding literally to co-operate. Rather, it is one which was put in place by evolutionary biology. It is interesting to note, incidentally, that Rawls himself is not unsympathetic to this idea. (See Rawls, 1971, pp. 502–3.)

Does this mean that a biological approach sits comfortably with what just about any modern moral philosopher would want to claim about obligations? Almost certainly not! Indeed, to be candid it probably intensifies worries that many have about social contract theories. For the evolutionist, sentiments must track biological consequences, and this point must apply equally to moral sentiments, even though they may be distinctive. But if one thing is certain to the evolutionist it is the following: not all social interactions are going to have the same pay-off. All other things being equal, your best reproductive investments are going to be in helping close kin. Then, probably, more distant kin and those non-relatives who offer most likelihood of reciprocation. Biologically, it makes more sense to co-operate with those in a position to co-operate and with a common interest in co-operation (Wilson, 1978). Finally, one reaches an outer limit, where one is dealing with strangers and, indeed, where the possibilities of danger from the unknown may well exceed any virtues of possible reciprocation.

What all of this seems to mean, from a biological perspective, is that not only will one's feeling of affection fall away as one moves beyond one's immediate family but so also will one's sense of moral obligation. It is virtually a truism that one loves one's children more than one loves some unknown stranger; but the evolutionist's position seems to imply also that one will feel a greater sense of moral obligation towards one's own children than towards some unrelated child. Even with non-relatives there will be a moral differential, with a stronger sense of obligation within one's own society than towards those without.

But this seems flatly to go against what has been argued by many moralists, among them Peter Singer. He argues that our obligation to the unknown starving child in Africa is no less than our obligation to one of our own children (Singer, 1972; for a slightly different view, see the conclusion of Article 23, WORLD POVERTY.) Of course, he loves his own children more than he loves the children of others, but this is not quite the point. He asserts that we have identical obligations to all.

I am not sure how one can resolve a disagreement like this other than by appealing to people's feelings and asking them to examine themselves deeply and carefully. Of course, we do feel that we have obligations to others but given the care and attention that we lavish first on our own children and then on those within our neighbourhood, it seems pushing a philosophical thesis to the point of extremity to suggest that all of the time we think that we are behaving in a grossly immoral way. Were you to learn of me that I give 90 per cent of my income to some charity like Oxfam, whilst my children have to eat at the Salvation Army soup kitchen, it is unlikely that you would think me a candidate for sainthood. You would rather be indignant at my failure to discharge my proper obligations. In this context, it is worth remembering the stark moral message of Dickens's great novel *Bleak House*. Mrs Jellyby spends all her time concerned with the welfare of the natives of some faraway African country. Dickens responds savagely that her first obligations are to her own family which she neglects, then to the unfortunates in her own society, like Jo the crossing boy, and then and only then to those beyond one's societal boundaries.

The evolutionary ethicist is *not* arguing that one has no obligations whatsoever to people in other parts of the world. Thanks to modern technology we are all brought much more closely together. But he or she does argue that it is foolish to pretend that we have an equal obligation. Indeed, he or she would argue that once we recognize the limited nature of our moral sentiments, we will probably all be much better off recognizing that, in dealing with other people, proper attitudes are often those of enlightened self-interest rather than mystical and unfounded feelings of affection. (As it happens, nations – which have to take international relations seriously – are much less inclined to the pretence that they are dealing with each other on grounds other than self-interest. The evolutionary ethicist takes this as confirmation of the position; but see also Article 34, WAR AND PEACE.)

What now of justification? What can one say here? What of meta-ethical foundations? One suspects that it is at this point that many traditional philosophers will fall away. However much empathy might be felt for the kind of position which has been articulated thus far, the traditional thinker will argue that to think that a genetic account of the evolution of morality says anything about justification is to leave an unfilled gap. At best one's position is incomplete and at worst one smashes into the is/ought barrier. In the end, therefore, one is still no further along than is the traditional evolutionary ethicist. (Rawls says this.)

Perhaps so. But, possibly there is a third option. This is the option which suggests that there is no foundation to ethics at all! This is not to say that substantive ethics does not exist, but, it is to say that the supposed underpinning is chimerical in some sense or another (Murphy, 1982; Mackie, 1977; Ruse, 1986). Is it not the case that sometimes, when one has given a causal explanation of certain beliefs, one can see that the beliefs, themselves, neither have a foundation nor could ever have such a foundation? At least, so argues today's evolutionary ethicist. Once we see that our moral beliefs are simply an adaptation put in place by natural selection, in order to further our reproductive ends, that is an end to it. Morality is no more than a collective illusion fobbed off on us by our genes for reproductive ends.

It must be noted that the qualification 'collective' is very important here. One can certainly distinguish between sensible ethical beliefs like 'Don't hurt old ladies' and crazy ethical beliefs like 'Be kind to cabbages on Fridays'. The whole point about ethics is that we are all in it together. If we are not, then some can cheat and the rest of us lose out in the evolutionary game. Ethics has its own standards and rules, just as do baseball or cricket. Yet, contrary to the beliefs of some devotees, just as baseball and cricket tell us nothing about the real world, in the sense of the world 'out there', neither does ethics. For this reason, the question 'What ought we do?' and 'What do we (as a group) think we ought to do?' collapse into each other.

The position which is being articulated here is a form of 'ethical scepticism'. (See Article 35, REALISM, and Article 38, SUBJECTIVISM.) It is important to emphasize that the scepticism is not about the substantive claims of ethics. No-one, least of all the evolutionary ethicist, denies the existence of these. The scepticism is about the foundations which supposedly lie beneath substantive ethics. The claim is that sometimes, once you have given a causal analysis of why people believe certain things, you see that the call for reasoned justification is illicit. The messages of spiritualism, satisfying (as they do) people's anxieties and needs, are a case in point. Ethics is another. Moral claims are simply adaptations. There is neither place for, nor need of, rational justification.

What of the objection that, even though evolution may have led us to think in moral ways, this does not deny that some objective foundation for morality yet exists? After all, to take a popular analogy, your evolved organs of sense are unlikely to make you conscious of an approaching train, if such a train is not really approaching. (Nozick, 1981, makes this objection.) The evolutionary ethicist's counter is that morality is not like trains. If you would be a better co-operator by believing the very opposite to what we understand by morality, then so be it. Try a thought experiment. Suppose evolution had led us to believe, not that we should be just and fair and so forth, but rather that we should be unjust and unfair and so forth. Suppose also that evolution made us aware that others felt the same way about us. Taking a leaf from the Cold War of the 1950s, we might end in an uneasy alliance of co-operation, not unlike our differently based present state. But, who is to say that we are truly right and our inverse world truly wrong? There is no guarantee that evolution has directed us to believe precisely that which coincidentally happens to be objectively true. That way lie thoughts of directed, progressive evolution. At the very least, an objective morality is irrelevant, which is surely a contradiction in terms.

Morality remains without foundation. Yet, to ask one final question: Why does such a thesis as is being argued for here seem so intuitively implausible? Why does it seem – or so it appears to many people – so ridiculous to argue that morality is no more than an illusion of the genes? Why does it seem so silly to suggest that moral claims are on a par with the rule in cricket that there should be six balls to an over? (Actually, it is not quite on a par with such a rule, since a moral claim is imposed on us by our genes, whereas a cricket law is imposed on us by our predecessors and could, in principle, be changed. Witness the great changes that have occurred in cricket in the last thirty years.) There is a simple answer and when seen it adds to the evolutionist's case rather than detracts from it. The simple fact is that if we recognized morality to be no more than an epiphenomenon of our biology, we would cease to believe in it and stop acting upon it. At once, therefore, the very powerful forces which makes us co-operators would collapse.

507

Unfortunately, from a biological point of view, although some of us might get an immediate gain, most of us would be losers.

It is important, therefore, that biology should not simply put moral beliefs in place but should also put in place a way of keeping them up. It must make us believe in them. What this means is that, even though morality may not be objective in the sense of referring to something 'out there', it is an important part of the experience of morality that we think it is. Its phenomenology, if you like, is that we believe it to be objective. In the words of the late John Mackie, we are led to 'objectify' morality, in thinking that morality is something imposed on us rather than a matter of free choice (Mackie, 1979). Hence, we are led to obey it and thus it works. If, when I interact with you, I realize that I could simply pull out of the deal if I so wish, then very shortly that is precisely what I will be doing. But, if as is the case, I think that morality is truly binding on me – and even the fact that I can recognize its base does not alter the psychological feelings that I have – I am led to continue in moral ways. (Obviously, no-one is claiming that we are always moral. The whole point is that we do have the choice to be moral or not to be moral. Where we have no choice is in the beliefs that we have. I can decide whether or not to steal. What I cannot decide is whether stealing is right or wrong.)

In short, the claim is being made that when people like G. E. Moore argued that morality is a non-natural property or some such thing, they were correctly identifying an important aspect of our experience of morality. It is not simply something which we choose or decide on, like the clothes we put on. Yet, at the same time the evolutionist argues that Moore was wrong in his analysis of the objectivity of morality. It is rather something subjective or non-cognitive. Where it differs from other subjective feelings is in having an aura of objectivity about it. Just as the Freudian argues that those who deny his or her explanation thereby confirm it, so the evolutionist argues that those who find his or her explanation implausible support the very point which is being made!

v Conclusion

A promising new approach to ethics asks as many questions as it gives answers. Certainly, there is much yet remaining to be unpacked from evolutionary ethics: about the interplay between biology and culture, for instance; about where it should be positioned with respect to the great thinkers in the history of ethics. (David Hume is my favoured father-figure.) And about the way or ways in which knowledge of our biological state might help us to avoid the taking of short-term routes to pleasure to avoid long-term disaster. But these and other questions must wait for the future. Now it is enough if the reader is convinced that biology is not quite so irrelevant to our morality as most of us have for so long assumed.

References

Darwin, C.: *The Origin of Species* (London: John Murray, 1859).

Dawkins, R.: *The Selfish Gene* (Oxford: 1976); 2nd edn (Oxford: Oxford University Press, 1989).

de Waal, F.: *Chimpanzee Politics* (London: Cape, 1982).

Goodall, J.: *The Chimpanzees of Gombe* (Cambridge, Mass.: Harvard University Press, 1986).

Hamilton, W. D.: 'The genetical evolution of social behaviour, I', *Journal of Theoretical Biology*, 7 (1964a), 1–16.

——: 'The genetical evolution of social behaviour, II', *Journal of Theoretical Biology*, 7 (1964b), 17–32.

Hume, D.: *Treatise of Human Nature* (1738); ed. L. A. Selby-Bigge (Oxford: Clarendon Press, 1978).

Huxley, T. H.: *Evolution and Ethics*, ed. J. Huxley (London: Pilot Press, 1947).

Kropotkin, Prince: *Mutual Aid: A Factor of Evolution* (London: Heinemann, 1902).

Lieberman, P.: *The Biology and Evolution of Language* (Cambridge, Mass.: Harvard University Press, 1984).

Mackie, J.: *Ethics: Inventing Right and Wrong* (Harmondsworth: Penguin, 1977).

——: *Hume's Moral Theory* (London: Routledge and Kegan Paul, 1979).

Maynard Smith, J.: 'The evolution of behaviour', *Scientific American*, 239: 3 (1978), 176–93.

Midgley, M.: *Evolution as Religion: Strange Hopes and Stranger Fears* (London: Methuen, 1985).

Moore, G. E.: *Principia Ethica* (Cambridge: Cambridge University Press, 1903).

Murphy, J.: *Evolution, Morality and the Meaning of Life* (Totowa, NJ: Rowman and Littlefield, 1982).

Nozick, R.: *Philosophical Explanations* (Cambridge, Mass.: Harvard University Press, 1981).

Rawls, J.: *A Theory of Justice* (Cambridge, Mass.: Harvard University Press, 1971).

Ruse, M.: *Taking Darwin Seriously* (Oxford: Basil Blackwell, 1986).

Spencer, H.: *Principles of Ethics* (London: Williams and Norgate, 1892).

Sumner, W. G.: *The Challenge of Facts and Other Essays*, ed. A. S. Kelle (New Haven: Yale University Press, 1914).

Trivers, R.: 'The evolution of reciprocal altruism', *Quarterly Review of Biology*, 46 (1971), 35–57.

——: 'Foreword', *The Selfish Gene*, R. Dawkins (Oxford: Oxford University Press, 1976).

van den Berghe, P.: *Human Family Systems: An Evolutionary View* (New York: Elsevier, 1979).

Wilson, E. O.: *Sociobiology: The New Synthesis* (Cambridge, Mass.: Harvard University Press, 1975).

——: *On Human Nature* (Cambridge, Mass.: Harvard University Press, 1978).

Further reading: a guide

Herbert Spencer's ideas can be found (at very great length) in his *Principles of Ethics*. W. G. Sumner's views are given in his collection of essays, *The Challenge of Facts and Other Essays*. Prince Kropotkin's major work is *Mutual Aid: A Factor of Evolution*.

The classic critique of traditional social Darwinism is by T. H. Huxley. His essay, together with a (pro-evolutionary ethics) essay by his grandson, Julian, comes in *Evolution and*

Ethics. G. E. Moore, *Principia Ethica*, shows the philosophical gaps in Spencer's arguments.

Of the many books dealing historically with social Darwinism, the definitive starting point is Richard Hofstadter, *Social Darwinism in American Thought* (New York: Braziller, 1959). Useful additions and correctives can be found in Cynthia Eagle Russett, *Darwin in America* (San Francisco: Freeman, 1976). The English scene is well covered by Greta Jones in *Social Darwinism and English Thought* (Brighton: Harvester, 1980).

Turning to our own age, the scientific background is presented by E. O. Wilson, most fully in his majestic *Sociobiology: The New Synthesis*, and in a more popular form, relating specifically to our own species, in *On Human Nature*. Richard Dawkins's provocative *The Selfish Gene* is compulsive reading. A more pedestrian overview of the science can be found in my *Sociobiology: Sense or Nonsense?* (2nd edn; Dordrecht: Reidel, 1985). As you will see, I have changed my mind completely about the relevance of evolution to ethics. Highly pertinent to the empirical case for the biology of our morality are two recent books on the chimpanzees: Franz de Waal, *Chimpanzee Politics*, and Jane Goodall, *The Chimpanzees of Gombe*.

Those who think the new biology revitalizes evolutionary ethics include John Mackie, 'The law of the jungle', (*Philosophy*, 53 (1978), 455–64); Jeffrey Murphy, *Evolution, Morality and the Meaning of Life*; and Michael Ruse, *Taking Darwin Seriously*. Sympathetic, but still critical, are Peter Singer, *The Expanding Circle: Ethics and Sociobiology* (New York: Farrar, Straus and Giroux, 1981) and Roger Trigg, *The Shaping of Man* (New York: Blackwell, 1982). Strongly hostile is Philip Kitcher, *Vaulting Ambition* (Cambridge, Mass.: MIT Press, 1985).

Also see:

Isaac, G. L.: 'Aspects of human evolution', *Evolution from Molecules to Men*, ed. D. S. Bendall (Cambridge: Cambridge University Press, 1983), pp. 509–43.

Singer, P.: 'Famine, affluence and morality', *Philosophy and Public Affairs*, 1 (1977), 229–43.

45

Marx against morality

ALLEN WOOD

i Introduction

MARXISTS often express a contemptuous attitude toward morality, which (they say) is nothing but a form of illusion, false consciousness or ideology. But others (whether they consider themselves Marxists or not) often find this attitude hard to understand. The Marxists condemn capitalism for exploiting the working class and condemning most people to lives of alienation and unfilfilment. What reasons can they give for doing so, and how can they expect others to do so as well, if they abandon all appeals to morality? The Marxist rejection of morality, however, begins with Marx himself. And it is, I will contend, a defensible view, a natural consequence, as Marx says it is, of the materialist conception of history. Even if we do not accept Marx's other views, his attack on morality raises significant issues concerning the way we should think about morality.

ii Marx's anti-moralism

Marx is habitually silent about the sorts of issues which interest moralists and moral philosophers. But from what he does say, it is clear that this silence is not due to benign neglect. His attitude is rather one of open hostility to moral theorizing, moral values, even to morality itself. Against Pierre Proudhon, Karl Heinzen and the German 'true socialists', Marx regularly employs 'morality' and 'moralizing criticism' as epithets of abuse. He bitterly condemns the Gotha Programme's demand for 'just wages' and 'just distribution', asserting that such phrases 'confound the realistic outlook' of the working class with 'outdated verbiage' and 'ideological trash' which his scientific approach has rendered obsolete (MEW 19: 22, SW 325). When others do prevail upon Marx to include bland moral rhetoric in the Rules for the First International, he feels he must apologize to Engels for it: 'I was obliged to insert two phrases about "duty" and "right" ... ditto about "truth, morality and justice", but these are placed in such a way that they can do no harm' (CW 42, p. 18).

Marx regularly describes morality, along with religion and law, as forms of ideology, 'so many bourgeois prejudices behind which lurk just as many bourgeois interests' (MEW 4, p. 472; CW 6, p. 494–95; cf. MEW 3, p. 26; CW 5, p. 36). But he does not condemn only bourgeois ideas about morality. His target is morality itself, *all* morality. *The German Ideology* claims that the materialist conception of history, by exhibiting the connection between moral ideology and material class interests, has 'broken the staff of all morality', irrespective of its content or class affiliation (MEW 3, p. 404; CW 5, p. 419). When an imaginary critic charges that 'communism does away with all morality and religion instead of forming them anew', the *Communist Manifesto* replies not by denying that this charge is true, but instead by observing that just as the communist revolution will involve a radical break with all traditional property relations, so it will also involve the most radical break with all traditional ideas (MEW 4, p. 480–81; CW 6, p. 504). Evidently it is Marx's view that just as doing away with bourgeois property will be one task of the communist revolution, so 'doing away with all morality' will be another. Marx even goes so far as to side with moral evil against moral good. He insists that in history 'it is always the bad side which finally triumphs over the good side. For the bad side is the one which brings movement to life, which makes history by bringing the struggle to fruition' (MEW 4, p. 140; CW 6, p. 174).

Some, such as Karl Kautsky, have interpreted such remarks as pleas for the 'value freedom' of Marxian social science. But that reading is both implausible and anachronistic. It is not at all what the passages themselves say. And the idea that science should be 'value-free' was largely a neo-Kantian invention; Marx wrote at a time, and in a tradition, which was both unfamiliar with and unsympathetic to it. No reader of Marx could possibly deny that he makes 'value judgements' about capitalism, and Marx never attempts fastidiously to segregate his scientific analysis of capitalism from his angry condemnation of it. When Marx accuses capitalism of stunting human potentialities, stifling their development and preventing their actualization, he avails himself unashamedly of judgements about people's needs and interests, and even of a (recognizably Aristotelian) naturalistic framework of ideas concerning the nature of human well-being and fulfilment.

Judgements about what is good for people, what is in their interests, certainly are 'value judgements', but they are not necessarily *moral* judgements, since even if I care nothing about morality at all, I may still be interested in promoting the interests and well-being of myself and others whose welfare I happen to care about. It would be entirely consistent for Marx to reject morality and nevertheless advocate the abolition of capitalism on the ground that it frustrates human well-being, so long as his concern with human well-being is not based on any moral values or principles. Marx's attack on morality is not an attack on 'value judgements', but it is a rejection of specifically *moral* judgements, especially those involving the ideas of right and justice.

iii   Historical materialism

It is the materialist conception of history which Marx credits with 'breaking the staff of all morality'. Historical materialism treats history as divided into epochs, each characterized fundamentally by its *mode of production*. A mode of production consists of a set of *social relations of production*, a system of economic roles assigning effective control over the means, processes and fruits of social production to the occupants of some roles and excluding the occupants of other roles. These differences between roles are the basis of *class* differences in society.

On the materialist theory, social change comes about because society's *powers of production* are not static but change, and on the whole tend to grow. At any stage of their development, the employment of the powers of production and their further growth are facilitated more by some social relations than by others. No one set of production relations has a permanent advantage over all others in this regard; instead, at different stages of the development of productive powers, different sets of social relations are better suited to promote productive development. Eventually, any given set of production relations becomes obsolete; they become dysfunctional in relation to the employment of the productive powers, and they 'fetter' their further development. A *social revolution* consists in a transformation of the social relations of production which is required by and for the growth of the powers of production (MEW 13, p. 9; SW, p. 183).

The mechanism by which social relations are adjusted so as to promote the development of productive powers is the *class struggle*. The social relations of production divide societies into groups, determined by their roles in production and their degree and type of control over the material instruments of production. These groups are not themselves classes, but they become classes as soon as there exists a political movement and an ideology representing their *class interests*. The interests of a class are based on the common situation of the class's members, and especially on its hostile relation to other classes. Generally speaking, members of those classes which control the conditions of production have an interest in retaining their dominance, and those over whom this control is exercised have an interest in wresting it away from those who have it. These individual interests, however, are not directly class interests. Since classes are not just categories of individuals but social and political organizations or movements bound together by ideologies, the interests of a class are always something distinct from the interests of the class's individual members. In fact, Marx identifies the interests of a class with the political interests of the movement which represents the class (MEW 4, p. 181; CW 6, p. 211).

Ultimately, the interests of a class consist in the establishment and defence of the set of relations of production which assign control of production to the members of that class. But it does not follow from this that class interests are simply the self-interest of the class's members, or that class interests are pursued in the form of egoistic interests. For in a war between classes, as in a war between nations, victory is sometimes possible only through the sacrifice of individual interests. The individuals who are called upon to make such sacrifices see themselves as fighting for something greater and worthier than their self-interest; and in this they are right, for they are fighting for the interests of their class.

iv Ideology

This greater and worthier thing, however, is seldom presented to them *as* the interest of a social class. Instead, a class shapes from its material conditions of life 'a whole superstructure of different and characteristic feelings, illusions, ways of thinking and views of life' (MEW 8, p. 139; CW 11, p. 128) which serve its members as the conscious motives of the deeds they do in its behalf. When these feelings, thoughts and views are the products of a special class of mental labourers working in the class's employ, Marx has a special name for them: *ideology*. The products of ideologists – of priests, poets, philosophers, professors and pedagogues – are, on the materialist theory, typically ideological. That is, the content of these products can best be accounted for by the way in which it represents the world-views of particular social classes at a particular time and serves the class interests of these classes.

In a well-known letter to Franz Mehring, Friedrich Engels describes ideology as 'a process carried out by the so-called thinker with consciousness, but with a false consciousness. The real driving forces that move him remain unknown to him; otherwise it would not be an ideological process. Thus he imagines to himself false or apparent driving forces' (MEW 39, p. 97; SC p. 459). According to this, the chief illusion in any ideology is an illusion about its own class basis. This is not ignorance, error or deception about the individual psychology of one's actions. When ideologists think they are being motivated by religious or moral enthusiasm, very often they really are – Engels does not mean to claim that they are necessarily victims of the sort of self-deception which occurs when I act self-interestedly but deceive myself into thinking I am acting from moral duty or philanthropic love. But the question is: what does it really mean to act on moral, religious or philosophical grounds? What is the relation of such actions to the social life of which they are a part? When we act from such grounds, what are we really doing?

When they are motivated by ideologies, people do not understand themselves as representatives of a class movement; but they are just the same. They do not think of class interests as the fundamental explanation of the fact that these ideas appeal to them and to others; but that is the correct explanation nevertheless. They do not act with the intention of promoting the interests of one social class as opposed to others; but they go right on doing so, and sometimes all the more effectively just because they truly have no such intention. For if they truly knew what they were doing, they might not continue to do it.

v Ideology as unfreedom

The Marxist attitude toward ideological false consciousness reflects the fact that it is taken to be a form of *unfreedom*. On the most obvious and superficial level (where, in the English-speaking liberal tradition, issues about freedom usually remain) freedom is taken away from us when we are frustrated in the pursuit of our goals by external obstacles, such as prison bars and threats of violent harm. Going a little deeper, we may also recognize internal obstacles (such as compulsive desires and incapacities) as destructive of freedom. If we go deeper still, we may see that ignorance can be unfreedom, when our intentions are formed without accurate knowledge of the way our actions affect the outcomes we care about, or without correct ideas about the range of alternatives open to us. The threat to freedom posed by ideology is something like this, yet not quite the same, since it is quite possible for victims of ideology to be fully informed as regards the things they care about. The problem is that the full significance of our actions may extend beyond what we care about, even beyond what we are capable of caring about, because it extends beyond what we understand about ourselves and our actions. I act from religious motives, for example, but I promote the interests of a certain class without realizing that I am doing so. When this happens I am unfree in what I do because the meaning of my actions eludes my free agency; because it is not *I* as a thinking and self-knowing being who does it. This is not the unfreedom of being unable to do what I intend; in fact, one could describe it as the unfreedom of being unable to intend what I do.

I am fully free in this respect only if my actions have what we may call 'self-transparency': I know these actions for what they are and I do them intentionally in light of this knowledge. When a certain system of ideas is socially available to me because of the class interests it serves and my actions are motivated by it, then I can be fully free in performing those actions only if I understand the role which class interests play in my actions and choose those actions in light of that understanding. But if the system of ideas itself inhibits such an understanding by disguising or falsifying the role played by class interests in its own genesis and effect, then it destroys self-transparency of action of those who act on it; it undermines their freedom.

Self-transparency of action is not merely a theoretical value. For knowledge is subversive: if we clearly understood the social basis and significance of what we do, we would not go on doing it. Humanity may be unacquainted as yet with any social way of life which could be led self-transparently by its human participants. If Marx is right, then all societies based on class oppression – and that means every social order which history records, including our own – depend for their stability on the fact that their members are systematically deprived of the freedom of social self-transparency. The oppressed can be kept in their place only if their ideas about that place are suitably mystified; and the system might be threatened even if the oppressors acquired excessively accurate ideas about the relations which benefit them at others' expense. Revolutionary classes can more effectively enlist the support of other classes, and even that of their own members, if they present their class interests in a glorified form. Ideology is not a marginal phenomenon, but essential to all social life as it has existed up to now.

vi Morality as ideology

In the light of this, it should not be surprising that Marx regards morality, along with law, religion and other forms of social consciousness, as fundamentally ideological. Morality is a system of ideas which both interprets and regulates people's behaviour in ways which are vital for the workings of any social order. It also has the potentiality for motivating them to make large-scale social changes. If the history of past societies is fundamentally a history of class oppression and class struggle, then it is only to be expected that the prevalent systems of moral ideas would take the form of ideologies through which class warfare is being simultaneously waged and disguised. In this way, Marx thinks that historical materialism has 'broken the staff of all morality' by revealing its foundation in class interests.

Perhaps we are not surprised to find Marx attacking morality in this way, but we may think his position exaggerated and needlessly paradoxical, even if we grant him for the sake of argument that historical materialism is true. Some moral precepts (such as minimal respect for the lives and interests of others) seem to have no conceivable class bias, but apparently belong to any conceivable moral code, since without them no society at all would be possible. How can Marx want to discredit these precepts, or think that historical materialism has discredited them? Further, if all class movements need morality, then apparently the working class will need it too. How can Marx want to deprive the proletariat of an important weapon in the class struggle?

To reject morality, however, is not necessarily to reject all the behaviour morality enjoins and advocate the behaviour it prohibits. There may be some patterns of behaviour common to all moral ideologies, and we might expect moral ideologies to emphasize them, since it helps to disguise the class character of the ideology's more characteristic features. If people must do and refrain from certain things in order to have a decent social life, then Marx would certainly want those doings and refrainings to continue in the communist society of the future. But Marx would not want them to be done *because* some moral code enjoins them, since moral codes are class ideologies, which undermine the self-transparency of the people who act on them.

Perhaps the fear is that without moral motives, nothing will prevent us from falling into the uttermost barbarism. Marx does not share this fear, a first cousin of the superstitious fear that if there is no God, then all is permitted. The task of human emancipation is to build a human society on rational self-transparency, free from the mystification of morality and other ideologies. Marx knows that at present we have no clear conception of what such a society would be like, but he believes that humanity is equal to the task of bringing one into being.

Marx has powerful reasons for refusing to exempt working-class moral ideologies from these strictures. The historic mission of the working-class movement is human emancipation; but every ideology, including working-class ideologies, undermines freedom by destroying self-transparency of action. Marx rails against moralizing within the movement because he regards the 'realistic outlook' brought to it by historical materialism as indispensable for its revolutionary task (MEW 19, p. 22; SW, p. 325).

vii Justice

Marx supplements his attack on working class moralizing with an account of the justice of economic transactions.

The justice of transactions which go on between agents of production rests on the fact that these transactions arise out of the production relations as their natural consequence. [The content of a transaction] is just whenever it corresponds to the mode of production, is adequate to it. It is unjust whenever it contradicts it. (MEW 25, p. 351–2; C 3, p. 339–40).

A transaction is just whenever it is functional within the existing mode of production, unjust whenever it is dysfunctional. From this it follows directly that the exploitative transactions between capitalist and worker, and the system of capitalist distribution resulting from them, are perfectly just and violate no-one's rights (MEW 19, p. 18; SW, p. 321–2; MEW 19, pp. 359, 382; MEW 23, p. 208; C 1, p. 194). But equally, once we see that this is what it means for capitalist exchanges and distribution to be just, we will no longer take the fact that they are just as any sort of defence of them.

As Marx tells us, his conception of justice rests on the way in which moral norms arise out of relations of production. It is not an account of justice which either a defender of the system or a moral critic of it would give, and it is not intended to be a conception of justice which captures the way in which social agents think about the justice of the transactions they regard as just. But it is an account which intends to identify what in fact regulates their usage of terms like 'just' and 'unjust', and in this way it anticipates certain features of some contemporary philosophical theories of reference. According to these theories, people's use of a term like 'water' refers to H_2O if people's use of this term is regulated by the fact that the substance they refer to is H_2O, even if they would not accept this as an account of what they mean by 'water' (because, for instance, they have no concept of H_2O, or because they have superstitious folk-beliefs about the nature of water). Analogously, Marx holds that people's use of terms like 'justice' and 'injustice' of economic transactions is regulated by the functionality of these transactions for the prevailing mode of production, and hence that these are the properties of the transactions to which such terms refer – even though understanding justice and injustice in this way has the effect of depriving these terms of the persuasive force they are usually taken to have. In Marx's view, it is only moral ideology which makes us regard moral properties such as justice as inherently or necessarily desirable. (Once we come to understand what justice really is, we will acquire a more sober view about how desirable it is.)

viii Morality and rationality

There are some conceptions which are essentially self-defining, through an activity which is associated with them. Scientific rationality, for example, is not limited to what people have called 'science' in the past, because the activity of science consists in criticizing itself, rejecting its present content and giving itself a new one. What has in the past been considered 'rational' behaviour, even the very criteria of rationality, may be subjected to self-criticism and now treated as less than rational. In modern culture, there has been a strong tendency simply to identify morality with practical reason, and consequently to regard moral reasoning too as a self-critical and self-determining notion. On this view, all errors in moral thinking are errors in the content of particular moral beliefs; 'morality itself' always (perhaps even 'by definition') transcends all moral errors, at least in principle.

Marx's view of morality involves the denial that morality can be regarded in any such way. If there is a kind of practical thinking which is self-correcting in this manner, morality is not it. The reason is that morality, moral concepts and principles, moral thoughts and feelings, have already been appropriated to quite a different sort of task with quite a different method of operation. Along with religion and law, the essential tasks of morality are social integration and class advocacy, its essential method is ideological mystification and self-disguise. A morality which understood its own social basis would be as impossible as a religion which founded itself on the clear perception that every belief in the supernatural is a superstition.

ix The illusion of impartial benevolence

We can see why this is so if we attend to one fundamental feature of morality as such. It is characteristic of moral thinking to present itself as founded on such things as the will of a universally benevolent God, or a categorical imperative legislated by pure reason, or a general happiness principle. Whatever the theory, morality is depicted as the standpoint of impartial or disinterested well-wishing, which takes account of all relevant interests and gives preference to some over others only when there are good (impartially based) reasons for doing so. It is this feature of morality which renders it fundamentally ideological.

No doubt people can *think* they are behaving in such a manner, and a particular action may even actually be impartially benevolent as regards the immediate interests of the small number of people whom it immediately affects. As long as we think only of our particular actions and their immediate consequences, as morality encourages us to do, there is no general problem about achieving the impartiality it demands. But morality also encourages us to think of our actions as conforming to a moral code which is valid for others as well as for ourselves. When we do this, we implicitly represent our actions as conforming systematically to principles of impartial benevolence which we imagine as possibly effective on a large scale. It is at this point that the illusory character of moral impartiality becomes evident. For in a society based on class oppression and torn by class conflict, there can be no socially significant and effective form of action which has this character of impartial benevolence. Actions which are commended as 'just' (because they correspond to the prevailing mode of production) systematically promote the interests of the ruling class at the expense of the oppressed. Actions taken to overthrow the existing order, which may be commended by some revolutionary moral code, advance the interests of the revolutionary class at the expense of other classes.

According to Marx, the most pervasive characteristic of ideology is its tendency to represent the standpoint of one class as a universal standpoint, the interests of that class as universal interests (MEW 3, p. 46–49; CW 5, p. 59–62; MEW 4, p. 477; CW 6, p. 501). This is precisely what moral ideologies do: they represent actions which benefit the interests of one class as disinterestedly good, as actions in the common interest, promoting the rights and well-being of humanity in general. But it would be an illusion to think that this deception could be remedied by some new moral code which succeeds in doing what these class ideologies only pretend to do. For in a society based on class oppression and torn by class conflict, impartiality is an illusion. There are no universal interests, no cause of humanity in general, no place to stand above or outside the fray. Your actions may be subjectively motivated by impartial benevolence, but their objective social effect is never impartial. The only actions which do not take sides in a class war are actions which are either impotent or irrelevant.

All this is just as true of the working class as of any other. Marx thinks the working-class movement is in the interests of 'the vast majority' (MEW 4: 472; CW 6: 495); but working-class interests are the interests of one particular class, not the interests of humanity in general. Marx does believe that the working-class movement will eventually abolish class society itself, and thereby achieve universal human emancipation. But its first step toward this must be to emancipate itself from the ideological illusions of class society. And that means that it must pursue its class interest in its own emancipation consciously as its class interests, undistorted by ideological illusions which would portray its interest in a glorified, moralized form – for instance, as already identical with universal human interests. Marx thinks that it is only by becoming clearsighted about itself in this way that the revolutionary proletariat can hope to create a society which is free both from ideological illusions and from the class divisions which create the need for them.

x Can Marx do without morality?

Marx was a radical thinker, and his attack on morality is clearly one of his most radical ideas. The Marxian idea of a revolutionary social movement and even a radically new social order which would abolish all morality was intended to shock, frighten and challenge its audience, to test the limits even of what it could conceive. Perhaps it is understandable that many who are sympathetic to Marx's critique of capitalism should find this idea useless, barely intelligible, embarrassing, and that they should think the only viable or sympathetic interpretation of Marx is one which reads it entirely out of his texts. Marxist anti-moralism combines badly with the widespread notion that the monstrous atrocities which have disillusioned our century (and for which self-proclaimed Marxists have borne no light burden of responsibility) have been due fundamentally to calamitous *moral* failures on the part of politicians, parties and peoples. The notion itself may be highly dubious – typical of the sad human tendency to react first with moral blame toward whatever we hate and fear but do not understand. But to those for whom it is second nature, a Marx who attacks morality is easily groomed as someone whose thought leads straight to the purge, the gulag and the killing fields.

But this way of thinking rests on some erroneous assumptions, and some invalid reasoning. To reject morality is not necessarily to approve of everything morality would condemn, nor is it even to deprive oneself of the best reasons for disapproving of it. We may reject morality and nevertheless have a rational, humane outlook – as Marx did. Morality is not the only possible remedy for the abuses which Marxism has suffered, nor is it even, I venture to say, a very good remedy. Fanatics continue to prove every day that even the purest moral intentions cannot prevent us from committing the most monstrous crimes unless we successfully employ our intelligence along with our moral fervour. Thus a better remedy might be simply to address the human intellect seriously to deciding whether our means will in fact achieve our ends, and whether our ends truly answer to our considered desires.

But the fear will be that without morality we have no way of trusting our desires. Why should we bother to overthrow capitalist oppression, or avoid the nightmares of totalitarianism, if, on reflection, we don't happen to want to? What if our own self-interest happens to lie on the side of the oppressors? What, if not morality, could provide the necessary counterpoise? But it is a basic tenet of historical materialism that the human motivation which is most powerful in human affairs, and explains the fundamental dynamics of social change, falls neither into the category of self-interest nor that of morality. Marx regards self-interest as an important human motive, but he thinks the self-interest of individuals as such is too varied in its effects to effect any world historical transformation. On the other hand, a high-minded concern for the universal interest or for justice in the abstract is going to achieve results only if it serves as the illusory pretext for the promotion of definite class interests.

It is these class interests themselves which are the real driving forces of history. Class interests are far from impartial – they do not aim at the general welfare or impartial justice, but at the achievement and defence of a certain set of production relations, those which signify the emancipation and dominance of a certain social class under given historical conditions. It is solely to the class interests of the revolutionary proletariat that Marx means to appeal in advocating the overthrow of capitalism and the establishment of a more emancipated and more human society. Marx does think that proletarian class interests will appeal to some who are not themselves proletarians but who have risen to a theoretical comprehension of the historical process (MEW 4, p. 472; CW 6, p. 494). This appeal arises from an informed identification with a concrete historical movement, not from crude self-interest, and even less from any impartial commitment to moral principles and aims which the movement is thought to serve. Those who join the proletarian cause with the latter attitude have not risen to a theoretical comprehension of the historical movement; they have simply been caught in the snares of moral ideology.

It is evidently from Hegel that Marx derives the idea that abstract (Kantian) morality is impotent, and that the motives which are historically effective always harmonize individual interests with those of a larger social order, movement or cause. (Similar neo-Aristotelian – or neo-Hegelian – ideas have recently been defended by Alasdair MacIntyre and Bernard Williams, among others.) But Hegel (like these more recent philosophers) attacks 'morality' only in a narrow sense, while trying to save it in a larger one. He locates the harmony of individual interests and social action in 'ethical life', which remains something distinctively moral by the fact that its ultimate appeal to us is supposed to be the appeal of impartial reason. The system of ethical life is a system of right, duty and justice, which actualizes the universal good; it even includes 'morality' (in the narrower sense) as one of its moments.

Marxian class interests, however, are not 'moral' even in an extended sense. They are the interests of one class which stands in a hostile relation to other classes, and they can be advanced only at the expense of the interests of their class enemies. All this holds, moreover, as much for proletarian interests as for those of any other class. To represent working-class interests as universal interests or as something impartially good (as happens when they are treated as a morality) is for Marx a paradigm of ideological falsification – and an act of betrayal against the working-class movement (MEW 19: 25, SW 325).

xi Has morality any future?

There is one passage in *Anti-Dühring* in which Engels contrasts the ideological moralities of class society with an 'actual human morality of the future' (MEW 20, p. 88; AD, p. 132). This passage conflicts with the anti-moralism characteristic of Marx (and of Engels too, in many other passages). But we ought to be clear about just where the conflict lies, and how profound it really is. There is a direct conflict between the claim that there will be morality in future communist society and the *Communist Manifesto*'s assertion that the communist revolution will 'do away with all morality instead of founding it anew'. But perhaps the conflict does not go very deep after all. Morality thinks its principles are impartial and universally human, and that following them will give your actions a justification which transcends the conflicting interests of particular individuals and groups. The Marxian view is that this cannot be done as long as class society exists, and that the fundamental ideological deception of morality is the way it passes off particular class interests as universal interests. But Marx and Engels think that after class society has been abolished, it will be possible for individuals to relate to each other simply as human beings, whose interests may diverge at the margins but are fundamentally identified through their common participation in a fully human social order. It is the classless society, therefore, which will actually accomplish what morality deceptively pretends to do. And on this ground, it may be understandable that Engels should speak of the 'actual human morality' of future society, even though this involves a revision in the more characteristic (and clarifying) Marxian concept of morality as essentially the false pretence to universality found in class ideologies. The point not to overlook, however, is that Engels regards this 'actual human morality' as something *future*, not something available to us now, while we are still the prisoners of class society and its inevitable conflicts. Engels is emphatic in denying that there are any 'eternal truths' about morality. He plainly thinks that the principles of an 'actual human morality' – belonging as they do to a future social order – are as unknowable by us as the scientific truths which will belong to some future theory which lies on the far side of the next major scientific revolution. Nothing in Engels's remarks gives any comfort to those who would use moral standards to criticize capitalism or guide the working-class movement.

xii Conclusion

Marx's anti-moralism is not an easy idea to accept. It is not clear how we could think of ourselves and our relations with others entirely in non-moral terms. If all morality is an illusion, then a clear-sighted person must be able to go through life entirely without moral beliefs, moral emotions, moral reactions. But is it possible for anyone to do this? Yet Marx's anti-moralism is far from being his only shockingly radical proposal for humanity's future. After all, communism as Marx conceives it would abolish not only all morality, but also all religion, law, money and commodity exchange, along with the family, private property, and the state. Marx's anti-moralism actually appeals to some of us – as it surely must have appealed to Marx himself – precisely *because* it is such a radical, dangerous and paradoxical idea – especially since, as I have been trying to argue, it is at the same time a disturbingly well-motivated idea in the context of Marx's materialist conception of history.

Yet even if we are not persuaded by historical materialism, Marx's critique of morality raises some troubling questions for us. Do we pretend that we understand the real social and historical significance of the moral standards we employ? Can we be sure that we would still accept those standards if we did understand their significance? In the absence of such understanding, how can we suppose that a devotion to moral ends and principles, which we so closely associate with our sense of self-worth, is compatible with the autonomy and dignity which we want to ascribe to ourselves as rational agents? And what sort of life, individual or collective, might there be without morality? What does it look like, that territory which lies (in Nietzsche's uncanny phrase) beyond good and evil?

Modern moral thought sees itself as essentially critical and reflective, not merely preaching traditional morality but questioning received moral ideas and seeking out new ways of thinking about both our individual lives and our collective life. Marx belongs to a radical tradition of modern thought about morality – a tradition which also includes Hegel, Nietzsche and Freud – thinkers who have made us painfully aware of the ways in which the moral life involves us inevitably in irrationality, self-opacity and self-alienation. What this tradition suggests is the enigmatic and abysmal possibility that it may not be feasible for modern moral reflection to go all the way with its critical thinking without undermining the *moral* character of that thinking. To paraphrase Marx (MEW 1, p. 387; CW 3, p. 184): what may turn out to be Utopian is a merely reformist thinking about morality, which hopes to make repairs in the structure of our moral convictions but still to leave the pillars of the house standing.

References

Writings of Marx and Engels are cited in both the German and a standard English translation. All translations presented here, however, are my own. I use the following system of abbreviations:

MEW *Marx Engels Werke* (Berlin: Dietz Verlag, 1961–66), cited by volume and page number.
CW *Marx Engels Collected Works* (New York: International Publishers, 1975–), cited by volume and page number.
C Marx, *Capital* (New York: International Publishers, 1967), cited by volume and page number.
SW *Marx Engels Selected Works* in one volume (New York: International Publishers, 1968), cited by page number.
SC *Marx Engels Selected Correspondence* (New York: International Publishers, 1965), cited by page number.
AD Engels, *Anti-Dühring* (Moscow: Progress Publishers, 1962), cited by page number.

Kautsky, K.: *The Materialist Conception of History*, trans. J. Kautsky (New Haven: Yale University Press, 1988).

Further reading

Brenkert, G.: *Marx's Ethics of Freedom* (London: Routledge & Kegan Paul, 1984.)
Buchanan, A.: *Marx and Justice* (Totawa, NJ: Rowan and Littlefield, 1982).
Cohen, G. A.: *Karl Marx's Theory of History: A Defense* (Princeton: Princeton University Press, 1978).
Cohen, M., Nagel, T. and Scanlon, T., eds.: *Marx, Justice and History* (Princeton: Princeton University Press, 1980).
Elster, J.: *Making Sense of Marx* (Cambridge: Cambridge University Press, 1985).
Geras, N.: *Marx and Human Nature* (London: New Left Books, 1983).
Henry, M.: *Marx: A Philosophy of Human Reality* (Bloomington, Ind.: Indiana University Press, 1982).
Kamenka, E.: *The Ethical Foundations of Marxism* (London: Routledge & Kegan Paul, 1972).
Lukes, S.: *Marxism and Morality* (Oxford: Clarendon Press, 1984).

Miller, R.: *Analyzing Marx: Morality, Power and History* (Princeton: Princeton University Press, 1984).

Nielsen, K.: *Marxism and the Moral Point of View* (Boulder, Col.: Westview Press, 1989).

Nielsen, K., and Patten, S., eds.: *Marx and Morality* (Guelph: Canadian Association for Publishing in Philosophy, 1981).

Wood, A.: *Karl Marx* (London: Routledge & Kegan Paul, 1981).

46

How could ethics depend on religion?

JONATHAN BERG

IN THE light of the venerable and intimate association between religion and ethics, it is only natural that the question arises whether ethics depends on religion in any essential way. The circumstantial evidence abounds: ethical norms form a large part of religious teachings, which, for their part, correspond closely to the norms of secular ethical theories. But does that mean that ethics depends on religion? And if so, how?

i God and the moral good

One simple way to think of ethics as depending on religion will be mentioned only to be immediately set aside. One may reason that if God created the universe and everything that is in it – absolutely *everything* – then he created, *inter alia*, the good. Were it not for him there just would not be any such thing as goodness. So ethics, being essentially concerned with the good, would depend directly on God for its very existence. Assuming, at least for the sake of argument (perhaps too generously), that dependence on God carries with it dependence on religion (religion being something like a theory – or *the* theory – of God), it would follow, then, that ethics depends on religion. But this trivial kind of dependence on religion is far too common to be of much interest. For in this way *everything* would depend on religion, from physics and mathematics to physiology and psychology. (See William Frankena's remarks on a similar view attributed to Dietrich von Hildebrand in Frankena, 1981, p. 309).

A more interesting way to construe ethics as depending on religion would be on the basis of a 'Divine Command Theory' of ethics, identifying the moral good with God's will or with what God commands. In its strongest form this is a theory about the very meanings of the words – what Jonathan Harrison has called a 'linguistic' theory. The idea would be not merely that God's will and the good happily coincide, which would typically be taken for granted (inasmuch as God is good), but rather, that they are one and the same, that to be morally good just *is*, by definition, to be as God wills.

One problem with such a strong version of the Divine Command Theory, where the expression 'good' just *means* the same (roughly) as the expression 'as God wills', is that it then becomes a seemingly empty tautology that God is good. God's great goodness would be no more remarkable than, say, a circle's roundness. Though some theologians might embrace this result, it would not be acceptable

525

to theists who take the assertion that God is good as more significant and informative than the assertion that circles are round. (See Article 37, NATU-RALISM.)

In any case, this linguistic version of the Divine Command Theory runs into trouble with the apparent fact that many people have beliefs about what is morally good *without* having the corresponding beliefs about what God has willed. That is, there seems to be no shortage of atheists and agnostics who, despite their lack of belief in God, do not suffer from any lack of moral beliefs. Defenders of the linguistic Divine Command Theory might dig in their heels and deny that there really are such people. Those who appear to be moral-minded atheists, one might venture, either are not really atheists or do not really have beliefs about the moral good. One might say, for instance, that those who believe there is order in the universe, or who believe in their own conscience – or hold any beliefs at all that they cannot rationally justify – therefore believe in God, even though they, themselves, would be disinclined to put it that way. But as Frankena says of similar arguments, whatever victory they may win, 'it is a hollow and verbal one' (Frankena, 1981, p. 311). For in whatever sense of the words these people might be correctly said to 'believe in God', clearly there is also an ordinary, everyday sense in which they do *not* believe in God, as evident from their sincere pronouncements. And this latter, ordinary sense is the relevant one here; construing belief in God differently could only make the theory trivially true, merely by definition, void of any significant content. (Alternatively, on the grounds that synonymous expressions are not interchangeable *salva veritate* in belief ascriptions, one might simply deny that the good's being defined in terms of God indeed precludes having beliefs about the good without having beliefs about God.)

Another way to deal with the problem posed for the Divine Command Theory by the existence of moral non-theists is suggested by Robert Adams, who, biting the bullet, restricts the scope of his 'modified' version of the theory to 'Judeo-Christian religious ethical discourse' (Adams, 1981, p. 319) and suggests that what theists and non-theists mean by moral terms 'may well be partly the same and partly different' (p. 342). That is, faced with the undeniable existence of moral-minded atheists and agnostics, Adams concedes that the Divine Command Theory cannot be a correct account of what we *all* mean by moral terms. So from the very start he sets for himself the more modest task of developing the theory only as an account of what he and like-minded theists mean by moral terms, hoping subsequently to show that what the theists mean and what the non-theists mean is at least in large part the same, despite some significant differences.

An easier route for Divine Command Theorists might be to abandon the linguistic version of the theory in favour of a more modest extensional version, holding that although 'the good' and 'God's will' do not *mean* the same thing, they *amount* to the same thing – that is, God wills whatever is good, and whatever God wills is good. This yields the intended equivalence without requiring the troublesome semantic claims.

But even in this weakened form, the Divine Command Theory still arouses many objections. For one thing, much of what God is often taken as commanding, from ritual practices to sabbath observance, does not seem to be a matter of what is most commonly thought of as morality. (Of course, what is commonly thought is not necessarily right.) Insofar as it is possible to distinguish a conception of morality properly pertaining only to some of God's commands, such as those about murder and theft, but not to other divine commands, such as those requiring the performance of rituals, the Divine Command Theory founders.

Apart from this problem of whether the requisite equivalence actually obtains, the Divine Command Theory faces deeper problems, traditionally seen as arising from the dilemma put by Plato in the *Euthyphro* (10a): 'Do the gods love holiness because it is holy, or is it holy because they love it?' Or in terms of the present discussion, does God command (or will) the good because it is good, or is it good because he commands (or wills) it? The question can be understood as one of priorities. If God wills the good because it is good, then the good is somehow prior to God's will (though not necessarily temporally prior). On this view something is first of all good, and it is in virtue of its being good that God wills it; his will is somehow determined or directed by its goodness. This would be a theory of 'divine psychology', of what it is that moves God or motivates him to will the things he wills. It is a reply to the question, 'Why does God will what he wills?' On the other hand, if what is good is good because God wills it, then God's will is prior (in the relevant sense) to the thing's goodness – as if the thing is not good to begin with, but only becomes good as a result of God's willing it. This would be a meta-ethical theory, about the nature or essence of goodness. It is a reply to the question, 'What makes a thing good?' (Harrison, 1971, provides an extended exposition along these lines.)

The main objection raised against the first theory, explaining God's will in terms of the good, is that it seems to infringe on God's sovereignty or omnipotence, making him subject to some independent moral norm. Any such constraints on God's freedom and power would be objectionable to those who maintain that there can be no limit whatsoever on what God can will or command. In reply there are basically two ways to argue that God's omnipotence is not infringed: either on the grounds that he nevertheless *could* will other than the good, or on the grounds that although he cannot will other than the good, his not being able to does not preclude his being omnipotent. The first of these replies would have it that God commands the good not out of any inability to do otherwise, but only because he freely *wants* to. He certainly has the power in him, on this view, to choose otherwise, but being as benevolent as he is, he wills – freely – the good. (See Nelson Pike's 'Omnipotence and God's inability to sin', 1981.)

The second way of reconciling God's omnipotence with his willing only the good is taken by R. G. Swinburne, proceeding on the basis of a distinction between necessary and contingent moral truths (Swinburne, 1974). Necessary moral truths are understood to be moral truths which cannot but be true; they are true in every possible (consistently conceivable) set of circumstances, regardless of which circumstances actually happen to obtain. These would include general principles of conduct, such as that one ought to keep one's promises (suitably qualified). Contingent moral truths are those that are true on account of particular actual circumstances. For instance, if it happen to be the case that I promised my neighbour not to make noise on weekends, and if it also happens to be the case that operating certain power tools makes a lot of noise, then under those circumstances it would be a contingent moral truth that I should not operate those power tools on weekends. Though this contingent moral truth is just an instance of the necessary moral truth that one ought to keep one's promises, it is contingent because it is an instance of the general principle only in virtue of circumstances that could have been otherwise. This distinction allows Swinburne to argue that at least *necessary* moral truth cannot infringe on God's omnipotence by restricting his will, no more than the logical truth can. Just as God's inability to make a round square does not detract from his omnipotence, neither does his inability to command that (in general) one ought not to keep one's promises. (As for *contingent* moral truth, Swinburne's view will come below.)

On the other horn of the dilemma of the *Euthyphro* was the view that the reason the good is good is because God wills it; his willing the good (and nothing else) is what *makes* it good. To this the principal objection has been that it makes goodness too arbitrary. For if goodness comes down to nothing but being willed by God, then since anything could, in principle, be willed by God, it follows that anything could, in principle, be good. Even such things as cruelty for its own sake could, on this view, be good – and *would* be good had God so willed. Adams cites William of Ockham as accepting this consequence, explicitly mentioning 'theft', 'adultery', and 'hatred of God' as things that would have been good had God commanded them (*Super 4 libros Sententiarum*, II, 19) – a position Adams suspects likely to be found 'somewhat shocking, even repulsive' (1981, p. 321). (See Article 11, MEDIEVAL AND RENAISSANCE ETHICS.) Rejecting this consequence as unacceptable for its failure to accord with common usage of moral terms (at least among like-minded believers), Adams endeavours to salvage the Divine Command Theory by modifying it in a way that would avoid this unacceptable result. To this end he proposes to temper the link posited between God's will and the good by resting it in a certain way on the assumption that God loves us. While accepting as a logical possibility that God *could* command cruelty for its own sake, Adams avoids concluding that cruelty for its own sake would therefore be good or permissible. For if God commanded cruelty for its own sake, it would not be true that he loves us; but without the assumption that God loves us, explains Adams, our moral concepts (or at least his own) would simply 'break down', thereby *not* allowing the conclusion that under such incomprehensible circumstances (as those in which God commanded cruelty for its own sake) cruelty for its own sake would not be wrong.

For Swinburne the second horn of the dilemma is the place to hang contingent moral truths. That cruelty for its own sake is wrong is probably a necessary moral truth, so that God could not make cruelty for its own sake good, even if he wanted to. But it would only be a contingent moral truth that it is wrong to throw babies off tall buildings (barring highly unlikely extenuating circumstances). For we could imagine a bizarre world in which throwing babies off tall buildings had consequences radically different from those it actually has, in our own world –

physics and physiology might be so different, that being thrown off a tall building would be beneficial, pleasurable, or even necessary for healthy growth. In full control of such contingencies, God could freely have the world one way or the other, making throwing babies off tall buildings good, bad, or neither, however he wills. So the arbitrariness of goodness ensuing from the good's being determined simply by God's will seems not to cause offence, so long as only contingent goodness, as given by contingent moral truths, is being considered.

So what is the fate of the Divine Command Theory? Though the theory seems hard to maintain as a general theory of meaning, a suitably qualified version could be plausible for theists prepared to accommodate the dilemma of the *Euthyphro*. Depending on one's intuitions about God and about morality, one might simply accept that God's choices are constrained by morality, or on the other hand, that what in fact strikes us as morally repugnant would actually be virtuous were God to command it. A number of ways have been suggested for making such positions easier to swallow. One could argue that the moral constraints on God's choices come from God, himself (Pike), or that such constraints are in effect necessary truths, not to be thought of as genuine limits on God's power (Swinburne). Or one could argue that the conviction that God loves us renders incomprehensible the very idea of God's commanding things we find morally repugnant, such as cruelty for its own sake (Adams), or that what is good depends on God's will only because of God's power to determine what is contingently true (Swinburne). (As in any philosophical discussion, of course, there are other lines of argument not discussed here, and for all the objections and replies considered there are further objections and replies, that for now must go unmentioned. For more extensive discussion of these and related matters, see the suggestions for further reading, below.)

ii God and the moral knowledge

This discussion of how ethics might depend on religion has concentrated so far on links that might be thought to obtain between God and the good. But since it is (alas!) one thing for an act to be good and quite another for us to *know* that it is good, it may be that only the latter depends on God (or religion). That is, while an act's being good or not may have nothing to do with God, our *knowing* whether it is good or not might depend on God. To whatever extent moral knowledge depends on God, ethics could be said to depend on religion *epistemologically*.

Again there is a trivial kind of dependence to be set aside from the start. God could be said to be the source of moral knowledge in the same way that he is the source of *all* knowledge. Apart from creating the universe and everything that is in it, it is he who endowed us with the capacity to know whatever we know, moral and otherwise. But the more interesting question in the present context is whether or not there is some specific way that moral knowledge, in particular – as opposed to astronomical knowledge, say – depends essentially on God. One could still take a simple way out by arguing that moral intuition is divinely inspired, whether the inspired individuals realize it or not. But as an answer to the question at hand, this would be no more satisfying than the previous one.

The most straightforward way to view moral knowledge as depending on God would probably be by holding that it is impossible to have any moral knowledge without having some knowledge of or about God. Although such a view does not require the Divine Command Theory, they would obviously go well together. In any case, the prevalence of moral non-theists once again seems to pose a problem. For there seem to be plenty of people who know, for instance, that murder is wrong, without knowing (without even merely believing) anything about God at all.

Short of denying the sincere atheistic or agnostic pronouncements of these prima facie moral theists (an option seen, in the above discussion of the linguistic version of the Divine Command Theory, to lack plausibility), those who would insist that moral knowledge depends on knowledge of or about God have at least two main lines of defence. One would be to loosen the connection between moral knowledge and the requisite knowledge of or about God, enough to accommodate the individuals in question. This could be accomplished by allowing that they need not, themselves, have the requisite knowledge of or about God. Rather, it would be enough for them to be suitably influenced, perhaps even very indirectly, by those who *do* have the requisite knowledge. In this vein one could argue that moral non-theists – and many or even most theists, too – gained their moral knowledge from duly qualified theists, perhaps through a chain of many generations. (Such a picture, though with regard to theists, is presented at the beginning of *Pirkei Avot*: 'Moses received the Law at Sinai and passed it on to Joshua, who passed it on to the elders, who passed it on to the prophets, who passed it on to the people of the Great Assembly.') Or one might say that the moral non-theists were taught their moral knowledge by a society morally informed by theists. The problem with such a line (as with some of the other positions mentioned above) is that it provides at most a causal account of non-theists' moral knowledge, offering only an explanation of how it came to be that these non-theists wound up with moral knowledge. All this could show is that ethics is causally dependent on religion, which is not to say that it depends on religion in any *essential* way. Those who maintain that ethics depends on religion generally have some more substantial connection in mind.

Alternatively, one could try to defend the view that moral knowledge depends on knowledge of or about God, by denying that moral non-theists actually have moral *knowledge*. Regardless of the sincerity and fervour with which they affirm and argue for their correct moral beliefs, such as that murder is wrong, non-theists could be held incapable of having any genuine moral knowledge; their correct moral views could be seen as no more than just serendipitously true beliefs. The issue here is about justification. Their moral beliefs would fall short of moral knowledge for want of sufficient justification, owing to their lack of the requisite knowledge of or about God. To make this view more palatable, one need not relegate the status of a non-theist's moral belief to that of mere lucky guesses. The moral beliefs of non-theists could be compared to the beliefs non-physicists have about sub-atomic particles, the beliefs therapists have about what it is like to undergo experiences they, themselves, never had, or the belief of children parroting their parents. In each case the relevant beliefs may well be correct and may well be had with good reason (more or less), but the believer is just not in a position to give a full enough justification of his beliefs for his having them to count as full-fledged knowledge.

This position, that the moral beliefs of non-theists are too lacking in justification to count as moral knowledge, is vulnerable to two strong objections. One objection is that this view just runs roughshod over common sense, or at least common parlance. For we would typically say of almost any sane adult that he knows that murder is wrong, no matter what he thinks of God. Certainly Bertrand Russell knew that murder is wrong, despite his well-known atheism. To dismiss all this as mere *façon de parler* would require tremendously compelling argument. Secondly, in denying the possibility of justifying moral beliefs without appeal to God, the position in question entails the rejection of every single rational non-theistic theory of ethics. Kant, for example (like so many others), argued that moral knowledge can be obtained by reason alone. Those who would refuse to recognize as adequately justified any moral beliefs not derived from knowledge of or about God, would have to refute the whole vast range of arguments put by Kant and all others who ever proposed a rational basis for ethics! (Indeed, on Kant's view one's reasons for acting morally must be the right – rational – reasons; moral actions cannot be prompted by any ulterior motives, such as the desire to obey God, but must be done simply on account of their intrinsic accord with unconditional, self-imposed moral principles.)

iii   God and moral motivation

Conceding that knowledge of or about God may not be necessary as a reason for moral knowledge, one may claim that it is necessary nevertheless as a reason for moral *behaviour*. This turns on a distinction between justification and motivation. One might argue (as many have, throughout the history of ethics) that whatever reasons there might be in support of various moral principles, the only reason to behave morally is that God rewards the good and punishes the evil, whether in this life or in some other. The underlying question here is 'Why be moral?' And the answer being considered is that there is no reason to be moral, except for the promise of divine reward and the threat of divine punishment.

There are at least two different ways to understand the claim that God's approval (or disapproval) is the only reason for being moral. It might be put forth on the assumption that the justification of moral principles falls short of providing sufficient reason for following them – as if one might concede, for instance, that stealing is wrong, without feeling any compulsion to refrain from it. Generally, however, when people justify a moral principle, giving reasons for following it is exactly what they mean to do. In fact, it would be hard to think of what a justification of a moral principle – that one ought not to steal, say – would look like, if it did not provide reasons for following the principle – reasons for not stealing. Reasons for morality – for behaving morally – may thus be seen as inherently superfluous, like reasons for doing what is desirable (and recognized as such). (See Kai Nielsen's 'Is "Why should I be moral?" an absurdity?' (1958) and Article 35, REALISM.)

A different way of interpreting the claim that the prospects of divine reward and punishment are the only reasons for moral behaviour would be as an empirical claim about human psychology. Thus construed the claim would be that human beings, as a sad but simple matter of fact, are just not moved to refrain from wrongdoing and to do what is right, unless they fear God's wrath and seek his favour. But then the claim seems patently false. For despite the many people of whom it is true – people who are moved to moral behaviour only by considerations of divine reward and punishment – there are perhaps just as many, if not more, who behave morally with no regard whatsoever to divine reward and punishment. One may protest that moral behaviour not inspired by thoughts of divine reward and punishment is not rational, but this just brings us back to the question of justification (considered above). (See also Article 16, EGOISM.)

iv   Preaching and proving

In considering arguments on how ethics might depend on religion it may be useful to keep in mind just what and whom the arguments are aimed at. Almost all the discussion here (and traditionally) has been about the compatibility of theism with theistic theories of ethics, especially Divine Command Theories. The major concern has been to reconcile beliefs and intuitions about morality with beliefs and intuitions about God and his goodness and power. Naturally these arguments have the most significance for those who share the beliefs and intuitions whose joint consistency is at issue (e.g. that there exists an omnipotent, benevolent God whose will is identical to the good). Of somewhat more general significance are arguments intended to establish a theistic theory of ethics on the assumption that God exists and has the attributes generally attributed to him. (See, for instance, Baruch Brody's 'Morality and religion reconsidered', 1974.) Such arguments are directed to virtually all theists, whether they already hold a theistic theory of ethics or not. These arguments cannot, however, prove to a non-theist that ethics depends on religion. The most they could show him is that *if* God exists, with the usual divine attributes, then ethics *could* (in the case of the consistency arguments) or *would* (in the case of the arguments from theism) depend on religion.

References

Adams, R. M.: 'A modified divine command theory of ethical wrongness', *Religion and Morality*, ed. G. Outka and J. P. Reeder (New York: Anchor/Doubleday, 1973). Reprinted in *Divine Commands and Morality*, ed. P. Helm (Oxford University Press, 1981).

Brody, B.: 'Morality and religion reconsidered', in his *Readings in the Philosophy of Religion: An Analytic Approach* (Englewood Cliffs, NJ: Prentice-Hall, 1974), Reprinted in *Divine*

Commands and Morality, ed. P. Helm (Oxford University Press, 1981).

Frankena, W. K.: 'Is morality logically dependent on religion?', *Religion and Morality*, ed. G. Outka and J. P. Reeder (New York: Anchor/Doubleday, 1973). Reprinted in *Divine Commands and Morality*, ed. P. Helm (Oxford: Oxford University Press, 1981).

Harrison, J.: *Our Knowledge of Right and Wrong* (London: Allen and Unwin, 1971).

Kant, I.: *Groundwork of the Metaphysic of Morals*, trans. and analysed by H. J. Paton (New York: Harper and Row, 1964).

Nielsen, K.: 'Is "Why should I be moral?" an absurdity?', *Australasian Journal of Philosophy*, 36 (1958), 25–32.

Pike, N.: 'Omnipotence and God's inability to sin', *American Philosophical Quarterly*, 6 (1969), 208–16. Reprinted in *Divine Commands and Morality*, ed. P. Helm (Oxford: Oxford University Press, 1981).

Pirkei Avot: in *The Ethics of the Talmud: Sayings of the Fathers*, ed. R. T. Herford (New York: Schocken Books, 1962).

Plato: *Euthyphro*.

Quinn, P. L.: *Divine Commands and Moral Requirements* (Oxford: Oxford University Press, 1978).

Swinburne, R. G.: 'Duty and the will of God', *Canadian Journal of Philosophy*, 4 (1974), 213–27. Reprinted in *Divine Commands and Morality*, ed. P. Helm (Oxford: Oxford University Press, 1981).

William of Ockham: *Philosophic Writings*, ed. P. Boehner, (Indianapolis: Bobbs-Merrill, 1977).

Further reading

Baier, K.: *The Moral Point of View: A Rational Basis for Ethics* (Ithaca, NY: Cornell University Press, 1958).

Brandt, R. B.: *Ethical Theory* (Englewood Cliffs, NJ: Prentice-Hall, 1959).

Helm, P., ed.: *Divine Commands and Morality* (Oxford: Oxford University Press, 1981).

Outka, G, and Reeder, J. P., Jr., eds.: *Religion and Morality: A Collection of Essays* (Garden City, New York: Anchor/Doubleday, 1973).

Sidgwick, H.: *The Methods of Ethics* (1874); 7th edn (1907); reprinted (New York: Dover, 1966).

Toulmin, S. C.: *The Place of Reason in Ethics* (Cambridge: Cambridge University Press, 1950).

47

The implications of determinism

ROBERT YOUNG

i What determinism is all about and why it is supposed to matter ethically

DETERMINISM is a doctrine that makes claims about the nature of the world, or, if you prefer, it is a metaphysical doctrine. For our purposes we will understand the doctrine of determinism to assert that the state of the entire universe at any particular time is linked by way of causal laws to the states of the universe both before and afterwards. Or, to put the point in a more rough and ready way: all states of the universe are the result of prior sufficient conditions and are in their turn sufficient for the later states of the universe. Thus if someone (perhaps God or maybe a 'superscientist') were to have perfect knowledge of the state of the entire universe at a particular time, and of the causal laws governing the operations of the universe, the state of the universe at any future time (or, indeed, any past time) could be *deduced*. (For further discussion of the doctrine of determinism see Honderich, 1988.)

In this essay I will concentrate on the supposedly fearful ethical implications of the truth of determinism. First, however, I must put aside one argument for supposing that determinism cannot be true. In my brief characterization of determinism I mentioned the idea of a perfect knower. This may seem to suggest that the doctrine of determinism is an epistemological doctrine (a doctrine about what can be known), rather than the metaphysical one I suggested at the outset. However, if the world is deterministic, that it is will be true whether or not there is a perfect knower, or indeed a knower of any sort. This point must be insisted on because there have been many (such as Lucas, 1970) who have thought to attack the doctrine of determinism and its putative ethical implications by arguing that there are conceptual obstacles to the prediction of human action that are unparalleled in the case of physical events like hurricanes and the orbits of satellites. They conclude that to suggest that human decisions and actions could be determined is incoherent. Goldman (1970) has convincingly shown, however, that both physical phenomena and human activities can be determined without it being possible for us to predict them.

I shall also ignore the sceptical view that the very idea of a complete description of the state of the entire universe at a certain time is incoherent and presume, for the sake of argument, that we can make coherent sense of it. If we suppose it to be sensible, among the elements which comprise the state of the universe at any time, or the states at different times, will be human thoughts, decisions, actions and the like. What many people believe is that if determinism is true, this threatens just such human activities. In particular it seems to many that if our decisions and actions were determined they would have no practical effect on the world and would be mere epiphenomena. Worse still, our lack of freedom would signal that we were in no position to shape the moral character of our world. The reason is that were determinism to be true, human beings would have no more control over what happens to them than does a salmon returning to its spawning grounds or a cog-wheel in a piece of machinery.

Now even though many find this idea persuasive it is easily refuted. Unlike returning salmon, and unlike pieces of machinery, people sometimes act intentionally. This intentionality in behaviour of persons is enough to show that such behaviour is not merely a tropism like the 'turning' of a sunflower toward the sun. Suppose that this be agreed. Won't it nonetheless be true, if determinism is true, that our intentions are determined and, if so, won't it follow that our behaviour is *outside our control?*

As agents who act intentionally we would be different from sunflowers, moths flying into candles, returning salmon and so forth, but we would still lack a crucial capacity if it was not *ultimately* up to us how we behaved. Since it would not be we who ultimately determined the courses of our lives (but instead the circumstances making up the conditions sufficient for our various decisions and actions) we would lack the capacity to be free because we would lack the capacity to decide anything or do anything other than what we in fact decide to do.

The sentiment is humorously captured in a limerick by M. E. Hare:

> There once was a man who said 'Damn!
> It is borne in upon me I am
> An engine that moves
> In predestinate grooves;
> I'm not even a bus, I'm a tram.'

It is not hard to see how various flow-on effects can be derived from such a conclusion. For example, it is widely, even if not unanimously (see Frankfurt, 1969), thought that being able to do otherwise is necessary for moral responsibility. But if determinism is true, it seems that no-one can do otherwise and so no-one can be morally responsible for any decisions or actions. If moral responsibility (not merely causal responsibility) is a prerequisite for guilt, blame, punishment and the like, and likewise for credit, praise and reward, then no-one will properly be subject to punishment or reward since strictly no-one will be blameworthy or praiseworthy. Social sanctions to be employed against the socially disruptive would still be needed but would require a different rationale to the one with which we presently operate (based as it is on a presumption that wrongdoers are responsible for their wrongdoings, a presumption which can, of course, be rebutted if there are shown to be suitable excuses).

Some even go so far as to say that if determinism is true and we, therefore, are not free agents, morality itself becomes of no account. Moral nihilism, the doctrine that nothing moral matters, is said to follow from our lacking freedom because our inability to exercise control over the moral quality of our behaviour evacuates all moral significance from that behaviour. (On 'nihilism' see also Article 38, SUBJECTIVISM.)

It will help bring these various contentions into clearer focus if we have before us a more formal statement of the course of the argument from the truth of determinism to the denial of freedom, responsibility and the significance of morality. Here is one statement of the argument:

1 If human decisions and actions are determined, then for all such decisions and actions, there are antecedently sufficient causal conditions.
2 If there are (antecedently) sufficient conditions for all decisions and actions, then decisions and actions are necessitated by these conditions.
3 But if decisions and actions are necessitated, no-one acts freely; that is, no-one is able to decide or act differently from the way he or she does.
4 Since it is required *inter alia* of morally responsible decisions and actions that agents act freely – that is, that they be able to decide or act differently from the ways they do – if determinism is true no-one ever decides or acts morally responsibly.
5 If no-one ever acts freely or morally responsibly many moral (and legal) practices lose their justification, and thus morality itself can have no objective foundation.

ii Three traditional responses to the problem

The task now is to assess the soundness of this argument. The obvious place to start is with the issue of how determinism bears on freedom. My statement of the argument implies that the relation between determinism and freedom is one of incompatibility. Those who think that it can't both be that determinism is true *and* that we are free are, accordingly, known as *incompatibilists*. A moment's reflection will make clear that there can be incompatibilists who think we have every reason to believe that the world is deterministic and therefore conclude that we cannot be free, and incompatibilists who are convinced that we are free and therefore conclude that determinism must be false. And indeed both kinds of incompatibilists exist. The former are known as 'hard determinists' (because they take a hard line on the implications of determinism). The argument sketched above is one many hard determinists would fully support (cf. Skinner, 1971), but there are others who would jib at step 5, namely, the claim that nihilism follows from the truth of determinism. These latter adopt a form of utilitarianism of a crude instrumentalist sort, so that where behaviour is modifiable by reward or punishment, positive or negative reinforcement and so on (cf. Edwards, 1961) we can consider it 'morally' good, but only in the same way as we consider our well-trained companion animals to behave well when they are properly responsive.

Incompatibilists who are convinced that we are free and hence that determinism is false are known as 'libertarians' (not to be confused with political libertarians, who seek to minimize the role of the state). They accept that if determinism were true – step 1 in the argument above – the subsequent steps would indeed follow. But, they claim, determinism is false because on some occasions at least, we act freely. The most common versions of libertarianism are *contra-causal* ones (Campbell, 1957). According to contra-causal libertarianism, while we inhabit a world that is largely deterministic, on those occasions when we act freely we act without being determined by states or events (such as our desires) which it is plausible to think operate deterministically. Rather, our selves act 'in opposition to' or, perhaps, transcend such deterministic forces. Though this is vague, and seems to suggest that when we act freely we (our inner selves?) have the power to act contrary to the laws of nature, the best sense that can be made of the idea is to see it as the claim that when we act freely our actions are rationally, but not deterministically, explicable. Taken this way the claim is that *reasons* are radically different from *causes* (compare Kant; see Article 14, KANTIAN ETHICS). It is a common objection (Hobart, 1966) that a libertarian freedom, being uncaused, would be valueless because if free decisions and actions are just fortuitous or random outcomes, to decide or act freely is not to be in control. By placing the emphasis on the rational rather than the causal explication of decisions and actions, contra-causal libertarians can evade this common objection. Not so another group of libertarians, the existentialists. Existentialists from Kierkegaard to Sartre have proclaimed that to be fully human is to make radical choices; that is, choices that not only are not determined but choices for which no rationally persuasive support can be offered. Only by making such choices and eschewing all talk of excuses can we make ourselves responsible agents.

Other libertarians contend that since free actions have unique status they are best understood as being caused in a unique way, namely by an agent who is not himself or herself caused to act in this way. This is known as *agent-causation* libertarianism (Chisholm, 1964; van Inwagen, 1983). This move breaks the deterministic chain, understood as one event causing another event, but has seemed to most contemporary philosophers to depend for its explanatory power on an obscure and perhaps not even coherent idea of causation. One further proposal that has had some contemporary influence is that free actions are intelligible because they fit with our choices and purposes (Wiggins, 1973). Though this is plausible enough, it is unlike the contra-causalist's claim that free decisions and actions are rationally but not deterministically explainable, in that there is nothing specifically indeterministic about it. It therefore could equally be said by *compatibilists*.

'Compatibilists' reject the argument outlined earlier as unsound. In doing so they do not have to claim that determinism holds, only that should it hold, its doing so is compatible with our being able freely to decide and act. Compatibilists have employed various strategies in the process of defending their shared conviction that we can be both determined and free. Perhaps most famously there have been attempts to show that even in a deterministic world we could decide and act differently from the ways in which we in fact decide and act, *if only* we

537

should choose to do so or should want to do so. These so-called 'hypothetical' analyses of the requirement for being morally responsible – see step 4 in the argument outlined earlier – have been vigorously criticized. Of these criticisms, one that many find persuasive is as follows: if determinism is true, the laws of nature, taken in conjunction with a statement of the conditions of the universe at any time before my birth, entail every true statement about my behaviour. But surely I could have refrained from behaving in these ways only if I could have falsified the laws of nature or altered the states of the universe which were true prior to my birth. Since I could not have done either of these things, no hypothetical analysis of my capacities could be devised to show that I could have done them (van Inwagen, 1983). The reply that a compatibilist disposed to the hypothetical analysis would make is obvious: that I had the capacity to choose and act differently is not gainsaid by the claim that I lack the capacity miraculously to overturn the laws of nature or to do the impossible in altering the past. My having the capacity to choose and act differently from the ways I in fact do (or have done) *is consistent with my not exercising the capacity*. Accordingly there is no incoherence in the suggestion that my capacity to act differently (an unexercised capacity) is just the capacity so to act that past situations would have been other than they in fact were had I exercised that capacity. Had I, on occasion, behaved differently, then, on the assumption that determinism is true, the past would have been different.

A second compatibilist strategy has been to set aside hypothetical analyses of statements like 'she could have done otherwise', in favour of taking sentences ascribing powers to perform particular actions to be presumptively true in the absence of the sorts of factors which would defeat the exercise of such powers (Goldman, 1970; Dennett, 1984). Thus, for example, if it is said that I can mow my lawn, that will be presumed true unless it can be shown that there is present some defeating factor (such as my being in a coma, my being subject to a post-hypnotic command not to mow my lawn, the lawn being covered with snow, there being no mower in working order ...). Such defeating conditions are, of course, often taken to be defeating conditions of moral responsibility even when determinism is not the focus. But the crucial claim here is that since the truth of determinism (or its falsity) seems to make no difference to the accuracy of this understanding of what we can or cannot do, compatibilists of this persuasion contend that it is not determinism as such that robs us of the power to do things other than those we do. Rather it is the particular defeating factors that have that effect. Certainly in a deterministic world there will be a deterministic account of the presence of a defeater on any particular occasion (consider, for instance, the post-hypnotic suggestion mentioned above). But that only goes to reinforce the point that not all deterministically produced states of affairs are incompatible with our being free to act as we choose or desire. Only some are. (It is worth noting that though, as we have seen, compatibilists who adopt this second strategy reject the hypothetical analysis approach, a sophisticated hypothetical analysis could be supplemented with the defeating conditions account (Young, 1979; Dennett, 1984).)

iii   Some contemporary attempts at reorienting the debate

In a famous contemporary contribution to the debate Peter Strawson contends that our interpersonal attitudes and behaviour are premised on the idea that (mature) people are free and are responsible for their actions (Strawson, 1962). He argues that, to a very great extent, our personal reactions and feelings depend upon, or involve, our beliefs about the attitudes and intuitions of others and of ourselves. Thus when we see someone's behaviour as unintentional or compulsive we do not experience normal *participant reactive attitudes* like resentment and moral indignation, but instead take the *objective* or clinical attitude characteristic of impersonal relations. Where, however, the actions of others display the goodwill, ill-will or indifference they intend, there is a range of participant reactive attitudes which is appropriate just because of our involvement or participation with others in interpersonal relations. Thus it is that gratitude, goodwill, resentment, moral indignation and so forth are so integral to our concept of ourselves and others as persons, that we could not abandon them in the way urged by the hard determinist. The hard determinist, in effect, insists that we judge the significance of these reactive attitudes from the objective or impersonal standpoint, a feat which it is impossible to carry out in our interpersonal dealings with others. So whether determinism is true or not, our view of ourselves and of the place we accord to the reactive attitudes is not negotiable. Hence the truth of determinism does not render nugatory claims about freedom, moral responsibility, moral obligation, praise, blame and punishment. Though Strawson's contribution can, therefore, be seen as a strategy for rejecting incompatibilism, it is more accurate to see it as an attempt at reorienting the debate to make it focus on what is essential to the moral life and not on the intellectual niceties of metaphysics.

There has been a further such reorienting of the debate in Harry Frankfurt's work (1971, 1987). Frankfurt accepts that to *act* freely is fundamentally a matter of doing what one wants to do, but argues that it is misleading to think that something similar holds for freedom of the *will*. One can be free to do what one wants but not have a free will. To enjoy freedom of the will is to be free to want what one wants to want, or, more precisely, to have the will one wants. Such a view of freedom of the will is, he contends, neutral with regard to the truth of determinism. Whether it is because of a deterministic process or because of chance (luck) that we have the will we want is not the issue. (A libertarian will be apt to see this as a tendentious way of stating matters.) What is it to have the will we want? It is to have the capacity to form effective second-order volitions, that is, to be able to want a certain desire to be our will. An unwilling drug addict who has conflicting first-order wants (to take a certain drug and to refrain from taking it), does something he wants to do, whichever of these desires is the one he finally acts on, but if it is to take the drug he can truly say it is not of his own free will that he does it since he identifies with the desire to refrain. By contrast an addict who does not care about her will, and so has no second-order volitions relating to her desire for drugs, lacks a free will because of her wanton lack of care about her will. This is an appealing idea because it suggests (especially as regards those

539

whose behaviour is to be regarded as compulsive) that it is impairments in people's capacity to deliberate rationally that obstructs their freedom, rather than any deterministic structure the world may have. Nonetheless it has been criticized on the ground that in being unconcerned about the aetiology of people's second-order volitions it implausibly leaves it open for, say, the citizens of Aldous Huxley's *Brave New World*, whose motivations are programmed for them, to count as having free wills (Watson, 1975; Slote, 1980). If so, the proposal would need to be shored up in such a way as to give higher-order desires, acquired in the way they are in the Brave New World, a different status from those acquired through reflective evaluation by the agent on her desires (Young, 1986). This would reinstate the agent's effective control over her own behaviour, but equally would put back on the agenda the issue of whether, when reflective evaluations are determined, they can themselves be appropriately regarded as under the agent's control. Compatibilists believe the regress that looms here can be halted; incompatibilists, as we have previously seen, deny that it can. Put another way: compatibilists think it possible for us to regard ourselves as responsible, moral beings, even if it should turn out that we, along with everything else in the universe, are determined beings; incompatibilists hold that we can't both be responsible moral beings and determined beings.

iv Moral responsibility, rewards and punishments, nihilism

It is worth reminding ourselves that although whether people act freely and responsibly cannot be detached from the sorts of metaphysical questions we have been considering, it is our concern with ethics that motivates those questions. In particular, to the extent that we can regard someone as a free, responsible agent of an action, we can morally assess both the action and the agent. If Jacinta was morally responsible for her actions in driving dangerously and causing injury to Cedric, her behaviour is morally condemnable and she herself is seen to be morally deficient in that she took insufficient account of the interests of others in behaving as she did.

We saw earlier that according to Strawson we cannot contemplate setting aside our reactive attitudes even if, as incompatibilists contend, such attitudes would be objectively unjustifiable in a deterministic world. Let's suppose Strawson is right. Let's also suppose that determinism is true (and known to be true). Hard determinists have wanted to say that, given the truth of determinism, the reactive attitudes can have at best an instrumental role, namely one of social control (Edwards, 1961). Misbehaviour won't be immoral behaviour (because those who misbehave will not be able to do anything else). But it will still need to be controlled if the interests of those who don't pose a social problem are not to be subject to intolerable risk of being interfered with by miscreants. In the extreme, a form of social control involving the isolation of those who pose a severe risk of causing death, bodily harm or damage to the property of others would be justifiable according to such hard determinists. It would be more accurately thought of as a form of quarantine – we do take steps to protect ourselves against carriers of contagious diseases even though they aren't usually considered responsible for posing a threat to society. Alternatively, therapeutic treatment may be linked with attempted rehabilitation as a substitute for punishment. Either approach would be justifiable instrumentally in terms of the benefits exceeding the costs.

Though it is an underlying assumption of our everyday *moral* practices that most offenders are fully responsible – the exceptions being some minors, certain psychiatrically disturbed individuals and so forth – a good deal of contemporary penology does see *legal* punishment as unjustifiable for reasons like those offered by hard determinists. According to such views, in addition to the truth of determinism showing that none of us is the free, responsible agent our moral and legal practices presume we are, we have a host of empirical grounds for the view that traditional penal practices are unsuccessful and need to be replaced with more effective strategies. Even if no-one deserves to be punished, and the usual forms which punishment takes have little to recommend them, we still need to protect the law-abiding from those who, because of their individual psychology or the sociology of their situation, break the laws (Murphy, 1973).

Article 32, CRIME AND PUNISHMENT, should be consulted on the moral issues punishment raises. One point worth some comment here, however, is that in relation to punishment an alliance is possible between libertarians and certain compatibilists. Libertarians insist that unless an individual is the ultimate cause of a particular action, it is inappropriate to punish him or her (though it may be appropriate, nonetheless, to provide an alternative form of institutionalization to protect the community, such as a psychiatric facility, or to provide therapeutic rehabilitation). But on matters like excuses such as ignorance and inability there is no reason why compatibilists need disagree with libertarians. Where compatibilists (such as Mackie, 1977) have adopted an instrumentalist approach to the moral reactive attitudes of praise and blame and to the legal ones of reward and punishment, they have done so more often than not because of their denial of the objectivity or realism of claims about moral wrongdoing, and not because of any wish to embrace a bloodless form of freedom. Compatibilists who are meta-ethical subjectivists or relativists (see Article 38, SUBJECTIVISM, and Article 39, RELATIVISM) likewise tend to reject any retributivist foundation for punishment and propose instead a wholly consequentialist one. But once again this does not require them to line up with hard determinists who reject the relevance of ideas of moral fault to the use of social sanctions. That is why they can unite with compatibilists who are moral realists (see Article 35, REALISM), with thinkers like Strawson and Frankfurt, and with libertarians, in insisting that morality does matter and hence that nihilism is to be rejected.

References

Campbell, C. A.: *On Selfhood and Godhood* (London: Allen and Unwin, 1957).
Chisholm, R. M.: 'Human freedom and the self', *The Lindley Lecture*, 1964; reprinted in *Free Will*, ed. G. Watson (Oxford: Oxford University Press, 1982).

Edwards, P.: 'Hard and soft determinism', *Determinism and Freedom in the Age of Modern Science*, ed. S. Hook (Collier Books, New York, 1961).

Frankfurt, H.: 'Alternate possibilities and moral responsibility', *Journal of Philosophy*, 66 (1969) 829–39.

——: 'Freedom of the will and the concept of a person', *The Journal of Philosophy*, 68 (1971) 5–20, reprinted in *Free Will*, ed. G. Watson (Oxford: Oxford University Press, 1982).

——: 'Identification and wholeheartedness', *Responsibility, Character and the Emotions: New Essays in Moral Psychology*, ed. F. Schoeman (Cambridge and New York: Cambridge University Press, 1987).

Hobart, R. E.: 'Free will as involving determination and inconceivable without it', *Mind*, 43 (1934) 1–27; reprinted in *Free Will and Determinism*, ed. B. Berofsky (New York: Harper and Row, 1966).

Honderich, T.: *A Theory of Determinism: The Mind, Neuroscience, and Life Hopes* (New York: Oxford University Press, 1988).

Huxley, A.: *Brave New World* (1932); (Harmondsworth: Penguin, 1955).

Kant, I.: *Foundations of the Metaphysics of Morals*.

Lucas, J. R.: *The Freedom of the Will* (Oxford: Oxford University Press, 1970).

Mackie, J. L.: *Ethics: Inventing Right and Wrong* (Harmondsworth: Penguin, 1977).

Murphy, J. G., ed.: *Punishment and Rehabilitation* (Belmont, Cal.: Wadsworth, 1973).

Skinner, B. F.: *Beyond Freedom and Dignity* (New York: Knopf, 1971).

Slote M., 'Understanding Free Will', *Journal of Philosophy*, 77 (1980) 136–51.

Strawson, P. F.: 'Freedom and resentment', *Proceedings of the British Academy*, 48 (1962), 1–25; reprinted in *Free Will*, ed. G. Watson (Oxford: Oxford University Press, 1982).

Watson, G.: 'Free agency', *Journal of Philosophy*, 72 (1975), 205–20, reprinted in *Free Will*, ed. G. Watson (Oxford: Oxford University Press, 1982).

Young, R.: 'Compatibilism and conditioning', *Noûs*, 13 (1979), 361–78.

——: *Personal Autonomy: Beyond Negative and Positive Liberty* (London and New York: Croom Helm and St Martin's Press, 1986).

Further reading

Dennett, D.: *Elbow Room: The Varieties of Free Will Worth Wanting* (Oxford: Clarendon Press, 1984).

Goldman, A.: *A Theory of Human Action* (Englewood Cliffs, NJ: Prentice-Hall, 1970).

van Inwagen, P.: *An Essay on Free Will* (Oxford: Clarendon Press, 1983).

Watson, G. (ed.), *Free Will* (Oxford: Oxford University Press, 1982).

Wiggins, D.: 'Towards a reasonable libertarianism', *Essays on Freedom of Action*, ed. T. Honderich (London: Routledge and Kegan Paul, 1973).

Young, R.: *Freedom, Responsibility and God* (London: Macmillan; New York: Barnes and Noble, 1975).

Afterword

PETER SINGER

IT WOULD be easy to think of ethics as a field in which, since ancient times, proponents of opposing views have been engaged in unending disputes without prospect of resolution. After all, does not each culture have its own ethical tradition, hopelessly at odds with all the others? And even within the narrow confines of modern Western philosophical ethics, are there not irreconcilable differences about what is good, or obligatory? Worse still, philosophers cannot even agree about what we are doing when we make such ethical judgements: whether we are describing some kind of moral reality, or expressing our attitudes, or prescribing what is to be done.

The contents of this *Companion to Ethics* may seem to confirm such a view. A quick summary might go like this: in the first part, we see how little we know about the origins of ethics, how ethics in small-scale societies takes forms very different from those it takes in our own, and how the most ancient ethical writings already reflect a variety of views about how life is to be lived. Then the great ethical traditions are put on display; and we find divergence of opinion not only between the different traditions, but within each tradition itself. The history of Western philosophical ethics shows how, from the earliest Greek thinkers to the present day, old philosophical positions have resurfaced at intervals, and old battles have had to be fought out all over again in more modern terms. When, in Part IV, the volume moves from the past to the present, we are presented with many theories of how we ought to live, and about the nature of ethics, all plausible, but all disagreeing with every other approach. Since we conclude with a set of challenges to the viability of the entire enterprise of ethics, we will surely close the book in a sorry state of confusion, not knowing what to think about any of it.

As I complete the editing of this volume, however, I am left with a quite different impression. If ethics is a jigsaw puzzle, then we are now at the stage where we have laid out all the pieces, and are beginning to see the outline of the picture. For ethics is *not* a meaningless series of different things to different people in different times and places. Rather, against a background of historically and culturally diverse approaches to the question of how we ought to live, the degree of convergence is striking. Human nature has its constants and there are only a limited number of ways in which human beings can live together and flourish; indeed, as the opening essay of this volume argued, some of the features common to the nature of human beings in different societies are common to the nature of

543

any long-lived, intelligent social mammals, and are reflected in our behaviour as they are reflected in that of other primates.

Hence what is recognized as a virtue in one society or religious tradition is very likely to be recognized as a virtue in the others; certainly, the set of virtues praised in one major tradition never make up a substantial part of the set of vices of another major tradition. (Exceptions tend to be short-lived, societies in the process of decay or self-destruction.) Moreover within each tradition, the same oscillating currents can be observed: there are periods in which the emphasis is on the performance of conventional duties, obligations or roles; then a great reformer will appear, urging that we have become so far steeped in obedience to the rules, so conventional in our ways of thinking and acting, that we have forgotten the higher goods by which the moral conventions themselves must be justified. Thus Buddha stressed egolessness rather than observance of the Hindu rituals of his day, as Mozi argued that we should follow universal love, not the particular duties specified by Confucianism, and as Jesus taught that love of God and neighbour was more important than following the letter of the prevailing Jewish moral law.

Granted, this oscillation might be seen as no more than a recurring, insoluble conflict between an ethic based on rules and one based on consequences – a conflict that, as the articles that make up Part IV show, is still very much part of contemporary ethics. But we could also see these two views of ethics as ineliminable aspects of a complete account of the nature of ethics. Any attempt to explain or understand the phenomenon of ethics must give each tendency its proper place; and although such an explanation of ethics would not in itself justify any particular ethical theory that tries to answer the question of how we ought to live, a better understanding of the nature of ethics would at least make it easier for us to see what kind of answer that question might need to have.

The applications of ethical theory to practical issues in Part V show disagreements about many specific points, but they share an implicit assumption: that even the most difficult practical ethical issues are amenable to discussion and argument. According to at least some views of the nature of ethics, reasoning about ethics should be no more profitable than reasoning about matters of taste. Yet could anyone say that the arguments in the articles in this section generally – not here and there on specific points, but systematically and as a whole – fail to make progress towards the goal of better reasoned conclusions about world poverty, the environment, euthanasia, abortion, and all the other issues covered in this part of the book? I take a much more positive view of the achievements of applied ethics; a view which acknowledges that we can agree on some standards of good and bad reasoning in ethics, as in other areas of our intellectual life. I think the essays in Part V support that view.

It was in reading over Part VI, on The Nature of Ethics, however, that I was most struck by the unexpected extent to which writers who had started from quite different places all seemed to be heading in the same direction. Consider the implications of the following set of articles. For Michael Smith, defending a realist view of ethics, the kind of objective moral reality that can be consistent with the action-guiding nature of ethics is to be found not in some set of queer facts about the universe, but in the reasons for action that we would accept if we were reasoning under certain idealized conditions. The objectivity of morality, then, comes down to the possibility that if we were all reasoning under such conditions, we would reach the same conclusions. Jonathan Dancy, writing about intuitionism, another realist or objectivist view of ethics, denies that intuition provides a means of perceiving moral facts. Instead Dancy settles on the most plausible version of intuitionism as one which regards moral 'facts' as reasons recognized in the exercise of our practical judgment. James Rachels approaches these questions from the opposite direction. He starts with a subjectivist account of ethics that takes feelings of approval as the basis of ethical judgment. Yet Rachels finds this and successive more refined versions of ethical subjectivism unsatisfactory, because they do not allow sufficient scope for disagreement and reasoned argument about ethics. Rachels's final attempt at an adequate formulation of subjectivism is one in which our individual feelings of approval are so constrained by requirements of impartiality and reasonableness that the outcome is scarcely to be distinguished from the objective notion of reasons for action reached by Smith and Dancy. Moreover, as Rachels himself notes, this conclusion is in important respects close to that of universal prescriptivism, the ethical theory proposed by R. M. Hare, which requires us to carry out our moral reasoning under the constraint of universalizability. Hare himself, in his article on universal prescriptivism, argues that this constraint can suffice to lead us to agreed conclusions about how to act, conclusions that are based on a method of reasoning supported not only by utilitarians and by Kant, but also by the 'Golden Rule' that, as the articles in Part II have shown, is central to several of the great ethical traditions.

This is, admittedly, a selective drawing together of common themes. The conclusions of the articles on naturalism and relativism do not fit quite so neatly with those of the other articles in Part VI; but at the same time their conclusions are not, strictly, incompatible with the common approach that I have identified. To defend this common approach against some of the more radical challenges posed by the articles in Part VII one would need to show that these challenges could be met by, or somehow accommodated within, a view of morality that draws on the common core. Whether that can be done is not a question that can be answered here; but the prospects strike me as encouraging. I persist in thinking that the puzzle of ethics is starting to come together, and that few, if any, pieces are missing.

Index

COMPILED BY MEG DAVIES

Note: Page references in **bold** type indicate chief discussion of major topics. Where names of contributors to the *Companion* are indexed, the references are to citations in articles other than their own articles.

desires 73, 147, 284
in Buddhism 60
in Chinese ethics 76, 80
in Greek ethics 126–7, 316, 461
role in action 400–2, 403–4, 405–9, 414–16, 449
sexual 316, 317, 321, 323
and virtue theory 251, 252
determinism 534–41
hard 536, 539, 540–1
in Kant 176, 180
deterrence 366, 368, 369–70
nuclear 385, 390
development, and aid 275–6
development, moral,
in Christian ethics 94
definition 471–4
and historical context 471–2
in Islam 116
and psychological development 64, 74, 464–74, 494
stages 465–8, 494
Dewey, John 154, 439
dharma,
in Buddhism 65
in Hinduism 43, 44, 45–9, 54, 56
in Jainism 51
Diggs, B.J. 186, 192
dignity of person, *see* respect for person
Dionysius the Areopagite 136, 138
'dirty hands' 233, 373–82
disagreement, moral 435–8, 440, 444–5, 448–9
discipline, in Islam 116
discrimination,
in war 387–90
see also racism; sexism; speciesism
dishonesty 34, 331
disinterestedness, *see* action, disinterested
divorce 97, 250, 316
dolphins, and humanity 308
Donagan, A. 211, 212–13, 215
double effect principle 209, 215, 300
Douglass, Frederick 263
Downie, R.S. 363
Drucker, Peter 360
dualism 6–7, 38, 315–16
dukkha (unsatisfactoriness) 59–60, 63
Duns Scotus Eriugena 136, 139, 140, 142
duty,
beyond borders 279–80
in Buddhism 62, 65

in Christian ethics 96
in Confucianism 70
in Hinduism 46, 47, 48–50
perfect/imperfect 178, 179
positive 216–17
prima facie 219–28
proper 223–5
role-specific 328–9, 544
and utilitarianism 245
and virtue theory 250, 256
see also deontology; help; Kant, Immanuel; obligation; poverty, world, alleviation; *dharma*
Dworkin, Ronald 262

Ecclesiastes, and meaning of life 37
Eckhardt, Meister 142
economics, as model for moral theory 477
ecosystems, moral status 287, 288, 289, 290, 291–3
Ecumenical Movement 93, 104
education, moral 459
Edwards, Jonathan 256
Efros, Israel 83
egalitarianism 20, 72, 247, 334–5, 341, 346–7
biotic 288
egoism 197–204, 328, 531–2
in Chinese ethics 74
in Christian ethics 96
and common good 200, 203
enlightened 7
ethical 201–3
in Greek ethics 127
in Indian ethics 44, 46
psychological 197–9, 203
and punishment 72
rational 191, 201–4, 284
and social contract 4–5, 7, 8–9, 10, 12
egolessness, in Buddhism 58, 59–60, 67, 544
Egypt, evidence of ancient ethics 16, 29, 33–5, 37
eliminatism 253, 254–5
Eliot, T.S., *Murder in the Cathedral* 96
Emile, Rousseau 491
emotion, *see* feelings
emotivism 262, 421, 422, 436–9, 455
ends,
in Hinduism 45, 47–8, 56
of just war 386
and means 205, 210, 276, 391, 393, 460–1, 497
in themselves 20, 27, 125, 178–9, 191, 307, 357
see also purushartha

enemy, in Christian ethics 95
Engels, Friedrich 322, 514, 521–2
enlightenment, in Buddhism 58, 67
Enuma elish creation epic 30
environmental ethics 544
animal-centred 286–7, 289–90, 291
definition 284–8
'everything' 288, 289, 290–2
and holism 288–9, 291
human-centred 285–6, 289–90, 291
justification 285, 289–93
life-centred 287–8, 289, 290, 291
envy, in Buddhism 64
Epicureanism 121–2, 316
Epicurus 121, 122, 123, 126–7
epistemology, moral 143, 223–4, 480, 483, *see also* knowledge, moral
equality,
and animals 254, 286–7, 347–8, 350
human 65, 80, 149, 188, 190–4, 254, 265, 310–12
of income 97, 335
of opportunity 97, 333–5, 336, 338–41
original position 191–3
racial 333
sexual 97, 212, 322, 325, 333, 335
in Buddhism 65
in Greek ethics 129–30
in Judaism 37, 84
in Mesopotamia 32–3
and utility 247, 346
of value 346
equilibrium, reflective 482
equivocation 94
Erasmus, Desiderius 376
eros 98–9
error-theory 421, 422, 426–7, 429
eschatology and ethics 38–9, 102
essentialism 492–3
ethic, female 491–9
Ethics: Inventing Right and Wrong, Mackie 253
ethics,
justification 506–7, 543
theistic 479
eudaemonism 52, 62, 123–5, 141–2
eudaimonia 122–4, 125, 130–1, 142
euthanasia 170, 294–302, 544
actions/omissions 297–8

551

equal consideration principle
286–7, 327, 328, 335,
339–41
in Hinduism 47
national 384, 385
and rights 264
welfare 244–5
Interests and Rights, Frey 344
intermarriage, forbidden 37,
38
internalism 415–16, 458
intimacy,
in personal relationships 327–
8, 330–2
and sexuality 318–19, 321,
325
intolerance, in Christianity 103
*Introduction to the Principles of
Morals and Legislation*,
Bentham 242, 348
intuition 411–12, 423, 461
in Chinese ethics 70, 71–2, 73,
75, 76–7, 79, 81
and God 529–30
in Hindu ethics 48
and moral theory 477, 478,
483–5
intuitionism,
arguments against 418–19
and Christian ethics 104, 135
and deontology 211–12, 215
as descriptive 452–3, 455,
459, 461
in mathematics 419
in medieval ethics 139–40
in modern ethics 150, 151–3,
223, 225, 278, 421, 545
moral attitudes and behaviour
413–14
and pluralism 411, 413
and relativism 454
irrationalism 455–6
irrealism 402–4, *see also*
emotivism; non-
cognitivism; prescriptivism;
projectivism
is/ought gap 423–5, 427, 459,
501, 506
Islam,
contemporary issues 116–17
ethics 106–17
foundational values 106–11
influence on Jewish ethics 87
and other religions 109–10,
111
philosophical approaches
113–15
and rights 267
Shi'a tradition 115–16
Sufi tradition 116
theological and traditional
approaches 111–13, 114

Ismaili Muslims 115
isolation, moral, in politics 381

Jaggar, Alison 323
Jain ethics 51–3, 54, 55, 310–
11
James, William 442
Jamieson, Dale 347
Jerome, St 135
Jesus Christ 91–2, 94–100, 101–
3, 316, 544
Jewish ethics 82–9, 212
early 35–9
literature 83–9
medieval 87–8
rabbinic 87–8
see also Judaism; sexuality
jihad 109
Job, and sin and punishment 36–
7
John, Gospel of 94, 97, 102
Johnston, Jill 323
Jonah, and treatment of
foreigners 38
Judaism 82–3, 254, 294
and Christianity 91–2, 100–1
early 35–9
and Islam 107, 109, 110, 111
medieval 87–8
modern 88–9
see also Jewish ethics; sexuality
judgement, moral,
and intuitionism 415–16,
418, 454, 545
logic 438
meaning 445
and naturalism 421, 422–5,
429, 453, 455
and prescriptivism 451–3,
455–60
and prima facie duties 221,
224–5
and realism 400–8, 543
and relativism 444–5, 453–4
and subjectivism 432–4, 437–
40, 454–5, 458, 545
jus ad bellum theory 386–7,
388
jus in bello theory 386, 387–8,
390
justice 5, 56, 190–1
in ancient Egypt 33, 35
in Buddhism 62
in Chinese ethics 72
in Christian ethics 97–100
commutative 359
conventional 162–3
corrective 98
distributive 98
and egoism 201
in Greek ethics 123, 124, 125,
127, 129, 162–3, 373

in Hinduism 46
in Islam 108, 114, 117
in Judaism 36–8, 85, 87
in Kant 178, 179, 184
and love 98–9
in Marxism 517–18, 520
in Mesopotamia 30, 32
in modern Western ethics
150–1, 153, 155–6, 281
natural 162–3
as natural duty 191–2, 193,
195
and natural law 164, 259
and politics 373, 378
and preferential treatment 334
and punishment 367
and risk of war 394
social 274–5, 278, 279
visible/hidden 25
see also punishment
justification,
in consequentialism 235,
238–9
see also belief, moral;
judgement, moral

Kabbalah 88
kamma, and causation 61
Kant, Immanuel,
and animals 7
and autonomy of man 147,
156, 251
and contract theory 188, 191–
5
critique 219–20
on duty 50, 151, 177–8, 179,
180, 181–3, 219–20, 256
ethics 175–81, 457, 494, 545
influence 9, 155–6, 252
and Kantian ethics 175, 176,
183–4, 249, 497, 521
and 'Kant's ethics' 175, 181–
3
and moral law 46, 151, 153–
4, 177–9, 180, 460–1, 484
on reason 175, 176, 180, 184,
252, 455, 531
on sanctity of life 294
see also knowledge; respect for
persons; will, freedom of
Kantianism, *see* Kant, Immanuel,
and Kantian ethics
karma,
in Hinduism 45, 46–7, 50, 56
in Jainism 51, 53
Kautilya 49
Kautsky, Karl 512
Kennedy, John F. 373
Kheel, Marti 352
Kierkegaard, Soren 537
killing 306, 307, 308–10, 313